Sparks

★

AMERICAN
★
RUSSIAN
★
RELATIONS
★
1781 - 1947

★

AMERICAN

★

RUSSIAN

★

RELATIONS

★

1781 - 1947

★

William Appleman Williams

1971

OCTAGON BOOKS

New York

Reprinted 1971
by special arrangement with Holt, Rinehart and Winston, Inc.

OCTAGON BOOKS
A DIVISION OF FARRAR, STRAUS & GIROUX, INC.
19 Union Square West
New York, N. Y. 10003

MAY 8 '72

LIBRARY OF CONGRESS CATALOG CARD NUMBER: 70-154671

ISBN-0-374-98581-2

Printed in U.S.A. by
NOBLE OFFSET PRINTERS, INC.
NEW YORK 3, N. Y.

★

TO

Fred Harvey Harrington

★

To the many friends and colleagues who have given encouragement and counsel in the preparation of this volume the author has personally expressed his deep appreciation and gratitude. He herewith wishes to acknowledge, however, his debt to the Research Committee of the Graduate School of the University of Wisconsin for their grant in 1949–50 which made possible the central portion of his research in manuscript materials.

Grateful acknowledgment is made to the following publishers for permission to quote excerpts from their copyrighted material:

THOMAS ALLEN, LTD., Toronto, Canada, and HOUGHTON MIFFLIN CO., Boston, for permission to quote from THE GRAND ALLIANCE by Winston Churchill, 1950; THE HINGE OF FATE by Winston Churchill, 1951; and CLOSING THE RING by Winston Churchill, 1951.

CAMBRIDGE UNIVERSITY PRESS, New York, for permission to quote from THE DEVELOPMENT OF THE SOVIET ECONOMIC SYSTEM by Alexander Baykov, 1947.

THE COUNCIL ON FOREIGN RELATIONS, INC., New York, and FOREIGN AFFAIRS for permission to quote from "The Sources of Soviet Conduct" by George Frost Kennan, FOREIGN AFFAIRS, Volume XXV, No. 4 (July, 1947), 566–82.

HARCOURT, BRACE AND CO., New York, for permission to quote from THE FAR EASTERN POLICY OF THE UNITED STATES by A. Whitney Griswold, 1938; and THEODORE ROOSEVELT: A BIOGRAPHY by Henry F. Pringle, 1931.

HARPER & BROTHERS, New York, for permission to quote from SPEAKING FRANKLY by James F. Byrnes, 1947; THE CHALLENGE TO ISOLATION, 1937–1940 by William L. Langer and S. Everett Gleason, 1952; ROOSEVELT AND HOPKINS. *An Intimate History* by Robert E. Sherwood, First Edition, 1948; TIME FOR DECISION by Sumner Welles, 1944; WHERE ARE WE HEADING? by Sumner Welles, 1946; and SEVEN DECISIONS THAT SHAPED HISTORY by Sumner Welles, 1951.

HOUGHTON MIFFLIN CO., Boston, for permission to quote excerpts from HENRY ADAMS AND HIS FRIENDS. *A Collection of His Unpublished Letters,* compiled and with a biographical introduction by Harold Dean Cater, 1947; and LETTERS OF HENRY ADAMS, *Vol. II, 1892–1918* by Worthington C. Ford, 1938.

THE MACMILLAN CO., New York, for permission to quote from THE SOVIET IMPACT ON THE WESTERN WORLD by Edward H. Carr, 1947; THE MEMOIRS OF CORDELL HULL by Cordell Hull, 2 volumes, 1948; RUSSIA IN FLUX by Sir John Maynard, edited and abridged by S. Hayden Guest, 1948; EUROPE IN DECAY. *A Study in Disintegration, 1936–1940* by Lewis B. Namier, 1950.

McGRAW-HILL BOOK COMPANY, New York, for permission to quote from I WAS THERE by Admiral William Leahy, 1950.

RINEHART & CO., New York, for permission to quote from DEPRESSION DECADE. *From the New Era Through the New Deal* by Broadus Mitchell, 1947.

CHARLES SCRIBNER'S SONS, New York, for permission to quote from THE FOREIGN POLICIES OF HERBERT HOOVER, 1929–1933 by William S. Meyers, 1940.

THE VIKING PRESS, New York, for permission to quote from THE LOYALTY OF FREE MEN by Alan Barth, 1951; and THE FORRESTAL DIARIES by Walter Millis with the collaboration of Eugene S. Duffield, 1951.

CONTENTS

CHAPTER

1 A REALISTIC ROMANCE   3
2 EXPANSION CONSTRICTS A FRIENDSHIP   23
3 RENDEZVOUS WITH REVOLUTION   49
      1. Opportunity Knocks but Three Times   49
      2. A Revolution Challenges the House of Morgan 80
4 A TOKEN OF SYMPATHY   91
5 THE BIRTH OF CONTAINMENT   105
6 SOWING DRAGON'S TEETH IN EASTERN EUROPE   131
      1. In Moscow and Washington   131
      2. At Paris   157
7 THE LONG, LEAN YEARS   177
8 THE TRAGEDY OF THE THIRTIES   231
9 CODA: THE SOPHISTRY OF SUPER-REALISM   258
   BIBLIOGRAPHY   285
   REFERENCE NOTES   289
   INDEX   347

★

AMERICAN

★

RUSSIAN

★

RELATIONS

★

1781 - 1947

The only answer for the desire for a better human life is a better human life.

Raymond Robins

Peace is a cut above war: her calls are more drastic, her dangers take more facing, her grand adventures are more full of beauty and strangeness.

Charles Edward Montague

1

☆

A REALISTIC ROMANCE

Our attachment to the United States is *obstinate, more obstinate than you are aware of.*

Count Rumiantzov to John Quincy Adams,
October, 1810

Russia and the United States may remain good friends until, each having made the circuit of half the globe in opposite directions, they shall meet and greet each other in the regions where civilization first began.

Secretary of State Seward to Cassius M. Clay,
May 6, 1861

☆☆

"It was an ironic moment in history," said Secretary of State Cordell Hull of the recognition of the Soviets by the United States in November, 1933.[1] True, the Russian had become the revolutionist and had achieved formal recognition some twelve years sooner than his earlier American counterpart; but neither John Quincy Adams nor Tsar Alexander I would have been confused by the conversations that occurred in Washington during the winter of 1933–34. Alexander might well have smiled had he overheard President Franklin Delano Roosevelt's greeting to Soviet Ambassador Alexander Troyanovsky—"I welcome you personally, Mr. Ambassador, with especial satisfaction"—for the Tsar had received Adams with equal warmth —"I am so glad to see you here."[2] These were but the verbal and visible expressions of a far more significant parallel. Both Adams and Alexander would have recognized that the threatened disruption of a mutually acceptable *status quo* had once again dulled the antagonisms engendered by the conflict of two destinies—both expanding and both avowedly manifest.

American-Russian relations have been determined in large measure by the interplay of three factors. From 1781 to the present both nations have adjusted policy with regard to the conflict between each country's territorial and economic expansion and the actual or potential value of each nation to the other in terms of a world balance of power. Prior to the Bolshevik Revolution of November, 1917, ideological considerations were clearly secondary. But after that date the considerations noted above were complicated by Washington's reaction—economic, social, and political—to the Revolution. For the existence of a Marxian state forced the West to formulate an answer to the challenge inherent in that fact. Yet Washington's response to the Bolshevik Revolution only intensified the policy toward Russia that was formulated a generation earlier. A review of American-Russian relations from 1781 to 1917 reveals that the early friendship between the two countries was at first blurred and then destroyed in the heat of a struggle in Northeast Asia. The Bolsheviks did not disrupt that loose and informal entente—it was ruptured along the rights of way of the South Manchurian and Chinese Eastern Railways between 1895 and 1912. Though certain groups made strenuous efforts to effect a *rapprochement* from 1917 to 1937, the break remained until temporarily fused in the heat of a new struggle to preserve the *status quo*.

During the hundred years that followed United States Minister to Russia Francis Dana's unsuccessful efforts to secure recognition from Empress Catherine—he waited in the diplomatic antechamber some twenty-seven months—the relations between the United States and Russia were in large measure cordial. This unusual and interested friendship was simple in design. Russia gave way every time her territorial expansion clashed with that of the United States in order to preserve their common front against Great Britain. And during the critical years of the mid-nineteenth century the United States took care to preserve credit in St. Petersburg for similar reasons. Indeed, had the Continental Congress of the United States not been so enamored of formal alliances these mutual interests might well have been recognized some twenty years earlier.

The instructions given Dana by the Continental Congress were admirably brief and direct, and it is easy to comprehend their intent. But they were most unrealistic—a hopeful expression of a need. Dana was charged with three tasks: (1) to "use every means which can be devised" to secure formal admission to the League of Armed Neutrality; (2) "to engage her Imperial Majesty to favor and support the sovereignty and independence of the United States"; and (3) to conclude a treaty of amity and commerce "agreeable to the spirit of those existing between the United States and France." [3] As to membership in the League, that was impossible for the simple reason that the United States was a belligerent.[4] Nor could an eager and overt response to the other aims be expected.

Catherine was then engaged in a program of expansion that irritated at least one raw nerve on the edge of Britain's own empire—Turkey—and she was in no position to risk further antagonism. England's position was unequivocal: her representative warned that it "was not sound policy" to risk a sure thing for an unknown quantity.[5] Catherine's refusal to receive the impatient Dana is quite understandable. But just as she chafed under England's control, so did she give Dana assurances for the future. The colonial victory was near in June, 1783, and Dana was promised recognition when the peace treaties were signed.[6] Russia made it clear that she would move as soon as England accepted the fact of American independence.[7]

But victory over England caused even so ardent a representative of the commercial interests as Alexander Hamilton to act on a short-range view of the situation. Britain's defeat "removed the primary object" of Dana's mission, declared Hamilton, and he counseled his return to the United States.[8] The Congress concurred, Dana was recalled, and there were no further direct negotiations between the two governments until Napoleon Bonaparte reminded each of the other's existence.

Early in 1798 both the United States and Russia acted against the threat of French expansion. The United States broke relations with her recent, and vital, ally and prepared for war. At the same time a Russian representative approached Rufus King, the American minister in London, with a view to furthering two broad policy concepts.[9] Russia's immediate concern was to consolidate the opposition against France. But the heart of the matter was St. Petersburg's desire to reach an understanding with a naval power through which she could protect herself against England's control of the sea. This mutual interest in the expansion of neutral rights—so as to remove naval stores from the wartime contraband list, for example—caused a flurry of excitement and a series of exploratory conferences. When, however, it became apparent that the United States would patch up its quarrel with France, the talks were abandoned.[10] Russia's first fear was the expansion of France and for the moment, at least, she was allied with England.

The collapse of these negotiations did not alter the basic community of interest between Russia and the United States. Recognition of this fact was greatly facilitated by the personal friendship between President Thomas Jefferson and Emperor Alexander I, both of whom acceded to power in 1801. Jefferson made the first move when he appointed Levett Harris, an old political friend from Pennsylvania, as consul at St. Petersburg. Russia's response was immediate. Harris was admitted to full standing at court and became the object of "flattering attention." [11] A more practical demonstration of Russia's desire for closer relations soon followed. Alexander intervened to save an American ship that had been captured after grounding on the coast of Tripoli. Jefferson personally thanked the Emperor and at the same time spoke of his hope for increased trade between the two countries through a policy of "more liberality . . . in voluntary regulations." [12]

During the next two years Jefferson assiduously cultivated Alexander's early liberalism in the firm belief that as long as Alexander ruled, Russia would be "the most cordially friendly to us of any power on earth." [13] As Jefferson acknowledged to his new friend, they held "a common interest in the neutral rights." It was a source of "great happiness," continued the President, to know that Alexander would give "protection" to these rights through a "correct definition" whenever peace should be concluded.[14] To William Duane, an American friend who questioned this policy, Jefferson was even more explicit. Duane was advised, in "confidence," that he had "not appraised correctly" Russia's "value to us." [15]

England's blockade of Europe, May, 1806, and Alexander's truce for time with Napoleon, July, 1807, quickened the tempo of American-Russian relations. The British move severely disrupted American trade, and Alexander's concern with neutral rights immediately became vigorous when England extended the blockade to include her former ally. Alexander and Jefferson moved independently to extend their personal friendship. In June, 1808, Russia dispatched a chargé d'affaires to the United States; but Jefferson had appointed a minister to the court at St. Petersburg before that news reached Washington. Alexander was advised that the purpose was to promote "useful intercourse and good understanding." [16] A more forthright explanation was given Duane. "I thought it a salutary measure to engage the powerful patronage of Alexander at conferences for peace," Jefferson amplified, ". . . it is prudent for us to cherish his good disposition, as those alone which will be exerted in our favor when that occasion shall occur." [17] Alexander, to be sure, understood the more formal wording. He assured Minister John Quincy Adams that Russia would not submit to the "intolerable" English regulation of "fair and lawful commerce" between nations. Adams answered with the promise that the United States would do all it could—consistent with its policy of non-entanglement—to "contribute to the support of" the Tsar's "liberal principles." [18]

Yet even before Adams arrived in St. Petersburg the long struggle around the northern perimeter of the Pacific Basin had begun. The Russians had developed an extensive fur trade along the northwest coast of North America during the eighteenth century and in 1799 formally organized it as a monopoly under the Russian-American Company. The company's patent granted it sole rights down to fifty-one degrees north latitude. But by May 17, 1808, the competition offered by American interlopers had become so intense that Russia officially protested. St. Petersburg proposed that American traders be advised to secure their furs solely from agents of the Russian-American Company in the future. But Russia did not press the request and it was ignored for two years.[19]

Adams, meanwhile, moved to secure Alexander's assistance for American commerce. Although the Baltic States supported Washington's interpretation of neutral rights they were under close surveillance by Napoleon's troops—and Bonaparte's Continental System classed American ships as enemy vessels subject to seizure. Adams counted a total of fifty-two such prizes during his voyage to Russia. His first official maneuver was to request Russian pressure to effect their release. It was a bold move, and Adams openly relied on the Emperor's "good will" toward the United States. The Russian foreign minister did not think much could be done, but Alexander "judged differently," and the Danes were advised that Russia desired to have "the American property restored as soon as possible." Then came American ships detained in Russian ports through French pressure. This was a far more daring demand, for Russia was tacitly Napoleon's ally. But once again—this time because of Russia's own need—Adams was successful. "It seems you are great favorites here," acknowledged the defeated French diplomat; "you have found powerful protection." [20]

And most valuable, the Frenchman might have added. For Russia's determination to maintain her friendship with the United States as a check against Great Britain was a key to American expansion in the Northwest. Not only did Russia decline to make a serious issue of competing claims; Russia ultimately withdrew entirely from the region. During the interlude the Tsar's policy afforded Adams an opportunity to squeeze England on the Oregon question. Early in January, 1810, Russia reopened the discussion of American penetration into the Russian-American Company's territory and requested Washington to prohibit further American trade with the natives.[21] The United States recognized that such an agreement would seriously impair its own claims (and ambitions), and when the Russian representative confessed his lack of authority to name a demarcation line, the discussions in Washington were terminated. "The limit," Adams was advised for future guidance, "should be as little advanced southwardly as may be." [22]

The warning was unnecessary. John Quincy Adams was a vigorous exponent of manifest destiny, and had no inclination to delimit American expansion on the North American continent.[23] Nor did the unusual and generous, if necessary and diversionary, request that America handle the "trade from the Russian settlement on the northwest coast of America to China" deter him from a blunt challenge. Straight to the point was his request on the Russian claims—"point them out to me." That, he was told, would "require some consideration." [24] At their next meeting on the issue, Adams politely reminded the Tsar's agent of their mutual concern with freedom of trade, and again raised the boundary question. As for that, responded the Russian, it would be best to defer such issues so as to avoid all pretext for "jealousy or uneasiness." [25]

Another clash between the spearheads of expansion did not occur until Adams had become Secretary of State. For the time being Washington fell back on Jefferson's earlier formula and offered to conduct trade in the Northwest on a "mutually liberal" basis. Russia accepted the proposal.

"It is the interest of Russia," reiterated Alexander's spokesman, "to encourage and strengthen and multiply commercial powers which might be the rivals of England, to form a balance to her overbearing power." [26] It was "probable," Adams advised the court shortly thereafter, that the rivalry between the United States and Great Britain would lead to war.[27] This was unwelcome news to Russia, coming as it did when her relations with France had begun to deteriorate. Alexander was disturbed when, on the eve of his preparations for the expected attack, he learned that Adams "had no doubt" as to the certainty of war.[28] But on June 25, 1812, Napoleon invaded Russia and the Tsar's immediate concern was armed resistance.

Three months later Alexander learned that his fears had materialized. He had meanwhile concluded peace with England—but now it was of little significance. The Tsar was "much concerned and disappointed to find the whole benefit which he had expected his subjects would derive commercially" from the move was "lost." [29] He quickly offered to mediate a settlement. President James Madison, well aware that Russia hoped to derive "advantage from the *neutral* interference with British monopoly in [her] trade," quickly accepted the offer. "We shall endeavor," he wrote Jefferson, "to turn the good will of Russia to the proper account." [30] The move was successful. Although England declined the Tsar's formal offer—"because," as Secretary of State James Monroe noted, "she wished to prevent a concert between" the United States and Russia—London did propose direct negotiations with Washington.[31] For a time Russia continued to press her mediation offer, but after Napoleon's retreat from Moscow the Tsar relaxed his efforts and took no part in the Anglo-American peace talks at Ghent.

Alexander, however, was not idle. With Austria, Great Britain, and Prussia, he made vigorous efforts to secure the final defeat of Napoleon. These nations formed a four-power alliance on March 1, 1814, and restated the terms in the Treaty of Paris on November 20, 1815. Alexander considered these treaties insufficient to insure the future peace of Europe and organized a further guarantee—the Holy Alliance, signed on September 26, 1815, by Austria, Prussia, and Russia. But Viscount Castlereagh, England's foreign minister, refused to accept Alexander's proposed extension of the original treaties. The old agreements had been formed to defeat France, he maintained; and though they contained "some few regulations not strictly territorial" there was no provision for the "Government of the World, or for the Superintendence of the Internal Affairs of other States." Castlereagh had no intention of limiting England's "due faculty of independent action." [32] For Alexander, this rebuff was an added incentive to secure the adherence of the United States to his Holy League of Allied Sovereigns.

This plan was delayed by a quasi-formal rupture in relations with Washington caused by the misconduct of the Russian consul general in

Philadelphia. The consul's arrest and brief confinement in jail on a charge of rape precipitated a bitter debate over the extent of consular immunity. The Russian representative in Washington broke off relations, October 31, 1816, and the Tsar refused to receive Harris in St. Petersburg. Despite these dramatic reactions, the entire affair was settled on the basis of the American contention that consular privileges did not include the violation of local laws. The Russian minister who so abruptly terminated relations was recalled, and the newly arrived American minister was welcomed into the Tsar's Imperial Circle during the New Year's Ball.[33] The unprecedented honor was symbolic of Alexander's determination to retain—and extend— his friendship with the United States.

The instructions given Pierre de Poletica, the new Russian minister to the United States, reflected this resolve.[34] Poletica's first task was to secure the entrance of the United States into the Holy Alliance. The Tsar had some reason to hope for success in the matter. Various peace societies had been organized in the United States after 1815, and these organizations gave enthusiastic support to Alexander's League—that "wonderful alliance." The Tsar was understandably pleased with such a response from the very object of his diplomatic attentions, and he assured his American supporters that he would continue to work for the "blessings of peace." [35]

Secretary of State John Quincy Adams, the man with whom Poletica had to deal, did not share his countrymen's enthusiasm for Alexander's plans. The Tsar's correspondents, he remarked privately, might "find themselves under the necessity of corresponding with attorney generals and petit juries at home." [36] This threat to invoke the Logan Act of 1798— passed to punish a Philadelphia Quaker who also sought peace—was never carried through. To Poletica, Adams was far more tactful. The Russian plan was to hold out the guarded promise of support against Great Britain if Washington would join the Alliance. Make the proposal on the grounds of "their own interest," Poletica was advised. The Russian envoy did just that during three interviews with Adams, but the Secretary had no intention of limiting his freedom of action and therefore declined the invitation. Poletica concluded that the only course was to "postpone indefinitely the question." [37] Indefinitely became forever.

Poletica's second effort—to persuade the United States to withhold recognition of the new South American republics—was equally unsuccessful. The confidential warnings Adams had received as to the possibility that the Holy Alliance might intervene on behalf of Spain were reinforced by the Alliance's declaration of May 12, 1821, which held that reform "must emanate only" from God's chosen monarchs.[38] Neither Russia's acceptance of American expansion at Spain's loss (Adams' Transcontinental Treaty of February 22, 1819, severely trimmed Madrid's claims in the trans-Mississippi West) nor Poletica's effort to revive the old neutral rights' controversy with England was of any avail. Adams refused to modify his support of the South American revolutionists.[39] More important than the Secretary's abstract—or specific—approval of South Americans ("We shall derive no improvement to our institutions by any communion with theirs.") was his concern with territorial *and* commercial expansion.[40]

Adams had manifested his expansionist sentiments while at the court of the Tsar. It was "a nation coextensive with the North American continent, destined by God and nature to be the most populous and most powerful people ever combined under one social compact" that he foresaw in the summer of 1811. Nor did he have any doubts as to the justification of General Andrew Jackson's invasion of Florida seven years later. "If the question is dubious," he judged, "it is better to err on the side of vigor." Shortly thereafter he further emphasized that the world "must be familiarized with the idea of considering our proper domain to be the continent of North America." [41] Equally clear was his determination to preserve and extend the right of commercial penetration overseas. The principle of the most-favored nation, Adams instructed his agents, must be "assumed as the basis of negotiation." [42] First came France, and he held out until Paris accepted the formula. In another instance Adams employed discriminatory legislation to secure what he considered "the great foundation of our foreign policy." Such coercion was used in an effort to break down Great Britain's colonial preference system.[43]

It is understandable, therefore, why Adams grew disturbed over new reports of Russian interest in the Northwest. Soon after he took office as Secretary of State in September, 1817, he was advised that Russian activity in the area was on the increase. Adams discounted these early alarms, however, and advised the American minister to Russia that the area could never "form a subject of serious difference, or jarring interest" between the two nations.[44] The Secretary soon changed his mind. Late in 1818 a departmental agent in California filed a report—considerably exaggerated—that the Russians were about to seize San Francisco Bay. Soon thereafter St. Petersburg denied a rumor that Spain was to cede her California claims to the Tsar, but the American representative emphasized his own belief that Russia was on the move.[45] By this time Adams was most concerned; doubly so because he was under fire from Western politicians who were exceedingly anxious to secure the Columbia River Valley.[46] And the Tsar provided them with a second issue.

On September 4, 1821, Alexander signed a militant edict which closed the northern Pacific from the Kurile Islands off Siberia around to the fifty-first parallel on the American continent. All foreigners were prohibited from trading and fishing; and no foreign ship could approach within one hundred and fifteen miles of the coast. Nine days later he renewed the

charter of the Russian-American Company and extended its domain south
to the new demarcation line. These moves appear to have been prompted
more by the company's effective pressure at court than by any serious desire
on Alexander's part to extend his holdings in North America.[47]

Western congressmen viewed the matter in a different light. Less than
a week after the Tsar's ukase reached Washington—it was passed on to the
Washington *National Intelligencer* the day it arrived—they pushed through
a resolution demanding information on foreign claims to the Pacific Coast.[48]
This pressure, coupled with the Administration's own concern in the matter, forced Adams to deal with a question apt to create "jealousy or uneasiness." "It is not impossible," judged the editor of Niles' *Weekly Register*, "that we may get into a dispute with Russia in regard to our claims." [49]

President James Monroe had foreseen such a development. The "only
circumstance in which a difference of interest is anticipated between the
United States and Russia," he wrote in 1816, "related to their respective
claims on the Pacific Ocean." At that time he considered the forty-ninth
parallel to be a "satisfactory" boundary. But by 1822, so Adams advised
the Russian minister, the President had changed his mind. Russia's preten-
tions to the fifty-first parallel, specified the Secretary, occasioned some
"surprise"; and equally disturbing was Russia's claim to jurisdiction over
the high seas "beyond the ordinary distance." [50]

Russia answered that the United States had settled with Spain at the
forty-second parallel, and between that and the Tsar's line there were
some five hundred miles. The new line, moreover, was roughly halfway
between the American-Spanish settlement and Madrid's old claim to the
sixtieth degree. As for the limitation on navigation, Russia declared that she
had adopted the restriction only in a final effort to control the illegal American traders. After all, so the argument ran, Russia controlled both shores
of the ocean area in question—she could declare that entire surface a
closed sea.[51]

Adams did not immediately press the issue with his usual vigor. For
one thing, Washington desired to avoid any undue strain on the old friendship. More to the point was the fact that Alexander was arbitrating a dispute between London and Washington. The Treaty of Ghent provided for
the restitution of any "possessions" taken after the war had ended. Compensation for slaves deported after that date was claimed by the United
States on behalf of certain of its citizens. The Tsar had been called in to
settle the affair when the two powers failed to agree. In such a ticklish
matter it was unwise to antagonize the judge. At this juncture the Russian
minister announced his return to St. Petersburg on leave of absence. Adams dropped his reserved attitude and (without word of the Tsar's decision
in the dispute with England) advised Russia of "the impossibility that the

United States should acquiesce either" in the announced restriction of trade or the new boundary.[52] But this belated firmness in no measure satisfied the Secretary's critics.

The pressure for more vigorous expansion in the Northwest mounted steadily through the remainder of 1822 and 1823. Very shortly the Westerners picked up support in New England—Adams' own bailiwick. The Boston shippers (concerned with the fur trade to China) and the Massachusetts whaling interests signified their concern early in 1822; and their campaign gathered strength when Russia's firmness became general knowledge. The Newburyport *Herald* used a play on words to indicate its militance. The editor first noted that the Russian minister cited "Techine-*off*" and others with similar names as "the authority by which he hopes to urge us *off* and warn us *off*." He then pointed out that the American suffix appeared to be "*on*," and cited "Madis*on*" and "Jeffers*on*" as examples. "Jacks*on*," the editorial concluded, was one "who will, no doubt, dash *on* towards Columbia River and take *off* the heads of all the *offs* that can be sent to oppose him." [53] Niles' *Register* was no less forceful. "The question of war or peace will entirely depend upon the will and interest of Russia," was the flat assertion, for the claims, "if persisted in, must necessarily lead to a maritime war." [54] This concern with Russia's activity in the Northwest was underscored at the end of 1822 when a Massachusetts representative supported Western demands for immediate action.[55]

Nor did the clamor taper off with the new year. Niles' *Register* called the edict "preposterous" and assured its readers that the United States frigate in the Pacific was "an able negociator." One of the Baltimore *Chronicle*'s readers composed a ditty to express his sentiments.

> "Brother Jove must look out for his skies,
>   let me tell ye,
>   Or the Russian will bury them all in his
>   belly."

Not to be outdone, Niles declared that Alexander's army was "composed of slaves" who were a "more stupid race of men than the black slaves of America." [56] By June, 1823, both Adams and the new Russian minister, Baron de Tuyll, were understandably upset. Tuyll asked Adams to counteract this unfavorable comment immediately after his arrival. Finally, in response to the Russian's complaint about an article in the Boston *Sentinel*, Adams agreed to take action. As was his custom, the Secretary wrote "a paragraph on the subject" which soon appeared as an editorial in the *National Intelligencer*. Adams emphasized that "the well-known moderation" of Alexander would assure a favorable settlement of the issue. Tuyll responded with profuse "thanks." [57]

Adams was merely marking time—his pro-expansionist sentiments remained unmodified. The Secretary, no doubt, was aware of another aspect of the situation. His presidential possibilities would be seriously damaged unless he moved to satisfy the widespread geographic as well as economic demands for action against Russia. In January, 1823, the Maine legislature had indicated support for him, and by April he was "seriously spoken of" as a candidate.[58] True, Adams had declared that only "the wishes, ardent and active, of others" would make him available; but when an opponent began to gain strength in New England he warned himself "to persevere." [59] Shortly thereafter he stepped up his offensive against both England and Russia.

The Secretary's strategy was obvious—play London and St. Petersburg against each other to Washington's advantage. The first step was to formulate instructions for the American minister in Russia, as the dispute had been transferred to the Tsar's home grounds. Adams desired to admit "no territorial right" on the entire continent, but the Cabinet finally resolved to "offer to agree to a boundary line for Russia at 55°" in return for unlimited trade with the natives. That the Secretary disliked the compromise was evident. Three weeks later he ignored the cabinet decision and advised Baron de Tuyll that the United States would "contest the right of Russia to *any* territorial establishment on this continent." And still later, on July 22, he again ignored the Cabinet. "There can, perhaps, be no better time for saying, frankly and explicitly, to the Russian Government," he instructed his agent in Russia, "that the future peace of the world, and the interest of Russia herself, cannot be promoted by Russian settlements upon any part of the American continent." [60] The Monroe Doctrine, it would appear, began to take shape in response to Russian—not British—action.

During these same weeks Adams proposed to Great Britain that the two countries jointly oppose the Russian claims. This policy was based on a bold bluff—the tacit assumption that London had abandoned all claims to the Columbia Valley. The Secretary blandly suggested that England join the United States to hold Russia at the fifty-fifth parallel and at the same time agree to stay north of the fifty-first. The "finger of nature," explained Adams, "pointed to this settlement." [61] Both sets of instructions were on their way by the end of July, 1823. Russian activity on the Northwest coast had aroused considerable opposition on the part of interested parties in the United States—parties who found John Quincy Adams most sympathetic to their demands for resolute action.

Adams was to push his policy still further. While he had been engaged with the problem of the Northwest coast, France had intervened in the Spanish rebellion on behalf of the conservatives. This development further modified Washington's approval of the current revolutionary spirit in South America. Members of the Administration had never been enthusiastic over the idea of a Cuban revolution, and the new intervention by France

heightened their concern. Far better that Spain retain a precarious hold
on the island than have it taken over by France—a strong power. That,
Adams fretted, might well repeal "the law of political gravitation" which
he confidently expected (sooner or later) to bring Cuba under American
control.[62] Small wonder, then, that he opposed Monroe's idea to secure
British co-operation against transatlantic intervention on the basis of a
mutual promise not to annex the island.

England's uneasiness, meanwhile, caused her to make the first move.
The precedent established by France greatly disturbed the British Foreign
Office. London's interest in the freedom—commercial as well as political
—of the Spanish colonies had been voiced as early as 1812. In that year
Castlereagh advised Madrid that unless commercial freedom was extended
to the colonies "without loss of time, their separation from the parent state
[was] inevitable and at hand." [63] The desired condition had been attained,
but it, like the status of Cuba, was apt to be forcibly revised if France
should move on from intervention in Spain to a new bid for empire.

This fear recalled American concern for Cuba. That, in turn, suggested to the British the possibility of joint action to forestall further
French action. The British foreign minister turned to the American representative in London. "What do you think your Government would say,"
he queried, "to going hand in hand with England in such a policy?" "I am
unable to say," parried the American agent, and referred the matter to
Washington.[64] This exchange occurred in mid-August, 1823, but the time
lag in communications coupled with Monroe's private consultations on the
matter delayed full cabinet discussions until the first week in November.

Russia raised the issue more directly. On October 16, 1823, Baron de
Tuyll advised Adams of Alexander's Doctrine of Non-Recognition as applied to the new Spanish American nations. The Emperor, continued Tuyll,
was pleased to note that Washington's policy of neutrality had been continued after recognition. That declaration of neutrality, shot back Adams,
"had been made under the observance of neutrality by all the European
Powers to the same contest." The interview concluded shortly, but the
Secretary's curtness carried over for a considerable time. Two days later
he prepared an answer to the Russian that formed the basis of all future
discussions concerning the Holy Alliance. As one of the *"Christian* Nations *of Christians,"* Adams taunted the Tsar, the United States was "satisfied" that the colonies "had become irrevocably Independent of Spain."
On that basis, concluded the Secretary, the United States had received and
would "continue to receive and send Agents Diplomatic and Commercial"
to the nations in question.[65]

This tentative answer to Tuyll was not discussed until the Cabinet
gathered to consider the British proposal. Adams viewed London's overture, whatever its form, to be aimed "really or especially against the ac-

quisition to the United States of any part of the Spanish-American possession." He did not care to discuss the "expediency" of such annexation at the moment—the point was to "keep ourselves free to act as emergencies may arise, and not tie ourselves down." That issue clarified, Adams presented his draft of an answer to the Tsar. "It would be more candid," he calmly announced, "as well as more dignified, to avow our principles explicitly to Russia and France, than to come as a cock-boat in the wake of the British man-of-war." The Secretary then read his draft message. Objections were immediately raised over the "sarcastic" tone, and the discussion that followed failed of any conclusion. Instead, Adams was instructed to seek amplification of the Russian note.[66]

The next two weeks were filled with a long series of conferences between Adams and Tuyll. Cabinet discussions continued concurrently. The Secretary, who no more believed that the Holy Alliance would restore Spanish sovereignty in South America "than that the Chimborazo will sink beneath the ocean," concentrated on Russia. The news that British ardor for a joint declaration had cooled considerably—Paris had given way in the face of a unilateral warning from London—simplified Adams' problem. Almost simultaneously, moreover, the Russians further antagonized Adams. Tuyll presented a new note which the Secretary viewed as "an 'Io Triumphe' over the fallen cause of revolution, with sturdy promises of determination to keep it down." [67]

The vigor of his earlier message aroused so many doubts that the final form remained indefinite for three days. In one sense the original draft was a full-length—and quite didactic—essay on republican principles. The Secretary summarized them in the second paragraph as if for a schoolboy. This "hornet of a paragraph" caused prolonged cabinet discussion, and was finally omitted by Adams.[68] The deletion in no manner altered the meaning of the final draft, as Adams made it quite clear that "the Monarchical principle of Government is different from theirs in the United States." As for the case in point, Washington would maintain relations with the new states. "Relations the more important to the interests of the United States," Adams amplified, "as the whole of those emancipated Regions are situated in their own Hemisphere, *and as the most extensive, populous and powerful of the new Nations are in their immediate vicinity; and one of them bordering upon the Territories of this Union.*" [69]

Alexander was the only figure to be so honored with a private note. That fact underscores the Secretary's preoccupation with Russia. Only Adams' unusual zeal in the matter could have prompted his complaint that "the cream of my paper" had been skimmed. But the Russian minister clearly understood what he heard, even though Adams thought it "a fabric without foundation." He immediately assured the Secretary that "it was not necessary, nor could it be useful, to enter upon a discussion" of such different opinions. Tuyll took care to emphasize that point.[70]

"Difference of principle," he told Adams, "did not necessarily involve hostile collision between them."

Those words were an oblique admission that Alexander was in no sense poised to invade the Western Hemisphere. Of sympathy and concern for Spain there were plenty, but little imminent danger.[71] Adams knew that to be the case. His militance was due to other factors. Obvious, of course, was his personal eagerness to answer Alexander's statement of political principles. And whatever the degree of his awareness of the growing trade with Spanish America there can be no question of his intense concern with the Northwest boundary question.

The fact that President Monroe emphasized the Holy Alliance and the problem of South American intervention in his message to Congress on December 2, 1823, tended to obscure the boundary issue. Only the Philadelphia *National Gazette and Literary Register* connected the message with opposition to Russia. The New York *Spectator* did not think it concerned the Russian-American Company. Niles' *Register,* whose extreme distaste for Alexander and the Holy Alliance ("most foul conspirators") was of long standing, could only lament that the real motivation had not been made clear. "There must," puzzled the editor, "be some special *reason* for putting it forth." [72] Curiously, he missed one of the best clues—his own earlier campaign against Russian claims. The Russians, however, clearly understood the President's language.

This became apparent when the boundary dispute was reopened in St. Petersburg on February 9, 1824. By that time the British had spotted the trap—one jaw at fifty-five degrees, the other at fifty-one—set for them by Adams and had refused to participate in three-way negotiations.[73] But Monroe's message did not cause the Russian retreat. As early as June 24, 1823, a spokesman for the Tsar made it clear that Alexander had "already had the good sense to see that this affair should not be pushed too far." The American agent could not have been too surprised, then, by the Russian's opening proposal. Let us, he suggested, "waive all discussions upon abstract principles of right and upon the actual state of facts and settle the differences in a manner conformable to [our] mutual interests." [74]

The United States accepted this proposal and negotiations opened immediately. Russia shortly agreed to freedom of trade and navigation throughout the Pacific subject only to the provision that permission be secured before the traders came ashore. To the third American stipulation—"the boundary line within which the Emperor Paul had granted exclusive privileges to the Russian Company, that is to say, latitude fifty-five"—Russia offered resistance. She desired to limit the access of foreign ships north of the boundary and to shift that line to fifty-four degrees forty minutes. Prolonged discussion ensued on these points, and it was not until April 17, 1824, that the convention was signed. As the agreement gave rise to a heated dispute in later years certain clauses should be clarified.

Article I guaranteed freedom of navigation, fishing, and trading on the Pacific Ocean and along its shores "saving always the restrictions and conditions determined by the following articles." Article III explicitly established the line fifty-four forty as a boundary. The United States agreed not to make "any establishment upon the northwest coast of America, or in any of the islands adjacent" north of the agreed parallel. Russia was to observe similar restrictions south of the line. Article IV, however, caused trouble. It specified a reciprocal right to "frequent without any hindrance . . . for the purpose of fishing and trading with the natives" the coast above and below the boundary for a term of ten years. Both parties had already agreed, however, that this reciprocity could "not be extended beyond the said term but by mutual consent." It was, observed Niles' *Register*, an "honorable and advantageous" settlement.[75]

But the American minister in St. Petersburg claimed he had settled spheres of interest rather than a boundary. All areas but those of actual Russian settlement he considered to "fall into the general category of unoccupied places upon the coasts of the great ocean." The State Department adopted this interpretation—despite the previous understanding about renewal—when Russia began to exclude American traders upon the expiration of Article IV. But Washington did not press its case until an American brig was forced to sea by armed Russian vessels. Secretary of State John Forsyth termed the act "most unfriendly," and a serious crisis appeared imminent. The Secretary's protest was somewhat ill-advised, for the fact of Russian settlements at the point in question left St. Petersburg in the clear even under an American interpretation of the treaty.

Forsyth's real object was to prevent Russia from integrating her claim to sovereignty north of latitude fifty-four forty. It is even possible that he stood in the vanguard of the later movement to squeeze England out of Oregon (Fifty-four Forty or Fight!) and extend the United States north to the Russian line. But if such was the case the Secretary soon discovered that he had overreached himself. The territory was but sparsely settled and the epidemic of "Oregon fever" was some five years in the future. Forsyth's flurry of excitement soon died out: in part because other issues (Texas, for example) demanded more attention, but primarily because American trade in the area was "too inconsiderable to attract much attention." [76]

That statement could not have been applied to the revolt of Russian Poland in 1830. Americans immediately expressed sympathy for the rebels and later collected funds for the cause. The money reached Poland too late to be of issue, but the anti-Russian tone of the American press did cause a minor incident. The Russian minister was ordered to ignore the expressions of unfavorable opinion in the United States, but he violated his instructions when the Washington *Globe*, generally considered the Administration's mouthpiece, joined the attack on Tsar Nicholas I, who had succeeded Alexander in 1825. His offensive official protest ultimately provoked a demand that the document be withdrawn—though the Secretary of State had registered no complaint when he saw it prior to delivery. Russia expressed regret and soon withdrew, unofficially, the agent who had erred.[77]

Russia's view of the matter was obvious—newspaper complaints in the United States were far less important than the official protests received from Great Britain and France. The situation offered the United States a splendid opportunity to conclude the long-sought-after treaties dealing with commerce and neutral rights. American Minister James Buchanan began to push the issue soon after his arrival in June, 1832; but the Tsar was "very reluctant to ruffle England . . . by any novel arrangement upon the claims of neutrals and maritime rights." [78]

After further delays caused by the Polish revolt and the new high tariff passed by Congress—the famous "Tariff of Abominations"—Buchanan did negotiate a separate commercial treaty in November, 1832. The minister's considerable tact, skill, and finesse—he proposed the treaty be signed on the Tsar's birthday—contributed in large measure to this success. But in the matter of a neutral rights convention the Tsar's hesitance to offend Great Britain could not be overcome. In confidence, Russia did give Washington "formal assurance" that when the United States was at war she would observe "strict neutrality," and "observe the most favorable principles" when at war herself.[79] Little more could have been asked.

Russia collected her first dividend on this policy of "obstinate" attachment to the United States during the Crimean War. As in the past, controversy between the United States and Great Britain was a major factor in the situation. Disputes and differences over Cuba, Central America, the Oregon territory, and fishing rights along the North Atlantic coast heightened the old disagreement over neutral rights. More significant in view of later developments was the Russian support of American plans for economic expansion in the Near East, the Southwest Pacific, and North China.

The Russian representatives in Washington, an ambitious pair with a preference for dramatic diplomacy, conceived grandiose schemes to make the United States an active ally of Russia. Their first plan (1853–54) was to engineer a dispute between England and the United States over neutral rights. Secretary of State William Marcy's comment that indications of forthcoming Anglo-French intervention in Latin America tended "to Russify us" no doubt encouraged them; but England checked the maneuver—by accepting Washington's dictum that the flag covered the cargo—and their own superiors warned them to avoid any move that might antagonize the United States. Russia preferred to build up credit for future needs.

This policy also secured certain immediate gains. Washington allowed the sale of Russian ships interned after the outbreak of war, protected a ship built for Russia in New York after it had put to sea, and demanded the recall of the English minister who led a recruiting campaign for the British Army from his office in the Legation.[80]

Led by Senators Charles Sumner, chairman of the Senate Foreign Relations Committee, and Hamilton Fish, the Senate pressed the President to offer his good offices to end the war. Russia was at first skeptical of Washington's motivation. Later, when St. Petersburg evidenced more confidence, the matter hung fire because of American hostility to England. "Defiant" Sebastopol no doubt won many hearts, but the "old dislike of Great Britain" and Southern (and Northern) sympathy for the system of serfdom were equally important in the formation of this attitude. The London *Times* blamed such belligerence on the "ranting and vindictive fury of Irish rebels and Cuban filibusterios" and retaliated in kind. The British fleet, warned the editor, could well "summer in the Gulf of Mexico." Speculation as to the offer of mediation continued throughout the war but no formal offer was ever made.[81]

Nonetheless Washington and St. Petersburg exchanged quite tangible expressions of understanding. The American consul in Hawaii advised the Russians of a forthcoming Anglo-French attack off Siberia—a warning that enabled the Tsar's fleet to score a brilliant victory. For her part, Russia made it known that she would not protest if the United States annexed the Hawaiian group. And when Secretary Marcy indicated interest in offering competition to the British economic penetration of Persia it appears that Russia responded favorably. More explicit was the Tsar's assurance that he would no longer support Spain against the United States. But the most significant exchange occurred shortly after the Crimean War was over. Commercial groups in the United States inquired as to their reception in northern Manchuria and on Sakhalin Island. They were advised that the door was open.[82]

Some forty years later the heirs to this assurance arrived in force, and their vigor led to a mutual antagonism that ultimately disrupted the informal entente of the middle fifties. For the time American-Russian relations remained firm. Nothing strengthened the bond more than Russia's "unequivocal assurance" of support for the Union after the outbreak of the American Civil War. Russia's first act set the tone for the next four years. On August 24, 1861, Washington and St. Petersburg signed a maritime treaty that—when England and France recognized the Southern Confederacy as a belligerent—automatically classed Northern privateers as pirate vessels subject to discrimination. The Russian minister called this to the attention of Secretary of State William H. Seward—much to the latter's consternation. "I never thought of that," he confessed. Thanks to the Russian's astuteness, the unpleasant consequences were avoided by the simple device of delayed ratification.[83]

Throughout the remainder of the Civil War Russia maintained her support of the North. The Tsar and his advisors no doubt entertained a sincere desire to see the Union preserved as a bulwark against Britain, but other considerations also influenced Russia's decision. Chief among these concerns was the well-planned Polish revolt of 1863. England and France had gone on record in favor of some measure of Polish autonomy as early as 1815, and the French Emperor's plan to erect an independent Polish state had been well known even before the Crimean War. Urged on by public sympathy for the Poles, London and Paris filed an official protest against the Tsar's fierce measures of retaliation. Unperturbed by its rejection, England and France then requested the United States to sign a second note. In the face of considerable American support for the Poles —Senator Sumner added his weight to the religious, political, and financial campaigns in their behalf—Secretary Seward declined to join the Anglo-French front.

Whatever the extent of his personal sympathy for the Poles, Seward candidly admitted that there was "an insurmountable difficulty in the way of any active co-operation with the governments of France, Austria, and Great Britain." [84] That difficulty, clearly, was the principle of intervention. For if Seward intervened in Poland he would surrender far more important ground at home: and not only with reference to the Civil War, still in progress. Spain reannexed the island of Santo Domingo a month after Fort Sumter was fired on, and France invaded Mexico in force shortly thereafter. Seward moved very slowly in response to this challenge to the Monroe Doctrine—he wanted no French alliance with the Confederacy—but he did "not propose to surrender anything." [85] Nor, it should be noted, did pro-Polish Senator Sumner.

At this juncture portions of the Russian fleet dropped anchor in the ports of New York and San Francisco. Actually the ships had been sent to seek refuge in the United States as Russia seriously feared war with France and England over Poland. But that made no difference at the time. Nor did the fact that a supposedly influential minority (congressmen and newspaper editors) warned of the Tsar's selfish motives. The Russian move not only shifted American attention from the Polish revolt, but created a positive pro-Russian enthusiasm. "God bless the Russians!" cried the Secretary of the Navy, and Seward no doubt felt likewise. Public response can be gauged by the fact that a Russo-American alliance was openly discussed. The later destruction of the myth that the Russian ships arrived solely to aid the North has tended to obscure the important fact that Russia's steady and staunch support of the Union was of considerable moral and material significance.[86]

Nor were Americans of the time indifferent to that aid. Their appreciation was dramatically expressed when Tsar Alexander II narrowly escaped assassination in April, 1866. The "deep regret" of the Congress was recorded in a joint resolution that also indirectly congratulated the Tsar on his earlier emancipation of the serfs. Assistant Secretary of the Navy Gustavius V. Fox, who was commissioned as a special agent to deliver the message, also stressed emancipation as the act of an "enlightened sovereign." Fox's mission was tendered a particularly cordial welcome which seemed to extend the old friendship. These interchanges, Alexander commented, "are as conducive to their reciprocal interests as to the good of civilization and humanity." [87]

A more material exchange in terms of reciprocal interests occurred the following year when Russia sold Alaska to the United States. Several considerations moved St. Petersburg to make the transaction, among them the steady decline of the Russian-American Company. Trade revenues decreased sharply prior to the American Civil War, and an attempt to open up the mineral resources of the area collapsed by 1854. Both the Crimean War and the Civil War drove home to the Russians the fact that their hold on the territory was extremely precarious. That England fretted about its sale to Washington offered little consolation. Neither did Secretary Seward's well advertised views on American expansion.

Russian representatives no doubt recalled the Secretary's many outbursts of expansive oratory during the years of his service as a United States senator. A strong supporter of Commodore Matthew C. Perry's use of the threat of force against Japan, Seward publicly advised the United States to "command the empire of the seas." Particularly the Pacific, which he felt would become the "chief theater in the events of the world's great hereafter." His later proposals were no less direct. In 1867 the Secretary asked for no more than a guarantee against internal rebellion in exchange for an effort to take "possession of the American continent and the control of the world." [88]

Together with the steady colonization of Oregon, these sentiments made the Russian minister in Washington quite "uneasy." Nor were observers in St. Petersburg any less disturbed. "They have taken California, Oregon," runs the paraphrase of a memo to the court in 1860, "and sooner or later they will get Alaska. It is inevitable. It cannot be prevented; and it would be better to yield with good grace and cede the territory." This deference to the expansion of the United States into contiguous areas was paralleled by similar Russian plans. "Russia, too," amplified the same correspondent, "has a manifest destiny on the Amur, and further South, even in Korea."

Both Russia and the United States had already profited from the troubles of the Manchu Dynasty in China, but Russian gains had been the more tangible. Through the middle decade of the nineteenth century China was torn by the Taiping Rebellion. This civil war was complicated by two acts of Anglo-French intervention—to gain new concessions, and to secure their ratification. Though officially neutral, Washington supported the intervention and then collected equal benefits by virtue of an earlier most-favored-nation treaty. Russia also remained neutral, but for "friendly services" rendered during the treaty negotiations she regained her old title to the territory north and east of the Amur and Ussuri rivers. To this area Russia now turned her attention.

Late in 1866 the Russian court reviewed the entire problem of Alaska for the last time. The collapse of the Russian-American Company and the low level of domestic finances both contributed to the decision to sell. But more important was the growing fear that "Russian America was a breeder of trouble between America and Russia." Perhaps the main consideration was presented by the Tsar's brother. "Russia," he advised again, "should devote her energies to the development of the Amur." The deal was completed a year later in Washington. On the night of March 29, 1867, final negotiations were completed. Perhaps Seward's enthusiasm for the acquisition of territory is best revealed by the fact that he insisted that the agreement be signed then and there. He dropped his hand of whist, aroused the needed assistants, and closed the deal at about four o'clock in the morning.[89]

The treaty of transfer met strong minority resistance in Congress, and was not ratified for more than a year. The fierce struggle for control of Civil War Reconstruction policies, Seward's personal enemies, rumors of bribery, and opposition by those who considered the area worthless all contributed to the delay. But the descendants of the men who supported John Quincy Adams in his tiffs with the Tsar rallied to Secretary Seward's cause. New England shippers vouched for the value of Alaska and westerners warned that "great dissatisfaction" would follow a failure to ratify. This pressure was effective: and where more was needed the Russian minister apparently supplied cash as a substitute. The final acceptance of the treaty moved the editor of the New York *Herald* to forecast the future. The "young giants," he wrote, are "engaged in the same work—that of expansion and progression." They "must ever be friendly," was his conclusion: "the colossi having neither territorial nor maritime jealousies to excite the one against the other. The interests of both demand that they should go hand in hand in their march to empire." [90] But the young giants were not to agree.

2

☆

EXPANSION CONSTRICTS
A FRIENDSHIP

Eastern Asia now appears, without much doubt, to be the only district likely soon to be able to absorb any great manufactures, and accordingly. . . . Whether we like it or not, we are forced to compete for the seat of international exchanges, or, in other words, for the seat of empire.

Brooks Adams, February, 1899

I have not the slightest objection to the Russians knowing that I feel thoroughly aroused and irritated at their conduct in Manchuria; that I don't intend to give way.

Theodore Roosevelt to John Hay,
July 18, 1903

☆☆

The transfer of Alaska was indeed the great divide in the contour of American-Russian relations. For the United States it marked the final advance on the continent prior to a large-scale effort to penetrate the markets of Asia. To Russia it was the symbol of a decision to concentrate on the effort to gain an Asiatic outlet on the Pacific. Both decisions reflected the increased tempo of industrialization in each nation. That was the factor overlooked by the editor of the New York *Herald* in his prognostications of 1867. For the financial and industrial powers of the United States soon came to dominate their domestic market and looked abroad for new opportunities. That movement—the overseas expansion of American economic forces—ultimately clashed with Russian activity along the Amur; and though their respective interests might conceivably have been fruitfully harmonized, the final result was bitter antagonism.

Curiously enough, just such economic activities had a part in the opening stages of this steady disintegration of the old informal entente. The coincidence is unusual. One of the most vigorous supporters of Seward's purchase of Alaska was Perry McD. Collins, promoter of a trans-Pacific telegraph line. Collins' plan was taken up by the Western Union Telegraph Company in 1863; and two years later an expedition embarked from San Francisco to begin a route survey along the Amur. A member of that small party was George Kennan who in later years aroused the American public against the injustices of Tsarism and opposed the Soviets with equal vigor.[1] In conjunction with a militant campaign against Russian persecution of religious and political minorities it was Kennan who conditioned the American public to accept Washington's anti-Russian policy at the turn of the century.

Kennan's campaign was not the product of his first trip to Russia. When he embarked for Siberia in 1865 he was but twenty years old and, although an experienced telegraph operator, a man preoccupied with a serious personal problem. A traumatic experience of early childhood left him, in his own words, with a "secret but deeply rooted suspicion that I was physically a coward"; and he did not recover from the shock of that admission for many years. Kennan considered the problem solved during his Siberian venture, but whatever the degree of his psychological compensation the incident casts considerable light on his later sympathy for the strong, powerful, and successful—whether they were individuals or nations. It may also provide a clue to an understanding of "his tremendous will to power." "To this," commented a friendly observer, "there seems to be no limit." [2]

After his return from Russia in 1868, Kennan wrote a short piece for *Putnam's Magazine*, expanded it into his best seller *Tent Life in Siberia* (twenty-odd printings), and then embarked on a tour of the Caucasus. On his return to the United States, Kennan served a short stint in the law department of the Mutual Life Insurance Company and then became Supreme Court reporter for the Associated Press. Within seven years he was night manager of that organization's office in the nation's capital. Despite the heavy responsibilities of the position, Kennan undertook a long series of lectures about Siberia which carried him to the "great cities and little hamlets" alike. It was the "palmy time of the lyceum lecture," and Kennan reached the top of the circuit when he was invited to give the Lowell Institute Lectures in Boston.[3]

These lecture tours were directly responsible for Kennan's second visit to Siberia in 1884. In the course of his lectures he openly stated his belief that the "Russian Government and the exile system had been greatly misrepresented" in an unfavorable manner. Other observers, however, challenged Kennan's view. The issue began to crystallize when Kennan presented his interpretation "fully and frankly" in an address before the American Geographical Society of New York in 1882. The prolonged newspaper "controversy" that followed culminated in a heated debate between Kennan and his chief opponent in April, 1884. Kennan remained adamant in his views and the discussion appeared to have reached an impasse, but shortly thereafter the *Century Magazine* offered Kennan a commission to study the situation firsthand and report his findings. Kennan immediately accepted the offer and embarked for Russia in October of the same year.[4]

Kennan's long, depressing journey through the prisons of Siberia changed his mind. His detailed and impassioned reports explained his conversion to the readers of the *Century* and to those who waded through his two-volume study, *Siberia and the Exile System*. Avowedly conservative, Kennan was most attracted to the liberal group of exiles. His preference, however, did not blind him to the fact that even "some of the best, bravest, and most generous types of manhood" could be revolutionists. Though decrying terror, he acknowledged that "an essentially good and noble matured man" could adopt such a policy under Tsarist persecution. Kennan's candor was paralleled by an evangelistic determination to bestir the United States to action in support of the exiles.[5]

The broad plan conceived by Kennan was to create interest and concern by a second cross-country lecture tour and then focus that pressure through a special organization—the Friends of Russian Freedom. He found ready enthusiasm for his denunciations of Tsardom not only among Russian exiles, but also in the groups of urban social workers and leading intellectuals. Mark Twain, Julia Ward Howe, and James Russell Lowell were among the leaders of American thought who responded favorably to Kennan's program with both their emotions and talent. "If such a government cannot be overthrown otherwise than by dynamite," sobbed Mark Twain during one of Kennan's stirring speeches, "then, thank God for dynamite." [6] A poet admirer hailed Kennan as an "unflinching Dante of a later day." [7] The Russian Government, however, responded with something less than equal enthusiasm to Kennan's new antagonism.

St. Petersburg was, no doubt, disturbed that the courtesy extended to Kennan during his survey had borne such bitter fruit. It was a hard blow to see an earlier apologist mould adverse public opinion in both the United States and England. More disturbing, perhaps, was the fact that Kennan's writings were reprinted in pamphlet form and smuggled into Russia to give strength to those who would resist the Tsar. This literature, according to at least one Russian observer, dealt "the first crushing blow" to the myth of the Tsar and helped prepare the way for the abortive revolution of 1905.[8]

An official reply to Kennan, written by a member of the Russian legation in Washington, appeared in the *Century* itself. An open defense of autocracy and paternalism was coupled with an appeal to the old "bridge of sentiment" between the two countries.[9] Kennan replied with a public challenge as to the character of that old relationship. Russia's appeal must be held invalid, he stated flatly, since the prior cordiality had been based on neither a "similarity of institutions, nor upon affectionate esteem and good will." [10] It should be pointed out that Kennan did not demand that the United States conduct its own foreign relations upon these premises—nor Japan either, for that matter. Kennan was to make his position quite clear on those questions in the future; but for the present he divided his attention between the exiles and a second problem that was also touched upon in his acrimonious exchange with the Russian official.

This was the disturbing question of the persecution of Jews in Russia. The fact that the Tsarist spokesman mentioned the issue in his article clearly indicated that the problem was of considerable public importance during the years of Kennan's exposé of Siberian prisons. It had been the subject of diplomatic concern for some years before. By 1875, according to one Russian witness, "emigration to America and other countries had considerably increased." [11] The issue first arose when those who fled religious persecution began to return to Russia as citizens of the United States. The Russian Government, among others, denied the validity of this expatriation and treated those who returned as nationals. As early as 1873 the policy led to conflict with Washington, and during the next three decades the dispute became most embittered.

Discrimination against an earlier citizen of Rochester, New York, initiated the long argument. When Theodore Rosenstrauss returned to Kharkoff as an agent of the Singer Sewing Machine Company he found his efforts to establish what was to be known as the Theodore and Company opposed by a well-executed campaign of delay and restriction. He immediately applied to the United States Ambassador for aid, and Washington authorized an official protest in his behalf.[12] Nothing came of the effort, and Rosenstrauss appealed "in the name of humanity" to the American public to keep him from being "placed on the same footing as a common Russian laborer." [13] This move, coupled with continued pressure by the Ambassador, led to considerable agitation.

In 1879 United States Representative Samuel S. Cox of New York used the case as an example of the necessity to amend the old treaty of 1832. His resolution languished in committee, but within three years a vigorous protest movement began to exert steady pressure on the Congress. Public meetings were organized in New York, Philadelphia, and other centers from which petitions poured into Washington. Cox felt strong enough to demand—and get—a file of correspondence relative to Rosenstrauss' plight.[14]

But the agitation accomplished little. Meanwhile the struggle to survive had discouraged Rosenstrauss. A direct appeal to the President brought small solace and no relief.[15] The constant surveillance gave him the sense of being "haunted," and he made a last desperate request of the American Ambassador—secure Count Tolstoy's personal intercession.[16] The Ambassador complied, but Tolstoy had no political influence at the court of Nicholas II. Nor was the case of Rosenstrauss unique. Many others wrote of the long battle to re-establish themselves. All their reports were the same: it was a desperate existence filled with "hot sobs and tears." [17]

St. Petersburg was well aware of the unfavorable reaction in the United States, and disturbed enough to plant a quasi-official article in the *Century* even before the reply to Kennan. The earlier spokesman admitted that feeling ran "high" but blamed the socialists and other anti-property groups for the outrages. More revealing of those high officials who turned their backs on the pogroms was the claim that the persecutions were directed at "a parasitical race." [18] The *Century*'s editors replied bluntly— "Russia's most apparent duty is to civilize herself." [19] This view apparently was shared by a rather sizable heterogeneous pressure group in the United States.[20] The issue was not forced, however, until 1893, when the extradition treaty signed in 1887 finally came up for Senate approval.

American disapproval of Tsarist domestic policies intruded, meanwhile, in the discussion of famine relief during the crisis of 1891–92. Famine and resulting pestilence throughout large sections of European Russia elicited a sympathetic response from Americans who enjoyed a bountiful harvest. The Congress refused—ostensibly on the grounds of states' rights—to appropriate transportation funds, and the entire program was carried through by private finances. The debates revealed that more than states' rights were involved. Russia, declared some congressmen, should not be aided until the persecutions were halted.[21] Similar arguments were advanced by those who opposed the extradition treaty.

The bitter campaign to defeat ratification served to unite Kennan's campaign with that of the anti-pogrom group. In the meantime, the latter organization had gathered new strength. Further persecutions called forth a "small committee" of prominent citizens to direct the fight. Financier Jacob H. Schiff, "undisputed head" of Kuhn, Loeb, and Company, General Lewis Seasongood, Jesse Seligman, and Oscar Straus sponsored independent research on conditions in Russia and convinced President Benjamin Harrison that the United States "had a right to remonstrate." [22] Harrison noted the problem in his message of December, 1891, and the next year both major parties expressed indignation in their party platforms. Other groups added their weight to the opposition and by April, 1892, the House of Representatives declared that it was time to move beyond expressions of sympathy and "be of great practical service." [23] To sign the treaty, Kennan declared, would be a grievous error. Beyond the fact that Russia did not have "an honorable government," to do so would "violate every right for which the Anglo-Saxon race has fought." [24] Others opposed these views.

To some, the growing unrest in the United States was a consequence of admitting such Russian political refugees. As proof of their argument they pointed to the Haymarket Riot and to the attempted assassination of Carnegie Steel executive Henry Clay Frick during the fierce Homestead Strike of 1892. The major spokesmen in the controversy were Kennan and John Bassett Moore. Moore not only defended the treaty as one acceptable under international law—pointing to the Anglo-Russian treaty which covered the same question—but indirectly voiced the fears of the political conservatives. "Any government," he argued, "will be despotic when assailed by assassins. The dagger and the bomb are the international arguments of anarchy." [25] Whether in consideration of Moore's argument or no, the Senate proceeded to ratify the treaty. Kennan's supporters immediately organized the Society for the Abrogation of the Russian Extradition Treaty and continued the fight with even greater vigor. Despite a flood of petitions from such widely separated points as Colorado, Wisconsin, Louisiana, and New York, the treaty remained in force.[26] But far more important pressures were at work to split Washington and St. Petersburg. The forces of American and Russian economic expansion were edging into conflict in the area just south of the Amur River.

After their gainful manipulation of a policy of neutrality during the Anglo-French intervention in China that accompanied the Taiping Rebellion, both the United States and Russia opened competition for ascendency in Manchuria. In 1882 Washington's naval agents opened Korea as they had opened Japan some thirty years before, and that move set the stage for Tokyo's implementation of Western techniques of expansion in North China. In twelve short years Japan declared war on China and began to give her own interpretation to the newly declared independence of Seoul. Russia, again thwarted in moves for a European warm-water outlet, had meanwhile turned east. As an American agent observed, she found Vladivostok "closed by ice from four to five months in the year," and so began to evidence interest in Korea and the northern coast of the Yellow Sea—areas which, in the mind of that same agent, "more clearly meet her requirements." [27] Her first desire, naturally, was to prevent Japan's pre-emption of those areas.

Tokyo's victory over China forced Russia to act prematurely. Neither her trans-Siberian communications system nor her program of naval expansion was completed, but Japan's demand for Korean "independence" and the outright cession of the Liaotung Peninsula—including the fine harbor at Port Arthur—forced St. Petersburg's hand.[28] The Russian foreign minister argued that it was imperative to acquire an "ice free port on the Pacific" and to secure "a part of Manchuria as a right of way for the Trans-Siberian Railway." The Tsar "absolutely" agreed,[29] and Russia asked Great Britain, France, and Germany to join in an open demand that Japan surrender the Liaotung Peninsula. London declined to participate in the move, but Tokyo—on the advice of her military authorities—surrendered the fruit of armed victory.[30] Japan's displeasure was ill-concealed.

Russia's next move did little to relax the tension. As a step in the further development of his program of peaceful economic penetration in Manchuria, Russian Finance Minister Serge U. Witte guaranteed, with the aid of France, China's huge war indemnity to Japan.[31] He then began negotiations through the Russo-Chinese Bank—"a slightly disguised branch of the Russian treasury"—to control the railroad development of Manchuria.[32] Difficulties quickly developed on two fronts. Witte's plan to run the trans-Siberian cutoff through the heart of Manchuria was opposed by other members of the Russian court on the grounds that it was politically and militarily dangerous. Because of the Tsar's enthusiasm for expansion in the Far East, Witte downed his domestic opponents. But foreign opposition was not so easily overcome.

The United States, for one, was beginning to manifest a growing interest in the economic life of North China. Official agents had "not failed on all proper occasions to urge on the Chinese authorities the pre-eminence of Americans in railroad construction"; feeling as they did that it "would be much to be regretted" if the market was lost by default.[33] American capital, represented by the American Trading Company, the American Sugar Refining Company, the Bethlehem Iron Works, the Cramp Shipbuilding Company, the Union Iron Works, the Chase National Bank, other syndicates of American bankers, industrial corporations and railroads, and the American China Development Company, was likewise becoming more active.[34] One of the latter's first plans was "the construction of a railway through Manchuria" to supplement the exploitation of the "mines and forests" in the area. When an agent approached the Russians, however, he met a blunt rebuke. St. Petersburg had "no intention" to include any foreign group in its railway plans.[35]

This reply was underscored by the negotiation of a new Russo-Chinese treaty in June, 1896. In return for a fifteen-year military guarantee against another Japanese attack, China granted the Russo-Chinese Bank a concession for a trans-Manchurian railroad. To secure her flank, Russia then signed an agreement with Japan concerning Korea. Ostensibly a guarantee of that nation's independence, the protocol was more an understanding as to the conditions of competition for final control. These gains disturbed American representatives in the area, but they advised that the "good will of Russia" would provide the best guarantee for American interests.[36] But another round of concessions—extracted in this instance at the initiative of Germany—heightened American concern for the future.

Germany's successful demand for economic concessions in Shantung Province as compensation for the death of two missionaries spurred the New York Chamber of Commerce to petition the President for aid. It demanded "prompt and energetic" action to preserve and protect the "important commercial interests" of American citizens in China.[37] Russia's next move no doubt upset them even more. Using both Peking's grant to Germany and China's inability to make the last payment to Japan as leverage, St. Petersburg demanded a lease on Port Arthur and further railroad concessions. China momentarily stalled the drive by floating a loan in London but the issue was merely postponed.

American representatives were most apprehensive. The final partition of China, they feared, was at hand. At best, Russia would become a "formidable competitor for the trade of China's millions of buyers and sellers." Quite possibly the situation would deteriorate much faster. If that occurred, they feared that the "greatest markets of the world, which we are just grasping, will be lost to us." [38] These dire warnings appeared to be prophetic when Russia pushed through her demands for Port Arthur and the railway concessions. Only St. Petersburg's assurance that "equality of opportunity" would be preserved and her indications that American capital would be welcomed in the development of the newly won sphere of interest eased Washington's dissatisfaction.[39]

An understanding of this character between the United States and Russia might well have developed during the next two decades—the arrangement was considered as late as 1912—had it not been for the concurrence of four factors which heightened the competition and deepened the antagonism between the two countries. Of primary importance were the policy decisions made in Washington and St. Petersburg. The pressure exerted on the State Department and the White House by various economic interests for a vigorous policy confirmed and invigorated the broad view of American expansion held by the key members of the government. Theirs was a policy avowedly designed to secure American supremacy in Asia. In St. Petersburg the long struggle between Witte, who advocated the economic penetration of North China, and retired Captain of the Guards A. M. Bezobrazov, who advised "an aggressive, militant policy in Manchuria and Korea," was decided in favor of the latter when Tsar Nicholas II removed Witte from office in August, 1903.[40]

The friction between Russia and the United States, sharp as it was under these circumstances, was increased as a result of the action of England and Japan. Tokyo, at first concerned with the domination of Korea, later moved west to challenge Russia in Manchuria. England, in an attempt to prevent her own isolation, both in Europe and in Asia, wooed Washington and Japan with promises of aid against Russia. In this setting Washington's determination to press trans-Pacific expansion, coupled with a grievous miscalculation as to European developments, led to a decision to join England in support of Japan.

That move gave Tokyo, already a participant in the economic division of China, the leverage she needed to bolt and bar the open door. Too late did Washington acknowledge the fact of Russia's economic adolescence. Trapped by its miscalculations, Washington had only two possible counter-moves—independent action or the belated re-establishment of a loose entente with Russia. But Tokyo, expansive with success and fortified with power, could threaten either nation with further encroachments upon their special interests.

The first and most critical period of this disintegration of American-Russian relations spanned the years from the outbreak of the Spanish-American War to the close of the Russo-Japanese conflict. The United States crushed the shell of the Spanish Empire with ridiculous ease, but it was far more than a back-yard war: it was the first skirmish of a diplomatic revolution that lasted some fifteen years. Of major significance in this realignment was Britain's persistent effort to win the support of the United States. In the campaign to win friends and then influence them, London's courtship of Washington began during the Venezuelan crisis of 1893–97. When the United States vigorously supported Venezuelan boundary claims the British Foreign Office was at first disposed to give its one-time colonies a lesson in diplomacy; but the strength of public and parliamentary sentiment against these tactics, and the fact that Germany's mistimed bluster emphasized Britain's isolation in her war against the Boers, combined to make London most conciliatory. When Congress jammed through the declaration of war against Spain a year later, London openly supported Washington with enthusiasm.[41]

Not so Russia. St. Petersburg was content to see the United States stretch out across the Pacific to Hawaii (that would prevent "the formation of a second Malta or the strengthening of Japanese naval power"), but the acquisition of the Philippines was another matter.[42] Together with signs that London's strategy was effective, the consequences of this development caused serious apprehension in St. Petersburg. "Having entered upon the path of conquest, and perhaps not always being selective in their policies," forecast the Russian minister in the United States, "they cannot fail immediately to create a multitude of enemies and give occasion for serious complications."[43] When President William McKinley fell in with the "march of events"—which he felt "rules and overrules human action"—and annexed the Philippines, the Russians anticipated Washington's expansion in "ever wider circles."[44]

Russia's fears were not entirely groundless. Secretary of State Hay not only desired to push the American economic penetration of Asia but openly expressed strong anti-Russian sentiments. This Russophobia was in part, no doubt, a consequence of his long-standing desire for closer Anglo-American relations. An intimate member of the group of American intellectuals and politicians that was openly Anglophile, Hay was an obvious target in the British effort to align the United States against Russia in the Far East. With such men as the historian Henry Adams, diplomats John W. Foster—who as Secretary of State had openly approved the abortive attempt to take over Hawaii in 1893—Richard Olney, Whitelaw Reid, Henry White, William Woodville Rockhill, and John Russell Young (the latter two had served as State Department representatives in China), and expansionists Henry Cabot Lodge and Theodore Roosevelt, Secretary of State Hay offered a ready ear to London's suggestions.[45]

Opposition to Russia in the Far East had long been one of the cardinal points of English policy. Early in February, 1898, Joseph Chamberlain, British Colonial Secretary, opened his drive to "adopt a more decided attitude in regard to China." "The Russians," he wrote, "have done us at every turn." His plan was to approach the United States and Germany for aid and then demand Russia to open both her leased territory and ports "to all." If Russia refused, Chamberlain was prepared to "make her go if necessary." [46] With great regret Hay, then serving as United States Ambassador to Great Britain, declined the overture, even though he felt that "the interests of civilization are bound up in the direction the relations of England and America are to take in the next few months." "I could not accept it," he later explained, "because I knew that unspeakable Senate of ours would not ratify it." But "ever since," he continued, "I have been laboring to bring it about without any help, and succeeded as far as was possible for one power to do." [47] These British contacts—his friendship with Lord Charles Beresford, roving spokesman for the British version of the open door, was another—continued to influence Hay after he became Secretary of State in September, 1898.

Hay's own American friends conditioned him along similar lines. William Woodville Rockhill, intimate friend and old China hand, was installed as director of the Pan-American Union to be readily available for consultation; and he exercised an important influence on the Secretary. Rockhill's ideas also reached Hay through Alfred E. Hippisley, an Englishman he had come to know during their earlier service in China. Nor to be overlooked is the Russophobia of Dr. Jacob Gould Schurman, president of Cornell University and chairman of President William McKinley's Philippine Commission, whose counsel was influential at the White House. But after all these factors have been reviewed it remains to account for Hay's receptiveness to the English suggestions. Or, in another sense, to explain the Secretary's concern with American economic expansion in Asia. This, there is strong reason to believe, stemmed from his desire to implement a broad foreign policy most clearly expressed by Brooks Adams. Long slighted as a somewhat eccentric and asocial brother of the more famous Henry Adams, Brooks Adams appears to have greatly influenced the entire membership of Henry's famous salon at 1603 H Street in Washington, D.C.[48]

By no means does this imply that Henry or the others were unimportant. Henry understood both Brooks's broad analysis of world history and the policy for the United States derived therefrom (and no doubt made minor contributions in the course of its development)—but his role was that of transmitting Brooks's ideas to those in power. Brooks Adams' interpretation of world history—that human society oscillated between "barbarism and civilization"—was published as *The Law of Civilization and Decay* in 1895, but it had been the subject of discussion in Henry's group for at least two years prior to that date. When published, Henry took pains to see that the book reached "all the hands worth considering," including those "of the Supreme Court and the Cabinet." [49] But by that time Brooks had already begun to seek a way to modify the sine curve he had established as law.

Brooks Adams was appalled by the implication of *The Law*. His interpretation made it quite clear that the last stage before a society either reverted to barbarism or collapsed was marked by intense centralization and "economic competition." [50] This was clearly a frontal attack on the American philosophy of inevitable progress, indicating, as it did, that concentration would soon reach its highest level in the United States. This realization spurred him to feverish activity in an effort to determine under what conditions, and by what action, the fate of disintegration could be avoided. He brushed aside Henry's warning that he was beginning "to monkey with a dynamo" and from 1895 on primarily concerned himself with the search for a formula which would avert chaos.[51]

More and more he inclined to two conclusions: that the next centralization of world economic power would occur in New York, and that the expansion of the United States into Asia was the only technique by which *The Law* could, in effect, be repealed. The problem then became Russia, since in his view England was already becoming an economic vassal of the United States. But Brooks did not believe that Russia would acquiesce in American control of Asia; so the question became how to defeat that great economic entity and take control of China.[52] Well aware of his brother's new interest, Henry shared Brooks's concern with St. Petersburg. "I fear Russia much!" he admitted to Brooks; and then concluded that "you ought to be—like your grandfather—minister to St. Petersburg." [53] But Brooks Adams was concerned with action, and soon published a policy recommendation.

In February, 1899—eight months prior to Hay's open-door circular note—Brooks Adams presented his proposals. In the past, he began, American industry's "liberal margin of profit" had been "due to expansion" across the continent. In the drive to control that market, industry had been "stimulated" to produce a surplus. "The time has now come," Brooks went on, "when that surplus must be sold abroad, or a glut must be risked. . . . Eastern Asia," he pointed out, "now appears to be the only district likely soon to be able to absorb any great increase of manufacturers." There was no choice, at least so Brooks Adams concluded, but to compete for that "seat of empire." [54] This strident call for expansion fell on important ears.

By virtue of his brother's long friendship with Rockhill and Hay, Brooks Adams' ideas had long been familiar to those men. Soon after Hay returned from London to take up his duties in the Department of State, he and Henry Adams began their daily walks at four in the afternoon.[55] The time was spent "discussing the day's work at home and abroad." They "diagnosed the whole menagerie," as Henry recalled, and "killed and buried, in advance, half the world and the neighboring solar systems." But Russia plagued them constantly. "What *can* you do?" Henry inquired rudely; and Hay confessed, in moments of despair, that the "only comfort after all is in your cheerless scheme of the correlation of forces." [56] Obviously Hay did not really believe himself in these moments of fatalism, for all the while he actively sought to implement Brooks Adams' answer to the dilemma.

There were others who advised collaboration with Russia. Charles Denby, Jr., United States chargé d'affaires in Peking, warned that America's "worst antagonists" in China were the English and concluded that "our friendly relations with Russia should be enhanced." [57] Two successive United States ambassadors to Russia also urged Washington to work with Russia. Equally significant, both England and Russia, and their respective protagonists, waged a public struggle for the allegiance of the United States through the summer of 1899.

A pro-English spokesman led off with the claim that the "very heart" of the question was whether an "Anglo-Saxon or Russian civilization" was to expand in Asia. "All the arguments against imperialism," concluded this writer, "fall before the . . . duty" to expand Anglo-Saxon culture.[58] A quasi-official Russian spokesman answered immediately. Taking note of the unfavorable opinion created by Kennan and the accounts of religious and political persecutions, he admitted that Russians were not perfect but suggested that Americans try the shoe for size. Would they, he asked, "insist that their treatment of the Indians is in strict accordance with their ideal of liberty?" "No," he answered. It was time, he warned, for the United States "to emancipate herself from England's political tutelage. . . . May Heaven preserve America from the curse of Western imperialism with which England is now tempting her." [59] Naturally the British replied in kind.

The first counterblast argued that while Russia was an "autocracy," China was actually "a democracy in all but name." But this British sympathizer also defended the expansion of "men of Caucasian race" in Asia as a "necessity"—it brought "wealth and prosperity to previously decaying regions." This was the important consideration. "Flattering as it may be . . . to have on hand two suitors," the writer was sure that the United States would support the policy of "free competition for all." That, the reader was assured, would exist "wherever British influence predominates." [60] Shortly thereafter came an open appeal on racial grounds. "It is," argued this spokesman, "as Senator Lodge points out, the conflict of the Slav and the Saxon." [61] Interesting as they are, these exchanges had little bearing on Washington's final decision.

The articles actually did no more than acquaint the public with various arguments that had long since been aired in discussions at the top level. Likewise, the policy-making group had its own ideological spokesman in the person of Brooks Adams, who had presented a far more rational analysis and interpretation of the forces pressing for expansion. But most important of all were the economic groups that demanded government assistance in the expansion of their Asiatic markets; theirs was the activity on which Adams based his analysis.

The pressure that had been exerted by the American China Development Company, the New York Chamber of Commerce, and others was increased in late 1898 and early 1899. Enoch Emery, the "pioneer American merchant of Siberia" and the "largest importer of American goods into" that area, reported in November, 1898, that the Russians were about to close all Siberian ports.[62] In January, 1899, a petition from the Pepperell Manufacturing Company of Boston—endorsed by other business interests and supported by Senator Lodge—requested action to remove the "danger of being shut out from the markets of that portion of North China which is already occupied or threatened by Russia." [63] And a bit later the South Carolina cotton mill owners declared that their "prosperity" depended "on the China trade." [64]

But American agents on the scene continued to emphasize the importance of closer relations with Russia. These men argued that the development of American-Russian trade would lead to further collaboration and even greater markets. Chargé d'Affaires Herbert H. D. Pierce reported from St. Petersburg that while the Russians expected "due profits" from their Manchurian railways "all treaty rights of foreign powers with China will be fully respected." [65] Ambassador Eathan A. Hitchcock negotiated at length for a large exhibition to acquaint the Russian market with American goods. The plan was to transfer the American display from the Paris Exposition of 1900 to St. Petersburg or another central point. Hitchcock approached the main exhibitors, "all of whom [were] in hearty accord with the idea." The negotiations broke down over the request for a "reduction" in transportation rates and customs dues, but Pierce was not discouraged.[66]

As late as October 11, 1899, he pointed out that there was a large market for such new articles as "bicycles, tools, hardware . . . elevators . . . pianos . . . stoves . . . street railways . . . automobiles . . . mills for the manufacture of lumber . . . mining machinery . . . and metal-working machinery." Equally important was the further extension of the market already penetrated by American raw cotton (most of it transhipped via England and Germany), the "Worthington pump . . . the Baldwin Locomotive Works . . . and the Westinghouse air brake." This trade, Pierce urged, was "of very great importance"—of more significance than Russia's threat to American trade in China.[67] American consular agents, who thought Russia "a world large enough to command the attention of the leading manufacturers and exporters of the United States who are seeking a market for their surplus," provided the facts to support this interpretation.[68] Nor were other Americans unmindful of such developments.[69]

But Secretary Hay disagreed. The Pepperell petition was on his mind and he directed Pierce's new superior, Ambassador Charlemagne Tower, "to act energetically in the sense desired by the numerous and influential signers" of that document.[70] Tower in turn thought it most "gratifying" when Russia declared the commercial facilities at Port Arthur open as a free port.[71] Hay's next and all-inclusive move in that direction was given serious consideration in St. Petersburg. Russia responded to the Secretary's open-door notes of November, 1899, with a plea for precise clarification. Tower bluntly told St. Petersburg that the "propositions had been made in behalf of American commerce and industry"; but Russia, clearly anxious to "maintain the relations subsisting between the two countries . . . went a great way, as Russian diplomacy goes," to reach an understanding.[72]

Hay was not satisfied with St. Petersburg's offer to make "a general public statement that Russia has replied favorably . . . and renews the assurance that all privileges conceded to any foreign country within the sphere of influence shall be guaranteed to the United States." [73] Rather did the Secretary blandly announce that all answers were "final and definitive." [74] His bluff worked, for England naturally supported the move and neither Japan nor Russia ventured a public protest. Russia had underestimated Hay's grasp of his own plans. "You do not yourself see the vast portee [sic] of them," exclaimed the Russians at one point.[75] That such was not the case soon became apparent.

For a time the two nations appeared to follow the same policy in response to the anti-foreign aspects of the Chinese Boxer Rebellion of June, 1900. While both powers sought to give the impression publicly that they favored the withdrawal of military units used against the Chinese, the fact was that both nations maintained their armed forces in China. Hay, conscious of America's economic stake in Manchuria, did not choose to discuss with St. Petersburg the Russian assurances that she would evacuate every "single inch of territory." [76] Such promises, he exploded in a display of fierce hostility, "are as false as dicer's oaths." [77] This deep-rooted prejudice contributed in no small measure to the ultimate failure of the Secretary's policy. More willingness to test the less belligerent, and more realistic, interpretation offered by his own agents, and an effort to strengthen the growing economic bonds with Russia might have paid greater dividends for the United States—and China.

For on September 11, 1900—before Hay's outburst against the Russians—Chargé Pierce in St. Petersburg submitted a long review of Russian internal affairs in which he reported that Finance Minister Witte might well assume direction of Russian foreign policy. This development, he continued, offered a "fair basis for entertaining the belief that if in the past there existed an intention to absorb Manchuria, that policy may now have been reversed." [78] This view was essentially accurate: Witte did oppose the annexation of Manchuria, and though Russian troops occupied large areas of that country in October, 1900, Witte, aided by protests from Japan, England, and the United States, did temporarily defeat the grandiose plans of the imperialist clique at the Russian court and negotiate an agreement to withdraw Russian troops in three stages over a period of eighteen months.

This point demands emphasis. Some have claimed that Washington knew little—if anything—of this early struggle for control of policy in St. Petersburg, or of the return engagement between Witte and his opponents that resulted in the former's dismissal in 1903.[79] Yet Pierce's "lengthy dispatch," which made it clear that the situation was in flux, appears never to have been considered as a basis for action designed to support Witte in his contest for power in St. Petersburg. Rather was Washington's policy conditioned by an intense antipathy for Russia and motivated by a determination to preserve the dominant position of American trade in Manchuria. The first of these considerations so controlled the formulation of a policy designed to secure the second that the United States ultimately surrendered its initiative to Japan.

As Pierce indicated, Witte's position was insecure from the very beginning. Witte who, when his power was sufficient, worked through Count V. N. Lamsdorff, the acting foreign minister after August, 1900, was opposed by two groups, both of which desired to substitute a militant policy for the finance minister's plan of economic penetration and development. Leader of the opposition was A. M. Bezobrazov, a retired Captain of the Guards and "a well-known figure on the St. Petersburg stock exchange." [80] In the winter of 1897–98 Bezobrazov picked up an old concession granted by the Korean Government for the exploitation of timber along the Yalu River and with this as bait opened a campaign to undercut Witte's influence with Tsar Nicholas II. By May, 1898, the captain had interested the Tsar on two counts—personal economic gain and the extension of Russia's empire in the Far East.

Witte, who refused to accept Bezobrazov's argument that Russia's influence would be extended only through complete domination of Korea and Manchuria, thwarted this first move in August, 1899. But the Boxer uprising gave another opponent, Minister of War General Kuropatkin, an opportunity to press his plan to occupy Manchuria and then wring further concessions from China. As Witte moved to check this maneuver, however, Bezobrazov secured the Tsar's approval for an East Asiatic Industrial Company that would be used to occupy northern Korea. The character of Bezobrazov's plans is best revealed in a candid letter to a fellow conspirator: "Either we must dominate the position and strengthen our political position or we will fall into the hands of the Jewish crooks and European diplomats." [81] Witte again checked the captain only to be outflanked by Admiral E. I. Alexeiev, another adventurer whose position in Port Arthur gave him comparative freedom of action.

Going beyond his instructions, Alexeiev forced a harsh agreement on the Chinese forces at Mukden. By this treaty the Chinese were to surrender a major portion of their sovereignty over Manchuria. Witte refused to accept this document when it arrived in St. Petersburg, but General Kuropatkin carried the day with a revised version that merely added economic concessions to Alexeiev's original demands. Confronted with these conditions, China appealed to the other powers for assistance.

Japan informed Washington that it would "insist on *status quo ante* in Manchuria," and Hay gave quick support to her position.[82] Suddenly Hay apparently indicated that he would retreat if assurances were given that American "trade would not suffer and that the door would remain open." [83] Yet at the hour the Secretary made these remarks to the Russian Ambassador another note of protest had already been despatched to St. Petersburg. As indicated by his specification to Russia, a clue to Hay's insistence on the open door is found in the trade reports. Exports from the United States totaled more than a third of all Manchurian imports— "greater than those of any other nation." But Russia was not the chief competitor. "Her trade interests here," reported an on-the-spot observer, "are nominal." Japan and England were the nations that formed, with the United States, an oligarchy in control of the region's foreign trade. For a moment the ambassador in Russia seemed to feel that this very fact offered an opportunity to link up with Russia in Manchuria and develop "most desirable and important" economic and political relations. The result, he realized, would be an entente of "inexpressible potency." [84]

This thought was quickly disregarded, and the ambassador advised a union with Japan and England against Russia. Washington never seriously considered any other policy. True, Witte's proposals to China of February, 1902, were acceptable to Washington *if* Russia did nothing to injure "the commercial interests of the United States" or to "diminish" China's capacity to meet her "international obligations." [85] But the United States vigorously opposed the grant of privileges for industrial development to the Russo-Chinese Bank.[86] American interests were obviously interpreted to mean the preservation of the existing control over Manchurian trade held by groups in the United States. No efforts were made to negotiate any mutual development of the area. China, somewhat encouraged for the time behind these "categorical protests of America and Japan," refused to sign the treaty.[87]

This failure further reduced Witte's influence with the Tsar. At the moment, of course, the just-published Anglo-Japanese Alliance of January 30, 1902, strengthened him against Kuropatkin, whose proposals for militant expansion he opposed. On April 8, 1902, Witte concluded an agreement to evacuate Manchuria within eighteen months. But the Bezobrazov-Kuropatkin-Alexeiev triumvirate—whose members had concluded long before that they could "not 'cook porridge' " with Witte—recovered quickly and moved to effect the Finance Minister's dismissal.[88] Within a year Bezobrazov was appointed state secretary and Alexeiev became military commander in the Far East.

Witte maintained his position long enough to carry through the first withdrawal in Manchuria, but the band of adventurers canceled the second and instead re-enforced the Korean border, re-entered areas around Mukden, and retained all the other occupied territory. Witte made one of his last stands in a meeting called on April 8, 1903, to discuss further penetration in Korea. No decision was reached, and Witte's position seemed to improve when Kuropatkin broke with Bezobrazov on the Korean issue. But the captain first outmaneuvered the General and then, on August 28, 1903, successfully concluded the "long intrigue" against Witte.[89] At the close of a routine meeting the Tsar advised Witte that he was dismissed.

In conjunction with Theodore Roosevelt's earlier (and quite fortuitous) elevation to the presidency and the Anglo-Japanese Alliance, Bezobrazov's victory over Witte was the crucial blow to peace in North China. Theodore Roosevelt began to assume direction of foreign relations soon after he became President in September, 1901. Only in part was Secretary Hay's progressive illness responsible for this development. An exponent of Social Darwinism and a close friend of Captain Alfred Thayer Mahan (whose theory of an industrial mercantilism influenced TR considerably), Roosevelt believed in a vigorous foreign policy. Two other considerations are important for an understanding of the President's policies: he was a regular member of the Adams-Hay Anglophile society and a close friend of Brooks Adams.

One who believed that American interests in the Far East coincided with England's, Roosevelt's association with Brooks Adams re-enforced both his determination to take the lead in world politics and his anti-Russian bias. Brooks and Roosevelt had been friends for many years prior to the publication of *The Law*, but that event intensified what had been a casual relationship among the elite. The key to this quickening of their friendship was a common reaction to the determinism of *The Law*.[90] This is apparent in the review of the volume written by Roosevelt at the special request of Brooks. Roosevelt, who had "a very firm faith" in the philosophy of steady progress, admitted it would be "very hard" to repeal *The Law*, but did "not think it . . . impossible." [91]

Brooks thought that a re-emphasis of the "martial man" (who would control and dominate the centralization and economic competition of the last stage prior to disintegration) was the only possible solution, and of course Roosevelt agreed. "Peace is a goddess," he declared in June, 1897, "only when she comes with sword girt on thigh." And as Roosevelt advised Hay, he and Brooks discussed the possibility of "heading some great outburst of the emotional classes" as early as 1899.[92] Even so, Brooks was disappointed that Roosevelt did not move faster in Asia after he became President.

Brooks no doubt was moved more by impatience than discouragement. The "permanent establishment of a wider market for American products" was a central theme of Roosevelt's first message to Congress in December, 1901. With reference to China, he amplified, that meant "not merely the procurement of enlarged commercial opportunities on the coasts, but access to the interior." The President's final warning to the nation—"build and maintain an adequate navy or else . . . accept a secondary position in international affairs"—was taken (as Roosevelt carefully acknowledged) from Brooks, by whom it had "been well said." [93] The tempo of Roosevelt's action, moreover, soon increased.

China, Brooks Adams carefully pointed out, was "the great problem of the future," and that area was "uppermost" in Roosevelt's mind.[94] It was, moreover, the "corrupt, tricky, and inefficient" Russians (Brooks termed them "ignorant, uninventive, indolent, and improvident") who early antagonized the President.[95] His enmity was fed by the efforts of Bezobrazov's group to prevent the Chinese from acceding to Washington's demand during the spring and summer of 1903 that Peking open various treaty ports and consulates in Manchuria. Only prolonged pressure forced Alexeiev to give way and admit that it was "necessary" to make some concession.[96] During the course of the negotiations Roosevelt dropped all pretense to impartiality. "I have not the slightest objection to the Russians knowing that I feel thoroughly aroused and irritated at their conduct," he advised Hay, and "that I don't intend to give way and that I am . . .

growing more confident that this country would back me in going to an extreme in this matter." [97] But Roosevelt's anti-Russian policy did not (contrary to his own interpretation) elicit general approval in the United States until a new series of Jewish pogroms in Russia called forth counter-demonstrations against the Tsar.

"Russia must have new outlets for her population seeking commerce," wrote the editors of the *Outlook* in June, 1900, and others shared this view. One quasi-official Russian writer argued that it would be wise for St. Petersburg and Washington to keep a careful watch on the "slumbering dragon" that was China; and another held out the opportunity for the United States to play "an important role" in the "economical awakening of Siberia, and particularly of its richest part—the basin of the Amur." [98] Josiah Quincy, namesake of an earlier opponent of American expansion, questioned the entire basis of opposition to the "natural and legitimate character" of Russian influence in Manchuria. He revived the arguments that earlier Americans had used to justify their own advance across the continent. Russia's "frontier coterminous with that of China," thought Quincy, called for "a frank recognition on our part of the fact that Russia is the dominant factor in the settlement of the Chinese question." [99] But the *Review of Reviews* reflected the new character of American expansion. For a time the editors viewed any move to "depart in any measure" from the old "cordial relations" with Russia as "a most serious blunder"; but the "growing Manchurian trade" of the United States caused them at first to waver and then join the anti-Russian front.[100]

Others supported this position from the first. The time had come, wrote one, for England and Japan to stop Russia—"a determined and relentless enemy." [101] Reverend Gilbert Reid, American religious spokesman, indicated that the sentiment against Russia was due to "the ambition to expand American trade throughout the whole of China." [102] An English politician, the Right Honorable Sir Charles W. Dilke, M.P., agreed. "Rivals we must be in trade; but we have . . . everything to gain . . . by co-operating in maintaining order throughout China." [103] William Barclay Parsons, chief engineer of the American-China Development Company, was more candid. "We should awake to the realization of our opportunities," he cried, "and unite for the invasion, not only of China, but of other Oriental lands as well." [104] H. L. Nelson, editor of *Harper's Weekly*, agreed that it was time for the United States to pull its own weight in the destruction of "Chinese exclusiveness"—"that barbarous and stupid custom." [105] Once again, however, public discussion followed a decision that had already been made in Washington.

In many respects, Washington's policy in the Far East resembled the analysis and recommendations advanced by Brooks Adams. The United States, he warned, "could hardly contemplate with equanimity the successful organization of a hostile industrial system on the shores of the Pacific." [106] Brooks recommended "preventing the industrial development of China." To accomplish this, he wrote, "the trust must be accepted as the cornerstone" of the move to "consolidate within" so that the nation could more efficiently "expand without." So far, Adams thought, Washington had been successful. "She has long held South America closed; she is now closing China; and while thus caging Europeans within their narrow peninsula, she is slowly suffocating them with her surplus." [107] But there was dangerous opposition.

If Russia and Germany combined, for example, they might well offer a challenge in both South America and Asia. That, Brooks Adams feared, would close the "outlet" for America's surplus.[108] The obvious enemy was Russia, "the vast monster," but if Japan should prevail, "the situation would remain substantially unaltered." Of course, Brooks admitted, the United States could live in peace if Washington was not "too grasping," but he made it clear that he thought "aggression" to be in the nation's "best interest." There was "little to be urged," he carefully pointed out, "by way of a precedent against the logic" of such a decision. But for success the United States would need a quick-striking army and, "more especially," a large navy.[109]

This analysis influenced people of importance other than Theodore Roosevelt. William Woodville Rockhill, who continued on as Roosevelt's advisor, shared the President's anti-Russian sentiments, but Henry Adams took care to re-enforce this attitude with his brother's militant views. Senator Lodge, one of Roosevelt's closest friends, publicly acknowledged his debt to Brooks. Russia, he agreed, was "potentially an economic rival more formidable than any other organized nation." [110] Senator Jonathan P. Dolliver was another who gave Brooks Adams credit for his view of the situation. There was little or nothing in the policy of the United States, he admitted, "to warrant us making any claim to higher motives than those which have actuated the people of other countries." As Brooks made clear, Dolliver went on, our interest "in the affairs of China is one that relates mainly to [the] opportunities to sell in that country the products of [our] factories and farms." [111] But the general public did not share these open expressions of opposition to Russia until a fresh outbreak of pogroms helped focus attention on that country.

Somewhat earlier the United States responded to an appeal to aid the victims of another Russian famine.[112] But the violent outbreak against members of the Jewish faith that erupted in Kishinev over the Easter holidays in 1903 led to the rise of considerable antagonism toward Russia among the general public in the United States as well as among members of the Jewish faith. St. Petersburg's official explanation that "the fault must be with the Jews" [113] did little to quiet the growing protest movement organized by Oscar Straus' "small committee," [114] the Jewish Publication Society, and the Independent Order of B'nai B'rith. Two New York papers financed another on-the-spot investigation and others wrote of the bitter prejudice in the Tsar's court.[115]

Another writer suggested that economic problems were at least partially responsible for the outbreaks and proposed that the major powers join in the "ransom of Israel," or that Russia herself "provide territory" for the creation of a new nation.[116] But his plan was overwhelmed by the enmity created by the seventy-seven protest meetings staged throughout the United States. Such prominent figures as social worker Jane Addams, lawyer Clarence Darrow, politician Carl Schurz, Anglophile diplomat William G. Choate, and financiers August Belmont, John F. Dillon, and Jacob Schiff played important roles in the movement.[117]

Former President Grover Cleveland was the principal speaker at a major rally staged by Straus in Carnegie Hall. After this meeting Straus and Schiff directed a pressure campaign that culminated in personal interviews with Secretary Hay and President Roosevelt, who was asked to "use his good offices" to put an end to the discrimination in Russia. Congress was called upon to denounce any treaties that denied equal treatment to all American citizens in Russia. This broad campaign was quite effective. The Baltimore *American* seemed to reflect the general atmosphere when it declared that to speak of any friendship—old or new—with Russia was the "limit of absurdity." Straus was no doubt correct when he observed that the massacres "seriously prejudiced public opinion here against Russia." [118]

The coincidence of this adverse sentiment with the outbreak of the Russo-Japanese War in large measure explains the general support accorded to the policy formulated by Roosevelt and the State Department some years before. The war itself was the result of a collision between Japan's expansionist plans and Bezobrazov's imperialism. Viewing the Tsar's dismissal of Witte as a dangerous omen, Tokyo proposed to St. Petersburg that Russia's claims in Korea and North China be settled by negotiation. To Japan's demand for recognition of her "preponderating interest in Korea," Alexeiev and Bezobrazov countered with a proposal to reserve northern Korea for future decision.[119] Tokyo, secure in her new entente with England and advised that in case of war Washington's policy "would be benovolent toward Japan," abruptly terminated the discussions with a surprise attack on the Russian fleet at Port Arthur.[120] President Theodore Roosevelt was "thoroughly well pleased." [121]

Roosevelt had been equally displeased a short time before, however, when United States Minister to Korea Horace N. Allen attempted to convince him that the United States should support Russia. At firsthand Allen had watched Tokyo advance from a guarantee of Korean "independence" to a demand for recognition of her "predominating interests," and the experience bred a "continual nervous terror of the Japanese." Sure that there would be "trouble on the Yalu and possible bloodshed," Allen made a special trip to the United States in the summer of 1903 in an effort to convince his superiors that the United States "should aid the Russians, in Manchuria at any rate." Upon his arrival in Washington he made a few preliminary contacts and then "went to Dep't and started things."

Rockhill was the first road block. Unable to move this close advisor to the President (who was "sure that the Japanese should be supported"), Allen by-passed him and went directly to the President. Quite bluntly Allen told Roosevelt that "he was making a mistake regarding Russia." Roosevelt called in Rockhill and the three men thrashed out the issue that same evening. In the first place, Allen argued, Russia would not voluntarily give up Manchuria any more than "we should evacuate Texas or, to make the example better, Hawaii." Co-operation with Russia, moreover, would give the United States a dominant position in that "great commercial field."

Most important, and Allen did his best to emphasize the point, Japan already had Britain's support—if Roosevelt added his then Tokyo would have no reason for restraint. But why, Roosevelt appears to have demanded, back a loser? "Simply because Russia 'wanted us to have all her trade we could handle,'" insisted the envoy to Korea, while 'Japan was just the opposite and would make us increasing trouble until we might have to cross swords with her.'" Roosevelt, however, was sure that he had everything well in hand.[122]

The President's plan—in close harmony with that of Brooks Adams—was "to exhaust both Russia and Japan" and so neutralize Manchuria to America's advantage.[123] Despite a brief flurry of interest in Allen's bold effort to point out the fallacy of such a policy, the President's decision seems to have been generally accepted *after* the war began. "Japanese trade ideals are necessary to world commerce," agreed the *Outlook*, and added that Tokyo was "really America's protagonist." James J. Hill, fellow railway magnate of Edward H. Harriman, advised the farmer to support the "development of the Oriental demand for our wheat and flour" —a view shared by the now anti-Russian editors of the *Review of Reviews*.[124]

Many others, including former Ambassador to Russia Andrew D. White, Oscar Straus, Senator Albert J. Beveridge, and Paul S. Reinsch, soon to become American minister to Peking, agreed that the past friendship with Russia was more myth than reality and concluded that Japan had "fought our battle as well as her own." American newspapers generally agreed with this conclusion.[125] And a visit from Standard Oil representatives, who feared for their markets in the Far East, put Roosevelt "in a still more warlike mood than before." [126] Standard's concern probably stemmed from apprehension over the possibility that the company's future growth in Asia would be limited by Russian competition.[127]

Roosevelt was also supported by George Kennan, who became so enamored of the Japanese that he graced them with honorary membership in the "Anglo-Saxon" race. "The Japanese," he agreed with another writer of similar ideas, "to all intents and purposes are Aryans." [128] Kennan wasted little sympathy on the Koreans—they were "so abominably dirty" and "lacking in virility." On the whole, he concluded, Korea was a "Degenerate State" and he urged the Japanese—with their "coolness and perfect neatness"—to step in and "resolutely *take* control." [129] As for the Chinese, Kennan thought they lacked "the brains of a Siberian Korak" and needed a "change in their moral character." [130]

Kennan developed such a "profound admiration" for Japanese courage, cleanliness, efficiency, and planning that he came to prefer them to the Russians. "For the reason that Japan . . . is civilized and modern," as he explained, "while Russia . . . is semi-barbarous and medieval," Kennan acknowledged that he would "unhesitatingly" support the former.[131] His sympathy for Russia by no means disappeared, however, and he openly organized revolutionary cells among the prisoners of war interned in Japan. With the co-operation of the Japanese Minister of War and aided by an agent sent out by the Friends of Russian Freedom, Kennan waged a long program of "education and enlightenment" that—so at least he claimed—converted 52,500 Russian soldiers into "revolutionists." This activity—Kennan termed it "a moral duty"—was but one cause of Russia's growing bitterness toward the United States.[132]

Taking particular note of the "active anti-Russian agitation" in the American press, the St. Petersburg *Vzestnik Evropy* warned that "it should not be forgotten that back of the Japanese stands England, and that the United States is ready to act with England." The *Novoye Vremya* acknowledged Kennan's part in the creation of unfavorable opinion in the United States, but also gave credit to the "armies of missionaries" active in China. A bit later the same paper developed the analysis still further. Europe had been "crowded out of America by the Dingley tariff," the editors declared, as a preliminary move to overseas expansion. This expansion had been initiated by Hay, who "placed the knife at the throat" of Spain and "grabbed . . . the Philippine archipelago, that magnificent outpost of China." Next came Roosevelt, the agent of the "mighty oligarchy which has long ruled America . . . the owners of the trusts, the kings of industry, the renowned circle of four hundred." [133] Nor was Russia unaware that American bankers led by Jacob Schiff—who took "pride" in the fact that he had "been able to bring to naught" all Russia's earlier attempts to secure loans in the United States—joined the English to finance Japan's entire war effort.[134] St. Petersburg was openly antagonistic.

This American aid to Japan contributed to Roosevelt's rapidly increasing uneasiness. His careful plan had gone awry—Allen's forecast began to look uncomfortably accurate as Tokyo rolled on through victory after victory. "I wish I were certain," he worried in December, 1904, "that the Japanese at bottom did not lump . . . all of us, simply as white devils . . . to be treated politely only so long" as it served their own interest.[135] Roosevelt was ready to stop the whole affair on another count. Both Brooks Adams and Roosevelt's diplomatic trouble-shooter, businessman George von Lengerke Meyer, who the President, in his growing fear, shifted from Italy to St. Petersburg, warned that a revolution in Russia would be disastrous no matter what the final result. A weakened Russia would further strengthen Japan while a reinvigorated Russia would threaten the Manchurian claims of all the interested powers.[136] Either possibility seemed imminent as the Tsarist bureaucracy began to break down under the strain of war. Roosevelt confided his fears to some—to others his problem was quite obvious.

For his part, Henry Adams was near hysteria lest his brother ("who runs about and instructs the great") would precipitate a full-scale catastrophe. "We shall sink or swim with" the Tsar, he cried, "half crazy" over the prospect of a revolution in Russia.[137] Roosevelt, too, was afraid. "I earnestly hope," he admitted to Meyer, that "the Tsar will see that he must at all hazards . . . make peace . . . and then turn his attention to internal affairs." [138] Japan was no less a problem. "What they will do to us hereafter when intoxicated by their victory over Russia," he confessed, "is another matter." [139]

First went Korea, which Roosevelt privately abandoned in January, 1905. That decision was formalized in the "agreed memorandum" signed by Secretary of War William Howard Taft and Japanese Prime Minister Katsura on July 29, 1905. In return for a guarantee of the Philippines, Washington recognized Tokyo's suzerainty over the Land of the Morning Calm.[140] But Roosevelt's vital need was to halt the war before Japan completely crushed the Russians in the Far East.[141] The President went through the motions to accomplish this end, but other forces decided the issue. Both powers were near exhaustion: France, Russia's financier, called a halt, as did the Anglo-American bankers who backed Japan.[142] These pressures re-enforced the belligerents' own decision. The Tsar was anxious to steady his tottering throne, and Japan's own military leaders, well aware that Siberia promised a fate similar to Napoleon's, left the field of battle to return to Tokyo and demand peace.[143]

Yet the Peacemaker of Portsmouth refused to acknowledge his failure. Though quite aware that his efforts to modify Japan's demands in no manner threatened her fruits of victory, Roosevelt ignored the significance of Tokyo's truculence. Still confident that he could "count absolutely on their doing what they said they would," the President—who proudly claimed the title of realist—seems to have forgotten that the Japanese left the peace table firmly entrenched in Manchuria.[144] The Russian fleet was destroyed—a surprising oversight for such an ardent disciple of Mahan— and the Japanese Army was fanned out to a point north of Mukden to protect Port Arthur and its connecting railroad (and related economic concessions) north to Chang Chun.[145] But Theodore Roosevelt was, in his own words, "far stronger pro-Japanese than ever." [146]

Roosevelt's great inflexibility was no doubt a factor in this failure of a policy designed to pre-empt Asia as an American market; [147] but the plan itself was basically unsound. The undue emphasis on the menace of Russia was an important contributing error. At no time a serious competitor in the markets of either China or Manchuria, Russia was nevertheless designated the principal enemy. In turn, this attitude led Washington to back its two leading competitors against a power that Roosevelt himself considered "inefficient" and one he thought Japan "would probably whip" on the sea.[148]

But the President failed to note the contradiction in this policy until too late. For Russia had, before 1903, helped serve American interests by checking Japanese expansion, but a weakened Russia could not resist a militant and confident Japan that threatened force in answer to nebulous American promises.

3
☆
RENDEZVOUS WITH
REVOLUTION

1. OPPORTUNITY KNOCKS BUT THREE TIMES

Our policy in Manchuria has won us the ill will of Russia, irritated
Japan, and failed of support in France and Great Britain.

E. T. Williams, August 28, 1910

I cannot too emphatically reiterate my conclusion that the sympathetic co-operation of Russia is of supreme importance: for . . . she can
never withdraw from participation in Far Eastern Affairs or maintain an
attitude of indifference toward them.

William Woodville Rockhill, January 30, 1911

☆☆

From the Treaty of Portsmouth to the Revolution of March, 1917,
American-Russian relations were of a double character. Washington's
efforts to delimit Japanese expansion and simultaneously extend the area of
American economic penetration in the Far East further alienated St. Petersburg and accelerated the formation of the Russo-Japanese entente. The
secret treaty signed by Foreign Minister Serge Sazonov and Baron Motono
on July 8, 1912, was the last stone in Japan's great wall around Manchuria. In the same year Washington unilaterally terminated the commercial treaty of 1832. Abrogation symbolized the economic and political differences in the Far East and Persia and was the result of renewed re-
crimination over Jewish persecution and political extradition.

At the same time the steady increase of American investment in
Russia (which expanded rapidly after the outbreak of World War I) was
reflected in the activity of a group that desired to broaden the area of
American-Russian co-operation. Thus while official Washington hailed the
March Revolution as an event that would lead to more cordial relations no

move was made to further a *rapprochement*. Rather did the group that held an economic stake in Russia's future make both a more realistic appraisal of the revolution and a concerted attempt to prevent Russia's total collapse. In the final analysis it was Raymond Robins, Midwestern progressive politician and one of Theodore Roosevelt's most ardent admirers, who initiated and led the effort to rebuild the old American-Russian bloc—this time against a resurgent Germany and an expansive Japan.

Russia's weakness at the close of the Russo-Japanese War offered Washington an earlier opportunity to regain the initiative lost to Japan. Driven out of Korea and South Manchuria, Russia had two problems: limit or forestall Japan's economic and political exploitation of her victory and at the same time protect North Manchuria. Tokyo's desire, naturally, was to integrate South Manchuria within her own sphere and then, if possible, secure further gains. Russia's dilemma was of no mean proportions— should she make the best of her defeat and sign with Japan, or risk an effort to re-establish an understanding with Washington?

Without effective power, St. Petersburg could do little more than initiate feeble overtures and hope for the chance to exercise a positive choice. Russian Foreign Minister Alexander Izvolski, who recommended "with insistence a conciliatory attitude toward Japan" because of his lack of confidence in the intentions of the United States, emphasized the "helplessness" of Russia's position against an armed Japan.[1] Others in St. Petersburg, however, spoke of the "historical necessity" for a "Russian-American *rapprochement*."[2] Both the State Department and some American economic groups spurned these overtures and formulated policies that lessened the chance of reconciliation.

Four considerations are of particular importance to an understanding of the complex pattern of American-Russian relations between 1905 and 1912. A primary factor was the character and purpose of the policy proposed by Brooks Adams (and others) and translated into action first by Secretary of State Hay and then by President Theodore Roosevelt. That Adams and Roosevelt employed exceedingly militant language to enunciate their plan to dominate the Far East tends to obscure the fact that both men considered diplomacy a major weapon in the battle to achieve supremacy in the Pacific. For neither Roosevelt nor Adams abandoned his efforts— either during or after the Japanese victory over Russia in 1905. Thus to view Roosevelt's two agreements with Japan—the Taft-Katsura Memorandum of 1905, which acknowledged Tokyo's control of Korea in return for a Japanese guarantee of the Philippines, and the Root-Takahira Agreement of 1908, which underwrote the territorial status quo, and the open door, throughout the Pacific—as written evidence of a strategic retreat is fallacious. Rather were these exchanges the manifestation of a determination, also reflected in Roosevelt's decision to send the United States battle fleet on an around-the-world cruise in 1907, to retain a fulcrum for Washington's lever of economic power with which—according to Brooks Adams —the final victory in Asia would be achieved.

No less significant, therefore, were the economic activities of two combinations of industrial and financial power in the United States which dominated American economic expansion in Asia. One of these, a working alliance between railroad magnate Edward H. Harriman, who also controlled an ocean steamship line, and Jacob Schiff, head of the banking firm of Kuhn, Loeb and Company, initiated this expansion into Asia in the period after the Russo-Japanese War. Harriman's desire to secure control of the Manchurian railroad system was backed economically by Schiff, who, in addition, entertained his own plans for financial and industrial operations in the area. For its part, the House of Morgan at first paid more attention to plans designed to control American-Russian trade and to obtain a share of loans to Russia. Then, as these early (1905–6) efforts produced no immediate results, Morgan joined Harriman and Schiff to finance a proposed railway in Southeast China. This enterprise held the House of Morgan's attention only briefly, and in 1912 the firm returned to the effort to penetrate Russia directly.

This economic activity provided the foundation for American diplomacy toward Russia from 1905 to 1912. Harriman's determination to obtain control of the Manchurian railways led him to seek Washington's active assistance—through the administrations of Presidents Theodore Roosevelt and William Howard Taft—to overcome Tokyo's opposition to any project that would weaken Japanese dominance in Manchuria. Working through Willard Straight, his personal agent who also functioned as chief of the Far Eastern Division of the Department of State during a critical stage in the effort, Harriman was able, first, to negotiate tentative arrangements with China and Russia which would—when pushed through over Japanese resistance—give Harriman control of Manchurian railways; second, manipulate a commitment on the part of the United States Government to support overseas economic expansion.

But Harriman and Straight underestimated the determination of President Taft and Secretary of State Philander C. Knox to re-establish American political power in Manchuria. Taft and Knox, supported by their bureaucratic aides in the State Department—men whose handling of routine affairs and function as advisors gave them significant influence in policy-making decisions—seized the Harriman economic plan as soon as the rail magnate died in 1909, and, ignoring Harriman's emphasis on collaboration with Russia, sought to use it as the weapon with which to effect Washington's supremacy over *both* Tokyo and St. Petersburg. But Japan's strong position in Manchuria enabled Tokyo to use Washington's overt bid for control of the area as a means to extract further concessions from Russia.

Preoccupied with their own bid for supremacy, Taft and Knox did not see the consequences of their failure to work with Russia until too late to check Japan.

Yet in any review of these developments a third factor must be kept constantly in mind. For at the same time Morgan, Harriman, and Schiff ostensibly co-operated in the attempt to penetrate China, a vigorous fight was being waged between Morgan and the Harriman-Schiff team for control of the vast Russian market for industrial products and the immense field in Russia for potential direct investments in, and possible control of, Russian railways, life insurance, mines, and other concessions. Bitter competitors during earlier and contemporary phases of domestic economic activity, particularly the battle for control of American railroads, these financial giants carried their private war abroad as they attempted to reap new profits and gain more power through overseas economic expansion. Though he had apparently achieved a favored position in St. Petersburg, Harriman's death in 1909 gave Morgan an opportunity he exploited in subsequent years—but not to the extent that either financier had originally anticipated.

But none of these three considerations can be understood outside the context of Russia's persistent effort to re-establish the old pattern of collaboration with the United States—this time against Japan. From the time of the Russo-Japanese War to the last hours before Washington, in 1912, abrogated the commercial treaty of 1832, Russia sought an understanding with the United States—economic *and* political—to oppose jointly Tokyo's steady pressure on the mainland of Asia. Yet St. Petersburg's uneasiness that Washington, too, entertained broad plans for expansion led to equal emphasis being placed on an effort to co-operate with American economic interests; a program designed to tie the hands of imperial-minded politicians in Washington. But as St. Petersburg was to learn, the American financiers not only sought to drive extremely hard bargains in private negotiations but—and more important—lost control of their official allies in the government. When that occurred Russia was forced to abandon any efforts to achieve a community of interest with the United States in the Pacific and by necessity sought some measure of safety through a series of alliances with Japan.

The first of these Russian overtures to Washington came after the Japanese military victory at Mukden in 1905. Aware that Tokyo was in a position to stage an invasion of Siberia, St. Petersburg considered selling the island of Sakhalin to the United States. This, thought some at the Tsar's court, would not only remove the chance of Tokyo seizing the island and thereby outflanking the Siberian coast, but would also strengthen common interests with the United States. The Russian Ambassador in

Washington quickly pointed out that the United States Senate would no doubt refuse even to consider the transaction, and submitted an alternate proposal. "It would be better," wrote Ambassador Cassini, "to limit ourselves to the proposition of American concessions on this island which might be more acceptable, since American capitalists are making their exodus from Korea."

Cassini's plan was eagerly taken up and expanded by his superiors in St. Petersburg. In the first days of April, 1905, a scheme was devised whereby concessions in Sakhalin would be leased to an American—a move designed to obtain Washington's intervention on behalf of the American national if Japan threatened to occupy the island. Then, if the ruse worked, the concession would be developed in a regular fashion. But after serious consideration Tsar Nicholas II ruled that his subordinates had "better turn it down" because President Roosevelt's pro-Japanese sympathies were too strong: Roosevelt might well tell all to the Japanese rather than support the American investor.[3]

St. Petersburg made a more concerted effort to carry through the same broad plan—an alliance with American economic interests—after Japan's victory later in 1905. Desperately in need of financial assistance at the end of the war, Russia hoped to underwrite her own recovery and at the same time lay the foundation for future protection against a renewed attack by Japan. Thus ex-Finance Minister Witte, then serving as Russia's chief delegate to the Portsmouth Peace Conference, approached J. P. Morgan early in September, 1905, to negotiate a loan for Russia. Great confusion has surrounded these meetings because Witte also spoke with Jacob Schiff of Kuhn, Loeb and Company who played a leading role in financing the Japanese war effort—in part because of his bitter opposition of Tsarist treatment of Jews in Russia. Unable to obtain, from his point of view, a satisfactory guarantee of an immediate reversal of Tsarist policy on this issue, Schiff refused to participate in a loan to Russia. But this was not, as often presumed, the reason Russia failed to secure American aid.

Indeed, Morgan was more than willing to discuss economic assistance to St. Petersburg despite Schiff's opposition. But Morgan's terms were high: Russia was to promise not to negotiate any loans with Schiff in the future, and also guarantee the industrial corporations of the United States "special advantages" in all Russia's future purchases abroad. This latter specification was almost as confining as the restriction aimed at Schiff, for through the techniques of the holding company, mutual memberships on various boards of directors, and outright ownership the House of Morgan controlled industries—agricultural machinery and steel, for example—that would receive the bulk of Russian orders. In a real sense, therefore, Morgan's demands—if granted—would have given him the means to challenge Germany and France for their respective industrial and financial leadership in Russia. Witte left Portsmouth with this proposal under consideration.[4]

During this same period the new Russian Finance Minister V. N. Kokovtsev engaged an American, Judge Charles Mayer, to circulate the capitals of Europe in search of similar economic aid. As a consequence of his own efforts as supplemented by those of Witte, Mayer, and Eduard Netzlin, president of the Bank of Paris, Kokovtsev assembled an important group of bankers from London, Paris, Berlin, Amsterdam, and New York in St. Petersburg on October 15, 1905. Not unexpectedly, Kokovtsev used this opportunity to discuss Morgan's offer to Witte with the Morgan representatives who came to St. Petersburg to study the possibility of a consortium to finance Russia.[5]

These negotiations between Witte and Morgan on one hand and between Kokovtsev and the projected banking group—in which Morgan would hold membership if the plan matured—both failed, but for different reasons. Morgan's offer to Witte was declined because Kokovtsev considered the conditions laid down by the American financier to be too severe. "Of course," Kokovtsev phrased his oblique refusal to Morgan of October 31, 1905, "there can be no objection to granting your firm the desired financial and banking business with the unavoidable condition that this would not hinder the freedom of the Russian Minister of Finance in relation to those financial establishments in America with which we now stand in relations." As for Morgan's specification concerning the placement of Russian industrial orders, Kokovtsev indulged himself in a bit of irony. "I recognize all the significance and the outstanding value of establishing the closest possible trade relations between Russia and America. I have worked toward this end with all the powers at my disposal, but I cannot help but affirm that the industry of Russia is insufficiently developed to satisfy all the demands of your firm, guided [as Russia is] by the same emblem which guides all Americans—America for the Americans." But Kokovtsev did indicate that he would turn to America if the "needs of Russia brought on the necessity of turning to foreign industry." [6]

Kokovtsev's negotiations with the international banking group momentarily developed more favorably. With American participation, the projected Russian consortium agreed to grant a loan of one and a quarter billion francs; but the financiers quickly backed away when the Russian Revolution of 1905–6 appeared to threaten the Tsarist Government. "All bankers declared with one voice and very decisively," Kokovtsev wrote Witte on January 6, 1906, "that it would be completely impossible to go through with the credit operation" under the circumstances. A bit later Netzlin told Kokovtsev that the effect of continued instability in Russia "on the French market was that of a sudden thunder [clap]." [7]

But toward the end of 1906, when the Revolution had proved to be abortive and Tsarist rule was re-established, Kokovtsev and Netzlin began to plan anew. Netzlin's interest was centered on his scheme "to shift the financial center of the world from London to Paris" with the aid of Kuhn, Loeb and Company in the United States.[8] This project appealed to Kokovtsev on two grounds: it offered him an opportunity to circumvent Morgan's severe conditions by dealing with Schiff, and at the same time strike an economic alliance with American capital that might lead to political collaboration with Washington against Tokyo. While Netzlin's plan failed to materialize, Kokovtsev did begin to explore the possibility of interesting American financial powers in Russian, Siberian, and Manchurian developments.

Kokovtsev's shift of attention from Morgan to Schiff led into an equally complex set of negotiations with Schiff and his ally Harriman over railroad plans for the Far East and, later, conversations with Schiff about the possibility of internal concessions in Russia. In 1905 and 1906 Kokovtsev's concern with affairs in Manchuria and Korea was heightened by the Tsar's insistence that the Finance Ministry assume all the obligations of the old Bezobrazov lumber concession in northern Korea. Bezobrazov, a court conspirator in the years before the Russo-Japanese War, had used this project as a lever to pry Nicholas II from under the influence of Witte, who opposed the grandiose and militant plans for expansion pushed by Bezobrazov and his allies at the court.

But when Japan moved into Korea as a consequence of Russia's defeat in 1905, the whole Bezobrazov affair had to be liquidated in some manner. Kokovtsev tried to turn the situation to Russia's advantage by selling the lumber rights and other concessions obtained by the Bezobrazov crowd before the war to Americans. In this manner the Finance Minister hoped to implement his basic plan of co-operation with the United States against Japan. Though never successfully executed, the project did serve to re-enforce Kokovtsev's idea of further operations of a similar character.[9] During 1905 and 1906, in fact, Kokovtsev had carried on exploratory talks with Judge Charles Mayer and others who were interested in the chance to obtain a contract to build the Khabarovsk to Vladivostok section of the trans-Siberian Railway and industrial concessions within Russia.[10] Again nothing came of these conversations, but they do help to explain Kokovtsev's receptiveness to the overtures of Edward H. Harriman, who wanted a share in the future of the trans-Siberian and other railways in Manchuria.

The first move was made by Harriman, whose broad project was an around-the-world transportation system. "We'll girdle the globe," he explained enthusiastically to Lloyd C. Griscom, United States Ambassador to Japan. In such a plan the network of Manchurian railways—the Russian-controlled Chinese Eastern and the Japanese-dominated South Manchurian —was a crucial link. Access to the trans-Siberian was also of major importance, but Harriman hoped that Russia's recent defeat would make it "comparatively easy" to convince St. Petersburg "to transfer control to an American company." Russia had considered selling the Chinese Eastern as early as 1887, but none of the periodic revivals of the idea ever led to serious negotiations. Similar rumors of sale had been heard with reference to the trans-Siberian. But two reasons led Harriman to make his first overtyre to the Japanese. He thought that Tokyo's financial weakness would enhance his chances to obtain the South Manchurian railway. More important, he had joined Jacob Schiff, who helped finance Harriman's railroad empire in the United States, to back Japan's war effort, and he anticipated the extension of that successful relationship.[11]

Despite the outbreak of demonstrations against the Portsmouth Treaty, touched off by Japan's failure to secure an indemnity from Russia, that accompanied Harriman's negotiations in Tokyo during September and October, 1905, he did conclude a preliminary agreement for equal control of the South Manchurian and the "development of all industrial enterprises in Manchuria." Harriman was well pleased, but this understanding was quickly canceled in the face of "great opposition" from Japanese Foreign Minister Komura. Harriman, however, was by no means defeated.

Long before, the railway magnate had tucked an ace up his sleeve. This insurance took the form of a young, brash, and ambitious man named Willard Straight who had served in the Far East as a reporter for the Associated Press and as private secretary to Edward V. Morgan, President Roosevelt's choice as successor to the troublesome Horace Allen. Straight not only shared Morgan's friendship with Roosevelt but was known to Harriman, who "needed to have a man like Willard Straight scouting for him in Manchuria." When Japan moved in to guarantee Korea's independence it was quite natural, therefore, that Straight was sent to the next line of defense—Manchuria—as Consul General at Mukden. Immediately the young official opened a vigorous campaign to halt the Japanese advance in that area.[12]

The concern was well warranted. Even before the war ended Japan controlled the "bulk of the trade" and enjoyed a "practical monopoly" of shipping services to Korea. Though Americans dominated the Manchurian market at the outbreak of hostilities, Japan made it quickly and officially clear that she expected victory to give her "a predominant position" in the area. "The economic loss sustained by us on account of the war," promised Count Okuma, "will be more than balanced by the profit we shall derive from the economic exploitation of Manchuria." Nor was Tokyo slow to activate her plans. For many months after the end of the war American property holders in Port Arthur and Dalny—among them the American Trading Company and the Boston Steamship Company— suffered considerable "anxiety," for Japan used the occupation to redirect Manchurian exports.[13]

A depression further hampered American merchants when they resumed operations, but that was not the primary reason why they lost control of the market. By the end of 1907 the Japanese cotton export syndicate, the Mitsui Bussan Karsha, controlled imports at Dalny, and with the aid of special credit arrangements other Japanese were "gradually taking over" even the market for clocks at Newchwang.[14] That the Standard Oil Company, the British-American Tobacco Company, and some United States exporters of rails to the Japanese-controlled South Manchurian Railway continued to offer active competition did not alter the fact that Theodore Roosevelt's faith in Tokyo's allegiance to the open door was something less than justified.

As a technique of opposition Straight chose the "investment of a large volume of American capital," a plan he had discussed with Harriman. Even before he completed the reorganization of the consulate, Straight opened negotiations with the Chinese for an immediate railroad extension from Hsinmintun to Fakumen "with the idea of eventually carrying the extension . . . to . . . Aigun on the Amur River." Himself a "man with a mission"—that of empire building—Straight anticipated, and incurred, Japanese opposition and the displeasure of his immediate superior, Minister to China William Rockhill.[15] Nor did the enthusiastic young consul's close connections with Harriman, other economic powers, and the Roosevelt Administration produce immediate results.

The first blow was Harriman's inability to take up the Fakumen project because the financial panic of 1907 made it impossible to raise "the necessary funds." Of equal import was Roosevelt's belated admission that he had failed to preserve the "abrasion fronts" in Manchuria. His own fear of the Japanese was supplemented by the rising anti-Japanese agitation on the Pacific Coast that "strained Japanese-American relations almost to the breaking point." Frankly worried, Roosevelt became "horribly bothered" by the "infernal fools in California." [16] He first negotiated a guarantee for the Philippines in return for recognition of Japan's "suzerainty over" Korea. The President next calmed the West Coast Japophobes as best he could and then arranged a gentleman's agreement with Tokyo under which Japanese immigration would be severely restricted.[17]

But Roosevelt, ever aware of Brooks Adams' warning not to appear " 'opulent, aggressive, and unarmed,' " was "anxious" to assure the Japanese that he was "not afraid of them." Some years after the crisis he recalled that "it was time for a showdown"—a recollection supported by an exclamation at the time. "Thank Heaven," he wrote Secretary of State Root, "we have the navy in good shape." Clearly, his dispatch of the fleet on a world cruise was designed to remind Japan that her destruction of the Russian fleet had not swept the seas. But neither Roosevelt's diplomatic maneuvers nor his show of force helped Consul Straight in Mukden. Tokyo's authority in Manchuria was based on occupation, and as early as February, 1907, American observers reported further Japanese infiltration into the area.[18]

Nor did the fact that other nations acquiesced in Tokyo's victory make Straight's task any easier. France led the procession with an agreement to "support . . . the respective situation and the territorial rights of the two Contracting Parties in the Continent of Asia." This move "supplied the formula" by which Izvolski began to overcome the "objections of certain groups" in St. Petersburg that favored an American orientation.[19] His first treaty, July 30, 1907, was one "to sustain and defend the maintenance of the *status quo* . . . by all the pacific means." The character of the *status quo* was, moreover, explicitly defined in a secret convention.[20] Japan's position was further strengthened a month later when England and Russia signed a truce in Persia, Afghanistan, and Tibet. For this agreement between London and St. Petersburg gave Japan an even greater area of freedom of action under the Anglo-Japanese Treaty of 1902. Consul General Denby at Peking neatly summarized the situation: the "open door in China," he wrote, "has at present . . . less hope of realization than at the time it was first conceived." [21]

Yet the pro-American group in St. Petersburg was far from overpowered. Through Paris in October, 1907, they sent "a feeler in the nature of a proposal by suggestion" for a Far Eastern convention with the United States. Secretary of State Root apparently "showed a good deal of interest in the suggestion," but only as another means to guarantee the Philippines. No consideration was given to the idea of real collaboration with Russia, and no response was ever made to this overture from St. Petersburg.[22] Despite Washington's indifference toward Russia and further evidence of Japan's strong position—London also refused to support her nationals in the Hsinmintun-Fakumen project when Tokyo protested—Willard Straight continued his efforts to expand American influence in Manchuria.

Though his militant activities called forth a specific inquiry by the Japanese Ambassador in Washington, Straight pressed on to a discussion of "the investment of American capital in China" with Secretary of War Taft. Taft was interested, but "didn't seem very optimistic." [23] Straight was undeterred and continued his negotiations with the Chinese. On August 11, 1908, the consul's persistence was rewarded by a Chinese request for American aid to establish a Manchurian bank to underwrite industrial developments in that area and to finance a railroad north to Aigun. Not too surprising, given Straight's vigorous activity in support of such a plan, was the Chinese specification that the proposal be forwarded to Harriman.

At this same time the Department of State ordered Straight to return to the United States on furlough. But there was more behind the Department's generosity than either the protests of the Japanese or a concern for the welfare of foreign service agents. "The reason," explained a key member of the State Department, "is as follows: 'Wall Street' is feeling confident again and is looking for the investment of capital in foreign lands. It has turned to Manchuria and wants the latest advice on the situation up there, probably, I assume, in the nature of Railways or the exploitation of the country through the central Manchurian Bank Scheme." [24]

At first glance Straight's success seems to have ended when he and the Chinese representative discussed the plan with Roosevelt and Secretary Root. For at the time of Straight's return and the Chinese representative's arrival in the fall of 1909, Roosevelt and Root were negotiating with the Japanese. Tokyo, acutely conscious that Straight's plan would link Harriman with the Russians in Manchuria, had immediately initiated discussions with Washington on learning of Straight's success in arranging a new draft agreement for a line north through Manchuria. Roosevelt and Root responded very cautiously, and in the Root-Takahira Agreement of November, 1908, agreed to do no more than underwrite the "existing *status quo* in the region of the Pacific Ocean." But to many observers this has appeared to be an American retreat. Straight helped confuse the issue by his oft-quoted remark that the deal was, "like the Korean withdrawal, . . . a terrible diplomatic blunder to be laid at the door of T.R." [25]

This view fails to account for the key fact that Roosevelt and Root directed Straight to arrange talks between the Chinese and Harriman *at the same time they negotiated with the Japanese*. To be sure, the President and the Secretary of State were not yet ready to return openly to the offensive in Asia, but neither did Washington entertain the faintest notion of giving Tokyo "a free hand in Manchuria"—as one writer has maintained. Indeed, the Department of State observed that "it really looks as if American interests in the Far East were going to assume a pretty definite shape." As for Straight, his angry judgment was the product of Washington's failure to provide immediate and active support for Harriman's Aigun project. Far from being Washington's responsibility, the factor that did disrupt the plan to push back into Manchuria behind cover supplied by the Chinese was the death of the Emperor and Empress Dowager of China —an event that forced the Chinese representative to break off negotiations with Harriman and return to Peking. [26]

This second setback was modified by developments during the winter of 1908–9. In November, 1908, at the end of his neatly timed furlough, Straight moved back into the State Department to take charge of the Far Eastern Division, a key spot from which to co-ordinate relations between the financiers and the government. Then came new indications that Russia might sell the Chinese Eastern; overtures immediately followed up by Harriman, still bent on his railroad plans in Manchuria despite Japanese opposition. The financier's position was strengthened by Japan's military activity in southern Manchuria which, despite the Russo-Japanese Treaty of 1907, increased the tension between Tokyo and St. Petersburg. Of similar importance was the fact that in March, 1909, the more militantly expansionist wing of the State Department bureaucracy moved into power with, and was strengthened by, the inauguration of President William Howard Taft. He, it is vital to note, kept Straight as chief of the Far Eastern Division until after the organization in June, 1909, of a formal American financial group to push economic penetration in Asia.

Russia's interest in the sale of the Chinese Eastern stemmed from two factors: economically the property was in "bad shape," a situation that re-enforced St. Petersburg's inclination to support Harriman's plan to outflank Tokyo in Manchuria through control of the line. Harriman's second failure, in the spring of 1906, to reach an agreement with Japan over the South Manchurian led him "to feel around" for a plan capable of "extinguishing Japanese interference." Harriman's goal seems to have been control of the Manchurian railways without *conscious* or *preconceived* political overtones. Yet Japan's continued intransigence forced him to seek an understanding with Russia. He and Schiff began, therefore, to maneuver for an opening around Straight's twice-negotiated project of a loan to China for Manchurian industrial development and the railroad north to Aigun.[27] For coupled with control of the Chinese Eastern this north-south Aigun line would give Harriman the power to by-pass Tokyo's South Manchurian and control Manchuria's transportation system.

Russia was aware of this situation through the reports of Gregory Wilenkin, the Russian Finance Ministry's agent in the United States, whose range of information was broadened and whose ease of entry into the key economic and social circles in the United States was enhanced by virtue of his marriage to an American woman. St. Petersburg responded quickly when, in the summer of 1908, Wilenkin recommended to his superiors, Finance Minister Kokovtsev and Minister of Foreign Affairs Izvolski, that Schiff and Harriman be approached on two counts: Russia's need for funds, and a plan to maneuver Japan into selling the South Manchurian, along with Russia's Chinese Eastern, ostensibly to China, but actually to a syndicate controlled by Schiff and Harriman. Izvolski not only approved Wilenkin's plan but carried through on the political implications of the project by proposing, in late December, 1908, a tripartite pact between China, the United States, and Russia to settle "all questions concerning Manchuria and the Pacific Ocean area in general." [28] Concerned rather with plans to re-establish American supremacy in Manchuria, the State Department ignored this overture.

Wilenkin, meanwhile, opened negotiations with Schiff in the fall of 1908. Having turned away from Morgan because of the stiff conditions he specified for aid, the Russians still faced the problem of Schiff's antagonism over the Jewish issue. In two talks with Schiff, Wilenkin suggested that the American financier go to Russia "to form for himself an opinion as to the situation." In reply, Schiff "gave a written agreement to go if Kokovtsev would invite him" for discussions on loans to Russia and "removing the restrictions on Russian Jews." Yet when Kokovtsev failed to follow through with the invitation Schiff continued his discussions with Wilenkin.

Two considerations would appear to explain Schiff's apparent retreat from the advanced position he had taken on the issue of pogroms in Russia, first in his talks with Witte in 1905, and then with Wilenkin in late 1908. For when Schiff's vigorous support of Japan during the Russo-Japanese War is recalled—action that brought him into conflict with Morgan, at least in the early stages of the war—the question immediately arises as to whether Schiff shifted ground there also. He did not; and Schiff's insistence that Japan participate in Wilenkin's projected purchase of the Manchurian railways offers the first clue to his position. For Schiff viewed Wilenkin's plan in a vastly different light than did either the Russian financial agent or his superiors in St. Petersburg.

Schiff explained to his friend Baron Takahashi, head of the Yokohama Specie Bank, that Tokyo's concurrence "would place Japan in a position where, with the passing out of the hands of Russia of the Chinese Eastern Railway, the influence of the latter would become so much further removed from both China's and Japan's borders." Thus Schiff hoped to avail himself of the "colossal financial opportunities in the railroads of Manchuria" that St. Petersburg offered—but through an alliance with Japan rather than Russia. At the same time, he saw the "prospects of large financial, commercial, and political gains" also offered by the Russians as an opportunity to be probed in its own right.[29]

But Schiff's grandiose plans were frustrated by Japan—the very power in which he placed so much confidence. Keenly conscious of her key position, Japan spurned Schiff's advances. Tokyo "would not consider the sale of the South Manchurian" and advised him "to abandon all further activity in this connection." As will be seen, Schiff was exceedingly slow to realize that he had misplaced his trust in Japan, but St. Petersburg had no illusions on that issue. Little matter that the Tsar thought Wilenkin's plan "excellent," for Russia could not move in the face of Tokyo's opposition. Japan's warning to Schiff immobilized Russia. Wilenkin was advised in the spring of 1909 that it was absolutely necessary "to adopt a waiting attitude in order that the initiative . . . would not appear to have come from the Russian Government or any of its agents."[30] The implication, clearly enough, was that St. Petersburg hoped Washington would pick up the idea and provide political support for the economic maneuver. But this expectation was to prove futile, for Washington had no plan to cooperate with Russia—or Japan.

Russia's sudden hesitance to push ahead stemmed from the fear that Japan was staging a new attack aimed either at North Manchuria or the Siberian Maritime Provinces. In the last days of April, 1909, Tsarist agents warned that Tokyo could overrun the area that very spring. The reports took on added meaning when Japan extracted new concessions from China during the next months.[31] But Tokyo's further expansion also brought new warnings from Washington's representatives both in China and Russia, the character of which bore a marked resemblance to the earlier advice of Charles Denby and Horace Allen.

The first hint came from Peking on August 23, 1909, when the Chinese were reported "now more anxious than ever to secure concrete American and other non-Japanese interests in Manchuria" as a check on Tokyo. Within ten days word came from St. Petersburg that "distrust of the Japanese" was steadily "increasing." Now, the agent suggested, "it would seem as if the time were ripe for informal discussion of this question," for "responsible persons" in the Russian Government looked to just such an agreement as "a check upon the ambitions of Japan in Asia." A bit later the new Ambassador to Russia, William Rockhill, verified these reports and asked instructions as to his "future course of action." [32]

Simultaneously, the old Harriman-Straight plan to buy the Chinese Eastern, then build a new line north to Aigun, and so outflank Tokyo, was again revived. Despite their many reverses, neither Harriman nor Schiff "[was] willing to abandon the idea of participating in the profits of railway development in China." [33] But Straight, who remained Harriman's personal agent in these plans, had meanwhile engineered Washington's more active involvement in the effort to penetrate China economically.

Formally, of course, the Department of State did ask Harriman and Schiff to admit Morgan to their counsels and become the agency of American participation in Chinese railway loans. But two aspects of this development need to be analyzed closely. Of immediate note is the basic nature of the relationship: Morgan joined Harriman and Schiff. The fact that Harriman and Schiff initiated Straight's recall from Mukden in 1908 (" 'Wall Street' is feeling confident again"), and the consideration that Straight had official approval to negotiate a private loan for reentry into Manchuria while Roosevelt and Root talked to the Japanese about the *status quo*, make it difficult to accept the view that Straight suddenly stopped representing Harriman when he returned to duty in the State Department in November, 1908, as chief of the Far Eastern Division. President Taft and Secretary Knox unquestionably supported economic expansion, but to conclude—as one writer has—that they took the initiative "to attempt to force American capital by diplomatic pressure into a region of the world where it would not go of its own accord" simply does not correspond with the known fact that Harriman and others—the International Banking Corporation, for example—had been trying to get into Asia since 1905.

After his double rebuff by Japan, Harriman consciously sought to gain entry via China and in co-operation with Russia. Of prime importance is the consideration that Straight, although he resigned his department job ostensibly to serve the combined Morgan-Harriman-Schiff group, first went to Paris to meet Harriman, then negotiating with the Russians and their Paris banker Netzlin for the purchase of the Chinese Eastern. "I want to use Straight," Harriman advised Henry P. Davison of the House of Morgan, "for some purposes of my own." This emphasizes that Straight, although representing Morgan for purposes of the Hukuang Loan, laid a primary stress on pushing through Harriman's Chin-Ai project. When Harriman died before the operation could be executed, Straight found it necessary to brief *both* Schiff and Morgan on the entire concept of collaboration with the Russians for control of the Chinese Eastern.

For not only was Schiff's interest centered on the Manchurian loan aspect of the Harriman-Straight scheme, but in all probability, Morgan had been taken into the Hukuang project without being briefed on the primary purpose of the entire plan: manipulate Washington's official support for the Manchurian enterprise. If for no other reason than to protect his own position, therefore, Straight had to make a major effort to get Morgan to take over Harriman's role in the Chin-Ai negotiations. In addition Straight was most anxious to identify himself with the House of Morgan for prestige and economic reasons.[34] These considerations suggest strongly that the lack of confidence and the active "dissention" within the Hukuang Consortium—of which later observers spoke—was not solely the consequence of the failure to penetrate China proper.

In any event, Harriman's need for political support, both in Washington and St. Petersburg, to push through his Manchurian railroad plans in the face of Japanese opposition was clearly the major impetus behind the Straight-directed formation of a formal group to participate in Chinese loans. But Taft, Knox, and the State Department bureaucracy did not, like Harriman, place primary emphasis on co-operation with the Russians to carry through a plan that was basically economic in original conception. This became evident when Harriman convinced the Russian Finance Minister to recommend the sale of the Chinese Eastern, despite Foreign Minister Izvolski's fears that the move would touch off a new Japanese attack on Russia in the Far East.[35] For Harriman's negotiations, which reflected the influence of those in St. Petersburg who inclined toward an understanding with Washington—for which Harriman's project might have provided an economic foundation—were not supported by the policies implemented by Taft and Knox. Rather did the President and the Secretary of State, once armed with an economic lance, attempt to open Manchuria to American penetration for the purpose of achieving political supremacy in Asia.

President Taft's oft-quoted remark of 1912 that his foreign policy was "an effort frankly directed" to the increase of American trade was in no sense an over-enthusiastic judgment after the fact. Two years earlier he noted that it was of the "utmost importance" to pursue a policy of "active intervention to secure for our merchandise and our capitalists opportunity for profitable investment which shall insure to the benefit of both countries concerned." Taft's appointment of Philander Chase Knox, a corporation lawyer most sympathetic to overseas economic expansion, as Secretary of State exemplified the President's early intention to revert to Roosevelt's pre-Portsmouth policy—vigorous and determined expansion in Asia. Knox's first act was to reorganize the State Department "in the interests of business and finance." [36]

Already in existence, by virtue of Secretary Root's earlier but less thorough reorganization, was the Far Eastern Division. With Willard Straight, the key figure in this division was William Phillips, a career diplomat who became the first chief of the division in March, 1908, just prior to Straight's return from Mukden. Educated in a private school and at Harvard, Phillips became a member of the Anglophile group around Hay and Henry Adams at an early date. "Close to Roosevelt," Phillips served his apprenticeship as Joseph H. Choate's private secretary when the latter was Ambassador to England from 1903 to 1905. From that job Phillips moved to the Peking Embassy for a tour of duty and then into the State Department. In subsequent years he played a vital role in the formulation and execution of American policy toward Russia. From the very beginning he advocated a vigorous policy in the Far East and served as liaison between the Department and the House of Morgan, Harriman, Schiff, and other financial interests.[37]

Phillips was the one who explained to Rockhill that Straight was recalled from Manchuria in 1908 because " 'Wall Street' is feeling confident again." Not unexpected, therefore, was Phillips' view that Roosevelt's policy of a *modus vivendi* with Japan was a temporary expedient to be circumvented as soon as possible. "The Department," Phillips summarized for Knox, who placed great trust in Phillips, "has in view the general extension of American influence in China so that when the commercial interests and exporters of the United States turn their attention more vigorously toward securing the markets of the Orient, they will find those of China open to their products and the Chinese public favorably disposed toward American enterprise." [38] In the meantime Phillips helped push financial penetration.

This desire to achieve dominance in Asia explains Washington's failure to support Harriman's efforts to work with St. Petersburg. Rockhill, transferred from Peking to St. Petersburg because Knox considered "that by far the most important post and where we have real problems to overcome," was advised to assume "a receptive attitude" to the overtures from Russia, but neither Knox nor his associates had any intention of following up St. Petersburg's proposals. Beyond the basic plan to "assume a bold front" in Asia, several considerations help explain this decision.[39] Not only did Roosevelt's militant Russophobia linger on in Taft's administration, but neither Washington nor the financiers grasped the essence of Harriman's object—weaken Japan's grip on Manchuria by supporting Russia.

Similarly, the legacy of Anglophilism and their own preoccupation with the Far East tended to blind the policy makers in Washington to the fact that Britain's central concern now was the rising power of Germany, and that London would not risk losing the support of Tokyo and St. Petersburg on that issue, particularly in view of the price England had paid in China, Tibet, Persia, and Afghanistan. As for the technique to be employed, Washington fell back on Secretary Hay's concept of the open door, which seemed to offer the best chance for American capital "to compete successfully with other foreign capital in the investment field in China." [40] But these investments, the State Department was quick to point out, would "give the voice of the United States more authority in political controversies in that country." [41]

These considerations are best exemplified in President Taft's militant insistence that American capital be admitted to a proposed Chinese railroad loan and Secretary Knox's scheme to "neutralize" the Manchurian railways with American capital. For coupled with the death of Harriman in September, 1909—midway between these two offensives by Washington —the development of these maneuvers reveals the manner in which the President and the State Department seized control of a policy initiated by one group of financiers—Harriman and Schiff—and then sought to use an expanded economic potential to achieve political supremacy in Asia. Essential to an understanding of the first phase of this pattern is an awareness of Straight's return to the Department as chief of the Far Eastern Division in November, 1908.

His first task had been to help conduct negotiations between Harriman and the Chinese for consummation of Straight's own draft agreement for a Manchurian bank loan and the railroad north to Aigun. These conversations, which were "making satisfactory headway," were disrupted by the death of the Empress Dowager of China.[42] Harriman, who dealt directly with the Russians concerning the Chinese Eastern, concluded that a similar technique would prove more successful with the Chinese. He asked Straight

to leave the Department and go to Peking to settle the question of a contract for the line north to Aigun which would, when combined with an
agreement with St. Petersburg, complete a Harriman-Russian squeeze play
against the Japanese.

Instead, Straight chose to remain in the Department to see what could
be done from that key position when Taft replaced Roosevelt. In late May,
1909, Straight saw the chance he sought to link official diplomacy to the
economic penetration of China. For England, France, and Germany had all
but completed final arrangements to finance and construct a net of railroads in South Central China tentatively known as the Hukuang Railways despite the fact that London, Paris, and Peking had earlier admitted
the right of American capital to a share in the operation. Straight seized the
opportunity to initiate diplomatic support for economic activity in China.
Ostensibly, he "started the row" over events in South China, but the move
was designed to clear the way for a full-scale challenge to Japan in Manchuria.

As for the Hukuang project, the Department, with Straight still chief
of the Far Eastern Division, invited the House of Morgan, the First National, and the National City Banks to join Harriman and Schiff as agents
of American participation. Taft's approval was not surprising, for the President remarked at the beginning of his term that his foreign policy might
"well be made to include active intervention to secure for our merchandise
and our capitalists opportunities for profitable investment." [43] The opportunity to effect that "active intervention" had come with reference to the
Hukuang railways, but Straight and Harriman kept their interest focused
on Manchuria.

Thus when Straight left the Department in June—after Washington
was committed to the principle of diplomatic support for economic intervention—he did not proceed directly to Peking to push the Hukuang operation. First he stopped off in London to argue the American case for participation in that loan before the European bankers. Unsuccessful there,
Straight went on to Paris to join Harriman, then negotiating for purchase
of the Chinese Eastern from Russia. After his talks with Harriman, Straight
proceeded to China—but for two purposes. Of primary import was the
plan—"I want to use Straight for some purposes of my own," Harriman
had advised the House of Morgan—that called for Straight to re-negotiate
the contract for the Aigun line while Harriman handled the purchase of
the Chinese Eastern. Of distinctly secondary importance to Harriman and
Straight was the Hukuang project.

Not so with President Taft, Secretary Knox, and others in the Department. Far from being a plan to collaborate with Russia, Washington's concept was American supremacy. Thus when Straight's talks with
the European bankers did not achieve the desired results—immediate ad-

mittance to the Hukuang loan—Taft took matters into his own hands on July 15, 1909. The President, who had "an intense personal interest" in the question, bluntly demanded that China grant "equal participation" rights to the American group. The President may have "saved the prestige of the administration"—a consideration apparently as important as the "promotion of the welfare of China"—but the railway project failed to survive the jostling.[44]

More important—Taft's militance undermined the influence of Finance Minister Kokovtsev's pro-American group in St. Petersburg. For Baron Rosen, the Russian Ambassador to the United States, did not miss the meaning of Taft's action. The President's protest to China, Rosen advised his superior, Foreign Minister Izvolski, was "not called forth simply by the desire to grant a group of American banks participation in a small railroad loan." Rather did the act appear to Rosen as the "first step" toward the broad "expansion of the sphere of American interests in China." [45]

Rosen's judgment was shortly verified. For when Harriman died, September 10, 1909, on the eve of Straight's successful negotiations "for the financing, construction, and operation of a railway from Chinchow to Aigun," the President and the Department of State seized Harriman's old plan as a means to reassert American political power in Manchuria. To carry through the project as conceived by Harriman, either Schiff, Morgan, or Washington would have had to pick up the thread of negotiations with the Russians. But only St. Petersburg continued to think in those terms. For Straight, now isolated by virtue of his resignation from the Department and Harriman's death, had no independent power. His only opportunity was to convince Harriman's associates in the Hukuang operation to shift their attention to the Aigun contract and purchase of the Chinese Eastern.

Most revealing at this point is the fact that Straight had to explain the whole Harriman project to *both* Schiff and Morgan. Henry P. Davison of the House of Morgan later agreed that Straight did "exactly the right thing" in pushing through the Aigun contract despite Harriman's death, but at that critical moment neither his firm nor Schiff stepped in to continue negotiations with St. Petersburg. Straight did his best to keep that key aspect of the plan alive, but to no avail. In great detail he explained both to Morgan and Schiff that "American capital would be used to bolster waning Russian prestige in the Orient, besides insuring for themselves the political support of the Russian Government in their enterprises in Manchuria and Mongolia." There would "be no question" about the use of American construction materials on the Aigun line, he amplified, but stressed the fact that the real goal was "ultimate acquisition of the Chinese Eastern Railway." For the time being Straight's new superiors declined to act on this urgent request that they continue talks with Russia.[46]

Straight's inability to refocus the attention of Morgan and Schiff on the need for alignment with Russia was of especial significance in the light of St. Petersburg's continued overtures to the United States. Clearly, the Finance Minister could not sustain his holding action against Japan without American aid. If such aid was not forthcoming, moreover, those who held that Russia's only chance to avoid another war with Japan was in alignment with Tokyo could proceed to implement that policy with little effective opposition from the pro-American group. "During the month of October," therefore, "the Russian Government inquired . . . whether the United States would be disposed to welcome Russian co-operation in future railway loans to China." Ever since the conclusion of the war with Japan, reported an American agent in explanation, Russian distrust of Japan "has been constantly increasing. At present it would seem," he suggested, "as if the time were ripe for the informal discussion of this question by the two governments"—for accommodation "would serve . . . as a check upon the ambitions of Japan which are now seen to be boundless." Rockhill verified these observations, as did another advisor, who thought the reports to be "very interesting and provide food for serious consideration on the part of Department officials." Washington's "very clear expression of a disposition entirely favorable" was not borne out, however, as subsequent events were to reveal.[47]

Nor was Russia's concern eased by this general reply. St. Petersburg could not square the character of Washington's policy toward Russian influence in northern Manchuria with Harriman's efforts to buy the Chinese Eastern. Taft and Knox had revived, and pushed belligerently, the old issue of Russian authority in Harbin, a vital economic and administrative center along the Chinese Eastern. President Roosevelt tried to force American entry there earlier; and despite a warning that Tokyo held her "position in Manchuria in a far tighter and more lasting grip than the Russians did before the war," Knox returned to the attack with particular vigor. This action "no doubt" strengthened Izvolski's position against the pro-American group, as did the report of another Russian observer who held that St. Petersburg "cannot rely on the active support of America." This was St. Petersburg's chief concern, for Japan was in a position to use force if Russia publicly sought a new alignment with the United States.[48] St. Petersburg realized that a prior understanding— economic—or political—with Washington concerning Manchuria was vital if Tokyo was to be checked. Otherwise, Japan would have to deal only with Russia.

Secretary Knox was *not* ignorant of this Russian fear. On November 2, 1909, an American representative advised that without American support the Russians might well be driven "to make common cause with Japan." On November 10, 1909, Straight warned Morgan that Russia could decide to "make a pact with Japan" unless "some understanding" was rapidly effected. Straight's information came from a Russian representative in Peking, and the news caused the New York group to accept Davison's view of the situation and give Straight "permission to go ahead . . . [and] negotiate with the Russians." But Straight decided to wait until China formally ratified the Aigun project—with the result that "no negotiations were started." As Straight's official biographer admits, this was a "crucial mistake." [49]

For whatever the reason behind Straight's decision to delay reopening talks with the Russians, it could hardly have been the thought that Washington would initiate the move. When Straight talked to the Russian spokesman in Peking, a State Department representative was with him whose response to the news that Izvolski might push through an agreement with Japan was a preview of events to come. Washington, this agent replied, was "committed to certain principles" that would be upheld "no matter whether the opposition came from Russia and Japan acting individually or together." The principle, of course, was the open door—purpose of which in this context was to regain Washington's influence in Manchuria. Against this background the significance of concurrent events in St. Petersburg becomes clear. [50]

For Washington had no serious interest in the Russian concept of cooperation against Japan. Rather did Knox view the situation as an opportunity to seize control of the Manchurian railways and associated economic developments. Rockhill was advised to maintain a receptive attitude. Meanwhile Washington prepared a projected coup. Quite unaware of these plans, Rockhill approached Izvolski during the first two weeks of November "about the necessity for Russia to go hand in hand with the United States in regard to Manchurian affairs." Though the State Department knew of Harriman's plan, and Russia's interest therein, these instructions to Rockhill were not conceived as a response to the suggestions from St. Petersburg. Their character is revealed in Knox's directive to Rockhill to make "shrewd and discreet use" of an entirely different plan that the Secretary hoped to present to the Russians as a *fait accompli*.

This project was Washington's scheme for control by neutralization as financed by a Morgan-Schiff combination—a proposal that stemmed from the old Harriman-Straight contract for the construction of the Chin-Ai line. For, as Knox reasoned, Chinese approval of the Chin-Ai contract gave the United States and Britain the power with which to defeat both Russia and Japan. The Secretary overlooked one important factor: neither St. Petersburg nor London could afford to antagonize Tokyo unless strengthened by an accord with Washington. The motivation behind Russia's overtures was the need for help against Japan, while England sought help from St. Petersburg against Germany—and guarantees for her own stake in

China from Japan. Under these circumstances all three countries viewed the Secretary's plan as a squeeze play designed to win Manchuria for American capital. Yet Knox drove ahead, determined to secure control.

This Knox plan of November, 1909, to neutralize the Manchurian rail system—*or build the Chin-Ai line with England*—was the final manifestation of developments that began as early as June, 1908, when Straight was on his way back from Mukden in response to Wall Street's revived interest in Manchuria. "The Manchurian situation," State Department bureaucrat Phillips explained to Rockhill, then in Peking, on June 3, 1908, "has changed a bit of late, for Germany has *very confidentially* shaken hands with us and is in complete accord with our views. We have approached Great Britain, and are endeavoring to get her to place a consul at Harbin. Russia, on her part," Phillips went on in a manner that pointed to the target of Washington's attack, "has been very active in trying to enlist the sympathies of Europe to her side, with, we are told, a certain amount of success. However," Phillips concluded, "if the United States, Great Britain and Germany can stand together out there we shall be able to assume a bold front."

A year later, while Straight worked to get diplomatic support for Harriman, another member of the State Department reminded Secretary of State Knox of this old plan. The timing was significant, for the revival came after Straight's first move to commit Washington to the principle of intervention in support of economic activity in China. If the "understanding" with Germany and Great Britain could be expanded to include France, Knox was advised on June 19, 1909, then Manchuria would become a "promising field and from [both the] commercial and the political point of view." On October 18, 1909, two weeks after he learned of China's approval of the Chin-Ai contract and one day after he had sounded the British on support for the project, Secretary Knox ordered a subordinate to prepare a full report on "our interest in Manchurian matters," giving particular attention to mining properties and what territorial and administrative rights went with control of the various railroads.

Against this background the Secretary then proposed to Great Britain *alone* on November 6, 1909, that the Manchurian railways be united under nominal Chinese control through a foreign loan "upon such terms as would make it attractive to bankers and investors." Knox acknowledged that the plan would "require the co-operation of China and of Japan and Russia," but he did not explain his failure to consult those nations. Instead, he suggested that if the first proposal was not accepted, "the desired end" would be attained if London and Washington carried through the Aigun project. London replied that the first suggestion was, for the present at least, "undesirable." As for the second, Japan would have to be admitted as a partner before it was given further consideration.[51]

Two considerations indicate that Knox consciously sought to duplicate Secretary Hay's bluff of 1899. First is the fact that Washington knew of Harriman's plan and, further, was well aware of St. Petersburg's fear of Japanese intentions in Manchuria and of Russia's consequent overtures for collaboration with Washington. Yet despite this knowledge Knox not only failed to consult Russia first but actually directed Rockhill to be "shrewd and discreet" while he sought England's prior approval. When confronted by London's refusal to go along, the Secretary merely followed his own advice. On December 14, 1909, Knox presented his plan to Germany, France, China, Japan, and Russia, with the sober announcement that London approved in "principle," and requested each to acknowledge his "like favorable consideration" of the plan. He admitted that this request was motivated in large measure because the Aigun project was the subject of "publicity and uninformed discussion" in London, St. Petersburg, and Tokyo—discussion which might "tend to greatly prejudice if not . . . entirely defeat" the proposal.[52] The Secretary's fear was well grounded.

As Knox noted, Tokyo was deeply concerned over the possibility of a Russo-American agreement. The Russian Finance Minister's trip to the Far East in October, 1909, motivated in large measure by his tentative arrangement with Harriman for the sale of the Chinese Eastern, prompted Japan to suggest "a closer understanding for the protection of the Russo-Japanese interests." The Japanese press began to dwell on the need for a "counterweight against American designs in Manchuria."[53] Those were the days when Rockhill followed his instruction to "foster the idea of Russian co-operation"—a move that, since it was not backed by any definite commitment, did little more than move Tokyo to propose a "formal alliance."[54] However strong may have been the desire of the Tsar and the Finance Minister's group to reach some understanding with the United States, the unmistakable character of Japan's offer could not be ignored. Foreign Minister Izvolski phrased his answer to the Kokovtsev argument very simply: if Russia joined any plan to push Japan out of Manchuria without firm assurances of American support, the result for Russia would probably mean "pushing her to our borders."[55]

Russia could do little but reject neutralization in the face of Japan's pressure. This fact has led many to conclude that there was no chance to counter Tokyo;[56] but closer examination reveals that Russia continued to seek an alignment with the United States for some two years. Deeply afraid that Japan would launch a second attack—this time aimed at eastern Siberia—St. Petersburg made a third overture to Washington in 1911. But the State Department once again ignored the suggestion in favor of continued efforts to secure unilateral control. Knox not only misled Rockhill on the neutralization scheme; after that project failed the

Secretary disregarded both St. Petersburg's open appeal and the Ambassador's pointed warning that co-operation with Russia was of "supreme importance." [57] By the time Washington began to realize the validity of Rockhill's recommendation domestic pressures in the United States and Japan's growing strength combined to forestall even a belated response to the Russian proposal.

The Secretary's instructions to Rockhill to withhold official verification of the Chin-Ai plan intensified Russian suspicions. When Tokyo advised St. Petersburg that Knox's "proposition" made it "imperative to enter immediately" into negotiations, Izvolski made a great point of the fact that he "was the last to be informed" of the Aigun project. Rockhill had little choice but to take the blame for the failure of Knox's scheme, but the Secretary engineered the maneuver as the pivot of the entire plan.[58] Even the Harbin dispute was a secondary matter. "From our point of view," Knox explained, "the railway neutralization plan will settle the Harbin question, and is infinitely more important." Control of the railroads, of course, would bring administrative supremacy in Harbin and other central points.[59]

Izvolski bluntly told Rockhill that neutralization "was still another manifestation of the hostility the United States had constantly shown Russia in the Far East, for the last ten years." Under Tokyo's constant prodding, and with Great Britain's approval, the Russian foreign minister shortly rejected neutralization, January 21, 1910, on the ground that it did not "sufficiently guarantee that the new order of things will have a satisfactory result from a financial standpoint." Only slightly veiled was his reference to the Russo-Japanese Treaty of 1907. To accept neutralization, Izvolski wrote, while "relinquishing for this purpose a system that has been tested, would only be possible with a certainty of obtaining favorable results." Neither the character of Washington's negotiations nor Japan's military activity in southern Manchuria suggested a favorable result.[60]

But Russia did not immediately reject the Aigun proposal. Izvolski considered himself "entitled to expect that the final conclusion of the Chinchow-Aigun Railway loan will not take place before" Russia expressed her views or offered "counter-proposals." Knox responded with a lame explanation of Rockhill's behavior and asserted Washington's right and intention to act "independently." The intensity of this determination to push through the Chin-Ai plan is best revealed, perhaps, by the extreme ideas that crossed the mind of the Department of State. On February 14, 1910, Knox directed Rockhill to concentrate on the Russian Finance Minister, a move apparently designed to rally the opposition to Izvolski. But a day later Rockhill learned that the Department was "about to attempt" the removal of Izvolski from his position as foreign minister. This plan to overthrow the ministry of another country centered on the use of economic force. "The Department," Rockhill was told, "thinks it possible to shake Izvolsky [sic] off his perch through French banking interests." [61] Montgomery Schuyler, United States chargé d'affaires in St. Petersburg, killed the scheme before any action was taken, but the concept and the intent provide an interesting commentary on Secretary Knox and his aides in the Department.

Rockhill's attentions to the pro-American group centered around the Finance Minister came too late to save the Aigun project but may have played a part in the formulation of Russia's alternate proposal. At the end of February, 1910, St. Petersburg, supported by France and Great Britain, rejected Knox's plan but proposed the joint construction of a line cutting northwest from Peking through Kalgan, Urga, and joining the trans-Baikal Railway at Kiakhta.[62] If the interest of Taft and Knox had been primarily focused on either the promotion of economic enterprise or the checking of the Japanese advance across Asia this line—which would have helped achieve both those objectives—was a realistic substitute for the Chin-Ai railroad. But Washington manifested little interest in the Russian counter-proposal—rather was control in Manchuria the goal.

Russia's opposition to the Aigun project does "not seem unreasonable." [63] "Such a railroad," St. Petersburg declared, "would be exceedingly injurious both to the strategic and to the economic interests of Russia." Russia's Kalgan-Kiakhta proposal, meanwhile, met a "very cold reception in Japan." [64] Both Rockhill and Straight made efforts to work out a compromise but Washington failed to offer the anti-Izvolski faction any definite assistance. Thus unanswered, Izvolski's two arguments—fear of economic and political penetration by the United States and the "possibility of war with Japan"—led to a new treaty with Tokyo on July 4, 1910.[65] Sir Edward Grey, British Foreign Secretary, was "very much satisfied," and concluded that "there can be little doubt that the policy adopted by the U.S.A. in China hastened if it did not bring about this arrangement." [66]

Perhaps the most extreme statement of Russian reaction to the policies of Taft and Knox came from Gregory Wilenkin, agent of the Russian Finance Ministry who handled many of Russia's early efforts to effect an alliance with American economic interests that would lead to political collaboration. "The aggressive actions of America in Manchuria reminds one," he wrote on March 1, 1910, "somewhat of the active policies of Russia in Manchuria and Korea up to 1904. The relation of Japan to it is the same as Russia up to the war. The parallel is so clear," Wilenkin pointed out, "that one Japanese has recently compared . . . [the American policy] with the activity of Messrs. Abara, Bezobrazov . . . and others. If America will continue its adventurist policy in Peking," Wilenkin prophesied in conclusion, "it will lead her to war with Japan." St. Petersburg viewed

Jacob Schiff's speech of a few days later as further proof of Wilenkin's analysis. For Schiff publicly acknowledged that his earlier talks with Wilenkin had been designed to aid the Japanese. Now, suddenly "much mortified" by his miscalculation of Tokyo's intent, Schiff turned in anger on both countries. As might be imagined, Izvolski's supporters did not miss the opportunity to dramatize Schiff's earlier plans to aid the Japanese.[67]

But Izvolski's diplomacy served only to strengthen Japan, a result that revived the efforts of those who sought an accord with the United States. Before the treaty of Japan was signed, in fact, Rockhill reported the Finance Minister's suggestion that neutralization be approached as a "private" operation. "If you serve us again the same dish," was the advice, "it must be with another sauce." This hint reflected the views of those who thought that Russia's "primary desire"—"to gain time" against Japan— could be most effectively secured by collaboration with Washington. Once again Wilenkin was the agent chosen to push the project. But he "did not make much of an impression" during his hour conference with Secretary Knox in June, 1910.[68] Even the "rather remarkable change of policy on the part of the management of the South Manchurian Railway"—a shift that gave Tokyo's large railroad supply orders to the British after years of priority for firms in the United States—did not modify the Secretary's disinterest.[69]

Another American responded in a manner that foreshadowed the later rise of direct investments in Russia. This was John Hays Hammond, an economic giant who was also an old friend of Witte. The ex-minister of Russian finances still thought in terms of economic collaboration with the United States and in 1910 asked Hammond to take the lead in a program of this character. Hammond, who had been convinced that "American commercial interests in the Orient would be best served by a Russian victory in the Russo-Japanese War," agreed to do what he could.[70] The industrial financier's close relations with President Taft—Hammond was president of the Republican League as well as a personal friend—inspired great hopes in a large section of official St. Petersburg. He discussed plans for irrigation projects, facilities for grain storage, and municipal improvements at great length, and with "great success," with the Tsar and other Russian leaders. Coupled with Japan's continued re-enforcement of her Manchurian garrisons, Hammond's program re-enforced the Tsar's earlier inclination to favor an alignment with the United States. "I succeeded in getting from the Tsar and his government great opportunities," Hammond summarized, "for the investment of American capital and the employment of Americans in the economic development of that country." [71]

Rockhill supported Hammond with enthusiasm. "If carried through successfully as now seems probable," he cabled in December, 1910, "it

will prove of great value to the future relations of the two countries." [72]
Russia also responded favorably. First came official support for the construction, railroad, and mining concession obtained by Rear Admiral
Colby M. Chester from the Turkish Government. President Taft, who took
"a most keen interest" in the project, asked St. Petersburg to help overcome
German opposition—a request the Russians, wary of Berlin's advance toward Persia as well as Japan's militance in Manchuria, were ready to
grant.[73]

More significant was St. Petersburg's request to have the Atlantic
Fleet visit the Russian naval base at Kronstadt in the early summer of 1911.
Russia gave the fleet a gay welcome that emphasized the purpose of the
invitation. This, as the State Department recognized, was "intended to
afford an opportunity for this Government to indicate its intentions with
respect to the possibility of more cordial understanding and co-operation
with Russia." The Tsar minced no words in a conversation with Rockhill.
"This co-operation *must* be brought about," he declared.[74] Later came
news that Russia's proposal for the trans-Siberian cutoff from Lake Baikal
through Kalgan and Urga to Peking "still held good and that it was made
in all friendliness." But there was also "restlessness" in St. Petersburg due
to the fact that neither Hammond nor Washington had yet responded to
these efforts "to determine whether the United States is disposed to accept its co-operation on the basis of loyal mutual consideration, or whether
[Russia] must be (in Mr. Izvolski's phrase) 'forced into the arms of
Japan.' " [75] Within a year, moreover, the latter had occurred, and these
overtures to the United States were forgotten.

Two factors contributed to this rapid deterioration of relations and
Japan's further victory in 1912: Washington's decision to press expansion
in the Near East coupled with renewed efforts to penetrate Manchuria and
China; and the success of the campaign organized by Jacob Schiff to
abrogate the Treaty of 1832. The friction in Persia grew out of the Anglo-
Russian Convention of 1907—London's effort to reconcile her need of
Russia in Europe with her fear of St. Petersburg's expansion toward India.
After 1864, when the British obtained a telegraph concession in Persia,
the two nations rapidly extracted further preferential treatment. Russia,
who already controlled Persia's tariff, added a railroad concession in
1874, monopoly fishing rights on the coast of the Caspian Sea, and during the next decade both countries established banks in Persia. The pattern of penetration roughly followed geographical proximity, a characteristic reflected in the division of oil rights at the turn of the century. A
Russian secured control of the petroleum in the five northern provinces and
the British received exclusive concessions "covering the rest of the country." [76]

Germany's economic advances in the region and her hints that the door of opportunity should be left open in Persia were important factors in the formal division of the country along those lines. London was disturbed by Germany's continued interest in the buffer area staked out between British and Russian spheres. England's concern played into the hands of Russian efforts "to secure a maximum of influence and advantage without causing an open breach in the entente with England." [77] The United States became involved at a secondary level when Berlin protested the appointment of a Frenchman to direct Persian finances, which had been bolstered by a loan on the Paris market in 1909. London suggested an American for the post, and though the new Russian foreign minister feared that Persian agreement indicated a desire "not" to acquiesce in the partition he finally accepted the British proposal. [78]

At first the State Department was not sure that "the game would be worth the candle." [79] Huntington Wilson, another of the Secretary's pro-expansionist advisors, thought that the "most important subject of study should be the question of how we can turn these Russian and British apprehensions to our advantage either in Turkey or in the Far East." [80] But the American Ambassador in Persia was also an ardent expansionist, and he "strongly" advised that "regardless of trouble or expense a great success be attempted." His view carried the day. The State Department advised Persia that it would "be happy to communicate the names of the persons the bankers may recommend" as experts to administer the finances of that nation. This decision was made despite explicit knowledge that Russia was "not sympathetic" to the plan—she regarded it "as merely an entrance for our political policies." [81]

In response to Persia's formal request for "disinterested American experts," therefore, Washington suggested W. Morgan Schuster and several assistants. Schuster's active "desire to be selected" was fulfilled largely by virtue of his earlier service as one of President Taft's "immediate subordinates in the Philippines." [82] The American, who was granted "direct and effective control of all financial and fiscal operations of the Persian Government," soon encountered bitter opposition from Russia. [83] His economic program threatened Russian influence at four points, and St. Petersburg opened a long campaign that ultimately effected his resignation.

Schuster, who thought that "international politics are intimately connected with international finance," proposed to reform the tariff, establish a sub-treasury system backed by a special, and rather sizeable, military force, and float a £4,000,000 sterling loan calculated to redeem Persia's indebtedness to Russia, which was St. Petersburg's most effective lever on Persian policy. Nor did the Russians respond favorably to Schuster's intention to float the loan through the Seligman Brothers of London, whose representatives in the United States were known to have supported Schiff in his opposition to Russian loans. Likewise unsatisfactory was Schuster's plan to use the remainder of the money for a construction program that included eight major railroad lines.[84]

Despite clear warnings from representatives in London and Teheran, the acting foreign minister in St. Petersburg—Sazonov was in Paris—proceeded to use the return of the earlier deposed and exiled ruler of Persia, Mohamed Ali—in whose preparations for re-entry into Persia some Russian officials had at best acquiesced—and Schuster's tax program as issues around which to provoke intervention. The American's personal manner and his refusal to compromise did little to ease the tension. Whether unusual or not, the high sense of responsibility exhibited by Russian representatives in England and Persia ultimately prevented an open breach with London.[85] An ultimatum, however, did effect Schuster's resignation and return to the United States, where he was welcomed as something of a hero.[86]

Apparently Russia's opposition to Schuster was due in part to his Jewish religion, and it is certain that his return to the United States coincided with the climax of the long campaign to effect some tangible retaliation against Tsarist persecution of his co-religionists and the extradition of political refugees.[87] After the failure of his talks with Witte in 1905, Schiff warned Roosevelt that "something must . . . be done and done soon" to rectify the situation; and in subsequent years the financier played a major role in the drive to abrogate the Treaty of 1832.[88] Roosevelt's administration, and others, felt that the United States should act with great circumspection, and despite further outbreaks in 1906 the problem did not become a major issue for five years.[89] But when it came, Schiff's final drive served to destroy whatever remained of the opportunity to establish closer relations with Russia.

Schiff used the intervening years to strengthen his position. During the presidential campaign of 1908 candidate Taft promised his "special attention" to the problem, and Root assured Schiff that he, too, wanted "complete revision and amendment" of the existing treaty. Democratic politicians made similar promises.[90] Yet no immediate action was taken even though Representative Henry M. Goldfogle set the stage with a joint resolution that called for a new treaty. A major reason for this caution was the Administration's desire to effect a solution by negotiation, particularly in view of the almost total lack of incidents after 1906.[91] But Schiff and his supporters—who included Kennan, whose *Free Russia* the financier had "aided"—slowly generated broad support for their campaign.[92]

This pressure became effective early in 1911 when abrogation was first demanded in Congress. By December the issue was beyond control.[93]

At the end of the first week of that month the National Citizens Committee for Abrogation, headed by former Ambassador to Russia Andrew D. White and William G. McAdoo, staged a huge rally in Carnegie Hall that seemed to force the issue. Among those who spoke was Woodrow Wilson, governor of New Jersey, and dark-horse candidate for the Democratic presidential nomination in 1912. Wilson joined the cry for abrogation and suggested that only then could the United States consider "upon what terms, if any, of mutual honor our intercourse may be re-established." [94] Within ten days after this rally the Congress demanded, and secured, abrogation.

The House of Representatives passed a belligerent resolution two days before the New York demonstration, and Taft's principal concern became an effort to effect the termination without a major incident. But demands similar to those of Representative William Sulzer, who cried out for "more decisive action," seemed to preclude such a development.[95] Nor did the petitions that flowed in from many states bespeak a spirit of compromise. Yet there were those who cautioned moderation. Representative Samuel W. McCall warned against "the cry of the jingo," and pointed out, in agreement with his colleague George R. Malley, that arbitration was far more sensible. Another reminded his listeners—apparently few in number—that the United States practiced similar discrimination against "citizens of the Far East." [96]

The President's concern was based on similar observations made by members of the Department and representatives abroad. "Russian friendliness and co-operation in the Far East," cabled Rockhill in the early stages of the agitation, "seem highly important and their value will increase steadily with Japanese expansion." But abrogation, he warned, would "seriously" imperil Washington's influence. Then, in answer to a specific request for his extended view of the matter, Rockhill prepared one of his most significant dispatches. "I cannot too emphatically reiterate my conclusion," he wrote on January 30, 1911, "that the sympathetic co-operation of Russia is of supreme importance. . . . I have reason to believe," he continued, "that the Russian Government would at least be sympathetic with the purposes of the United States in these regions if it were confident of their sincerity, and convinced that the American Government would loyally and consistently respect Russia's established interests and make no unfriendly use of the resulting increase of its influence in Asiatic affairs."

Against this background the Ambassador then gave his estimate of the consequences of abrogation. "At this critical juncture when Russia is reconsidering her relationship to Far Eastern questions, and hesitating between a policy of coercion and one of co-operation with the United States . . . I fear that the proposed Congressional Resolution . . . might precipitate this Government's decision against the policies with which the

United States is identified." As for any moderating impact on Russia's domestic legislation, Rockhill cautioned that it was "quite futile" to anticipate any result of that character.[97]

Rockhill's estimate was verified some nine months later, in the heat of Schiff's final push for abrogation. On September 25, 1911, the new Ambassador to Russia reported that St. Petersburg wanted to settle the issue by arbitration and then take up the question of Manchurian railways in three weeks.[98] Shortly thereafter Secretary Knox recorded his own skepticism as to any positive results of abrogation. "If, then," he wrote President Taft, "we make this drastic protest against the exercise by Russia of the very principle which we assert against other nations as a fundamental right incident to our sovereignty and independence, we must answer to the charge that we demand more than we will grant." [99] From St. Petersburg came a last-minute warning of serious import: the Ambassador's "profound personal conviction that abrogation of the treaty means an alliance between Russia and Japan." [100]

These estimates moved Taft to a belated effort to arrange mutual termination and renegotiation, but the proposal came too late. Russia interpreted the suggestion as a direct affront. The best the President could effect was a more moderate resolution that justified the action in less belligerent terms. Whether arbitration could have solved the problem at that late date is questionable, for to emphasize the ticklish question of prestige came the news that Japan had again re-enforced her army in Manchuria.[101] Coupled with the embittering episode of abrogation this development ended any chance that Russia's overtures of 1910 and 1911 would lead to collaboration between St. Petersburg and Washington in Asia. As for the restrictive legislation in Russia—there is no evidence that abrogation served to improve the situation in the slightest.

John Hays Hammond reported another consequence directly: "The resultant ill-feeling destroyed any hope of carrying out my plan of obtaining American capital for Russia." Wilenkin, who had worked with Hammond in these plans, broke with Schiff over abrogation. "I belong to an orthodox Jewish family and remain faithful to my religion . . . ," Wilenkin explained to Schiff, "but I thoroughly believe that the solution of the Jewish question in Russia lies in Russia." [102]

A similar result occurred in Asia. The bankers, in fact, sought to disentangle themselves from the Department's policy after the fiasco of neutralization. Then they threatened to dissolve the syndicate, but Secretary Knox convinced them to try again: "but only on the understanding that they would be under no obligation to seek or accept contracts which aroused the irreconcilable opposition of other powers." [103] When China applied for a loan to underwrite currency reform and the industrial development of Manchuria, the financiers tried to avoid their earlier failure by inviting all the powers to participate.[104] The ensuing period of "fruitless negotiations" emphasized Japan's ascendancy in North China. Finally, convinced that they were "not yet in a position to make any profit out of their endeavors," the Americans abandoned the field of battle. They did not resume competition in the area until the Russian Revolution of 1917 destroyed the Japanese-dominated "anti-American front" in Manchuria and left the United States openly opposed to both the new Soviet state and Tokyo's continued expansion.[105]

2. A REVOLUTION CHALLENGES THE HOUSE OF MORGAN

What! Raymond Robins, that uplifter, that Roosevelt shouter? What the hell is he doing on this mission?

William Boyce Thompson, June, 1917

Yet the collapse of the effort to arrange an accord with St. Petersburg and the failure to penetrate Asia did not end the relations between American capital and pre-Bolshevik Russia. Rather did abrogation and the end of the first consortium mark a change in the character of the relationship. After 1912 the House of Morgan turned from the effort to secure profits in Asia to a more careful cultivation, and protection, of direct investments in, and trade with, Russia. By a curious quirk in history a figure who helped push through abrogation also did much to bolster the Morgan effort to protect their stake in Russia. For Raymond Robins, who was militantly active in one phase of the agitation that ended the Treaty of 1832, also helped lead the House of Morgan's campaign to preserve the non-Bolshevik Provisional Government of the March, 1917, Revolution.

Part of the strength of the abrogation movement stemmed from the earlier agitation against the extradition of Jan Janoff Pouren and Christian Rudewitz. Russia's demand for Pouren's return on grounds that he was a non-political offender aroused the northeastern seaboard to feverish action in his behalf. Kennan's Friends of Russian Freedom moved to his defense supported by the Political Refugees Defense League and the Pouren Defense Committee. Their activity became almost frantic when Pouren was held guilty of theft, arson, and attempted murder, and ordered surrendered to the Russian embassy. The new wave of protest brought an official Russian complaint against the "violent agitation," but to no avail. Coupled with political considerations inherent in a presidential campaign, the well-organized pressure campaign and new evidence adduced by Pouren's lawyers effected a new hearing at which the earlier decision was reversed. The fact that St. Petersburg was assessed the cost of the proceedings did little to ease the situation.[106]

Nor did the case of Rudewitz, which attracted equal attention west of the Alleghenies. Agitation on behalf of Rudewitz—more clearly an actual revolutionary—centered in Chicago, a stronghold of the rising progressive movement. Though several national figures, including Jane Addams and Clarence Darrow, were active in his defense, it was Raymond Robins, known then only on the local scene, who engineered the refugee's release. Robins had no intimation of the fact, but his defense of Rudewitz was the first phase of his activity as a central figure in American-Russian relations from the administration of Woodrow Wilson to that of Franklin Delano Roosevelt. His fighting speeches for Rudewitz appear in retrospect as but a minor episode in a career that involved him in the military, financial, and diplomatic decisions affecting the two nations.

In 1908 Raymond Robins was a prominent catalyst in the social and political ferment in Chicago. A man who organized and led a strike in a Tennessee coal mine at the age of nineteen, Robins knew the haunting fear of economic insecurity. His first response to that experience was militant labor activity, devotion to Henry George, and successful political action in San Francisco on behalf of William Jennings Bryan in the presidential election of 1896. The taste of fame and the jangle of success, however, momentarily obscured these experiences and he joined the stampede to fortune in the Alaskan gold rush of 1897–98. But the last frontier was a refresher course in the proximity of death, the constancy of man's exploitation by man, and the fact that men had to work together if they were going to alter society. Robins arrived in Chicago in 1901, determined to use his modest fortune to implement the social gospel through trade unionism and political action.[107]

In the next six years Robins contributed considerable evidence in support of the formula. From the day he walked into Chicago Commons and "volunteered for residence and any work that might be assigned him," Robins was "in the storm center of the city's most tempestuous moments." [108] Within a month he attracted attention by his defense of Abraham Isaak, a victim of Chicago's hysteria after the assassination of President William McKinley. A firm belief that the "only safe vote for reform was the labor vote" led him to activate his mine union membership, a move that gave him political potential as well as the friendship of John Mitchell, national president of the United Mine Workers. Robins earned a spot on the UMW committee that negotiated with President Roosevelt during the great anthracite strike of 1903, and was chosen to present the appeal for arbitration to the President.[109]

Though Roosevelt impressed him considerably, Robins remained a Bryan Democrat for the time. His whirlwind courtship and marriage of

Margaret Dreier—soon to begin her long service as national president
of the Women's Trade Union League—did not keep him from "active and
aggressive" participation in municipal politics. Physically assaulted by
political enemies during his battle against the gas and traction interests,
Robins recovered quickly and helped lead the fight to improve the lot of
Chicago schoolteachers. Just prior to the Rudewitz case he was the principal speaker at the American Federation of Labor's national protest meeting against the Supreme Court's decision in the Danbury Hatter's case.
The decision must "peaceably" be reversed, he declared, and suggested
organized political action as the democratic technique.[110] This was the
plan Robins used to defend Rudewitz.

But more was needed than his rousing speech before the huge rally
of November 29, 1908. For this reason Robins took advantage of his contact with Roosevelt and made two trips to Washington to press the President for action. Coupled with Secretary Root's preoccupation in Latin
America and agitation in other quarters, these efforts were successful.[111]
Robins turned back to domestic affairs but his contacts with Roosevelt ultimately led him into the President's third-party campaign of 1912 and, a
bit later, accounted for his far deeper involvement in American-Russian
relations.

The pattern of these developments approximated the structure of
American politics. For it was through Roosevelt's close association with
the House of Morgan that Robins first became an unofficial diplomat. And
despite the belligerent reaction on the part of some groups in Russia to
the abrogation of the commercial treaty, the American stake in Russia
continued to increase after that action. From the days when Colonel Samuel
Colt unsuccessfully attempted to peddle his revolver to the Russian Army,
economic relations between the two countries were of considerable importance.[112] That a large portion of American exports entered Russia by
way of Germany and other countries tended to obscure this relationship,
as did the fact that the extent of direct investment in Russia was generally
unknown.

Cotton exports accounted for the largest segment of this invisible trade.
In 1910, for example, statistics revealed that Russian imports were but
$38,000,000, "whereas the American cotton used by the mills alone
amounted to approximately $50,000,000." [113] But other American goods
entered Russia in the same manner. Raw iron, copper, lead . . . pipes and
wire, zinc . . . joiner and carpenter's wares . . . parts of machinery . . .
[and] instruments and appliances" went in via a "curiously indirect" route
through England and Germany.[114]

The direct export trade, the bulk of which was handled by three export syndicates in New York, was not insignificant. Almost all products
of American industry were sold in Russia: Worthington pumps, leather

goods, locks and clasps, typewriters, nails, cement, " 'Walkover Shoes,' " tools from, among others, the Bullard Machine Tool Company of Bridgeport, Connecticut, the "higher grades of cosmetics," mining and construction machinery, the "largest share" of private firearms, and even bicycles, roller skates, and fishing tackle. Steinway piano agents did a "thriving business" in St. Petersburg, as did the American plumbing company that secured the contract for the Winter Palace. In another field exports from the Baldwin Locomotive Works and the steel industry made both the trans-Siberian and the Chinese Eastern Railways "in all essentials" American lines. And in 1896 the Westinghouse Company was awarded a monopoly contract to supply air brakes for Russian passenger trains.[115]

In subsequent years the operations of Westinghouse reflected the movement toward direct investment in Russia. The Baldwin Locomotive Works took a first step in that direction when it leased designs and provided technical guidance for a plan in conjunction with the Sormovo Machine Works.[116] Westinghouse and a competitor, the New York Air Brake Company, which was to supply brakes for Russian freight trains, next built factories near St. Petersburg and Moscow. During the Revolution of 1905 the New York firm requested, and received, through the United States Ambassador, the intervention of the Russian Government to help break a strike.[117] Sometime later the New York company sold out to the International Harvester Company, which not only controlled the Russian market for agricultural machinery, but became the largest American firm in Russia. Likewise, the Singer Sewing Machine Company established a plant near Moscow.[118]

American-Russian economic relations also reflected the growing financial control of industry in the United States. For despite J. P. Morgan's inability to reach an economic agreement with Witte in 1905—a failure conditioned by St. Petersburg's refusal to agree to Morgan's strict specifications that Russia's future business in the United States be done through his firm—the House of Morgan not only dominated the American economic scene but gave "a great impetus" to the rise of direct investments in Russia.[119] Interests in the Westinghouse Company, General Electric, the American Telephone and Telegraph Company—which had "close connections" in Russia—and a share in the credit arrangements for direct trade only served to complement Morgan's control of International Harvester and his monopoly of the large American life insurance business in Russia. In the early years Morgan's New York life shared the field with the Equitable—a Harriman-Schiff company—but after 1909 the latter also became Morgan property. A large number of Russian railway securities were also absorbed in the American market.[120] But the new emphasis on direct investments did not solve the problem that abrogation of the Treaty of 1832 created for those who engaged in direct trade.

These interests, moreover, quickly brought pressure to bear on Washington to forestall critical consequences. Most active in this respect were the manufacturers and exporters of agricultural implements, one of whom reported "great damage" to his business.[121] Cyrus McCormick's similar expression of concern helped quicken official reaction. "I should be very pleased," replied Knox, "to have a representative of your company consult with the Department in regard to the interests of the American manufacturers." Russia, meanwhile, had already passed on a "very strong hint" that she also was anxious to open negotiations for a new treaty.[122]

But the leaders of the abrogation movement acted quickly to prevent any developments of this character. "We need not make haste in pushing forward these negotiations," advised Oscar Straus, who thought that Russia would "find it to her advantage to come to an understanding." This reminder was doubly effective, timed as it was to coincide with the opening stages of the presidential campaign in 1912. "Complications of the political situation," Knox concluded, necessitated a more circumspect approach. Those who opposed any *modus vivendi* maintained their opposition, and the only makeshift arrangement that could be effected was to trade through the loophole in an old tariff law. Section II of the Act of 1909 provided an opening of this nature if neither country established new discriminations, and by mutual agreement the ruse was used.[123]

But the need for a wider avenue of trade immediately confronted President-elect Woodrow Wilson, even though he admitted that "he was unfamiliar with the details of 'the critical character of the situation with regard to the relations between' " the two countries.[124]

Perhaps mindful of Wilson's concern with domestic reform, Russia did not wait for the President to make the first move to regularize direct trade. Early in 1913 the Government in Petrograd—St. Petersburg was renamed in 1912—sent a special mission to the United States for that express purpose.[125] Not until three years later did Wilson respond, but the President's selection of David R. Francis, St. Louis grain dealer and Democratic politician, as Ambassador to Russia in 1916 was prompted, in large measure, by the need to negotiate a new commercial treaty. Francis, who controlled the St. Louis *Republic* and held considerable railroad securities in the United States—and had manifested a "passing interest" in the American economic penetration of Korea—quickly became "absorbed" in his job. But though he discussed the problem with the financier, an acquaintance of "fifteen or twenty years," before sailing, Francis was perturbed by Morgan's desire to handle Russian loans through the British offices of his firm.[126] This policy made it difficult for American exporters to arrange satisfactory credit and was largely responsible, in Francis' view, for England's great influence at Petrograd.

Francis had little need to solicit orders for American firms. Trade with Russia, which quickly recovered from the slight recession of 1912, jumped sharply after the outbreak of World War I. Exports of 22.7 millions in 1912 (26.5 in 1913) increased to 658.9 in 1917.[127] To help finance these purchases Russia floated loans in "aggregate over $96,000,000" through Morgan's New York Office. In addition, some $86,000,000 was supplied by Morgan through the British.[128] Morgan representatives also dominated the American-Russian Chamber of Commerce organized in the spring of 1916. The National City Bank, the New York Life Insurance Company, the Chase National Bank, the Guaranty Trust Company, and the First National Bank supplied the new organization with "officers and directors." In Russia, Baron Rosen, former Ambassador to the United States, headed a group organized to promote "friendly relations—business and social"; while Morgan men dominated the Russian-American Chamber of Commerce in Moscow and Petrograd.[129]

"Russia is an inviting field for American business enterprise," remarked Dean E. F. Gay of the Harvard School of Business Administration, a comment that reflected considerable opinion.[130] Ambassador Francis agreed, but continued to worry about British influence. He thought London should be reminded that it "is only able to finance Russia . . . by the assistance she gets from the United States." [131] The Ambassador might better have used his energy to obtain more aid, for Russia was near economic collapse.

The strain of the World War opened cracks in the Russian economy as early as December 6, 1914, when a "lack of shells and munitions at the front" was reported. By the time Francis arrived, Russian pig-iron production had actually decreased and coal and oil supplies were "far from adequate." [132] It was indeed a "tragic situation"—one that forced a high Russian official to confess that "the reasons for our failures are too basic to hope for their elimination during this war, even though their eradication would begin immediately." [133]

The impact of these Tsarist failures reached both the army and the home front by the end of 1915. First came "general discontent with the 'rear,' " and by January, 1917, the chaplains in the Russian Army began to "complain of the difficulty of their position." [134] At the same time, so reported the police, the circumstances of civilian life were so desperate that the "industrial proletariat of the capital [was] on the verge of despair." [135] By February, 1917, the "lack of bread" crystallized the "complete distrust" in the government and "spontaneous and irrepressible" strikes rocked both Petrograd and Moscow.[136] The Tsar was correctly warned that the "deplorable lack of organization and leadership" in his government might be disastrous.[137] On March 11, 1917, he prorogued the Duma and ordered the workers back to their benches—but the Government's troops joined the strikers. Three days later a provisional government under Prince G. E. Lvov assumed the responsibilities of government. President Wilson was aware that Russia was a weak link in the Allied front. Walter H. Page, Ambassador to Great Britain, suggested that the Russians lacked "staying qualities" as early as October, 1914. By January, 1916, the President's most trusted advisor, Colonel Edward M. House, wrote that Russia might well be knocked or bargained out of the war. During the following fifteen months House repeatedly warned his chief that both France and England were "greatly alarmed over the Russian situation." [138] Wilson was also advised of the suggestion to pressure the Tsar into granting reforms by "withholding, in the final settlement, some of the things which [Russia] so earnestly desires." [139] But the simple fact was, as the British acknowledged early in 1917, that the assistance offered to Russia fell "very far short of her undoubted requirements." [140]

Nor did the Wilson administration have any reason to believe that the Revolution of March, 1917, would provide a cure-all. American Minister to Sweden Ira N. Morris reported that the extreme socialists were well within reach of power, and that Russia's continued participation in the war would be "more doubtful" if they took control. Ambassador Francis agreed with Morris and added that the Lvov Government needed funds "badly." Financial assistance was "so vital," acknowledged Secretary of the Treasury William G. McAdoo, "that the very life of the new Government may depend upon it." [141] Despite the enthusiasm and confidence displayed on the surface, it is clear that Wilson and his advisors knew the situation was extremely critical. This concern led to an early decision to send a mission to Russia to survey the situation and make policy recommendations.

Such figures as Oscar Straus, Henry Morgenthau, Senator Henry Cabot Lodge, Charles R. Flint, and Eliot Wadsworth pressed Wilson with advice. [142] But the President turned to his own select circle for guidance on the Russian question. Colonel House, Charles R. Crane, Secretary McAdoo, Cyrus H. McCormick, and Secretary of State Robert Lansing, who in turn relied heavily on William Phillips and Richard C. Crane, were the men whose judgment Wilson valued. [143] In the main, Professor Samuel N. Harper of the University of Chicago supplied the information upon which these early decisions were based.

Harper's importance stemmed from his close relationship with Charles R. Crane, plumbing magnate and onetime Progressive who was particularly close to President Wilson. Crane's "romantic" interest in Russia— which was buttressed by certain material considerations, including investments in the Westinghouse Company—was primarily responsible for Harper's career. Crane helped stimulate the professor's original interest in Russia, and for several years heavily subsidized Harper's chair and department at the University of Chicago. [144] Of equal importance was the fact that Crane's son, Richard C., was Lansing's personal secretary. Since his father and the Secretary shared a fundamental ignorance of Russia it was natural that all concerned should turn to Harper for advice.[145]

Crane's influence was considerable. At his suggestion Harper served as Ambassador Francis' personal advisor during the latter's early months in Russia and the Administration relied on Harper for background on the March Revolution.[146] He likewise participated in the ticklish discussions as to the personnel of the proposed commission. Both the final composition of the mission itself and the directive issued by Wilson revealed a tragic failure to face the issue in Russia. As chief emissary to a socialist revolution in a nation mentally and physically tired of war, Wilson chose ex-Secretary of State Elihu Root, a conservative corporation lawyer of legalistic leanings. "I convinced myself," Wilson explained, "that he was genuinely and heartily in sympathy with the Revolution." This was hardly the case. Root expected to be "awfully bored" on the "damned expedition"—an attitude that explains, perhaps, the "large package of novels . . . and . . . two cases of Haig and Haig" he took along.[147]

Other members of the Root Mission included Charles Crane, the romantic businessman; John R. Mott, Y.M.C.A. official; Cyrus McCormick, who built reapers in Russia and was also "enthusiastic over" social-welfare work because it "increases efficiency"; Samuel Bertron, Wall Street financier; James Duncan, seventy-nine-year-old vice-president of the American Federation of Labor who later lectured the Petrograd workmen on the importance of Union labels; [148] Charles E. Russell, the capitalist socialist; and two military officers.

Only three members of the group were in any sense qualified for their task. Basil Miles, secretary to the Mission, had been personal secretary to George von Lengerke Meyer, President Theodore Roosevelt's Ambassador to Russia. Colonel William V. Judson, army engineer appointed through the personal intervention of his old friend Postmaster General Albert S. Burleson, had served as American military observer during the Russo-Japanese War. Harper, who trailed along at the urging of Charles Crane, was a student of Russian history, and attempted to remedy the situation by briefing Crane, McCormick, and Mott.[149]

Despite continued warnings from Ambassadors Francis and Morris and the receipt of a blunt "hurry-up" cable from Michael M. Podolsky, a member of the Provisional Government, President Wilson and Secretary Lansing conceived of the Mission as one primarily designed to "show our interest and sympathy." Faced with unpleasant reality, Wilson and his advisors practiced self-deception. They were to find that easy road built on quicksand.[150]

Of further significance was Harper's effectiveness in having all references to Russia's weakness screened from the public. Privately he was frank to admit that America's "failure to give material support" increased the danger of a Russian collapse.[151] But he worked hard to get Frederick H. Dixon, editor of the *Christian Science Monitor,* and Roy W. Howard, head of the United Press, to stop using so much unfavorable news.[152] Both men fell in line. Harper began to write articles for the *Monitor* and the UP asked him to "criticize and suggest on their service from Russia." [153] This phase of Harper's work was made easier when George Creel's Committee of Public Information ruled that "speculation about possible peace is another topic which may possess elements of danger." Taking no chances, Harper asked Arthur Bullard, the *Outlook*'s home-front correspondent, whom the Committee on Public Information was sending to Russia, to "put some pressure on our newspapers." [154] For his part in the campaign, Richard Crane, Lansing's aide, inspired at least one false news article when a reporter told him that "he was hard up for a story." [155] This evidence would appear to indicate that Harper's pressure was partially responsible for the optimistic response accorded the Provisional Government in the press of the United States.[156]

Neither these acts of self-deception on the part of certain members of the Wilson administration nor the conscious distortion of the news by Harper and his associates was completely effective. For almost simultaneously another group of influential Americans, keenly aware of Russia's grave weakness, conceived their own plan to forestall a complete collapse in Petrograd. Early in April, 1917, financier Henry P. Davison and mining magnate William Boyce Thompson—both closely associated with the House of Morgan—met in New York to discuss the problem of "strengthening" the Provisional Government.[157] Their concern was understandable, for the House of Morgan not only had an important stake in American-Russian trade and large direct investments in Russia, but also, by 1917, had immense sums tied to the Allied cause in the war.

Without formal membership in Wilson's administration, Davison and Thompson at first lacked either direct influence at the White House or independent authority to undertake their plan to sustain the Provisional Government. Within a short time after their New York conference in April they secured the necessary power as a consequence of Wilson's tendency to choose Wall Street figures for wartime leadership in Washington—in this instance to head the American Red Cross War Council. Cleveland H. Dodge of the National City Bank engineered the preliminary moves and then advised Wilson that "Mr. J. P. Morgan and several members of his firm" were "willing to permit Mr. Davison" to direct the Red Cross war effort "provided it [was] entirely acceptable to the President." Davison acknowledged that he was "ready to go ahead," and Wilson approved the appointment.[158] During the period of these negotiations, moreover, Davison had already made his first efforts to get a man into

Russia. With the help of Eliot Wadsworth, another Morgan man serving the Red Cross, Davison submitted a double request to Wilson and the State Department to send a Red Cross man to Russia with the Root Mission. But the Department sided with Root, who was "not in favor" of the idea, and Davison's first effort was defeated when the President agreed that "it would not be wise." [159]

The setback was no more than a short delay. Less than a month later the "question of sending a mission to Russia was discussed" at the third meeting of the Red Cross War Council on May 29, 1917. Davison again applied through Phillips for presidential approval but Wilson remained hesitant. The President wanted "to be very sure just what the errand of the commission was to be, and just what it would attempt." But Lansing's "hearty accord" with the idea moved the President to acquiesce.[160] It is doubtful that Davison ever worried over Wilson's delay. He was busy selecting personnel early in May. When Theodore Roosevelt, his first choice to head the Mission, declined the honor, Davison picked Dr. Frank C. Billings, a leading Chicago physician recommended by Harper and Crane. But Roosevelt was never one to be left out entirely. Acting on the suggestion of Frances A. Kellor, his secretary, he asked that Raymond Robins, his "true friend," be included.[161]

Roosevelt's request might well have been a gesture of appreciation for Robins' loyal support in the years after 1908. Party loyalty kept Robins in the Democratic party through the early part of 1912, but a luncheon conference with Wilson provoked him to rebellion. Robins got the impression that Wilson felt that "I'm a tremendous person and you don't seem to appreciate it yet." [162] The Midwesterner concluded that such high levels of awareness were beyond him and broke party ranks to support Roosevelt's third-party campaign. Roosevelt gave Robins a responsible role in the campaign—an expression of trust the latter repaid with personal and political loyalty. Robins even ran for United States senator from Illinois in the next off-year election, 1914, in an effort to keep Roosevelt's machine in motion.

Supported by such local and national figures as Victor Freemont Lawson, editor of the Chicago *Daily News;* Charles R. Crane; Harold Ickes; United States Senators Robert L. Owen, Oklahoma Democrat, and George W. Norris of Nebraska; and even Wilson's Assistant Secretary of Agriculture Carl S. Vrooman, Robins was generally credited with the defeat of the Democratic candidate—who had Wilson's endorsement.[163] Nor was that all; when it became apparent in 1916 that the GOP regulars, including William Boyce Thompson, who never supported Roosevelt, would have none of Roosevelt, Robins meekly followed him back into the fold. This party switch cost Robins a considerable portion of his prestige among old-line Progressives. He crossed violently with ex-Progressive Bainbridge

Colby—later to serve Wilson as Secretary of State—when the latter branded Roosevelt a "traitor." But the Democrats wanted Robins too—"of special importance because of his . . . influence with the labor vote"—and made strenuous efforts to recapture his loyalty. Robins chose to stand with Roosevelt, a decision with important consequences.[164] And one of the first was Roosevelt's recommendation to Davison.

Davison agreed that it was "important" to have Robins along, and in a short time reported that the State Department had no objection to Robins making the trip. Both Roosevelt and Davison were "more than delighted." [165] Robins found himself a member of a complex group when the Red Cross Commission to Russia went aboard the *Empress of Asia* at Vancouver on July 5, 1917. "Poor Mr. Billings believed he was in charge of a scientific mission for the relief of Russia. . . . He was in reality nothing but a mask—the Red Cross complexion of the mission was nothing but a mask." [166] William Boyce Thompson, the mining magnate who was interested in the possibilities of Siberian concessions, was paying for the entire venture. Weeks earlier he had advised his agents in North China and Manchuria to stand by for orders. The discovery of Robins, an old political enemy, as a member of his group upset Thompson considerably.[167]

"What! Raymond Robins, that uplifter, that Roosevelt shouter! What the hell is he doing on this mission?"

The Root Mission, meanwhile, was preparing two sets of reports. Root publicly advised the American people that Russia was out of danger, but such double talk had no place between friends.[168] The "fundamental question," he wrote Billings on July 21, 1917, is "whether Russia is going to be able to continue the war." Root also enclosed a memo from Basil Miles who warned that the "bread problem in Petrograd" was a political factor of "vital importance"; unless solved it might well lead to "the downfall of the present regime and . . . possibly the total withdrawal of Russia from the war." [169] Every man in a position of authority knew that Russia was about to collapse. Both Raymond Robins and the United States were about to be tested in the twentieth century's rendezvous with revolution.

4

☆

A TOKEN OF SYMPATHY

I think that our policy should be based on the hypothesis that Russia will go from bad to worse. . . . No other course is safe.

Secretary of State Lansing, August, 1917

I personally appreciate the token of sympathy and of strength which you show you desire to give.

Premier Kerensky to William Boyce Thompson,
August, 1917

☆☆

In August, 1917, the United States determined to abandon Russia of the March Revolution until the "normal process" of revolt ran its course and order was re-established "by arbitrary military power." Conceived in indifference and conditioned by a lack of insight, this policy was strengthened by a belief that Kerensky compromised "too much" with the radicals, a conviction that there was "nothing we can do," and the conclusion that some "dominant personality" would ultimately "end it all." Despite many warnings from varied sources that this policy was extremely dangerous to the interests of the United States, Washington refused to modify the analysis until after the Bolsheviks seized power in November, 1917.[1]

The primary opposition to this policy came from a small group of men of greater insight and of less faith in a "natural law" of revolutions. Accepting the fact that Russia was torn by revolution, they argued that a policy of indifference and enmity would not only threaten America's security but would also destroy the forces of moderation and drive the revolution either to the extreme Right or Left. They were unable to penetrate either the fog of indifference or the armor of inaction. Washington was aroused only by the crash occasioned by the disintegration of the Provisional Government.

During the months of May, June, and July, 1917, the United States

91

acted with considerable vigor in an effort either to help or force the Provisional Government to continue the war and destroy its Bolshevik opposition. Even before President Wilson gave the Root Mission its last briefing on May 14, the John F. Stevens Railroad Commission left Washington to help rehabilitate Russia's transport system. To supplement this technical aid the first of several official credits was extended two days later.[2]

In Petrograd, Ambassador Francis used open threats in his effort to reactivate the Russian Army and silence Lenin and Trotsky. Though he advised his chief assistant, Consul General Maddin Summers, on March 15 of the peace party within the government, Francis seemed unable to understand that the Russian people had little inclination to continue the war. When Foreign Minister Pavel Miliukov reiterated Russia's demand for control of the Dardanelles Straits—a Tsarist price for war—he aroused great popular opposition. The Bolsheviks did not instigate the demonstrations, but immediately took the opportunity to assume leadership of the anti-war sentiment.[3]

Francis called on Miliukov and Minister of War Alexander Guchkov at six-thirty in the evening on the day of these protest parades and issued an ultimatum. Unless they "gave better evidence of established government," Francis bluntly warned, he would ask his government "to make specific demands before furnishing credit or supplies." The Ambassador airily dismissed their reply that the situation was difficult in view of the fact that the "workingmen desired to control" the government. Impossible, Francis shot back: "it would lose them the respect of the Russian people and all of the Allies as well as their own self-respect."[4] The tension was eased when Miliukov's followers organized a successful counter-demonstration.

The incident illustrates the basic dilemma that confronted American policy makers. Reality forced Francis, and others, to report that conditions in Russia were in "a very unsatisfactory shape." The "general unsettled conditions, both economic and otherwise," made it obvious that the situation was "growing more grave all the time." Yet the blunt truth confused and bewildered Francis, and he turned to Vladimir Ilich Lenin, leader of the Bolsheviks, for a scapegoat. It was impossible, reflected Francis, that the Russian people wanted peace. All the clamor, he concluded, must be the work of Lenin. Francis first joined Sir George Buchanan, British Ambassador and former confidant of the Tsar, to urge the arrest and execution of Lenin. Failing there, the American Ambassador then began to grasp at any evidence—no matter what its source or character— and opened a long campaign to type Lenin a German agent and to credit him with Russia's unrest and desire for peace.[5]

Wilson, Lansing, and others in Washington faced the same problem. With Harper in Russia advising Francis and the Root Mission, Lansing turned to George Kennan and Counselor of the State Department Frank Polk for help and understanding. Kennan, who shared the Secretary's deep conservatism, accepted Lansing's bid with "great pleasure." But Lansing found little cause for hope in Kennan's counsel. To the file of ominous reports from abroad Kennan added an admission that he could not, in contrast with his earlier views, "see much that is encouraging in Russia." There was a strong urge for peace, he pointed out, and the Socialists would use it "in order that they may proceed undisturbed with their plan for turning Russia upside down with the proletariat on top." That, he was quick to point out, was "the crazy plan of unbalanced brains," but it might take the "inexperienced Russian peasants a good while to find out." [6]

Little wonder that Lansing—who advised Francis that the pressure for peace could well "interfere with Russia getting her share from the loans extended the Allies"—eagerly endorsed the British plan for propaganda "to persuade the Russians to attack the Germans with all their might." The plan was to use the Monk Illiador, a close friend of Grigori Rasputin (earlier a notorious influence at the court of Tsar Nicholas II) and a "wonderful mob orator," to rally support around the Czech forces then in Russia after their desertion from the Austrian Army. Despite considerable interest, the plan was not undertaken. But Lansing did take time to tell the editor of the Chicago *Tribune* that he "very much" appreciated the latter's thought that it was "best not to print" a story of the concerted effort among newspapermen to kill the International Socialist Conference in Stockholm—called to oppose the war—by "ridicule and distortion." Lansing contributed to the failure of the Conference by refusing to issue passports to the American delegates. [7]

At the same time Washington and London increased their pressure on the Provisional Government. Weak as it was—"We are tossed about like debris on a stormy sea," Premier Lvov admitted to General Kuropatkin— the Allies repeatedly urged Petrograd to launch a major assault on the Eastern Front. The July offensive was undertaken in large measure in response to slightly veiled ultimatums from London, Paris, and Washington. But within three weeks after the Russians committed their weakened and poorly supplied forces to battle, July 17, 1917, the German counterattack crushed the Russian Army at Tarnopol and forced Prince Lvov's resignation. The situation was extremely critical, and it appeared that Lenin, who previously warned the Provisional Government that "No party has a right to refuse power, and our party does not refuse it," would make his bid for control. A section of the Bolshevik party pressed for militant action but Lenin refused to act prematurely, even in the face of party opposition and extreme personal provocation.⁸ From the Bolsheviks' point of view Lenin's judgment was vindicated when a weakened Provisional Government reformed under the leadership of Alexander Feodorovich Kerensky.

Francis was relieved and hopeful; he mistook Bolshevik discipline for weakness. On July 23 House pointed out the consequences of further American indifference and inaction. "The time is . . . short and means everything," he cautioned. "I do not think we can devote too much attention to the Russian situation, for if that fails us our troubles will be great and many." Arthur Hugh Frazier, State Department representative in Paris, warned of the "profound repercussions" of the Revolution in western Europe. But the Administration was content to mull over the idea of counterpropaganda while it awaited the return of the Root Mission.⁹

Root, McCormick, and Bertron saw and admitted privately that Russia was on the verge of collapse but they did not so report to the people of the United States. Two other members of the Mission, however, endeavored to act in the crisis. Charles E. Russell realized almost immediately that the Committee of Workmen and Soldiers, the organization of more militant revolutionaries which exerted tremendous pressure on the Provisional Government, was of significance in the development of the Revolution and began to campaign against the Bolshevik effort to assume leadership of the group. Russell asked to stay behind and continue his work. Francis was opposed. Of the opinion that the workers already had too much influence, the Ambassador argued that Russell was wrong, and warned that he "might make trouble" if allowed to stay. The ability and experience of Colonel Judson, military representative on the Root Mission, however, impressed both Root and Francis, and at their request he was reassigned to the Embassy in Petrograd as head of a special military mission. His first official act was to report on the imminent danger of Russia leaving the war.¹⁰

On August 7, 1917, the American Red Cross Commission arrived in Petrograd. Everything was "running smoothly." Thompson had reached a "thorough understanding" with Billings; McCormick had wired a special contribution; and Thompson's men were on the prowl for food and other supplies. "I am sure you will welcome the opportunity to be of service," one of them wrote to a business ally, "for you know how tremendously important it is . . . that our people should take the lead." There is reason to believe that Lansing understood and approved the real nature of the mission. Thompson knew he was entering a critical situation and went in "full of enthusiasm"—prepared to act. With one eye on Japan—"If for any reason Russia should fall down, look out!"—he advised Dwight Morrow, another Morgan representative, to prepare to provide "large sums"; for "only the most strenuous efforts on the part of the United States would keep Russia from concluding peace within the next six months." ¹¹

On August 8, 1917, critical audiences were granted in Petrograd and

Washington. Kerensky received Thompson and the Root Mission was welcomed home by Wilson and Lansing. The decisions that resulted from the
conferences differed as widely as the locales. Thompson was "favorably
received." This was not surprising, for in the course of the interview Thompson personally subscribed for 500,000 rubles "at 85" of the new Russian
Liberty Loan. The move was but a gesture: Thompson had in mind a
Morgan syndicate to purchase 5,000,000 rubles of which he personally
would take 20 per cent. Grateful for any small favor, Kerensky expressed
his personal appreciation for Thompson's "token of sympathy." [12]

Thompson's vigor was not mirrored in Washington. After his "long
interview" with the Root Mission, Lansing declined to modify his pessi-
mism. The Secretary, fully aware of "the strong opposition developing
against" Kerensky, was "astounded" at the Mission's optimism. He was,
moreover, and in marked agreement with Kennan, "very skeptical" of
Kerensky because the latter compromised "too much with the radical element of the revolution." "From the first" Lansing felt that any efforts to
maintain a middle ground "would be a failure." The only course, the Secretary confided to his diary, was to act on the hypothesis that Russia will go,
"from bad to worse . . . prepare for the time when Russia will no longer
be a military factor in the war," and sit back "until some dominant personality arises to end it all." [13]

In conjunction with the arbitrary refusal of Ambassador Francis and
President Wilson to acknowledge the fact of Russia's progressive deterioration, Lansing's self-addressed policy statement explains the Administration's failure to act in the face of tragedy. During the following six weeks
the President and Lansing were well aware that both Russia and the Allies looked to America for positive leadership. British Foreign Minister
Arthur H. Balfour admitted that only the United States could handle the
job and offered to subordinate British interests and personnel. Colonel
House, McCormick, Ambassador Francis, and many others urged Wilson
to act—at least to open a publicity campaign in Russia.[14]

But Wilson confined himself to pleasant and meaningless answers.
The President was far more concerned lest John F. Stevens, director of the
railroad commission, overstep his authority. "It is important," he dictated
to Lansing, "that the impression should not be created that he and his
associates represent or speak for the government of the United States."
The President was to modify his view of the usefulness of the Stevens group
within a year, and in any event his earlier concern was unwarranted for
dissension, as well as other interests, quickly made a joke of the Commission's first efforts. In August it "began to break up." Some members returned home. Stevens and several of his friends, however, went back to
Siberia to prepare for the new struggle with Japan for control of the Manchurian railways.[15]

Meanwhile the Red Cross Commission began to act on its assumption that Russia could be saved. Although Thompson and Robins regarded each other with considerable suspicion, they quickly reached a tacit agreement to share leadership of the Commission. Within a week after Thompson's interview with Kerensky they completed their initial survey and formulated plans to supply medicine, clothing, and condensed milk to the large urban centers. They also began to work closely with the Provisional Government in matters of transportation and sanitation.[16] But the greatest problem was that of food; and Thompson turned to Robins for a solution. Robins knew the situation was critical. "The bread, meat, milk and sugar lines," he wrote his wife on August 18, "last all day and far into the night. . . . Not since the first great winter in the Yukon have I seen bread and food generally so much the center of men's lives. . . . As go these lines," he prophesied, "so goes the Provisional Government." Desperate as the issue was, Robins did not concede the future. "There is here a great quiet power. The Russian will find himself in the next thirty years, and he will be the dominating figure in this Far Eastern situation." [17]

After their initial surveys were completed, Thompson and Robins held several joint conferences with Ambassador Francis, Kerensky, and other members of the Provisional Government. The result was a two-point program: reinvigorate the Revolution by fighting Germany, its greatest enemy; and at the same time re-establish the normal flow of food into the cities and to the army. Robins was assigned strategic jobs in each task force. Kerensky personally asked him to speak before the workers and the Army. Robins was hesitant about becoming so involved, but Thompson ordered him to comply. Thompson also detailed him to serve as liaison with the Provisional Government, and to go into the provinces and get food. For himself, Thompson accepted responsibility for the propaganda program. On August 29 he advised Red Cross Director Davison of the plan and asked him to secure President Wilson's active support.[18]

The President was not unaware of the Commission's work when he granted Davison an interview. Ambassador Francis and Harper both cabled of the group's "great success." Charles Crane advised his son, still serving in the State Department, that Robins made the "best impression on the workmen of any" American who had yet arrived. Secretary of War Newton D. Baker—who had asked his old friend Robins to do what he could to break up the contraband ring headed by pro-German Russians—added his "own strong judgment" that the mission should "be urged to put forth very great efforts." [19] Nor did Wilson, as some have claimed, lack either adequate information or counsel. For six months he received regular reports from both his official outposts and his personal advisors. Colonel House and Francis both warned that the crisis was quickening. In addition, Colonel Judson advised Burleson and the Army War College that the situation was "very bad." [20] But the Wilsonian calm was not easily ruffled.

The President advised Davison that he was "greatly interested" in Thompson's estimate of the situation and his plans but did not think it wise to "recommend aggressive action at this time." Davison also had to tell Thompson that his own House of Morgan "did not desire at this time" to act on the plan for a bond syndicate.[21] Thompson was discouraged; but he drove ahead, trusting that Wilson would act in the near future. He ordered Robins to make a loop through the Ukraine and Siberia to expedite the delivery of grain to the cities. Thompson then cabled Morgan to transfer "one million dollars" of his own funds to the Russian Minister of Finance. Morgan complied, but Thompson advised Morrow privately that it might "be necessary to have twenty times that much." He then submitted huge requisitions to the Red Cross War Council for medicine and food for the urban women and children. These preparations made, Thompson turned to the implementation of his propaganda campaign. But Colonel Judson was not too optimistic. "I sometimes wonder," he wrote Burleson bitterly, "whether this is all appreciated at home." [22]

While Thompson was thus occupied, Robins was out among the peasants. At first he quite naturally worked with the local representatives of the Kerensky Government. They were very cordial and friendly—"but they delivered no grain." Time and again when he returned for an explanation they shrugged and advised him to "see the soviet." Robins concluded that the Provisional Government had no power, and so wired Thompson for permission to deal with the local soviets. Thompson's answer was an order.

"You were sent to get the grain," he wired. "Get the grain." Robins immediately began to deal with the local committees. For a time he was successful. But suddenly all co-operation ceased. Robins discovered that he had been labeled a Wall Street representative who was sending the grain out of Russia instead of on to Moscow, Petrograd, and to the Army. He called the peasant leaders together, explained his position, and argued that to preserve the Revolution they had to fight Germany. To ease their suspicions he suggested that each soviet send a guard with its quota of grain. The proposal was accepted and deliveries were resumed.[23]

While Robins argued that the Revolution must be delayed to save it, the movement was challenged from another direction. Russian General Lavr G. Kornilov's abortive coup was in full swing when Robins finally had returned to Petrograd. Judson, his natural conservatism re-enforced by a growing fear that Russia would leave the war, "fervently wished" that Kornilov would win out and establish order and discipline. Other Allied representatives were similarly blinded by the character of their associations in Russia and through their desire for order. Without a second thought they reasoned from their western backgrounds that Kornilov would have considerable support. But the middle class, which many times supplied the strong man, simply did not exist. "As for the mass of the rank and file, it was clearly against Kornilov." Even the general's own Cossacks refused to fight.[24]

Robins was well aware that the peasants and workmen had no reason to support the man on horseback. "We're on a volcano," he warned Thompson. "Kerensky's got no power. . . . Underneath all," he explained, "is the fact that the binder . . . is gone and.each group is doing what seems right in its own eyes." Only if the integrity of the Revolution was restored, he argued, could Russia be integrated and reinvigorated. The task, Robins readily admitted, would not be easy. For one thing, those of "little imagination"—and there were "many English and Americans" in that group— would "turn . . . to the old order." As a result these Allied representatives would, "consciously or unconsciously, become friends of the reaction and add to the cry . . . for the dictator." But, Robins argued, "Revolutions never go backward. . . . Costly and discouraging as it is, we must work our way through and forward, not down and backward."[25]

While the embassies hid their disappointment and congratulated Kerensky on his magnificent show of strength—to which the Bolsheviks contributed no little—Thompson and Robins carefully reviewed the Kornilov episode. Through the entire affair they were out on the streets, going back and forth between Kerensky's Winter Palace and Smolny, a former finishing school for girls of the Tsarist circle, where the Bolsheviks had their headquarters. As the two men compared notes they realized that it had been "from Smolny and not from the Winter Palace" that Kornilov's defeat was directed. They both realized that the crisis had deepened, not eased.[26]

Coupled with the long-standing desire for peace and the absence of any effective opposition, the growing unrest over the land question steadily provided the Bolsheviks with raw material for a new revolt—or, as Lenin put it, the facts for "an objective analysis and estimate." The Bolsheviks had just demonstrated that they were capable of effective and militant leadership. Nor was their leader unaware of the situation. "It would be wrong," wrote Lenin on September 12, "to think that we have departed from the task of the conquest of power by the proletariat. Not at all. We have approached much nearer to it."[27]

Forced to admit that Kerensky's government "had not reached down its roots into the life of Russia," Robins submitted three recommendations for action. The "organization of public opinion in America friendly toward Russia" was of primary importance. Of equal significance was the organization of public opinion in Russia to support the war and so save the Revolution. Materially, Robins advocated large-scale relief work and the "encouragement of large government loans." Robins' trip convinced him that America was "more popular with the Russian people than any other nation," and he wanted to retain that position. Sentiment and humanitarianism, however, were not the only considerations.

"Taking the purely commercial view," Robins noted that Russia was the "greatest possible field for commercial enterprise, the investment of capital and the consumption of manufactured products" in the world. Even though American investments might "for the time being seem to have been wasted," Russia's future good will would constitute an investment that would "pay in the next fifty years $100 for every dollar contributed." Close economic ties might well, he analyzed, "be a determining factor . . . insofar as the question of the Far East is concerned." There could be "no effective menace from Japan, however militaristic and imperialistic," if Russia and the United States stood together. In September, 1917, Robins was "confident" that there were enough men in America "with vision and understanding" sufficient to insure the co-operation with Russia that he considered so "necessary and boundlessly fruitful for the better future of Russia, America, and the world." [28]

Robins' cogent analysis and the Kornilov episode brushed aside all Thompson's remaining doubts and spurred him into a total commitment. Neither Thompson nor Robins was unaware of the stakes. After the final decision was taken the two men admitted the risk.[29]

"It means," Thompson pointed out, "that if we fail you get shot."

"Colonel, if I get shot, you will get hung."

"I wouldn't be surprised," admitted Thompson, "if you are damn right."

In close harmony with Ekaterina Konstantinova Breshko-Breshkovsky, an early opponent of the Tsar fondly christened "the Grandmother of the Revolution," Bullard, the Committee on Public Information's fieldman, and members of the Provisional Government, Thompson opened his propaganda campaign. Ambassador Francis had already given his unofficial but personal sanction to the program. The principal objectives were the "continuation of the war," the "establishment of civil order and civil liberty," and the defeat of the extremists. The technique was to "corner the paper market . . . and choke off the Bolshevik press." [30] In addition to his responsibilities on the food front, Robins was assigned to the speaking campaign. With Sasha Kropotkin, daughter of Prince Peter Kropotkin, the philosophic anarchist whom Robins had known in the United States in 1905, as his interpreter, Robins campaigned vigorously among the soldiers and workmen. He altered the earlier Allied propaganda line—that the Allies were going to win the war in a walk. To that the peasant had responded, "Well, if that's so, let's go home." Robins told them that their revolution, their land, and their access to political power could come only if Russia helped defeat Germany. To keep him up to date on current politics Robins employed a large staff that reported to him each morning. Correspondents, other Americans, and Russians from all walks of life assisted him in this manner.[31]

Robins also conferred with Kerensky and other ministers with a view to establishing a special food commission. The plan was to have P. P. Batolin, "a sort of embryo Armour, a man who had a fleet of ships on the Volga" and some 800 peasant banking agencies under his control, head the agency with Robins as his chief assistant. But the appointment was "delayed from day to day" and ultimately Kerensky postponed the whole program indefinitely.[32] The only material aid Robins could supply came from the Red Cross. Thompson's huge orders of condensed milk, which helped save the lives of many children in the winter of 1917–18, were particularly valuable.

Thompson realized that his million would provide no more than a stop-gap almost before his first subsidized papers began to appear on the streets of Petrograd. After talks with Frederick M. Corse, Petrograd manager of the New York Life Insurance Company, and H. Grosvenor Hutchins, vice-president of the New York Bank of Commerce, Thompson prevailed upon the latter to return to Washington and attempt to jar the Administration awake and get aid. At Robins' request, Professor Harper, who was also about to return to the United States, agreed to brief Theodore Roosevelt on the situation.[33]

Hutchins arrived in New York on September 19, and within four days completed long conferences with Davison, Morrow, Colonel House, Thomas L. Chadbourne, counselor of the War Trade Board, Vance McCormick, chairman of the War Trade Board, and John Ryan, president of Anaconda Copper. "There was much interest in certain quarters, but there followed days of heartbreaking delay." Ryan gave a special dinner for the War Industries Board. No one offered to add his support to Thompson's program. Chadbourne's wife gave a quiet luncheon for Miss Helen Woodrow Bone, a presidential house guest, hoping she would whisper in Wilson's ear. The luncheon went off as scheduled, but no White House interest was manifested.[34]

Thompson, meanwhile, reported that the work was "well started" in Russia. But he admonished Hutchins to hurry—he needed to know what he could rely on "without delay." Suddenly, moreover, Thompson and Robins found it necessary to use "desperate" measures to keep Kerensky's head above water. Just before Hutchins arrived in New York the Bolsheviks issued a call for a Democratic Congress to meet on September 27, 1917. It was obviously a maneuver to seize power, and Thompson turned to Robins for advice.[35]

"Pack the convention," suggested the veteran of 1912 and 1916. Working feverishly with Breshkovsky and Nikolai Chaikovsky, a peasant co-operative leader, Robins proceeded to do just that. The Bolsheviks found themselves a minority when the Congress convened. The critical vote came on a Bolshevik motion to bar all bourgeois delegates. Trotsky's hard, driving speech, in which he attacked the war and the government's refusal to distribute the land, almost turned the tide. But Robins, watching from his private box, countered with a near-hysterical anarchist who swung the convention back to Kerensky.[36]

Thompson, aware that Hutchins had been home for three full weeks, wired Davison for "immediate support or all efforts may be too late. . . . You *must*," he pleaded to Hutchins, "put it over." Thompson's fellow Wall Streeters helped him turn the screws up tight. Allen Wardwell wired Francis Stetson, of Stetson, Jennings, and Russell, to see Dwight Morrow with reference to the "serious situation." Young Thomas D. Thacher cabled his father at the important law firm of Simpson, Thacher, and Bartless to do likewise because "immediate action [was] necessary." The delay unnerved Thompson. "We cannot conceive," he cried, "how the responsibility for failure to act . . . can willingly be assumed by any Americans." [37]

As an added effort, Thompson had Breshkovsky cable Wilson for aid. To make sure the message was not garbled by diplomatic phraseology Thompson sent Davison a simple English translation. But the President could be neither hurried nor brought to see the crisis—even though Davison personally briefed Wilson on the meaning of the message. When he leisurely responded three weeks later, Wilson chose to ignore the issue completely. "Intellectual development and moral firmness," wrote the President, are the most helpful aids to national progress.[38] Robins did not quote from this message in his speeches to the workers and the Army.

There is absolutely no question but that President Wilson was fully apprised of the critical situation. Lansing, House, and Francis all warned the President that Russia's condition was "certainly critical." Judson cabled of the "gradual disintegration of the power of government in all directions," and recommended vigorous support for Thompson. But the War College decided, in a very revealing memorandum, that "the English and the French, rather than the Russians, are our natural allies." Judson's cables were ignored. Even the Provisional Government's own admission that events were "threatening the very existence of the Russian Republic" did little to excite Wilson.[39]

Twenty-three days after Hutchins' arrival in New York, Vance McCormick of the War Trade Board finally reached the President with Thompson's message. Wilson thought it unwise for Thompson to continue, but in the same breath said it would be all right to see the Committee on Public Information concerning the program. The President, it appears, was not at all pleased with a man who spent a million dollars and asked for more. George Creel, chief of the CPI and close to Wilson, was enthusiastic over Thompson's plan. He secured Hutchins an appointment with Wilson—but not until twelve more days were lost. Even then it was futile, for Wilson completely misconceived the entire idea. He assured Thompson of the need for someone to represent the "fraternal interest of America," but cautioned that the United States "cannot go too carefully." [40]

Almost as an afterthought Wilson finally acted. He approved the appointment of Edgar Sisson, ex-Chicago *Tribune* editor and Creel's personal preference for the job, as special Committee on Public Information agent in Russia. He endorsed, reluctantly, an appropriation of $250,-000 to finance Sisson's work. His orders to Sisson were to stress America's "friendliness . . . unselfishness . . . and desire of helpfulness." No details were supplied—Sisson was not even warned of Russia's perilous condition. The President appeared confident that the "war aspects . . . would take care of themselves if a bond were forged" between the two peoples. Nor was there any mention of the "growing Bolshevik sentiment throughout the country." Sisson's commission was "to study conditions." Hutchins was "not enthusiastic" over the Administration's response to Thompson's appeal.[41]

Thompson, meanwhile, had no alternative but to curtail the entire program. The delay had been "very embarrassing." On November 1 Kerensky admitted that Russia was worn out and confessed that the future was unpredictable. The Bolsheviks won a majority in the Petrograd Soviet two days later. On November 3, 1917, the State Department lied in a bold effort to cover its negligence and complete failure to act in the crisis. "There has been absolutely nothing," read the press release, "in the dispatches received . . . from Russia nor in information derived from any other sources whatever, to justify the impression . . . that Russia is out of the conflict. . . . At the same time," Washington went on, "this Government, like those of the Allies, is rendering all possible assistance." Little wonder that Thompson was "deeply grieved and chagrined." "It was sickening and it was terrible," recalled Judson.[42]

In dramatic contrast to the State Department's behavior, Thompson and Robins made a last desperate bid to save the Provisional Government. On the night of November 3 they conferred with British General Alfred Knox; General Nueselle, his French opposite; General Judson; General Nevslakovsky of the Russian General Staff; and David Soskice, acting for Kerensky. Robins opened the proceedings with a summary of the reports he had from his agents, and then added his own observations. His review was pessimistic. All information indicated that the Bolsheviks were rapidly gaining control of the important military units. If Kerensky was to survive, Robins made clear, the Provisional Government had to win the support of the soviets.

Robins also acknowledged an earlier misjudgment. During the summer and early fall he felt that Thompson's propaganda program would turn the tide against the Bolsheviks; but during the long days while waiting for Wilson to act Robins concluded that words were of themselves insufficient. The only solution, he concluded—and he urgently recommended it to the group—was to distribute the land to the peasants immediately. This was the only chance, he argued, to cut the ground from under Lenin. It might, moreover, make possible a regeneration of the Russian Army.

"Distribute the land in Russia today and in two years we'll be doing it in England!" Knox shouted.

Thompson interrupted to support Robins but the Britisher would not be stopped. He delivered a long tirade against the Provisional Government and the cowardly Russian soldier. General Nevslakovsky broke in long enough to strike back with a dignified protest and then left, Soskice going with him. Their exit made the conference pointless, for without Russian concurrence the talk meant nothing. But General Knox was not concerned.

"I am not interested in stabilizing Kerensky. I do not believe in Kerensky and his government. It is incompetent and inefficient and worthless. You," he turned to Robins, "are wasting Thompson's money."

"Well, if I am, the Colonel knows all about it."

"You ought to have been with Kornilov," the general retaliated.

"Well, General," commented Robins, "you were with Kornilov."

Knox was momentarily trapped, and Robins pressed his advantage.

"We could not have added a whole lot to the Kornilov adventure, could we?"

"Well," confessed the general, "that may have been premature, but the only thing in Russia today is Soninkov Kaledines and a military dictatorship. These people have got to have a whip over them." [43]

The wrangling continued for several hours—always to the same point. Either distribute the land or stand by and watch a new revolt. But the Allied military representatives were pursuing the phantom of Napoleon. Members of the American Embassy were chasing their own will-o'-the-wisps. Consul General Summers gave an excellent summary of the entire situation. "We are too prone here," he admitted to his good friend Counselor Frank Polk, "to see things as we would like to see them and to believe that what we wish to happen is or may be happening." A constitutional monarchy was best for the Russians, Summers advised, and the people would have to learn that "communism cannot find a place in modern times." [44] He provided a good resume of his own social philosophy, but in doing so he also revealed the failure of American officials in Russia to acknowledge, the question of approval aside, the reality around them.

Within a week Lenin and the Bolsheviks seized power. For a time Allied observers believed that they "could not hold on very long." Kerensky retreated southward to rally his forces, but encountered instead "a decidedly hostile atmosphere." After their defeat at Tsarskoe Selo, Kerensky's Cossacks lost interest in civil war and negotiated with the Bolsheviks. Nor did the Army rally to Kerensky's support. A few days later, disguised as a sailor and hidden behind "automobile goggles," Kerensky "drove off toward Luga" in a car provided by Ambassador Francis. In Petrograd, meanwhile, Lansing's dominant personality had arrived, but Lenin's politics were not of the character the Secretary of State had anticipated.[45]

5

☆

THE BIRTH

OF CONTAINMENT

Any movement [against the Bolsheviks] . . . should be encouraged even though its success is only a possibility.

Secretary of State Lansing, December, 1917

The poorest service that can be rendered Russians by Americans, whether in Russia or at home, is to lose hope in her future, to stupidly and blindly turn back.

Raymond Robins, September, 1917

☆☆

Washington was bewildered, confused, and angered by the Bolshevik coup. Rather than shake itself awake and come to grips with reality, the Administration at first tried to ignore the existence of Lenin's government. But the failure of the counterattacks by Kerensky and the Moscow Committee of Safety indicated that the Bolsheviks could not be wished away. Yet the policy ultimately formulated by Washington was based in part on the assumption that Lenin would miraculously disappear, and that the Soviet Government would—because it should—collapse. The main points of American policy were quickly evolved and implemented. They were, moreover, consciously formulated.

These cornerstones were: (1) as long as the Bolsheviks remained in power the United States would refuse to establish normal intercourse and would under no circumstances recognize Lenin's government; (2) Washington would do all in its power to aid any serious and conservative leader or group whose aim was the destruction of the Soviet Government. The origins of this policy were obscured by publicity that presented Russia's withdrawal from the war as the product of Lenin's role as a German agent. The de-emphasis, almost to the point of exclusion, of Russia's economic collapse made it possible to type the Bolsheviks as unscrupulous representatives

105

of German militarism. But in fact none of the policy makers based their antagonism to the Soviet Government on this argument. Their basic motivation was an intense opposition to what they considered an effort "to make
the ignorant and incapable mass of humanity dominant in the earth";
and a steadfast refusal to admit the hard fact that the Russian Revolution
of November, 1917, was a revolution—not a parliamentary election—or
recognize the reality of the Bolsheviks' seizure of power, or to acknowledge
that Lenin would not stand by and theorize about his defeat.[1]

The sources of American policy are of especial significance when
considered in relation to the armed intervention of the United States in
Russia, both European and Siberian. For American intervention in Russia is usually explained as a move designed solely to forestall Japanese expansion in Manchuria and Siberia. Yet this analysis of the origins of intervention is gravely misleading. True, Washington did oppose Tokyo's
efforts to exploit both American preoccupation in Europe and Russia's
weakness during World War I; but to account for American intervention
in Russia on that ground alone is to evade the question of why Washington did not collaborate with Lenin, who took the initiative to seek an alliance
with the United States for the specific purpose of opposing Japan. Instead,
the United States delayed intervention until the Wilson administration
found a Russian to support who was not only anti-Japanese but also anti-
Bolshevik. Indeed, the search for an acceptable anti-Bolshevik—Admiral
Aleksander Kolchak was finally chosen—was the factor that delayed American intervention from February to July, 1918.

This basic anti-Bolshevik character of intervention underlies, in turn,
the failure of the United States to collaborate with the Soviet Union against
Japanese expansion from 1920 to 1922, during Tokyo's invasion of Manchuria in 1931, and later, when Japan began to wage hostilities against
China in 1937. For the corollary of Washington's opposition to the Soviet
Union's economic and social programs was the old pre-World War I American policy of attempting to secure supremacy in Manchuria through economic penetration under the open-door policy. And though publicly explaining its actions as steps taken to help China against both Japan and
the Soviet Union, Washington actually sought to assume control of the
Chinese Eastern Railway. In the attempt, as will be seen, the United States
even tried to deny China the right to participate in joint operation of the
line.

Formulated in the first months of 1918, this policy of antagonism to
Soviet Russia had three other important results. Any and all efforts to
emphasize the national problems faced by the Bolsheviks in the early days
of their rule—considerations which would restrict and modify the application of their theoretical program—were automatically discounted and ig-

nored. Instead, antagonism led to intervention, which enabled the Bolsheviks to use nationalism as their own rallying cry. The consolidation of Bolshevik power, an event considerably abetted by intervention, only deepened the enmity of American policy makers and heightened their determination to outlast the Soviet state. The decision "to promote tendencies which must eventually find their outlet in either the breakup or the mellowing of Soviet power" was not reached in 1945 or 1947—it was an established policy as of January 31, 1918.[2]

Many forces helped establish this policy toward Soviet Russia in the winter of 1917–18, but the men in Washington needed no prompting. As a political theorist, Wilson, who believed in a "slow process of reform," considered revolution a "puerile doctrine"; and as President of the United States viewed actual revolutions as events that in "other states should be . . . prevented." [3] Neither Secretary of State Lansing nor his career foreign-service assistants in the State Department made any move to quarrel with this estimate as applied to the Bolshevik Revolution. Long neglected in investigations of American foreign relations, these bureaucrats played important roles in policy formulation.

For by 1917 the United States was a highly industrialized nation, and one of the consequences of that development had been an increase in and an extension of the power of the national government. As the duties and responsibilities of the elected officials increased through the years after 1900, more and more authority was delegated to members of the appointive and civil service bureaucracy. By their day-to-day handling of routine affairs and through their function of supplying information to higher officials—who made the major decisions—these bureaucrats exerted a significant influence on the character of national policy. Nor was their importance restricted to instances where they had direct ties with special groups outside the government, as has been seen in the case of Willard Straight, who functioned as agent for the financial institutions of Kuhn, Loeb and Company and the House of Morgan at the same time he served as chief of the Far Eastern Division of the State Department. As men conscious of their power these bureaucrats made decisions both in terms of their personal attitudes and from the point of view of a special-interest group within the government.

In 1917, and thereafter, too, these men in the Department of State—unknown to the general public and tucked away safely beyond the reach of even an aroused congressman—formed a tightly knit team. With reference to American policy toward Soviet Russia, several of them deserve specific consideration because of their importance. The influence of Samuel Harper has been noted, and when he returned from Russia he merely renewed old friendships with William Phillips, Frank Polk, Richard Crane, and Basil Miles. But Harper found himself considerably restricted by professional duties throughout the academic year 1917–18, and he was not intimately involved in policy decisions until June, 1918.

Meanwhile the others functioned smoothly. Frank Polk, a graduate of Yale and Columbia, was a New York lawyer appointed counselor of the State Department when Robert Lansing was moved up from that job to replace William Jennings Bryan as Secretary of State. Phillips, of course, had been an important link between the Department and the financiers in the days of Dollar Diplomacy, and he continued to exercise a significant influence in the years after the Bolshevik Revolution. But while Polk and Phillips should not be underestimated, Basil Miles was the figure who gradually became the leader in the Department's day-to-day routine. His increased influence was in part a product of earlier experience in American-Russian relations. Miles dropped his business career to serve as private secretary to George von Lengerke Meyer (Theodore Roosevelt's businessman diplomat) when the latter was sent to Russia in 1905 as Roosevelt's special representative to the Tsar. Both Miles and Meyer, who viewed the great mass of Russians as "not much superior to animals with brutal instincts," were members of Roosevelt's social and political circle—and the President's intense dislike of Russia is well known.

This background became more important when, after Meyer was recalled from Russia in 1906, Miles stayed on in Russia as Third Secretary in the Embassy until May, 1907, when he returned to the United States to manage the Washington, D.C., office of the United States Chamber of Commerce. He resigned that post to be appointed special assistant to Ambassador Francis, who later reminded Lansing that "the principal object of my appointment as advised by yourself and President Wilson was to negotiate [a] treaty on commerce and navigation." Miles was raised to Minister Plenipotentiary early in 1917, and after service as an aide to the Root Mission was called home to be a special advisor on Russian affairs. Shortly after his return in September, 1917, he took over the Russian desk in the Department of State and was designated chief of the Division on Russian Affairs. President Wilson considered him a "capital" member of the State Department.[4]

Russian affairs were also of vital concern to the Departments of War and Treasury, but "most everything" was handled by the State Department and decisions were "largely influenced by the recommendations of its ambassadors and its chiefs." Within the State Department Miles, Phillips, and Polk reigned supreme. The Secretary turned to them constantly. Polk "worked closely" with Phillips and "made a good team" with Lansing. These aides screened all the reports from abroad, made oral and written summaries to the Secretary and other departments, and filtered the stream of people who provided additional information or endeavored to influence policy. In most instances they drafted the messages to American representatives in Russia.[5] No matter what the Secretary's personal inclinations, he was limited in large measure by the interpretations and decisions of these advisors. But there was no conflict between Lansing and his advisors in the matter of policy toward Russia.

Both President Wilson and Secretary Lansing received a steady stream of cables that reported and verified the Bolsheviks' consolidation of power and the continued demonstrations for peace. Burleson and Baker both supplied Wilson with Judson's analysis of the situation. The crisis might well, warned Judson, "put Russia . . . out of the war," and pointed out that this would "lead everywhere to an accentuated struggle between extreme socialism and severe reaction." Colonel House and other diplomatic representatives all wrote similar, if less acute, dispatches.[6] But the State Department blandly announced that Lenin would soon be overthrown and that Russia would remain active in the war. Secretary Lansing assured the Ambassador of the Provisional Government that the United States would recognize him indefinitely. Later a report hinted that a blockade would be established until "a stable government" was effected. This report was officially denied, but the Treasury Department suspended further cash advances and all shipments to the Provisional Government were halted.[7]

By the end of November the Administration had outlined its policy toward Russia. Francis was brought up to date by a report from Lansing on his talks with Jules J. Jusserand, the French Ambassador to the United States. Lansing considered him the "most accomplished" foreign diplomat in Washington, and one with whom it was "never . . . necessary to guard against tricks or deceptions." [8] They discussed the question of a general agreement not to recognize the Bolsheviks, and the French drive for intervention, launched with a gentle probing action in the west, found a soft spot. In Petrograd more resistance was encountered. American representatives in Russia proved themselves far more resilient than the group in Washington. Immediately following the actual coup they renewed their efforts to keep Russia in the war. At the same time they began to organize into two groups with reference to the Bolshevik Government.

The immediate objective of the Robins group was to keep the Eastern Front intact. The morning after the Bolsheviks occupied the Winter Palace Robins began an exploratory trip through the city. His first objective was to check the rumors that Kerensky had gathered a strong force in the suburb of Gatchina and was about to depose Lenin. Neither that visit nor the remainder of his scouting trip impressed Robins with the strength of the counter-revolution. But Thompson, bombarded with reports that Lenin and Trotsky were German agents, was not convinced, and Robins agreed to gather more information. He asked Thompson, however, for permission to change the guards at the Red Cross warehouse. Thompson refused. Robins asked him if that was an order. Reluctant to disregard Robins' advice, Thompson said no. On the way to Smolny, Robins engaged the Red Guards to protect the supplies of food and medicine. As a result, the Red Cross "never lost a pound of anything" during the remainder of its work in Russia.[9]

The second and last session of the Second Congress of Soviets opened at Smolny at eight in the evening. Robins was an interested observer. He stayed until five the next morning, through all the debates on peace, the land question, and the fierce struggle to establish a coalition. Back at the Hotel Europa he reviewed the meeting for Thompson.[10]

"Chief, we have got to move pretty fast. Kerensky is as dead as yesterday's 7,000 years."

Thompson was still bothered by the German agent thesis, and Robins was unable to satisfy his doubts. Robins pointed out, however, that the Bolsheviks were in power and that a decision must be reached as to whether the Red Cross would stay in Russia or abandon the field. Robins argued that the only way to find out where the Bolsheviks stood was to talk to them. Thompson agreed, and authorized Robins to visit Smolny. Robins was handicapped, however, by the violent anti-Bolshevism of his interpreter, Sasha Kropotkin. Not only was she a political enemy of those in power, but she was deeply involved emotionally in the counter-revolution. Her contacts, so valuable during Kerensky's days in office, were now a definite handicap. After long consideration Robins selected Alexander Gumberg, a Russian-American from New York.

Gumberg was an important if quiet member of the American colony in Russia from the date of his arrival in the early summer of 1917. Long a resident of New York's East Side, Gumberg had a "deep love" for America, even though it had offered him most of its worst and little of its best. Although many of his friends developed a romantic and emotional attachment to the November Revolution, Gumberg's central purpose was, and remained, to help build strong relations between the two nations. The limitations imposed upon him by America thwarted him at every turn. Automatically associated with the extreme left wing, and discriminated against in other ways, Gumberg had been denied the opportunity to make an individual contribution. When he returned to Russia as the representative of a New York manufacturing concern, however, it appeared that his unique background would be utilized.

His "thorough understanding of the situation in both" Russia and America made him of the "greatest possible assistance" to Charles Edward Russell and the rest of the Root Mission. When Russell was denied permission to remain in Russia, he strongly recommended Gumberg to John F. Stevens of the Railroad Commission. Stevens declined to avail himself of Gumberg's services, but Gumberg became an observer who occasionally did work for Bullard of the Committee on Public Information and Charles Smith of the Associated Press.

Robins and Gumberg knew each other through the long discussions among the American group during the months of August, September, and October. Gumberg provided more accurate information than the others who had reported to Robins, and was the only American to warn of the impending collapse of the Provisional Government. Though not a Bolshevik, Gumberg did have access to Smolny through his brother and by virtue of his acquaintance with Trotsky, who published a Russian-language newspaper in New York before his return to Russia. Robins turned to Gumberg for help in securing his first appointment with Trotsky and then, on November 10, employed him as a personal secretary. The two men complemented each other to an unusual degree. Robins accepted Gumberg as an equal, valued his advice, but made his own decisions. Gumberg, on the other hand, was given an excellent opportunity to use his knowledge and experience to help build a bridge between Russia and the United States. The association thus formed lasted until Gumberg's death in 1939.[11]

Robins held his first interview with Trotsky on either the tenth or the eleventh of November. Robins, a devoted follower of Theodore Roosevelt and himself no further left than any enlightened reformer, did not discuss the fine points of Marxism with one of its high priests. But both men were political realists. "I won Trotsky," Robins recalls, "by putting my case absolutely on the square. By not hiding anything."[12] Robins advised Trotsky that he was there because he would be dealing with those in power, no matter who they were, because he wanted to continue Red Cross activities and keep Russia in the war. He also wanted to gauge Bolshevik power and determine whether Lenin and Trotsky were German agents or sympathizers.

Robins verified the fact of Bolshevik control and concluded that they were "very peculiar" German agents. Dealing directly with Trotsky, Robins secured the transfer of some thirty boxcars of Red Cross supplies to Jassy, Rumania; and had a large quantity of condensed milk and other supplies conveyed from Murmansk to Petrograd, after General Frederick C. Poole, head of the British Economic Mission, told him to write them off as lost. Later, Trotsky co-operated with Robins to hold up a large contraband train destined for Germany at Viborg, and on Robins' request sent the material to Murmansk where it was guarded by the British Fleet. Thompson was convinced. "My emphatic belief," he cabled Davison, "is that [the] present Russian situation is not hopeless for the Allies."[13]

Official American representatives were not of the same mind. Francis, who originally hoped the Bolsheviks would try to form a government because "the more ridiculous the situation the sooner the remedy," refused to have any contacts with Smolny; and on November 19 appealed to the people of Russia to "remove the difficulties that beset your pathway." Consul Summers was likewise concerned with "all classes of Russians standing for law and order." Judson first sided with this group and notified the chief of the old Russian General Staff that the newspaper report of an embargo "correctly states the attitude" of the United States. Lieutenant Colonel Monroe C. Kerth joined the French and British military representatives to protest "categorically and energetically" against any separate armistice.[14]

Meanwhile Thompson prepared to return to the United States and attempt to modify American policy. The decision was made soon after the Bolsheviks consolidated their power in Petrograd and Moscow, and on November 19 Robins provided Thompson with a long letter of introduction to Theodore Roosevelt. The letter symbolized Thompson's determination to effect a shake-up in Washington, for in earlier years the financier bitterly opposed Roosevelt on the grounds that he was too radical. Thompson originally planned to leave via Siberia and proceed directly to Washington. But Thomas W. Lamont, also of the House of Morgan, strongly advised Thompson to come to London and confer with Colonel House; and at the last moment Thompson agreed to this plan. He left Petrograd on November 28, 1917, having promoted Robins to the rank of colonel in command of the Red Cross unit. Thompson's last official act was to deny Judson's statement that supplies from America would be stopped and to dissociate the Red Cross from the American military's ultimatum.[15]

Judson, however, had already concluded that the Bolsheviks were without question the de facto government of Russia. He also realized that his primary objective—to prevent peace on the Eastern Front—could hardly be gained by a policy of blind antagonism to the Bolsheviks. Knowing of Robins' success in dealing forthrightly with Smolny, Judson turned to him for advice. On November 27 they had a long conference during which Judson requested Robins to question Trotsky on the proposed armistice with Germany. On the same day Judson also wrote a second and more conciliatory note to Trotsky.[16]

Several factors contributed to the establishment of this relationship between Robins and Smolny and of the close co-operation between Judson and Robins. First was the fact that Sisson, who arrived on November 25, found the Ambassador "without policy except anger at the Bolsheviks." But for the time Francis failed to implement his policy. So intense was his emotion that he could not bring himself to share the realism of George Buchanan, the British Ambassador and a fellow conservative. Buchanan hated the Bolsheviks with a deep malice, but saw and admitted that Russia should be released from her war commitments. "Every day we keep Russia in the war against her will," he warned, "does but embitter her people against us." In no sense, of course, did Francis agree with William Chapin Huntington, American commercial attaché, who recognized that the Bolsheviks touched "a deep yearning," and that the embassies "with their fear" of recognition were "making fools of themselves." [17] But in the early days of the revolution Francis did not commit himself so thoroughly and effectively to the cause of counter-revolution as did his Consul General, Maddin Summers.

Summers entered the Foreign Service shortly after he completed his schooling at Vanderbilt and Columbia. He switched from bank clerk to consular clerk in July, 1899, and remained in the Foreign Service. Save for one brief stint in Belgrade he served exclusively in Spain and South America until August, 1916, when he was detailed to Moscow. Shortly thereafter he married Natalie Goraynoff, the daughter of a Russian noble. Summers was a highly competent and efficient officer of the Foreign Service; but as a man to interpret and maintain relations with a revolutionary government he was less than qualified. The limitations imposed by his narrow conservatism were further increased by associations stemming from his marriage. Summers' opposition to the Bolsheviks hardened when Natalie's family lost both its land and laborers through the November Revolution. Ruin and Bolshevism were "synonymous" to Consul Summers; and he drove himself without limit in an effort to destroy Smolny.[18]

The Embassy itself, moreover, suffered from serious demoralization. The cause was the Ambassador's conduct. The fact that Charles Crane spoke "well" of Francis did not alter the fact that the Ambassador was both indiscreet and exceedingly indifferent to the responsibilities of his position. The Ambassador's failure began, according to Harper, on the trip to Russia. Aboard the *Oscar II* bound for Petrograd was a group of passengers "distinctly open to suspicion" as German agents. One of these was an especially attractive and intelligent woman, Madame Matilda de Cram, who was "very friendly" with Francis by the time the group reached Russia. Her continued association with the Ambassador caused the Embassy staff "much anxiety." Francis refused to hear the charges or modify his conduct.[19]

Through the months of October and November, 1917, the relationship between Madame de Cram and Francis continued and, possibly, matured. She was constantly in the Embassy. She heard policy discussed, and was many times in the rooms where cables were coded and deciphered. At least one letter report was given to her by Francis for her perusal. When she was detained for some cause, the Ambassador called on her. Madame de Cram's influence was greater than that of any official member of the Embassy staff—and probably exceeded that of the combined group. Judson, J. Butler Wright, Embassy counselor, Colonel Kerth, Captain E. Francis Riggs, and Robins all knew the situation firsthand. When Francis was careless with cipher codes and the secret material disappeared, these men launched their own investigation. They quickly discovered that Madame de Cram was on the secret suspect list of the Inter-Allied Passport Bureau. Some member of the Embassy staff then notified the State Department. The Department fired back a blunt warning that Madame de Cram was suspected both of espionage and connection with the Black Tom Plot, and directed Francis to suspend all relations with the woman immediately.

Francis was enraged. He termed the informer a "willful liar" and continued the association. Finally Judson, acting in desperation, called on the Ambassador personally. Judson recited the long record of evidence and even showed Francis the dossier from the Passport Bureau. Francis was personally pleasant, but Judson left knowing that he had made absolutely no impression. The matter became the "subject of gossip" in Washington, but Francis continued the relationship on through 1917 and well into 1918.[20]

These important considerations were re-enforced by Robins' growing insight into the Revolution itself. Familiar with the writings of Marx long before he arrived in Russia, Robins assumed, in the early days of November, that Smolny would follow the guidebook. Indeed, he was quite aware that Lenin's speeches and writings were filled with exhortations to the workers of the world and promises of the revolution to come. These developments, coupled with Trotsky's co-operation on the questions of Red Cross supplies and contraband, convinced Robins that the cry of German agent was misleading.

This did not mean that Robins was in sympathy with Bolshevism. His record of opposition to socialism, and of support for Theodore Roosevelt and Charles Evans Hughes, was long and vigorous. Robins' analysis of the Revolution did indicate, however, that Germany would be denied any large-scale exploitation of Russian resources unless they conquered the nation. As he continued to press Trotsky on this question of contraband, Robins began to see the full implications of the dilemma in which Smolny found itself. Although theoretically and ideally committed to world revolution, the principal problem faced by the Bolsheviks was the consolidation of their power in a nation state. Trotsky acknowledged the seriousness of the situation when, later in November, he approached Robins and suggested the use of American troops to stop the contraband traffic. For all their huzzahs for international revolt, the Bolsheviks knew that to survive they must capitalize on one of three opportunities: war fatigue in Russia, the conflict between Germany and the Allies, or the struggle between the United States and Japan in the Far East. Though the Allies "refused" this first offer from Trotsky it was renewed several times as German aims in Russia became clearer.[21]

Robins, in turn, realized that Smolny's problem presented a great opportunity to Allied diplomacy. Two main options presented themselves. Full-scale opposition might well destroy Smolny. But that was militarily well-nigh impossible: American resources were committed on the Western Front. And on another level the Congress had declared war against Germany—not Russia. On the other hand, Bolshevik weakness could be exploited, not only in terms of world politics, but to modify the Bolshevik's domestic program. This, to Robins, presented the only realistic possibility. He felt it would be more productive to work for firm American-Russian relations, which would serve both to stabilize world politics and to give the United States the greatest influence with the Revolution, than to allow reactionary forces to triumph or to muddle through and be confronted by a Soviet government that had won out on its own.

This estimate of the situation led both Robins and Judson into a diplomatic no-man's land where they were useful but expendable. After his long talk with Judson on November 27, Robins saw Trotsky about the armistice proceedings. Trotsky exhibited considerable interest in the possibility of reaching some agreement; and Judson went back to Francis and reopened their old argument about establishing some working contact with Smolny.[22] Judson insisted that the Bolsheviks were the de facto government, and argued that the peace sentiment would force them at least to negotiate with the Germans. Given that situation, the only realistic policy was to attempt to insert a clause in the settlement that would immobilize German troops in the East. Francis, under pressure from Sisson and others who supported Judson's plan, and aware that the British were considering a similar move, granted Judson's request and gave him official authorization to talk with Trotsky.[23] Judson first approached the British and French for their support. General Knox, at first "rather favorable" to the idea, was overruled by Buchanan. The French had no sympathy for the idea. They were "implacable," noted Judson, and appeared to be "more bent upon expressing their opinion than upon substantial accomplishments." As a result, Judson made the trip alone.[24]

On December 1, 1917, Judson held a forty-minute interview with Trotsky. Judson, who "made it clear at the outset that at the present time he had no right to speak in the name of the American Government," desired "to clear up certain misunderstandings" and exert some influence on the scheduled peace talks between Russia and Germany. Trotsky voluntarily recognized that Russia had "a certain obligation to her Allies," and was further "very amiable and very responsive" to Judson's program to hold German troops on the Eastern Front. The armistice commission, agreed Trotsky, "would be given instructions accordingly." In parting, Trotsky assured Judson that the "allies of Russia would have further opportunity to examine into and offer suggestions as to said terms."[25]

Judson and Robins were enthusiastic and prepared to exploit the opportunity. Judson's experience convinced him that Robins' interpretation of the Revolution was accurate, and he prepared a vigorous program to take advantage of the fact that the United States was the "only Allied nation possessing the confidence of Russia sufficiently to act." His aim was to "extract a broadening of its foundations from the Soviet Government" and at the same time keep Russia in the war. Judson requested authorization to express the United States' "friendly appreciation" of the "desperate situation" and to make it meaningful by offering to co-operate in the operation of the trans-Siberian railway system and to carry through with "assistance on a larger scale of every other character." [26]

Judson's optimism was not warranted. For on the day of his interview with Francis, the Ambassador was advised that it was "most unwise" for him to "take any sort of initiative." After the Department reacted unfavorably to the news of Judson's talk with Trotsky, the Ambassador was to save face by denying that he authorized the visit; on December 3, meanwhile, Francis refused Judson's request to see cables between Washington and the Embassy. Judson assumed that the information contained in the State Department cables would enable him to "better advise" the War Department and to make his communications "more harmonious" with those of the Ambassador—a state of affairs Judson thought might be of "obvious advantage to our Government." [27] Ambassador Francis did not agree.

Washington also had other ideas of what constituted its obvious advantage. "By the first of December" the Administration forced itself to acknowledge the "temporary success" of the Bolsheviks. Three days later the President and Lansing found themselves united in "disappointment and amazement" against the "class despotism" in Petrograd. Lansing prepared and submitted to Wilson a long memorandum on Russia. In essence it was an embittered attack on Smolny that concluded with a strong recommendation not to recognize the Bolshevik Government because of its class origin and structure. The President (who thought that "a great menace to the world had taken shape") "approved in principle," but "did not think that it was opportune to make a public declaration of this sort." [28]

This decision was made *before* the reports of Judson's trip to see Trotsky reached Lansing. When the Secretary did learn of the interview, on December 4 and 6, he acted with more dispatch than at any time since the March Revolution. He talked with Secretary of War Baker "on recalling Judson from Petrograd," conferred with Phillips on the same problem, and also discussed the situation with Wilson. The result was the following cable sent to Francis on December 6, 1917: [29]

Referring press reports received here last few days concerning communications of Judson with Trotsky relative armistice, President desires American representatives withhold all direct communication with Bolshevik Government. So advise Judson and Kerth. Department assumes these instructions being observed by Embassy.

The following day Lansing again conferred with Wilson on Judson's "conduct in Petrograd," and then unburdened himself to his diary. "The correct policy for a government which believes in political institutions as they now exist and based on nationality and private property," he wrote, "is to leave these dangerous idealists alone and have no direct dealings with them." The Secretary was appalled at what he termed an effort "to make the ignorant and incapable mass" dominant in the world. Nor did he grasp the counter-revolutionary import of nationalism. The "only possible remedy," he decided, was for a "strong commanding personality to arise . . . gather a disciplined military force . . . restore order and maintain a government." Generals Alexei Kaledin and Mikhail Alexeev, formerly the Tsar's Chief of Staff, who had gone to South Russia immediately after the Bolshevik coup, were noted as the most promising candidates for the position of savior.[30] *As these events of early December, 1917, make unmistakably clear, neither Lansing nor Wilson formulated policy toward Russia on the premise that Lenin was a German agent.* This fact cannot be overemphasized, for later commentary, both official and scholarly, presented intervention as either anti-German or anti-Japanese in origin.

These counter-revolutionary forces in South Russia rapidly became the focus of American interest. Phillips, Polk, and Miles all shared Lansing's opposition to Smolny and supported his December 10 recommendation to Wilson. The best "hope" was a "military dictatorship"; and the "only apparent nucleus . . . sufficiently strong to supplant the Bolsheviks" appeared to be the group around Kaledin.[31] Further conferences, during which Secretary McAdoo indicated his support of the project, resulted in the preparation of a highly confidential memorandum outlining American policy in support of the counter-revolutionary forces.

This document, to which Wilson gave his "entire approval," was sent on to Oscar T. Crosby, Treasury representative on the Inter-Allied Finance Council, for the guidance of American representatives in Europe. The problem had been "carefully considered," Crosby was advised, to the conclusion that "any movement" against the Bolsheviks "should be encouraged even though its success is only a possibility." Kaledin and Kornilov were singled out for special consideration. As yet it was "unwise" and impossible to give open financial aid, Crosby was cautioned, but Kaledin should be advised that Washington was "most sympathetic with his efforts." Britain and France, furthermore, should be approached on the matter of finances. Obviously, Crosby was warned, it was of particular importance to act "expeditiously" and secretly. This policy decision, it should be noted, was made on December 12, 1917, ten days *before* a similar decision was made by England and France during a conference in Paris. Of especial significance is the fact that Wilson and Lansing both acted, not from a belief that Lenin was a German agent, but from an avowed opposition to what they considered the goals of the November Revolution." [32]

The dates in question become even more important when considered in relation to the activities of William Boyce Thompson after he left Russia. The House of Morgan's influence in England became readily apparent when Thompson was taken aboard H.M.S. *Vulture* at Bergen, Norway, after he missed his regular connections. Lamont, who arranged the battleship ride for Thompson, was upset when the latter arrived in London too late to catch Colonel House and Vance McCormick, but did arrange conferences with high members of the British Government. After his initial interview with Ambassador Page, Thompson saw Lord Reading; Admiral Hall, head of British Naval Intelligence; Sir George Clark, Balfour's representative; John Buchan, British propaganda chief; and Lord Carson of the War Office. All were impressed with Thompson's knowledge and analysis of the situation. Carson told Thompson to inform Wilson that he would "go just as far as he will and further," and that finances were no problem. [33]

On either December 13 or 14 Thompson had lunch with Prime Minister David Lloyd George at 10 Downing Street. He was in no sense awed by the Welshman's high office. "Because of their shortsighted diplomacy," Thompson told Lloyd George, "the Allies since the Revolution have accomplished nothing beneficial, and have done considerable harm to their own interests." It promised little, he continued, to treat Russia as an outcast; for very possibly the Bolsheviks were the key to the entire war. Firm contacts with them should be established, Thompson argued, for two reasons. Any chance to reconstitute the Eastern Front must be exploited to the limit. Equally important was the fact that the Bolsheviks were fighting for their very existence, and as yet had been unable to translate their theories into action. Internally they were struggling with necessities; and internationally they were searching for security. "Let's make them our Bolsheviks," Thompson suggested. [34]

Lloyd George seemed to accept the proposal. He expressed agreement with Thompson's suggestions to send representatives "democratic in spirit," and to constitute an inter-allied commission to carry on relations with the Bolsheviks as a de facto government. Thompson was also asked to express Lloyd George's agreement to President Wilson. [35] Thompson and Lamont left for the United States the next day as guests aboard a British transport. They arrived in New York on Christmas Day and hurried on to Washington to complete their errand.

But Lloyd George, meanwhile, followed Thompson's advice in a peculiar manner. True, he selected Robert Bruce Lockhart, who served in the British Embassy in Russia during 1904–5, to go to Russia; and Lockhart, who had been trying to influence Lord Alfred Milner to adopt a policy similar to Thompson's, appeared to be a logical selection. He was, moreover, charged with the "responsibility of establishing relations." But, in Lockhart's words, "I was to have no authority." This is not surprising, for on December 22, 1917, Lord Milner agreed, on behalf of England, to support the forces of counter-revolution. Lockhart's mission would appear to have been part of the plan "to avoid the imputation as far as we can that we are preparing to make war on the Bolsheviki." On December 23, 1917, England and France signed a formal agreement to support Alexeev and to split Russia into respective spheres of influence. Thompson's advice became a mite distorted in its execution.[36]

In Russia a similar situation existed. Robins and Judson continued their work to keep Russia in the war. Consul Summers led the forces of containment and destruction. The prize at stake was the concurrence of Ambassador Francis who had yet effectively to implement any policy— even his own anger. For a time it appeared that Robins and Judson would succeed in their efforts to have the United States take advantage of Smolny's tenuous position and endeavor to establish a firm relationship with Russia on the basis of mutual self-interest.

Sisson offered his support to Robins and Judson immediately upon his arrival in Petrograd. He approved the policy that motivated Judson's visit to Trotsky and cabled Creel so to advise the President. Creel found Lansing and Wilson unreceptive, and was ordered to rebuke Sisson. But in the meantime Sisson had received Creel's advice to "co-ordinate all American agencies in Petrograd and Moscow." To Sisson this was a "plain order," and he began to interpret the cable liberally. Apparently he was "taking himself quite seriously," for he continued to irritate Francis. Lansing again brought the matter to Wilson's attention; and the President seems to have reminded Creel of his earlier orders. In any event, Creel took occasion to assure the President that Sisson understood that he was "not to touch the political situation." [37]

Sisson did not evidence this understanding. Robins shared with Sisson the services of Gumberg and secured for him Bolshevik co-operation in the distribution of various speeches and other propaganda. Some time during the middle of December Robins proposed the use of Bolshevik propaganda against German troops. With Sisson he worked out the plan and put it into operation. During this period Sisson gave every indication that he shared Robins' determination to "use the possibilities yet remaining" to establish "an authoritative Allied co-operation in Petrograd." [38]

Consul Summers viewed the situation in a slightly different manner. On December 15, following private talks with right-wing General A. A. Brusilov, Summers personally dispatched De Witt Clinton Poole, consul at Moscow, to approach Alexeev and Kaledin. Summers acted on his own initiative, and before he received any word of Washington's decision of December 12. Poole spent the rest of December sounding out these White leaders. Both he and F. Willoughby Smith, American consul at Tiflis, gave Alexeev, Kornilov, and Kaledin strong moral support.[39] Lansing ordered Smith, who was "in close touch and working unanimously with" these leaders, to make duplicate reports to Crosby in London. Summers and Poole recommended that the United States "should immediately" support this movement as the "only salvation." "The Russia we welcome as a democratic nation," wrote Summers, "is in the South." [40]

This performance by Summers may have contributed to Francis' mid-December failure of nerve. The Ambassador, for all his antagonism to the Bolsheviks, realized that Wilson's policy of non-intercourse with Smolny placed the United States in a ridiculous position. When the Washington cable arrived he promised Robins that he would "stand between you and the fire." Almost immediately his courage wavered; and he asked whether Red Cross personnel were included in the President's order. The Department quickly advised Francis that they were, and so to advise Robins.[41]

Working in close co-operation with Judson, Robins meanwhile received "assurances from Trotsky" that Russia would insist that Germany hold her troops on the Eastern Front if the armistice was extended. They scored again when Trotsky gave the United States credit for holding up a rumored Japanese intervention in the Far East. In view of these developments, both men considered Summers' policy extremely dangerous. Judson, whose cables were ignored by the War Department, viewed the mission to Kaledin as "absolutely futile and ill-advised." Robins thought the move would "simply mean civil war," and might well develop to Germany's advantage. The United States was "becoming isolated," warned Judson, by its "position of apparent repulsion of the Soviet Government." [42]

This fact, coupled with his own regretful admission that Bolshevik power was "undoubtedly" supreme in Russia, made Francis willing to overlook the Department's non-intercourse order to Robins. The Ambassador was willing "to swallow pride, sacrifice dignity, and with discretion" establish regular contact with Smolny. Judson, realizing this was a key opportunity, wrote a vigorous letter to the Ambassador urging him to take the lead. German influence is unopposed, Judson began, principally because the United States had no communications with the Bolshevik Government. "The terrible responsibility for this deplorable condition, fraught with untold danger" to the world, rested, declared Judson, upon himself and the Ambassador. It was their responsibility, he pointed out, to inform Washington and to recommend appropriate action. "Do not stand on dignity," he concluded. "It is necessary that the United States adopt at once a broad Russian policy." [43]

For the moment Francis agreed, and requested permission for Robins to continue his relations with Smolny. The request officially appeared to be dictated by Red Cross requirements, but the true purpose was as indicated. It was fortunate that the façade was employed, for Phillips was upset by Francis' earlier willingness to establish working relations with the Soviets. Noting that the Ambassador appeared to be "thoroughly depressed," Phillips warned Lansing that Francis needed "a tonic in the form of a Departmental instruction." The Secretary agreed, and on December 29 Francis was advised that recognition was "not considered" a present possibility. The same day Lansing authorized Robins to continue his visits to Smolny on Red Cross business.[44]

Francis interpreted the approval in the same sense as the request. This was important, for on December 27 the negotiations at Brest-Litovsk were disrupted over the question of occupied territories. Adolf Joffe expressed Soviet willingness to withdraw from Poland, Lithuania, Courland, and other Baltic areas pending local plebiscites unhampered by occupying forces. Germany retorted, through Richard von Kuhlmann, that she considered those nations to have signified their preference for Germany. The plebiscite, Kuhlmann amplified, would "ratify the will already expressed." [45] The meaning was clear, and Smolny realized it was being forced to choose between a German-dictated peace or a renewed war, which without help would mean the destruction of Bolshevik power.

Robins' entire forecast was being verified, and he hurried to Smolny to exploit the break in the weather. Trotsky was "enraged" and exceedingly worried by the German proposals. His primary concern was "what America will do" if negotiations terminated. Robins immediately informed Judson, and together they "hastened" to the Embassy to inform Francis. After hearing their report, the Ambassador gave them full authority to "go to Trotsky and inform him that [the United States] would render all assistance possible." Even the British and French admitted it was a great opportunity and agreed to support the decision.[46]

The opportunity thus offered to the United States by virtue of Smolny's primary concern with its own existence was so challenging that both Francis and Washington momentarily overcame their fundamental antagonism and considered the possibility of reaching some *modus vivendi* with the Bolsheviks. Despite evidence of the benefits that would thereby be gained, the United States refused to abandon its program of support for counter-revolution. That active intervention would be the final decision was indicated in Francis' cable of January 1, 1918. On that afternoon and evening Sisson, after conferences at the Embassy, attended the meeting of the Central Executive Committee of the Soviets of Workers', Soldiers', and Peasants' Deputies called to discuss the crisis. He reported to Francis, Robins, and Judson that "the speeches all indicated a spirit of readiness to resume the war if the Germans did not yield." Francis agreed to cable Washington that he would "take any step . . . necessary to prevent separate peace." [47]

Unknown to Robins and Judson, the Ambassador was "inclined" to think that if such a peace proved unavoidable "it should favor Germany to [the] extent possible in order to make it the more unacceptable not only to the allies but to pacifist and proletariat throughout the world." Francis then inquired if the Department agreed. The arrival of the cable in Washington prompted Basil Miles to write a short note to Phillips. "I had not thought this last sentence requires answer," he remarked.[48] Neither did Phillips, Polk, or Lansing. Nor, in the last analysis, did President Wilson.

On the same night the long arm of Lansing reached Russia in the form of Judson's unconditional recall. The interview with Trotsky on December 1, 1917, aroused the Secretary's intense anger; and at his request Secretary of War Baker agreed to withdraw Judson. Always one "eager to say what seemed to be the truth," Judson paid a high price for his integrity.[49] It is possible that Secretary Lansing's personal satisfaction was extracted at a rather high cost to the interests of the United States.

Judson was stunned, and for more than a week took little vocal part in the rapid sequence of events. Robins continued the effort to conclude an understanding with Smolny on his own. His arguments still reached Francis, but Judson's withdrawal unnerved the Ambassador. "Surely our interest is to prevent peace," cabled Francis to Lansing; but he "would not presume to commit [the] Department." Still, the Ambassador "might consider it advisable to commit myself to recommend assistance . . . for sincere rigorous prosecution of war." [50] The Ambassador did just that on January 2, promising Robins that he would cable for help if Smolny was forced into war. Two cables were drafted and initialed by Francis for Robins' use in discussion with Trotsky.

These stand-by messages gave both Robins and Trotsky definite reason to believe that the United States was seriously interested in agreement. Francis signed the following statement, drafted by Robins, which would appear to be reasonably definite.[51]

If upon the termination of the present armistice Russia fails to conclude a democratic peace *through the fault of the Central Powers and is compelled to continue* the war I shall urge upon my government the fullest assistance to Russia possible, including the shipment of supplies and munitions for the Russian armies, the extension of credits and the giving of such advice and technical assistance as may be welcome to the Russian people. . . .

Two days later the Ukrainian Rada, a separatist government, opened negotiations with Germany; and on January 5, 1918, Kuhlmann informed Trotsky that Germany would no longer negotiate on the basis of no annexations and no indemnities.

The Bolsheviks were desperate. Trotsky argued to Lenin that the negotiations had to be dragged out to provide time for either a revolution in Germany and Austria, or for the Allies to promise assistance. Lenin was very skeptical, and agreed to the plan only on condition that Trotsky himself did the delaying. "At his insistence" Trotsky left for Brest-Litovsk on the night of January 5.[52] Events likewise moved toward a climax in Washington. Acting at least partially under the immediate pressure of Colonel House, Lansing, Lord Balfour, and Sisson—who cabled Creel that there was a need for "internal evidence" of Wilson's concern for the Russian situation—President Wilson delivered his Fourteen Points Speech on January 8, 1918.[53]

With pointed reference to the parleys "in progress at Brest-Litovsk," Wilson enunciated his conception of the "only possible program" for world peace. The subsequent struggle over the implementation of this program and the development of Washington's policy toward Russia have tended to obscure the character of Wilson's references to Russia. In view of the President's later actions these are of particular interest. It is clear, for example, that Wilson viewed the Bolsheviks as the legitimate "Russian representatives" who were speaking as the "voice of the Russian people" at Brest-Litovsk. The President considered, moreover, that they "were sincere and in earnest." Aware that Russia was "prostrate and all but helpless" before "the grim power of Germany," Wilson carefully specified his policy.[54]

The evacuation of all Russian territory and such a settlement of all questions affecting Russia as will secure the best and freest co-operation of the other nations of the world in obtaining for her an unhampered and unembarrassed opportunity for the independent determination of her own political development and national policy and assure her of a sincere welcome into the society of free nations under institutions of her own choosing; and, more than a welcome, assistance also of every kind that she may need and may herself desire. The treatment accorded Russia by her sister nations in the months to come will be the acid test of their good will, of their comprehension of her needs as distinguished from their own interests, and of their intelligent and unselfish sympathy.

The President's remarks indicate a momentary disagreement with Lansing on Russian policy. Or more exactly, perhaps, an occasion when Wilson's sympathy with the deep urge for economic and social reform actually influenced a policy statement. For on January 2, 1918, Secretary Lansing repeated his earlier argument that the Bolsheviks could not be recognized in any manner because they were "a direct threat at existing social order." The Secretary viewed their *Appeal to the Toiling, Oppressed, and Exhausted Peoples of Europe* as a call "to the ignorant and mentally deficient"—to Lansing a "very real danger in view of the social unrest throughout the world." He was also opposed to any broad program of national self-determination. It was, in Lansing's opinion, "utterly untenable" to hold that either Ireland or India should break away from the British Empire. This long and urgent memorandum did not—quite obviously—

set the tone for Wilson's address. But the Secretary's loss of influence was only temporary.[55]

Shortly after the President expressed his "heartfelt desire and hope that some way may be opened whereby we may be privileged to assist the people of Russia," Lenin wrote his analysis of Smolny's predicament and, feeling that aid from the Allies was no more than a foolish hope, concluded that Russia had to sign the peace. On January 11, however, Gumberg managed to obtain an interview with Lenin for Robins and Sisson. The two men requested Lenin's co-operation in spreading Wilson's speech across Russia and into Germany. Lenin considered the statement "a great step ahead toward the peace of the world" and assured them that he had no objection to its distribution. He also asked as to the implementation of the speech—an inquiry not answered. Lenin, faced with the reality of German military might, was aware that words are not immediately effective against bullets. But for the time being the Bolsheviks refused to accept the dictates of Germany—and Lenin did not publish his views on the matter.[56]

Beyond the fact that it secured the distribution of Wilson's speech in Russia, this interview was important because it exerted a critical influence on the division of American personnel in Russia. Sisson emerged from the conversations with the conviction that it was a "mistake for anyone to believe that our political democracy can merge with this industrial democracy." Trusting to the always-dangerous procedure of thinking other people's thoughts, Sisson concluded that Lenin considered himself "the Great Destroyer." Sisson shortly embarked on a vigorous campaign to fight Lenin as a German spy, but by his own admission the label was composed of "only popular catchwords." [57] Sisson's opposition to the Soviet Government was grounded in his conviction that industrial and political democracy were irreconcilable.

Robins emphatically dissented from this interpretation. The result, in Sisson's mind, was the "Robins grouch." Within three weeks the disagreement resulted in Sisson's switch to the side of counter-revolution. Robins, on the other hand, proceeded to exploit the initial contact with Lenin in every possible manner. During the remainder of his stay in Russia, Robins became one of the few foreigners to gain Lenin's trust. It was established, by Lenin's own admission, on the same terms as Robins' relationship with Trotsky. "Robins represents," remarked Lenin in 1918, "the liberal bourgeoisie of America." [58] Neither Lenin nor Robins had any delusions as to the other's position—but they were not hypnotized by ideology.

At Brest-Litovsk, meanwhile, Trotsky delayed the negotiations by insisting on the principle of self-determination. Germany's Major General Max Hoffman angrily pointed out that "the victorious German armies [were] on Russian territory"—an argument difficult to refute—and on

January 18 Trotsky suspended further talks and returned to Petrograd. On January 21 and 22, 1918, the situation was debated at length by Bolshevik party leaders.[59]

"The situation in which the Socialist Revolution in Russia finds itself," Lenin began, "is to be taken as the point of departure for every definition of the international task confronting the new Soviet Government. . . . It would be a mistake," he amplified, "for the Soviet Government to formulate its policy on the supposition that within the next six months, or thereabouts, there will be a European, to be more specific, a German Socialist revolution." That, declared Lenin, would be a "blind gamble." "The only true inference to be drawn from this is that from the time a socialist government is established in any one country questions must be determined not with reference to preferability of any one imperialistic group but solely from the point of view of what is best for the development and consolidation of the socialist revolution which has already begun."

The arguments for a revolutionary war might give "satisfaction to those who crave the romantic and the beautiful," Lenin concluded, but they had no relation to reality. The only policy was to sign the peace and save the revolution. Joseph Stalin, then no more than a second-level member of the policy-making group but the man who was to become Lenin's ultimate successor, supported the latter's interpretation in 1918 as well as in later years. "There is no revolutionary movement in the West," Stalin argued in January, 1918, "there are no facts; there are only potentialities, and we cannot take into account potentialities." With this and other support Lenin stalled those who counseled a revolutionary war. But Trotsky's policy was also supported, and he prepared to test the project of "no peace, no war." [60]

The Constituent Assembly, meanwhile, was dissolved. The Bolsheviks' determination to push the revolution through to what they considered the socialist phase was implemented in this instance by an intense campaign against the Assembly among the soldiers and workers of the capital. That the workers "rather inclined to an indifferent skepticism" toward the meeting was a measure of their success; as was the fact that although the Second Baltic Squadron "swore not to go against it," the sailors viewed an active defense of the Assembly as "another question." Small wonder, then, that there was no resistance when the Assembly was dissolved on the pretext that "the guard is tired." [61]

Despite his opposition to Lenin, Sisson concurred with Robins' report that the act was accepted "without important protest." The judgment was verified by the Bolsheviks' political opponents. As members of the Conservative as well as the moderate Socialist parties agreed, the people seemed "equally unwilling to rescue the Provisional Government or to join the Bolsheviks." More forthright was a leader of the latter group's admission,

a few years later, that "we could not drive them against the Bolshevik movement." Actually, the dissolution of the Constituent Assembly was a re-
flection of the existing situation in Russia, and not a call to civil war. The
Allies, despite their public claims to the contrary, had a very intimate knowledge of that fact.[62]

Perhaps aware that his policy was somewhat unrealistic, Trotsky asked
Robins as to the chances of American recognition before he left for Brest-
Litovsk. Robins told him frankly that there was no such possibility, and
Trotsky was left to sally forth to attack the Germans with oratory. Meanwhile Judson prepared to leave, his requests to remain unanswered. To the
last a voice unheard, Judson cabled on the day of his departure that the
United States might "lose many chances to serve [its] own interests" unless
"friendly intercourse . . . not involving recognition" was quickly established.[63]

This farewell warning was ignored in Washington. Wilson's interest in
the proceedings at Brest, so evident in his speech of January 8, proved to
be limited to verbal concern. The President acknowledged that Russian
power appeared to be "shattered"; but when the Bolsheviks were forced
by that very fact to continue the negotiations he exhibited no interest in
extending material aid. Brest-Litovsk was rationalized as further proof of
Bolshevik treachery. The President chose to remain passive until there
was "something definite to plan with and for." This choice, coupled with
the State Department's view that statements of principle answered any requests for aid, and their decision to avoid any acts that would damage the
cause of counter-revolution, meant that Washington had turned its back
on any policy designed to influence developments within the Soviet Government—save in a negative sense.[64]

The decision was due neither to a misunderstanding nor to a lack of
information. When Wilson prepared his warning that policy toward Russia
would be the "acid test" of Allied diplomacy, he had at hand a multitude of
reports and suggestions. In addition to the advice of Colonel House, Lord
Balfour, and Creel that some statement on Russia was needed, the President
had similar messages from Lansing, William C. Bullitt, another State Department advisor, Phillips, Robins, and a long letter from William Boyce
Thompson. Phillips viewed Bullitt's conclusion that "Today the iron is
hot!" as of "great importance," and considered the primary issue to be
"how best to take advantage of the present hostility of the Bolsheviks to the
German Government." House, after conferences with Thompson and Lamont, advised "an expression of sympathy" and the offer of "our financial,
industrial, and moral support in every way possible." Creel forwarded
Thompson's letter, a long review of his talks in London—including Lord
Carson's message to the President—that closed with the argument to influence the Soviets in the direction and interests of the United States. All

these arguments were discussed at the White House on January 7, 1918, and clearly helped shape Wilson's speech of the following day.[65]

During the same period the United States took the first steps toward intervention and acquiesced in the British blockade of Russia. The arguments of John K. Caldwell, consul at Vladivostok, Richard Washburn Child, another of the President's many advisors, and the British for some show of strength in the Far East were thoroughly discussed by Wilson, Baker, Lansing, and Secretary of the Navy Josephus Daniels. Caldwell wanted military action to comply with the "numerous requests" he had received "from better-class Russians for foreign intervention and protection to enable them to organize." Lord Robert Cecil of the British Foreign Office was "uneasy" about the military stores at Vladivostok. Child argued that the Germans would soon overrun Siberia—an area some 4,000 miles from Brest-Litovsk—and proposed that Japan be allowed to intervene *"at once."* The President seems to have followed the advice of the Department's own Basil Miles. Miles's plan was to "continue . . . support of elements of law and order in the south, but . . . not exploiting Russia to carry on a civil war." The inherent contradictions of this advice would appear obvious, but Wilson thought it "a sensible program." In any event, the cruiser *Brooklyn* was ordered north on January 3, 1918.[66]

Lansing's reply to the French proposal for direct intervention made it apparent that Miles had convinced everybody. The "anarchy" in Siberia moved Paris to suggest, on January 8, a "military mission" to protect the supplies at Vladivostok from "German influence." Lansing did not think armed action would be wise in view of the "present conditions in Siberia." It might, the Secretary pointed out, "result in uniting all factions in Siberia against" the White Russian forces. Clearly, the decision was reached, not in terms of the danger of German occupation, but on the basis of what action would offer the most support to the forces of counter-revolution. The Department's decision to co-operate with the British embargo on goods to Russia was reflected in the American Red Cross order "to hold up all orders for Russia which have not yet been placed." "Our neglect to place additional orders," explained George W. Hill, assistant director of Foreign Relief, "will automatically stop shipments to Russia." [67]

Spurred on by Robins, William Boyce Thompson opened the long campaign to gain a hearing for the argument that intervention was not in the best interests of the United States. Wilson professed himself "much interested" in Thompson's argument, but the initial effort to gain a personal audience through the offices of Secretary of the Treasury McAdoo, Polk, and Supreme Court Justice Louis D. Brandeis was unsuccessful. But Thompson was encouraged by the President's message of January 8 and redoubled his efforts to reach the White House.[68]

Far more significant than his public speeches was Thompson's suc-

cess in organizing a group of interested public figures. He called on
Theodore Roosevelt and reviewed the Russian situation in detail. Roosevelt
was momentarily convinced, writing Robins that he would, "of course,
govern my conduct and my utterances hereafter absolutely by it." This
was not quite true, as events proved—Roosevelt later wrote "that the
United States should join with Japan and support the White Russians"—
but for the time being the former President passively supported Thompson.[69] More important was the support Thompson gained from United States
Senators William E. Borah, William M. Calder, Robert L. Owen, William J.
Stone, and other prominent figures including Hugh A. Cooper, director of
a large engineering corporation, and later important in relations with
Russia.

"Night after night" these men discussed the critical need to revise
American policy. Thompson hammered away at the futility and danger of
the Administration's recent decision. Borah, who earlier objected "to the
Hamletic program of thinking too much upon the deed," led Owen, Calder,
Stone, and Cooper in a direct assault on the White House. Others wrote of
Robins' significance and urged that his important associations with the
Bolshevik leaders be extended.[70] As a result of this pressure, Senator Owen
—who broke party ranks to support Robins in the latter's campaign for
United States senator in 1914—was asked to prepare a written policy recommendation. Owen suggested that the Bolsheviks be acknowledged as a de
facto government, and implied that the efforts of Robins should be given
full support. Thinking that the tide was about to turn, Thompson wrote
again for an interview. But Wilson's request for a departmental opinion
on Owen's suggestions was answered by Basil Miles, who thought it "quite
impossible" to follow the senator's recommendations. Thompson was advised that the President had a "cold," which limited conversation. Evidently Lansing was likewise handicapped, for he abruptly ended his substitute interview before Thompson had a chance to present his views.[71]

Robins, meanwhile, extended his contacts with Lenin and extracted
surprising concessions from the Soviet Government. His talks with Lenin
during the week of Owen's offensive in Washington resulted in the transfer
to Switzerland of Ivan A. Zaklind, Trotsky's assistant, who had co-operated
with anarchist threats against the American Embassy. He also negotiated
the cancellation of John Reed's appointment as Soviet consul in New York.
But Robins, growing more hopeless as the days dragged by without word
from the United States, was only mildly encouraged by the arrival of Bruce
Lockhart from England on January 30, 1918. It was well that Robins was
groping in the dark, for had he known of Wilson's "cold" he might well
have given up entirely.[72]

For it is apparent that by the end of January, 1918, President Wilson
had accepted—"for other than military reasons"—the principle of inter-

vention as the basis of American policy toward Russia. It is likewise clear that the other reason, which Secretary of War Baker later chose to "refrain from discussing," was a decision to implement a policy designed to support counter-revolution against the Soviet Government.[73] At the time, the policy was not clearly revealed because armed intervention did not follow immediately. Later, when that tactical step was taken, the basis of the original decision was obscured by the fact that Washington also desired to prevent further Japanese expansion on the mainland of Asia. But, as Wilson's interest in the various anti-Soviet governments in Siberia—and active support to one of them—indicated, intervention was an attempt to restrict Japan within the limits imposed by the decision to oppose the Soviets.

6

☆

SOWING DRAGON'S TEETH
IN EASTERN EUROPE

1. IN MOSCOW AND WASHINGTON

> When every evil rumor becomes foundation for distrust, cooperation
> is impossible.
>
> *Raymond Robins, April, 1918*

☆☆

Through the spring of 1918 the Robins group continued its efforts to take advantage of the Soviet Government's precarious position and thereby gain a favored position for the United States. With French and British representatives who shared this estimate of the situation, Robins tried to capitalize on the antagonism and fear engendered by the actions of Germany and Japan. These efforts produced tangible gains both in terms of special interests of the United States and the stated interests of the Allies. Despite verbal encouragement from Ambassador Francis, Robins concluded that Washington had no intention to modify its anti-Soviet policy. For that reason he determined to return to the United States where— so he thought—his reports would serve as an antidote to the misleading information that constantly re-enforced an American policy which seemed, in turn, to lead to the progressive hardening of Soviet policy, both domestically and internationally.

Robins correctly evaluated Washington's position. Although Wilson's February, 1918, approval of military intervention was temporarily withdrawn, it gave the green light to Tokyo, London, and Paris. Washington's determination to depose the Soviets resulted, moreover, in a decision to recall Robins from Russia. The immediate cause of this action—which coincided with Robins' own decision to withdraw—was the Ambassador's recommendation against co-operation with the Bolsheviks. The incident which was used to justify the recall was the protest of Consul Summers, whose vigorous activity in behalf of the White Russian forces was paralleled by a strong personal and professional dislike of Robins.

Robins' return coincided with the full-scale drive for American military intervention. Working with Senator Borah and others, Robins proposed an economic program designed to tie the Soviets to the United States and at the same time deny Germany the opportunity to re-establish her economic and political supremacy in Russia. Such a program, Robins argued, would also help thwart Japanese designs in the Far East. But the Robins group was unable to compete successfully against another economic program sponsored by an organization around Professor Harper—a plan primarily designed to exploit Russia economically and to establish the White forces as the political rulers of Russia.

For a short period Harper and his associates, working through Colonel House, did attract the President's interest. But Wilson and Lansing's opposition to the Soviet Government gave the French and British a focal point upon which to exert pressure in their effort to implement Washington's decision of December, 1917, to support anti-Bolshevik forces. In conjunction with Washington's growing fear over Japan's freedom of action in northern Manchuria, Siberia, and China, this pressure moved Wilson to lay aside the plan for economic intervention and support military action. From this choice it was but a step to a decision to choose—and then actively support—a Siberian counter-revolutionary who also opposed the Japanese. Once committed to armed intervention, Washington found it necessary to support a similar venture undertaken by the British in North Russia and, to a far smaller degree, the operations of the French in the South.

Defeated in the battle of the pressure groups, Robins became a victim of the mounting hysteria which culminated in the Red scare of 1919–20. Quickly convinced that public statements did little to change policy, the Robins group turned to the more effective work of organizing political opposition. With strong emphasis on the Russian question, these men concluded that the defeat of Wilson was vitally necessary to further the best interests of the United States. As a result of this decision Thompson personally revived the sagging Republican party congressional campaign of 1918. Encouraged by this success, the Borah-Robins group attempted to force the withdrawal of American troops from Russia. But President Wilson, then in Paris, maintained his support of the anti-Soviet forces, and it was not until 1920 that Robins, Borah, and Thompson were able to launch a new attack on that policy.

The fact of German aggression and Russia's fear of Japanese encroachment provided a significant opportunity for Allied representatives to conclude an agreement with the Soviets. All of the Allied embassies rejected the opportunity. Pride, fear, personal and official antagonism, and "in part" the "emotional impulses" of those involved were all responsible for this decision. As a result, the efforts to negotiate an agreement were made by Robins, Lockhart, and the military attachés of France and the United States —Jacques Sadoul and James Ruggles and E. Francis Riggs. Robins, by virtue of his extended dealings with Trotsky and his recently established association with Lenin, was the leader of the group, and the man to whom the Soviets turned in their apprehension.

Trotsky's refusal to agree to German territorial demands on February 10 gave these men an important opening. The Germans, their appetite whetted by successful dealings with the Ukrainian Rada, recovered quickly from the shock of Trotsky's action. "Dumfounded" on the tenth, they determined, in a special conference on the thirteenth, to denounce the armistice and "prevent Russia from being enforced by the Entente." Moving quickly, the Germans then violated the armistice and reopened their offensive in the East.[1] The Soviets were near panic. They first voted to stand by Trotsky's formula of no peace, no war; but the German advance gave meaning to Lenin's terse warning that they could not "joke with war," and on the night of February 18 the Soviets acknowledged that they were "forced to sign the treaty." The Germans continued to advance on Petrograd. On the twenty-first the Soviets declared that the nation was "in great danger," and decreed that all "forces and resources of the country shall be devoted wholly to the revolutionary defense." [2]

At this juncture Sadoul, who worked with Robins after the Soviet overtures of January, took the initiative and offered French aid. Trotsky readily accepted, and on the following day the French proposal was formally acknowledged through Lenin's vote, cast in favor of accepting the aid "of the imperialist robbers of the Anglo-French coalition." Until the aid materialized, however, there was no choice—other than "signing the death sentence of the Soviet Government"—but also to accept the German terms of February 23.[3] But the Germans continued to advance to insure "the protection of Finland, Esthonia, Lithuania, and the Ukraine." Lenin responded with an order "to delay demobilization of the Red Army . . . to gather and arm detachments . . . to transport arms into the interior of the country." Ambassador Francis, who considered the Russians "incapable of great movements or great achievements," prepared to retreat eastward. At the same time he repeated his earlier recommendation that the Allies take "immediate possession of Vladivostok, Murmansk, Archangel." But when travel arrangements bogged down, Francis turned to Robins for help. Going directly to Lenin, Robins secured special authorization for the movement, and the Ambassador and his staff were safely in Vologda on February 28, 1918.[4]

Robins immediately returned to Petrograd to continue negotiations for Soviet resistance to Germany. Lockhart's interview with Lenin on March 1 provided an encouraging welcome. Lenin, though he made it quite clear that he had no intention to be "made a cat's paw for the Allies," was prepared to "risk co-operation with the Allies." He candidly told Lockhart, moreover, that he was "quite convinced that your Government will never see things in this light"—but the negotiations continued. Trotsky sent Sadoul to Francis to determine the position of the United States. The Soviets, "convinced that a real peace with Germany was impossible," and "concerned about the Japanese," inquired as to "what help they [could] count upon, particularly immediate help from the Allies." Francis responded with assurances that he would "recommend moral and material co-operation provided organized resistance is sincerely established." As proof of his sincerity, the Ambassador dispatched Ruggles and Riggs to negotiate with Trotsky.[5]

Before they arrived, both Robins and Lockhart discussed with Trotsky the possibilities of active collaboration. Lockhart called on Trotsky during the morning of March 5, and found the Soviets particularly disturbed over the continued reports of Japanese intervention. The Germans, cabled Lockhart, gave the Allies their greatest opportunity in Russia; but if Japan was allowed to enter Siberia, the situation would become "hopeless." This "long conversation" did not produce any tentative offers or commitments. It was Robins who extracted a written statement from Trotsky and Lenin.[6]

Early in the afternoon of March 5 Robins called on Trotsky to discuss the disposition of Red Cross supplies in view of the German advance. Trotsky brushed aside the query and bluntly asked Robins if he wanted to prevent ratification of the Brest-Litovsk Treaty. Robins, skeptical in view of Lenin's arguments for acceptance of the terms, replied that he was interested; but only in terms of a written statement.

"You want me," Trotsky shot back, "to give you my life, don't you?"

"No;" rejoined Robins, "but I want something specific."

Robins further specified that Lenin must agree, in his presence, to the entire transaction. Trotsky acquiesced, and late the same afternoon Robins, Lenin, and Trotsky thrashed out the terms of the final draft. In brief this document was a formal inquiry concerning "in particular and especially in what way would the assistance of the United States be expressed" if *any one* of four circumstances materialized. If the Soviets refused to ratify the treaty; if Germany broke the treaty and resumed its offensive; if the Soviets "would be compelled by Germany's behavior to repudiate" the treaty and resume military operations; or if Japan, acting with Germany or alone, "would make [an] attempt to take Vladivostok and [the] Eastern Siberian Railroad." It was further stipulated "that the internal and foreign policy of the Soviet Government continues to be directed by [the] principles of international Socialism."[7]

This document, so clearly the result of a coincidence of self-interests, inspired a period of feverish activity. Robins immediately advised Lockhart, who grasped the significance of the document immediately and wired London to accept the offer. Harold Williams, leading English newspaper correspondent; R. R. Stevens, National City Bank representative in Russia; and Charles Smith of the Associated Press also urged the United States and Britain to seize the opportunity. Robins first transmitted the message to Francis at Vologda, noting it was of "utmost importance"; dispatched a copy to the War Department; and then cabled Thompson to do all in his power to secure its acceptance. These affirmative responses prompted Robins to request Lenin to delay the Fourth All-Russian Soviet, so that replies could be received from London and Washington. Lenin complied and postponed the opening session two days, from March 12 to March 14.[8]

Robins then left Petrograd for Vologda to brief Ambassador Francis and to establish headquarters for his operations during the forthcoming congress in Moscow. Robins arrived in Vologda late on the night of March 8, only to discover that Francis knew nothing of the interview with Trotsky and Lenin. With Ruggles and Riggs in Petrograd, it had been impossible to decipher Robins' message, which had been sent over the military wire. Robins gave Francis the original document, filled in the background of the negotiations, and brought the Ambassador up to date on events in Petrograd. Then, no doubt relieved that the congress would not convene for another seven days, Robins proceeded to Moscow.[9]

In Petrograd, meanwhile, the military representatives opened their talks with Trotsky. On the basis of Trotsky's proposals, and armed with Ambassador Francis' warrant of authority, the American officers "officially promised" aid. As Riggs noted, the "question of ratification [of the Brest-Litovsk Treaty] was really immaterial. The only real point was the amount of effort and enthusiasm put into the formation of a new resistance for the future." Ruggles learned of Robins' success the same day and cabled the Army War College that he "most strongly" recommended an immediate and positive answer. Within the next two days Lockhart, Sadoul, and Riggs all saw George Chicherin, acting Commissar of Foreign Affairs, who reported that the Soviets were "convinced that war with Germany [was] inevitable." "Now," he pointed out, "was the most favorable moment for a demonstration of Allied sympathy."[10]

All these men thought such a demonstration would be forthcoming. None of them questioned the integrity of their superiors. There is considerable evidence, however, to indicate that no section of Allied officialdom—whether in Vologda, Washington, London, or Paris—ever considered these negotiations more than a ruse to conceal momentarily the basic policy of support to the forces of counter-revolution. At no time was there any divergence of opinion between Washington, London, or Paris as concerned the primary goal—the overthrow of the Soviet Government. Rather was full-scale intervention delayed by two purely tactical considerations. The first concerned the question of means, and centered on the problem of whether active military assistance should be given to the Whites. More important was the fact that the United States delayed formal action in the hope that some solution could be evolved for its peculiar dilemma. Washington desired the overthrow of Lenin, but it wanted to avoid a price that included Japanese ascendancy in the Far East. In the end, the policy makers found themselves caught in a net of their own weaving.

After the split between Sisson and Robins that began after their interview with Lenin on January 11, Sisson nourished his anti-Sovietism slowly, and it was not until February 2 that he moved to make his break with Robins complete. On that day he discussed with Robins a set of documents purporting to show that Lenin and Trotsky were German agents. Similar documents were offered for sale in Petrograd as early as July, 1917; but Robins, after intensive investigation, concluded that they were forgeries. Sisson saw them as a means to help depose Lenin, and immediately opened a drive to secure their official acceptance. Between February 8 and 11 he broke completely with Robins and began to work with the anti-Lockhart forces in the British Embassy and with Ambassador Francis himself.[11]

Sisson's switch removed whatever doubts Ambassador Francis might have harbored on January 2, when he authorized Robins to work for some definite agreement with the Soviets. Francis joined Sisson and on February 8 reported to Washington that he was "absolutely" convinced that Lenin and Trotsky were German agents. From that date forward the documents became the principal weapon in Francis' propaganda arsenal. He did not, of course, tell Robins of his decision—that might "impair his effectiveness." Robins, meanwhile, warned that the events of January, February, and March rendered the theory of German control "no longer tenable"; and Bullard of the Committee on Public Information told House of the "ambiguous and mysterious persons" hawking the material on "all sides." [12]

These warnings were ignored. The campaign of the documents rolled on through 1918—a campaign that abetted the development of a symbol equation which linked Russian Bolsheviks to all American critics of developments within the United States—an equation that was part of the Red scare. Sisson, meanwhile, dashed back to the United States on March 4; but in Russia the diplomatic corps carried on in grand style. Directed by Francis, the group was able to "force down the price" of the documents from 25,000 to 17,000 rubles. The money was obtained from the Russian branch of the National City Bank, which, in turn, was reimbursed by the Embassy.[13] This great effort was not the reason for intervention. These documents, which were used to justify intervention as an auxiliary attack on Germany, were no more than a screen.

The primary objective of Ambassador Francis was the destruction of the Bolshevik Government, and his negotiations via Robins, Ruggles, and Riggs were a blind to cover this goal. Francis authorized Ruggles and Riggs to work for the creation of an army, but only so that it could, "by proper methods" of course, be "taken from Bolshevik control." The Ambassador did "not" reveal this plan to either Robins or Riggs.[14] Thus did Francis knowingly and purposely work for the overthrow of the Soviets. That he misled his own agents appears to have bothered him very little.

Washington, which had been worried by Francis' indecision in January, offered no criticism of the Ambassador's policy. Early in February, when the Ambassador cabled that some shift in policy might be advisable, Phillips adroitly suggested that it would be well to avoid "compromising the position of the Government" unless the Ambassador was in "personal danger." This appeal to the personal vanity of Francis was not immediately successful, for a few days later, after Robins won another point at Smolny, Francis wired that he was "endeavoring to establish . . . working relations" with the Soviet Government. This evidence of Robins' success upset Basil Miles and he suggested to Phillips that the Ambassador needed "instructions." "He may splash over," Miles fretted, "if we don't look out." [15] Miles's fear was ungrounded. For despite strong recommendations from many sources, neither Lansing nor Wilson was disposed to support any efforts to co-operate with the Soviets.

Not through ignorance did Washington choose to disregard the advice of Robins. Thompson's efforts to gain a hearing were quickly opposed by strong forces led by Ralph Easley, executive chairman of the National Civic Federation, who charged that Thompson was "stirring up the animals." Another of the same group complained to Harper about the "drool" that Thompson was handing out, and urged the professor to "go after 'em." [16] The attack on Thompson was the first round of the National Civic Federation's long and bitter campaign against recognition of the Soviet Government. Organized in 1896 by Marcus A. Hanna, the formidable economic giant who exerted tremendous influence within the Republican party, and by Samuel Gompers, labor's *laissez faire* philosopher and perennial president of the American Federation of Labor, the National Civic Federation soon abandoned its original precepts. By 1903 its early support for unionization was gone—replaced by opposition to socialism and the union shop. But Gompers, no less opposed to socialism than Hanna, remained a leader of the organization and helped lead the campaign against the Soviets. His attitude was doubly important because of his close relationship with President Wilson and, later, with Secretary of State Charles Evans Hughes. Yet in the critical days of 1918 Wilson was not without counsel of another character.

Bullard of the Committee for Public Information and Davison of the Red Cross War Council both advised Wilson of Robins' view that collaboration with the Soviets was feasible; and Colonel House warned that "it would be a great political mistake to send Japanese troops into Siberia." The President's attention was also called to similar reports and recommendations made by Colonel Judson. These efforts secured an agreement from Wilson that Robins could remain in Russia "for the present until things clear up a bit." But the President's decision to stand with his anti-Soviet advisors was not long delayed.[17]

Wilson's basic antagonism to the Soviets assured Lansing of the opportunity to conduct Russian affairs with little restraint. Wilson indicated that he shared the Secretary's great concern for the *status quo* when the President approved a policy recommendation prepared by Gompers. Important in itself as the fundamental statement of the American Federation of Labor's long-term policy of bitter opposition to the Soviet Government, the reception given Gompers' proposal emphasized the labor leader's influence at the White House. Though Gompers admitted that the Soviets were "undoubtedly" the de facto government of Russia, he warned against any friendly overtures. Wilson thought the advice a "very proper basis" for official policy, and Lansing, who sympathized with Gompers' concern about socialism, shared the President's "deep concern" over events in Russia.[18] Both men, moreover, agreed that any aid to the Soviets was "out of the question." Miles formalized this anti-Soviet policy in his memo of February 19, 1918. Any attempt to accommodate the ideas of "economic freedom" and "political freedom" was "idle." "They are wholly different," Miles declared, "and cannot be reconciled." The idea that democracy was "an equal division of power," declared this advisor, was professed only by those who "lived in the shadow." [19]

Coupled with strong pressure from London and Paris, these sentiments resulted in Wilson's written note of February 28, 1918, in which he assured the Japanese of his "entire confidence" in their projected intervention. *As per instructions,* the document was shown to the British, French, and Italians. The British forthwith "practically requested" the Japanese to "go ahead." As London phrased it, Japan would "be compelled to take action in her own interests." Lansing's diary bears testimony that the Secretary had "gained only a little" from his interview with Judson.[20]

This Wilson Memorandum of February 28, 1918, is of especial significance because it indicated the President's decision to acquiesce in Japan's further penetration of the Asiatic mainland despite his "uncomfortable impression" of Tokyo's object. Japan had already taken advantage of the war in Europe to force China against the wall. Tokyo's twenty-one exorbitant demands, made early in 1915, threatened to destroy any remaining semblance of Chinese economic and political integrity. Also clear, of course, was the fact that Japan's maneuver, if successful, would close and board over the open door. Wilson's "grave concern" over these developments was shared by Lansing, then counselor of the State Department.

But Lansing was prepared—as early as March, 1915—to give Tokyo "an opportunity to develop southern Manchuria through Japanese emigrants into that region" in return for two compensations. Japan, he suggested, would have to agree to register "no further complaint in regard to legislation affecting land tenure in the United States," and also "reaffirm explicitly the principle of the 'Open Door,' making it particularly applicable to the territories affected by the [21] demands." But Lansing found the "growing material power of Japan" difficult to check. Though concerted action prevented execution of the Twenty-one Demands, the United States was forced to acknowledge "that Japan has special interests in China, particularly in the part to which her possessions are contiguous."

That admission, formulated by Lansing in November, 1917, led to an interesting exchange between the Secretary and the Chinese minister, who was "particularly disturbed" over the phrase. Lansing replied that "geographical propinquity necessarily gave nations special interests in their neighbors," and added that "the axiom held good the world over." The Chinese minister offered "no comment" in reply to the Secretary's explanation. Washington also found it difficult to provide an answer when its interests, other than those that stemmed from territorial propinquity, were challenged by Japan in North China.[21]

The fact that Japan was "deeply stirred by the growth of American business in Siberia" during the years 1908–11 is the clue to this problem. Worried by this competition, Tokyo viewed the Root and Stevens missions as evidence of a concerted American effort to monopolize trade in that area. Her eye already on a greater Asia, Japan thought to counter American economic penetration by armed force. The Bolshevik Revolution, moreover, "provided the Japanese imperialists with a large, discontented Russian element willing to help in the promotion of interventionist schemes." The careful cultivation of a supposed German menace to Tokyo became a favorite device to gain support for the plan. The "charges and excuses changed from time to time, but the reason remained the same"—domination of northern Manchuria and eastern Siberia.[22] These considerations provoked immediate opposition to the President's approval of Japanese intervention.

Colonel House led a determined effort to reverse Wilson's decision. After conferences with Senator Root and others, House warned the President by mail and telephone of the "danger of the proposed Japanese intervention." The situation was "exceedingly delicate and dangerous," and threatened that "fine moral position" established by virtue of Wilson's leadership. More to the point was House's suggestion that Tokyo be maneuvered into an agreement "to leave the settlement of all Siberian questions to the council of peace." [23] As was to be made abundantly clear, "the Japanese-American struggle for control of the railways constituted the basic economic aspect of the Allied intervention in Siberia." [24] But equally important was Washington's opposition to the Soviet Government, which allowed Japan to retain the initiative given her by Theodore Roosevelt in 1904–5. For acting alone, the United States was unable effectively to delimit Japanese expansion without recourse to war.

Wilson gave way under the pressure from House, and on March 5, 1918, dramatically reversed himself and issued a formal statement against intervention. He was "bound in frankness to say" that if Japan intervened she must give "the most explicit assurances" that the peace conference would exercise the final authority in disposing of the occupied areas. Equally important was Wilson's fear that such intervention "might play into the hands of the enemies of Russia and particularly of the enemies of the Russian Revolution." This was Lansing's earlier argument, and the Revolution referred to, obviously, was the March revolt. These developments determined the fate of Robins' negotiations with Lenin and Trotsky.[25]

In the meantime, Ambassador Francis accepted responsibility for the Soviet inquiry concerning aid against Germany. But the Ambassador did not transmit the entire contents of the Soviet document to Washington until some eighty-nine hours after Robins arrived in Vologda at midnight on March 8. Even then he did not note the need for speed; nor did he stress the importance of the inquiry. The fact that the Soviets provisionally accepted the Allied landing at Murmansk on March 5 was also ignored by Francis. At the end of the dispatch in which he finally advised Washington of the Soviet action, Francis revealed his entire attitude by remarking that "if the Department thinks above questions require reply in addition to President's message" he would transmit it to the Soviets via Robins.[26]

The reference to Wilson's message concerned the President's short note to the Congress of Soviets, which Robins delivered to Lenin. Wilson expressed his "sincere sympathy" for the Russian people, but noted that the United States was "unhappily not . . . in a position to render the direct and effective aid it would wish" to deliver. Actually, this note bore very little relation to Russian developments—and absolutely none to the Soviet inquiry of March 5. It was conceived in the mind of Colonel House, whose "thought [was] not so much about Russia as . . . to seize this opportunity to clear up the Far Eastern situation but without mentioning it or Japan in any way." When an edited version of the Soviet note reached Washington on March 15, moreover, the State Department had already decided that there was, "in fact, no Russian Government to deal with." [27]

The document from Lenin and Trotsky nevertheless aroused some interest in the first four days after its receipt. Harper was "asked for an opinion," and though he does not reveal his judgment, the fact is that Basil Miles noted on the nineteenth that Wilson's note was an "adequate" answer. Wilson, who finally got a copy of Francis' abridged version of the Soviet inquiry on the same day, was of a like mind.[28] Thus was the Soviet request casually considered and filed away. It was an opportunity to establish some working relation with Moscow, but it is apparent that no one in authority ever seriously proposed to explore the possibilities thus offered.

The Soviets, "convinced that the most consistent Socialist policy may be harmonized with the strictest realism and most level-headed practicality," waited until the last minute to ratify the peace. Lenin, who trusted Robins as an "honest man" and one who did not hide his differences of opinion, delayed his speech until the second night of the congress. Before he spoke, Lenin asked Robins and Lockhart if they had any word from their governments.[29]

"Nothing," Robins was forced to admit.

"I am now going to the platform," Lenin answered, "and the peace will be ratified."

But as Riggs noted, formal action on the Brest-Litovsk Treaty was of small significance. The Germans continued to advance all during the spring, moving on from Kiev to take Kherson on April 8. Later in the same month they staged a coup in conjunction with the wealthy landlords and peasants of the Ukraine, and by May 8 had reached Rostov-on-the-Don. The Robins group tried hard to exploit this advance and secure from the Soviets a formal bid for joint action against Germany. Their first success came on March 18, when Trotsky agreed to supplement Ruggles and Riggs—who "did actually drill some detachments"—with a French military mission. Trotsky then "made a formal request for help," and it seemed that the opposition of the formal diplomats was about to be overcome. But the French Ambassador supported Bullard, Summers, and others who "strongly" advised against such collaboration. The entire plan was "wrecked" when the French "intervened," and only the United States— thanks to Robins—emerged with its reputation relatively untarnished.[30]

Robins worked hard to foster this constant Soviet tendency to turn to the United States. His primary aim was to keep the Eastern Front alive and at the same time lay the foundation for an expansion of American-Soviet economic relations that would in turn provide a firm basis for future relations. To this end he negotiated an agreement with Trotsky whereby the latter requested American railroad aid and supervision "in the reorganization of the country." He also arranged a large sale of platinum, vitally needed in the American war effort, to the United States.[31] But Robins' most successful effort was to persuade Lenin to exempt the International Harvester Company, the Singer Sewing Machine Company, and the Westinghouse Brake Company from the provisions of the decree that nationalized all industry.[32] These were the immediate consequences of his long talks with Lenin during which they worked out a comprehensive plan for fostering and expanding Soviet-American economic relations.

Robins hoped to accomplish three objectives via such economic integration of the two countries: the stabilization of the American economy, assistance to the Russian people, and the creation of a peculiarly effective relationship between the United States and the future development of the Soviet Government. The first move in this direction was a "specific request" by the Soviets for permission to send an economic commission to the United States.[33] All these developments occurred *after* the Treaty of Brest-Litovsk was ratified, but their significance was ignored both by Ambassador Francis and the policy makers in Washington.

Actually, of course, Robins was flying a diplomatic solo; for Francis had absolutely "no intention" to work for more thorough collaboration with the Soviets. Robins' entire position was, moreover, rapidly undermined by a coalition of counter-revolutionary enthusiasts headed by Consul General Maddin Summers. An early and vigorous proponent of intervention, Summers naturally feared that Robins' successes would mean the ultimate disintegration of the White forces. In addition, the formal diplomat was "very unhappy" about the ease with which Robins effected results without protocol. Summers was supported by other members of the Embassy staff, various officers of the Foreign Service stationed at other posts throughout Russia, and high officers in both the French and British embassies.[34] At the same time, moreover, the anti-Soviet forces were aided by the sudden activity of David B. MacGowan, American consul at Moscow who was on special duty in Siberia.

MacGowan, a former newspaperman, had grandiose plans for the economic control of Russia—plans that interested William C. Huntington, commercial attaché and good friend of Professor Harper. All the "important financial groups in America," MacGowan advised Francis, "should be consulted" as to the formation of a giant "international trust." The aim was to "secure for the world supplies of steel, coal, copper . . . grain, fats, and the like." The plan would necessarily "require a free supply of labor from China." But the Russian people, MacGowan carefully pointed out, "should be made to understand from the start that the International Trust was a work of civilization." [35]

While he waited for this plan to be acted upon MacGowan reinvigorated the German agent theory of the Bolshevik Revolution. He reported that the Soviets were arming "large numbers" of German and Austrian prisoners of war in Siberia to be used against the White forces. Francis eagerly accepted the veracity of these reports despite the thoroughgoing research sponsored by Robins and Lockhart that proved the reports absurdly exaggerated. MacGowan's prisoner story, which was only the first of his many efforts to commit the United States to more vigorous intervention in Russia, re-enforced Francis' determination to avoid any further collaboration with the Soviets. Washington made the task very easy. "Do not," ordered Lansing, "give Soviet promises [of] military support." [36]

Francis endeavored to keep Robins ignorant of his real aim—the overthrow of the Soviets—but the Ambassador's failure to act on any of the pending Bolshevik overtures ultimately moved Robins to protest vigorously. "Just as we begin to get co-operation, all the military missions working with Soviet power," he asked, "is Washington to credit discarded forgeries of German control?" If so, he continued, "why are we wasting time here?" Intervention, he warned, would "not help the Western Front and [would] lose Russia permanently." Robins was momentarily encouraged by Francis' apparent willingness to mollify the Soviets over the combined Japanese-British landing at Vladivostok on April 4, 1918. Robins, in return, tried to improve the Ambassador's position with the Soviets, but made it clear to Francis that "the most dangerous crisis" had arrived. If Japan's intervention was allowed to stand, "all American advantages are confiscated." [37]

But on April 15, when Francis ordered the military representatives to stop working with the Soviets, Robins concluded that "unless such co-operation between governments" was sustained his "useful work" would be ended in two weeks. "When every evil rumor," he cabled Thompson, "becomes foundation for distrust, co-operation is impossible." Francis, however, made no effort to respond to Soviet Foreign Commissar Chicherin's request "to define in definite form . . . the attitude of the United States to the Government of the Russian Federated Soviet Republic and to all attempts of separate representatives of America to interfere in the internal life of Russia." Within the week Robins decided to return to Washington to try to help revise the "micawber policy" that, in his opinion, was becoming daily "more impossible." [38]

Robins judged the situation accurately, for the façade of co-operation was about to collapse. The senior military representatives of the United States, France, England, and Italy "unanimously" decided—against the advice of their junior officers—that the "intervention of Japan is more than ever necessary." Lockhart—who by his own admission lacked "the moral courage to resign and take a stand which would have exposed me to the odium of the vast majority of my countrymen"—concluded that "the time had come" to "impose" intervention if the Soviets refused to "invite" such aid. Francis, who "for months past" had favored intervention, stopped pretending to support Robins and cabled his official recommendation for direct action. Lenin was well aware that the opposition had crystallized. When informed that Balfour declared that the Japanese were "intervening to help the Russians," the Soviet leader pertinently inquired as to "which Russians?" [39]

Washington, officially declaring that it knew "nothing whatever" of any efforts to "promote improved relations" with the Soviets, prepared to withdraw Robins—he had expended his usefulness as a decoy. Both Francis and Summers provided Lansing with a ready-made excuse. The Ambassador's protest over Robins' cables to Thompson concerning policy were quickly supported by the State Department. The key event was Summers' request for a transfer. The Consul General's antagonism toward Robins flared up anew after an official rebuke from Francis and a direct request from Summers' friend MacGowan, who did not appreciate the Robins-sponsored investigation of his German prisoner tale. "Could you see your way clear," MacGowan bluntly proposed, "to aiming [at] the same goal"—the recall of Robins. The day after he received this inquiry Summers requested an early transfer. "There can be," explained Summers, "no co-operation between Robins and myself." The entire question, amplified Francis, was "opened by Summers who bitterly hates Bolsheviks." [40]

Francis was "sincerely sympathetic" with Summers' discomfort, and Lansing immediately conferred with Polk and others "on getting Raymond Robins out of Russia." The "conditions which have embarrassed you," he cabled Summers, "will unquestionably show early improvement." Acting through General Tasker H. Bliss, Lansing ordered Robins to "leave Russia immediately." The Consul General's untimely death—from a "brain hemorrhage"—denied Summers the opportunity to work for the victory of the counter-revolution unhampered by any opposition. [41]

In company with Louis E. Brown, Chicago Daily News correspondent who later sought to influence Colonel House, and Gumberg, Robins left Vologda on May 15 for the United States. En route to Vladivostok Robins received Davison's long-delayed cable advising him that his recall had been "reconsidered," and that it was "desirable" that he remain in Russia for at least three weeks. But Francis' quick protest, and the fact that Robins was already in Siberia, made it easy for Washington to order him to continue his journey home, and to refrain from speaking publicly until further notice. [42]

The major opponent of the efforts to involve the United States in active counter-revolution had finally been removed. Francis, however, wanted a sure thing. The Ambassador cabled Melville Stone of the Associated Press, his "close friend," that Robins was a near-Bolshevik who should be ignored. Taking no chances, Francis reminded Stone that his paper "owns membership in [the] Associated Press." Then, trusting that the

United States was "making all possible preparations for Allied intervention," the Ambassador publicly denied that any "authoritative proposition" had ever been made to the Soviet Government. But there was really no need for this precaution. Secretary Lansing, most pleased with the Ambassador's "extraordinary ability in conducting affairs," and his "full grasp of the present situation," had no intention of modifying American policy. Nor did President Wilson. "Everything," wrote Acting Consul General Poole, "has worked out splendidly." [43]

Robins returned to the United States with two main objectives: to forestall intervention and to secure acceptance of his plan to influence the development of Soviet policy through economic aid. By the time of his interview with Secretary Lansing, however, American policy was so rigidly established that there was no possibility for Robins to succeed. Others had already proposed similar if less well-developed plans only to have them spurned by the Wilson administration. Charles H. Smith, a member of the Stevens Railroad Commission, suggested a comparable program in January, 1918. Though approved by various American and British officials, Smith's plan was ignored. Thomas G. Masaryk, leader of the Czech nationalist movement, suggested a like move; but it, too, was disapproved. Robins had no need to question those men, for Thomas Thacher, fellow member of the Red Cross group, experienced a like rebuff in Washington.[44]

Thacher, recalled from Russia in March, 1918, by Thompson in an effort to strengthen the Washington campaign, was totally ineffective. He returned via London, where he attempted, without success, to emulate Thompson's earlier influence. His London effort was a long memorandum of April 12 which argued that the Allies "should discourage Japanese intervention" and give the "fullest assistance" to Soviet efforts to organize against the Germans. Upon his arrival in the United States, Thacher amplified these recommendations with a proposal for economic aid that clearly reflected the talks between Robins and Lenin.

After making the rounds of other officials with Thompson, Thacher tried to secure an interview with Wilson through William Kent, member of the United States Tariff Commission. Kent was "deeply interested" in Thacher's evaluation and proposals, and considered it of "great importance" that both Wilson and Lansing avail themselves of Thacher's counsel. "I haven't time," responded Wilson, and passed the buck to Lansing. The Secretary interviewed Thacher on May 28, and crossed him off the list as a Wall Street lawyer "in favor of" the Soviets. Thacher took advantage of the opening to submit a written report urging that an economic commission be sent to Russia to aid "in reorganizing and reconstructing its internal affairs." [45] Lansing, however, manifested little interest in this particular economic plan.

Nor was the Secretary of State of any mind to give Robins a serious hearing. The Administration's entire attitude toward Robins was revealed by its welcome. Basil Miles, still worried even though Robins was out of Russia, asked Lansing for permission to search Robins' luggage when he arrived in Seattle. The Secretary thought it an excellent idea, and told Miles "to make it thorough." After being so received, Robins met Thompson and Thacher in Chicago and proceeded directly to Washington. His first appointment was with Secretary Lansing on June 26, 1918.[46]

Lansing concentrated assiduously on the job of "polishing his pince-nez" while Robins briefly outlined his program of an economic commission. Then, as Robins began to make a full report, the Sécretary cut him short and shunted him off to the British and French. The significance of this move, which delivered Robins to the leading lobbyists for intervention, was obvious. Lansing, urged on by Miles and supported by the entire State Department, had no intention of exposing himself to any information contrary to his own views. Robins did not miss the meaning of the maneuver; and after Reading told him that "things are different now," he concentrated on an effort to reach President Wilson with his recommendations.[47]

Robins first saw United States Senators William E. Borah and Hiram Johnson, two Progressive leaders with whom Robins had worked in the years preceding the outbreak of the war. In a series of long conferences with these old political friends Robins reported on events in Russia and elaborated his plan of economic aid and influence. Necessary to the preservation of the Eastern Front and the establishment of a secure peace, Robins argued, was a strong understanding with Russia. Only in that matter could Germany and Japan be restrained in the future without recourse to war. Intervention, he cautioned, "unless welcomed by the great mass of the Russian people would be destructive in principle of the entire basis of President Wilson's democratic war policy."

Aware that intervention was aimed at the Bolsheviks as well as Japan, Robins also pointed out that the United States had an invitation to assume a privileged position with reference to the Soviet Government—a position that would give Washington an unusual opportunity to influence events in Russia. Robins took care to point out two factors of particular importance in this connection: that so far the United States had not incurred the militant hostility of the Soviets; and, further, that the Bolsheviks were governed "not by theory, but by the unyielding necessities of life." A program of economic aid, he concluded, would lead "to the modification, adjustment, and softening of the hard and impossible formulas of radical socialism." Both Borah and Johnson were convinced that Robins' evaluation was correct. They accepted him as their principal advisor and opened a drive for the recognition of the Soviets as the de facto government of Russia and for the speedy establishment of close economic relations. Thus began Robins' "tremendous influence" with Senator Borah.[48]

Robins also saw Theodore Roosevelt, Secretary of War Newton Baker, and other figures close to Wilson in the effort to gain a hearing before the President.[49] But the door of the White House remained closed. Even Tariff Commissioner Kent—who was "greatly impressed" by Robins and "sincerely" hoped Wilson would grant an interview—was ineffective. Perhaps it was because the Tariff Commissioner was a bit outspoken. Kent was "convinced" that "much of the information reaching this country through our diplomatic channels is colored by fear and hysteria and to a certain extent begotten by social prejudices." In view of Wilson's expressed fears and opinions it is doubtful whether the President was pleased by such a judgment. It is clear, of course, that the State Department had no use for Robins. Professor Harper, who worked closely with Miles, also exercised all his talents and influence against Robins. A "bit afraid" of Thompson and a "bit disappointed" in Robins, Harper "came out frankly against" the latter and spent a good portion of the summer of 1918 "following him around" in a perpetual counterattack. "Don't worry about Robins," wrote Harper, "his goose is cooked." [50]

Beyond the fact that this concerted campaign to discredit Robins and his ideas re-enforced Wilson's antagonism toward the Soviets, the President's attitude toward Robins may well have been the critical factor in his refusal to consider the latter's recommendations. Coupled with their earlier personal differences, Robins' refusal to rejoin the Democratic party after supporting Theodore Roosevelt in the presidential campaign of 1912 quite possibly irritated the President. In addition, Bainbridge Colby, with whom Robins differed bitterly over support for Roosevelt in 1912, was very close to Wilson. But whatever its source, Wilson clearly revealed his prejudice against Robins when he returned the latter's written recommendations for an economic aid program to Secretary Lansing. "The suggestions," Wilson confessed, "are certainly much more sensible than I thought the author of them capable of." But the President did nothing to verify his statement that he differed "only in practical details." [51]

The President's temporary withdrawal of his February approval of intervention did not signify any intention of letting the Russians settle their own affairs. He instructed the State Department to keep a close watch on counter-revolutionary activities in Siberia, noting that it would afford him "a great deal of satisfaction" to give support to the most promising group. General Gregory Semenov attracted his interest at an early date, and Wilson inquired as to "whether there [was] any legitimate way" the United States could assist the White general. In the lull before the full power of the drive for intervention reached the White House, however, a distortion of the Robins plan momentarily attracted the President's attention.[52]

White House interest was captured by a program that was a direct consequence of the economic penetration of Russia by American interests prior to the Bolshevik Revolution. While enjoying the war-sponsored trade boom, American firms kept a sharp eye on postwar possibilities. An article in the *Iron Age* as early as January, 1917—"Russia, the Most-Promising After-the-War Market for American Products"—reflected this interest and foreshadowed considerable speculation as to the best means of expanding the prewar trade totals. The Morgan-backed Russian-American Chamber of Commerce reported that upward of 2,500 firms contemplated the expansion of existing markets or entrance into the field. Representatives of the Provisional Government encouraged this interest, and assured the United States that its capital would receive "the warmest welcome in Russia." Nor was the response limited to financial circles. One source noted that "businessmen share with bankers the hope and expectation that Russia would become a far greater factor in the American market than ever before." [53]

Some observers considered a "decisive transition from the communal regime to a system of private ownership"—that would encourage the "investment of surplus capital in the various Russian industries"—to be a prerequisite both for Russia's advancement and the expansion of American returns. The advent of the Bolsheviks naturally re-enforced such views, and opposition to their program became a dominant theme in the business community. The American-Russian Chamber of Commerce symbolized this antagonism in its honorary dinner for Prince Lvov, former Premier of the defunct Provisional Government. Lvov asked the organization to help overthrow the Bolsheviks—an act, he assured the group, that would give American capital access to Russia. Long before Lvov's public request, however, attempts were made to implement a similar program in conjunction with Washington's anti-Soviet policy.[54]

These efforts ultimately failed for two reasons—Wilson's preference for military intervention against the Bolsheviks, and dissension among those who advocated economic penetration. The President's decision did not prevent the final acceptance of a plan to enter Russia economically, but it did deprive that effort of energetic support by the Government. Whatever hopes the group had to enter Russia behind armed force were dissipated in an internal struggle for control of the venture. This division was apparent even in the first nebulous plans formulated in April, 1918.

One plan began to take form in the American-Russian League organized by Herbert L. Carpenter and supported by the National Chamber of Commerce, the American Federation of Labor, and one wing of the American-Russian Chamber of Commerce. But the return to the United States of Frederick M. Corse, who had served as manager of the Russian division of the New York Life Insurance Company for sixteen years, led to immediate complications. Corse, who considered Bolshevism no more than "conscious, organized loot," naturally desired to have the Morgan-backed American-Russian Chamber of Commerce control the entire opera-tion. He immediately began to work toward this goal through Harper and McCormick. Thacher's proposals, no doubt passed on through Crane, served to crystallize the effort in which Harper initially served as liaison between both groups.[55]

Harper thought Thacher's proposal an "excellent summary" and wrote Carpenter and others of his high hopes for action. "Does it not make you boil," he fumed, "to think of the opportunities . . . we did not seize?" For a brief time Harper considered Robins "just the man" to handle the Russian end of the plan and thought it "most unfortunate" that Robins was scheduled to return to the United States. His "word of welcome" was quickly withdrawn, however, when he discovered that Robins did not share his own ideas of "economic penetration."[56]

Long before that time "a good many people" were thinking along the lines of economic penetration. Largely through the efforts of Harper, Crane, McCormick, and Corse the plan rapidly gathered strong support. As early as June 8 Secretary of Commerce William Redfield knew "confi-dentially, but indirectly," of the State Department's interest in the idea. Four days later Colonel House received a suggestion to place Herbert Hoover, wartime food director and head of the Belgian Relief Commission, in charge of the venture "as part of an intervention plan." "Enthusiastic over the suggestion" (as was Lansing), Hoover was quite "willing to serve." Thus encouraged, House sent the proposal on to Wilson with the recommendation that it would, "for the moment, settle the Russian situa-tion." Lansing, equally worried by the clamor for intervention and the fact that it would be a "grave error" to give Japan a free hand in Asia, agreed that it was "the only practical plan."[57]

Both the Secretary and the President were in an unenviable situation. Deeply anti-Bolshevik, Lansing and Wilson wanted to act but feared the consequences if the Japanese were allowed to put an army along the Man-churian railways and in Siberia. Yet from all sides the pressure to inter-vene mounted steadily. London, Paris, Rome, and Tokyo all demanded action—and the cry was echoed by former President Taft, various vocifer-ous senators, and the American-Russian Chamber of Commerce. The problem, Lansing confessed, "bade fair to develop into a most distressing situation," and he counseled the appointment of Hoover to head the eco-nomic mission in the hope that it would, "for the time being, dispose of the proposal of armed intervention." Wilson appeared to agree, and dele-gated Redfield to take charge and "organize an original kind of relief ex-pedition."[58]

Redfield moved quickly, and a tentative program was reviewed at a

White House conference less than ten days later. The Merchants' Association of New York suggested that "exiled Russian businessmen" be trained as "efficient and instructed business agents"—a plan Wilson thought "most intelligently conceived and the objects sought are excellent." Such pressure, and Wilson's ruling that the commissioners would "have to operate on their own private account," moved Redfield to protest that the whole scheme smacked of economic exploitation. He suggested, instead, a special Government agency to direct the enterprise.

But Wilson stood firm. Strong recommendations from other interested parties may have given him confidence. R. D. McCarter, onetime President of the Westinghouse factory in Moscow—and incidentally one of Hoover's close business friends—warned that intervention was "absolutely necessary." "Armed intervention," wrote McCarter, is "prerequisite to the . . . building of grain elevators . . . refrigerator plants and cars . . . railway improvements . . . new railways." The plan, he concluded, would be "an excellent investment"—though for whom he did not specify. Of a similar mind was August Heid, manager of the Vladivostok office of the International Harvester Company. In any event, the President advised Redfield that the plan should be managed "through the Russian-American Chamber of Commerce and . . . the firms of which the Secretary of State spoke the other night who are directly interested in trade in Russia." That Redfield accepted his defeat gracefully can be seen in the composition of the proposed mission: Corse and E. C. Porter of the American-Russian Chamber of Commerce; Walter F. Dixon of the Singer Sewing Machine Company; Charles M. Muchnic of the American Locomotive Sales Corporation; and M. A. Oudin, foreign manager of the General Electric Company. But the President had a "reasonable confidence . . . that the whole matter may be kept within the bounds of fairness and right dealing." [59]

Secretary Lansing, though not worried about exploitation of the Russians, was quite miffed over Redfield's new authority. He wanted to be top man, "whatever may be the most effective agency for penetration in Siberia, whether industrial, commercial, social, or political." Lansing's fears were ungrounded, for the President considered the economic mission no more than a secondary aspect of active military intervention. By "early in July" it was known that the United States intended to "co-operate with the British Expeditionary Force in Russia." [60]

This decision grew from Wilson's determination—"I don't think you need fear of any consequences of our dealings with the Bolsheviki, because we do not intend to deal with them"—re-enforced by strong domestic and foreign pressure. As early as the end of May the matter was "receiving very careful consideration," and during the next forty days Wilson was bombarded with advice. Francis and the Allied ambassadors urged that the

landing come "as swiftly as possible." Postmaster General Burleson prepared a thirteen-page memorandum in favor of the idea; members of the
Root Commission urged "decisive action," and the French and British
pounded away at House and Lansing.[61]

During the flurry of excitement over the plans for economic penetration the negative reactions of House, Baker, and the high military prevented any clear decision. Baker wanted to "take everybody out of Russia . . . and let the Russians settle down and settle their own affairs."
House, constantly worried about the Japanese, supported the economic
mission under Hoover. General Peyton C. March, who warned against a
"merely sentimental" solution to the problem, considered intervention
"neither practical nor practicable," for it "would not divert a single German division from the Western Front." Though "urged" by Ambassador
Francis and the British to support the plan, General John J. Pershing refused to authorize the transfer of any troops from his command in France.[62]
But early in June the action of the Czechs in Siberia set the stage for intervention.

Nominally on their way to the Western Front via Siberia—though the
French had not provided any transportation—the Czechs first began to arrive in Vladivostok on April 4, 1918, the day the Japanese landed their first
troops in that city. The latter event aroused new Soviet fears, and Trotsky
—"unquestionably motivated by the imminent threat of a Japanese landing
at Vladivostok"—ordered the complete disarmament of all Czech forces
in Russia. The Czechs, who had already determined to proceed to the
Pacific, refused to obey the new order. They were immediately supported
by France and the United States. Ambassador Francis, who planned "to
encourage these men to disobey the orders of the Soviet Government,"
shared Poole's enthusiasm—the Acting Consul General was "glad from
a political point of view." But the Czechs needed little encouragement,
and "starting with the fall of Omsk on June 7 and Samara on June 8,
they systematically helped to establish anti-Bolshevik governments in the
towns of Siberia." Small wonder, then, that Minister to China Paul Reinsch
warned that "it would be a serious mistake to remove the Czecho-Slovak
troops from Siberia." [63]

President Wilson's reaction to these developments revealed the depth
of his determination to undertake military action against the Bolsheviks.
For even while he discussed economic intervention with Redfield, Wilson
began to formulate a plan for joint action with Tokyo. In Reinsch's cable
about the Czechs, the President saw "the shadow of a plan that might be
worked, with Japanese and other assistance." By the time Redfield's plans
were well under way the Czechs, with the tacit collaboration of Japan,
England, and the United States, had seized Vladivostok. Within three days
the French, who "bitterly" denounced Robins for his efforts to reach an

understanding with the Soviets, carried the Supreme War Council in an approval of Japanese action.

Intervention suddenly became an "urgent and imperative necessity." Urged on by Kennan, who thought Washington had "already shown too much consideration for the claims and feelings of the Bolsheviki," Secretary Lansing forgot his squabble with Redfield. "I do not think," he confided to his diary, "that we should consider the attitude of the Bolsheviki." Even Colonel House forgot his fears and concluded that Japan should be allowed to "expand in nearby Asiatic, underdeveloped countries." Though it was acknowledged that the re-establishment of an Eastern Front was "physically impossible," the President and his advisors agreed, on July 6, 1918, to intervene in Russia with force.[64] The Czechs, in effect, offered Wilson a means to implement his earlier decision of February 28, 1918.

While Wilson admitted that intervention "would add to the present sad confusion in Russia rather than cure it," the President nevertheless considered that to "help the Czecho-Slovaks consolidate their forces" and to "steady any efforts at self-government or self-defense in which the Russians themselves may be willing to accept assistance" was a "sufficient justification" for intervention. Nor did the President mean "to wear the least color of criticism" against what other governments might "think it wise to undertake." It was his "hope" to supplement such armed action with economic and educational work, but that program would "not be permitted to embarrass the military assistance." Though "fretted with the Japanese attitude," Wilson was through "sweating blood" over Russia. His anti-Bolshevism had fully matured, and it was to condition all his future actions. Senators Borah and Johnson dissented vigorously from the decision, but to little avail. The most prophetic judgment came from a newspaper correspondent in Russia. "The Allies," warned the representative of the Manchester *Guardian*, "are sowing dragon's teeth in eastern Europe." [65]

For a time Harper tried to push the plan for economic penetration. Batolin, the businessman detailed to work with Robins in September, 1917, became the central Russian figure in this plan. Sent on to the United States by Stevens—who considered him "thoroughly reliable"—Batolin began to collaborate with Harper early in August. By mid-September both men were "in consultation with the various Government officials." Together they saw House, who was enthusiastic and promised to do what he could to make Batolin's visit "worth while." Corse, who was "trying to get a coterie of bankers organized . . . who would take hold of Russia in a large way," and McCormick were also busy. The State Department encouraged the group and for a time it appeared that Harper's protégé might "form a nucleus around which something [would] be done."

But Wilson's indifference—"the military forces should go in before the economic"—was re-enforced by internal dissension within the group itself. Harper and Corse broke with Carpenter when, in their opinion, he developed the "big head." More significant, however, was Corse's complaint that Carpenter's American-Russian League had "stolen the thunder" from his own American-Russian Chamber of Commerce. Even the fact that Carpenter helped effect the final break between Thompson—who stood by Robins—and his old Wall Street friends did not decrease the tension. With the help of Gompers and Easley of the National Civic Federation, Carpenter first eased Mrs. Robins out of the League; and then Thompson was "asked to resign." But Harper was discouraged, and when offered the chance to conduct "informal classes" on Russia for State Department personnel he "accepted eagerly." [66]

Corse and McCormick continued the fight against Carpenter and ultimately were successful. Successful, that is to say, in the sense that they controlled what remained of the grandiose plan for economic penetration. McCormick, who also served on the board of directors of the National City Bank, carried the brunt of the battle, mainly because he had direct access to Wilson and others in the Administration. Though McCormick wanted "to act as soon as possible," the President could not be rushed. Even active intercession by Lansing and Vance McCormick—a relative who was chairman of the War Trade Board—failed to speed the plans. Not until October was the Russian Bureau, Incorporated, created as a division of the War Trade Board and empowered to encourage "private capital to engage in trade in Russia and Siberia." Since Washington had embarked upon a policy "actively hostile to the de facto Russian Government," trade was restricted to non-Soviet areas.

Whatever the contrast between this half-hearted gesture by Wilson and their original hopes, Corse and McCormick took advantage of the opportunity. By mid-October the National City Bank established a branch in Vladivostok at the "invitation" of August Heid, the International Harvester agent who became the Russian Bureau's representative in that city. Secretary of War Baker's opinion that the United States had no right "to use military force to compel the reception of our relief agencies" did not deter McCormick from requesting an "increase in the number of Allied soldiers placed . . . to do police duty." But Wilson was preoccupied with efforts to counter Tokyo's efforts to dominate the Manchurian railways, preparations for the Peace Conference in Paris, and the Borah-Johnson attack on intervention; and it was many months before McCormick and Corse could report any tangible gains.[67]

The Robins group, meanwhile, continued its fight to effect a more realistic Russian policy. Though the work of Harper's group severely restricted Robins' public effectiveness, the latter continued to advise Borah and Johnson, who constantly criticized Wilson's policy from the floor of the Senate. If their efforts had been limited to verbal attacks it is doubtful that the Administration would have been greatly concerned. "In this day, when intolerant newspapers imperatively demand immediate and complete endorsement of prevailing opinion," Johnson admitted candidly, "it is a dangerous and a delicate thing to speak of Russia, or to inquire concerning our activities there." But two other developments in which Robins played a significant role caused Wilson and his advisors serious concern. The first was the Republican party's victory in the November, 1918, campaign for congressional seats; the second was intimately connected with the consequences of the Administration's endorsement of Sisson's documents that purported to prove Lenin and Trotsky to be German agents.[68]

Faced by a critical shortage of funds, Will Hays, chairman of the Republican congressional campaign of 1918, asked Robins to help raise the needed money. Convinced that there could be no shift in American policy toward Russia until Wilson was removed, Robins accepted the chance to help prepare the ground for a Democratic defeat in 1920. Aware that Thompson shared his views, and that he was severely "shaken" by Wilson's refusal at least to hear their arguments, Robins arranged a meeting with Hays at the Union League Club in New York. Hays opened the discussion with a direct appeal for funds. But Thompson seemed unresponsive to a request based on stock political arguments. Robins then reviewed their Russian experiences and asked Thompson to assist on the basis that it would help change Wilson's Russian policy. Thompson answered with silence. Only as the group was about to break up did Thompson act—"my feeling against Wilson on account of his action in Russia made me jump in." With $450,000 guaranteed by Thompson, the Republicans went on to win control of Congress in November, 1918. It was, as Hays noted, very "timely aid." [69] The more so since it gave Borah and Johnson added strength in the Senate—strength that began to worry Acting Secretary of State Frank Polk.

The Wilson administration provided the opponents of its Russian policy a rallying point when it allowed Sisson to stamp his documents with the Seal of the United States. For though these documents provided the cornerstone in the foundation of symbol meanings upon which rested the great Red scare, their publication also gave the Robins group and its supporters an issue around which to organize a counterattack. Though by no means the only critical factor, this domestic opposition to Wilson's Russian policy did exert an influence on the decisions made in Paris. In this complex pattern of developments, moreover, the earlier attitude of the American press was uppermost.

Prior to the Bolshevik Revolution of November, 1917, the left wing of American politics was linked to Germany and labeled disloyal. Not only was this true of the International Workers of the World, whose militant opposition to the war re-enforced the earlier antipathy of the dominant economic groups, but also of the left wing of the American Socialist party. After that party's emergency convention in St. Louis in April, 1917, its members who refused to support the war effort were quickly typed unpatriotic. Nor was the attack merely verbal, as dramatically illustrated by the arrest, conviction, and imprisonment of Eugene Debs for opposition to the draft. Against this background the constant rumors that the Provisional Government would seek peace served to link Russian Socialists to their American sympathizers—and both groups to Germany. Washington's refusal to grant passports to those Socialists who desired to attend the Stockholm Conference was but a case in point. Equally important was the progressive identification of all domestic American critics—be they strikers or those who proposed legislative curbs on free enterprise—with this so-called disloyal group.

From these symbol definitions it was but a step to identify Americans who offered objections to various developments in their own country with Russian Bolsheviks—whom "the overwhelming majority of papers" treated as German agents. Since the press effectively played down the fact of Russia's economic and military collapse it was quite easy to explain the Treaty of Brest-Litovsk within the same symbol equation. Nor did the members of the Wilson administration take any measures to correct this highly distorted presentation of world events. Rather did they tacitly use the equation to help effect their intervention against the Soviets—an intervention fundamentally grounded in antagonism to the latter's social and economic program. Coupled with the consideration that intervention was supported by "most of the papers" of the United States, it can be seen that public opposition to Wilson's Russian policy subjected one to grave risks.[70]

No better illustration of that fact can be offered than the case of Jacob Abrams and his associates who openly sought to effect the recall of American troops from Russia. The Abrams case, moreover, was the incident that reinvigorated the Robins group. Late in August, 1918, Abrams, Molly Stiemer, and four others were arrested on the charge of having violated the wartime espionage act by their distribution of a leaflet that exhorted the workers of America to end the "crime" of intervention. Consciously aware that it would be labeled pro-German—evidence of the degree to which the symbol definitions noted above had become operative—the group took particular care to record its "hate" for "German militarism." Before the case came to trial, however, the Administration sanctioned the official publication of the Sisson Documents.

For more than a week after the date of release, September 15, the press of the country was particularly excited over this proof of the conspiracy between Lenin and the Germans. Those who questioned the validity of the documents were generally ignored. Nor did Wilson and Lansing act to withdraw the documents when they learned, early in October, that the British had come "to the definite conclusion that they were forgeries." Robins, who had no desire to repeat his experiences of the early summer—when his views were distorted and misrepresented—at first declined to participate either in the public controversy over the documents or in the Abrams trial. But when he learned that part of the evidence against Molly Stiemer was the fact that she quoted him in opposition to intervention, Robins acted.

The court, as a matter of fact, first attempted "to compel" Robins to appear through Judge Henry D. Clayton's "order for Mr. Robins' arrest." Robins "evaded" the service of the subpoena and came into the courtroom of his own free will. But once on the stand the judge ruled that his testimony was "immaterial" and refused to let him answer any significant questions. Molly and her associates, who the New York *Times* admitted were "not . . . particularly dangerous to the country or its institutions," were given heavy sentences. Judge Clayton, in the opinion of the same paper, deserved "the thanks of the city and of the country." [71] Two who disagreed with that opinion were Supreme Court Justices Oliver Wendell Holmes and Louis D. Brandeis.

The Abrams case was not heard by the Supreme Court for more than a year, an interval during which the fear and hysteria of the Red scare replaced serious discussion and evaluation as a technique of public administration and personal judgment. Even professional historians warped their perspectives, as the actions of Professors Harper and John Franklin Jameson—Harper's more famous colleague who was managing editor of the *American Historical Review*—readily indicate. The head of the Committee on Public Information, an intimate friend of Sisson, called upon them to subject the documents to a thorough test in view of the public furor over their validity. Though Harper privately admitted that he did "not like the way he [Sisson] uses the term German agent," both he and Jameson publicly endorsed the material.[72] It is not surprising, therefore, that a majority of the Supreme Court accepted the story as fact.

But Justice Holmes was not only "stirred" by the case; he maintained and exercised both his integrity and his powers of analysis. At an early date he pointed out that "an actual intent to hinder the United States in its war *with* Germany must be proved" to sustain a verdict of guilty. Or, as he later wrote, an "intent to prevent interference with the revolution in Russia might have been satisfied without any hindrance to carrying on the war in which we were engaged." Save for Brandeis, the other members of the court declined to cut through to the heart of the question. Rather did they rationalize their verdict through the Sisson Documents. The troops were sent to Russia, declared the majority opinion, "as a strategic operation against the Germans on the eastern battle front." [73] It would seem apparent that the majority failed to analyze the President's *aide-mémoire of* August 3, 1918.

By the time of that decision the value and effect of intervention were seriously questioned in many quarters. In October, 1918, however, the Robins group could do little more than probe for a weak spot in the Administration's policy. But Senator Johnson had no doubts as to the fundamental issue. On December 12, 1918, he demanded information as to whether, among other things, the Committee of Public Information "as administered by Mr. Creel, has been engaged, not in developing facts as to our people, but in justifying a course subsequently pursued at variance with our words." The attack was bold, and it upset the State Department. "Frankly," cabled Polk to Lansing, "I am disturbed over the situation." [74] But decisions made in Paris would be difficult to change from the floor of the Senate—as Senators Johnson and Borah were to learn. And at ten-thirty on the morning of December 14, 1918, President Wilson arrived in Paris.

2. AT PARIS

The question now arose whether we ought to include in the new terms of the armistice other problems, such as that of Poland.

PRESIDENT WILSON suggested it might be unwise to discuss a proposal of this sort on its individual merits, since it formed part of the much larger question of . . . . how to meet the social danger of Bolshevism.

From the minutes of the meeting of the
Supreme War Council, January 12, 1919

President Woodrow Wilson's deep desire so to order the affairs of the world that individual men would never again organize themselves for the planned creation of chaos is a matter of record. But despite his total commitment—physical as well as intellectual—to that effort, the scattered shambles of Berlin, London's East Side, Stalingrad, Manila, and Hiroshima were to document the discrepancy between Wilson's desire and its fulfillment. Yet that difference cannot be satisfactorily explained by references to a group of "willful men," the inadequacy of the plan, the vengeance of the victors, the vindictiveness of the vanquished, or even the petulance of the President himself. To be sure, those considerations were important; but as a few men have hinted, and as the record verifies, the critical factor at Paris was the Russian problem.[75] For the conflicting interests that were resolved by an armed truce rather than by a decision to delimit national expansion all impinged upon the question of what to do with Soviet Russia.

The policy of the United States toward the Soviets exemplified the victory of those domestic forces that, though generally labeled isolationist, in fact desired the further and unrestricted overseas expansion of American economic and political power: those groups that demanded freedom of action and at the same time sought to avoid being charged with responsibility if their intervention or expansion provoked international friction. Nor did these opponents of the League of Nations achieve their victory only after overcoming the constant and vigorous opposition of President Wilson. Far more significant than the President's refusal to compromise on the final draft of the Versailles Treaty in his fight with the Senate was the manner in which he handled the various aspects of policy toward Russia. Wilson's solution to that problem signified his choice to stand with those who opposed him. At heart he may well have disagreed, but in the hour of decision President Woodrow Wilson "cast in his lot with the rest." [76]

That decision revealed the touchstone of the President's foreign policy —the attempt to use economic and military force to create and guarantee the life of foreign governments modeled on his concept of the economic and political system of the United States. Intervention in Russia was but another phase of a policy that included the manipulation of an arms embargo during the Mexican Revolution—a revolution that desired, among other considerations, to nationalize the country's natural resources—and Wilson's own efforts to revise the character of the German Government as a condition for the execution of an armistice in November, 1918. The President's active aid to Admiral Aleksander Kolchak was an attempt to implement that policy in two other respects—the limitation of Japanese expansion in the Far East and the actual destruction of the Soviet Government.

Conditions were far from ideal for the success of this plan. Many other problems made demands on Wilson's energy, necessitated the expenditure of influence, and, equally important, lowered the level of the reservoir of effective power at his disposal. The strong desire of the majority of the people of the United States to return to peacetime pursuits seriously restricted his efforts to aid those forces he preferred in Russia, and elsewhere; as did the personal and political opposition to the President and his party. Another broad conflict was the consequence of Wilson's great emphasis on the creation of a League of Nations. Both the President and Colonel House evidenced a preference to concentrate on the superstructure of that institution—with the result that several of the foundation stones were neither square nor well mortared. Other specific problems—reparations and Czechoslovakia, for example—demanded both his attention and a portion of American power to effect a solution.

With particular reference to the Russian question, Wilson was not only troubled by the low morale among the forces of intervention, but also by the constant challenge to the venture offered by the Robins group. The President's critical decision was concerned neither with pressure politics nor the ethnic geography of Central Europe. The dilemma was far more profound—as Wilson himself was well aware. Bluntly put, the question was whether he had the courage to face the challenge of the Bolshevik Revolution. His own words bear tragic witness to his failure of nerve.[77]

The essential tragedy of Wilson's failure lies in the fact that he realized and acknowledged that the Soviets represented a desperate attempt on the part of the dispossessed to share the bounty of industrial civilization. More, he knew they must be given access to that share if further resort to violence was to be forestalled. Yet this keen insight was first dimmed then ultimately beclouded by antagonism to the Soviets and the conscious desire to expand American influence abroad. For a time, however, Wilson appeared ready to offer a positive answer to the Bolshevik challenge.

No single source can be credited with the origin, late in 1918, of official interest in a plan to oppose Bolshevism through economic aid and reconstruction. Interest in an approach of that character was undoubtedly inspired by the proposals of Charles Smith and Thomas Masaryk; stimulated by Thacher and Robins; and intensively cultivated by that portion of the business community led by Harper, Corse, and McCormick. That none of their suggestions was adopted formally obscures the impact they made on official thought. But without question their recommendations influenced later policy.

The successful conclusion of the war against Germany emphasized the deep antagonism toward and fear of Bolshevism shared by Lansing and Wilson. "We must not go too far in making Germany and Austria impotent," the Secretary fretted as early as October 26, 1918. As one who considered "Democracy *without* education" a "greater evil" than "Autocracy *with* education," Lansing was extremely worried by the social unrest in Europe. In his fervent search for a technique of opposition he began to think in terms of "food" as an instrument of policy that would complement "arms and ammunition." Perhaps the concept was but the product of the Secretary's own interest in McCormick's proposals as re-enforced by a long review of the problem, but a memorandum by William Christian Bullitt may well have been a catalytic element.[78]

Young William Bullitt, the son of a wealthy Philadelphia family, was one of the numerous advisors clustered around the White House and the State Department in preparation for the peace conference. From an early date his somewhat romanticized concept of the Foreign Service and his intense, if also nebulous, liberalism helped re-enforce an active interest in the Russian problem. Early in the summer of 1918 he suggested the creation of a special commission to study the question with an eye to the elimination of "indecision." [79] That particular recommendation was not acted on, but his formal memoranda of November 6 and 8 may have helped effect a temporary modification of the policy of armed intervention.

From his observation that "famine and economic disorganization are the parents of Bolshevism," Bullitt suggested that the United States take the lead and work with the "labor leaders and moderate socialists . . . to establish a basis of co-operation against Bolshevism." He likewise underscored the dangers of negative opposition. "If the governments of the world form a holy alliance against Social Democrac in Europe," Bullitt warned, "the entire moderate socialist groups . . . will stand with" the Bolsheviks. Lansing found the suggestion was "worthy of consideration" and sent it on to Wilson; but the Secretary recommended caution—the "danger of compromise with any form of radicalism" raised "strong reasons" for the rejection of the plan. Lansing's personal opinion never wavered: "Bolshevism must be suppressed." [80]

President Wilson not only shared Lansing's thought—or perhaps it was originally the President's—that Germany should not be weakened, but also feared that the "dangers of Bolshevism" would be "likely to show themselves in this country" at an early date. A warning to that effect was, to Wilson at least, the product of "a rare and true insight into the near future." But the President was challenged by the proposal to defeat Bolshevism through the distribution of food and other aids to economic rehabilitation. "Soon after the Armistice," in fact, he took occasion to stress that "the necessity of feeding Germany arose not only out of humanity but out of its fundamental necessity to prevent anarchy." Herbert Hoover, with whom Wilson discussed the situation, was equally determined to "entirely eliminate the incipient Bolshevism in progress." [81] That Wilson accepted the concept and sought to secure its adoption as official allied policy became even more evident after the peace conference began serious work.

Wilson's attempts to defeat Bolshevism through economic measures were paralleled by several maneuvers that appeared designed to end military action in Russia. But at no time did he have a definite plan of action; rather were the moves a consequence of his realization that the Soviets posed a question to which armed intervention offered no real answer. Other considerations strengthened his sense of urgency and helped, as in the last days of December, 1918, to re-enforce the President's inclination to act. None of these moves produced a solution—for in each case Wilson declined to carry through the enterprise.

There is no better example of the interactions of these factors than the Buckler Mission of December, 1918–January, 1919. Wilson's confidence in economic countermeasures was re-enforced by several other developments soon after his arrival in Europe. A disturbing element was Lansing's warning that the morale of American troops in North Russia—landed to support the English-dominated intervention—was "not good and further weakened by considerable friction with the British." Then from Washington came news of Johnson's successful demand for a hearing on intervention—a gain that some thought heralded "great pressure . . . for the immediate withdrawal of our troops at Archangel and [in] Siberia." Quite possibly another bit of bad news—that Japan's "extensive military activities in Siberia" threatened the open door—further persuaded Wilson to make a favorable reply to Maxim M. Litvinov's Christmas Eve appeal for an end to intervention.[82]

But Litvinov's message would have made an impact on the President even if the other considerations had been absent. "The principles proclaimed by you as a possible basis for settling European questions, your avowed efforts and intention of making the settlement conform to the demands of justice and humanity," Litvinov wrote, "induce and justify me to send you this statement." The Soviet spokesman then made two points: that the Bolsheviks had "never been allowed to put fully their case and answer the charges made against them"; and that the Terror "was not the cause but the direct result and outcome of Allied intervention." There were two choices open to the Allies, Litvinov continued.

"One is continued open or disguised intervention . . . paralyzing the economic development of the country for long decades." The second, for which the Soviets requested consideration, was "impartially to weigh and investigate the one-sided accusations . . . to come to an understanding with the Soviet Government, to withdraw the foreign troops . . . to raise the economic blockade . . . and to give her technical advice how to exploit her national richness in the most effective way, for the benefit of all countries badly in need of foodstuffs and raw materials. . . . The dictatorship of toilers and producers is not an aim in itself," Litvinov concluded, "but the means of building up a new social system. . . . One may believe in this ideal or not, but it surely gives no justification for sending foreign troops to fight against it." [83]

Litvinov touched a tender spot—the discrepancy between words and actions—and President Wilson's reflex was vigorous. On January 7, 1919, shortly after his return from Rome, the President directed William H. Buckler, a roving trouble-shooter attached to the American Embassy in London, to proceed "at the earliest possible moment to Stockholm" to meet Litvinov. But the move was *in no sense* the product of a decision to "come to an understanding with the Soviet Government." This fact cannot be overemphasized. The action was taken in line with the attempt to forestall the strong French pressure for the recognition of a counter-revolutionary government, but at the same time defeat Bolshevism by non-military means.[84]

On the same day that Buckler was ordered to Stockholm, Wilson opposed a French effort to increase the number of Allied troops in Russia.

The President's view was neatly summarized by General Tasker Bliss, one of his most confidential advisors at Paris: "troops in sufficient numbers . . . could prevent *Bolsheviks* from crossing [a given] line, but . . . we could not prevent *Bolshevism* from crossing . . . Bolshevism fed on ignorance and hunger." Or as Wilson wrote Lansing three days later, "The real thing with which to stop Bolshevism is food." The only purpose behind Buckler's journey was to gather information. There was no thought that a settlement would be effected.[85]

But mere antagonism to the Bolsheviks offered no solution to two problems: one general and one that Washington faced alone. No effort was required to establish the fact that all parties in Paris disliked the Soviets; but discussions as how best to act on that unanimity revealed deep differences. By no means the least important source of the diversity was Washington's dilemma of how to squeeze the Japanese out of Siberia yet at the same time help depose the Soviets. Though he did not share the President's concern for American interests in the Far East, British Prime Minister David Lloyd George was troubled by the resistance to further intervention evidenced in his own country—and especially within his own political party. Under these circumstances the Peace Conference leaders easily agreed that Russian prisoners of war would not be repatriated to areas controlled by the Soviets, whom "we did not like," and that Russia would not participate in the Peace Conference since the Soviets were the de facto government— but both Wilson and Lloyd George opposed the plans for full-scale military intervention proposed by Georges Clemenceau, French Premier.[86]

French determination to destroy the Soviet Government was never in doubt. From the day of Lloyd George's candid admission that while it was "possible that the Bolsheviks did not represent Russia" he was certain that none of the foreign-backed counter-revolutionary groups could claim that role—and protested any effort to "select" the latter as delegates to Paris—the French sought to involve both England and the United States in full-scale war against the Soviets. Nor did Wilson's support for the British proposal to invite all Russian groups to Paris modify Clemenceau's opposition.[87] Although the French Premier failed to achieve his goal he did frustrate Wilson's attempts to solve the question—or, more exactly, he encouraged the President to abandon his own program. There is no doubt but that the President was the one who ultimately gave way, but before he did so Wilson left clear proof that he understood the crisis.

"There was throughout the world," Wilson cautioned on January 16, 1919, "a feeling of revolt against the large vested interests which influenced the world both in the economic and in the political sphere." To his mind the "way to cure this domination was . . . constant discussion and a slow process of reform; but the world at large had grown impatient of delay." If the French representative, and, perhaps, even others, winced at these comments, they no doubt felt grave dissatisfaction at the President's concluding remarks. "Bolshevism was therefore vital," he bluntly warned, "because of these genuine grievances." To drive home the point he revealed that "British and American troops were unwilling to fight in Russia because they feared their efforts might lead to the restoration of the old order." The French plan contained the sources of its own failure, for "part of the strength of the Bolshevik leaders was doubtless the threat of foreign intervention. With the help of this threat they gathered the people around them." These brief remarks on January 16, 1919, left no doubt but that Wilson understood the appeal of the Soviets. But the insight was never translated into action.[88]

The key to the President's failure was his desire to preserve and increase American influence in China, Manchuria, and Siberia. Washington's opposition to Japan's plans in Asia was re-enforced throughout the fall of 1918. Tokyo strengthened her garrison in Siberia, rushed in commercial agents, and manipulated various counter-revolutionary leaders in an attempt to secure a stranglehold on the general economic life of the area, and in particular sought access to northeastern Asia's jugular vein— the Chinese Eastern Railway. Washington employed economic sanctions in an effort to weaken Tokyo's position, but the temporary Japanese retreat in January, 1919, was more the result of internal pressure. The "growing intensity of the social struggle" in Japan was dramatized by the rice riots of July and August, 1918, and helped effect a short-term victory for the more moderate elements in Japanese politics. Washington exploited these developments to push through her version of an Inter-Allied Agreement for the Supervision of the Chinese Eastern and the Siberian Railways.[89]

This agreement was no more than a new version of the old Knox neutralization scheme and had the same objective—American control of the railroads. Ostensibly a multi-nation group appointed to run the railroads until a stable Russian government came into existence, the Inter-Allied Railway Committee was "actually a mere front for the management of the whole railway enterprise by John Stevens," the American railroad specialist who became head of the Technical Board. "In fact, it could be said that the railway plan was found acceptable to the United States only because it was understood that John Stevens would be named as president of this Board." But acceptance did not imply satisfaction, and Wilson approved the plan only "as the best that can be obtained." [90]

The Inter-Allied plan—unsatisfactory as it was—may well have influenced Wilson to press for a non-violent solution in Russia. The same day that Washington was notified of his reluctant approval, Wilson submitted Buckler's report as testimony in opposition to the pro-intervention witnesses at Paris. Earlier the French offered their former Ambassador to Russia who, while he admitted that "it could not be stated that the majority were opposed to the Bolsheviki," did make much of the opposition of the "well-to-do classes." He was followed by another of Clemenceau's protégés, the former Danish minister to the Tsar's court, whose idea of the "proper policy was to destroy the centers of Bolshevism by capturing Petrograd and Moscow." [91]

Buckler's report gave evidence of the same social orientation, but in his case modified by a willingness to acknowledge the Soviets' right to exist. He advised Lansing that the Soviets were "prepared to compromise on all points, including the Russian foreign debt, protection to existing foreign enterprises, and the granting of new concessions in Russia." The "conciliatory attitude of the Soviet Government is unquestionable," Buckler stated flatly. The special agent cabled House that "agreement with Russia can take place at once, obviating conquest and policing and reviving normal conditions as disinfectant against Bolshevism." His full report, submitted to the Big Five by Wilson on the morning of January 21, 1919, repeated this estimate of the situation.[92]

At three o'clock that afternoon Wilson joined issue with Clemenceau. The President acknowledged that all were "repelled by Bolshevism, and for that reason they had placed armed men in opposition to them"; but reiterated his conviction that "by opposing Bolshevism with arms they were in reality serving the cause of Bolshevism." For that reason he felt that if his colleagues "could swallow their pride and the natural repulsion which they felt for the Bolsheviks, and see the representatives of all organized groups in one place, it would bring about a marked reaction against Bolshevism." Clemenceau initially opposed the proposal "because we would be raising them to our level by saying that they were worthy of entering into conversation with us." But faced with the fact that "some 150,000 additional men would be required, in order to keep the anti-Bolshevik Governments from dissolution," the French Premier acknowledged that he could not guarantee any volunteers. When Lloyd George tartly remarked that the Soviets "would not be crushed by speeches," the French and Italians gave way and authorized Wilson to issue the invitations for the abortive Prinkipo Meeting. Again, it must be emphasized that the move was never conceived as an effort to reach agreement with the Soviets. The delegates, Wilson made clear, "should merely report back to their Governments the conditions found." As Lansing acknowledged a few days later, the plan "was the direct consequence of a recognition of the impossibility of military intervention." [93]

The intimate relationship between that fact, Wilson's Prinkipo proposal, the vigorous opposition to intervention led by the Robins group, and the bitter struggle between Washington and Tokyo for pre-eminence in Asia became clear within a very few weeks. Two days after Wilson's invitation to the groups in Russia was dispatched, the President learned that Johnson's December attack on intervention had led to the rise of a "critical spirit in Congress." Not only was intervention challenged, but specific charges were leveled at various aspects of American policy. Attacks on the activities of McCormick's Russian Bureau, Incorporated, were complemented by the blunt charge that Ambassador Francis had been "hopelessly incompetent." As New York's Representative Fiorello H. LaGuardia phrased the charge, the "personal conduct and associations of our Ambassador with certain of his friends of Teutonic tendencies" contributed no little to the current failure of American policy. Ever resourceful, Acting Secretary of State Polk took advantage of an oversight in the phraseology of LaGuardia's inquiry to escape a possible charge that he lied when he denied the accusation.[94]

But it was a near miss—too near, in fact—and Polk was worried. The opportunity to control the Manchurian railways was in jeopardy, he wired, because the opposition was strong enough to defeat an appropriations bill authorizing the necessary funds. "I am taking the liberty of stating the case so boldly," Polk explained, "so the President and yourself may have all the facts before you before he commits himself to supply the money for this purpose from his private fund." Wilson proved equal to the crisis, however, even though the strength of the opposition caused him to camouflage the counterattack with considerable care. But the private discussions of the high command were quite candid.

Wilson's first thought was to reveal the sources of his Russian policy "fully and frankly, though in confidence," to the members of Johnson's committee of inquiry. Polk was instructed to explain that control of the railroads was vital on three counts. They were "a principal means of access to and from the Russian people and as affording an opportunity for economic aid to Siberia where the people are relatively friendly and resistant to Bolshevik influence." Of like importance was the "potential value of this railroad as a means for developing American commerce particularly from the west coast of the United States to Russia." But that ultimate gain —"giving practical effect to the policy of the open door"—could not be exploited, Polk was to make clear, until Japan's troop movements and "commercial activities" were counterbalanced by "administration of the railway by Stevens as a Russian employee." The President thought a blunt explanation of this sort would prepare Congress "to appropriate the funds necessary."

Polk did not agree. "I am convinced," he cabled back, "that I would not be given any consideration. . . . The first question to be asked," he amplified, would be "what is the Russian policy?" Johnson, the acting Secretary, went on to add, had "considerable support . . . on the ground that our men are being killed and no one knows why they are still there." Polk considered the criticism "unjust," but since the Siberian project was "only a part of the whole Russian problem," the situation was very ticklish. For all the Administration's congressional leaders were agreed that "if the Russian question were thrown into Congress at this time, it would probably jeopardize all the appropriation bills."

"In view of [the] situation," the President withdrew his plan to tell all and substituted a less direct proposal. Polk was advised to implement the Inter-Allied Railroad Agreement with State Department funds for the time being. Whether or not the Bolsheviks were finally defeated, Lansing explained, "it is essential that we maintain the policy of the open door with reference to the Siberian and particularly the Chinese Eastern Railway." [95] This directive clarified two other aspects of Washington's policy in Asia. The Administration had already tried to speed consummation of the new consortium negotiations, initiated by Wilson in November, 1917, as a second technique designed to delimit Japanese gains in Asia. This effort was ultimately frustrated by Lamont, who broke with Thompson on the question of Russian policy and approved Japan's demand for special privileges along the South Manchurian Railway and in Mongolia.[96] Clearly, the marked correlation between Wilson's effort to complete the agreement and intervention was not a coincidence.

The President's reversal of his earlier refusal to back the Taft-supported consortium also foreshadowed Washington's reaction to China's protest against American domination of the Manchurian railways. "China," the State Department curtly answered, "should cooperate fully and without reservation in making effective the principles agreed upon by Japan and the United States." Though Washington successfully opposed Peking's continued efforts to participate in the Inter-Allied administration of the railroads, as was China's treaty right, the United States was the ultimate loser. For coupled with the decision to attempt to isolate and prevent the consolidation of the Soviet Government, Washington's brusque treatment of China left the United States all but impotent in the face of Japan's continued militance in the Far East.[97]

Wilson shortly abandoned his insight into the Bolshevik Revolution— with it went his inclination to tolerate the existence of the Soviet Government—and actively began to support the forces of counter-revolution. An indication of the President's final stand came during the breakdown of the Prinkipo project. Nominally accepted by the Big Five, the plan actually had many enemies. One of the "major sensations of the Peace Conference," Wilson's call for the meeting earned him "bitter comment," particularly from the right wing of French politics. Together with representatives of all anti-Bolshevik groups in Paris, the French fought the project from its inception. Various Americans in Paris also opposed the idea. Straus, McCormick, and Hoover all conferred with the French and the "group of refugee statesmen." And in England the extreme conservatives organized a major counterattack.[98]

These opponents no doubt took joy in opposition to the plan manifested in the United States. Those who had access to mediums of mass communications were well-nigh unanimous in their antagonism to the Bolsheviks. Jerome Davis, head of the Y.M.C.A. program in Russia, defended the project, as did the New York *World*, but the *Outlook*'s review of opinion indicated that the moulders of American thought were quite set against the effort. Nor did Wilson's selection of Professor George Herron as one of the American delegates modify this opposition. A long-time friend of the President, who used him as a listening post in Switzerland, Herron was generally typed as a political radical. Actually, his "revolutionism was of the mind only." His Russian associations were Pavel Miliukov, who wanted to validate the imperialistic treaties concluded between the Tsar and the Allies, and Baron von Wrangel, the French-sponsored counter-revolutionary in South Russia. But the newspaper and periodical press of the country waged an ugly campaign against Herron—whom they condemned as "not even an American in the best sense of the word." [99]

More significant was the opposition within the President's own confidential circle. Soviet acceptance of Wilson's invitation placed the Big Five in an uncomfortable position—for none of the other factions agreed to send delegates. The British conservatives took advantage of the awkward situation and sent Winston Spencer Churchill to Paris to maneuver the Allies into full-scale intervention. Churchill had served the British war effort with distinction—though his daring plan to force the Dardanelles Straits failed of success—and had a flair for dramatic plans and rhetoric. His arrival was expertly timed to coincide with the eve of Wilson's scheduled departure for the United States. Churchill wasted little time (the hour was six-thirty in the evening)—with preliminaries—"if only the Bolsheviks were to attend the conference, it was thought that little good would come of the meeting."

Wilson replied that he "had a very clear opinion about two points." First was that foreign troops "were doing no sort of good in Russia. They did not know for whom or for what they were fighting." The second—and equally revealing—was that what "we were seeking was not a *rapprochement* with the Bolsheviks, but clear information." For Churchill's suggestion to furnish "volunteers, arms, munitions, tanks," and other supplies to the White forces, Wilson had a ready answer. "Conscripts could not be sent and volunteers probably could not be obtained. He himself felt guilty in that the United States had in Russia insufficient forces, but it was not possible to increase them. It was certainly a cruel dilemma." The only feasible answer, concluded the President, was to withdraw the troops.

Yet in the final moment before the meeting adjourned Wilson remarked that "he would cast in his lot with the rest." [100]

But the President balked somewhat when he learned what the rest had in mind. With Wilson safely at sea the delegates in Paris let down their hair. Churchill suggested a plan whereby the Soviets would be forced to halt their victory in the field as a condition of the conference. Clemenceau, who "favored the policy of encirclement; the policy of setting up a barrier around Russia," offered a more direct solution. The delegates were assembled, he noted, "to get out of" an "awkward situation"—the best procedure was to make "no further reference" to Prinkipo. Colonel House admitted that he had "never been in favor of the Prinkipo proposal" and agreed that the "question to be decided was how to finesse the situation against the Bolsheviks." Balfour likewise "thought it was necessary to take steps to put the Bolsheviks in the wrong." Churchill came up with a second plan: let the project die and use the time to prepare "a definite war scheme." Lansing agreed with the plan to kill the conference but objected to Churchill's war plan—an objection clarified by General Bliss.[101]

"It is quite certain," Bliss warned other delegates, that the United States would not join any new war on Russia "so long as the present general conditions elsewhere continue to exist." For one thing, the general amplified, the people were unable "to focus their undivided attention on Russia." But if the delegates "could make final and definitive peace *at once*," he went on, then the "people of the United States might come to see that peace in Russia is the only thing necessary to secure universal peace; that her present condition is the only thing that menaces the peace of the world." Bliss was quickly supported by a cable from Wilson that warned "it would be fatal to be led further into the Russian chaos." [102] But the President did nothing to reactivate the Prinkipo plan.

He finally abandoned the effort to make peace with Russia when the findings of his own mission left him no choice but opposition or co-existence. In a sense, Wilson trapped himself. With pseudo-secrecy—contrary to the usual view, Lansing told *both* England and France of the plan—he dispatched William Bullitt to Russia on a new mission to gather information upon which to base a decision. But when that information pointed to a settlement with the Soviet Government, the President sought another solution. Bullitt, who advised the withdrawal of "all American troops at Archangel as soon as possible," was briefed on his mission when the Prinkipo failure became evident. In company with Captain Walter Pettit of Military Intelligence and Lincoln Steffens, progressive journalist, he left Paris on February 22 and arrived in Petrograd on March 10, 1919. He was greeted with expressions of "full confidence in the good will of the American

Government" on behalf of the Soviets, and requested Lansing and House to "suspend judgment" until he could file a full report.[103]

The heart of Bullitt's report was a plan for peace "drafted by Litvinov, approved by Lenin, and handed to Bullitt by the latter on March 14." That the Soviets considered the mission "very important" was clearly revealed in their proposal. Their conditions were: (1) an armistice with all factions in "full control of the territories which they occupy at the moment"; (2) the "economic blockade to be raised" and relief supplies sent in "on equal terms to all classes of Russian people"; (3) the Soviet Government to have "unlimited" access to all Russian railways and ports; (4) a "general amnesty to all political opponents" by all factions; and (5) the withdrawal of all foreign troops and the end of all foreign assistance to non-Soviet governments. In addition, Bullitt was assured of Moscow's "unequivocal" readiness to "pay the foreign debts." There was "no doubt," Bullitt concluded, "of the sincerity of this proposal, and I pray you will consider it with the deepest seriousness." [104]

The report and its implications were no doubt considered, but the Soviet proposal was never discussed at a meeting of the Paris Peace Conference. Though Bullitt gathered the impression that the top layer of American policy advisors thought it "highly desirable" to accept the Soviet overture—an interpretation verified by others—Lansing nevertheless ordered Pettit to "withdraw from Russia immediately." On the second morning after his return Bullitt conferred with Lloyd George, whose enthusiasm decreased in direct ratio to the amount of food he consumed at breakfast. By the end of the meal it was apparent that the British Premier, troubled more by indecision than indigestion, would not act. But there was still the President, who had gone on record that he viewed the Russian question as "the acid test" of Allied diplomacy—and who understood the fundamental issues at stake. Bullitt waited hopefully for his scheduled interview, but it never occurred. The President "had a headache" and canceled the meeting. Together with his "cold" that prevented the conference with William Boyce Thompson in January, 1918, Wilson's apparent susceptibility to everyday ailments would seem to have played a vital role in American relations with Russia.[105]

But neither the President's headache nor the fact that House, to whom Wilson delegated the future of Lenin's proposal, quickly dropped his reputed support for the plan altered the fact that Wilson's failure to act on the overture signified his final decision to attempt the forceful overthrow of the Soviet Government. William Bullitt was wrong when, in his letter of resignation, he claimed that the Russian problem had "not even been understood." [106] Wilson understood the question—he merely failed to translate comprehensions into a positive policy. From the date of his headache, Wilson actively aided Admiral Kolchak, acquiesced in the overthrow of Bela Kun's Bolshevik Government in Hungary, helped the counter-revolution in South Russia, maintained an American economic embargo against the Soviets, tacitly aided Poland's efforts to secure new territory in the Ukraine, and in the last hours of his administration approved a plan calculated to maneuver Lenin out of power. That opposition to Japan's penetration of Siberia was a concurrent policy did not modify Washington's bitter antagonism toward the Soviet Government.

Wilson's attempt, through half-measures at best, to effect the modification of Kolchak's reactionary regime rather than the moderation of the Soviet's domestic program illuminates his final choice. When the project to feed Russia broke down with Lenin's refusal to accept the Allied condition that the Red Army cease all military operations—a demand sponsored by Hoover—and the refugee government's angry cry that "the feeding of the starving population is not a solution of the Russian question," the President turned to the Siberian admiral.[107] Though Wilson fretted about Kolchak's extreme conservatism, that consideration was overlooked for the simple reason that the admiral was, in the eyes of the United States, a well-nigh perfect instrumentality. His anti-Bolshevism was never in doubt, nor his willingness to pay Russia's old debts, and he was bitterly opposed by the Japanese. Tokyo's favorite was Cossack General Grigorii Mikhailovich Semenov, "exclusively backed by the Japanese after October, 1918." Japan's scheme was to use Semenov to prevent Kolchak from defeating the Soviets and thereby gain control of Siberia for themselves.[108]

Wilson tactfully explained this to the Big Four on May 9, 1919, when the Japanese delegate was absent. He phrased the charge as a suspicion, but made clear his belief that "the Japanese would be glad to have a collision between the Cossacks and American soldiers." The situation left the United States with a clear choice—"Take sides with Kolchak and send in much stronger forces" or "withdraw." Tokyo, however, would no doubt enlarge her own garrison if Washington took the former course. The President's suggestion "to clear out of Russia and leave it to the Russians to fight it out among themselves" was no more than a token gesture, for he then reintroduced his earlier proposal to question Kolchak on his domestic program as a preliminary step to more active aid. British and American pressure for recognition of Kolchak helped keep the idea current while the question of a blockade against the Soviets was settled.[109]

Washington later denied participation in the blockade, but on May 9, 1919, the Big Four agreed—with Wilson in attendance—that any modification of the economic sanction "would not apply to Bolshevist Russia." When Kolchak began to suffer military reverses, the United States wavered a bit and noted that a "legal" blockade could not be established. But two devices solved the President's "difficulty of being without constitutional

authority to prosecute an act of war." Pressure was exerted on the neutrals
to prohibit all trade with the Soviet Government as a supplement to the
State Department's "refusal to issue licenses for shipments to Soviet Russia." The British summarized the situation with delicate understatement:
"The United States Government made a distinction between fighting Russia and being at war with Russia." [110]

But though he frankly admitted that the anti-Soviet forces "could
be broken down at any time by our failure to support them," Wilson declined to risk the destruction of Kolchak in return for guarantees of a
more liberal policy on the admiral's part. The Soviets, the President
added, were "perfectly correct in claiming that the Allies were supporting
Kolchak and Denikin, and not putting pressure on them to stop fighting."
Nor, he might have added, to force them to change policies that gave the
Bolsheviks "increasing popular support as Kolchak's regime disclosed to
the people its real nature and purpose." To be sure, the President had
"misgivings" about the admiral's politics and even suggested economic
coercion to change them. He accepted, however, Kolchak's assurances that
all was well in Siberia as "a very good proclamation." Not recognition,
assuredly, but a satisfactory answer to a query made to specify "certain
conditions under which they would continue to send supplies and munitions
to the anti-Bolshevik forces." [111]

The move satisfied the articulate anti-Bolsheviks in the United States
but provoked the resignation of two advisors, historian Samuel Eliot Morrison and economist Adolf A. Berle, Jr., who were "fundamentally opposed" to Wilson's Russian policy. Little affected, Wilson released shipping
space to the counter-revolutionaries in the South—whose ultimate defeat,
wrote an American agent, was due to their failure "to win active support of
the people"—and approved further aid to Kolchak. The House of Morgan
supplied the funds with which the admiral bought locomotives, ammunition, and other supplies.

The President offered "no objection" when a combination of the
Equitable Trust, the National City Bank, and English firms negotiated
a large loan to finance the anti-Bolshevik forces. Their fears as to repay-
ment—the agreement was not completed until late 1919—were no doubt
calmed by word from the State Department that the United States was
"committed to support Kolchak." Washington's bet on the admiral was
never collected. The Administration was deeply disappointed. "I wish you
to know," Lansing explained to Kennan, "that it was not lack of sympathy which prevented the employment of a large active force in Siberia.
. . . We were bound hand and foot by the circumstances." [112]

Herbert Hoover's performance against the Bolsheviks was somewhat
more successful than that of the formal diplomats. Whether the nationalization of the Ural mining properties in which he held a large interest con-

tributed to his deep antagonism to the Soviets is an unknown factor, but Hoover's role in the anti-Soviet campaign left little doubt of his hatred of Moscow. Representatives of the firm, which grossed profits of 6,000,000 rubles in 1916, actively supported Kolchak in Siberia, but the American Food Administrator made his move with reference to affairs in Hungary.[113] One who judged Bolshevism "utter foolishness as a basis of economic development," the former engineer thought the Soviet Government would "fall of its own weight"—but he was not averse to the manipulation of food supplies to speed the inevitable.[114]

Particularly in cases where certainty was so slow afoot—as in the case of Bela Kun's Bolshevik Government in Hungary. Bela Kun's persistent clutch on power posed a difficult problem for the Big Four. He obeyed their ultimatum to cease military operations—and benefited by the rise in national sentiment that accompanied later attacks by Rumania. When the economic blockade maintained by the Allies failed to break his government, the situation became especially critical in view of the general unrest in Central Europe. On July 1, 1919, Hoover reviewed the crisis. Normal commerce on the Danube, he explained, was "one of the chief clues to settling the entire Central European problem." To remove the blockade, however, was "impossible with Bela Kun in power at Budapest." The Big Four, Hoover summarized, "would either have to negotiate with Bela Kun or throw him out by force of arms." British and American economic advisors favored the latter option and Hoover was "convinced that the two French divisions at present in the southeast of Europe were fully capable of accomplishing this act." [115]

Even though he acknowledged that Bela Kun "had, by careful redistribution, managed to feed the population tolerably well . . . [and] had saved the Allied and Associated Powers considerable expenditure" despite the blockade, Hoover viewed the Hungarian Bolshevik "as an economic danger to the rest of Europe." While certain American representatives thought force was the "only remedy," Hoover disliked the idea of French authority in Budapest and engineered the non-violent overthrow of Bela Kun. The plan, naturally enough, involved Hoover's food relief agent in Hungary, one Captain T. T. C. Gregory, who co-operated with his British counterpart. Involved negotiations with anti-Kun forces in Hungary and considerable discussion in Paris evolved an elaborate scheme—a coup against Bela Kun would be timed to coincide with a public announcement that the Allies would welcome a non-Bolshevik government. Peace negotiations, free commerce on the Danube, and an end to the blockade would be promised to the new government.[116]

The Big Five approved the plan on July 26, 1919, and the coup was successful. Bela Kun's defeat moved Hoover to recommend "a relaxation of the blockade, the opening of the Danube, and the supply of foodstuffs to

Hungary." But only if the new government did "what the Council wished." The final victory of an extremely conservative group in Hungary was not, however, held to be a danger to the economic life of Central Europe. Hoover's antagonism toward Moscow was by no means mitigated. He later aided the unsuccessful White attack on Petrograd prior to the collapse of intervention in 1920.[117] Then, from his position as Secretary of Commerce under Presidents Warren G. Harding and Calvin Coolidge, Hoover joined Secretary of State Charles Evans Hughes in efforts to prevent the consolidation of the Soviet Government.

This shift in the character of America's opposition to diplomatic and economic measures was the consequence of the failure of armed intervention. Kolchak's collapse again posed the old dilemma: fight an open war against Moscow or withdraw. Though John Stevens of the Inter-Allied Railroad Administration warned that a retreat would give Japan the fruits of the world war in the Far East, Washington had little choice but to order General Graves to evacuate his forces. The Robins group sparked the blast of opposition—both in Congress and across the nation—that helped move the Administration to a policy of withdrawal. But the parents and close friends of American soldiers began to protest vigorously in the summer of 1919. Most important was Secretary of War Baker's decision that evacuation was a "military necessity." Baker's view was crucial for the simple reason that neither Bainbridge Colby, the new Secretary of State, nor his assistants would have abandoned Kolchak unless overruled.

Colby, who believed in the open door as a technique of American overseas expansion, left little doubt as to Washington's bitter hostility toward Moscow when he reassured the Polish Government that the United States "strongly recoils" from recognition of the Soviets. Washington refused to exert strong pressure on Poland to accept the Bolshevik peace proposals of early spring, 1920, but did give a "good deal of assistance" to Warsaw from the time the Soviets began to drive the Poles out of Russia. Colby did not want a second "advance into Russia," as he thought a second Polish invasion would create further "undeserved support to the Bolshevik regime." But the Secretary made clear his "hope" that the Soviets would "soon" collapse. His was a policy, Colby later admitted, predicated upon the assumption "that Russia was an enemy state." From the promise of Wilson's speech of January 16, 1919, to the reality of Colby's note of August 10, 1920, was the measure of the failure of American policy toward Russia.[118]

Unlike Wilson, Robins refused to abandon the ideal. "I would never expect, sirs," Robins explained to hostile senators who sought to label him a Bolshevik, "to suppress the desire for a better human life . . . no matter how ill founded in political fact and political experience, with force. The only answer for the desire for a better human life is a better human life."

Membership in the Republican party offered no safety in the Red scare, as Robins soon learned. The subject of "a rather extended file" in the War Department's Division of Intelligence and also shadowed by agents of the Federal Bureau of Investigation, Robins realized that public opposition to the Wilson-Colby policy was of little effect. His conclusion was verified by a friend who discussed the wisdom of such intransigence with the Secretary. "For about two hours," the informant wrote, "he denounced Russia with a wealth of expression I have never seen equaled." [119]

Robins retreated to backstage politics. With William Boyce Thompson and Will Hays, Robins went to work to secure the Republican presidential nomination for Senator Hi Johnson. When the deadlock between General Leonard Wood, Governor Frank Lowden, and Johnson resulted in adjournment, Robins made his decisive move. Aware that Philander Knox was a sick man, Robins suggested to Boies Penrose—Pennsylvania politician who exerted tremendous influence in the party—that they compromise on a Knox-Johnson ticket. Penrose agreed, and Robins hurried off to get Johnson's approval. The senator, however, was not interested; and on the ninth ballot Warren G. Harding was nominated. Thoroughly disgusted, Robins told Hays he would not participate in the campaign and boarded a train for the East.[120]

Hays belatedly realized that Robins meant business. Not until Thompson personally intervened did Robins agree to reconsider his decision to "sit this one out." He held several long conferences with Harding and on the basis of a strictly *quid pro quo* agreement Robins finally entered the field. In return for Robins' support, Harding agreed to veto every attempt to repeal the La Follette Seaman's Act; to work for better labor conditions in the steel industry; and to reopen the entire question of American policy toward Soviet Russia. The understanding was not, naturally enough, general knowledge; but the old-line Progressives knew that something was afoot. Edward A. Ross, the sociologist, was one, thought Robins, who "had been had," and expressed disappointment. But Robins, searching for some means to turn up the dragon's teeth, made the best horse trade he could negotiate.[121]

Other forces, soon to link up with the Robins group, meanwhile effected the end of the embargo on trade with Russia. Though other members of the business community who opposed economic relations with the Soviet Union retained control of the American-Russian Chamber of Commerce for the time being, the pro-trade group, strengthened by some 100 exporters of heavy machinery, exerted enough pressure to force the State Department to take the first steps toward modifying the restrictions that "stood in the way of trade and communication with Soviet Russia." [122] When these economic interests joined forces with the political strength represented by Borah and Robins, the advocates of recognition were ready to challenge Hughes and Hoover.

Yet the course of American-Russian relations from 1920 to 1933 was not to be without irony. For the inability of President Herbert Hoover—who thought the Soviet economic system was "utter foolishness"—to meet either the economic problems of the depression of 1929 or the Manchurian crisis of 1931 played a vital role in the ultimate recognition of Moscow. A closer tie with the Soviet Union was sought for two reasons: to help save American capitalism and as a result of Washington's final awareness that Japan could not be stopped in Asia without Moscow's assistance.

7

☆

THE LONG, LEAN YEARS

Europe cannot recover its economic stability until Russia returns to production. . . . That requires the abandonment of their present economic system.

Secretary of Commerce Herbert Hoover,
March 21, 1921

So long as you have a hundred and fifty million people outlawed in a sense, it necessarily follows that you cannot have peace.

United States Senator William E. Borah,
October 10, 1925

☆☆

The three Republican administrations that succeeded President Woodrow Wilson are generally labeled isolationist, but for those in quest of an understanding of American foreign relations during those years the term is dangerously misleading. Foreign policy under Presidents Warren G. Harding, Calvin Coolidge, and Herbert Hoover was consistent in active intervention designed to preserve and extend American influence abroad. In two vital areas, moreover, the concept of a sharp shift in policy after the inauguration of Harding is not validated by the record. Both Wilson and his successors used—and sought to refine—two tools forged long before their advent to the White House: the open door as a technique of economic penetration and political influence, and opposition to Russia in the Near and Far East. Coincident with his plans for the League of Nations, Wilson reorganized the consortium to further American influence in Manchuria and China. And it was under Wilson—not Harding—that the policy of bitter antagonism toward Soviet Russia was formulated and implemented.

During the years of Republican rule this opposition continued to be grounded in economic and social considerations. The increased emphasis that came to be placed on the issue of propaganda was no more than a new

177

expression of the basic fear and opposition. Certainly Secretaries of State Charles Evans Hughes, Frank B. Kellogg, and Henry L. Stimson entertained few illusions as to the reality of interference—either abortive or successful—in the domestic affairs of other states. Mexico, Nicaragua, and China offered ample evidence that Washington's concern was not the principle of intervention but rather the economic and political character of the interference. As in the years of Wilson's administration, this antagonism toward Moscow not only conditioned the form of efforts to regain lost ground in Asia, but also exerted an important influence on relations with Europe.

The policy of non-recognition with respect to Soviet Russia was implemented in three principal areas: relations with China and Japan, involvement in the Near and Middle East, and in trade relations with the Soviets. The myth of isolation is seen to be somewhat less than unassailable when viewed in the light of American activity in the Far East; at the conferences of Genoa, the Hague, and Lausanne; and in the world struggle for oil. Likewise, American policy in these instances reflected the desire to prevent the consolidation of the Soviet state. Washington's attempt to proscribe further Japanese expansion—a concern primarily focused on control of the Chinese Eastern Railway and associated rights of exploitation—offers an excellent example of the complications involved in any effort to pursue both goals at once.

Forced to formulate foreign policy within the confines of a program of broad economic retrenchment, Great Britain offered little concrete assistance in Asia. Nor did France, anxious to preserve her own interest, and principal, in the Chinese Eastern, provide major support. In these circumstances Washington's animosity toward Moscow was the critical weakness in any plan designed to hamstring Japan. As for concern in China's future, Washington's vigorous opposition to Peking's efforts to weaken the structure of extraterritoriality and foreign rights further dimmed any illusions that perchance survived the days of Taft and Wilson.

Nor did Secretary Hughes leave any doubts as to the intensity of his anti-Sovietism during the international conferences called to deal with European problems. With the aid, explicit direction, and corrective advice supplied by various economic interests and Secretary of Commerce Hoover, the Secretary of State sought to extend the open door to Russia and to use economic pressure to effect a fundamental change in the economic structure of the Soviet Union. Despite these efforts, Soviet-American trade continued to expand and influenced the immediate future of American-Russian relations. For in this area came the consolidation of forces which prepared the way for the ultimate recognition of the Soviet Union in 1933.

From 1920 through 1923 there was little co-ordination between the economic groups that engaged in trade with Russia and the small circle of men who viewed recognition as the first step toward a collaboration that could secure world peace. Immediate economic problems of the postwar recession motivated a segment of both capital and labor to demand regularized trade with Russia as early as 1920, but their campaign was unsuccessful. And by 1922 the leadership of the American Federation of Labor squashed the labor agitation for recognition. Certain financial and industrial circles, and the cotton exporters, however, retained their interest in closer economic relations. Late in 1923 Alexander Gumberg began to organize these groups as a cohesive force for recognition. From the co-ordination of his efforts with those of Raymond Robins and Senator Borah—aided, to some degree, by the activities of Louis Fischer, Walter Duranty, and other journalists—came the strength behind the senator's long fight for recognition.

There was never, to be sure, an exact community of interest between the Borah group and the economic forces. Save for a few exceptions the latter were concerned either with short-term economic gain or the creation of a relatively small but steady return on investment. Gumberg, Borah, and Robins, while quite conscious that trade with Russia would exert a stabilizing influence on the American economy, were primarily concerned to effect collaboration to preserve the peace. But though the crash of 1929 and the failure of Washington's go-it-alone policy to restrain Japan greatly facilitated co-operation between the two groups, President Herbert Hoover declined to modify his extreme hostility toward the Soviet Union. As a result, Washington did not respond to Moscow's steady overtures for a *rapprochement* until November, 1933. Hoover's inflexibility was but the final expression of an antagonism toward Moscow that defeated the attempt to secure recognition in 1921.

Though the Supreme Allied Economic Council ostensibly removed the embargo on trade with Moscow on January 16, 1920, the State and Treasury Deparments co-operated to render the formal action quite meaningless. International trade requires credit and shipping space—neither of which was immediately authorized by Washington. The Soviets were likewise refused permission to use gold in payment for goods purchased in the United States. This ruling, handed down as a unanimous decision by State and Treasury, set the pattern for many years. That shipping space became available did not alter the fact that later Soviet attempts to float bond issues or deposit bullion on account were frustrated with monotonous regularity.[1]

Washington based the decision on the grounds that both bonds and gold were stolen property—the product of illegal decrees of confiscation and repudiation—a rationalization that overlooked the long record of similar repudiation throughout the world, including the United States. At one time Moscow, apparently wearied of this omission of certain aspects of economic history, satirically inquired if the victorious North gave "compensation to the landlords of the southern states for the liberation of their slaves." [2] Washington's concern for pre-1917 property rights, however, was to plague American-Russian relations for many years.

While the Russian-American Chamber of Commerce, now headed by former Secretary of Commerce Redfield, the Morgan-sponsored committee to protect American investments in pre-Soviet Russia, and other groups supported the Department's program of economic restrictions, a small group of Americans continued its campaign to force Washington to relax the regulations.[3] Though primarily an organization of small industrialists and exporters, the American Commercial Association to Promote Trade with Russia did include the Lehigh Machine Company and was supported by William Boyce Thompson. Despite their pressure, and Moscow's promise of a "gigantic role" in the "reconstruction of Russian economic life," Washington refused to modify the restrictions.[4] Departmental representatives who observed that intervention "accomplished nothing," that Russia was "a power whose good will will be invaluable and with whom it would be wise to be friends," and that reconstruction was "impossible until Russia is opened to trade" were also ineffective.[5] Basically the economic restrictions were but one aspect of the avowed policy of antagonism; but a supporting factor was the consideration that large firms were either opposed or indifferent to trade prospects *immediately* after the war.

The postwar recession of 1921 dramatically altered both the character and the intensity of the demands to facilitate trade with Russia. "Thousands of men and women in this country are out of work," wrote the Erie Central Labor Union on January 16, 1921, in one of the earliest of an extensive number of demands that Washington modify its intransigence. The International Association of Machinists bluntly advised the Department that industry was "stagnated"; an interpretation verified by, among others, various locals of the Bakery and Confectionery Workers, the Brotherhood of Railway Clerks, Station Employees and Freight Handlers, the United Brotherhood of Carpenters and Joiners of America, and the Madison, Wisconsin, Federation of Labor—all of whom supported the argument, advanced by many branches of the United Mine Workers, that the "opening of trade relations with Russia would materially relieve the situation." [6]

These numerous petitions were not the product of a Bolshevik conspiracy. Unless, of course, Moscow is to be held responsible for the recession. As George W. Morris, a manufacturer of Christmas stockings phrased the complaint, business was "on the blink" and he wanted a "crack at the Russian market right away." His was a concern and an interest shared by the Baldwin Locomotive Works, the financial house of Kuhn, Loeb and

Company, and the foreign trade division of General Electric. The Department of State could hardly claim the pressure as coming from secondary or tainted sources. But the short-lived congressional inquiry that was launched did not effect a change of policy.[7]

Several groups supported Washington's refusal to open the credit channels. The Russian-American Chamber of Commerce, though still interested in "entrance into Russia" via Siberia, campaigned ceaselessly against trade. Other financial and industrial firms supported the argument that the Soviets had nothing to export.[8] Washington's most vocal and energetic assistance, however, came from the top leadership of the American Federation of Labor. Opposition to the Soviet Union was no new departure for Samuel Gompers or John Spargo, who retained his important position in the National Civic Federation; but Gompers may well have been especially upset when a local of his own Cigar Makers' Union joined the campaign for trade relations. Coupled with the current challenge to his leadership of American labor, Gompers saw in labor's militancy a trend to be opposed. On March 15, 1921, he asked Secretary Hughes for help in the matter—his specific request was a formal explanation of Washington's opposition to trade relations and recognition.[9]

Well aware that he needed a rationalization for his failure to respond to the pro-trade resolutions that continued to reach the Department in "some numbers," Hughes welcomed the inquiry from Gompers. Two other considerations also bothered Hughes. Herbert Hoover, now Secretary of Commerce, was perplexed by the conflict between his antagonism to the Soviets and his broad program for the expansion of American foreign trade. He was particularly worried by the news of a prospective trade treaty between London and Moscow. For if the pact went through, Hoover fretted, it would be "very unfair" to deny Americans the right to take Soviet gold in payment for exports.[10] Hoover's doubt was not modified by the Soviet's direct appeal for the "speedy establishment of friendly relations" that came less than a week later.

Soviet spokesman Maxim Litvinov noted that Moscow was "entirely absorbed in the work of internal reconstruction" and asked Washington to consider "the interests of both peoples which imperatively demand that the wall existing between them should be removed." Hughes used the note as a pretext for a belligerent policy statement. But the Secretary of State was a bit slow to respond, and Hoover was the first to advise Litvinov that negotiations could be opened only after the Soviets announced the "abandonment of their present economic system." Four days later Hughes agreed that no discussions could take place until there was "convincing evidence" that "fundamental changes" had been effected in the economic structure of the Soviet Union. The Secretary's later letter to Gompers was an anticlimax. Neither Gompers nor Spargo was chagrined, however, and used both statements in their campaign against recognition.[11] For its part, the State Department continued to answer only those letters that supported official policy.[12]

The Hughes-Hoover policy did not, quite obviously, square with Harding's campaign promises to Robins, and the latter arranged an early interview with the President to remind him of certain obligations. Harding, clearly in tow behind his two Secretaries, referred Robins to Hughes. The Secretary was completely indifferent to Robins' arguments and restated— in more vehement language—his public declarations with reference to private property. Robins recalls that Hughes's extreme position moved him to reply in kind. "Mr. Secretary," he shot back, "this interview reminds me of a story I heard in law school. If you've got the law, you pound it into the judge. If you've got the facts, you pound them into the jury. But if you've got neither, then you pound hell out of the table. Mr. Secretary, that's exactly what you're doing," and Robins walked out.[13]

The incident apparently upset Harding, for he sought to reach a compromise with Robins. Acting through Hoover, the President asked Robins to accept a policy of watchful waiting for the next months. But the interview with Hoover was merely the second scene of the act that opened at the State Department, and Robins turned aside in disgust. This decision, coupled with the fact that the domestic market began to spark recovery from the recession, gave Hughes and Hoover a clear field for maneuver. "Bitter attacks," summarized a White House memorandum of February 2, 1922, "have ceased." [14]

Robins did not actually abandon the battle for recognition, but Senator Borah's rear-guard action in the Senate was not a serious challenge to Hughes's supremacy. Borah saw an opening when White General Gregory Semenov—temporarily abandoned by the Japanese—arrived in Washington in April, 1922, to seek funds for further counter-revolutionary activity. Though militant in his anti-Sovietism, Semenov's record of violence against American troops in Siberia moved the American Legion, despite full sympathy with Hughes and Hoover, to attack the General vigorously. This turn of events prompted Borah to fire a salvo at the entire emigree organization centered around Boris Bakhmeteff, still accredited as Russian Ambassador by the State Department.

Semenov's unsavory character and Bakhmeteff's handling of the funds advanced to the Provisional Government gave Borah a large target, and for a short period his barrage caused considerable anxiety in official quarters. But Bakhmeteff's well-timed resignation forestalled a full-scale investigation of American policy and Borah was unable to shift attention to the more fundamental questions involved. The affair was of minor importance.

Washington had no thought to modify its opposition to Moscow. "Property rights," reiterated Hoover in mid-May, 1922, "are not a fetish. . . . Unless there can be assurance of the security of these rights of foreigners, there can be no process of exchange of goods or investment of savings." [15]

Rigid adherence to this blunt policy statement conditioned American action in no less than six series of international negotiations from mid-1921 to the end of 1923. At no time, however, did American action based on this principle effect the desired goal of modifying the Soviet economic system. Rather did this so-called isolationist policy seriously jeopardize any chance to solve international problems without recourse to war. That the end product was the near isolation of the United States has perhaps been responsible for the use of the term, but the character of Washington's policy was actually unilateral intervention.

Failure was nowhere more dramatically highlighted than in the Far East. In that area Hughes continued the Wilsonian attempt to ride three horses at once: anti-Sovietism, the restriction of Japanese expansion, and the consolidation of American control of the Chinese Eastern Railway. The first move in this effort was an attempt to use the consortium to purchase the railroad. London suggested the idea as a technique helpful "in controlling Japan, stabilizing China, limiting the Bolshevik menace, and publicly proclaiming the first step of the consortium to be of broad international value." [16]

Washington approved the plan because of the chance to have London exert influence on France, a line-up that could perhaps effect "such pressure as might induce" Japan to accept a minority position in the consortium.[17] But without the House of Morgan to provide the necessary cash the plan was impossible of execution, and the Department's strenuous efforts failed to modify Thomas Lamont's refusal to undertake the project without Japanese approval. Tokyo's lifeline ran from the Yokohama Specie Bank to the House of Morgan and on to the Department of State. Even had Lamont retained his earlier enthusiasm for an American-Soviet bloc in the Far East, however, the Japanese hardly could have been expected to blunder into such a well-marked trap. Nor did the French, who held back to push plans to refinance the railroad through a reorganized Russo-Asiatic Bank, support the projected coup. Neither was Paris anxious to pay her share of the cost required to transport the ill-fated Czech forces across Russia and Manchuria. "We seem," admitted a departmental advisor late in 1920, "to be left out in the cold." [18]

Though Hughes agreed that he was "frankly very close to being defeated in this matter," the Secretary made one last effort. The House of Morgan seemed to modify its opposition on August 2, 1921, but three weeks later the organization revealed the preconditions for its opposition to Japan.

Only if the Chinese would "be prepared to pledge the surplus revenues of all the Government Railroads in China, over and above the charges on the bonds issued for railway construction"—this to guarantee the Chinese Eastern loan—would the House of Morgan proceed.[19] The demand was so severe that Hughes dared not press Peking for acceptance—a development that forced the Secretary of State to consider an alternative to direct purchase of the line.

But neither Hughes nor his successors, including those who held the office in the decade of the thirties, were men without a choice. There were options available: firm collaboration with either China or Soviet Russia, or the formation of a multi-nation entente founded on a *rapprochement* with Moscow. But American policy—based on the fundamental aim to extend if possible, and preserve at all costs, the economic and political influence of the moment—could not be cut to fit co-operation with revolutionary governments in either Peking or Moscow. As a result the Washington Conference, an attempt to implement the third line of action so revised to exclude Russia, failed in execution—though the formal collapse of the effort was delayed for more than a decade. Contrary to the view that antagonism to Moscow was "secondary" to other aspects of Washington's Far Eastern policy until 1933, the determination to prevent the consolidation of the Soviet state was the very source of the failure of that policy.[20]

Moscow's chief concern was to overcome this antagonism in order to erect a stout barricade against Tokyo's further expansion. The United States, *Izvestia* pointed out on December 6, 1921, is the "principal force in the world." Lenin's earlier judgment that survival and recovery depended on "systematically utilizing this rivalry" between Tokyo and Washington was never modified. "All possible means will have to be employed," *Izvestia* re-emphasized, "somehow or other to come to an understanding with the United States." [21] Moscow was to hue to the same line—periodic threats of alliance with Japan not withstanding—until late in 1939.

Yet in view of Trotsky's public admission that the "inner soundness of the American bourgeoisie is still almost intact," Moscow's analysis was most un-Marxian.[22] *Izvestia*'s curious phrase of equivocation—"somehow or other"—admits as much. Within the Soviets' preferred system of theoretical analysis the fact of capitalist strength postulated the improbability of concessions on the part of Washington: an improbability verified by the public statements and official acts of Secretaries Hughes and Hoover. But the explanation of Lenin's insistence on the point is easily understood. Even the most romantic view, or theoretically pure analysis, of Soviet ability to direct the revolutionary spirit in China offered them little solace, for the fact of industrial weakness in both Russia and China was openly acknowledged. Alignment with the United States remained, therefore, the most practical defense against Japan. In Moscow's steady determination to effect collaboration with Washington is revealed the most significant effort to forestall Marxist inevitability in Soviet history.

As a solution to their dilemma the Soviets sought safety within a policy of co-existence—a revision of Marxism that placed primary emphasis on the nation-state.[23] The essence of co-existence was the new role assigned to extra-Russian centers of communism. Their principal function became not the seizure of power but the protection of the Soviet state—a permanent left jab in the face of capitalism and other nation-states. To be sure, if local conditions appeared to warrant an attempted coup, no restraint was offered; *but in no instance did the Soviet Union risk its own existence to insure the outcome of such a revolution.* For the non-Soviet world the significance of the policy became the degree of control theoretically abandoned by the Soviets to other states. Theirs became the option to rectify—or ignore—the situation that leads men to accept the dictatorship of the proletariat as the only means of salvation. From its very inception the focus of the policy of co-existence became the United States.

In 1921 the implementation of the policy took the form of a continued effort to effect some degree of co-ordination with Washington and at the same time strengthen relations with China. After the earlier overtures to Washington that culminated in Litvinov's appeal of March, 1921, Moscow tried to combine the need for economic aid and the necessity to end Japan's occupation of the Maritime Provinces through a program of concessions granted to American exploiters. The first grant went to Washington B. Vanderlip in late 1920. That Moscow confused this man with Frank A. Vanderlip of the House of Morgan is certain, but the Soviets entertained no doubts as to the purpose of the contract for the development of Kamchatka.

"Legally," Lenin pointed out, "Kamchatka belongs to us, but in fact has been grabbed by Japan. Should we offer Kamchatka to America, it is clear we will win." [24] Vanderlip, who actually represented an investment group composed of the Los Angeles *Times,* E. L. Doheny, the Union Oil Company, and a California bank and insurance company, wanted a grant to exploit natural resources. But his rights were conditional on a "binding agreement" between Washington and Moscow—an alignment that did not materialize.[25] Meanwhile the Japanese extended their area of intervention to include the northern half of Sakhalin Island and at the same time sought to seize control of the Far Eastern Republic centered in Chita, Siberia. Tokyo anticipated that control of this republic—which rose on the shambles of the Allied-supported White governments—would legitimatize her occupation of the entire area.[26] Together with the failure of the scheme to buy the Chinese Eastern, these Japanese gains forced Washington to formulate a new technique of opposition to Tokyo.

Moscow, to be sure, was quite ready to maintain the myth of the republic's independence—privately it was deemed a "makeshift creation" —if the camouflage would enable Washington to save face. First came a request for trade negotiations; but as Tokyo strengthened her control over Semenov's vanishing government, the Far Eastern Republic openly asked a "helping hand." [27] State Department advisors, acutely aware of Japan's gains, recommended the dispatch of agents to open negotiations with the buffer state. After some delay Hughes agreed, but specified that the men were sent "solely to secure information." The Secretary's hesitance was reflected in the Department's reaction to another warning from Charles Smith of the Inter-Allied Technical Committee that an understanding with Moscow offered the only effective answer to Japan's expansion. "It is time," judged a policy advisor, "that Smith is told to attend to his own business." [28]

Yet Tokyo gave no indication that her troops would be evacuated— to the contrary, her position was buttressed by the old alliance of 1902 with England. London was not only aware of Washington's desire to destroy this treaty, but there was considerable sympathy for the move in Great Britain. The fact that Lloyd George did not feel able to "withstand importunate inquiries" on the issue moved Britain to suggest that "all essential matters" in the Far East be discussed in conjunction with Washington's desire—the "question is vital here"—to effect a general reduction of armaments. Hughes accepted the proposal only to meet immediate opposition from Japan and the Soviet Union, to whom no invitation was extended. [29]

Japan's objection was obvious: she saw the conference as a technique designed by Washington and London to achieve her own isolation. Just as clearly, the Soviets protested the assumption that they would be replaced in the near future. Nor did they miss the implication that exclusion was a technique designed to facilitate that hope and expectancy. Chicherin bluntly told Hughes that "in no case" could he agree with the assumption registered a militant protest against "exclusion" from any discussion of Russia's interests as a Far Eastern power, and, for that reason, reserved "freedom of action in all circumstances." [30] Washington ignored Moscow's note and outflanked Tokyo with the announcement that all nations had accepted the invitation.

Tokyo countered with energetic efforts to force China to accept Japanese predominance in Siberia prior to the date set for the conference. Hughes became progressively more worried as he watched Japan tighten up the screws, but still hesitated to strengthen his ties with the Far Eastern Republic. Only repeated warnings from American representatives in the Far East convinced the Secretary that the move was "the only way to prevent cession [of] administrative or territorial rights to Japan." Finally, on October 4, 1921, Washington agreed to grant visas to a delegation from the republic for "commercial purposes." [31] The irony was undoubtedly unintentional, but that was the exact reason for the decision—only the purposes involved were those of the United States with regard to the Chinese Eastern and the hoped-for trade with a non-Soviet Russia. Other aspects of the struggle with Japan were given far more verbal and public attention during the conference, but the Chinese Eastern Railway was constantly in mind.

Though actual references to the issue were few in number—and composed but a tiny percentage of the written record—the conflict between Washington and Tokyo was clearly revealed. No less significant was the attitude adopted toward China. Hughes's problem was infinitely difficult: to effect the withdrawal of Japanese troops from Siberia yet at the same time prevent Peking from taking an active share in control of the railroad —either singly or through agreement with Moscow. To secure Japanese withdrawal was by far the easier task. From the first Hughes had London's support in his maneuver to force Tokyo to validate her written assurances of evacuation. Both the United States and Britain opposed the rising economic power of Japan in Asia; the former in anticipation of final penetration and the latter in terms of protection for existing investments. Japan's only real chance to sabotage the Far Eastern discussions was to capitalize on the indecision of France. Though not a major factor in the final outcome, Hughes's decision to admit Chita's representatives to the United States did strengthen his position.

Their very presence of necessity kept Japan from discounting all possibility of an understanding between Hughes and Chicherin; and Chita's expertly timed exposé of a purported agreement between Paris and Tokyo to continue intervention did not enhance the latter's chance to split her former allies. [32] But Japan's own militance was the paramount factor in France's final decision to support London and Washington. Two other considerations also contributed to the first-round victory scored by Hughes. Chita's skillful negotiations at the Dairen Conference not only gave Washington time to maneuver, but also helped provide proper circumstances for the Japanese business community to make known the fact that it "was tired of the expensive and unprofitable intervention on the continent." [33] By the skillful exploitation of auspicious circumstances Hughes achieved his first objective—Japan's unequivocal commitment to withdraw from Siberia.

But the Secretary did not fare so well in the attempt to retain control of the Chinese Eastern. With Japan effectively checked, Hughes sought to reconstitute the old Allied Technical Board—with Tokyo still included as a member—as a new instrument for the same purpose. The gap between a blunt admission of the goal and the previous public pronouncements of concern for China's integrity was too great, however, to allow direct action. Particularly was this the case in view of China's determination to reassert her rights under the old treaty of 1896 that provided for joint Sino-Russian control. Peking took the first step in this direction by concluding a new treaty with the Russo-Asiatic Bank, legal owner of the line. China was to take "supreme control" of the railway until final arrangements were concluded with a Russian government "recognized by China." [34]

By this action China undermined Washington's entire plan. For the power of recognition gave Peking the means to revive the treaty of 1896 and thereby end the situation that Hughes sought to use to justify the continued existence of the Allied Technical Committee. The Secretary was caught in a web of his own spinning. Washington's curt refusal to deal with Moscow gave the Soviets complete freedom of maneuver—an opportunity they seized in terms of collaboration with China to frustrate the Secretary's efforts to prevent China's resurgence. Hughes countered with the position: continued hostility toward Moscow while at the same time shifting the label "unstable" from the Soviets to China, whose slow-motion revolution appeared quite active in the postwar years.

"Under existing circumstances and until the situation is more stable," he counseled in December, 1921, the best plan would be a "temporary international conservacy controlled by a board of conservators or body representing the national interests which have furnished the money." Aware that China's "susceptibilities" were already aroused, the Secretary suggested that the police operations along the railway could be confided to the Chinese—but they "would have to be paid (and thereby controlled) by the conservacy." At the same time Washington began to counsel Peking that any arrangements with Moscow would be of "questionable validity." [35] China, however, planned to use the opportunity to regain her own share in the operation of the Chinese Eastern and the Secretary's warnings were ineffective.

Strengthened by the agreement with the Russo-Asiatic Bank, Peking steadfastly refused to acquiesce in the new plan for internationalization proposed by the Technical Sub-Committee on the Chinese Eastern Railway. Under the chairmanship of Elihu Root, who served earlier as Theodore Roosevelt's Secretary of State, the committee first brushed aside Moscow's "special protest" and then formulated a policy quite unacceptable to China. Money for the operation of the line was to be available only "if the funds provided are to be expended under adequate supervision"—a control defined to mean not only economic administration but a police force that would be "paid by and remain under the control of the finance committee." One departmental advisor characterized the plan very neatly—if unintentionally—as "the so-called Allied supervision." [36] For her part, China made "reservations" concerning this majority report. Peking accepted a separate injunction to give "better protection" and to make "more economical use of funds" but refused to initial the Root plan. The other powers, *now joined by Japan,* responded with an open threat—"the right to insist hereafter upon the responsibility of China for performance or non-performance of the obligations toward the foreign stockholders, bondholders, and creditors of the Chinese Eastern Railway Company." [37] Washington's concern for the integrity of China appeared to be active only in the absence of an agreement as to the division of the spoils.

These maneuvers for control of the Chinese Eastern offer a revealing insight into the contrast between public declarations and actual policy. From the first attempt to use the Chin-Ai contract as a lever to tip the Chinese Eastern into its own hands, Washington proclaimed the goal to be an open door. All subsequent moves in that direction were further labeled internationalization and described as efforts to aid China. Yet when the policy finally failed—and the railway appeared about to be recaptured by the two original owners—Washington not only sought a guarantee for an investment that could be classified only as risk capital, but even demanded the right to pass on the future management of the property. When China explained her action as one taken to prevent "a limitation of China's sovereignty," moreover, the American representative in Peking calmly replied that "this matter had been decided at Washington adverse to the Chinese view." By the logic of its own policy the United States was forced to view China's effort to reassert her authority along the railway as "not only obdurate but rude," and to claim that the costs of the Allied Technical Board would "constitute an eventual claim against the Railway." [38]

Nor was Washington able to do much more than register claims in the years that followed. One of the aspects of the antagonism to Moscow—determination to preserve private and government property claims—was primarily responsible. For the United States found the same issue at stake in the Chinese Revolution. A strong China could effectively challenge Western overlordship. As Hughes admitted, Peking's policy in the railway issue was "most inopportune as tending to create in the minds of the treaty Powers a doubt as to China's intentions with regard to the observance of its express obligations to foreign interests." [39] This refusal to acknowledge the power of the revolution in Asia left Washington with no option but to oppose the people of Asia. The same elements were at the core of Hughes's refusal to accept Moscow's overtures for collaboration against Japan.

Fully aware of her inability to fend off Japan alone, the Soviet Union continued to seek alignment with Washington. That fact became apparent in the concessions granted Henry Ford Sinclair for the exploitation of oil reserves in the Japanese-occupied northern half of Sakhalin; and in a similar concession given Charles Smith for development of the Amur River Basin. Quite aware of Sinclair's influence with President Harding, Moscow made the concession conditional upon a definite agreement with Washington. Likewise, the Soviets took particular care to point up Smith's view that the "object of Japan is to obtain complete control in the Far East, from Peking to Urga, and from Baikal to the mouth of the Amur." In open support of Radek's open bid for common action, Litvinov approached the banking firm of Dillon, Reed and Company with a concession to run Russia's share in the Chinese Eastern. As the Department of State privately admitted, "the Soviets have always been most anxious to establish relations with the American Government." [40]

But Washington ignored the obvious. Hughes, usually most co-operative in the protection of American investments abroad, refused to help Sinclair when the Japanese moved in on his concession. Nor was any attempt made to encourage Smith, probe the offer to Dillon, Reed, or take advantage of other overtures from Moscow. The Secretary's concern for "foreign interests" also proscribed any major attempt to aid the forces of the Chinese Revolution. The Soviets, however, were encouraged by the valid revolutionary situation in Asia. Not only did the conditions—landlords and foreign powers—facilitate the rise of Marxist leadership, but in that fact Moscow saw an opportunity partially to counterbalance Washington's rebuffs. Quite understandable, then, was the Soviet move to reinvigorate the group around Sun Yat-sen, who hesitated to compromise with the reactionary elements around Yuan Shih-kai—the leader with whom the consortium had earlier sought agreement.[41]

Moscow's interest came at a critical moment for Sun, whose accomplishments did not include the practical art of revolutionary organization. Though he rejected communism, Sun did accept Soviet leadership in that area of the movement's activity. By the end of 1923 Michael Borodin was well established as a tactical leader.[42] While he applied the principle of tight, disciplined organization to Sun's following—with the aid of Chinese Communists as well as Koumintang leaders—Moscow made a formal overture to negotiate all outstanding issues. In 1919 and 1920 the Soviets issued sweeping declarations renouncing Russian rights in China, but by November, 1922, the first flush of revolutionary enthusiasm was not only gone—Japan still occupied Manchuria. Both considerations were reflected in Moscow's new distinction between the "predatory" interests of the Tsars and those of a "local and just" nature based on the fact of a common border.[43]

This modification was far less important than the extension of Soviet influence in Mongolia—the issue over which negotiations collapsed late in 1922. Neither side considered the break to be final, and the talks were resumed in mid-1923.[44] Washington's fears, both for the future of the Chinese Eastern and with regard to Soviet influence in China, were not eased by an agreement that "the future of the Chinese Eastern Railway shall be determined by the U.S.S.R. and . . . China, to the exclusion of any third parties or party." Two months later this preliminary declaration was followed by Chinese recognition of the Soviet Union and a provisional plan for management of the railway. Washington's constant insistence that Peking observe the treaty of 1896 backfired, for the terms of the new treaty, May 31, 1924, assured Moscow a "preponderant influence" in the affairs of the railway and associated economic interests in North Manchuria.[45]

American diplomacy had come full circle from 1904. A weak China and Russia controlled a vital railway in the face of a militant Japan. Once again Moscow sought a defensive entente against the latter. Washington's initiative was even greater than before, for London was now, by necessity to be sure, a junior partner in the Far East. But there were two new factors: Moscow's economics and Peking's strengthened nationalism— Washington's reaction to which would determine the pattern of Asia's future. To neither challenge did the United States respond until too late. Basic aspects of that failure were nowhere more sharply outlined than in American policy toward the Soviets in Europe. Nor does any phase of Washington's policy more dramatically reveal the true character of what has been labeled isolation, but what was in reality an effort to exercise dominant power within a broad framework of freedom without responsibility.

For neither consciously nor unconsciously did the policy makers of the United States withdraw from the world during the years between World War I and World War II. Indeed, the Republican party—generally viewed as the political vehicle of the isolationists—initiated two of the more significant international conferences of the period. First came the Washington Conference on Far Eastern Affairs in 1922, designed to destroy the Anglo-Japanese Treaty of 1902 that had caused American Secretaries of State so much difficulty in implementing their own plans to penetrate China and Manchuria—and to extend American influence over the Chinese Eastern Railway. Five years later Washington called the Geneva Disarmament Conference of 1927 in a move to maintain the 5-5-3 ratio of naval power between, respectively, the United States, Great Britain, and Japan—a power ranking established at Washington in 1922–23.

Two of the Republican party's leaders—Charles Evans Hughes and Herbert Hoover—took the lead in pushing American political and economic intervention abroad. Certainly the maneuvers of the United States with relation to the economic conference at Genoa in 1922, the political conference on Near Eastern Affairs at Lausanne in 1923, and the unilateral actions taken in Central and South America cannot be described as withdrawal or isolation. In each of these instances the basic purpose of American policy was to attain certain unilaterally defined goals—economic and political—through the technique of intervention.

A characteristic of Washington's policy thus emerges with considerable clarity: unilateral intervention to preserve or extend the overseas power of the United States. A further aspect of American policy can be seen with equal ease—a refusal, in later years, to accept any burden of responsibility for the consequences, immediate or indirect, of arbitrary policies for the international community. Thus, for example, Washington held China solely accountable for Peking's move toward a *rapprochement* with Moscow in the early 1920s. In this instance the consideration was Washington's unwillingness to acknowledge that efforts to deny China a meaningful share in control of the Chinese Eastern Railway left Peking no other option. Or, in another sense, Washington's persistent claim that negotiations with the Soviet Union over the question of the Tsarist debt were impossible—a claim advanced on the grounds that Moscow declined to accept the American demands and conditions without further discussion.

To be sure, the Republicans held no copyright on this policy designed to push American interests without assuming any responsibility for the consequences. For with the rise of a militantly expansionist Nazi regime in Germany during the decade of the thirties, the Democratic administration of President Franklin Delano Roosevelt followed a similar policy as late as 1939. "Relatively unconcerned with the terms of appeasement so long as they did not touch American interests," write recent students of the period, Roosevelt "hoped for British success, and at the height of the Munich crisis used all his influence to insure further negotiation." A policy, conclude these same observers, "leaving no doubt that American official opinion wished the British success in their efforts, but without prejudging their methods, without taking a stand on any specific issue, without assuming any responsibility." To emphasize: far from isolation, the American policy of these interwar years was one characterized by decisions and actions taken with sole reference to unilaterally determined goals —decisions and actions for the consequences of which Washington disclaimed all responsibility.

Within this framework, therefore, both Secretaries Hughes and Hoover were active interventionists with reference to the Soviet Union. From 1920 to 1924, the years of vigorous diplomacy in the Far East, these men directed several operations that clearly revealed both their general aims and their immediate goals with reference to Moscow. Fundamental to an understanding of the Hughes-Hoover policy toward Russia is a close review of their exchange of letters in the early days of December, 1921. Hoover had just embarked on his energetic campaign to transform the Department of Commerce into a determined agency for the expansion of foreign trade and investment, and it was essential to correlate that program with the plans of the Department of State, for long years the leader in that movement. While Hughes did not consider the possibility of active collaboration with

Russia—as witness his refusal to support Vanderlip, Sinclair, and Smith —the Secretary of State did waver in the matter of indirect trade.

Late in 1921 Hughes advised Hoover that he was "disposed to agree" with a policy recommendation from the Russian Division of the Department of State that proposed the expansion of American foreign trade through the encouragement of German-Soviet trade in American cotton, rubber, and agricultural machinery. "A basis of co-operation with German officials and businessmen," read the memorandum, "should be laid out at once by removing from the German mind misapprehensions as to our friendly disposition, now that peace is signed, and our readiness to encourage indirect trade." [46] Hoover was quick to halt this proposed modification of the long-range plan to effect "fundamental changes" in the Soviet economy.

"I regret," the Secretary of Commerce replied, "that I cannot agree with this program as being in American interest." Well acquainted—from personal as well as official experience—with the upsurge of American penetration of Russia from 1912 to 1917, Hoover did not intend to abandon one of the fruits of victory in the world war—Germany's demise as the dominant foreign economic force in Russia. Quite candid in his admission that "Americans are infinitely more popular in Russia and our Government more deeply respected by even the Bolsheviks than any other," Hoover's plan was to exploit that fact to insure *ultimate* control of the Russian economy.

Hoover's reference to the famine relief program that he also directed was of particular significance. "The relief measures," he explained to Hughes, "will build a situation which, combined with the other factors, will enable the Americans to undertake the leadership in the reconstruction of Russia when the proper moment arrives." The Secretary of Commerce left no doubt as to his primary concern: "the hope of our commerce lies in the establishment of American firms abroad, distributing American goods under American direction; in the building of direct American financing and, above all, in the installation of American technology in Russian industries." Thus, once the Soviets were deposed—relations could be established only after "fundamental changes" were effected—did Hoover plan to replace Germany as the dominant influence in the Russian state.

Hoover's sharp rebuke—"I trust, therefore, that the policies initiated by this Department will be adhered to"—served to dispose of any short-range aberrations that Hughes may have entertained.[47] Proof of this fact came in the policy of the United States during the International Economic Conference held at Genoa, Italy, during April and May, 1922. Early in January of that year the Supreme Council, faced with the fact of Europe's economic lethargy, planned a conference to discuss, formulate, and activate plans for the reconstruction of Europe. The Cannes Resolution of January 6 documented the interest of the Allied Powers in the "revival of Russia" —but only on terms specified by the West. The proposed conference was conceived, in fact, largely in terms of the economic penetration of Russia by a giant international trust. After some hesitation Secretary Hughes decided against official American participation on the ground that Russian recovery was impossible until the Soviets abandoned their own economic program. But he was careful to place Richard Washburn Child, then American Ambassador to Italy, in "unofficial" attendance.[48]

Behind the Secretary's caution was his awareness that the conference clearly was to be the scene of a wild scramble for oil. The oil, of course, was located in the Soviet Union; and the struggle was between Standard Oil of New Jersey, the policy-making division of the undestroyed Rockefeller corporation, and Royal Dutch Shell of England. Standard, moreover, was Washington's chosen instrument in the drive for control of the world's oil. Though Hughes was intimately associated with the corporation before he became Secretary of State, there is no direct evidence to indicate that the relationship accounted for Standard's preferred position. But of the latter fact there is no doubt.

Standard asked for "the support and encouragement" of the State Department before Hughes became Secretary. But no action was taken until, in the words of the Department's representative in Persia, "the withdrawal of the British forces from North Persia" necessitated some action in support of those Americans who had a "lively interest in the possibilities of certain natural resources of Persia."[49] No less important was Moscow's renunciation of all Tsarist rights in Persia. As a backdrop for the Genoa negotiations, and in relation to Hoover's desire to replace German influence in Russia, Secretary Hughes's desire to take Russia's place in the old Anglo-Russian Convention of 1907 is extremely significant.

For while Persia "substantially escaped" Soviet interference during the interwar years the same cannot be said with reference to the United States.[50] The whole Schuster episode of 1911–12 was re-enacted over a period of six years, and early in the process Standard Oil's favored position within the Department became well defined. Schuster himself reappeared in a dual role during the course of the long struggle that developed between Sinclair and Standard Oil for dominance in North Persia. The former director of Persian finances functioned both as agent of the American-Russian Industrial Syndicate—which handled Sinclair's negotiations for a concession in Persia—and as the Persian Government's fiscal agent in the United States. Schuster's divided responsibilities naturally complicated Persia's efforts to float a loan during the fight between Standard and Sinclair over the old Russian sphere in the northern provinces—a battle that became even more involved when the Anglo-Persian Oil Company advanced strong claims to the concession granted an independent Russian in March, 1916.[51]

Standard's most astute move was to advance the financially desperate

Persian Government a loan of $1,000,000.[52] This gesture of generosity both served to sway the Persians and to place Standard in an excellent position to benefit from the Department's lack of enthusiasm for Schuster and Washington's keen desire to work a squeeze play against the Anglo-Persian. Indifference to Sinclair's efforts was revealed when the Persian Government dropped consideration of the Anglo-Persian claims to formulate a long-term concession for Standard. "May I urge that the company send one of its best men to represent it locally," wired the American chargé d'affaires in Teheran, "as the Legation has already gone as far as it properly can in pushing this matter through." [53]

Sinclair representatives arrived sooner, however, and the three-way battle continued. A possible clue to Sinclair's ultimate failure—though a prospective agreement was once formulated—lies in Schuster's dual role. Persia's near bankruptcy became a central pivot in the oil war, and Standard gained the upper hand when it became, as Thomas Lamont told Schuster, an "important client" of the House of Morgan. Lamont advised Schuster —in the latter's capacity as Persia's financial agent—that the House of Morgan would "probably take a five-million-dollar loan" if the Standard concession was approved. To complement Morgan's close connection with the British, meanwhile, Standard began to moderate the conflict with Anglo-Persian.[54] In these circumstances the United States provided another economic advisor for the Persian Government in the fall of 1922. For American-Russian relations this long struggle for the oil of North Persia had one paramount result—a "bitter memory in the minds of Soviet leaders," who viewed the affair as "proof of encircling capitalist imperialism." [55]

Certainly the close link between these maneuvers and events at Genoa did little to modify that interpretation. For the policy pursued by Hughes at Genoa was not only the product of Standard's advice, but was clearly designed to prevent the rehabilitation of the Russian economy under Soviet direction. Standard's concern in the matter stemmed from their purchase, in July, 1920, of "a joint and equal interest" in the old Nobel holdings in Russian oil. This new acquisition amounted to "about one-third of the Russian production, about 40 per cent of the Russian refinery business, and about 60 per cent of the distributing business." Not unexpected, therefore, was Standard's flat rejection, in December, 1920, of the Soviet offer of a fifty-year concession for the development of a large segment of Russia's oil reserves.[56]

Turned aside by Standard, the Soviets approached Royal Dutch Shell with a similar offer. A. C. Bedford, chairman of the Board of Directors of the Standard Oil Company of New Jersey, immediately asked the State Department for help. Their important investment, Bedford wrote, was "threatened" by the negotiations in London, and he asked Hughes to "make as quickly as possible such diplomatic representations to the British Government as will safeguard the American interest involved." The Secretary's quick response was a directive to investigate the question "discreetly but thoroughly." Long before the Cannes Resolution was passed, therefore, both Bedford and Hughes knew that the "real, moving driving power" at Genoa would be oil.[57]

By early 1922 the negotiations between Moscow and Dutch Shell convinced Bedford that more decisive action was needed. He first reiterated his old concern that Hughes insist upon "the return of all Russian properties to private owners"; warned the British that there must be no move, either privately or at Genoa, "to exploit the resources of Russia" through agreement with the Soviets; and then hurried to the United States to counsel Hughes personally.[58] Forewarned by these moves, Britain acted quickly to consolidate the position of Royal Dutch Shell. Lloyd George first proposed to drop the Cannes demand that Russia return all nationalized property to foreign owners if the Soviets would grant leases of ninety-nine years' duration in return. But Bedford quickly blocked that maneuver by an agreement with France and Belgium, who served as proxies for Standard at the conference table in Genoa. London then attempted a bold bluff and sent the famous Allied Memorandum of May 2 on to the Russians without approval by Paris and Brussels. By this time Genoa "reeked of oil," and the truth had seeped into the newspapers.[59]

The Memorandum of May 2 was a thinly disguised instrument of economic penetration. Russia's need for help was first postulated as the most serious question in Europe; a problem that required the most "sympathetic" attention. The remedy proposed was to "open the Russian market to foreign manufacturers and traders." This "international trust" would help Russia, but only under conditions that would "encourage enterprise." The principal requirements set forth were Russian recognition of "all public debts"—the Allies admitted "no liability" for counter-claims based on intervention—and Soviet agreement to "restore or compensate all foreign interests for loss or damage" that resulted from nationalization. A "mixed arbitrational tribunal" was specified as the agency of adjustment, and Russia was to pay all debts in "new Russian 5 per cent bonds."

These conditions would appear to satisfy the most rabid defender of private property, but the British modified the demands in Clause VII. This section removed any doubts as to the *immediate* purpose of the document. Restriction of the term "previous owner" to one who held interests "at the date of nationalization" transformed this broad set of definitions into an exclusion act aimed at Standard Oil. For Standard did not acquire the Nobel interests until long after the original decree of nationalization.[60] Neither Bedford nor Hughes intended to allow the maneuver to go unchallenged. The Secretary's determination to act was never in doubt, but Arthur S.

Millspaugh—the Department's economic advisor who soon resigned to take charge of Persia's finances—suggested a delay until Bedford arrived for consultation. "We shall be in a better position to draft instructions," Millspaugh pointed out, "after we get his information and views." [61]

Bedford's position was hardly in question. He merely advised Hughes to demand that "a fair and equal opportunity should be observed by all concerned." Hughes immediately delivered a vigorous protest to the British. The policy, as Bedford and Ambassador Child both admitted, was no more than the formulation of an "open door in Russia." Senator Borah rephrased this analysis. The issue at Genoa, he observed caustically, "was what amount of natural resources and raw material of Russia each one of the Allied powers could get ahold of." [62]

Britain's answer to the Hughes protest tended to confirm Borah's characterization. Determined not to surrender without a fight, London sought to use Moscow's reply to the Memorandum as a weapon against Washington. The Soviets entertained no illusions as to the character of the British note, but they wanted help in reconstruction and therefore proposed to use London's memorandum as a basis for further negotiations. British acceptance of this offer stepped up the tempo of Washington's counterattack. With the full support of the Cabinet, Hughes warned Child to be prepared to use his own judgment "to forestall separate and competitive dealings with the Soviet Union." Child, who opposed negotiations with Moscow "on account of the disciplinary effect it will have on Soviet Russia," carried out the Secretary's orders designed to insure the failure of the new conference called at The Hague. Hughes took the position that the Soviets could sit on the proposed commission of investigation only if they withdrew their proposal that served as the basis of the entire idea. [63]

Allied demands, judged Borah, "would have reduced Russia to a condition not dissimilar to that of Haiti at the present time, under the military rule of the United States." The whole affair, he concluded, "reminds us . . . that our peace is nothing but war carried on in a different way." [64] Royal Dutch Shell and Standard Oil evidently agreed, and to consolidate their forces they signed a manifesto on Soviet oil on July 24, 1922. Common ground was found in "holding the principle of the sanctity of private property inviolable." On that basis they solemnly promised not to enter into any negotiations with, or make any approach to, the Soviet Union with reference to concessions or the outright purchase of oil. [65] But the truce, as events were to show, was short-lived.

Hughes and Hoover, meanwhile, sought to exploit the opportunity presented by the final collapse of negotiations at the Hague. The opening was one the Secretary of State had in mind when he turned down the idea of a joint commission of inquiry. All that was needed to initiate this next scheme was Hoover's suggestion, on July 14, 1922, to send a "strong, technical mission to Russia to study the economic situation." Hughes promptly sought President Harding's approval, pointing out that the plan would be "of great value, first, in giving trustworthy information to our people, and, also, would apply the right sort of pressure to the Russian authorities to make necessary adjustments" in the economic structure of Soviet society. Harding needed another reminder before he authorized the plan, but that was the only delay.[66] "It would seem," Hughes explained to Ambassador Alanson B. Houghton in Berlin on the day of Harding's approval, "that the opportunity is ours to determine what can be done in a business way to improve economic conditions in Russia." He cautioned Houghton to avoid any suggestion that the United States was "starting a scramble for concessions." [67]

Neither Houghton nor Moscow was particularly interested in the Secretary's plan to diagnose Soviet "maladies" and recommend the "necessary economic remedies." The American Ambassador agreed with Batolin—a central Russian figure in earlier plans to penetrate Russia economically—who thought the plan would "tend directly to strengthen the group which now holds power in Russia." Houghton counseled delay in the hope that the Soviets would lose power. Chicherin responded to the Hughes plan with the remark that Moscow would welcome straightforward trade talks but could not agree to any investigation unless "a certain reciprocity was admitted." Noting that Washington no doubt took advantage of the activities of the Hoover-administered famine relief program to gather information on conditions in Russia, the Soviet Government expressed the desire to open trade talks whenever the United States decided that the "time has come for serious discussion." [68]

Houghton was "reluctant to proceed further," however, though he was quite certain a compromise could be reached. Hughes, who did not share the New York *Times*'s opinion that mutual study "would do both Russia and America good," approved his agent's lack of enthusiasm. "No discussions" of that character, he cabled Houghton, "can be permitted." The Soviets again expressed their willingness to negotiate but Washington considered the matter closed. This arbitrary decision further emphasized President Harding's secondary role in the formulation of foreign policy. "I should have preferred to indicate in a diplomatic way," he explained belatedly—and after further pressure from the Borah-Robins group—"that the investigation of the committee was to furnish the understanding essential to the proper consideration of the relations between America and Russia." [69] But the President did not press the point; and Hughes never conceived the move as one calculated to narrow the breach with the Soviet Union.

Coincident with the collapse of these negotiations came the first phase of Washington's participation in the Lausanne Conference on Near Eastern Affairs, called to write a peace treaty with Turkey, a German ally in World War I, and to settle the problem of who should control access to the Black Sea. As at Genoa, Hughes sent a delegation whose precise relation to the conference was ambiguous but whose purpose was plain—"to give support where it has interests in common with others and to oppose measures threatening such interests." [70] Though publicly he refused "to assume responsibility for the political and territorial adjustments which may be effected," the Secretary consciously exerted extensive influence in two areas quite difficult to separate from the political and the territorial.[71]

In view of the "extensive vested interests in Turkey" held by American citizens the Department gave strong support to British efforts to restrict severely any extension of Turkey's economic sovereignty.[72] Washington's role in this campaign to protect and maintain foreign interests—which included the question of refunding the Turkish debt and the conditions under which a new loan would be granted—had no direct relation to policy toward the Soviet Union. But the Department's attitude was significant because these negotiations formed the setting in which the struggle for the Dardanelles was waged. Here again the United States and Britain shared the same goal —freedom of action in the Black Sea.

President Wilson phrased the policy quite bluntly during conversations with Lloyd George some four years prior to the Lausanne Conference. To the British Premier's expression of concern in the matter Wilson replied that "Russia would be bottled up, owing to the fact that some other Power would hold the straits." [73] Perhaps the link between Wilson and Hughes was the advice of the United States Navy, then the most powerful military voice in the formulation of foreign policy. One thing is certain: the Navy prepared a detailed outline that the State Department followed with meticulous care.

This policy brief contained a peculiar contradiction. From an admission that no solution that set up an "artificial barrier" between Russia and the open sea could hope to achieve "permanency," the Navy advanced to the conclusion that all fortifications should be razed and control entrusted to the combined British and American fleets. "Attention is particularly invited," the blue-water strategists wrote in explanation, "to the fact that the general situation is that of a new and as yet unorganized market of prodigious size offering the greatest opportunity to trade enterprise." With equal candor they explained the relationship between this market area and their policy recommendations. "When there are no naval powers bordering on the Black Sea that maintain fleets of importance in that sea it is to the interests of other powers, and especially to those powers that have political or economic ambitions in the Black Sea to have the navigation of the Dardanelles open to their vessels of war. They are thus able to use at least the show of force to further their interests." [74]

Hughes followed the Navy line precisely. His representatives declared that the United States could not accept the position that the future of commerce in the Black Sea was an "exclusive affair of the States bordering upon it." "We assert," American spokesmen at Lausanne continued, "that it is the concern of all the nations of the earth." With the exception of Soviet Russia, they might have added. Though momentarily frightened by indications that Russia and Turkey would unite against this policy, London and Washington pushed through their plan to destroy all land fortifications and control the straits by superior naval power. [75] If the Soviets thought their surrender might make Washington more amenable to a discussion of outstanding issues, however, they were quickly disillusioned. Chicherin's request to reopen the negotiations for an exchange of economic missions was quietly ignored. [76]

Viewed within the framework of this steady antagonism toward the Soviet Union, the Russian phase of Herbert Hoover's periodic humanitarianism loses some of its altruistic glitter. There is no question that this huge, and successful, campaign to provide major relief for the victims of the Russian famine was the most constructive aspect of American-Russian relations during the early twenties. But also clear is the fact that credit belongs to two groups: those Americans who contributed their dollars to purchase the major portion of the food, and those American and Russian relief workers who solved the problems of distribution.

Hoover's original proposal for the relief of Russia, made in March, 1919, was never executed because the Soviets considered the political and military conditions too clearly aimed at their destruction, and because the White Russian leaders in Paris wanted military aid instead. Food and other economic aid were restricted to the anti-Soviet forces and the small states along Russia's western border. Moscow, meanwhile, sought to obtain relief through bilateral negotiations with the United States. No serious progress was made until the summer of 1921, when a multitude of circumstances effected the creation of the American Relief Administration's Russian Division under Hoover's direction. By then, the combination of intervention, civil war, the extremes of war communism, and the drought of the spring and summer brought widespread starvation. Outside aid was vital.

Maxim Gorky's appeal of July 15, 1921, was answered by Hoover's assurance of assistance on two conditions: the release of all Americans then held in Russia, and complete freedom of action for the relief workers. Soviet agreement was quickly followed by the arrival of the advance units of the American Relief Administration in Moscow on August 29, 1921. [77]

Support for the program came from many groups within the United States. Graphic coverage of the catastrophe by the American press—on-the-spot reports by H. G. Wells were given particular display in the Midwest, for example—helped to intensify and focus the response of the citizenry.[78] A sizable portion of the relief funds came from individual or group contributions. The congressional battle over appropriations revealed that the basic humanitarianism of certain groups was strengthened by more immediate concerns. Farm groups in particular saw in the projected federal purchase of grain stocks a partial solution for the loss of their war-sponsored foreign markets—a matter of no small concern in the fall of 1921. The shipping interests also viewed the program as a source of emergency revenue. Secretary Hughes momentarily relented to the extent of allowing the import of $10,000,000 of Soviet gold to help finance the program.[79]

Political considerations made their appearance immediately. Hoover's admission that the entire operation was an important phase of his broad plan to effect the ultimate Americanization of the Russian economy was not an isolated example. Hughes also saw the A.R.A. as a substitute for international negotiation. "Full information will be obtained in this way," he explained, "without the risk of complication through government action." Nor were the Soviets unmindful of these aims—a fact that no doubt contributed to their intense suspicion.[80] Yet the all-important consideration is that the aid was given and that the Soviets co-operated.

The most rational summary of the whole effort came from Professor Frank A. Golder, a close student of Russia, and a companion, both of whom served with the A.R.A. "We are convinced," they wrote, "that the Soviet Government tried to co-operate with us in-so-far as that was possible. Where it failed to do so the failure was generally due either to inability or to a misunderstanding of our point of view. At first the Soviet officers were suspicious of the motives of the A.R.A., but when they convinced themselves that the only object of the organization was to relieve suffering they gave us more confidence." [81] Equally significant—particularly so in view of Moscow's constant overtures for recognition—was the part A.R.A. played in the "surprising degree of good will toward America" manifested in Russia all through the interwar years.[82] The Hughes-Hoover policy was not designed, however, to strengthen either the official desire or the public sympathy.

Just that fact aroused Robins to make a final effort to hold Harding to his campaign promise of 1920 to review American policy toward Russia. His earlier rebuff emphasized the necessity to exert strong pressure to counterbalance the influence wielded by Hughes and Hoover. Early in December, 1922, therefore, Robins began to consolidate the forces for recognition. Vital to the entire effort was Borah's position within the Republican party. The senator's office became the general headquarters of the entire effort. Borah's conviction—constant since his talks with Robins in 1918—that a *rapprochement* with Russia offered the best foundation for the economic well-being of the American economy and the first essential for the preservation of peace was of critical significance, for as leader of the insurgent wing of the party the senator's effective political power was considerable.

Robins also had influence at the White House, but his major role was that of a co-ordinator who refused to acknowledge defeat. From the end of the short drive for recognition during the recession of 1921 through the major contest between Hughes and Borah in 1924 the issue was kept alive largely through the work of Robins. Other figures of importance also worked with the Borah group. Former Governor Goodrich of Indiana, who served with the A.R.A., contributed his influence and ability. Charles Smith also centered his efforts around the senator, and through his association with the Soviets no doubt helped build their confidence in Borah. Though never again a public figure in the movement, William Boyce Thompson continued to give help at various stages in the long battle.

But the most important single development in the entire program was the integration of Alexander Gumberg into the Borah group. For this Robins was personally responsible: a move in the steady co-ordination of the economic and political forces striving for recognition. The move was doubly significant, moreover, because Gumberg's emphasis on economic relations originally led him to seek recognition through Hoover. Robins first thought Gumberg might be effective, an attitude re-enforced by personal assurances of a vague character from the Secretary of Commerce. But as the nature of the Hoover-Hughes plan to inspect the Soviet economy became clear Robins grew suspicious. A second personal interview with Hoover verified his fears, and he warned Gumberg that the program was "impossible."

Gumberg's efforts to raise funds for famine relief led to an acquaintance with Goodrich, who shared Robins' view. "I am getting disgusted," Goodrich wrote after the Houghton-Chicherin talks, "with the whole Russian situation." Further information on that episode—gathered in direct negotiations with Hoover's agents—verified these estimates, and Gumberg acknowledged that his efforts were misdirected. He quickly began to co-ordinate his efforts with those of Robins, Borah, and Goodrich. Gumberg, wrote Robins to the senator immediately, "has my entire confidence. . . . I want you to know him and have his help in your splendid battle for an intelligent policy." [83] From the hour of Borah's acceptance of that recommendation Alexander Gumberg played a crucial role in the movement for recognition.

Gumberg's influence would have been considerable under any circumstances, but the link with Borah was vital. Gumberg's most important work was the careful cultivation of American-Russian economic relations —an effort that slowly created a powerful pressure for recognition in the

years after 1925. As that pressure gradually increased, Gumberg's connection with Borah provided the channel of political influence. Likewise
significant were Gumberg's associations with important pro-recognition
publicists: men who helped keep the issue before the public, and also served
as leaders of the small group of Americans who thought that American-
Russian collaboration might help secure the peace.[84] Thus Gumberg's integration into the Borah-Robins group served to consolidate the forces opposed to the existing policy toward Russia.

Within a month after the top command was so strengthened Borah
opened an attack on the Hughes-Hoover policy from the floor of the
Senate. But Hughes, who also had the support of certain business and financial quarters in addition to that given by the top leadership of the A.F. of L.,
was well prepared to maintain his position. The Secretary's spokesmen
in the Senate were headed by William H. King of Utah and Henry Cabot
Lodge. Hughes provided King with special ammunition from the Department's files and Lodge hammered away on the propaganda issue.[85] In
addition, the Department assigned agents to shadow Borah on occasion.
One, for example, attended a major rally on March 18, 1923, and reported
that Borah addressed an audience "composed mostly of Jews." Those "who
seemed to be of American extraction," the agent summarized, "were greatly
in the minority." [86]

Borah was also attacked by economic groups who saw in certain aspects of Russian trade a threat to their control of the domestic market, and
by those who demanded a return on earlier investments. A banker protested with reference to Russia's "external obligations"; and the lumber
and mining interests wrote to "remonstrate decidedly" against Borah's
views and what they considered his "grandstand plays to the radical element." Borah, aware that the business community was enjoying an un-
paralleled boom, wrote careful, patient letters in reply. "I regret," he advised an Idaho mining company, "to lose your support," but went on to
add that "I am going to do while I am here precisely what I think is
right. . . . I am not here to retain this office by prostituting my own in-
tellect." To former Ambassador Francis, who wrote of his desire to "depose" the Soviets, Borah replied with restraint that he was wholly "unable
to agree." But never did he stray very far from the principal theme. "I am
not," he assured another critic, "a believer in bolshevism nor in communism," and went on to reiterate his belief that recognition was "in the
interest of peace, in the interest of the restoration of Europe." [87]

Hughes and Hoover considered the new campaign strong enough to
warrant public opposition. "We want to help," declared Hughes, but repeated his condition that the Soviets must change their economic system
before the aid would be given. Hoover followed suit a few days later.[88]
These public declarations were not effective. Despite the open opposition

of Hughes and Hoover, Robins did secure from President Harding a partial payment on their verbal agreement made prior to the presidential campaign of 1920. In response to the pressure exerted by Robins and Borah through the first half of 1923, Harding authorized Robins to make a trip to Russia as the first step in a reconsideration of American policy. Although he was on his way to Moscow, Harding's death forced Robins to organize a new campaign.

Early in June, 1923, Robins wrote a long memorandum that was forwarded to Harding by Borah and Goodrich. "A review of the policy determining Russian-American relations," declared Robins, "is advisable." Gently Robins reminded the President of his promise and then called attention to the many declarations by Hughes which were, he assumed, "not issued without authority." Recognition, continued Robins, was necessary for the protection of American interests. Pointing to the fallacy of Hoover's own argument, Robins acknowledged that Russia was "the largest undeveloped and unappropriated purchasing and consuming factor in the industrial life of the world," but noted that the policy of the United States gave Germany a "tremendous advantage." The Hughes policy, Robins summarized, was "a continuing and growing menace to the economic welfare of America and to the general well-being and peace of the world." "I am not afraid," he concluded, in a direct answer to Hughes, "of any propaganda that may be carried on by Russia in this country." [89] That the critic should have had more faith in America than its rabid defenders was not, of course, a unique situation.

Robins pressed on to organize a petition signed by "those who have recently been in Russia," and then placed the issue squarely before the President. Harding gave ground and authorized Robins to make a confidential trip to Russia and report his findings. If upon his return Robins was satisfied conditions warranted recognition, the President agreed to reopen the question. "In spite of the stubbornness of some folks," Gumberg wrote, he believed that the "struggle for world peace through *rapprochement* with Russia will be crowned with success in the near future." [90] Robins was in Berlin by late July making final arrangements to move on to Moscow, but the entire plan collapsed when President Harding died on August 2, 1923. [91] Not only did Robins' mandate expire, but Borah urged him to come home to discuss the new turn in domestic politics. "Harding's death has changed the map of politics in our America, and also my plans," Robins advised a friend. He was assured that there would be "no occasion" for a statement concerning the confidential trip to Russia, and the real purpose behind Robins' trip never was made public. [92]

Rather was a new attempt made to change policy through an agreement with Calvin Coolidge, the new President. "We are now," judged Borah, "in a position to put forward a program, and to do so with success, of real progressive principles and policies." For a time it did appear that Robins and Borah would make headway with Coolidge. There were persistent rumors that Russian policy would be reviewed—rumors given substance by Coolidge's overtures to Borah for political support. Robins acted quickly, and early in November, 1923, discussed the issue thoroughly with the new occupant of the White House. Coolidge was interested but wanted to move slowly. Robins' first conclusion was that it would be "exceedingly difficult, in fact almost impossible, to get any consideration of international questions . . . just before the Presidential election."[93]

Yet this clear indication that Coolidge hoped to secure the Republican nomination for president in 1924 strengthened Borah and Robins considerably, and they moved to exploit the advantage. On December 1, 1923, Robins negotiated with the Republican National Committee over support for Coolidge and saw the President on the Russian question. The interview was "encouraging" and in all probability was responsible for the President's overture to the Soviets on December 6. "We hope the time is near at hand," declared Coolidge, "when we can act."[94] There was, as Robins noted, "a lot doing" on the next day. Robins first had lunch with Coolidge and then opened a broad campaign to re-enforce his position against the certain counterattack by Hughes. He spent the next ten days "burning up the wires" to organize further support while Washington waited for the Russian reply. Strategy conferences with Borah resulted in the senator's introduction of a resolution that declared for recognition. Robins planned a total commitment. "I must have," he wrote, "an affirmative step . . . or I will not help the Republican Organization as I have been pressed to do."[95]

Moscow's reply of December 16 was most conciliatory. The Soviets expressed a willingness to negotiate the debt matter and in other respects evidenced considerable moderation.[96] But Robins underestimated the determination of Hughes. The Secretary did not, apparently, consult President Coolidge before he bluntly advised Moscow that "there would seem to be at this time no reason for negotiation."[97] Robins had been outmaneuvered. Coolidge was overwhelmed. A week later he thought it "perfectly understandable" that one observer viewed the policy of non-recognition "as one of the most disgraceful chapters in American history." "If our institutions cannot stand discussion and criticism," wrote the critic, "we had better change them." When another—who had been in Russia during the Revolution—pointed to the "serious inconsistency" between the statements of Coolidge and Hughes, the White House required almost a month to formulate an answer. "Of course," finally came the reply, "the proposals . . . were in somewhat different forms. But, after all, they serve to present the three elements in this matter which the American Government regards as essential." No mention was made of the Soviet reply.[98]

Agreed that the Secretary's reply was "exceedingly unfortunate," Borah and Robins determined to fight the issue through to some decision.[99] The senator opened the bitter struggle in a long debate with Lodge. Robins, angered over Coolidge's "abject surrender to the witch hunters in the Russian issue," wanted to get a real hearing so they could either "force Mr. Hughes to surrender or drive him out of office." The plan was for a "giant contest," and Robins marshaled all the reserves.[100] Gumberg, Thompson, Goodrich, and others stood by to provide Borah with ammunition. The senator won the first round when he forced the creation of a special commission of inquiry and pushed through a resolution that directed Hughes to deliver any reports on Russia that had been received from Robins, Thompson, Goodrich, and others within the last six years.

The Secretary's response to this resolution indicated that he would use almost any means to prevent recognition. Without batting an eye, Hughes evaded the entire order. The resolution was intended to put the spotlight on the Robins Memorandum to Lansing of July, 1918—a report clearly within the specified time limit. The Secretary, who was quite aware that the memorandum was of particular significance, simply denied its existence to prevent its introduction as evidence. Nor did he see fit to make public the reports of Goodrich, who also challenged the policy of non-recognition. "It is pretty hard," conceded Borah, "to investigate a department which rares back upon its dignity." [101] To regain lost ground, Robins went directly to the White House.

Coolidge was polite, but Robins did "not get anywhere beyond kind words." The talk opened, Robins reported, "with me going direct to the Russian proposition. We went to the mat on both Gompers and Hughes." The President, however, had rapidly shifted ground in the face of Hughes's militant opposition and eased Robins into a "perfectly good social affair" aboard the presidential yacht. As for any real decision, "there was none." Robins was thoroughly disgusted—almost ready to "go to planting trees and sweet potatoes in Florida." He did not think himself strong enough politically to deliver an ultimatum, and that seemed to be all that would modify the situation. But within a week Robins returned to the battle.

Coolidge's behavior verified the fact that even if the President was not actually "dominated" by Hughes, the Secretary was without question "very influential"—enough so to effect indecision at the White House. Gompers and Spargo—who busied himself getting assurances for the "withholding of criticism" from various groups—next began to attack Borah openly, and Robins again warned his group to "bring up the reserves now on Coolidge." Borah and the others did what they could, but the President's curt refusal to consider the revival of Harding's plan to send Robins to Russia indicated that Hughes was winning the battle. A few days later Coolidge turned directly to Gompers for advice.[102]

Borah and Robins probably would have lost the campaign for recognition even if the struggle had developed fully, for Hughes and Hoover controlled the party machinery. But the whole affair was called off when the first of the scandals within the Harding administration—the fact of Attorney General Harry M. Daugherty's sudden wealth—became public knowledge. Borah was "fighting mad." In a blunt exchange with Coolidge the senator "demanded that Daugherty resign." Robins quickly agreed to "take no further step with the Administration except on the clear promise that Daugherty goes and at once." Other forces in the Republican party supported Daugherty "to the limit." [103]

The issue crystallized immediately, and the Borah group was forced to choose between the use of its influence to prevent the proposed whitewash of Daugherty or to continúe the drive for recognition. Coolidge himself posed the alternatives, and Borah and Robins dropped recognition.[104] They played an important role in the fierce behind-the-scenes struggle within the Republican party, but the superior strength of the pro-Daugherty group became only too clear in the result. To be sure, Daugherty's resignation was finally secured, but the wing of the party that excused or ignored the scandals remained in power. Apparently Secretary Hughes mislaid his zeal for reform, for he did not use his important influence to insure a thorough housecleaning. Nor did Hoover. As for American policy toward Russia—the fight over Daugherty sapped the strength of the drive for recognition.

"After Coolidge laid down on me I was maybe lessened in my zeal," recalled Robins, as he looked back across the years. His immediate reaction to the Republican ticket of 1924 verifies that recollection. "I want none of it!" he wrote Borah, and coined a phrase of derision: "Coolidge and Davis, The Morgan Golddust Twins." "I knew just how you would feel," the senator sympathized, "and I am sadly demoralized myself." Robins also sensed that the first great opportunity was gone. The chance to get the "inside track" to help Russia was lost, he concluded, and a *rapprochement* would have to await the "inevitable action of time and circumstance." [105] But no Bryanite or Bull Mooser could long trust to the inevitable, and though Robins devoted a major portion of his energies to other issues until 1933 he never abandoned the issue of recognition.

A flurry of interest in recognition during the fall of 1924 brought a "special" overture from Coolidge that led to further talks throughout the winter and spring of 1925. But the President refused to make a definite commitment and the plan never progressed beyond speculation. Borah and Robins, who continued to advise the senator, were momentarily encouraged by the resignation of Hughes and made the first moves in a new campaign. In the end, however, Borah was reduced to making speeches in the Senate —as ineffective an approach to policy modification as either of them could imagine. Though Frank B. Kellogg, the new Secretary of State, was by no means the power represented by Hughes, the State Department was "flatly opposed" to any change in policy and neither Coolidge nor Kellogg challenged that edict.[106]

"Is it not time," Robins retaliated, "to substitute sanity and common sense for hysteria and lying propaganda in dealing with the Russian Government?" His forthright challenge was ignored, as was his observation that "co-operation between Russia and America is the key to the solution of every international problem in the Orient." A bit later Robins played a vital, if quite unknown, role in the election of Hoover as President in 1928, but the contribution did not ease the former Secretary of Commerce's bitter hostility toward the Soviets.[107] In the meantime, Gumberg did more effective work for recognition.

Gumberg's contribution toward the recognition of Russia was the organization and expansion of the growing vested interest in American-Russian economic relations: trade, concessions, and contracts for technical assistance. Conditions conducive to this interchange were, of course, the product of the Soviets' need to create an industrial proletariat in Russia to conform to Marxist theory—and to strengthen Russia as a nation-state—and the desire of certain American financiers and industrialists to make a profit from the effort. Wartime destruction only emphasized that Russia was predominantly agricultural. Once the revolutions in the West had failed—and in place of communist governments in Austria and Germany there appeared the states of the *cordon sanitaire* created at the Paris Peace Conference—both Lenin and Stalin emphasized that the inevitable world revolution would be postponed indefinitely. Indeed, that very inevitability became identified with the survival of the Soviet state—even dependent upon that contingency. To strengthen and preserve the Russian nation became, then, the main Soviet goal. Domestically the problem was industrialization under Bolshevik leadership—the solution of which depended, in turn, upon international security. In the post-Versailles world, moreover, that security could be attained, and in case of an overt challenge, maintained, only through an alignment with one or more capitalist states.

Aware, by 1923–24, that the Soviets could in no sense be presented as about to overwhelm the world, and conscious that the rehabilitation of the Russian economy was well under way, the policy makers in Washington began to modify the tone—but not the character—of their public expressions of antagonism to Moscow. This shift from the heavy emphasis openly placed on economic considerations—as revealed in the comments of Hoover and Hughes in the early twenties—to the new stress on propaganda as the central issue in dispute between the United States and Russia did not indicate any change in the basic grounds of opposition. Rather was this variation on a theme designed as a tactical maneuver to sidestep more fundamental considerations; as, for example, the reason why Washington declined to accept the Soviet offer of December, 1923, to discuss the debt issue. This new public emphasis on Soviet propaganda, first apparent in the Hughes-Borah battle of 1924, was maintained in later years.

This continuity in the State Department's new explanation for the American failure to respond to Russian proposals reflected a similar carry-over of top personnel within the Department after Hughes resigned as Secretary early in 1925. Of particular significance was Robert Kelley, a career Foreign Service officer who rose to prominence as an expert on Russian affairs at the close of Coolidge's term and remained an influential advisor through the first term of President Franklin Delano Roosevelt. Considered by many within the Department to be *the* expert on the Russian problem in the history of the Department, Kelley's importance may well have paralleled that of earlier advisors—such as Basil Miles and William Phillips.[108]

Kelley's view of Soviet foreign policy is, therefore, of major relevance. At the close of 1923 Kelley concluded that Soviet policy was founded on the premise that "for an indefinite period of time two different systems of society must exist side by side." [109] The connection between that significant, though not-too-startling observation—others were aware of this development in Soviet theory—and the Department's heavy stress on the danger of propaganda requires some explanation. Kelley was certainly familiar with the Soviet concept of the futility of revolution out of context: of revolts which were not the consequence of the careful cultivation of unstable social conditions, but only the result of doctrinaire and formalized leadership.

Nor is there any reason to doubt that Kelley was aware of Moscow's hope to use non-Russian centers of communism as a means of helping to protect the Soviet Union during the development of a broad crisis within capitalist society. But neither of these fundamental aspects of Soviet theory and policy leads to a concern with propaganda. The Department of State's clamor about Soviet propaganda can be explained only in terms of a grave misjudgment as to the real problem—the steady internal adjustment of capitalist society that would indefinitely forestall the inevitable collapse as prophesied by Marx—or as a new move to gain support from various groups within the United States for a policy designed to prevent the consolidation of Moscow's power.

That the latter was the case becomes clear upon continued examination of the Department's policy. Or, for that matter, from a memorandum on the issues to be settled prior to recognition that Kelley prepared, and which the State Department sent on to Hoover, early in 1925. Soviet Russia, judged Kelley, was "a power of revolutionary and international character, based on a new social idea." The first requisite for recognition was not an agreement on the part of the Soviets to halt their propaganda highlighting the discrepancy between existing society and their new social idea but rather Russia's recognition, and ultimate payment, of past debts.[110] Faced with the problem of how best to effect the changes in the Soviet state necessary to secure payment of the debts—while at the same time expanding American trade—the Department settled on controls designed to prevent the extension of long-term credits to Moscow, credits usually considered essential for large-scale industrialization.

But as Gumberg was to demonstrate, Washington's plan overlooked one central factor—the strong tendency of the business community to formulate policy in terms of short-range gain. Certainly but a small portion of the economic community of the United States thought in other terms as they drove higher the index of American exports to Russia and sold their know-how to the Soviets for cash. To be sure, a small group of American financial and industrial leaders did accept Gumberg's thesis that collaboration with Russia offered the best guarantee of a prosperous peace. But the broad drive was for immediate profit; and after the crash of 1929 American economic interests gave particular attention to the Russian market as a means to take up the slack in domestic sales.

Before Gumberg became a controlling figure in American economic relations with Russia, however, various business organizations attempted to revive old connections in Russia and institute new relationships with the economic agencies of the Soviet Government. Three firms which had close economic ties with Tsarist Russia led the way. International Harvester and Westinghouse—whose Russian holdings had been saved from nationalization in 1917–18 through the efforts of Raymond Robins—both reached a temporary *modus vivendi* with regard to the operation of their plants in Russia. Westinghouse, moreover, reported that "excellent relations exist between employees and management" in the Soviet Union. Despite prolonged negotiations, neither firm accepted Soviet proposals as to the character of an ultimate settlement, and the Russian properties of these two firms were formally taken over by the Russians in 1924–25.

General Electric, meanwhile, also "decided to begin negotiations with Soviet Russia for the re-establishment of their business in Russia." These early talks did not bring immediate results, but General Electric's later private credit arrangements did allow the Soviets to make large purchases from the American firm despite Washington's ban on formal loans. Other Americans followed the efforts of Leslie B. Urquhart of England to recover his vast holdings in Russia, in which citizens of the United States were economically interested. Urquhart's negotiations with Moscow dragged on for many years, but Lenin's remark in the early 1920s—"Urquhart was too big a fish to let loose in the Soviet pond"—probably explains the Englishman's failure to recover his property.[111]

Despite this inability of large concerns to come to immediate understandings with the Soviets, smaller economic interests in the United States did secure concession contracts in Russia during these early years. American companies signed contracts to help produce asbestos in Russia, and the Russian-American Mining and Engineering Company obtained a concession in Soviet mica fields. Others in the United States were employed by Moscow to plan and manage experimental farms; and one American secured a monopoly of the sale of Soviet stamps abroad. A group of American workers, led by an old I.W.W. leader, helped push forward the industrial development of the Kuznets Basin.

The largest of these pioneer efforts was directed by A. J. Hammer of the Allied American Company. As the agent of more than thirty firms interested in trade, Allied American signed its first contract with the Soviets in July, 1923. Exporters of agricultural implements, cotton, metal products, and automobiles all benefited from Allied's operation. Hammer himself closed for a concession to provide all the pencils made in Russia. To help overcome the obstacle of Washington's ban on credit operations the International Garment Workers' Union established an exchange contract with the Industrial Bank of Moscow whereby American workers helped finance the construction of Russian clothing factories.[112]

Before World War I, the Russian textile industry depended on American cotton, and the same situation continued to exist during the first fifteen years after the Revolution. Yet without regularized arrangements to finance this trade the American cotton exports to Russia in 1923 were but a fraction of the prewar total. This was the first problem in American-Russian economic relations on which Gumberg focused his energy and ability. Aware that expansion of cotton exports depended on the extension of credit to the Soviets, Gumberg sought help from Thomas Thacher, one of the original members of the Thompson-Robins group in Russia. Thacher's legal work proscribed further activity in the political campaign to effect recognition, but he gave Gumberg assistance in the effort to facilitate trade. His primary contribution was to help establish Gumberg's association with Reeve Schley, one of Thacher's law partners and also a vice-president of the Chase National Bank. Gumberg's plan to by-pass Washington's ban on credits—which ended Schley's earlier effort to float Soviet securities on the American market—through a domestic credit corporation appealed to Schley as a source of constant income for the Chase National. With the bank's first loan of $2,000,000 Gumberg organized the All-Russian Textile Syndicate in December, 1923.[113]

Though primarily concerned with the cotton trade, the firm handled more than a third of all American-Russian trade during the next six years. Concurrently, moreover, plans were developed to establish an agency of the Soviet Commissariat of Foreign Trade in the United States. An early proposal was to enlarge the American office of Arcos, the Russian trade outlet in Britain, but the final decision was to consolidate Arcos-American and the Products Exchange Corporation, an American firm incorporated in England. The new firm, named Amtorg, was formally launched in mid-June, 1924.[114] This concerted campaign to revitalize American-Russian trade was successful. By 1925 exports to Russia, which totaled 7.6 millions in 1923 and 42.1 in 1924, jumped to 68.9—well over the most optimistic estimates for the best prewar years. As in the years before 1914, one of the most important items in this revived trade was agricultural machinery. "During the past three years," summarized an official report in 1927, "Russia has become one of the leading purchasers of American agricultural implements and machinery." [115] But direct trade was far from the only aspect of American-Russian economic relations.

Equally important was the entrance, in 1925, of major American firms into the concession market. First to "blaze the trail" was the organization of Stuart, James, and Cooke, consulting engineers. Approached by the Russians in 1925, Charles Stuart agreed to conduct an investigation of the Donetz State Coal Trust. In Stuart's words, his report to the Soviets was "highly critical, but well received." From that start the company secured further contracts—and the high esteem of Soviet authorities. Moscow later took the most unusual step of writing an open letter to the New York *Times* to "express its gratitude" to the firm.[116] Not all concession contracts negotiated between the Soviets and American firms were as mutually satisfactory as Stuart's; as evidenced by W. Averell Harriman's attempt to rationalize Soviet manganese production. Son of E. H. Harriman, who had worked to establish economic ties with Tsarist Russia in the 1906–9 period, W. A. Harriman had carried on his father's activities as a railroad and steamship power in the United States and, in addition, had entered the banking business. His role in American-Soviet relations was to continue into the years after World War II. His contract of June 12, 1925, with the Soviets gave Harriman, who also held interests in Polish zinc mines, the "sole right to exploit" the Chiaturi deposits in Russia for twenty years, during which period he was "freed from all taxes and excises with the exception of a very few." In addition, however, Harriman was required to construct a railroad to be used in the mining operations within three and a half years.

Moscow, happy to have the manganese resources pried from the control of the Krupp interests—who held them before World War I—also hoped the concession might facilitate recognition by the United States—a hope, and motivation, that accompanied every contract signed with American

firms. Almost immediately, however, the relationship with Harriman began to break down. Harriman, in fact, "barely succeeded in reaching
the minimum production" figures set by the agreement. Many factors contributed to the failure—both sides clearly shared the blame—but Harriman's economic calculations appear to have been quite faulty. Obviously
in the business to make money, Harriman seems to have counted on a
high-price policy backed by control of the market for manganese, as
Brazilian sources of the ore were not yet commercially developed. The not-
unexpected reaction was an attempt on the part of certain manganese purchasers to locate another supply. Bethlehem Steel supported Harriman
while the United States Steel Corporation began to develop the neglected
Brazilian deposits. Further contributions to Harriman's failure to make
a go of the operation were his lack of planning and the obligation to build
the railroad. Harriman's supporters stressed the lack of Soviet co-operation
—particularly among local Russian labor leaders. "The workmen," commented one of Harriman's representatives, "feel that they are the government." The final result of these differences was a negotiated abrogation of
the contract that brought Harriman a sizable payment from the Soviets to
compensate for his original investment.[117]

    While all concession holders added to Harriman's list of complaints
—and spoke at length of Soviet inefficiency, delay, and political influence—
his failure did not disrupt the broad development of American-Russian
economic relations. Gumberg's work, meanwhile, continued to be an important factor in the further extension of those relations. The Chase
National Bank's success in financing the sale of cotton to Russia was a
good advertisement of Gumberg's ability, and helped swell attendance at
a special luncheon called at the Banker's Club of America on December 10,
1925, at Gumberg's initiative, to discuss further expansion of trade with
Russia. As the Soviet magazine *Economic Life* observed, the meeting signified a "change in favor of the Soviet Union which may be observed in
business circles of the United States." Not atypical were the remarks of
Charles M. Schwab, powerful in the steel industry as well as a director
of the Chase National Bank, who declared himself "very glad" to see the
two countries again doing business. Somewhat later, in 1926, the National
Association of Manufacturers also began to evidence interest in the future
of the Soviet market.[118]

    This increased interest in economic ties with Russia gave Gumberg
and Schley all the power they needed to reorganize the old Russian-American
Chamber of Commerce. No dramatic change occurred below the level of
leadership—where the investment interests gave way to the commercial,
industrial, and commodity groups—and the old members renewed their
support. An active participant in the reorganization drive, for example,
was the Baldwin Locomotive Works. Schley's election as president of the

organization on June 24, 1926, symbolized Gumberg's successful efforts to spark the reinvigoration of economic relations as a force to effect a political *rapprochement* between the two countries. With justice as well as insight the organization chose Charles Smith, who had advocated strong economic and political ties with Russia since 1918, to serve as its representative in Russia. His efforts helped the group become "a powerful factor in the growth of Russian-American commerce."[119] Crucial, however, was Moscow's attitude. To open acknowledgment of America's industrial and technological leadership was added the Soviet's equally clear desire to effect a diplomatic reconciliation. On this foundation, and aided by the existing trade and early concession contracts, the Chamber's vigorous efforts to expand American-Russian economic relations were effective.

From 1926 to 1931 economic ties with the Soviet Union multiplied rapidly. One of the most interesting aspects of this trade was the result, not of the Chamber's promotion program, but of the struggle for oil between Standard and Royal Dutch Shell. These two oil companies' earlier pact to isolate, and then control, Soviet oil broke down when Russia's production began to reach world markets through the Naphtha Syndicate in 1924. Soon after Naphtha opened the Russian Oil Products, Ltd., in Britain as a saucy challenge to Shell's home office, the English company began a vociferous campaign against the new competitor as a purveyor of "stolen oil."

Standard Oil of New York, however, began to purchase from Naphtha in a move designed to cut prices against Dutch Shell in areas east of the Suez Canal. For by picking up Soviet oil at the eastern end of the Mediterranean Sea the Standard Oil Company of New York could slash transportation costs to markets in Asia and, if necessary, absorb any small additional losses taken to undersell Dutch Shell by markups in other areas. Standard of New Jersey's claim that it had no control over the actions of the New York branch of the firm did not deceive the British. "I realize," a Shell spokesman told an American diplomatic representative, "that this is but a preliminary skirmish and that the recent price war in India was merely a minor development in the main issue, which is of course the desire of both companies for a share in the potential production of Russian fields." His observation was verified a few years later when, after Naphtha refused to sell out—distributive apparatus and all—Standard Oil of New Jersey retaliated with a new boycott against Russian oil.[120]

Other aspects of American-Russian economic relations were more closely connected to Gumberg's efforts. Best known, perhaps, of those economic leaders who influenced Soviet economic life—and who were, at the same time, close associates of Gumberg in the battle for recognition—was Colonel Hugh L. Cooper. Cooper's major contribution to the industrialization of Russia was his part in the construction of the huge hydroelectric

power development of the Dnieper River. Cooper's vast experience in the design and construction of hydroelectric installations—the Missouri River
Power Company of Keokuk, Iowa; the Toronto Power Company at Niagara
Falls; and the Muscle Shoals project were but the largest of his earlier enterprises—no doubt accounted for the initial Soviet bid he received in 1926.
Cooper first won the competition with a German firm to provide the most
rational plan for developing power on the Dnieper and then directed the
vast Dnepropetrovsk dam project to final completion. "I am," he observed
in 1928, "a regular commuter between New York and Moscow."

Beyond the great importance of his contribution to Russia's economic
progress—in which other American firms, including the Newport News
Shipbuilding and Dry Dock Company and General Electric, shared—
Cooper became an active figure in the drive for recognition. On many occasions he stated publicly the implications of the Dnepropetrovsk contract,
but no more concisely than in July, 1928. "For the time being," Cooper
pointed out, "we have their confidence and unless this confidence is abused,
and if it is encouraged in a practical way, we can do more to advance peace
and create happiness in Russia and in Europe than can any other nation
or group of nations." [121]

Cooper's observation was particularly astute, for the successful implementation of Soviet plans for the creation of rationalized basic industries
was due, in many respects, to American aid.[122] Steel centers in Stalinsk,
Magnitogorsk, and elsewhere mushroomed with the assistance of the Freyn
Engineering Company of Chicago, the Arthur G. McKee and Company
of Cleveland, the United Engineering and Foundry Company, and Koppers Construction Company of Pittsburg. Another landmark of Russia's
gigantic struggle toward industrialization that later became both a center
and a symbol of resistance to Nazi Germany—the Stalingrad Tractor Factory—was built with the assistance of Albert Kahn, Inc., of Detroit and
the International Harvester Corporation.[123] The American engineer John
Calder also played a "considerable and valuable role" at Magnitogorsk and
Stalingrad. But many other Americans caught the spirit of the effort and
established common ground with their Soviet employers—as John Scott's
Behind the Urals readily attests. These engineers and technical advisors
found their talents employed through the whole fabric of the Soviet economy: from the Sewing Machine and Knitting Trust to those charged with
the production of oil, rubber, and paper.[124]

An important symbol of this collaboration was the $28,000,000 con-
tract signed in 1928 by the General Electric Corporation to provide technical assistance to the Soviets. General Electric earlier contributed to the
construction of the Leningrad power system, and later aid included work
on the Leningrad Electrical Institute and advice on high-voltage operations. Westinghouse and Western Electric were also active in the field.[125]

Sometime later Henry Ford agreed to supply designs and other technical assistance to the Soviet automobile and tractor industries. Though no Fords were entered in the Soviet road tests of 1925—Cadillac and Buick were the winners—Moscow wanted Ford's answer to the question of "how to work and achieve with the least outlay of effort and capital—the technique of mass production. Exchange of philosophies was not involved in the contract, and a Ford representative openly stated that "there was never any evidence of bad faith on the part of the Soviet officials." [126] Other technical assistance was given by the Radio Corporation of America, International Harvester, the Sperry Gyroscope Company, Ralph Budd, president of the Burlington, Chicago, and Quincy Railroad who first analyzed and then helped improve Soviet railways, and the Du Pont de Nemours Corporation.[127]

Generally associated with the concentration of industrial power within the United States, the Du Pont contribution to Soviet development was made in terms of increasing agricultural production. Stalin's conclusion that a failure to collectivize agriculture would jeopardize the future of the Revolution was perhaps the most far-reaching decision of the dictator's life. His resolute and ruthless determination to implement that decision was met by equal resistance on the part of many landowners and peasants. A man-made famine was a way station on the road to final victory—a price gravely close to defeat, as Stalin acknowledged in his speech on the dangers of being "Dizzy with Success," and in his "Reply to Collective Farm Comrades." Or in his remark to Churchill more than a decade later: "collectivization was all very bad and difficult—but necessary." Once the issue was decided, however, the Soviets turned to the United States for assistance vital to the achievement of greater and more stable agricultural production.[128] Du Pont's technical aid in the construction of fertilizer plants supplied a portion of that help, as did the Nitrogen Engineering Company. But the success of agricultural collectivization depended on more than chemical fertilizers, and Moscow sought help to solve the central problem of mechanization and rationalization.

Important in this Soviet agricultural program was Thomas Campbell who owned and operated the vast Campbell Farming Corporation in Montana. Originally a Morgan-financed operation of World War I, the huge Montana project was purchased by Campbell early in the twenties. His successful management of the enterprise prompted the first Soviet offer, in 1928, of a concession to establish a model farm in Russia. Campbell declined that offer but did agree to teach more than two hundred Soviet experts the techniques of mechanized, round-the-clock farming. An important ramification of this training—and Campbell's trips to Russia—was the further rise in orders for American agricultural machinery. Again, as in

industrial development, many other Americans made significant contributions to Soviet agriculture. George MacDowell of Kansas was awarded the
Order of Lenin, while the contributions of Arthur Powell Davis in irrigation and Howard J. MacDowell in production improvements brought similar
recognition.[129]

When the Russian-American Chamber of Commerce arranged a special
trip to Russia in the summer of 1929 an American magazine writer correctly noted that trade with Russia had become "respectable." From a "sort
of back-alley affair" economic relations with the Soviet Union achieved an
acceptance that was a "very painful thing for some people in Wall Street to
contemplate." As the writer emphasized, the members of the group around
William Boyce Thompson, who had led this revival of trade with Russia,
were "extremely influential Americans." [130] Though this writer failed to
connect the two developments, that economic influence was in measure responsible for the new vigor of Senator Borah's drive for the recognition
of Russia. Even before the significant luncheon at the Bankers' Club of
America in December, 1925, or the formal reorganization of the Russian-
American Chamber of Commerce, Borah's correspondence began to show
the effects of Gumberg's efforts to lay a firm foundation for American-
Soviet collaboration.

There were "at least a dozen representatives of business interests in
to see me within the last ten days," observed Borah on November 16,
1925, and that experience set a pattern for the next seven years.[131] A
factor in Borah's emergence as the political leader of this economic agitation for recognition was the senator's new attitude toward that activity.
After his failure to gather enough strength to force a modification of policy
under Hughes, Borah realized that his argument for a *rapprochement* to
help secure the peace was not particularly effective during a period of
postwar economic expansion. The senator began, therefore, to encourage
the business community to support recognition on grounds of self-interest.

But the new approach did not signify any change in Borah's long-
range goal—a fact clearly revealed in his answer to a request from Will
Hays, who had become the morals censor of the movie industry, for help
in selling American motion pictures in Russia. "Of course, Hays, as I said
to you," the senator answered on October 10, 1925, "I am only interested
in this question in the sense that it brings about a closer relationship between this country and Russia. I am thoroughly convinced that our policy
. . . is not only a mistake from an economic and business standpoint, but
even a greater mistake from the standpoint of exercising the proper influence with reference to some of the most vital world movements at this
time." [132] Time and again during subsequent years Borah hammered home
this theme.

Thus by 1931, when the depression caused a tremendous upsurge in the economic pressure for recognition, Borah was well established as the political spokesman for the movement. The especial significance of Borah's leadership became apparent when the statesmen of the business community—and their agents in the government—were unable to convince the American people that the depression was no more than an automatic readjustment of the capitalist economy. Perhaps their lack of success was due to their own lack of faith in the argument. For as the files of Senator Borah reveal, the American business community wanted help—and quickly. Letter after letter congratulated him for his stand on trade with Russia as an economic necessity and asked for recognition. The president of the General Motors Export Company after a Borah speech in December, 1930, wrote, "The things you said are, to my mind, so sound from the standpoint of their economics that they admit of no controversy." Borah was "delighted," of course, but privately very doubtful about the possibilities of recognition. Yet the pleas for help became more insistent.

And with reason. For in 1930, a year that saw a continued decline in the index of American production, the Soviet Union purchased 36 per cent of all agricultural implements exported and 50 per cent of all the tractors sold abroad. In 1931 Russia bought 65 per cent of the machine tool industry's exports—"which made the difference between collapse and survival" in that area of the economy. Not too unexpected, then, was a request from the Barnes Drill Company for a "better business relationship with Russia" that entered the senator's files along with similar letters from the Consolidated Machine Tool Corporation, the Hempy-Cooper Manufacturing Company, the Sundstrand Machine Tool Company, and many others. Borah answered all these urgent letters with a request that they maintain their pressure. Now and again he could not resist a touch of sarcasm, as in his reply to the Barnes Company: "I have been advocating that for ten years," he commented dryly, "in season and out of season." [133]

But the two critical problems—credit and recognition—seemed impossible of solution unless the Administration changed its views. Gumberg was particularly worried, for his intimate knowledge of American-Russian trade figures emphasized the danger. The sag was first noticeable in 1931 and Gumberg warned Borah of the future. "The increase in Russian purchases in Germany, England, and Italy," he pointed out, "is due primarily to the fact that those countries have granted the Russians much better credit terms than they are getting in this country." But the propaganda campaign of 1928 that presented the Soviets as about to collapse was not the cause of Gumberg's concern. In the first days of the depression, to be sure, American investors abandoned the discounted paper of Soviet purchasing firms as if it threatened even further failure. Only a few had the confidence to buy up the notes, but their venture brought a huge profit when Moscow met the obligations in full. By 1931 the problem was not a lack of confidence but rather the State Department's rule against credit operations.

The twin sources of the policy of no credits and non-recognition—President Hoover and policy advisor Kelley—were well known to Borah, Gumberg, and Robins. As early as April 15, 1929, Robins warned that Kelley was the man who re-enforced Secretary of State Henry L. Stimson's decisions. Stimson was in no sense an enthusiast for recognition, but Kelley stoutly resisted any inclinations the Secretary may have had in that direction. Kelley's position was not in question. His policy recommendations of 1923 were re-enforced in the winter of 1927–28. Then he again helped block another of Schley's proposals to extend credits to Moscow—in this instance for railroad construction. Supported by the New York Life Insurance Company and the first International Securities Corporation—two firms that held Tsarist loans—Kelley wrote that the Department "cannot view with favor" the proposal. Later in the year, however, Kelley quite approved Schley's plan to finance Moscow's payments to Harriman when the latter's contract was mutually abrogated.[134]

Borah shared Robins' concern, but saw little that could be done. Instead, the senator sought to refocus all the economic pressure for recognition on the President. "The difficulty of all this situation," he advised the United States Rubber Company, "lies with the Executive Department." [135] But neither economic pressure nor the first international consequences of Washington's policy of freedom without responsibility moved President Hoover from his determination to destroy the Soviet Union. For neither the deepening depression nor Japan's advance into Manchuria in 1931 moved the Executive Department to consider Moscow's constant overtures for collaboration in the face of that challenge.

Rather did developments in the Far East serve to dramatize Washington's concern for the system of foreign rights and its antagonism toward the Soviets. So deep was the concern for these rights in China, in fact, that the United States was unable to exploit the break between the Kuomintang and Moscow. The embargo on arms to China established at the Washington Conference began to trouble the Department as early as April, 1926—a year before the conservative wing of the Nationalists in China consolidated their power. "Tantamount to intervention to their detriment," was the American minister's bitter view of the impact of the restriction on the anti-Soviet group.[136]

Secretary Kellogg quite agreed and "undoubtedly desired" to give all possible aid to Chiang Kai-shek. Chiang, quite clearly, "had no wish to be cut off altogether from the Chinese upper bourgeoisie, or from the capital of the West." But Kellogg could not solve the problem so easily as did the American Chamber of Commerce in Shanghai, a group that simply declared that "the basic conflict in China was . . . that of the Western Powers and Japan against the Soviet Union." For one thing, Senator Borah was quite aware that major interference in Chinese affairs would risk the complete alienation of the Chinese people.[137] Borah had enough strength, moreover, to help prevent large-scale intervention.

But Chiang's victory only dramatized Washington's old dilemma in a new setting. His wing of the Kuomintang broke away from Soviet influence in April, 1927, and by the end of the year severed diplomatic relations with Moscow. While the hard core of Chinese communists trekked north to reorganize and gather new adherents, Washington sought an answer to a very difficult question. How, pondered Kellogg and later Stimson, does an outside power regularize relations with a revolutionary government whose international orientation is potentially valuable, whose cause has been aided both for that reason and its social conservatism, and yet whose nationalism threatens the economic interests that in turn form the basis of control over its international orientation? At some stage in the effort to solve that problem at least one departmental member must have concluded—at least temporarily—that through the open door had walked the contents of Pandora's box. If not, then certainly the Sino-Soviet dispute of 1929 made the fact abundantly clear.

For the seizure of the Chinese Eastern Railway by the forces of Chang Tso Lin's Manchurian government on July 10, 1929, left Washington no area of maneuver. That China anticipated approval by the non-Soviet world—and especially in the United States—became clear during subsequent negotiations. Equally apparent was the source of China's grave misjudgment as to the basis of Washington's antagonism toward Moscow. For on the issue of the seizure of the railway the Department of State's determination to collect past debts from Moscow converged with the concern to protect foreign rights in China. Nor did explanations based on the influence and interference of Soviet sympathizers alter the central issue. China, concluded the American minister, "forced the present issue by what is unquestionably intended to be an act of confiscation of the railway." [138] The move, far from invoking sympathy, only served to heighten the fear that further expressions of militant nationalism might well destroy the whole system of extraterritoriality.

When China spurned Moscow's proposal to negotiate in the atmosphere of the status quo ante, Stimson went into action. The threat to American rights in China was supplemented by the challenge to American prestige involved in an act that challenged the just-signed Kellogg-Briand Peace Pact.[139] In final form—the outlawry of war by public opinion—the pact no doubt differed radically from the original concept, but whatever the degree of this altered character Washington was ego-involved, so to speak. This is not to brush aside the intense sincerity of those responsible for the document or to discount Stimson's deep concern to localize the railway dispute.[140] But the Secretary's intervention was neither pro-Soviet nor was his fundamental motivation concern for the Kellogg-Briand Pact. At stake was the principle of economic intervention abroad. China's open defiance of that principle brought immediate countermeasures.

Stimson's first move was unilateral—strong pressure on China. The Nationalists' assumption of Washington's support was short-lived: the Secretary's firm refusal to offer his good offices unless Moscow joined the request clarified that point. China's admission that she "had not taken the matter seriously until Russia had severed diplomatic relations" left no doubt, moreover, that she expected a different reception at the State Department.[141] Nor, as subsequent developments showed, was Stimson in any sense pro-Soviet. Of particular import in any consideration of the Secretary's later actions was his awareness that neither side wanted war. Stalin's collectivization program provided trouble enough, and several Soviet leaders candidly admitted their concern that the dispute be settled as "the grain-stocking campaign would be upset and the internal situation complicated by war." [142] The Nationalists, for their part, could not risk the full weight of war on their shaky alliance with Chang's Manchurian government.

But even the shock of disillusionment at Stimson's attitude did not immediately temper Nationalist belligerence. Neither did the record of Washington's actions in the Far East nor Stimson's procedure help to modify Soviet skepticism as to the Secretary's intent. In mid-July he shifted his emphasis from unilateral pressure on China to an attempt to effect a multinational settlement. Stimson proposed that the railway be operated under the direction of neutrals while an international group gathered facts upon which final settlement would be based. China and Russia, meanwhile, would refrain from war. Thomas Lamont's interest in the acquisition of the Chinese Eastern through a reinvigorated consortium was by no means dead, but there is no evidence to suggest that Stimson's plan was another version of the old Knox neutralization scheme of 1909, designed to win control of the line for the United States.[143]

Coupled with the long history of American efforts to control the Chinese Eastern, the Secretary's failure to communicate the plan to Moscow aroused all the old suspicions. "Direct intervention . . . for the purpose of taking the Chinese Eastern Railroad into their own hands," came the immediate Soviet response. Nor did Stimson's use of the French as intermediaries modify Moscow's anger. "Nothing could have been more unacceptable," Washington learned soon after. Gumberg, then in Moscow to further strengthen trade relations with the Soviets, "tried to tell them that they were all wet in regard to their information as to American policy in Manchuria. However," he reported, "I always found myself arguing against this 'fatal' document." [144]

Meanwhile, the tension along the Sino-Soviet border mounted. Armed clashes seemed to shock both sides, and brought new efforts to freeze the *status quo* pending further negotiations. But Soviet "moderation" was balanced by Chiang's "evasiveness" and the *status quo* remained dynamic. Yet Stimson seemed quite unwilling to take further action even though the Nationalists began to fret openly over their row with the government in Manchuria. Within a week after the Secretary so advised the Chinese, however, Washington became very active. The clue to this sudden shift was word that Japan intended to "play the role of mediator." [145]

Stimson first advised Tokyo that a new appeal seemed necessary and then, on December 2, 1929, he released another note under the authority of the Kellogg-Briand Pact. This public repetition of the earlier secret move was not a brilliant maneuver. Quite aware that arrangements for a negotiated settlement were well advanced, Stimson declined to await results—despite his knowledge of Soviet internal stresses and the inability of the Nationalists and Chang in Manchuria to agree. Once again the Secretary used Paris as his relay station to Moscow. Soviet displeasure was immediate. "A pressure which nothing justifies," Litvinov snapped; "consequently it can in no way be considered a friendly act." [146] Though certainly not an effort to improve China's bargaining position, as Moscow claimed, neither was Stimson's move a contribution to the ultimate settlement effected in bilateral talks. Far more significant than either of the Secretary's references to the Kellogg-Briand Pact was his flat refusal to condone China's challenge to the whole structure of treaty rights in Asia. That refusal stemmed from the same roots as did the policy of non-recognition toward Soviet Russia.

The strength of those roots was revealed again and again during the remaining years of President Hoover's administration. A quick glance at Stimson's reaction to subsequent developments in the Far East might support the contention that the Secretary modified his view toward recognition and—particularly after the outbreak of war in Manchuria—desired to recognize Moscow but was restrained by Hoover. Close examination reveals that Stimson, too, turned his back on recognition. The Secretary clearly sought to proscribe Japanese expansion but neither he nor the President thought in terms of collaboration with the Soviet Union. The Administration's response to the strong economic pressure for recognition offers an excellent case in point.

Even before the impact of the depression brought impatient new converts into Borah's camp the Senator made his first move. Though not quite sure that his support was strong enough—"I have a feeling it is a little early yet"—Borah introduced another of his many resolutions for recognition on April 18, 1929. Stimson lost little time in reply. Within two weeks he publicly assured Matthew Woll that "no change is under consideration." Even so, Borah could muster considerable strength. In addition to the large segment of business interests that demanded recognition for economic reasons, the senator had new support on the floor of the Congress. This group included Representative Fiorello LaGuardia and Senators Bronson Cutting, William Brookhart, Burton K. Wheeler, and Geroge W. Norris, in addition to Hiram Johnson and Robert M. LaFollette, two earlier advocates of recognition.[147] But the Secretary of State also had strong re-enforcements: the National Civic Federation was now joined by other economic interests and a vigorous coalition of patriotic and fraternal societies.

This split within the American economy on the issue of recognition was not novel: many times before the raw-material producers opposed a trade policy advocated by the manufacturers and processors. Broadly grouped around two leading figures—Senator Tasker L. Oddie, Republican from Nevada, and Representative Hamilton J. Fish, Republican from Massachusetts—the wheat, lumber, asbestos, wood-pulp, coal, and manganese interests waged a militant battle to enact discriminatory legislation against those particular Russian exports. Whether Oddie's own real estate, financial, and mining activities in Nevada heightened his concern for the welfare of certain of the state's voters is an unknown factor, but his belligerence was never in question. His call was for a complete embargo on Russian trade. Representative Fish, meanwhile, dropped his earlier interest in trade with the Soviets. In 1926, after a special study of the question in Russia, Fish talked at length of the great promise and importance of trade; but by 1931 his views were altered. Though congressmen from many other states—Oregon, Arizona, Montana, Washington, and Pennsylvania—joined the drive, Oddie and Fish were the tactical leaders.[148]

Oddie's main attack came on the manganese front, where the sharpest conflict between the two economic groups occurred. Oddie, who blamed the Soviets for the depression in manganese production, won the first round when an embargo was placed on manganese imports. The American Iron and Steel Institute countered with a brief against the move—a counterattack that highlighted the congressional inquiry and the hearings before the tariff commission.[149] A five-year contract between the United States Steel Corporation and the Soviet manganese trust, signed in 1929, no doubt influenced the Institute's decision to contest the embargo. Neither Oddie's cry for "economic isolation" from Moscow nor the American Manganese Producers Association's insistence that the Russian ore be banned changed the hard facts at issue. Despite the depression—and cries of Soviet dumping—investigation revealed "a small increase" in American manganese production during 1930. Secretary of the Treasury Andrew J. Mellon concluded that the embargo was "not justified." [150]

Another bitter fight developed over Soviet lumber exports. Around this product arose most of the convict labor charges. The American Federation of Labor's estimate that Soviet labor camps cost one million Americans their jobs was followed by vigorous activity on the part of the American Coalition, organized in February, 1931, to oppose recognition and support the drive for a complete embargo on Soviet products. From the date of their resolution that declared a "national emergency" this group helped keep alive antagonism toward Russia. Other groups, the American Farm Bureau Federation was one, stressed the danger to American farm products. And Hamilton Fish used the radio to warn that further trade with Russia would cut raw-material exports.[151]

The pro-embargoists encountered considerable resistance, if for no other reason than America's industrialization. Even the National City Bank, long angry over the matter of Tsarist debts, confessed to "skepticism" about the dumping charges. The quite conservative *Outlook* also thought Fish and Oddie less than helpful. "They clutter the road, endanger Russian credit, and constitute a threat to Russian-American trade," concluded the editors.[152] Borah—certainly never one to ignore the abuses and excesses of the Soviet system—stood fast for "markets for our goods" and a move designed to stabilize the Far East. His patient, forthright efforts to reestablish relations with the Soviets gave him far greater influence, moreover, in negotiations to secure redress for Americans than did the policy of violent antagonism advocated by Fish, Oddie, Woll, and others.[153] Once again Gumberg's efforts—Thacher's law firm first helped the American Iron and Steel Institute wage the fight against the embargo—were of major importance. At one conference called to fight the restrictions, for example, the American-Russian Chamber of Commerce mustered the International Paper Company, the International General Electric, General Motors, Westinghouse, the Chicago Pneumatic Company, the American Tool Works, and the American Locomotive Company, among others. Against this power even Senator Oddie and Representative Fish could not prevail.[154]

In the midst of this wrangle over Soviet exports came the report of Stimson's decision to make a special study of relations with Russia. Hoover's curt comment that no policy change was contemplated failed to crush the hopeful. Schley quickly asked Stimson to verify the rumor that recognition was just around the corner. The Secretary gave the representatives of the American-Russian Chamber of Commerce a "very cordial reception" when they called at the Department, but offered little reassurance: the reports, he advised Schley, were "greatly exaggerated." [155] As the result of renewed Soviet overtures, however, Stimson actually was engaged in a review of the policy of non-recognition. His "own conclusions"—based on the traditional reasons and re-enforced by another memorandum from Kelley—were against recognition.[156]

At the close of the unsuccessful drive for trade restrictions on the eve of open hostilities in Manchuria came Hoover's blunt expression of his basic attitude toward Moscow. During an interview printed in the San Francisco *News* on August 13, 1931, the President acknowledged that his goal was the destruction of the Soviet Union.[157] But Tokyo's overt action to consolidate and extend her position in Manchuria changed the attitude of neither the President nor his Secretary of State.

To be sure, Secretary Stimson firmly declared Washington's refusal to recognize any act that impaired "the treaty rights of the United States or its citizens in China, including those which relate to the sovereignty, the independence, or the territorial and administrative integrity of the Republic of China, or to the international policy relative to China, commonly known as the open-door policy." No less clear was the explanation of his firmness. All the imposing evidence that Tokyo could—and did—marshall to explain and legalize the fact that there was no other example "of a country enjoying in the territory of a neighboring State such extensive economic and administrative privileges" did not alter the fact of Japan's continued advance through Manchuria.[158]

Whether Lieutenant Kawamoto of the Japanese Imperial Army thought the explosion on the South Manchurian Railway on the night of September 18, 1931, was the signal for a major Chinese assault is, in the last analysis, immaterial. One hard fact cannot be dissolved in any solution of legal rights: Japanese troops did not content themselves with a victory over the non-resisting Chinese in Mukden's North Barracks, but within a month attacked all the vital centers of Manchuria. A lieutenant's mistake could precipitate the first but not the second.[159] Nor was Japan in 1931 challenged by a power already embarked upon an armed assault on the world. Rather was this the first trial salvo for that later conflict.

"I find no evidence," cabled the only on-the-spot American observer on September 22, "that these events were the result of an accident nor were they the acts of minor and irresponsible officials." Even before he received this message, moreover, the Secretary warned Tokyo that "responsibility for determining the course of events" was hers "for the reason that Japanese armed forces have seized and are exercising de facto control in South Manchuria." [160] Washington's failure to implement this awareness is a complex of many factors.[161] Extremely significant, apparently, was Stimson's fear that precipitate action would give the military full control in Japan. Yet through their right of equal access to the Emperor they already exercised a virtual veto power, and the Secretary's awareness of the army's continued advance is clear. Whether Stimson was equally acquainted with the internal tensions of Japanese society—or realized their significance in terms of foreign policy—is by no means well established.

Important, too, was the bitter struggle between two policy advisors as to the degree of firmness with which the United States should act. But of crucial significance was Herbert Hoover's reaction to the crisis.

By the first week in December, 1931, the extent—and character—of Tokyo's march across Manchuria was not in doubt. The Japanese Army resumed the attack on Chinchow, and Stimson returned to the militancy of his early note. In this context President Hoover advised the cabinet of his views. "There is something on the side of Japan," he began, and then candidly revealed the degree to which he sympathized. "Suppose Japan had come out boldly and said: 'We can no longer endure these treaties . . . China has failed to establish the internal order these treaties contemplated. Half her area is Bolshevist and co-operating with Russia . . . Manchuria . . . is in a state of anarchy that is intolerable. . . . Beyond this with Bolshevist Russia to the north and a possible Bolshevist China on our flank, our independence is in jeopardy. Either the signatories of the Nine-Power Pact must join with us to restore order in China or we must do it as an act of self-preservation. . . .' America certainly would not join in such a proposal and we could not raise much objection." [162]

Stimson's strong pressure did force the President to give way and agree to a new, extended, and vigorous restatement of Bryan's old doctrine of non-recognition. Though the decision—reached after long consideration—to keep the fleet in the Pacific was no more than a gesture, the token was one of warning—as was the earlier concentration of the Asiatic Squadron at Shanghai. Yet at the hour of both these decisions Stimson knew quite well that the British were coldly unenthusiastic. So, too, did Tokyo. For on January 11, 1932, the London *Times* left no doubt about the matter. Published therein was the British answer to Stimson's request to apply the principle of non-recognition to Japan's violation of the Kellogg-Briand Pact—dramatic background material for those to write of Sir John Simon's later "fanatical devotion" to the Munich Pact with Hitler.[163]

One of the Secretary's harshest critics has seen "no reason" to expect Stimson to know Simon's attitude. The personalities and politics of British statesmen have seldom been state secrets. London's reply gave Stimson all the clues he needed. Since the outbreak of hostilities—London used the term "events"—Stimson was advised, Japan had given two assurances that she "would adhere to the open-door policy, and would welcome participation and co-operation in Manchurian enterprise." London did not, therefore, consider it necessary to address a formal note to Tokyo. A *Times* editorial filled in between the lines: "Nor does it seem to be the immediate business of the Foreign Office to defend the 'administrative integrity' of China until that integrity is something more than an ideal. It did not exist in 1922, and it does not exist today." [164] No man of Stimson's intellectual stature could have missed the meaning, and subsequent months left no doubt but that Japan, at least, acted on the revelation.

To change the British Cabinet was, assuredly, beyond the realm of possibility. But there was an opening that Stimson never probed—reconciliation with Moscow. He was aware, moreover, that others quickly sensed that possibility. Early in October the Secretary was advised that "the Chinese Government is very apprehensive of a rapidly extending sentiment of friendship for the Soviet Government and of a popular feeling that ordinary diplomatic relations should be resumed immediately as offset to Japanese aggressive designs and to develop effective action by the League of Nations." [165] But when he invoked the Kellogg-Briand Pact against Japan the Secretary did not discuss the matter with Moscow.

Far more isolated at the outbreak of hostilities even than Japan, who knew and calculated on certain attitudes in Washington and London, the Soviets responded with a vigor that might well have given Stimson considerable encouragement. Moscow, on September 23, 1931, openly declared that the Mukden Incident promised "imminent large-scale Japanese action of a military character." [166] Coupled with Tokyo's sharp refusal to consider a non-aggression pact, spurned twice between December 31, 1931, and mid-January, 1932, and the steady advance of the Japanese Army toward the Soviet border, the encroachments on the Chinese Eastern Railway sharpened Moscow's concern. "Reports of the re-enforcement of the Soviet Far Eastern army and of the hasty reconditioning of the Trans-Siberian Railway began to receive ample confirmation." Considerable evidence indicates that these countermeasures gave pause in Tokyo: an official statement "obviously designed to calm Russian suspicions" was followed by less challenging maneuvers by the Japanese Army.[167]

The Soviets, meanwhile, sought to strengthen their position in accord with Lenin's judgment of 1918 that security could be found only within the dynamics of the struggle between the United States and Japan. Whatever their theorists might prophesy for the future, moreover, the Soviets knew full well that Japanese militarism was of far greater immediate danger than American capitalism. This awareness motivated Moscow's strenuous efforts to induce the United States and China to effect a joint guarantee against further Japanese expansion. A formal proposal was made during the World Disarmament Conference in 1932, when the Soviets presented their plan to State Department representatives then in Geneva. Once again, as in the years between 1906 and 1912, Russia took the initiative to delimit Tokyo's plans to dominate Asia. As before, however, Washington spurned the overture: the Soviet proposal of 1932 was considered but briefly and then ignored.

But Moscow continued her courtship of Washington. In July, 1932, came a public bid for collaboration against Japan. Karl Radek's article in *Foreign Affairs* of that month argued one central point—in view of London's failure to act—Radek's explanation was grotesque—the only possible force of restraint was collaboration between Washington and Moscow. A bit later, the day after Tokyo recognized Manchukuo, *Izvestia* passed a judgment that was in reality a fond hope. Non-recognition, the Soviets declared, was a bit of "lifeless Byzantine etiquette" that would soon be disregarded.[168] The forecast was to be vindicated, but not until the party that held the allegiance of America's most constant spokesman for recognition had been voted out of power.

But Borah, aware of the Soviet proposals in Geneva, challenged Stimson before the election of Franklin Delano Roosevelt to the presidency in November, 1932. Late in August of 1932 he asked the Secretary seriously to reconsider the policy of non-recognition of Russia, particularly in view of the Far Eastern crisis. Together, Borah argued, the two nations might effect a moderating force on Tokyo. But left isolated and confronted with the reality of a Japanese Army along her border, he cautioned, Moscow might well have no choice but to repeat the Tsar's progressive surrender after the Russo-Japanese War. Quite aware that Washington's policy gave history every chance to repeat itself, Borah made one last effort to point out the dangers of missing the same road twice. Stimson's reply provided all-too-valuable evidence for those who claim that history has no lessons.

The Secretary's letter was at once a tribute to the virility of vested interests abroad, evidence of the power wielded by those who advise the statesmen, and a rave notice on Japan's performance in her self-created role as defender of the world against Bolshevism. Whatever the intensity of Stimson's inclination to recognize Russia in the spring of 1931, Kelley's review of the question most certainly dampened his ardor. Nor did Moscow's direct approach in 1932 modify the attitude—or the decision—of either the advisor or his senior. In reply to Borah the Secretary again revealed Washington's concern with the repudiation of debts and foreign holdings and propaganda. Recognition of Russia "in disregard of our previous emphasis upon that aspect of her history," Stimson argued, would be viewed as "political expediency" designed to "bring forceful pressure upon Japan." He neglected to mention that no formal response—save blunt refusal—was ever made to Moscow's overtures to negotiate these issues. But in any case, the Secretary explained, Russia would not give in to Japan because "their interests are too antagonistic for that." Once again, as in the years from 1906 to 1912, Washington sought to preserve the open door before it had been wedged open: to oppose Japan's use of force while at the same time denying the power of that force.[169]

One aspect of Stimson's reply cannot be challenged. Having consciously followed a policy designed first to destroy and then to alter the basic economic structure of the Soviet Union, Washington's cry for help would have been expediency—and also the measure of Washington's own failure. For the finger pointed at repudiation of debts and propaganda was proof of a lack of courage to enter the open market and demonstrate that the fundamental challenge of the Bolshevik Revolution could be met within a democratic society. Perhaps, indeed, there was reason for Washington's concern. Did not Woodrow Wilson acknowledge "a feeling of revolt against the large vested interests which influenced the world both in the economic and in the political sphere." But Wilson, though he failed to act upon his honesty, at least cut through the cant of debts and propaganda: "Bolshevism was therefore vital because of these real grievances." Wilson's failure had all the elements of tragedy: that of the men who succeeded him was only pathetic. With bitterness and passion Borah recognized his failure. "I do not think it is possible," he wrote, "to move things under the present administration. Better to sacrifice the American people than to sacrifice your prejudices." [170]

The final irony was quick to follow. For fifteen years Borah, Gumberg, and Robins advocated and fought for the recognition of Soviet Russia as a stabilizing force on the American economy and as an effective measure to strengthen world peace. They failed, and the act of recognition was a product of the very circumstances they hoped to help forestall. And likewise the cause of their small role in the final hours of decision. Herbert Hoover's disdain for the economic system of the Soviet Union was matched only by his confidence in an automatic version of capitalism. That vehicle proved not quite free of defects, however, and when Hoover did little more than pump the choke the passengers chose to employ another driver.

Franklin Delano Roosevelt's inauguration in March, 1933, denied Borah any further opportunity to change policy toward Russia, but all sense of continuity was not destroyed. Gumberg, Borah, and Robins had done the spadework that channeled domestic pressures for recognition and had helped familiarize the public with the issue. Roosevelt's decision to recognize the Soviet Union was primarily a product of domestic pressures and was given at least tacit approval by the public. But all too easily the Borah group would recognize the factors that kept recognition from becoming a positive factor in world history from 1933 to 1939.

8

☆

THE TRAGEDY OF
THE THIRTIES

To my mind the essential difference, and the precise difference between tragedy and pathos is that tragedy brings us not only sadness,
sympathy, identification and even fear; it also, unlike pathos, brings us
knowledge or enlightenment . . . to the degree that you are able to understand not only why they are ending in sadness, but how they might have
avoided their end. The demeanor, so to speak, of the story is most serious
—so serious that you have been brought to the state of outright fear for
the people involved, as though for yourself.

Arthur Miller, *On the Nature of Tragedy*

We have been standing apart partly on account of a trivial, measly,
insignificant item of indebtedness. When desperado-inclined nations see
two great countries, like yours and mine, floating along for years on account of that sort of trifling difference it's not surprising that international lawlessness is rapidly growing.

Secretary of State Hull to Soviet Ambassador Troyanovsky,
October, 1937

It had, however, unfortunately transpired that the ideological conflict
between the two countries had become stronger than common sense, upon
which he, the Reich Foreign Minister, had pinned his hopes.

Nazi Foreign Minister von Ribbentrop to Soviet Ambassador
Dekansov, 4 A.M., June 22, 1941

☆☆

The tragedy of the thirties lies in the failure of American leadership
to face boldly the challenge posed by the Soviet Union—both in terms
of domestic problems and the rise of Hitler's Germany and a militaristic
Japan. For though they stood in breadlines, or were deeply troubled by
their existence, and later scorned France and Britain for not halting Ja-

231

pan's drive into China and for not being men at Munich, neither the citizenry nor their leaders addressed themselves to the central problem—the state as an entity had survived and thrived during the transition from agrarianism to industrialization. That they were aware of the fact there can be no doubt. The laborer, farmer, businessman, both big and small, and the great amalgam who wore white collars or blouses all turned to the state for salvation. Not, to be sure, because the Leviathan sent them sprawling when their backs were turned; but because they were down and found no handholds by which to pull themselves up with frontier courage and resourcefulness. Yet though they knew the strength of the state they failed to ponder who should exercise that power—or in what manner for what purpose.

Nor did President Franklin Delano Rosevelt, whose first decision—the National Industrial Recovery Act—embodied an extreme centralization of power, access to which was limited to those who controlled the economy. Roosevelt shortly retreated from this extremely vulnerable position, no doubt grateful to the members of the Supreme Court for their breaking of the way. In this reaction was reflected, perhaps, Roosevelt's own awareness that great and vital as it was, his act of rekindling men's faith in their ability to determine their own future was not enough. The character of the future was equally important. But the challenge was never met with hard intellectual application—the New Deal became "grandly opportunist." [1] The first turn away from the NRA led to the most conscious effort to analyze the breakdown of the economy and formulate corrective policies. Financial manipulation, production controls, and protection for labor so that its power might come more nearly to balance that of capital were some of the reforms. All these acts extended the power of the state—yet the New Deal offered no basic framework within which these moves were co-ordinated.

When these steps did not mitigate the desperate need for direct relief—earlier met through the CWA, the FERA, and the WPA—a second shift occurred. During these years—roughly late 1934 to the fall of 1937—the New Deal struggled to develop a pattern of solution. Both economically and politically its concept of power shared by the state, business, and labor was fuzzy. Coincident with direct aid to private enterprise through the Reconstruction Finance Corporation came the Tennessee Valley Authority—a state-sponsored enterprise in which both capital and labor were to contribute and benefit. But both these moves concentrated more power in the state without effecting the one-sided division of power within the state. Nor did the resuscitation of a regional area revive the whole economy.

Neither labor, business, nor the New Deal—the white collarites were "politically voiceless"—offered positive leadership in the crisis of the recession of 1937. [2] Perhaps, as some contend, the twin proposals of Supreme

Court reform and seven TVAs constituted Roosevelt's plan to redress the
political balance and provide a permanent economic reorientation. If so,
the concept was quickly abandoned. For Roosevelt won his campaign
against the "Nine Old Men," but—more significantly—turned away from
the TVA approach when the recession of 1937 revealed the failure to
achieve recovery. Business critics pointed to this relapse as proof of the
New Deal's basic failure and demanded further freedom for themselves.
Labor, which owed its new strength to legislative protection provided by
the New Deal, formulated no meaningful option.[3] Rather did the New Deal
switch to an effort to reconstitute a competitive economy. The manifest
unreality of this approach and a candid acknowledgment thereof were
nowhere better documented than in the major investigation instituted for
that purpose. As one close observer has written, a "note of pathos pervaded
the hearings" before the Temporary National Economic Committee. This
was not strange, when the goal—to make *laissez-faire* capitalism operative
—was soon discovered to be most difficult of achievement in view of the fact
that the "door of opportunity is only theoretically open." Later events
clearly demonstrated that the state alone could push the door ajar. But this
fact became apparent long before the revelation that new businesses were
easiest founded through federal friends. For "the nation did not emerge
from the decade of the depressions until pulled out by war orders from
abroad and the defense program at home." [4]

   This failure of American leadership—New Deal, business, or labor—
candidly and courageously to explore the fundamental problem of economic policy, with all its political and social ramifications, was intimately
connected with the development during the same years of the situation
that gave Nazi Germany and Japan the opportunity to launch an armed
assault on the world. In those nations the state was seized by men who
promised economic salvation and an opportunity for the individual and
the group to realize their potential through a program of overt armed
conquest. In this context the Soviet Union confronted the West with a double
challenge. Domestically their economic approach was operative, and in
addition they proposed a plan of action designed to forestall the implementation of Hitler's program of recovery through loot and Japan's plan of
sustenance by empire. But to neither Soviet challenge did the West respond
until Berlin and Tokyo spelled out the validity of Moscow's warning with
rape in Shanghai and tanks in Prague.

   At the core of the West's failure to respond to the Soviet call for mutual
action against Hitler and Japan was its refusal to face the issues posed
by the Great Depression. In terms of relations between the United States
and the Soviet Union this lack of courage and intellectual discipline brought
three principal results. First, and already noted, was the New Deal's inability to formulate even a study of the economic and social problem—

"idle factories and idle workers"—much less grapple with the vital questions "as to what interests economic processes should serve, which institutions should be employed and which should give way, and what interest groups should be shorn of vested positions for the common benefit." [5]

Second—and a direct consequence of this failure—was that the basic premise of democracy—the availability of a meaningful choice to the electorate—was denied the citizenry. Not alone was the New Deal responsible for this development, as no opposition leadership rallied to the crisis and forced the administration in power to deal with this critical problem. Lacking, therefore, the intellectual firmness to pose and probe the central problem—and thereby test democracy on the strength of its fundamental proposition—the Roosevelt administration had no alternative but to conduct foreign relations within the same framework of evasion and ultimate deception.

Thus American policy toward the Soviet Union was concerned with propaganda and demands that Moscow pay a debt before collaboration against Nazi Germany and Japan could be seriously discussed. Washington was not hamstrung by a spirit of isolation abroad in the land, nor did the quite-understandable preoccupation with domestic affairs spring from the secret presses of the Chicago *Tribune* or the archives of the America First Committee. Denied positive leadership, the citizenry had no option but the pathetic consequence—attempted escape or individual opposition to the policies of the state. The latter course of action could, and did, save personal integrity for some—but it could not and did not forestall the callousness of neutrality toward Spain or the hyprocrisy of righteous indignation toward Munich.

Third, the failure of the nations of the West in Spain and at Munich limited their opportunity to exercise influence with reference to the domestic policies of the Kremlin, or to demonstrate clearly to the captured people of Germany and Japan that their leaders' policies of armed expansion to solve domestic crises would mean war against the United States, Great Britain, France, and the Soviet Union. Instead, the Soviet leaders were given solid grounds to wonder whether the West desired Hitler's destruction more than that of the U.S.S.R.; and both the Nazis and the military in Japan were given not only the chance to play upon that theme but the opening to bluff their own citizenry. The consequences in terms of Russia's internal development was a turn away from economic consolidation to preparation for war. Internationally the sequel was no more than a new—and more desperate—setting for the original problem.

Alexander Gumberg did not need a warning that these could be the consequences. As a matter of record, he received one from an astute observer of Europe in August, 1931, as Hitler began to bargain and bludgeon his way to power.[6] The date of this warning, moreover, makes clear the fact that hindsight is not the historian's staff of life. For Gumberg and his correspondent were but two of those who saw that a *rapprochement* between Moscow and Washington might forestall disaster. Another was Senator Borah, who thrust aside political differences when "advised" early in November, 1932, that President-elect Roosevelt was "favorable to re-establishing diplomatic relations with Russia." "I think it exceedingly important," he wrote Gumberg, "that we know the situation as nearly as possible." Gumberg, who arranged an interview between Roosevelt and Walter Duranty earlier in the summer, immediately advised Hyde Park of Borah's attitude. But back came news that Roosevelt was "not ready to commit himself," and Borah was left to do what he could to maintain the pressure for recognition during the long pause between Hoover's defeat and Roosevelt's inauguration.[7]

Early in February, 1933, however, Robins again began to play a more active role in the campaign for recognition. He first reported a general feeling, both in Washington and New York, that the new administration would probably recognize the Soviets shortly after inauguration. But the excitement of the One Hundred Days worried Robins—"if the step at a time approach is undertaken recognition will be sidetracked"—and he began to consider a trip to Russia. When the issue continued to be "clouded by delay and conflicting counsel," he left for Moscow, strengthened in his own decision by unofficial suggestions from various people close to Roosevelt and "with the blessing of a good many individuals." He sailed, appropriately enough, aboard the S.S. *President Harding*.[8]

Despite Robins' fears, the Roosevelt administration was keenly aware of the issue. Correspondence pertaining to the move reached Secretary of State Cordell Hull from his "first day in office," and these letters were but the continued expression of the old pressures for and against recognition. Most influential was the business community. Nor did their rising demands for action come as a surprise to the State Department. Their own summary of the strength behind Borah's last campaign made that abundantly clear. "I was greatly struck by the tremendous increase of interest in Soviet Russia," reported a departmental member on February 13, 1931, "among responsible editorial, banking, and commercial personages." His talks with "representatives of highly conservative commercial and financial institutions" brought significant conclusions. These economic leaders were quite aware that the Soviet Union had an economic policy—"in marked contrast to the government of the United States and the governments of other capitalistic countries which are apparently drifting along in the hope that something will turn up which will prevent the necessity of their taking any intelligent action to remedy defects in the present economic system." To the Department's representative this signified "a development which may reflect itself both in national and international politics and one which the Department should be prepared to take into consideration."⁹

A more accurate forecast would be difficult to find. Nationally the business community responded with a program designed to guarantee profits through a limitation of competition, power to raise prices, and authority to restrict production. These proposals, first adopted as the official program of the Chamber of Commerce in April, 1931, less than two months after the State Department's report was filed, became the foundation of the NRA, the New Deal's first attempt to end the depression.¹⁰ At the same time, moreover, these dominant economic groups pushed through the recognition of Russia, not as a measure designed to thwart Nazi Germany or Japan's Army Clique, but as a means to take up the slack in the domestic market through trade with Russia. The first success of this program came months before formal recognition, when the Reconstruction Finance Corporation granted a loan to finance cotton sales to the Soviet Union.

Representatives of this cotton trade with Russia, first organized by Gumberg in December, 1923, proposed the RFC loan in the last days of Hoover's term.¹¹ Though given formal approval at that time, the plan was not implemented until the summer of 1933. In late June and early July both William Bullitt—the man Wilson sent to Russia in 1919—and Raymond Moley, American delegates to the World Economic Conference in London, discussed the issue with Soviet Foreign Commissar Maxim Litvinov. By that time the idea—pushed also by the Soviets, Jesse Jones, head of the RFC, and Brookhart, now working with the United States Board of Trade —was "about completed." Later in July the loan, granted at 5 per cent, was formally announced by Jones. As the anti-recognition editors of the *Saturday Evening Post* observed, the advocates of recognition had "scored heavily." This was an accurate estimate, for while others laid plans to use the technique to boost their own trade, additional economic groups maintained the pressure to establish formal relations.¹²

Predominant in this movement for recognition of Russia were the machine-tool and agricultural-implement industries. Once again the American-Russian Chamber of Commerce helped co-ordinate the campaign. To be sure, many of the companies appealed directly to the Administration. The Sundstrand Machine Tool Company, for example, transferred its attention from Borah to Roosevelt, asking for recognition so that credits might be arranged to offset Soviet purchases in Germany and England. Others, including the MacDonald Engineering Company, Thomas Campbell—the master farmer who secured implement orders—and import firms did likewise.¹³ But Gumberg and others in the Russian-American Chamber of Commerce maintained strong pressure. They called on Hull as early as March 21, 1933, and later organized the machine-tool industry's request that the RFC grant new loans to exporters other than those shipping cotton.[14] Some businessmen gave support to other pro-recognition moves. Thomas A. Morgan of the Curtiss Wright Corporation and James D. Mooney of General Electric were two who helped direct a special study of the question.[15]

This strong domestic pressure for recognition served to emphasize Moscow's steady overtures to Washington. Though the Soviets placed a high priority on their continued ability to purchase American products and technical assistance, their central concern was Japan's armed expansion in the Far East. At the close of 1928, in fact, the State Department was fully aware of Russia's "repeatedly emphasized" hope for collaboration. The desire, it recognized, had been "current in Moscow for many years," but no response was made—not even to an open bid for "some common understanding in regard to the Manchurian problem." [16] Japan's awareness of the potential of the alignment was quickly revealed in answer to rumors that Roosevelt would recognize Moscow. "The Japanese," cabled Ambassador Joseph Grew, in March, 1933, "are somewhat worried over the possibility." With reason, for the Soviets discussed recognition almost entirely in terms of "a dangerous growth of the influence of aggressive militarist groups" and as a "correlation of forces with which the adventurous groups striving to break the peace would have to reckon." [17]

Secretary Hull later wrote, after World War II, that this aspect of recognition was uppermost in his consideration of the move. The exact degree to which this was the case is extremely difficult to establish, but there is enough evidence available to raise a serious doubt as to whether considerations of international politics overshadowed the significance of pressure from domestic economic interests. Even at that early date Hull and certain of his advisors were afraid that open collaboration might strengthen the military group in Tokyo—despite an open Japanese admission that they were "forging ahead with their plans of economic development, and they have no intention of retreating." In any event, the Department decided upon a "conscious intent" to soft-pedal the international aspects of recognition.[18] More revealing, perhaps, even than this hesitance to acknowledge the full strength of the Japanese militarists was the Department's own attitude toward Russia's overtures for recognition.

This was clearly revealed when—despite strong opposition from some groups—Secretary Hull and his associates began serious consideration of the problem in midsummer. Pressure against recognition was centered in the Allied Patriotic Societies, Incorporated, and in the two organizations still holding Tsarist debts—the Bondholders' Protective Committee and the American Committee of Creditors of the Soviet Union. "We not only commend the policy of non-recognition of the Soviet Government," the Patriots wrote as early as 1928, "but condemn the attempts of certain financial interests to compromise such a policy." In 1933 they gained vigorous support from all the earlier opponents of recognition. Republican Representative Hamilton Fish—who helped lead the attempt to place a complete embargo on trade with Russia—called at the State Department to give "fair warning" that he would fight any loans to Russia; the lumber interests expressed their "great anxiety" that they would "suffer competition"; the National Council of Catholic Women and the National Civic Council added their protests; and Louis A. Johnson—whose intense anti-Sovietism became especially meaningful after he became Assistant Secretary of War under President Roosevelt and, later, Secretary of Defense under President Harry S. Truman—presided over the American Legion's "monster demonstration mass meeting" against recognition in mid-April.[19]

Both Robins and Bullitt focused their energies against this campaign when they returned from their visits to Moscow. Robins made by far the more significant contribution toward recognition, but Bullitt's position within the Democratic party and as a member of the New Deal administration gave him more influence in policy-making decisions in Washington. Upon his arrival in Russia, Robins re-established his acquaintance with Karl Radek, an old Bolshevik of the 1917–18 period, and other Russian leaders, and reported that the Soviets viewed a *rapprochement* with Washington to be "of vast importance." His trip through the Ukraine and as far east as the rising industrial center at Magnitogorsk concluded with a "ninety-minute interview with Stalin" on May 13, 1933.

As Walter Duranty, New York *Times*'s correspondent in Russia, noted in his dispatches, Stalin picked his visitors "carefully" in 1933. The explanation of Robins' access to the Kremlin was his long campaign to effect economic and political collaboration with Moscow. "I knew of this in 1918," Stalin commented, "from the words of Lenin, and afterward on the basis of facts." Robins, who made it clear that he was "not a communist," stressed his desire—as a private citizen—to do what he could "by means of the granting of credits, by means of establishing normal relations between the two countries," to underwrite the mutual security of the United States and Russia. In this connection Robins emphasized the need for "tranquility in the Far East which nothing could promote more than the establishment of normal mutual relations with the Soviet Union." Stalin, keenly aware of the connection between Robins and Senator Borah's earlier efforts to effect recognition, acknowledged that Robins' analysis was "true." "May it be so," was Stalin's reply to Robins' final expression of hope that his trip to Russia might "perhaps promote the realization of the plan of *rapprochement* and co-operation between our two countries."

Immediately upon his return to the United States, Robins began to discuss his trip "with friends close to the Administration in Washington." Within a week Roosevelt was advised that Robins had information "you would do well to explore on the subject." But an old State Department opponent of Robins, William Phillips, intervened to delay the interview until mid-October, by which time the decision to recognize Russia had in all probability been made. Whatever influence Robins exerted came through his conversation with Hull, talks with other cabinet members, and an extended public report given over the entire network of the National Broadcasting Company.[20] Bullitt, though not received by Stalin, returned to exercise a more direct influence as "one of the chief advisors to President Roosevelt on the question of recognition." [21]

Yet in the last analysis both Hull and Bullitt followed the line laid down by Robert Kelley, departmental expert on Russia. Whatever modifications in the advisor's standard recommendations—made as early as 1923—moreover, were effected by those "who were doing business in Russia before the Revolution." Their pressure, it appears, led to Kelley's memorandum of July 27, 1933, that became the cornerstone of the Administration's position.[22] Kelley saw three primary obstacles to recognition: (1) "the world revolutionary aims and practices of the rulers of that country"; (2) the Soviet "duty" to acknowledge property and investments held by Americans in Tsarist Russia; and (3) "difficulties arising out of the profound differences between the economic and social structure of the two countries." [23] Hull, Bullitt, and other advisors accepted this broad analysis of the issue and laid particular stress on the questions of propaganda and the debt. Their plan of action was to "utilize every available means of exerting pressure on the Soviet Government" to secure satisfaction on these points. This proposal, Hull advised Roosevelt, would be facilitated because recognition was "greatly desired" by the Soviets—"they are apparently convinced that recognition by the United States would be a factor in preventing a Japanese attack on the Maritime Provinces." Nor did Japan's activities on the mainland of Asia modify Kelley's position. Recognition should not be granted, he continued, until the Soviets were committed in the matter of propaganda and debts. By this method, he amplified, the Department would retain "one of the most effective weapons" to gain the desired goal.[24]

Soviet Foreign Commissar Litvinov arrived in Washington late in 1933 to discuss recognition, with his attention centered on a somewhat different aspect of the problem: the twin danger posed by Hitler's triumph in Germany—followed by "unmistakable and prompt" improvement in German-Polish relations—and Japan's renewed militance in Manchuria. At the core of Moscow's response to these developments was the Russian suggestion to define aggression—first offered to the World Disarmament Conference on February 6, 1933.[25] The character of this document—"so uncompromising that the French themselves could not find fault with it"—offers a most revealing insight into the context of the later recognition agreement with the United States. An aggressor, read Litvinov's proposed definition, was one who engaged in any of the following acts: "(1) declaration of war . . . (2) invasion by its armed forces, with or without a declaration of war . . . (3) attack by its land, naval, or air forces, with or without a declaration of war . . . (4) naval blockade . . . (5) provision of support to armed bands formed in its territory which have invaded the territory of another State, or refusal, notwithstanding the request of the invaded State, to take in its own territory all the measures in its power to deprive these bands of all assistance or protection." Specifically aimed at Tokyo was the proviso against acts later justified—as did Japan before the Lytton Commission set up by the League of Nations to investigate the Manchurian crisis—on grounds of the invaded area's "political, economic, or social structure; alleged defects in its administration; disturbances due to strikes, revolution, counter-revolution, or civil war." [26]

Though not acted upon by the Disarmament Conference, this definition was incorporated into agreements with Russia's border states during the World Economic Conference in London during July, 1933. Thus Litvinov was most conscious of the plan, and the targets thereof—Japan and Germany—when he opened his talks with President Roosevelt on November 8. Despite the dearth of contemporary written records of these conversations there is considerable evidence that Roosevelt accepted the broad recommendation in Kelley's memorandum of July, but by virtue of the use of both the words *credit* and *loan* failed to establish a clear understanding with Litvinov on either the character or extent of debt repayments and the relation between the debt and financial support for future Soviet purchases in the United States. Certain it is that both words were used in these conversations—and the later debt conversations saw Washington cling to the former while Moscow stood fast by the latter.[27]

Though the debt issue became the central symbol, though not the underlying cause, of the later deterioration in relations, the United States also protested over the appearance of American communists at the Seventh Congress of the Communist International in 1935. The State Department seemed disturbed by the fact that certain resolutions adopted by the Congress pertained to the failure of its American membership. For this reason, therefore, there is need to examine the context as well as the content of Litvinov's letter to Roosevelt of November 16, 1933. A review of paragraphs two and three of that document reveals a striking resemblance to Litvinov's proposed definition of an aggressor state.[28]

This is in no sense to imply that Washington read or understood the document in these terms. Or, for that matter, to question in any respect the validity of Washington's later protest under the letter of the fourth paragraph. Nor is the point at issue Roosevelt's obligation "to adhere reciprocally" to the provisions of Litvinov's note "within the limits of the powers conferred by the Constitution and the laws of the United States."

The President had no powers under the Constitution, as then interpreted, to undertake any efforts to silence either the continued exercise of free speech in the newspapers, on the floor of the Congress, or by the various groups who campaigned ceaselessly for a quick rupture with Moscow. To be sure, it might be argued that as Commander in Chief of the Armed Forces Roosevelt had not only a right but an obligation to reprimand Rear Admiral Yates Sterling, Jr., for his open call in the summer of 1935 for an alignment with Hitler in a "great crusade led by Germany . . . not only forever laying the ghost of bolshevism, but for opening up the fertile land of Russia to a crowded and industrially hungry Europe." In the great tradition of Justice Holmes and Brandeis, Roosevelt concluded that in matters of fundamental democratic rights to err on the side of latitude was far safer than a policy of restriction.[29]

But none of these aspects of the issue is germane to the problem. Rather must a far more fundamental inquiry be directed to the State Department's interpretation of the pledge. For Washington had a Soviet assurance "not to permit the formation or residence on its territory of any organization or group" making claim to be the Government of the United States, or "groups having the aim of armed struggle against the United States, its territories, or possessions." Yet at the hour of Signor Mussolini's adventure in Africa the United States concluded that a major issue was raised by the Comintern meetings of 1935 in Moscow. One can but conclude that the Roosevelt administration determined, despite Soviet leadership in the organization of resistance to Hitler, Mussolini, and Japan, to press a highly legalistic issue to the point of serious aggravation.

For the main Comintern decision was not a call for revolution in America. Once again the millennium was postponed. "In the face of the towering menace of fascism . . . it is imperative," read the resolution of August 20, 1935, "that unity of action be established between all sections of the working class, irrespective of what organization they belong to, even before the majority of the working class unites on a common fighting platform for the overthrow of capitalism and the victory of the proletarian revolution." [30] Ambassador Bullitt knew this to be the tenor of the Congress, but he neglected to mention that there was "no important reference to the United States" until after he initiated the protest and apparently sought to magnify the problem.[31]

Both Bullitt's questionable conduct as Ambassador and Washington's attitude toward the basic problems involved were revealed with further clarity in the long and futile negotiations over the debt question. Yet the full significance of these attitudes cannot be understood without a brief survey of the background against which they were implemented as policy. For the dilemma of the debt spanned the years 1933 to 1938—from Hitler's rearmament through Mussolini's attack on Ethiopia, Nazi reoccupation of the Rhineland, a public display of those weapons in Spain, Japan's renewed assault on China, and Hitler's victory in Austria to the eve of the Munich Conference. These were the years during which Soviet Foreign Commissar Litvinov desperately sought to build some defense against the undisguised character of these events. The death, in 1934, of French Foreign Minister Louis Barthou, a Conservative who nevertheless viewed alignment with Russia as the key to defense against Hitler—was a harsh blow at the heart of Litvinov's hopes for a firm commitment from France. Nor was the situation eased by the strident calls for collaboration with Moscow sounded by the British Conservative, Winston Spencer Churchill. Churchill's vigorous rhetoric produced no visible change in the policy of His Majesty's Government until Spain had succumbed and Czechoslovakia had been denied the opportunity to resist.[32]

Nor was there a lack of correlation between international events after Barthou's death and domestic developments in Soviet Russia that followed the assassination of Sergei Mironovich Kirov, Secretary of the Leningrad Communist party, on December 1, 1934—two months prior to Barthou's death. For Kirov was not only one of Stalin's close personal friends—and perhaps one considered as a possible successor—but the leader of the intra-party group who counseled a policy of political conciliation as counterpart to the program of economic consolidation. The full significance of Kirov's assassination can best be understood in context— he was killed "as he sat in his office in Smolny to announce the Government's decision to abolish rationing and equalize food prices." [33] This decision, carried out despite Kirov's death, "was not only an event of great economic significance, it was politically and psychologically the transition to a new era . . . to a period of *consolidation*." [34]

In no sense did this or subsequent acts signify a decision to embrace the principles of nineteenth-century Liberalism—nor even a conclusion that the Marxist millennium was around the corner. Yet considered in conjunction with the West's failure to respond to Litvinov's program there can be no doubt that Kirov's assassination "had an important influence upon the course of events." Two results were immediate: trial before military tribunal was specified for crimes of political conspiracy, and the "treatment of political prisoners underwent a radical change." [35] Other implications were less dramatic, but nonetheless tangible. Their substance delineated an essential difference between Stalin's Russia and Hitler's Germany.[36]

The publication and official distribution of the works of Shakespeare, Zola, and Tolstoy, to name but a few, in Soviet Russia contrast sharply with the burnings of Heine in Nazi Germany. Perhaps more tangible— but hardly more significant—was the extension of the right to own private livestock, and the buildings therefore, laws "calculated to rehabilitate family life," and the economic emphasis on "improving the quality" of production.[37] Of similar importance was the increased emphasis placed on personnel. Rewards within the system, "both moral and material, were made for personal efforts and achievements, and did not depend on the type of work or its field of application; they were related to the *person*, not to the *nature of the job*." These developments did much to strengthen "a growing confidence . . . in the possibility, through personal efforts, not only of contributing to the growth of the country's productive capacity and prospects, but also in the direct and immediate possibility, through personal endeavor and by increased earnings, of improving one's own standard of living." [38]

Neither collectivization nor the Five-Year Plan was motivated by revenge for intervention or implemented as part of a plan to solve economic crises through armed conquest. The question is not Russia's sudden transformation according to Western concepts of the ideal society. That did not occur. At issue is her direction of movement. The Soviet Union's efforts to stabilize a revolution offered vital contrast to the character of Adolf Hitler's "New Order" and Tokyo's "Co-Prosperity Sphere." [39]

Washington was not unaware of these developments within the Soviet Union during the long disagreement over the debt. Secretary Hull received personal correspondence on the matter and advisor Kelley felt that Kirov's assassination was an act of those who opposed "the present conservative trend of Party policy both foreign and domestic." [40] These considerations did not modify Washington's unequivocal position that a financial settlement was "indispensable to the development of friendly relations." [41] In the implementation of this policy the State Department and its representatives used many techniques—from direct economic pressure to behind-the-scenes political maneuvers calculated to weaken the position of official Soviet spokesmen. If the lack of overt references to the Far Eastern situation during the conversations between Litvinov and Roosevelt was the product of the Department's "conscious intent," then that aspect of relations with Russia did not survive the camouflage. And the transfer of the American fleet from the Pacific to the Atlantic dramatized that fact for Japan's benefit.

For despite the resignation of Japanese General Araki, a leader of the Army clique, as Minister of War on January 22, 1934—an event not unrelated to Russia's increased confidence and strength in the Far East— Washington did not allow international developments to influence the debt talks.[42] Nor, for that matter, did numerous other events in this area: Stalin's blunt comment that Japan was a "grave danger," his request for "used steel rails" to strengthen the trans-Siberian, the view that recognition "gives pause to those in authority" in Tokyo, or Litvinov's proposal for a bilateral non-aggression pact—made in the context of Barthou's assassination.[43]

Rather did Bullitt advise the Russians that there would be no rails until the debt was settled. In a similar manner the Administration took particular care to insure that no loans would be made by the First Export-Import Bank, organized specifically to handle trade with Russia, while the issue remained unsolved.[44] The Johnson Act of 1934, passed to bar loans to nations in debt to Washington, did not bear upon the issue. Section Two, inserted by Administration forces, specifically exempted the Bank from the restrictive provisions of the bill. Secretary Hull personally explained that the Bank's own resolution against credit operations "was a part of the policy of the Executive branch of the Government in dealing with the debt situation." [45] Since this was the "general agreement from the beginning," Bullitt's recommendation to the same effect probably did no more than re-enforce an existing attitude. "It seems to me," the Ambassador cabled on March 21, 1934, "highly desirable that the Johnson Bill should be passed as soon as possible and that the Department should adopt a firm attitude with Troyanovsky." [46]

At this point the ostensible issue—the amount and interest thereon to be paid in answer to the demands of Tsarist creditors in the United States—rapidly became far more than an economic problem. To be sure, the question of interest remained a central issue in dispute, but the significance of the controversy shifted to other levels as well. The indefinite character of the Litvinov-Roosevelt conversations—a fact acknowledged in both Washington and Moscow—was quickly overcome when both nations spelled out their positions. Hull told Troyanovsky that he "could not for a moment justify to Russian creditors in this country a settlement for a given amount of money payable without any interest at the end of twenty years." That, to Secretary Hull at least, "was equivalent in a large sense to nothing at all." [47] Moscow's reply brought the differences into sharp focus. Litvinov proposed that the as-yet-idle Export-Import Bank advance a twenty-year credit for twice the amount settled upon as payment to Tsarist investors— $100,000 was specified—this fund to be used "when the Soviet Government needed cash to pay for purchases made in the United States and to bear interest at 4 per cent for the first four years and 7 per cent for the last sixteen. This satisfied one of Roosevelt's central concerns—that the money be spent to help revive the domestic economy—but was not sufficient in other respects.[48]

Hull's immediate reaction was extreme: "The proposal is so unreasonable not to say fantastic as to make unnecessary comment on the inadequacy of the total amount of indebtedness it contemplates and the inadequacy of the interest rates." His answer was to up the principal to $150,000,000—Litvinov and Roosevelt had agreed to settle on a figure between 75 and 150 million during their talks in November, 1933—and more than double the total interest rate.[49] Already antagonized and bitter over Hull's public statement that the Administration—not the Johnson Act—held up grants from the Export-Import Bank, Litvinov characterized the plan as "a taxation of Soviet trade." Bullitt replied with a slightly veiled warning that rejection of the offer would mean no credits whatsoever. Hardly designed to decrease the tension under any circumstances, Litvinov took the remark as "a badly advised threat designed to bring pressure on the Soviet Union." Even Bullitt was somewhat sobered by the conversation, and he acknowledged the grave importance of the "general construction of national policy in the decision we now have to make." But his recommendation was to discontinue talks with Troyanovsky in Washington.[50]

"You can be confident," Hull reassured Bullitt, that "there will be no negotiations here with Troyanovsky." Not only did the Secretary approve Bullitt's conduct but further suggested that he use Russia's "great apprehension" that failure to reach agreement would "furnish encouragement to Japan" as a bargaining weapon to supplement the inaction of the Export-Import Bank.[51] Within a few days Moscow, "most anxious to arrive at agreement," modified her proposals so that a difference of 5 per cent interest appeared to be the central problem. In a like spirit of compromise, Hull modified the amount of principal further to increase the prospects of settlement. But this counterproposal contained a new stipulation that posed difficulties more far-reaching than the rate of interest. Credit advances, Hull specified, "shall be liquidated in not more than five years." A day later he stressed the "great importance of a conclusion being reached." [52]

Next followed a new period of negotiation over the interest rate. Despite Bullitt's reply that "less than 10 per cent could not be discussed" in answer to Litvinov's suggestion of 7, this issue came to share importance with the question of the time for which credit advances were to be made. In the last days before this problem was clarified Bullitt suggested that Washington's discouragement of private credits might "prove to be an effective weapon." [53] But shortly thereafter Litvinov posed the crucial question—the international significance of Washington's position on the debt. This, in turn, revolved around the question of like payments to European investors in Tsarist Russia. Not only did a significant portion of this group reside in Britain and France, but their claims were far in excess of those held in the United States.

Yet these were the countries with which Litvinov sought agreement in order to forestall Hitler. Relations with London gradually improved, despite the bitter memory of the arrest, and ultimate release, of British engineers charged with economic sabotage in Russia in 1933 and opposition to this slow reconciliation from various groups within British society. A new trade treaty signed in mid-February, 1934, served as a prelude to British support for Russia's entry into the League of Nations.[54] At the same time, moreover, these gains in London strengthened Moscow in negotiations for a security pact with France. A conversation between Litvinov and Barthou in Geneva on May 18, 1934, was followed by a second meeting in Paris on June 27. From these talks came not only French support for Russia's entrance into the League, but behind that move was the concept of a Franco-Soviet military agreement.[55]

From Moscow on July 9, 1934, came Litvinov's frank review of his position. "We sincerely desire the best possible relations with the United States," he told Bullitt, "but we cannot jeopardize our relations with the rest of the world." Then, more explicitly, he explained that Hull's debt plan would lead European creditors—who had "shelved and forgotten" their claims—to "demand immediate settlements." This, in turn, would seriously undermine his progress in London and Paris. "The distinction with regards to the payment being only on the Kerensky debt," he pointed out, "might be good in a court of law but it is no good in international relations."[56] Soon thereafter came Bullitt's open report of Moscow's "obvious desire" to effect a settlement, and the concern to get rails for the trans-Siberian.[57] At the same time, moreover, the prospective traders with Russia made known their dissatisfaction with the failure to extend credits to Russia.

Late in March the American-Russian Chamber of Commerce discussed the issue with a group of bankers, and their "bitter" reaction was public knowledge soon thereafter. The Merchants Association of New York carried the issue directly to Roosevelt, as did others during the months of July and August.[58] Further dissatisfaction may have been made known, too, for by August 24, 1934, advisor Kelley was disturbed. Whether Litvinov's candid reference to events in Europe influenced his thoughts on the matter is not known, but he proposed that credits be advanced through the Export-Import Bank in order to avoid the charge that undue solicitation for the old investors was in effect discrimination against the traders. But he did not propose to alter the five-year limit on credits—save for a possible one-year extension for extensive industrial equipment.[59] Coincident with these reflections came another cable from Bullitt in further explanation of Moscow's concern to effect a settlement that would not antagonize France and Britain.[60]

Hull replied that there was "no difference" on the amount to be paid as principal, but that the issue of interest rates and the question of maturity time on credits remained outstanding. On these points the Secretary refused further compromise. Nor did Hull hold any brief for Litvinov's explanation of the international repercussions. "We are not responsible for the Soviets' relations with England and France," was his blunt reply.[61] Even a personal appeal from Troyanovsky failed to modify his intransigence. If "the United States, Great Britain, and Russia, without any alliance whatever, should speak or act simultaneously along similar lines on appropriate occasions," Troyanovsky argued on January 28, 1935, "it would be more calculated to quiet and restrain than any other steps the wild movements of conquest on the part of the army and navy people now in control of Japan." Hull was not moved: he "had gone to the outside limit." [62]

Three days later the Secretary terminated negotiations during a four-and-one-half minute interview with Troyanovsky. "I say this regretfully," Hull explained publicly, "because I am in sympathy with the desire of American manufacturers and agricultural producers to find a market for their goods in the Soviet Union, and with the American claimants whose property has been confiscated." Whether the Secretary's concern for the latter groups was adequately expressed in the word "sympathy" is no doubt a problem for the semanticists, but Troyanovsky did not miss the implications of the interview. That he "appeared crestfallen" as he left the Department was perhaps not unrelated to the quick reports of Nazi Germany's open expression of relief and encouragement over the failure of the negotiations. [63]

The export group was somewhat calmed by the shortly concluded (July 13, 1935) Trade Agreements Act under which the Soviet Union agreed to "purchase American goods to the value of $30,000,000." This economic bond, later strengthened in 1937, did help boost exports to a total of $86,-943,000 in 1940, but was not paralleled by collaboration in the field of international politics. [64] Whatever the full story—and it has yet to be told—the tension that developed between Bullitt and Litvinov did not facilitate a settlement of any kind. Nor, in all probability, did the fact that another American representative "discreetly reviewed developments" with "an outstanding opponent of Litvinov." [65] A more fundamental consideration was Litvinov's conclusion, as relayed by the Chinese, that "it was impossible to get the United States to involve itself in any effective way in international affairs either in Europe or the Far East." [66]

In terms of Litvinov's attempts to delimit the area of Hitler's activity this was an accurate judgment. Nor did Bullitt's open anti-Soviet campaign in France during these years provide any basis for a new estimate. Contemporary accounts of his action are verified in Bullitt's later acknowledgment that in mid-1935 he "argued at length with the French for the defeat of the Franco-Soviet pact then being negotiated." [67] Roosevelt's later appointment of Bullitt as Ambassador to France, despite Washington's knowledge of his conduct, was hardly calculated to reassure Moscow. Yet Washington could not completely ignore the character of subsequent developments in Europe. Though the Patriotic Alliance, the American Legion, and the lumber and manganese interests joined organized labor in a "determined effort" to withdraw recognition, their hue and cry could not quite drown the rumble of Hitler's tanks as he remilitarized the Rhineland on March 7, 1936, or the roar of General Francisco Franco's rebellion against the Spanish Government, launched four months later. Nor could they blot out the scratching of the pens that signed the Anti-Comintern Pact on November 25, 1936.[68]

By December, 1936, Washington considered it "a matter of real importance, if it can be done consistently with our self-respect, that friendly relations and co-operation should be restored, particularly in view of the Chinese-Japanese situation and the possibility of a world war starting in Europe." But the new Ambassador, Joseph E. Davies, was carefully cautioned to make no overtures. "Hold fast to the *festina lente* idea," he was directed by the Assistant Secretary of State. Almost immediately upon his arrival in Moscow the Soviets opened the question in conversations with Davies. Quite in keeping with his instructions, the Ambassador replied that the debt was "a matter of principle" and stressed Washington's view that the Soviets would have to take full initiative.[69] Taking the hint, Moscow reopened the question two weeks later, but Washington seemed quite content to make haste slowly.

Military circles in Japan did not share this philosophic view. On July 7, 1937, they launched a full-scale drive into China. "The Prime Minister, Prince Konoye, despite his avowals of regret, did not prevent the Army from marching on." [70] Though hardly more than a noble statement of hope, Secretary Hull's remarks of July 16, 1937, brought a quick response from Litvinov. Perhaps aware that his broad reminder of the 1934 overture for a pact with Washington would elicit no active response, Litvinov emphasized the importance of public expressions of agreement similar to the immediate exchange. On the same day *Izvestia* stressed the "instructive analogy" between 1931 and 1937. Then, argued the Soviets, Japan's success was a direct product of the "passivity of the Western powers" (here the writer charged the British with sole responsibility)— but now they had a second chance to "become a most important factor in the international situation." [71]

Two weeks later President Roosevelt seemed to indicate that he had in mind far more positive action than had his predecessor in 1931. Hoover flatly refused to consider economic sanctions at that time. On October 5, 1937, Roosevelt first drew an analogy of his own between war and an epidemic, noted that the community quarantines the patient in the latter case, and closed his comparison with the warning that "there must be positive measures to preserve peace." [72] Only slowly, and in response to League initiative, did Stimson come to accept a similar plan in 1931, but there was no doubt of his vigorous support for Roosevelt in 1937. Through a letter to the New York *Times* the former Secretary condemned the policy of "nervous jitters" and presented a vigorous argument for economic countermeasures. Britain immediately asked the President's specific intention, the League of Nations was greatly encouraged, and Litvinov was "extremely enthusiastic." [73] No doubt this support was in some measure a response to Tokyo's blunt statement of immediate purpose. "The sole measure for the Japanese Empire to adopt," Prince Konoye said to the Japanese Diet, "is to administer a thoroughgoing blow to the Chinese Army so that it may lose completely its will to fight." [74]

But other groups within the United States either considered Roosevelt's concern ill-warranted or opposed Stimson's challenge to shake off the jitters—or both. From the Chicago *Tribune* came the expected denunciation, followed by further vigorous opposition from others who had access to organized channels of communication. Far more vital was the lack of active support from within the President's official family. That the nation was surprised cannot be doubted, but one speech is not an airing of an issue—and that campaign was never waged. Yet not a few groups carried through the concept on their own. [75] Denied an opportunity to know and decide the issue, small wonder that the nation sought refuge in the not-uncultivated myth that "their own invulnerability was due to special virtue." [76]

Though Roosevelt failed to draw the issue boldly, he did not entirely abandon his concern to take more effective action. [77] His plan was to use the forthcoming International Far Eastern Conference at Brussels, Belgium, as a means to organize some form of positive collaboration between the United States, Britain, France, and the Soviet Union. Whether this conference he considered as "The Last, Lost Good Chance," the prelude to "The Last Frail Chance," or merely a second called strike against the Western Powers, the Brussels Conference was in reality the last stop on the "Road to Munich." The meeting in Brussels was the last time the United States and the Soviet Union met with France and Britain in an attempt to prevent what Winston Churchill termed "The Unnecessary War." [78] Behind Washington's failure to take a firm stand at Brussels was far more than the President's refusal to take up the challenge of his domestic critics.

For the Brussels Conference was the first event of that offset year (November, 1937–October, 1938) that began with the economic failure of the New Deal and concluded with British Foreign Minister Halifax's words to the Russian Ambassador on the first day of the Munich Conference: "We all had to face facts, and one of those facts was . . . that the heads of the German Government and of the Italian Government would not be willing in present circumstances to sit down in conference with Soviet representatives." [79] Nor was Washington unaware of the crisis. Hull told Troyanovsky in October that their "trivial differences over the measly, insignificant item of indebtedness" no doubt encouraged "international lawlessness"—but stood fast on the decision that all initiative, and com-

promise, must come from Moscow. At the same time, and in direct preparation for the meeting at Brussels, the State Department embarked upon a
study of recent events in the Pacific.

To what degree the official conclusions represented at least a temporary defeat for the group who sought "to prod the Department into
more militant action" is difficult to judge; but apparently the Department
"surveyed the Far Eastern scene with more disposition to allow that there
might be some admissible basis for Japanese action than ever before or
after." It thought in terms of giving Japan "a sense of economic and
political security"—but in a manner that "would prevent the Soviet
Union and China from misusing the chance they would get." [80] President
Roosevelt may have viewed the problem from a somewhat different angle,
for he seemed to stress the importance of halting Japan's active penetration of China. In correspondence with former Ambassador to Japan Lloyd
Griscom, who observed firsthand the consequences of a pro-Japanese policy
in 1904–6, and during conversations with Norman Davis, the delegate
to Brussels, he searched for an effective technique. Griscom proposed the
revival of a note sent to Russia and Japan in 1904. At that time Secretary
Hay notified Tokyo and St. Petersburg of his "earnest desire" that they
respect China's integrity. "Just before" Davis sailed for Brussels he discussed this approach with Roosevelt. Both were "impressed," the President
wrote Griscom, with the "possibility of using the interchange . . . as a
starting point for asking somewhat specific assurances or statements" at
Brussels.

Whether during these last-minute talks or while Davis was at sea,
the President abandoned whatever inclination he had to take a firm stand.[81]
His directive was "to do nothing at Brussels that would entail American
initiative to curb Japan." This alone was no doubt enough to account
for the fact that Davis "felt very keenly that he had not been properly
supported"—but his greeting in Europe could well have added to his
dismay. For Litvinov met him with the candid observation that "if the
Brussels Conference produced no results his own days in the Foreign Office were numbered, as Russia would go into isolation." [82] Davis quickly
warned Washington that the Conference would fail unless the United States
agreed to positive measures, but support was not forthcoming. Roosevelt's
hesitation to bring the issue out in the open was buttressed by more than
just the conclusions of the State Department, for by November, 1937, the
New Deal was troubled—and forced on the defensive—by the sharp recession that began two months earlier.[83]

Perhaps this economic jolt reminded the Association of American
Creditors that their holdings were still unrecovered, but in any event they
sought to use the crisis in Europe as a lever to pry a settlement from Moscow. Hull assured them, quite unnecessarily it might seem, that their claims

"have not been relinquished." [84] At the same time, others viewed a settlement as a means to weaken Hitler and Japan. Their proposal did not reach Hull, who thought the plan "a corker," until April, 1938, by which date Washington had ignored Litvinov's appeal of March 17, 1938, for a conference to discuss resistance to Germany and Japan.[85]

In the Far East, meanwhile, Russia took active steps to help China. Conferences in Moscow during January, 1938, led to the shipment of "considerable supplies" to Chiang during the remainder of that year and the next.[86] At the same time the Russians approached Washington for aid in a naval building program of their own.[87] This was the question first broached by Stalin when he talked with Ambassador Davies in June, 1938. After a brief review of the difficulties encountered in the matter, Stalin initiated a discussion of the debt. Davies acknowledged that his instructions "were not to bring up or urge the matter of debt settlement but strongly to take the position that we had done everything we were honorably committed or required to do and that so far as we were concerned it was a closed book, unless and until the Soviet Union wished to reopen the matter and fulfill its honorable obligations." Further meetings, during which Moscow pushed the matter "purely as a matter of clearing up the misunderstanding with the United States," led to negotiations in Washington. But the Senate's position on the broad question of debt settlement left the matter indefinite, and the State Department thought it "advisable to leave the matter open for the present." [88]

There were those in the State Department who took this attitude toward all relations with Russia. Whatever the result of the discussions, a new Ambassador was not named for many months.[89] During this interlude—in which Hitler traveled to Munich and, being given the green light, roared on through to Prague—Secretary Hull held two "basic discussions" with the Soviet Ambassador in Washington. Beyond the debt question, which Hull stressed, there were other causes for complaint. Russian monetary restrictions brought hardship to members of the Embassy and forced abandonment of the plan to build a new building. The Moscow consular district was restricted, as were other movements of official personnel. Far more serious was the issue raised by Soviet arrests of citizens of the United States then in Russia, their detention, and the extreme difficulty encountered in attempts to intervene in their behalf. Hull could not have emphasized Washington's dissatisfaction in much stronger language: the Department was forced "to consider whether the value to it of that mission is sufficient to warrant the maintenance of the Embassy on the present scale." [90]

Not until March, 1939, was Lawrence Steinhardt appointed as the new Ambassador. Two weeks before Stalin gave meaning to Litvinov's open warning to Davies at Brussels. Speaking to the Eighteenth Congress of the

Communist party on March 10, 1939, Stalin observed that the Soviet Union must "be cautious and not allow our country to be drawn into conflicts by warmongers who are accustomed to have others pull the chestnuts out of the fire for them." [91] "Persistently cold-shouldered" by London and Paris, the Soviets chose to adopt the policy of fending for oneself.[92] Litvinov lasted not quite two months, replaced by Viachislav Molotov on May 3, 1939. Though "the prospect of a German-Russian pact had long been in our minds"—as early as November, 1938—and "due significance" was given Litvinov's replacement, Hull took no steps to speed Steinhardt on his way.[93] "It is high time," the New York *Times* observed in March, when Steinhardt was appointed after the long delay, but the Ambassador did not arrive in Moscow until the end of the first week in August.[94]

Soon thereafter came the Soviet decision—based not only on the past policies of the West, but on the character of their proposals during the Moscow negotiations—to gamble on a truce with Hitler. Nor was the pact unrelated to Japan's probing of the Siberian border. For Lenin's version of Marxism—that safety was to be had by courting Washington within the dynamics of its struggle with Japanese militarism—was proven somewhat in error. Yet upon that estimate the Soviets based their policy from 1919 to 1939. The first essential was recognition, and Moscow's long campaign was formulated within the concept of mutual defense against Japan. Then came Litvinov's long series of efforts to render recognition meaningful—to no avail. The formulation that was justified by events in 1919 only threatened catastrophe two decades later. Nor did Stalin hide his fear and consternation: he laid both reactions quite bare in his speech of March 10, 1939.

Indeed, the theme pervades his entire report. World War I, Stalin noted, was concluded by two main treaties: Versailles for Europe and the Nine-Power Treaty in the Pacific. These two "main props" of peace were destroyed when "Japan tore up the Nine-Power Pact and Germany and Italy the Versailles Treaty." All three powers, he continued, "in every way infringe upon the interests of the non-aggressive States, primarily England, France, and the United States, while the latter draw back and retreat, making concession after concession to the aggressors." Stalin then recited the long list of German and Japanese encroachments in support of his analysis.[95] For Stalin the issue was survival, and the summer-long battle with Japan along the border between Manchuria and Outer Mongolia made him highly skeptical of England and France, who "had not thought out the military concomitants either of their own guarantees or of Russia's." [96]

When the Nazis seized the opportunity presented by Moscow's dilemma —the success of the Anti-Comintern Pact can stand upon this victory—the Soviets chose to risk a truce with Hitler, not only to forestall an early Nazi attack on Russia but as the way out of an actual engagement with Japan in the Far East. As for the United States, Roosevelt's warning to Stalin that Hitler "would turn on Russia . . . next" meant nothing in the context of the President's explicit qualification that "he was making no suggestion, much less any official indication of any desire on the part of this government . . . either to accept any responsibility or to give any assurances as to the possible course which Great Britain and France might undertake in connection with their present negotiations with the Soviet Union." Somewhat divorced from reality was Roosevelt's thought that his discourse on a situation of which Russia was quite aware, and in which Moscow was intimately involved, would alter the circumstances themselves: doubly so in view of Roosevelt's remark that he "was making no suggestion, *much less any official indication of any desire on the part of*" the *United States to act.*

Moscow, remembering that Roosevelt had been "relatively unconcerned with the terms of appeasement so long as they did not touch American interests," and conscious of Washington's refusal "to accept any responsibility" for the failure to take joint action with Russia—even in the Far East—answered that Russia "did not regard general declarations as sufficient." "We are not interested in declarations," Foreign Commissar Molotov replied to the President's message. "We are desirous that the present negotiations lead to a determination of the action to be taken under specific conditions or circumstances and that there shall be mutual obligation to counteract aggression." [97] When the West proved unwilling to enter into obligations of that character the Russian position became extremely precarious. "In so critical a situation the Moscow Government determined to do its utmost to safeguard its own security against possible Nazi attack." [98] In signing the Nazi-Soviet Pact of August 21, 1939, Stalin may have abandoned Leninism, but his own rule of thumb—the logic of facts is stronger than any other—was not violated. Japan had attacked in Asia and Hitler was about to march in Europe: the West had no plan of defense.

Kept in the dark by Hitler, Tokyo was stunned by this adverse turn of events. There exists no better measure of her dismay than Japan's approach to Roosevelt for "an alliance and agreement with them to go into Siberia and take it away from the Russians." This rather desperate Japanese reaction to the Nazi-Soviet Pact was short-lived, but Tokyo did approach Washington with a view to negotiations designed to stabilize the Far East. But the United States remained unwilling to assume any responsibility. "The future of American-Japanese relations is largely in the hands of Japan," Hull told Tokyo's representative at the end of August.[99] On the last day of the same month—in marked contrast to the American action —the Soviets lowered the age of conscription and extended the time of service for those already called to duty. At the same time, moreover, Moscow continued to support China's efforts to repel the Japanese—the Russian flow of supplies to Chiang "continued and perhaps even increased." [100]

But the Tragedy of the Thirties was yet to be played out. With an overture in Manchuria, the first act in Spain, a second at Munich, and the climax provided by the Anglo-French-Soviet negotiations in Moscow, the last scene was the Russian attack on Finland. Against the background of Washington's refusal to take a positive stand in the Far East—clearly revealed at the Brussels Conference in 1937, and again in Hull's remarks of August, 1939—and a similar decision at the time of the Munich Crisis, there was "no doubt that American official opinion wished the British success in their efforts, but without prejudging their methods, without taking a stand on any specific issue, without assuming any responsibility"—Russia had no reason to anticipate any meaningful collaboration with the United States against either Japan or Hitler in the foreseeable future. Yet Moscow was confronted with the immediate problem of a Nazi-dominated frontier. Unable, by the force of these circumstances, to forget for a moment that "the Munich deal had left the Soviet Government completely isolated," Moscow embarked upon a security program aimed "uniquely" against Hitler. [101]

Essential to this Soviet preparation against the Nazis was the integration of a defense line from Poland north to Leningrad. The same problem had been the issue between Russia and the Western Powers during the negotiations in Moscow through the summer of 1939. Even before that date—"in the spring of 1938"—the Soviets approached Finland to discuss mutual-security arrangements in view of the "possibility that Germany would begin a war against Russia, and that the left wing of the German front would land in Finland." Moscow initiated these talks in 1938 on "the premise that the Finns alone could withstand a German attack for only a short time." [102]

Bilateral negotiations between Moscow and Finland continued through the French-English-Russian conversations in Moscow. During this critical summer of 1939 Finland "did all it could" to secure the rejection of Moscow's conditions concerning "action intended to use the territory of one of the States in question [Finland, the Baltic States, and Poland] for aggression against it or one of the Contracting Powers [England, and France]." [103] But whereas the Nazi-Soviet Pact "caused no anxiety" in Finland, it was the product of considerable concern in Moscow. [104] Here was the very crux of the matter, as Stalin revealed in October. "But one cannot rely on it," Stalin observed during conversations with Latvia about the treaty with Hitler. "We must be prepared in time. Others who were not ready paid the price." [105] But to be ready north of Leningrad also exacted a toll in terms of relations with Washington.

For Moscow's determination to achieve what it considered to be minimum security arrangements against any attack in the Leningrad area was blocked by Finland's equal persistence in clinging to the idea of neutrality. But by the fall of 1939, neutrality, "without collective security, had become a meaningless concept and an untenable position." [106] On November 28, 1939, Moscow broke off negotiations with Helsinki, who up to that time had refused to withdraw Finnish troops from the border regions near Leningrad, and two days later the Red Army invaded Finland. Whether Moscow thought a sharp armed engagement would force Helsinki to give way to Russian demands—as a similar show of strength had ended Japanese attacks in the Far East—is not known with certainty. The Red Army's marked lack of early success against the Finns suggests that the Soviets thought in those terms; but if so, the Kremlin's calculation was gravely in error. Helsinki not only resisted stoutly but received immediate and enthusiastic support from the West.

On December 2, 1939, three days after the Soviet attack, President Roosevelt declared a moral embargo on shipments of materials and goods to Russia.[107] The speed of this action—which contrasted sharply with the timing of American countermeasures against Nazi Germany and Tokyo—was in part due, perhaps, to the immediately preceding tiff between Washington and Moscow over Soviet action in connection with the Nazi's capture of an American freighter, the *City of Flint*. Loaded with contraband bound for Britain, the *City of Flint* was taken by the Germans on October 9, and arrived in Murmansk two weeks later. Moscow's refusal immediately to force the Nazi prize crew to sail outward bound according to the provisions of maritime law moved Secretary of State Hull to "indignation and fury." [108] That the Soviets took the required action within a week did not mollify Washington.

Roosevelt, who described Moscow's campaign against Helsinki as "this dreadful rape of Finland," was especially anxious to take any action that would hurt Russia. "You see," he ordered Secretary of the Treasury Henry Morgenthau, Jr., on December 4, "that they stop buying aluminum." A bit later molybdenum, tungsten, nickel, and refinery equipment for the production of aviation gasoline were included under the moral embargo. Even then the President "was annoyed that no means could be found to add other items to the list." [109] Former President Herbert Hoover, supposedly an isolationist, was not satisfied by Roosevelt's policy. Hoover first demanded an explanation from Washington for "all this tenderness toward Russia," and then organized a special group to aid Finland.[110] An ironic bystander might well have recalled Hoover's comparative compassion for Japan in December, 1931. In those eight years America's fears to face the responsibilities of freedom had threatened the integrity of her democracy. For "when our actions do not, our fears do make us traitors." [111]

9
☆
CODA

The ancient Goths of Germany . . . had all of them a wise custom of debating every thing of importance to their state, twice; that is,—once drunk, and once sober:—Drunk—that their councils might not want vigour; and sober—that they might not want discretion.

Laurence Sterne: *Tristram Shandy,*
Book V, Chapter 17

ates has it in its power . . . to promote tendencies
lly find their outlet in either the breakup or the gradual
t power.

George Frost Kennan, 1947

The fate of the western world will turn on its ability to meet the
Soviet challenge by a successful search for new forms of social and economic action in which what is valid in individualist and democratic tradition can be applied to the problems of mass civilization.

Edward Hallett Carr, 1947

☆☆

Intellectual sleepwalking is the gravest danger of the atomic age. Man may
well stumble out the door of civilization thinking it the entrance to
the millennium. Even the most recent awakening did little to end the
confusion of illusion for reality. All can recall the mental paralysis that
accompanied the veneration of air power—until men started to walk
through the rubble. Yet the effects of that shock disappeared almost immediately. Those afflicted did no more than substitute the magic formula
$E = mc^2$ for the winged propeller as the badge of their dream-walking.
As before, their goal is perpetual peace and plenty; but once again their
paths vanish in the mists of unreality.

Three roads seem favored by the dreamers: the majority have chosen
Containment Avenue, another group prefers World Government Trail,
while a few risk sudden death on the one-lane express highway marked
Preventive War. The confidence of the latter group that their choice leads
to a modern Eden is easily demolished. With or without serious damage
to the industrial plant of the United States—both versions of this dream
are current—the reconstruction and administration of a severely damaged
and demoralized Western Europe and a de-industrialized Russia would be
neither immediate nor perfect. Edens are not created by atom generators in
the form of bombs.

* AUTHOR'S NOTE

To project this study beyond 1939 is a task impossible of execution: manuscript
sources of the character and extent that form the basis of the preceding chapters are
inaccessible to the independent scholar. For that reason the following pages are in
no sense a formal chapter on American-Russian relations after 1940. The essay is designed as no more than a review of the central features of recent relations between the
United States and the Soviet Union.

At first glance the other two groups of travelers appear to be groun̄ on hard reality. Certainly that is their claim. Yet the roadbeds they wandeȓ are far removed from the world they would save. Thus the world government group proposes the erection of international polling places prior to an agreement to hold an election. But the substitution of ballots for violence proceeds from one of two power relationships: complete control, or an agreement that certain basic aspects of the *status quo* will be respected by any victor. Equally certain, moreover, are two other facts. The Soviet Union will resist with force any effort by the United States to effect the first alternative; and the second condition can be satisfied only by the mutual accommodation of basic security demands that would, in turn, allow both nations, and the world, to turn to the solution of other problems.

However strange appears the coincidence, the failure to acknowledge those two considerations—the line at which the Soviet leaders will resist with force, and the foundation of a negotiated settlement—provides the link between those who propose world government and the men who formulate and administer American policy toward Russia. For the fallacies of world government are the fallacies of the policy of containment publicly enunciated by George Frost Kennan of the Policy Planning Division of the Department of State and acknowledged to be the blueprint of American policy. Between 1939 and 1947, others sought to establish the conditions for and then consummate a negotiated understanding that would give the United States, Russia, and the remainder of the world the security necessary if further attempts to improve human life were to be made. The theme of American-Russian relations from 1940 to 1947 was a slow modification of the antagonism and indifference of the late 1930s in the direction of accommodation, the breakdown of those efforts, and the substitution therefor of the policy of containment.

Mutual agreement on minimum security requirements forms the cornerstone of any negotiated settlement, and Hitler's continued assault on the world forced Moscow and Washington to face that problem with reference to their relations less than a year after the Nazi-Soviet Pact was signed. Moscow initiated discussions of the issue in terms of a post-Hitler world, moreover, immediately after the German attack on Russia. Progress toward accommodation was delayed by the necessity for Washington to adjust its policies to the fact of Soviet power. Not until 1943 did Roosevelt begin to modify—in terms of Russia's position both in Europe and Asia—his early assumption that Washington and London would dominate the postwar world. This revision of policy opened the way to the development and implementation of a new concert of power. Through the preservation and extension of that concert Roosevelt hoped to secure the peace and provide an atmosphere in which both the Soviet and non-Soviet world

ward the solution of common problems—economic, so-
. When the principle of negotiated settlement and adjust-
existing power relationships was abandoned for one that
only as a contest of power, initiative was surrendered to
iet Russia.

's position in January, 1940, was not, in many respects, un-
decision—in view of the Munich settlement and the West's
subsequent failure to accept reciprocal obligations against Hitler's next
attack—to attempt the unilateral solution of her minimum security requirements had so strained relations with Washington that Roosevelt "did
not feel that a visit to Moscow would serve any useful purpose." At the end
of the month, in fact, the President directed subordinates to "follow . . .
up" his suggestions to extend the moral embargo against Russia to include
gasoline shipments and deny sailing papers to vessels loaded for Soviet
ports.[1] But behind these and later attitudes was Washington's continued
antagonism toward Moscow and the parallel tendency to ignore Russia's
power in estimates of the future. For these reasons Washington declined
to make an all-out effort to exploit the meaning of Soviet policy in the
Russo-Finnish War and further failed immediately to modify policy in the
light of Hitler's assault on Moscow.

Secretary Hull was quite aware that the Russian peace terms to Finland
left the latter country independent—"in marked contrast to the results of
similar campaigns by Nazi Germany." [2] Nor could he have missed the
significance of Moscow's refusal to join Hitler in war against the West
when Paris and London prepared to give open military aid to Helsinki.
This latter development further emphasized the fact that it "was not easy"
to implement the Nazi-Soviet agreement. "For some time," reported the German Ambassador in Moscow in April, 1940, "we have observed in the Soviet
Government a distinct shift which was unfavorable to us." Both this change
and the "sudden termination of the Finnish war" he attributed to Moscow's determination "to avoid anything that might have furnished a pretext to the English and the French." [3] And the steady reports that Nazi
Germany would ultimately attack the Soviets were re-enforced by indications that Moscow anticipated the assault and hoped to stall for moie time
in which to make further preparations.[4] But the United States "had not
shared" British hopes that Russia could be wooed from Hitler, and Roosevelt and Hull were unwilling to do more than "wait and see what these
indications forebode." Washington's policy was not entirely negative,
but Hull's attitude—"do nothing that would drive her further into the
arms of Germany"—reflected his "strong bias against any negotiations
with Russia." [5]

Even Moscow's notable "change of attitude" that became apparent
in the summer of 1940 did not alter the Secretary's policy.[6] In February of

that year Molotov publicly referred to Japan as an enemy state and "remarked that it would not surprise him" to see the United States and Russia collaborate in her defeat.[7] Washington ignored this gesture. But Nazi
Germany's swift victory over France forced Stalin to modify his estimate
of the duration of his truce with Hitler; and the United States immediately
felt the effects of that revision. Moscow's earlier, and "violent," complaint
against Washington's cancellation of Soviet machine-tool orders was repeated. Secretary Hull, however, considered the move no more than another
of many "comparatively small items" that plagued relations with Russia.[8]
True, Hull did delegate Sumner Welles to explore the possibility of "some
real basis of agreement," but Welles's report that the "friendly relationship which is beginning to exist is unquestionably of real advantage to
this Government insofar as the Far Eastern situation is concerned" was
not enough—in the Secretary's view at least—to warrant support for
Britain's effort "to bring about a definite shift in Russian policy."[9]

On August 6, 1940, to be sure, the trade agreement between the two
nations was renewed; and, more importantly, discussions were initiated
with a view to establishing a three-way trade to aid China against Japan.
Moscow appeared ready to provide "such strategic materials as manganese, asbestos, platinum, and chrome"—a report that was greeted with
enthusiasm by such a stalwart conservative as Jesse Jones, head of the
Reconstruction Finance Corporation. But Hull exercised his "very strong
bias" against Russia most "vigorously" and the project was abandoned.[10]
His flat refusal to go along with London's suggestion to release to Moscow
the assets of the Baltic States—frozen after their reabsorption by Russia
in 1939–40—further emphasized his antagonism toward the Soviets.

The talks between Welles and Soviet Ambassador Constantine Oumansky ultimately collapsed when the Soviets "demanded much more in purchases of key materials" than Washington would allocate in view of commitments to London.[11] Britain's magnificent stand against the Nazis certainly justified this decision, but that fact should not lead to an assumption
that American policy toward Russia had undergone any serious modification. Washington's broad attitude remained unchanged: "make no approaches to Russia," and view "any approaches toward us with reserves
until the Russians satisfied us that they were not maneuvering merely to
obtain unilateral concessions for themselves."[12] Yet the negotiations with
Russia did modify Roosevelt's estimate of the future in one important
respect. On March 6, 1941, the President pushed through—against a faction "strongly represented in the State Department," one wing of the so-
called isolationists, and other "timid friends"—a version of the Lend-
Lease Act that would permit him to aid Moscow if the occasion arose.[13]

But Hitler's drive to the East of June 22, 1941, did not—as might have
been expected—immediately alter Washington's view of relations with Mos-

cow. Prime Minister Winston Churchill's quick welcome to Stalin as a partner in the common struggle against Hitler was a dramatic but hardly unexpected move. Churchill had advocated the same alliance previously, and for the same reason: the preservation of the British Empire. Roosevelt was clearly committed to similar support, but several factors contributed to the President's failure to respond with Churchill's vigor. Those who hoped to see the Soviets exhaust themselves in defense of the West were supported in their campaign against all-out assistance to Russia by the Catholics, some of the President's military advisors, and others who had no confidence in Moscow's desire, or ability, to fight through to final victory over Hitler. Roosevelt overruled this counsel, however, and agreed "to give all economic assistance practicable" to the Soviet Union.[14]

As added emphasis the President dispatched Harry Hopkins, his most trusted trouble-shooter, to Moscow to expedite the implementation of this decision. But Roosevelt's extension of Lend-Lease to Russia did not signify any fundamental awareness of Moscow's important role in any plans for the future. The character of the Atlantic Conference between Churchill and Roosevelt in August, 1941, bears strong witness to that fact. For implicit in the Atlantic Charter—drafted by Churchill and Roosevelt *before* the entrance of the United States into the war but *after* the Nazi attack on Russia—was the assumption that Britain and the United States would make the postwar settlement for "all the men in all the lands."[15]

To Churchill's inquiries about an international organization Roosevelt replied that "he himself would not be in favor of the creation of a new Assembly of the League of Nations, at least until after a period of time had passed and during which an international police force composed of the United States and Great Britain had had an opportunity of functioning."[16] Sumner Welles, an intimate participant in the formulation of the Charter, further documents the lack of serious reference to Russia. In 1946 Welles explained this absence on two counts: divided counsel as to Moscow's power of resistance, and "very slight" knowledge of "any" aspect of Soviet foreign policy.[17] Actually, as was later revealed, Roosevelt and Welles had specific information on both problems.

Harry Hopkins proceeded directly from his talks with Stalin to the meeting between Churchill and Roosevelt. Even had the Prime Minister failed to brief the President—an unlikely eventuality—Hopkins brought news that Russia "had been concerned, from the very beginning, with the political aspects of the enforced alliance." At the same time, moreover, his reports on Stalin's determination and confidence left "virtually no argument" on the question of a major commitment to aid Moscow. Stalin gave second priority to aluminum in his requests to Hopkins—not the act of a man "who feared imminent defeat."[18] Welles himself was concerned with the "vitally important question" of Russia's resistance before the mid-

Atlantic meeting. And Roosevelt was warned of the "vital importance that Stalin be impressed with the fact that he is not 'pulling the chestnuts out of the fire' for Allies who have no use for him or who will be hostile to him after the war and who will be no less enemies, in the event of an allied peace, than the Germans in the event of their victory." [19] But despite this knowledge the President continued to plan in terms exclusively British and American. From Welles's words of 1951 it would appear that neither he nor Roosevelt had yet accepted the Soviet Union as a power of major stature. Nor the fact that the Charter "would never in itself prevent future bitter controversies over frontiers and zones of influence." [20]

In December and January, 1941–42, furthermore, Roosevelt was again explicitly advised of Russia's minimum security demands, but rejected them without discussion or negotiation. Immediately upon his arrival in Moscow in late December, 1941, British Foreign Secretary Anthony Eden was approached with proposals to settle Russia's postwar European boundary. Moscow's desired settlement was a forthright challenge to the West— obviate the possibility of another German attack. Together with Stalin's earlier concern with reparations in kind, "particularly in machine tools," from Germany—a preoccupation known in Washington—these territorial demands could not but raise the specter of Munich and the Moscow negotiations of 1939. Eden was asked to agree to the Soviet border of 1941, "prior to the German attack," with certain modifications that would have, had they then existed, enabled Russia to proceed immediately to the assistance of Czechoslovakia in 1938. This frontier specification, to which Stalin "attached fundamental importance," was conditioned by one basic concern—security against another German attack.[21]

Thus by January, 1942, the United States was well aware of Russia's major postwar objectives: strategic security in Eastern Europe and economic plasma for the war-ravaged industrial system of European Russia, already occupied by the Nazis. These objectives were neither denied nor disguised by the Soviets, but the United States failed to formulate a policy in response until the opportunity to negotiate a firm understanding on both issues had been lost. Many factors contributed to this failure: Hull's reluctance to settle such problems in advance—and with Russia in particular—and openly anti-Soviet advice from within the State Department, for example, but the fundamental consideration was the attitude of President Roosevelt. For a time Roosevelt did see the need to reach specific agreements on the critical issues of security and economic recovery, but he chose, in the final analysis, to avoid any commitments that would limit the " 'freedom of action' which he valued so highly." [22]

In response to this first overture from Moscow, therefore, the United States directed Eden to decline all Soviet offers. He was to assure Stalin, of course, that Moscow "would participate no less than Britain and the

United States" in any final decisions, but no commitments were to be made. These instructions—which Churchill accepted in view of his fear that an approach to Roosevelt "might cause lasting trouble"—were based on the Atlantic Charter, a document formulated without Russian participation. The directive to Eden was written, furthermore, with the knowledge that exclusion from the Atlantic Conference intensified Russia's suspicions "that the British and ourselves aimed at excluding her from the peace and postwar settlement, and that we would not be prepared to take sufficiently harsh measures in that settlement to render Germany harmless." Britain openly admitted that "prior understandings" with Washington prevented any settlement of the issue—a revelation that spoke far more powerfully than Hull's verbal assurances for the future.[23]

Churchill faced the problem squarely when the Soviets reopened the question three months later. The Prime Minister specifically asked Roosevelt to acknowledge Russia's strength and formulate policy accordingly. "The increasing gravity of the war," he cabled, "has led me to feel that the principles of the Atlantic Charter ought not to be construed so as to deny Russia the frontiers she occupied when Germany attacked her." Doubly significant was Churchill's candid reminder that this "was the basis on which Russia acceded to the Charter." [24] But Washington answered Russia's insistence on territorial guarantees with a cable that "bluntly expressed" determination to prevent any agreement of that character. The policy, Hull maintained, was "logically" unassailable, but logic was not the cause of Russia's acquiescence.[25]

Far more influential was Washington's expression of "interest" in a second front at the critical stage of negotiations. This was Moscow's main military concern from the day of Hitler's attack; this reference to a second front eased the tension and was undoubtedly a vital factor in the conclusion of an Anglo-Soviet treaty that did not include territorial provisions. At the same time, however, Washington's adamant position reenforced Moscow's suspicions. By virtue of her winter successes against the Nazis, Russia could ponder the possibilities of a double option. For, as Stalin could well reason, even if no firm understanding was reached with the West the Red Army would ultimately secure the desired borders. Hardly strange, therefore, was Molotov's failure to broach the border question during his visit to Washington in June, 1942. Nor was Hull's emphasis on postwar postal conventions and the problem of civil air communications calculated to impress Moscow with Washington's sense of realism.[26]

Molotov was occupied with more critical problems: the second front and future collaboration with the United States and Britain. Roosevelt's first step toward a more realistic appraisal of the premises of collaboration enabled the two countries to progress toward a basic understanding despite a serious crisis over the second front. As for the second front, Molotov "put this question bluntly: could we undertake such offensive action as would draw off forty German divisions . . . ?" And the Soviet foreign minister "requested a straight answer." When General George C. Marshall answered "Yes," the President "authorized Mr. Molotov to inform Mr. Stalin that we expect the formation of a second front this year." In this context the official communiqué—which reported that "full understanding was reached"—meant but one thing to Moscow: a major assault upon Hitler's Europe.[27]

Churchill's decision to undertake a trip to Moscow to advise Stalin of the inability to implement this communiqué revealed the Prime Minister's clear understanding of the Russian interpretation of Roosevelt's answer. Stalin was "very glum" and "restless" when given the news—a combination that foreshadowed later Soviet reaction.[28] Roosevelt anticipated as much and warned Churchill that Stalin would be in "no mood to engage in strategic discussions of a theoretical nature." [29] Nor was the President in error: relations with Russia cooled dangerously.

The first months after Stalin learned that there would be no European second front in 1942 were characterized by "more and more questions from Moscow and very few indications of cordiality." [30] Resentment at what was considered a clear breach of faith re-enforced memories of 1918 and 1939, and this increased suspicion of the West was given the power of expression by the Red Army's victory at Stalingrad. The Soviets were strengthened in their confidence that minimum security requirements could, if necessary, be achieved unilaterally. This sense of isolation was "not lessened" by Ambassador Admiral William H. Standley's sharp accusation that Moscow hid the character and extent of American aid from the people of Russia.[31]

At this critical juncture Roosevelt's understanding of the power realities that would accompany victory matured rapidly. In his conversations with Molotov in June, 1942, the President officially expanded his concept of the postwar policemen to include Soviet Russia and China. Stalin's response was "full accord" save for the reservation "possibly" in connection with China. On this question the Soviet leader was supported by Eden, who for his part "did not much like the idea of the Chinese running up and down the Pacific." Ultimately, both Russia and England were to compromise on the admission of China—a power that they considered no more than an automatic vote for Washington.[32] Then, as relations with Moscow deteriorated, Roosevelt opened a detailed consideration of the structure of that power concert. The President first acknowledged that Russia "regarded the question of her western frontiers as not open to discussion"—a fact that Churchill had sought, unsuccessfully, to make clear some eighteen months earlier. The awakening came when Eden arrived in Washington shortly after Standley's verbal outburst. Eden's review of the situation was verified by unofficial conversations with Soviet representatives in Washington and London—all of which brought agreement that "the real decisions should be made by the United States, Great Britain, Russia, and China, who would be the powers for many years to come that would have to police the world." [33] But other developments dramatized the necessity to act on that conclusion without delay.

First came the rupture between Moscow and the Polish Government-in-Exile, an event that foreshadowed serious difficulties. The success achieved by former Ambassador Davies' special trip to Moscow—he arranged tentative plans for a meeting between Roosevelt and Stalin—was negated by the further postponement of the second front to May, 1944. Stalin made it quite clear that he was "not impressed" with this and other decisions made at the Trident Conference in Washington during May.[34] The recall of Soviet Ambassadors from London and Washington was swiftly highlighted by the formation, on July 21, 1943, of a "Free German Committee" headed by the survivors of Stalingrad. Of little encouragement in these circumstances was the War Department's opinion that Russia was "the decisive factor in the war." The *"most important factor the United States has to consider in relation to Russia,"* emphasized this memorandum of August 10, *"is the prosecution of the war in the Pacific."* [35] Not only was the military's counsel of significance at the time, but similar estimates of the situation were of equal importance in later decisions at Yalta.

The first consequence of this steady disintegration of relations with Moscow appears to have been a major policy fight within the State Department. Sumner Welles, who was particularly close to Roosevelt, shared in broad outline, if not in intensity, the President's determination to achieve a basic understanding with Britain and Russia. Another group agreed that definite plans were needed, but argued vehemently that they should be anti-Russian in character. Secretary Hull, however, stood by his original view that no settlement should be negotiated until victory was achieved. Whatever the day-by-day developments of the battle the final result was not unexpected—if unfortunate. Welles left the Department. The shift of personnel, however, did not solve the policy problem. Rather did Hull find it necessary to open discussions of the postwar settlement.[36] This decision represented a complete reversal of his instructions to Eden of December, 1941. Then the Secretary thought negotiations would be "unfortunate"—to Stalin in October, 1943, he declared that any official who was "opposed to formulating the fundamental policies for a postwar world until after the war is over, would be thrown out of power overnight." [37]

Hull made the adaptation necessary to avoid that eventuality but he did not fully execute Roosevelt's policy. He did, however, secure two presidential objectives in the Far East. Stalin agreed to attack Japan when Germany was defeated, and also accepted China as a member of the postwar policy group.[38] The full meaning of these Soviet decisions did not become apparent until the meeting of the Big Three at Yalta. Of more immediate consequence was Hull's seeming failure to carry through Roosevelt's policy on Poland. For during talks with Eden in March, 1943, the President left no doubt as to his position. Eden was disturbed because the Poles were "being very difficult" about their "very large ambitions after the war"— ambitions predicated on the assumption that Russia's weakness and Germany's defeat would enable Poland to "emerge as the most powerful state in that part of the world." Eden thought this "completely unrealistic," and Roosevelt agreed. The President made it clear that he "did not intend to go to the Peace Conference and bargain with Poland or the other small states; as far as Poland is concerned, the important thing is to set it up in a way that will help maintain the peace of the world." [39]

The Polish Government in London entertained other ideas. It demanded a new guarantee based on the position of 1939 that led to the final breakdown of talks between France, Britain, and Russia. In their counterattack against Hitler the Soviets were not to advance through Poland without prior approval, western troops were to be stationed there if an advance did occur, and the Warsaw-in-London Government "expressed reservations against a projected" Czech-Soviet alliance.[40] Hull sought to induce Moscow to re-establish relations with this government *prior* to any agreement on the border settlement: this despite Roosevelt's firm expression of opinion on the issue. The result was the loss of an opportunity to delineate a mutually acceptable settlement. For despite blunt warnings that the advance of the Red Army made it "desirable for the Government of Poland to reach a solution without delay," the London group refused to accept that demarcation of the eastern Polish border.[41]

Secretary Hull records that "in general we let the British take the lead" on the Polish problem, but the Secretary fails to note that Churchill's firm stand on the Curzon Line meant little to the London Poles in view of Washington's evasion and delay.[42] Churchill, quite conscious that the Red Army could well settle the question of Russia's western frontier, candidly discussed the issue with Stalin at Teheran.

"Are we," Churchill inquired in response to Stalin's emphasis on the danger of a resurgent Germany, "to try to draw frontier lines?"

"Yes," was Stalin's blunt answer.[43]

Their broad conclusion can be summarized as an agreement to move Poland west. Stalin accepted the Curzon Line as the basic line of demarcation in the east, with the Poles to be compensated "mainly at the expense of Germany." The British Prime Minister frankly advised Eden that he was "not going to break my heart about this cession of part of Germany to Poland." As for the London Poles, he continued, they "would be most unwise" to let the Soviet proposals "fall to the ground." The issue "of the utmost consequence" in Churchill's mind was the need to secure firm territorial settlements before the Red Army crossed Russia's border of 1940.[44]

Churchill's view did not appeal to the London Poles. They could, and no doubt did, argue that his stand on the Curzon Line contradicted England's pledge to Poland in 1939. But the London group was unwilling to acknowledge that specification of conditions for the advance of the Red Army, or Russia's future relations with Czechoslovakia, or the London Poles' own postwar ambitions had any meaningful relation to the conditions of 1939. Or, in another sense, the London group declined to face the consequences of Poland's 1934 treaty with Hitler and Warsaw's refusal, in 1939, to permit the Red Army to engage the Nazis on Polish soil. In response to the Teheran Conference, therefore, the London Poles proposed to discuss "all outstanding issues"—under which heading they classed the Curzon Line. Russia's reply was simple and final: Stalin and Churchill had settled that point at Teheran.[45]

Certain modifications in favor of Poland aside, read the Soviet note, Poland must accept the Curzon Line in the east and receive compensation from Germany in the west and along the Baltic coast. Churchill publicly supported this Russian stand. "I cannot feel," he advised Parliament on February 22, 1944, "that the Russian demand for reassurance about her western frontier goes beyond the limit of what is reasonable or just." In a blunt warning to the Poles, he noted that the advance of the Red Army made an agreement "indispensable." Churchill may well have hoped that these remarks would also remind President Roosevelt of his earlier remark to Eden "that, after all, the big powers would have to decide what Poland should have"—and his participation in the talks on Poland at Teheran.[46]

For, given the London Poles' refusal to accept the Curzon Line, Washington's quick agreement to serve as an intermediary in the proposed talks with Russia could only raise the question of whether Roosevelt would maintain his earlier attitude. This, as Churchill realized, was a critical issue. The foundation of the unity manifested at Teheran would crumble if Roosevelt did not act on his declaration that the Big Three should settle fundamental issues of security. Yet this is exactly what ultimately occurred —Roosevelt's failure to carry through on this fundamental decision of the Teheran Conference.

One pattern emerges from a review of the conference and the aftermath: the achievement of a general accord with reference to three broad problems—measures to be taken to forestall a third German assault on Europe, the character of future relations between the United States and Russia, and Russia's future position in Asia—followed by the progressive dissipation of the understanding in each area. As the developments with reference to Poland indicate, this disintegration proceeded in a sequence that roughly followed the order given above. In view of these considerations it is important to review carefully Roosevelt's concept of the Conference and his decisions in the first months that followed. Roosevelt's own strong sense that he established common ground with Stalin at Teheran is well known, and has been further substantiated by others after the fact.[47] But one very suggestive relationship in connection with the President's view of Teheran—and, more importantly, his entire approach to the postwar years —has been generally ignored.

This is the character and timing of Roosevelt's message to Congress of January 11, 1944. For here, with Europe yet to be invaded and the Philippines still occupied by Japan, is a militant extension of the New Deal—an Economic Bill of Rights. Prior to his specification of this plan for the future, the President reviewed the spirit and purpose of the meeting at Teheran. "The one supreme objective for the future, which we discussed for each nation individually, and for all the United Nations," Roosevelt emphasized, "can be summed up in one word: Security." But not security as an end. Rather as a means to what all three leaders made "abundantly clear" as their basic war aim. This, the President stressed, was the "resumption of peaceful progress by their own peoples—progress toward a better life." And the opportunity to make that effort toward a better life, Roosevelt pointed out, was contingent upon an understanding between the Big Three.

In words more courageous than those of any President of the United States since November, 1917, Roosevelt then acknowledged the challenge of the Bolshevik Revolution. "We have come to a clear realization," was his candid admission, "of the fact that true individual freedom cannot exist without economic security and independence." The elements of that foundation for freedom, the President continued, included the right to "a useful and remunerative job . . . to earn enough to provide adequate food and clothing and recreation . . . a decent home . . . [and] adequate medical care." This was a challenge that lesser men in the United States and the world at large had refused to face for a generation—and thereby had confessed their own lack of confidence in the democratic approach to the problems of an industrial society.

But to Roosevelt on January 11, 1944, this was the basic problem. "We must be prepared to move forward, in the implementation of these rights, to new goals of human happiness and well-being." There were, he cautioned, "grave dangers of rightist reaction in this Nation," and those dangers must not be allowed to materialize. Otherwise the war would have been fought in vain. "Indeed," the President warned, "if such reaction should develop—if history were to repeat itself and we were to return to the so-called normalcy of the 1920s—then it is certain that, even though we shall have conquered our enemies on the battlefields abroad, we shall have yielded to the spirit of fascism here at home." [48] The President's words were those of a man who believed that the Teheran Conference pointed the way to avoid that eventuality.

Yet the President failed to measure up to his own insight and under-standing. For in the last analysis he placed more value on the maintenance of unlimited freedom of action than upon the effort to stabilize the postwar relations between Great Britain, Russia, and the United States. To be sure, that failure to carry through was not marked by a single dramatic decision; and, indeed, both those who attack and defend Roosevelt do so on the assumption that he went all out to build and maintain the unity. But the policies of the United States toward territorial settlements in Europe, with specific reference to Soviet-American relations, and toward China, all characterized different phases of that indecision. Both Roosevelt and his successor, Harry S. Truman—and their critics, it might be noted—failed to see that freedom of action could not be maintained in every situation at all times; and, in addition, that to secure the initiative in a given area it was vital to deal with both aspects of the problem—external security and the internal answer to the challenge of the Bolshevik Revolution.

Thus the breakdown of the unity exemplified at Teheran occurred in a complex pattern. First came the wartime refusal to reach territorial set-tlements on the basis of Russia's 1941 proposals *before* the Red Army carried that frontier farther west. Then—once that opportunity had been lost—the failure to link resolution of the new problem with Russia's post-war economic needs, as revealed in her persistent demands for reparations in kind from Germany and Italy and her formal request for direct aid from the United States. In Asia, where the basic territorial commitments were made, the subsequent failure to validate them by facing the challenge of the Bolshevik Revolution in terms of China's *internal* development. Dis-integration was speeded by Roosevelt's apparent inability to realize that delay served only to decrease the number of possible options at his dis-posal.

For the President's on-again, off-again efforts to evade the relation-ship between military occupation and political influence only re-enforced Russia's lack of confidence in the West's objectives—particularly in East-ern Europe, the area of most immediate concern to Moscow. There re-mained, under the circumstances, but one way to secure Allied solidarity once Germany and Japan were defeated: use Russia's preoccupation with economic rehabilitation as the means to secure negotiated settlements. When this approach was abandoned—or, more exactly, ignored—the cold war was declared by default. For without negotiation the highly prized free-dom of action could be achieved only by force, a fact that was to be formalized in George Frost Kennan's policy of containment in 1947.

In the first months after Teheran, however, Prime Minister Churchill did his most to forestall that eventuality. That he understood Roosevelt to have committed himself to the Curzon Line at Teheran seems clear from his cable to the President on January 6, 1944. "As soon as I get home," he outlined, "I shall go all out with the Polish Government to close with this or something like it. . . . If I can get this tidied up early in February, a visit from them to you would cinch matters." [49] As good as his word, Churchill sent the London Poles to Roosevelt with a five-point program based on the Curzon Line. But Roosevelt and Hull, though they pointed to the advance of the Red Army as reason enough "to reach a solution without delay," would not commit themselves to the proposal. Under these conditions it is not too strange that the London Poles "would not accept the Curzon Line as a basis for negotiations with Russia." [50] While that line had been central in all discussions at Teheran, Churchill's most energetic efforts to translate the discussions into decisions were of little avail as long as Roosevelt and Hull refused to do likewise.

But the issue could not be evaded, for the Red Army was beginning to advance across southeastern Europe. And Moscow's initial attitude in the new situation only served to re-emphasize Russia's determination to secure her 1940 borders. On April 1, 1944, Gromyko frankly advised Hull that the penetration into Rumania "was the beginning of a full re-establishment of the border delineated in 1940"; but also took care to give assurances that no further extensions were planned.[51] Here was an open restatement of the aims given to Eden in December, 1941—again reiterated before the fact. The note was at once a reminder that Moscow had not forgotten Munich and another invitation to definitive negotiations. But Washington did not take the proffered initiative. Churchill, however, realized the significance of both the note and the advance of the Red Army.

Well aware that the successes of the Red Army posed the problem of a "showdown with the Russians" over the settlement to be effected in the Balkans and along the eastern Mediterranean, Churchill proposed a tentative arrangement pending further talks—Russian initiative in Rumania and British leadership in Greece. Moscow responded favorably but specified, in the words of Hull, that "before they could give any final assurances they would like to know whether the United States Government had been consulted, and whether we were in agreement with the arrangement." [52] Like the first, Moscow's second overture to Washington received no clear answer. Secretary Hull's opposition, "we . . . should do what we could to discourage it," was not backed by an alternative—not even a proposal for top-level discussions.[53] Churchill, however, extended the scope of the agreement to include Bulgaria and Yugoslavia, and then carried the issue directly to Roosevelt who finally approved the understanding for a three-month trial period.[54]

There was no question of not acting together, Churchill explained, but someone had to "play the hand." [55] But in subsequent months Roosevelt and Hull did little more than sit back and watch the game. "Numerous diplomatic cables" registered Washington's dissatisfaction as Churchill maintained the pattern of agreement; but even Roosevelt's earlier idea of "consultative machinery" failed to be implemented. [56] And protests were no substitute for direct negotiations. With no option but to keep on playing the hand, Churchill and Stalin added specific refinements to their understanding during talks in Moscow in October, 1944. "The march of events in southeast Europe," ran the laconic summary of the meeting, "was fully considered." Behind that histrionic verbiage—and the Prime Minister's wry comment that "We worked very hard"—was Churchill's effort to stabilize the situation before the advance of the Red Army rendered any reference to the Soviet proposals of 1941–44 completely unrealistic. Concerned "above all" with Greece, Churchill agreed to Soviet predominance in Rumania, Bulgaria, and Hungary in return for "joint" authority in Yugoslavia and British dominance in Athens. [57]

To ignore these commitments or the action taken under their provisions—as was later done, both by American policy makers and unofficial observers—is to distort gravely the causes of the subsequent rise of tension between Moscow and the West. "It is important," Roosevelt cabled Ambassador to Russia W. Averell Harriman on the eve of the Churchill-Stalin meeting, "that I retain complete freedom of action after this conference is over." [58] How, exactly, Roosevelt planned to exercise unlimited freedom of action in an area occupied by the Red Army is not clear. Later developments suggest, that perhaps he thought in terms of negotiations with Moscow on the questions of reparations and direct economic aid to Russia; but if so, he failed to carry through on the plan before his death. Nor did his successor, as will be seen.

Under these circumstances, therefore, Washington's later moves to exercise freedom of action in the Balkans only served, in effect, to disrupt an understanding to which the United States had acquiesced. "Had we made such a determined fight against the Anglo-Russian agreement as we had made successfully against the proposed territorial clauses of the Anglo-Russian alliance of May, 1942," concluded Secretary of State Hull, "it is possible that some of our later difficulties in the Balkans might not have arisen." [59] Like Roosevelt, Hull neglects to mention what lever he would have used to pry the Red Army out of the Balkans; but his admission that Washington failed to take a definite stand until after the British had acted in Greece under the terms of the Churchill-Stalin agreement is of critical importance.

For these Anglo-Russian talks of October, 1944, formed the basis of Moscow's understanding of the Yalta Agreement. This was especially so, for between October, 1944, and the Yalta meeting the British exercised their authority to quell—by major military action—internal disturbances in Greece. Through December and January, 1944–45, British forces engaged and defeated the Communist-led campaign against the Greek Monarchists. Moscow's rigid observance of the pact with London was acknowledged by Churchill himself. "Stalin adhered very strictly to this understanding during the thirty days' fighting against the Communists and ELAS in the city of Athens," the Prime Minister advised Roosevelt, "in spite of the fact that all this was most disagreeable to him and those around him." [60]

Thus when Moscow staged a similar unilateral intervention in Rumania during the Red Army's assault on Berlin, the President understandably "felt that the Rumanian situation did not offer the best test" of relations with Moscow.[61] Yet Washington's protests grew ever more militant, while at the same time no further discussions among the Big Three were initiated. To Russia, as her constant references to British action in Greece and her steady, but unsuccessful, efforts to link discussions of reparations from Germany with the dispute over Poland and the Balkans implied, the West's actions no doubt signified an unwillingness to abide by a reciprocal agreement.[62] In Washington, however, where the decision was made to ignore the Churchill-Stalin talks—and where the concept of negotiations around the question of economic rehabilitation was neglected or ignored—the Soviet actions were viewed as proof of a refusal to share control. Meanwhile, a similar crisis grew out of the Red Army's push across Poland.

Against the background of Moscow's firm stand on the issue of the 1940 border and the Polish Government-in-Exile's refusal to accept that basic line, the Yalta Agreement could not serve as an instrument of settlement unless it signified a settlement as to which Polish Government, London's or Moscow's, would serve as the basis of reorganization. That this was not the case soon became apparent. Article VII of the Yalta Agreement specified that the "Provisional Government which is now functioning in Poland should therefore be reorganized on a broader democratic basis with the inclusion of democratic leaders from Poland itself and from Poles abroad." Moscow read this line to mean the expansion of the government then in existence, whereas London and Washington claimed that an entire new government was intended.[63] In the atmosphere of the disagreement over Rumania the tension over Poland rapidly increased. Stalin demanded that any representatives picked by London or Washington must make a clear statement accepting the Cruzon Line and must further give evidence of "really striving to establish friendly relations between Poland and the Soviet Union." A reply to Stalin was being prepared when Roosevelt died on April 12, 1945.[64]

At the moment of his accession to office, therefore, Harry S. Truman inherited a policy predicated upon a unity among the Big Three that was severely strained. Washington's failure to meet the issue of the Red Army's advance across Europe prior to, or during the first stages of, that sweep produced two grave consequences. Equally serious as the fact of Soviet control was the result in terms of Moscow's reaction to Washington's intervention in the Churchill-Stalin agreement on the Balkans. In these circumstances President Truman had two alternatives: break with the policy of negotiated settlements among the Big Three and force the Red Army out of Eastern Europe, or negotiate a new agreement along the lines of the Churchill-Stalin arrangement of October, 1944. But as of April, 1945, the President had but one practical method by which to save the concept of a concert of power—America's economic strength.

Roosevelt recognized the potential of this power in terms of American-Russian relations as early as the Teheran Conference. He briefly discussed the significance of close economic relations with Stalin, who hoped they would be "greatly expanded." Yet their conversation at that time was no more than peripheral. "I am sorry I did not get time," Roosevelt wrote shortly after the meeting, "to talk with the Russians about the whole question of reconstruction in Russia." [65] At Yalta, a year later, Moscow indicated deep concern over this matter: it emphasized heavy "reparations in kind" from Germany, and stressed Molotov's hope "that the United States would furnish the Soviet Union with long-term credits." [66] Details of further conversations on a loan are not available, but there is evidence of Washington's acute awareness of the question. "I am convinced," wrote Secretary of the Treasury Henry Morgenthau, Jr., to Roosevelt on the eve of Yalta, "that if we were to come forward now and present to the Russians a concrete plan to aid them in the reconstruction period it would contribute a great deal towards ironing out many of the difficulties we have been having with respect to their problems and policies." [67]

Truman's basic decision—one that he later characterized as a "mistake"—was to use this economic power in an attempt to implement Washington's answer to various questions rather than as a tool of negotiation.[68] Nor was this decision delayed: it was made in April, 1945. Soon after his establishment in the White House, Truman assembled a group of advisors to discuss policy toward Russia. "The consensus of opinion among the group Truman had called together," reports Admiral William D. Leahy, "was that the time had arrived to take a strong American attitude toward the Soviet Union and that no particular harm could be done to our war prospects if Russia should slow down or even stop her war effort in Europe and Asia." Although Secretary of War Stimson "thought that the Russians perhaps were being more realistic than we were in regard to their own security," and another thought that the Yalta clause on Poland was open to "two interpretations," the majority pushed for a less adaptive policy.[69]

Ambassador to Russia Harriman took a particularly extreme stand. Aware that the Russians "probably wanted about $6,000,000,000 in credit from the United States" for economic rehabilitation and construction, Harriman had already decided to ignore this opportunity for a discussion of outstanding issues. Rather did he inquire as to whether "our basic interest might better be served by increasing our trade with other parts of the world rather than giving preference to the Soviet Union as a source of supply." And at the White House conference he proposed that Lend-Lease "should be limited exclusively" to war matériel.[70] Secretary of the Navy James Forrestal, who was particularly concerned with the Russian question, supported Harriman.[71] Truman's attitude appears to have been equally clear: he did not intend to let the differences over the Polish issue delay the San Francisco Conference, scheduled for later in the month. "He intended to go on," runs one set of notes on the President's remarks, "with the plans for San Francisco and if the Russians did not wish to join us they could go to hell." A bit later, in fact, Truman did tell Molotov that he would— if necessary—form the United Nations Organization of non-Russian States. And shortly thereafter Harriman's recommendation on Lend-Lease became policy.[72]

Yet the attitude here reflected did not immediately crystallize into a hard, inflexible policy. At the suggestion of one who had interpreted for Roosevelt in his talks with Stalin, President Truman sent Harry Hopkins back to Moscow "to talk things out directly with Stalin and Molotov." The particular problem was Poland, but the conversations revealed far more significant information than Moscow's views on that issue. With a frankness that may well have shaken Harriman who, as Ambassador, attended the meetings, Stalin stated his "impression that the American attitude towards the Soviet Union had perceptibly cooled once it became obvious that Germany was defeated, and that it was as though the Russians were no longer needed." Another of Stalin's remarks also might have jogged Harriman's memory. Inability to continue Lend-Lease, Stalin noted, "was one thing but that the manner in which it had been done had been unfortunate and even brutal." He wished to "make it clear that he fully understood the right of the United States to curtail Lend-Lease shipments," but warned that "if the refusal . . . was designed as pressure on the Russians in order to soften them up then it was a fundamental mistake." [73]

Hopkins returned to the Polish question that, he explained, "*per se* was not so important as the fact that it had become a symbol of our ability to work out problems with the Soviet Union." Again and again he stressed the point that the feeling of dissatisfaction with Moscow's policy "was a fact"—whatever "the reasons why this had occurred, or the merits of the case." In reply, Stalin emphasized three factors: the issue from his point of view, of course, was the fact that "in the course of twenty-five years the

Germans had twice invaded Russia via Poland." This was possible, he continued, "because Poland had been regarded as a part of the *cordon sanitaire* around the Soviet Union and that previous European policy had been that Polish Governments must be hostile to Russia." He then admitted the error of Moscow's unilateral actions, but pointed out that they "had arisen out of the presence of Soviet troops in Poland." As for the future, Stalin proposed the expansion of the Soviet-backed government along the lines of his earlier understanding with Churchill on the Balkans.[74]

These frank exchanges between Hopkins and Stalin, the subsequent meeting of the Big Three in Potsdam, Germany, July–August, 1945, and later discussions between the top foreign policy spokesmen of the three nations led to certain accommodations. Aspects of the disagreements over Rumania and Bulgaria, as well as Poland, were settled, and a bit later Moscow acceded to pressure from Washington and London and withdrew Soviet troops from northern Iran. The latter action was formally taken in response to a United Nations directive, but the initiative came from Washington and London. Often lost sight of, or not mentioned, in later months, however, was the fact of Moscow's retreat. Nor did the Red Army return when the Iranian Parliament refused, under strong pressure from the West, to ratify an oil agreement negotiated during the period of crisis—or despite the clear extension of Washington's military influence at the doorstep of Soviet oil fields. In a similar pattern—likewise ignored—Moscow gave Washington the initiative in China.

Stalin did not, contrary to one prevalent view, win China at Yalta. Rather did the Soviet position symbolize a conclusion that the government of Chiang Kai-shek would remain in control of China. This policy became apparent early in the war, when Stalin objected to Chiang's inclusion in the concert of Allied power; for, as with Churchill, Stalin had no great interest in giving Washington a "fagot vote," as the Prime Minister termed China's role, in all discussions.[75] In response to continued pressure, however, the Russians gave way and admitted China to full membership in October, 1943. The Soviets "seem genuinely to have thought in the war years that what they required was some measure of control, through the Chinese Communists, of the actions of the Kuomintang, which they assumed would continue to be the central Government, and also of some physical guarantees for their material interests in the border regions." [76]

Roosevelt revealed his awareness of the significance of Russia's actions during the Teheran Conference a month later. He saw quite clearly that nothing he could do would affect the fact that Russia had been and would continue to be a major Pacific power. At Teheran, therefore, the President spoke in terms of Russia's need for an economic outlet and then mentioned the possibility of an arrangement with respect to the Manchurian ports of Dairen and Port Arthur. Roosevelt went on to formulate an agreement founded on Russia's position in the Far East as re-enforced by three other important considerations: the view of the Combined Chiefs of Staff that Soviet aid was necessary to defeat Japan; Tokyo's attack on Russia in 1904; and the existing treaty between China and Russia concerning the Chinese Eastern Railway.[77]

The President had little choice but to accept the recommendations of the majority of his military advisors who "insisted" that Soviet assistance was vital.[78] The charge, later made by some, that Roosevelt should have gazed three months into the future of atomic physics is absurd. Nor was there any valid reason not to return the fruits of an earlier Japanese military excursion against Russia. Extensive criticism has been made, however, of the decisions affecting the disposition of Port Arthur and the Manchurian railway system.[79] These critics overlook several fundamental considerations. Of primary importance was Roosevelt's concern with future security against the power that challenged the nations of the Pacific basin to a trial by arms. Japan's long occupation and administration of the area had put down roots that could not be destroyed by mere military defeat. China, on the other hand, gave little evidence of the strength necessary to neutralize that vested interest. To recognize Russia's legitimate economic and strategic stake in Manchuria under conditions that specified "that China shall retain full sovereignty" was a solution far more conservative than to abandon the "cradle of conflict" to the winds of fate.[80]

Though seldom noted—either by the critics or the defenders of the Yalta decision—China never recognized Moscow's sale of the Chinese Eastern to Japan in 1935. Russia's act, read the Chinese protest, "does not in the least affect the validity of the provisions of the agreement of 1924, nor the status of the railway." [81] The treaty of 1924 specified, among other things, that the manager of the railway—"a purely commercial enterprise" —should be a Soviet citizen. On August 14, 1945, these provisions were re-stated in the agreement to consolidate the Chinese Eastern and the South Manchurian "as a purely commercial transport undertaking." [82] From George Frost Kennan, State Department career officer then on duty in the American Embassy in Moscow, had already come a significant summary of Soviet policy. Russia's attitude, he wrote on April 23, 1945, represented "a fluid resilient policy directed at . . . all the diplomatic and territorial assets previously possessed on the mainland of Asia by Russia under the Czars [and] . . . Domination of the provinces of China in central Asia contiguous to the Soviet frontier. Such action is dictated," Kennan concluded, "by the strategic necessity of protecting in depth the industrial core of the U.S.S.R." [83]

Moscow's later, and arbitrary, removal of industrial assets from Manchuria did not contribute, however, to American-Soviet collaboration in the Pacific. Nor, on the other hand, was Washington's unilateral occupa-

tion and administration of Japan a move calculated to promote collaboration. For, as Secretary of State James Byrnes "emphasized" to Forrestal
three months after Japan's surrender, "Stalin feels that he has been completely ignored on the question of Japan." [84] But in any event the Soviets
cannot be charged with responsibility for the fall of Chiang Kai-shek. Despite large-scale military aid from the United States—aid that helped
Chiang capture the communist capital of Yennan—the Kuomintang failed
to consolidate its hold on the country. After an extensive survey of the
situation General George C. Marshall announced his conclusion on January 7, 1947. "The salvation of the situation, as I see it," he wrote, "would
be the assumption of leadership by the liberals." [85] Behind that statement
was irrefutable evidence that Yennan's refusal to compromise was matched
by Chiang's failure to reform. But revolutions are not Sunday-school pic-
nics. The administration of Harry S. Truman failed to propose any fundamental solution to the crisis. Nor, it should be noted, did his vociferous
Republican critics. Arms for Chiang there were aplenty, but no serious
demand that Chiang rectify the abuses of his rule that cost him more men
than the weapons of the communists.

   Thus by 1947 Washington faced two critical problems: the Red
Army's presence in Europe, and Chiang's persistent refusal to meet the
basic challenge of the Chinese communists. In both cases Washington
failed to use its economic power in an attempt to solve the dilemma. Indeed, as early as the end of January, 1946, Secretary of State Byrnes reported that he "had discontinued the practice of having private meetings
with the Russians on various questions." The "Russian attitude," he amplified, "continued to be that they would like to discuss stability and
peace with the United States alone, although from time to time admitting
Great Britain to the conversations." Byrnes felt, however, that bilateral talks
produced "bad feeling among the rest of the United Nations"—but he
did not, apparently, give equal concern to the Russian reaction to his refusal to continue direct negotiations. [86]

   A similar, and related, reluctance to consider the consequences of a
policy is seen in Washington's steady opposition to Soviet reparation demands, while at the same time ignoring Moscow's specific request for a
major loan. That Stalin's reaction to the termination of Lend-Lease—a suspicion that the move was "designed as pressure"—was re-enforced when
the State Department "lost" Moscow's formal bid for a $6,000,000,000
loan became apparent during his conversations with Secretary of State
George C. Marshall on April 15, 1947. In response to Marshall's long review of the deterioration of relations, Stalin laid heavy emphasis on Washington's handling of the loan request. Ambassador to Russia General
Walter Bedell Smith admitted that Stalin "certainly had a good point

there," but no effort was ever made to seize the opening to renew top-level talks.[87]

The concept of negotiations around economic power had been abandoned. For that the loan document itself could be misplaced is conceivable —but that the issue could be mislaid for more than a year was the clue to Washington's entire attitude. By the time of the Marshall-Stalin exchange, moreover, those who controlled the content of mass communications in the United States had created an atmosphere in which "anyone who admitted the possibility of ever settling any dispute with the Soviet Government was likely to fall under suspicion of favoring 'appeasement.' " [88] There remained the power inherent in a temporary monopoly of the atom bomb. But Washington's atom diplomacy from 1945 to 1947 did little to rehabilitate the concept of a concert of power.

First came extension of the wartime policy to exclude Moscow from the pseudo-secret. Certainly that decision did little to modify Russian "suspicion of the ultimate purposes of the Western Powers." [89] Nor did the move to link abolition of the veto in the Security Council to the problem of international control of atomic energy. For the veto was at the heart of the entire concept that the Big Three should thrash out their differences in top-level discussion on all issues that affected their individual and collective security requirements. But efforts to modify the American plan in this respect were fruitless.[90] Though the plan for step-by-step control was logically unanswerable, it failed of adoption because there was no basic agreement between Moscow and Washington. And in terms of that agreement the vital document was not the report on the international control of atomic energy written by David E. Lilienthal and Undersecretary of State Dean Acheson; but rather an article authored by George Frost Kennan, then chief of the Policy Planning Division of the Department of State, that appeared publicly for the first time in the July, 1947, issue of *Foreign Affairs*.[91]

Kennan's article, a slightly modified version of an official paper submitted to Secretary of the Navy Forrestal early in 1947, documented the final crystallization of the "consensus of opinion" among those who met with President Truman in April, 1945. Kennan's opinion as to the proper policy to be pursued with relation to Soviet Russia seems to have formed the backdrop for American decisions as early as mid-February, 1946, when—in response to a request for his views on the Iranian situation, Ambassador Harriman being absent—he cabled a lengthy statement of his broad policy recommendations. This official dispatch differed in no major respect from either the special report to Forrestal a year later or the version sent on to *Foreign Affairs* with official clearance in the second week of April, 1947.[92] In addition, of course, Kennan's regular cables from

Russia—and his association with Ambassadors Harriman and Smith—leave little question as to his important role in establishing the context for formal decision making during the years 1945–47. This, to be sure, was nothing new in the history of American policy toward Russia, as the significance of other seemingly minor and little-known officials such as William Phillips, Basil Miles, and Robert Kelley made clear from as early as 1900—but Kennan's rise to power emphasized the great importance of the unknown career Foreign Service bureaucrat.

The exact date at which Kennan's formulation was consciously accepted as the explicit guide to future action is probably impossible to determine. Harriman's suggestion of April, 1945, to embark upon a policy of trade discrimination against Moscow certainly implies that containment was no novelty to him at that early date. For his part, Forrestal seems to have viewed Kennan's dispatch of February, 1946, as "exactly the kind of a job for which [he] had looked vainly elsewhere in the government"— ideas that "accorded very closely with those Forrestal had already been developing." Nor did Forrestal modify his views, even though he agreed with Generals Lucius M. Clay and Dwight D. Eisenhower and Harriman that the "Russians would not take steps leading to immediate war." As early as September 25, 1946, the Departments of State, War, and Navy discussed the possibility of using American economic aid in a more political manner than distribution through the United Nations allowed.[93]

In any event, Washington's reaction to Britain's inability to continue supervision of affairs in Greece leaves little doubt that Kennan's recommendations had been accepted—formally or informally. Of particular importance, therefore, was the meaning of Truman's speech to Congress on March 12, 1947, in terms of the old agreement between Churchill and Stalin. For that settlement could not be disassociated from Washington's unilateral action in Greece and Turkey. As a move limited to the reactivation of that understanding—and accompanied by discussions with London *and* Moscow—the Truman Doctrine might have led to an era of decreased tension. But, as formulated, the policy was world-wide in implication and unilateral in character. Decisive meaning was thereby given to Truman's *prior* decision, February 21, 1947, to by-pass the United Nations as an agency of economic relief.[94] And the officially approved publication in *Foreign Affairs* of Kennan's report to Forrestal revealed the final purpose of the Doctrine.[95]

This aim was to effect either a definitive change in, or the actual destruction of, the Soviet Government. Though Kennan's postulates, logic, and conclusions have been discussed at length there has been no clear exposition of the fundamental contradictions of his formulation. For this reason the article needs to be reviewed with care. To be sure, his point of departure in this analysis is an acknowledgment that the sincerity of

Soviet leaders cannot be questioned—that they do desire the betterment of life in Russia—but he immediately concludes that they have explained any lack of progress in that direction by the prior necessity to establish the security of the government.

Kennan's first problem, therefore, is an examination of the validity of this explanation. For a review of the facts, however, he substitutes a statement that enables him to label the argument no more than a rationale by which the Soviet leaders maintain themselves in power. No more, in short, than a technique of control. "Tremendous emphasis," Kennan writes, "has been placed on the original Communist thesis of a basic antagonism between the capitalist and Socialist worlds. It is clear, from many indications, that this emphasis is not founded in reality. The real facts concerning it have been confused by the existence abroad of a genuine resentment provoked by Soviet philosophy and tactics and occasionally by the existence of great centers of military power, notably the Nazi regime in Germany and the Japanese Government of the late 1930's, which did indeed have aggressive designs against the Soviet Union." There is, Kennan concludes, "ample evidence that the stress laid in Moscow on the menace confronting Soviet society . . . is founded not in the realities of foreign antagonism but in the necessity of explaining away the maintenance of dictatorial authority at home."

These comments and interpretations require further examination. A most noticeable omission is Kennan's failure to point out that capitalist leaders militantly opposed socialism, both verbally and more actively, long years before the existence of the Soviet state. He also neglects to mention the fact of Allied intervention in Russia—intervention primarily designed to destroy the Soviet Government. Nor does the reader find any reference to the avowed policy aims of Herbert Hoover—the "abandonment of their present economic system" on the part of the Bolsheviks—and Charles Evans Hughes, who conditioned recognition on "fundamental changes" in the Soviet economic system. Likewise peculiar is the use of the word "occasionally" and the chronology "in the late 1930's" to characterize the threat to Russia from Germany and Japan.

"Occasionally" can hardly be applied to an armed challenge that concerned the world for the majority of the interwar years. The phrase "in the late 1930's" does not correspond with Japan's activities in the intervals from 1917 to 1922 and from 1931 to 1941—or Hitler's from 1934 forward. Kennan's argument that neither Japan's occupation of eastern Siberia and subsequent attacks along the border between Manchuria and Russia nor Hitler's expansion in Central Europe was a threat to Soviet security contrasts strangely with his claim that Moscow was a dire threat when Washington had the only stockpile of atom bombs. Yet upon this questionable foundation Kennan proceeds to erect his entire argument.

But he immediately repeats the performance just reviewed. Kennan goes on to deal with two other factors that are important to an analysis of his policy recommendation. "The theory of the inevitability of the eventual fall of capitalism," he writes, "has the fortunate connotation that there is no hurry about it." And again: "the Kremlin is under no ideological compulsion to accomplish its purposes in a hurry." He points out, however, that the Soviet Government, "like almost any other government . . . can be placed in a position where it cannot afford to yield even though this might be dictated by its sense of realism." For this reason, Kennan emphasizes, "it is a *sine qua non* of successful dealing with Russia that the foreign government in question should remain at all times cool and collected and that demands on Russian policy should be put forward in such a manner as to leave the way open for a compliance not too detrimental to Russian prestige." These statements would appear to indicate that Kennan—despite his inaccurate and misleading presentation of past policies toward Soviet Russia—envisaged some careful effort to establish a basic security accommodation with Moscow. His actual conclusion, however, can hardly be described in that manner.

Rather does Kennan stress the use of "unanswerable force," a coupling of words that has no meaning save in a military sense. Nor is his formulation vague. The United States, he concludes, "has it in its power to increase enormously the strains under which Soviet policy must operate, to force upon the Kremlin a far greater degree of moderation and circumspection than it has had to observe in recent years, and in this way promote tendencies which must eventually find their outlet in either the break-up or the gradual mellowing of Soviet power." Kennan's choice of words further dramatizes his resort to force. Had he anticipated "a result to be expected," Kennan would have used the phrase "will eventually." Instead, he wrote "must eventually," an expression of obligation under "physical or logical necessity." [96] Men do not surrender states to the dictates of logic, as Kennan himself admits.

Thus Kennan disregards both his own warning about "tactless and threatening gestures" and his concern "to leave the way open for a compliance not too detrimental to Russian prestige." For his policy calls for the application of a steadily rising military pressure to challenge existing Soviet leadership. If implemented in the spirit of its formulation, the Soviet leaders could not be expected to reply other than by preparations for a short-range showdown. This would hardly bring a "mellowing" of internal controls in Russia. By the same token Kennan's proposals destroy the "fortunate connotation" in Soviet theory that there is "no hurry." A more classic *non sequitur* could hardly be conceived, even as an exercise in mental gymnastics. But the responsibility for the future of American-Russian relations cannot be classed as intellectual amusement, for upon their character depends the immediate future of the world.

And freedom is not nurtured by states preparing for war. Rather does it find more opportunity to flower in the atmosphere of mutual accommodation achieved and sustained through negotiated settlements. Here is the heart of Kennan's greatest failure—for his policy would, in fact, prove Marx to have been right. To "create among the peoples of the world generally," in Kennan's words, "the impression of a country which knows what it wants, which is coping successfully with the problems of its internal life and with the responsibilities of a World Power"—to do this the United States must demonstrate the courage to acknowledge the broad challenge of the Bolshevik Revolution, face its implications, and embark upon a conscious effort to prove Marx's *predictions* to have been in error. One must conclude, however, that Kennan and those who followed the course he charted were unaware of the challenge—and until that issue was faced candidly no effective response would be formulated to the challenge of Soviet power.

☆
BIBLIOGRAPHY

Publishing specifications for this volume posed two alternatives: severely cut the notes or sharply delimit the bibliography. The second option was chosen because the writer considered the source material more meaningful when correlated with the text. Extensive deletions were unavoidable; but every effort was made to keep the notes as rich as space requirements allowed.

MANUSCRIPT SOURCES

A. Official

The National Archives of the United States of America, 1890–1935.
Record Group 40: General Records of the Department of Commerce.
Record Group 43: Records of the United States Participation in International Conferences, Commissions, and Expositions.
Record Group 59: General Records of the Department of State.
Record Group 63: Records of the Committee on Public Information:
File CPI 1-A1: Correspondence of George Creel;
File CPI 3-B4: German Bolshevik Conspiracy;
File CPI 27: Russian Division;
File CPI 27-A1: Cablegrams and letters of Arthur Bullard.
Record Group 84: Records of the Foreign Service Posts of the Department of State.
Record Group 94: Records of the Adjutant General's Office.
Record Group 107: Records of the Office of the Secretary of War.
Record Group 151: Records of the Bureau of Foreign and Domestic Commerce.
Record Group 165: Records of the War Department General Staff.
Record Group 182: Records of the War Trade Board (World War I).

The Archives of the American National Red Cross, Washington, D.C.

B. Private Collections

Ray Stannard BAKER: Library of Congress.
Tasker Howard BLISS: Library of Congress.

285

William E. BORAH: Library of Congress.
Albert S. BURLESON: Library of Congress.
Calvin COOLIDGE: Library of Congress.
George CREEL: Library of Congress.
George GIBBS: Wisconsin State Historical Society, Madison, Wisconsin.
Alexander GUMBERG: Wisconsin State Historical Society.
Samuel N. HARPER: Harper Memorial Library, University of Chicago, Chicago, Illinois.
Herbert HOOVER: Material supplied through the courtesy of Suda L. Bane, Archivist of the *Herbert Hoover Archives.*
William V. JUDSON: Newberry Library, Chicago, Illinois.
George KENNAN: Material supplied through the courtesy of Dr. Charles Vevier.
Harry W. LAIDLER: The New York Public Library, New York.
Robert LANSING: Library of Congress.
Victor F. LAWSON: Newberry Library, Chicago, Illinois.
Salmon O. LEVINSON: Harper Memorial Library, University of Chicago.
Vance C. McCORMICK: Library of Congress.
Louis MARSHALL: American Jewish Archives, Hebrew Union College, Cincinnati, Ohio.
Raymond ROBINS: Brooksville, Florida.
William Woodville ROCKHILL: Material supplied through the courtesy of Professor Paul Varg and Dr. Charles Vevier.
Franklin Delano ROOSEVELT: Hyde Park, New York.
Theodore ROOSEVELT: Library of Congress.
Elihu ROOT: Library of Congress.
Charles Edward RUSSELL: Library of Congress.
Jacob SCHIFF: American Jewish Archives, Cincinnati, Ohio.
Graham H. TAYLOR: Newberry Library, Chicago, Illinois.
Thomas D. THACHER: The New York Public Library, New York.
William Boyce THOMPSON: Library of Congress.
Woodrow WILSON: Library of Congress.

C. Miscellaneous

Archives of the Chicago Daily News, Chicago, Illinois: Files on

Charles C. CRANE	William V. JUDSON
Samuel N. HARPER	Raymond ROBINS

SELECTED CORRESPONDENCE and INTERVIEWS

Correspondence

Norman ARMOUR	Joseph E. DAVIES
William C. BULLITT	Walter DURANTY

Correspondence

Will H. HAYS
Cordell HULL
Harold ICKES
Earl M. JOHNSON
George Frost KENNAN
Robert Bruce LOCKHART
William PHILLIPS

De Witt Clinton POOLE
Raymond ROBINS
Henry L. STIMSON
Raymond Gram SWING
Thomas D. THACHER
Allen WARDWELL

Interviews

Harold ICKES, March 9, 1950.
Raymond ROBINS, July 28–August 11, 1949.
Edward A. ROSS, April 12, 1950.
Henry W. TEMPLE, February 8, 1951.
Thomas THACHER, March 22, 1950.
Allen WARDWELL, March 22, 1950.

☆
REFERENCE NOTES

ABBREVIATIONS USED IN REFERENCE NOTES

AHR	*The American Historical Review.*
Amerika	*Amerika v Borbe za Kitai* by A. Kantorovich, Moscow, 1935.
Annals	*Annals of the American Academy of Political and Social Sciences.*
ARC	*Archives of the American National Red Cross*, Washington, D.C.
Atlantic	*The Atlantic Monthly.*
Bliss Mss.	*The Papers of Tasker Howard Bliss*, Library of Congress.
Borah Mss.	*The Papers of Senator William E. Borah*, Library of Congress.
Burleson Mss.	*The Papers of Albert S. Burleson*, Library of Congress.
Century	*The Century Magazine.*
China	*Treaties and Agreements With and Concerning China, 1894–1919*, compiled and edited by John V. A. MacMurray, 2 vols., New York, 1921.
Commerce	*Commercial Relations of the United States with Foreign Countries*, Departments of Commerce and State, Washington, D.C.
Consular	*Monthly, Weekly, and Daily Consular Reports*, Department of Commerce, 1880–.
Coolidge Mss.	*The Papers of Calvin Coolidge*, Library of Congress.
Creel Mss.	*The Papers of George Creel*, Library of Congress.
DGP	*Die Grosse Politik der Europaischen Kabinette, 1871–1914*, 40 vols., Berlin, 1921–27.
Digest	*The Literary Digest.*
Diplomacy	*Entente Diplomacy and the World: Matrix of the History of Europe, 1909–1914* by B. De Siebert and G. A. Schreiner, New York, 1921.
FDR Mss.	*The Papers of Franklin Delano Roosevelt*, Hyde Park, New York.
Gumberg Mss.	*The Papers of Alexander Gumberg*, Wisconsin State Historical Society, Madison, Wisconsin.
HAF	*Henry Adams and His Friends, A Collection of His Unpublished Letters*, compiled by H. D. Cater, Boston, 1947.
HAHR	*The Hispanic American Historical Review.*
Harper Mss.	*The Papers of Samuel N. Harper*, Harper Memorial Library, University of Chicago.
Harriman	*E. H. Harriman* by G. Kennan, 2 vols., New York, 1922.
Hearings	*Report and Hearings of the Subcommittee on the Judiciary of the U.S. Senate, pursuant to Brewing and Liquor Interests and German and Bolshevik Propaganda*, 3 vols., Washington, D.C., 1918.

289

House   The Intimate Papers of Colonel House, Arranged as a Narrative,
                 edited by C. Seymour, 4 vols., Boston, 1926–28.
JMH   The Journal of Modern History.
Judson Mss.   The Papers of William Voorhees Judson, Newberry Library, Chicago.
KA   Krasnyi Arkhiv, 104 vols., Moscow, 1922–37.
Lansing Mss.   The Papers of Robert Lansing, Library of Congress.
Levinson Mss.   The Papers of Salmon O. Levinson, Harper Memorial Library, Uni-
                 versity of Chicago.
LHA   The Letters of Henry Adams, Volume II, 1892–1918, edited by Worth-
                 ington C. Ford, Boston, 1938.
LTR   The Letters of Theodore Roosevelt, edited by E. E. Morrison, 4 vols.,
                 Cambridge, 1951–52.
Lytton   Manchuria, Commission of Enquiry into Sino-Japanese Relations,
                 League of Nations, Geneva, 1932.
MVHR   Mississippi Valley Historical Review.
NA   Archives of the United States of America, 1890–1935, Washington,
                 D.C. (followed by the Record Group number).
PPC   Papers Relating to the Foreign Relations of the United States, Paris
                 Peace Conference, 1919, 13 vols., Washington, D.C., 1942–48.
RAR   Russian-American Relations, March, 1917–March, 1920. Documents
                 and Papers, compiled and edited by C. K. Cumming and W. W.
                 Pettit, New York, 1920.
R of R   Review of Reviews.
R v M   Rossia v Manchzhurii, 1892–1906 by B. A. Romanov, Leningrad, 1928.
Record   The Congressional Record, Washington, D.C., 1874–1952.
Register   Biographic Register of the Department of State, Washington, D.C.,
                 1917–50.
Relations   Papers Relating to the Foreign Relations of the United States, Wash-
                 ington, D.C., 1862–1952.
Rivalry   American-Russian Rivalry in the Far East. A Study in Diplomacy and
                 Power Politics, by E. H. Zabriskie, Philadelphia, 1946.
Robins   Robins, conversations with author, July 28–August 11, 1949, Brooks-
                 ville, Florida.
Robins Mss.   The Papers of Raymond Robins, Brooksville, Florida.
Rockhill Mss.   The Papers of William Woodville Rockhill, material through the
                 courtesy of Professor Paul Varg and Dr. Charles Vevier.
Russell Mss.   The Papers of Charles Edward Russell, Library of Congress.
Schiff   Jacob H. Schiff. His Life and Letters by C. Alder, 2 vols., Garden
                 City, 1929.
Schiff Mss.   The Papers of Jacob Schiff, Hebrew Union College, Cincinnati, Ohio.
State   American State Papers, Class I, Foreign Relations, 6 vols., Washing-
                 ton, D.C., 1832–59.
Straight   Willard Straight by H. Croly, New York, 1924.

Supremacy　　　*America's Economic Supremacy* by B. Adams, New York, 1900, 1947.

Thompson Mss.　The Papers of William Boyce Thompson, with Notes and Other Material Supplied by Herman Hagedorn, Library of Congress.

TR Mss.　　　　The Papers of Theodore Roosevelt, Library of Congress.

Tribunal　　　　Proceedings of the Alaskan Boundary Tribunal, Convened at London, 7 vols., Washington, D.C., 1904.

Weltpolitik　　　Deutchland und die Vereingten Staaten in der Weltpolitik by A. Vagts, 2 vols., New York, 1935.

Wilson Mss.　　The Papers of Woodrow Wilson, Library of Congress.

Wilson Papers　The Public Papers of Woodrow Wilson, edited by R. A. Baker and W. E. Dodd, 6 vols., New York, 1925–27.

Chapter I: A REALISTIC ROMANCE

1. C. Hull, *The Memoirs of Cordell Hull* (2 vols., New York, 1948), I, 292.

2. Roosevelt to Troyanovsky, January 8, 1934, *FDR Mss.* (also *NA*, RG 59) ; Alexander to Adams, November 5, 1809, *Memoirs of John Quincy Adams, Comprising Portions of His Diary from 1795 to 1848*, edited by C. F. Adams (12 vols., Philadelphia, 1874–77), II, 51.

3. F. Wharton, *The Revolutionary Diplomatic Correspondence of the United States* (6 vols., Washington, D.C., 1889), IV, 201–2.

4. *Ibid.*, IV, 700.

5. Harris to Grantham, March 11, 1783, *Diaries and Correspondence of James Harris, First Earl of Malmesbury*, edited by the Third Earl of Malmesbury (4 vols., London, 1844), II, 38.

6. Wharton, *Correspondence*, VI, 494–95.

7. *Malmesbury Papers*, II, 36.

8. Wharton, *Correspondence*, VI, 437–38.

9. *The Life and Correspondence of Rufus King*, edited by C. R. King (6 vols., New York, 1894–1900), II, 463–64.

10. King, *Correspondence*, II, 552–53, 568–70, III, 29–30, 141, 165; *The Works of Alexander Hamilton*, edited by J. C. Hamilton (7 vols., New York, 1850–51), VI, 398.

11. J. C. Hildt, *Early Diplomatic Negotiations of the United States with Russia* (Baltimore, 1906), 36.

12. *The Writings of Thomas Jefferson*, edited by A. A. Lipscomb and A. E. Bergh (Memorial Edition, 20 vols., Washington, D.C., 1907), XIX, 142–44.

13. *Ibid.*, XI, 290–92.

14. *Ibid.*, XI, 103–6.

15. *Ibid.*, XI, 290–92.

16. *Ibid.*, XII, 153–54.

17. *Ibid.*, XII, 432–34.

18. Adams, *Memoirs*, II, 51–55.

19. *State*, V, 439, 453.

20. Adams, *Memoirs*, II, 81–82, 88, 143, 226.

21. *State*, V, 438–39, 441.

22. *Ibid.*, V, 440.

23. See note 41.

24. Adams, *Memoirs*, II, 151–52.

25. *Ibid.*, II, 179–80. The quotes are by Adams himself.

26. *Ibid.*, II, 271–72.

27. *Ibid.*, II, 290.

28. *Ibid.*, II, 362.

29. *Ibid.*, II, 401–2.

30. *Letters and Other Writings of James Madison* (4 vols., Philadelphia, 1867), II, 559–60.

31. *The Writings of James Monroe*, edited by S. M. Hamilton (7 vols., New York, 1903), V, 277–81.

32. Castlereagh, "Memorandum on the Treaties of 1814 and 1815," in C. K. Webster, *The Congress of Vienna, 1814–1815* (London, 1919), 166–71; Castlereagh, "Confidential State Paper of May 5, 1820," Appendix A in *Cambridge History of British Foreign Policy, Volume II, 1815–1866* (Cambridge, 1922), 622–33.

33. A long review of this episode is in Hildt, *Early Negotiations*, Chapter V.

34. W. C. Ford, "Correspondence of the Russian Ministers in Washington, 1818–1825," *AHR*, V 18(January, April, 1931), 309–45, 537–62; and below.

35. *Fourth Annual Report of the Massachusetts Peace Society* (Boston, 1819); *The Friend of Peace* (Boston, 1819), V 1:10:28; M. Curti, *The American Peace Crusade 1815–1860* (Durham, North Carolina, 1929), 27–28.

36. *The Writings of John Quincy Adams*, edited by W. C. Ford (7 vols., New York, 1913–17), VI, 280–81.

37. Ford, "Correspondence of the Russian Ministers," *AHR*, V 18:330; F. A. Golder, *Guide to Materials for American History in Russian Archives* (Washington, D.C., 1917), 34; Adams, *Memoirs*, IV, 370–80, 394–95, 404, 446–47.

38. W. R. Manning, *Diplomatic Correspondence of the United States Concerning the Independence of Latin American Nations* (3 vols., New York, 1925), III, 1851–52; G. Fr. De Martens, *Nouveau recueil des traités de l'Europe* (10 vols., Gottingen, 1817–42), V, 644.

39. Adams, *Memoirs*, IV, 390, 394–95, 404.

40. *Ibid.*, V, 324–25.

41. Adams, *Writings*, IV, 128, 209; Adams, *Memoirs*, IV, 107–14, 438.

42. Adams, *Writings*, VII, 437.

43. Adams, *Memoirs*, V, 123, 179, 195, 417–25.

44. Hildt, *Early Negotiations*, 114, 123.

45. *Ibid.*, 142.

46. For details of this western pressure see S. F. Bemis, *John Quincy Adams and the Foundations of American Foreign Policy* (New York, 1949), 495–98.

47. *Tribunal*, II, 23–31; *State*, IV, 857–61. A rumored version of these documents was

printed in Niles' *Weekly Register* as early as December 29, 1821. See note 74.

48. Proceedings of February 16, 1822, *Annals of Congress*, 17th Congress, 1st Session (Washington, 1821–22), I, 1073; the *National Intelligencer* printed a full copy "from an authentic source" on February 12, 1822 (Poletica delivered it to Adams on February 11, 1822), but had speculated as early as December, 1821, that the Tsar's action was taken in *response* to western pressure. See Niles' *Register*, February 12, 1822.

49. Niles' *Register*, December 29, 1821.

50. Monroe, *Writings*, V, 383; *State*, IV, 867; *Tribunal*, II, 32.

51. *State*, IV, 861–63, 863–65.

52. *State*, III, 745–48, IV, 407; Adams, *Writings*, VII, 245–46; *Tribunal*, II, 39–40; significantly, these notes appeared in Niles' *Register*, May 4, 1822.

53. Niles' *Register*, June 8, 1822; R. C. Cleland, "Asiatic Trade and the American Occupation of the Pacific Coast," *American Historical Association, Annual Report, 1914* (Washington, D.C., 1916), I, 283–89; S. E. Morison, *The Maritime History of Massachusetts* (Boston, 1921), 53.

54. Niles' *Register*, July 27, 1822.

55. *Annals of Congress*, 17th Congress, 2d Session, 414–20, 682–83.

56. Niles' *Register*, March 8, 1823, April 26, 1823, May 10, 1823, June 14, 1823.

57. Adams, *Memoirs*, VI, 143; Boston *Chronicle*, June 20, 1823; Niles' *Register*, June 21, 1823; Adams, *Memoirs*, VI, 151; *National Intelligencer*, June 30, 1823; Niles' *Register*, July 5, 1823; Adams, *Memoirs*, VI, 159.

58. Niles' *Register*, January 25, 1823, April 5, 1823.

59. Adams, *Memoirs*, VI, 132–37 (but see 308, 312, 323–24), 140, 159. For Adams' reaction to the western pressure see *Memoirs*, VI, 228.

60. Adams, *Memoirs*, VI, 157–58, 159, 163, 169–70; *Tribunal*, II, 42–51.

61. *Tribunal*, II, 53–56; *State*, V, 447–48.

62. Adams, *Writings*, VII, 373.

63. Castlereagh to Wellesley, April 1, 1812, in C. K. Webster, *The Foreign Policy of Castlereagh, 1812–1815* (London, 1931), 70.

64. R. Rush, *Memoranda of a Residence at the Court of London* (2 vols., Philadelphia, 1845), II, 10–13; Monroe, *Writings*, VI, 361–72.

65. W. C. Ford, "John Quincy Adams and the Monroe Doctrine, I," *AHR*, V 7 (July, 1902), 686, 692; Adams, *Memoirs*, VI, 179.

66. Adams, *Memoirs*, VI, 177–81.

67. *Ibid.*, VI, 186, 189–90.

68. *Ibid.*, VI, 199–204.

69. Adams to Tuyll, November 27, 1823, in Ford, "JQA and the Monroe Doctrine, II," *AHA*, V 8 (October, 1902), 41–44. Italics added.

70. Adams, *Memoirs*, VI, 203, 211, 214.

71. D. Perkins, *The Monroe Doctrine 1823–1826* (Cambridge, 1927), 126–35; on the competition for South American markets see J. F. Rippy, *Rivalry of the United States and Great Britain over Latin America, 1808–1830* (Baltimore, 1929); E. J.

Pratt, "Anglo-American Commercial and Political Rivalry on the Plata, 1820–1830," *HAHR*, V 11(1931), 302–35.

72. Philadelphia *Gazette and Register*, December 6, 1823; New York *Spectator*, December 6, 1823; Niles' *Register*, March 22, April 5, April 12, August 2, October 11, and December 6, 1823.

73. Rush, *Court of London*, II, 82–88.

74. *Tribunal*, II, 42–46, 56–65, 67–80; *State*, V, 453–57.

75. *Tribunal*, II, 69–92; Niles' *Register*, August 7, 1824.

76. *Tribunal*, II, 78–79; V. J. Farrar, "The Re-Opening of the Russian American Convention of 1824," *Washington Historical Quarterly*, V 11(1920), 83–88; *Tribunal*, II, 232–50; *Diary of George Mifflin Dallas, 1837–39*, edited by Susan Dallas (Philadelphia, 1892), 118; *Senate Document 1*, 25th Congress, 3d Session (Washington, 1838), 23–74; J. D. Richardson, *Messages and Papers of the Presidents, 1789–1897* (20 vols., New York, 1917), III, 488.

77. Golder, *Materials in Russian Archives*, 57; *The Works of James Buchanan*, edited by J. B. Moore (12 vols., Philadelphia, 1908–11), II, 298–305.

78. Buchanan, *Works*, II, 253–63; *House Document 111*, 33d Congress, 1st Session (Washington, 1854), 60–62, 76.

79. *House Document 111*, 58–59, 60–62, 75–76, 77–79.

80. Golder, "Russian American Relations During the Crimean War," *AHR*, V 31 (April, 1926), 462–76.

81. *House Journal*, 33d Congress, 2d Session (Washington, 1854), 55, 62; *Senate Journal*, 33d Congress, 2d Session (Washington, 1854), 63, 75, 146; *Congressional Globe*, V 30:76; *The United States Review* (August, 1855), 131; A. D. White, *Autobiography of Andrew Dickson White* (2 vols., New York, 1905), I, 455; London *Times*, April 28, 1854, March 1, 1855.

82. E. A. Adamov, "Russia and the United States at the Time of the Civil War," *JMH*, V 2(1930), 592; Golder, "Relations During Crimean War," *AHR*, V 31:3:467, 475.

83. E. D. Adams, *Great Britain and the American Civil War* (2 vols., New York, 1925), I, 171n.

84. *The Works of William H. Seward*, edited by G. E. Baker (5 vols., Boston, 1884), V, 382–83; *Charles Sumner, His Complete Works* (20 vols., Boston, 1900), X, 144; H. Blinn, "Seward and the Polish Rebellion of 1863," *AHR*, V 45(1940), 288–89.

85. F. Bancroft, *The Life of William H. Seward* (2 vols., New York, 1900), II, 430.

86. G. Welles, *Diary of Gideon Welles* (3 vols., New York, 1911), I, 443.

87. *Congressional Globe*, 39th Congress, 1st Session (Washington, 1866), 2443–44, 2562, 143; J. F. Loubat, *Narrative of the Mission to Russia in 1866*, edited by J. D. Champlin (New York, 1873), 88–90.

88. Seward, *Works*, I, 51–58, 236–50, 356, IV, 24–25, 356; Seward, quoted in V. J. Farrar, *The Annexation of Russian America to the United States* (Washington, 1937), 113; chapter heading from Seward to Clay, May 6, 1861.

89. Golder, "The Purchase of Alaska," *AHR*, V 25(1920), 413, 414–15, 416, 418, 424;

and see Golder's chapter in *The Pacific Coast in History,* edited by H. M. Stevens and H. E. Bolton (New York, 1917), 269–75.

90. Annexationist sentiment in *Russian America, Executive Document 177,* 40th Congress, 2d Session (Washington, 1866), 4, 25–28, 31, 141–42; New York *Herald,* April 29, 1867.

Chapter II: EXPANSION CONSTRICTS A FRIENDSHIP

1. *Russian America,* 25–28; G. Kennan, *Tent Life In Siberia* (New York, 1870), iii–v, 1–9; *Century,* V 36(1888), 625–31; and below.

2. *Atlantic,* V 79(May, 1899), 717–19; *Century,* V 36(1888), 625–31.

3. *Century,* V 36(1888), 625–31.

4. *Ibid.,* 3–4.

5. Kennan's series in the *Century* ran from 1888 to 1891; for his effectiveness see *Century,* V 42(1891), 958; W. V. Ellsworth, *A Golden Age of Authors* (Boston, 1919), 258–77; and *NAR,* V 153(1891), 596.

6. *Free Russia* (Friends of Russian Freedom publication), No. 2(September, 1890), 12.

7. *Century,* V 38:707.

8. M. Laserson, *The American Impact on Russia—Diplomatic and Ideological—1784–1917* (New York, 1950), 316.

9. *Century,* V 45(1892–93), 611–15.

10. *Ibid.,* V 46(1893), 461–72; and see *Ibid.,* V 40(1890), 636–37.

11. *KA,* V 14(1926), 162. For reaction in the United States see *Century,* V 46(1893), 359–62.

12. *Condition of Israelites in Russia. Executive Document No. 192* (Washington, 1882), 9–10.

13. *Ibid.,* 25.

14. *Record,* V 13:645, 738, 1240, 1258, 1325–26, 1628, 2026, 2044, 2096, 2141, 3532.

15. *Proscriptive Edicts Against Jews in Russia. House Document No. 470* (Washington, 1890), 67.

16. *Ibid.,* 72.

17. *Ibid.,* 76; *Relations, 1880,* 880; *The Abrogation of the Russian Treaty. House Report No. 179* (Washington, 1912), 7.

18. *Century,* V 23(1882), 905–20; *KA,* V 2(1922), 6, 43; *KA,* V 14(1926), 258.

19. *Century,* V 23(1882), 949.

20. *Executive Document No. 12. Report 1000* (Washington, 1892); *Record,* V 21: 2288–89, 2426, 2454.

21. W. C. Edgar, *The Russian Famine of 1891 and 1892* (Minneapolis, 1893).

22. O. S. Straus, *Under Four Administrations* (Boston, 1922), 106–7; *Schiff,* I, 14, II, 114, 116.

23. *House Report 1177. Committee on Foreign Affairs, April 23, 1892* (Washington, 1892), 1.

24. *Forum*, V 15(May, 1893), 291, 297; *Public Opinion*, V 15(June 17, 1893), 264.
25. *Forum*, V 15(July, 1893), 629–46.
26. *Free Russia*, V 3:11(June, 1893), V 4:2(September, 1893), V 4:7(February, 1894) ; *Record*, 53d Congress, 2d Session, 5499, 5666.
27. Breckinridge to Gresham, February 18, 1895, *NA*, RG 59.
28. *China*, I, 18–25.
29. *KA*, V 52(1932), 74–76; *R v M*, 69–70.
30. W. L. Langer, *The Diplomacy of Imperialism 1890–1902* (New York, 2d Edition, 1951), 181–86; *R v M*, 75–76.
31. Langer, *Imperialism*, 188.
32. Baron Rosen, *Forty Years of Diplomacy* (2 vols., New York, 1922), I, 198; *R v M*, 57–60; *Rivalry*, 29–32.
33. Denby to Olney, February 25, 1895, *NA*, RG 59.
34. Denby to Olney, May 25, September 2, 1896, *NA*, RG 59; *R v M*, 102–3; *Amerika*, 99–100; *Istoriya Diplomatii*, edited by V. P. Potemkin (3 vols., Moscow, 1941–45), II, 117–18; C. Cary, *China's Present and Prospective Railways* (New York, 1899), 14–17; *Commerce, 1896–97* (Washington, 1898), 21–22; and C. C. Campbell, Jr., *Special Business Interests and the Open Door Policy* (New Haven, 1951) also discusses this early activity.
35. Cassini to Lobanov, April 10, 1896, *Amerika*, 99.
36. Denby to Sherman, April 2, 1897, *NA*, RG 59; *Weltpolitik*, II, Chapter XI; *KA*, V 52:125–140.
37. *Weltpolitik*, II, 1017.
38. Denby to Sherman, January 31, 1898, same to same, February 14, 1898, same to same, March 8, 1898, same to same, March 19, 1898; Hitchcock to Sherman, February 8, 1898, all in *NA*, RG 59.
39. Hitchcock to Sherman, March 19, 1898, *NA*, RG 59.
40. D. S. Crist, "Russia's Far Eastern Policy in the Making," *JMH*, V 14: 3(September, 1942) :318; and below.
41. L. M. Gelber, *The Rise of Anglo-American Friendship: A Study in World Politics, 1898–1906* (New York, 1938) ; L. M. Penson, "The New Course in British Foreign Policy, 1892–1902," *Transactions of the Royal Historical Society, Series IV*, V 25(1943) :121–39.
42. *KA*, V 52:129; *Rivalry*, 197; *KA*, V 60(1933), 3–60; Laserson, *Impact*, 343.
43. Cassini to Lamsdorf, June 24, 1898, *KA*, V 52:138–39.
44. *Relations, 1898*, 907; Chicago *Times Herald*, October 14, 1898; *Amerika*, 94.
45. J. W. Pratt, "The 'Large Policy' of 1898," *MVHR*, V 19(1932), 219–42.
46. Chamberlain to Balfour, February 3, 1898, in B. E. C. Dugale, *Arthur James Balfour* (2 vols., New York, 1936), I, 252–53.
47. Hay to Lodge, May 26, 1898, in W. R. Thayer, *The Life and Letters of John Hay* (2 vols., Boston, 1915), II, 168; Hay to C—S—H—, October 29, 1900, *Letters and Extracts from Diary* (3 vols., Washington, 1908), III, 199.

48. A. W. Griswold, *The Far Eastern Policy of the United States* (New York, 1938), 68–69, emphasizes Hippisley's influence on Rockhill, but for a more thorough study see Professor Paul Varg's biography of Rockhill to be published by the University of Illinois Press (a mss. copy of which he kindly made available to this writer). T. Dennett, *John Hay. From Poetry to Politics* (New York, 1933), 289, but Brooks —not Henry—developed the policy.

49. Note the difference between H. Adams to Hay, June 18, August 30, November 7, 12, 1892, *LHA*, 11, 12, 19, 24–26; and same to same, October 18, 1893, *HAF*, 291–94; H. Adams to B. Adams, January 3, 24, 1896, *HAF*, 354–57.

50. B. Adams, *The Law of Civilization and Decay* (New York, 1896; London, 1895; New York, 1947), ix–xi.

51. H. Adams to B. Adams, of June 5, 1895, *LHA*, 69–70; of September [?], 1895, *LHA*, 82–84; of December 27, 1895, *HAF*, 352–53; of January 3, 1896, *HAF*, 354–55; of April 4, 1898, *LHA*, 162–63; H. Adams to E. Cameron, August 21, 1905, *LHA*, 460.

52. H. Adams to B. Adams, of June 5, 1895, *LHA*, 69–70; of February 18, 1896, *LHA*, 100; H. Adams to C. F. Gaskell, June 20, 1895, *LHA*, 72; of January 4, 1897, *LHA*, 119; see below.

53. H. Adams to B. Adams, June 5, 1895, *LHA*, 70.

54. B. Adams, "Commercial Future: New Struggle for Life Among Nations," *Fortnightly Review*, V 71(New Series 65, February, 1899), 274–83. This article became Chapter II of *Supremacy*.

55. For Henry's friendship with Hay and Rockhill see *HAF*, 452–60; *LHA*, 207, 214, 218, 269, 423.

56. H. Adams to Cameron, November 21, 1898; to Hay, June 26, 1900; and Hay to H. Adams, July 8, 1900, all in *LHA*, 190, 289–90, 292.

57. Denby to Sherman, April 2, 1897; Denby to Olney, January 10, 1897, both *NA*, RG 59.

58. *Outlook* (June 24, 1899), 431–32; *NAR*, V 168(1898), 190.

59. *NAR*, V 169(July, 1899), 6–32; for the importance of this article see Griswold, *Policy*, 71.

60. *NAR*, V 169(September, 1899), 329–48.

61. *Forum*, V 28(October, 1899), 178–80; *R of R*, V 21(January, 1900), 42–49.

62. *Consular*, (August, 1900), 492; Emery to Hitchcock, November 21, 1898, *NA*, RG 59; and see Campbell, *Business Interests*, 77.

63. Griswold, *Policy*, 60–1.

64. *Weltpolitik*, II, 1038–58, 1046.

65. Pierce to Hay, February 25, 1899; and see Denby to Olney, January 10, 1897, Denby to Sherman, April 2, 1897, all in *NA*, RG 59.

66. This effort can be followed in *Relations, 1899*, 591–97; *Weltpolitik*, II, 1023.

67. Pierce to Hay, October 11, 1899, *NA*, RG 59; *Weltpolitik*, II, 1046–47.

68. *Consular*, (March, 1899), 510; (January, 1888), 104–7; (August, 1889), 638–

40; (October, 1897), 274–77; (January, 1898), 34; (February, 1898), 236–37; (April, 1898), 390; (May, 1898), 36–37; (June, 1898), 236–37; (July, 1898), 471; (September, 1899), 149; (November, 1899), 404–8.

69. *Outlook* (December 10, 1898), 891–92; (June 3, 1899), 238–39; (June 17, 1899), 369–70.

70. Adee to Tower, March 8, 1899, *NA*, RG 59.

71. Tower to Hay, August 23, 1899, *NA*, RG 59.

72. Tower to Hay, December 28, 1899, same to same, February 12, 1900, *NA*, RG 59.

73. Tower to Hay, February 9, 1900, *NA*, RG 59.

74. Hay's Note of March 20, 1900, *NA*, RG 59.

75. Hay to Tower, January 22, 1900, *NA*, RG 59.

76. Pierce to Adee, August 30, 1900, *NA*, RG 59.

77. Dennett, *Hay*, 317.

78. Pierce to Adee, September 11, 1900, *NA*, RG 59.

79. *Rivalry*, 64, 85; A. L. P. Dennis, *Adventures in American Diplomacy, 1896–1906* (New York, 1928), 355.

80. Crist, "Russia's Far Eastern Policy," *JMH*, V 14:3:318.

81. Bezobrazov to Grand Duke Alexander, July 18, 1900, *R v M*, 393–94. On the struggle between Witte and Bezobrazov see, among others, Crist, "Russia's Far Eastern Policy," *JMH*; *Rivalry*, 84–100; *Fortnightly Review* (May, June, 1910), 816–31, 1031–44; V. Avarin, *Imperialism v Manchzhurii* (2 vols., Moscow, 1934) ; *KA*, V 2(1922), 5–117; V 18(1926), 30–48; V 14(1926), 1–49; V 17(1926), 70–80; and G. S. U. Witte, *Vospominania* (2 vols., Berlin, 1922–23).

82. Rockhill to Hay, January 23, 1901, *NA*, RG 59.

83. Hay, March 28, 1901, as quoted by Cassini, *R v M*, 304.

84. Miller to Squires, June 27, 1901; Conger to Hay, September 7, 1901; but see *Relations, 1902* and *1903* for a number of Miller's reports. On trade dominance by United States see *Consular*, (May, 1903), 455–58; (June, 1903), 173; (December, 1905), 103; (April, 1904), 8; (November, 1898), 397–99; and D. G. Munro, "American Commercial Interests in Manchuria," *Annals*, V 39 (January, 1912), 154–68.

85. Hay to Cassini, January 16, 1902, *NA*, RG 59.

86. Hay to Tower, February 1, 1902, *NA*, RG 59.

87. Polotivov to St. Petersburg, February 11, 1902, *R v M*, 347.

88. *KA*, V 18(1926), 34, 45; V 14(1926), 41–42.

89. Crist, "Russia's Far Eastern Policy," *JMH*, V 14:3:337; *R v M*, 340–45, 411; B. B. Glinskii, *Prolog Russko-Iaponskoi Voini* (Petrograd, 1910), 178–84.

90. See this writer's article, "Brooks Adams and American Expansion," in the June, 1952, issue of the *New England Quarterly* for a full review of this relationship.

91. Roosevelt, "The Law of Civilization and Decay," *The Forum*, V 22 (January, 1897), 575, 578, 579, 587; Roosevelt to Balfour, March 5, 1908, Bishop, *Roosevelt and His Time*, II, 107.

92. Roosevelt, Naval War College Speech of June 2, 1897, *The Works of Theodore Roosevelt, Memorial Edition* (24 vols., New York, 1923–26), XIV, 182–89; Roosevelt to Hay, June 17, 1899, *LTR*, II, 1021.

93. Roosevelt, Message to Congress, December 3, 1901: see first Roosevelt to Adams, September 27, 1901, *LTR*, III, 152–53; then *Record*, V 35:1:82, .83, 84, 86, 88, 92, and compare with *Supremacy*, 82, 103, 105, 131–32, 170, 192, 194. Also see *HAF*, 524–25, and *Selections from the Correspondence of Theodore Roosevelt and Henry Cabot Lodge, 1884–1918*, edited by H. C. Lodge (2 vols., New York, 1925), II, 135, and *LTR*, I, 644–49, 555.

94. *Supremacy*, 194; H. F. Pringle, *Theodore Roosevelt. A Biography* (New York, 1931), 372.

95. Roosevelt to Griscom, July 27, 1905: T. Dennett, *Roosevelt and the Russo-Japanese War* (New York, 1925), 241, 5; *Supremacy*, 179.

96. Kuropatkin to Lamsdorff, July 6, 9, 1903, *Amerika*, 151.

97. Roosevelt to Hay, July 18, 1903, Dennis, *Adventures*, 359.

98. *Outlook* (June 23, 1900), 417, (July 28, 1900), 730; *NAR*, V 170(1900), 605–6.

99. *NAR*, V 171(October, 1900), 528, 537, 541–42.

100. *R of R*, V 23(January, 1901), 8, V 23(April, 1901), 397–98.

101. *NAR*, V 170(1900), 892.

102. *Ibid.*, 641.

103. *Ibid.*, 643–44.

104. *McClure's Magazine*, V 14(April, 1900), 510.

105. *Outlook* (July 28, 1900), 730; *NAR*, V 170(1900), 871–83, V 174(1901–2), 315–28.

106. *Atlantic*, V 86(September, 1900), 310.

107. *Ibid.*, V 87(February, 1901), 157–65.

108. *Ibid.*, V 92(1903), 632–49.

109. *Ibid.*, V 88(1901), 154–55; *Supremacy*, 63, 78, 132, 96, 98, 151, 153, 155, 157, 179, 193, 170, 194.

110. *Scribner's*, V 31(1902), 571.

111. *NAR*, V 174 (1901–2), 594.

112. *Outlook* (August 12, 1899), 829–30.

113. Cassini's release to the Associated Press, May 18, 1893.

114. Straus, *Under Four Administrations*, 170–71.

115. *The Voice of Kishineff*, edited by C. Alder (Philadelphia, 1904), xxiv.

116. *NAR*, V 176(1904), 10–24.

117. Alder, *Voice*, 57, 116.

118. T. B. Mott, *Twenty Years as Military Attaché* (New York, 1937), 136–37; Straus, *Under Four Administrations*, 170–72; Alder, *Voice*, xiv; Baltimore *American*, June 6, 1903; *Schiff*, II, 116–23.

119. *KA*, V 2(1922), 80; *R v M*, 426–27.

120. Baron Eckardstein, *Die Isolierung Deutschlands* (Leipzig, 1921), 189.

121. Pringle, *Roosevelt*, 375.

122. F. H. H. Harrington, *God, Mammon, and the Japanese. Dr. Horace N. Allen and Korean-American Relations, 1884–1905* (Madison, 1944), 312–18.

123. *Rivalry*, 107; *Supremacy*, 193–94.

124. *Outlook* (January 9, 1904), 102–4, (January 23, 1904), 205–6, (February 20, 1904), 443–45; *R of R*, V 29:2(February, 1904), 133–37.

125. *Century*, V 68(1904), 412–20, 597–602, V 69(1905), 127–38; *NAR*, V 181(1905), 237–50, V 178(1904), 801–11; *Outlook*, V 68(1904), 815–17, (September 16, 1905), 117–18; *R of R*, V 31:1(January, 1905), 88–90.

126. *Weltpolitik*, II, 1178.

127. *Consular*, (October, 1880), 173, (February, 1886), 172–73, 256, (May, 1889), 16–17, (October, 1889), 196, (February, 1895), 310, (July, 1895), 505–7, (December, 1900), 478; and see Munro, "American Commercial Interests in Manchuria," *Annals*, V 39:154–68.

128. *Outlook* (June 18, 1904), 403, (August 10, 1912), 822.

129. *Ibid.*, (October 7, 1905), 307–15, (October 8, 1904), 363–69, (October 22, 1904), 465–72, (November 18, 1905), 669–73.

130. *Ibid.*, (March 31, 1906), 745, (April 7, 1906), 791; *Century*, V 34(1887), 263.

131. *Outlook* (January 14, 1905), 105–6, (August 13, 1904), 890–97, (October 29, 1904), 515–17.

132. *Ibid.*, (March 17, 1915), 622–26.

133. *R of R*, V 29(April, 1904), 455–56, V 30(October, 1904), 480–83, V 31(January, 1905), 96–97. Official Washington received the same information, see McCormick to Hay, February 9, 1904, of February 27, 1904, and Meyer to Hay, April 18, 1905, all in *NA*, RG 59. *Novoye Vremya*, August 17, 31, September 2, 7, 1905; Laserson, *Impact*, 327–35.

134. *Schiff*, I, 213–28, II, 119, 120–23, 124–28; *Weltpolitik*, II, 1190; *Amerika*, 165–66; *KA*, V 10(1925), 3–5; *Digest*, V 31(September 9, 1905), 335.

135. Dennett, *Roosevelt*, 47–50.

136. M. A. D. Howe, *George von Lengerke Meyer* (New York, 1919), 173–75; Bishop, *Roosevelt*, I, 399–400; *Supremacy*, 191.

137. H. Adams to E. Cameron, February 7, 1904, of January 10, 1904, of August 29, 1905, all in *LHA*, 423, 419, 461.

138. *KA*, V 28(1927), 190.

139. Pringle, *Roosevelt*, 380.

140. Dennett, *Roosevelt*, 112–14; Pringle, *Roosevelt*, 384.

141. Dennett, *Roosevelt*, 165–66, 195.

142. *Schiff*, I, 231–32; *Weltpolitik*, II, 1169–1256; *KA*, V 10(1925), 3.

143. Viscount K. Ishii, *Diplomatic Commentaries* (Baltimore, 1936), 69–72.

144. Bishop, *Roosevelt*, I, 418.

145. Yet Roosevelt summarized this point quite clearly in his letter to G. Harvey, September 6, 1905, Dennett, *Roosevelt*, 263.

146. Roosevelt to Rockhill, August 29, 1905, *Rockhill Mss*.

147. H. Adams to E. Cameron, February 23, 1902, *LHA*, 374.

148. Pringle, *Roosevelt*, 375.

Chapter III: RENDEZVOUS WITH REVOLUTION

1. A. Izvolski, *Recollections of a Foreign Minister. Memoirs of Izvolski*, translated by C. L. Seeger (New York, 1921), 4–5.

2. Meyer to Root, December 10, 1906, *NA*, RG 59.

3. Cassini to Lamsdorff, March [?], 1905, *Amerika*, 166; *R v M*, 547.

4. Witte to Kokovtsev, September 9, 1909, *KA*, V 6(1924), 45–47.

5. *R v M*, 526–27.

6. Kokovtsev to Morgan, October 31, 1905, *R v M*, 530ff.

7. Kokovtsev to Witte, January 6, 1906, *KA*, V 10(1925), 15; Kokovtsev, "Reports to the Tsar, January, 1905," *KA*, V 11–12(1925), 1ff.; Netzlin to Kokovtsev, July 28, 1906, *KA*, V 4(1923), 131ff.

8. Netzlin to Kokovtsev, November 30, 1906, *R v M*, 542–43.

9. *R v M*, 548–52.

10. *Ibid.*, 536–37.

11. On Harriman's tie with Schiff see O'Brien to Knox, November 1, 1909, *NA*, RG 59; *Harriman*, I, 119–30, II, 1, 4, 354, 369–72; *Schiff*, I, 133, and I, 25–26, 83, 114, 179–80, 183–85; *Straight*, 239. The present writer wishes to acknowledge the generous courtesies of Dr. Charles Vevier, who is engaged in a re-evaluation of the *Straight Papers* and associated materials, during the preparation of this chapter. L. C. Griscom, *Diplomatically Speaking* (New York, 1940), 261, 262; Rockhill to Foulk, February 28, 1887, *Rockhill Mss.*, material through the courtesy of Professor Paul Varg.

12. Soyeda to Harriman, October 30, 1905, Griscom to Harriman, no date, both in *NA*, RG 59; *Harriman*, II, 13–15, 16, 17–18, 20–22; *Straight*, 240, 135, 155, 200, 212, 214, 238, 235, 207; Harrington, *God, Mammon, and the Japanese*, 329; Dennett, *Roosevelt*, 302–3, 311–12.

13. *British Trade Journal* (London), August 1, 1904; *Consular* (July, 1905), 252–53; Rockhill to Root, July 18, 1906, Wilson to Secretary of State of November 22, 1905, of January 12, 1906, of January 18, 1906, all in *NA*, RG 59. Other American firms in the area included the Singer Sewing Machine Company, Swift and Company, and McNeil and Libby.

14. Rogers to Rockhill, July 6, 1906, Wright to Bacon, February 2, 1907, Straight to Rockhill, May 8, 1907, all in *NA*, RG 59; *Consular* (August, 1905), 23–29, (October, 1905), 51–56, (November, 1905), 157–59, (December, 1905), 103–8, (April, 1906), 119–28, (July, 1906), 58–61, (August, 1906), 130–31, (July, 1907), 3–4, (November, 1907), 22–25, (May, 1908), 138–39, (September, 1908), 27, (December, 1909), 10–12; *Commerce, 1908*, II, 479.

15. *Straight*, 207, 237, 238, 232, 214–42, 210, 235; *Harriman*, II, 24–25; Griswold, *Far Eastern Policy*, 138–39.

16. *Straight*, 242; *Harriman*, II, 25; *DGP*, V 19:1:112–13; on the West Coast anti-Japanese agitation see Griswold *Far Eastern Policy*, Chapters III, IX; Dennett, *Roosevelt*, 47, 50; T. A. Bailey, *A Diplomatic History of the American People* (4th ed., New York, 1950), 570.

17. Dennett, *Roosevelt*, 112–15; Pringle, *Roosevelt*, Chapter X; P. C. Jessup, *Elihu Root* (2 vols., New York, 1938), II, 18–31.

18. Fisher to Rockhill, March 26, 1907, *Rockhill Mss.*; Lodge, *Correspondence*, II, 135; Roosevelt to White, July 30, 1907, A. Nevins, *Henry White* (New York, 1930), 292–93; Bishop, *Roosevelt*, II, 249–50, 64.

19. White to Root, June 19, 1907, *NA*, RG 59; Japan *Daily Mail*, June 19, 1907; *China*, I, 640; E. B. Price, *The Russo-Japanese Treaties of 1907–1916 Concerning Manchuria and Mongolia* (Baltimore, 1933), 31; A. Gerard, *Ma Mission au Japon, 1907–1914* (Paris, 1919), 7, 12–13, 25–26.

20. *Korea: Treaties and Agreements* (Carnegie Endowment, Washington, 1921), 58; Price, *Treaties*, Appendix B, 107–11.

21. Denby to Secretary of State, December 21, 1907, *NA*, RG 59.

22. White to Root, September 20, 1907, Adee to Root, September 21, 1907, Root to White, October 21, 1907, Adee to Bacon, October 21, 1907, all in *NA*, RG 59; Fisher to Rockhill, March 26, 1907, *Rockhill Mss.*

23. State Department, "Memorandum. The Chin-Ai Railway Project, January 16, 1911," *NA*, RG 59; *Straight*, 251, 242–43, 251, 250, 258; *Parliamentary Debates, House of Commons*, V 185(March 3, 1908), 527; *Relations, 1910*, 269; *Straight*, 251, 250, 258.

24. Phillips to Rockhill, July 16, 1908, *Rockhill Mss.*

25. Phillips to Rockhill, September 19, 1908, *Rockhill Mss.*; *Relations, 1908*, 510–12; *Straight*, 276, 271.

26. Phillips to Rockhill of September 19, 1908, of January 9, 1909, both in *Rockhill Mss.*

27. Fisher to Rockhill, March 26, 1907, *Rockhill Mss.*; Rockhill to Knox, March 26, 1910, Phillips to Adee, September 16, 1908, both in *NA*, RG 59; *Harriman*, II, 22; *Straight*, 278–89, 299, 298; *R v M*, 563.

28. *Schiff*, II, 129–32, 133; *KA*, V 6(1924), 45–47, V 7(1924), 5–9; Straus, *Under Four Administrations*, 189–90; Witte, *Memoirs*, 161; Russian Foreign Ministry Memorandum, December 27, 1908, *R v M*, 562.

29. First see Guggenheim to Marshall, July 22, 1908, *Papers of Louis Marshall*; then correspondence between Wilenkin, Kokovtsev, and Schiff in *R v M*, 562–64; and also *Schiff*, I, 248–50; *Straight*, 279.

30. Cloud to Knox, June 24, 1909, Straight to Knox, August 3, 1909, both in *NA*, RG 59; *Straight*, 279; Kokovtsev to Wilenkin, March 21, 1909, *R v M*, 565, 563.

31. *R v M*, 562.

32. Rockhill to Knox of October 2, 1909, of September 21–22, 1909 (Rockhill's review of his interviews at the Russian court), *Rockhill Mss.*; Fletcher to Knox of

August 23, 1909, of September 6, 1909, Schuyler to Knox, September 27, 1909, all in *NA*, RG 59; *R v M*, 566.

33. *Straight*, 280; *Harriman*, II, 23.

34. Griswold, *Far Eastern Policy*, 146, argues in this manner. Harriman to Davison, July 21, 1909, Straight to Schiff, no date given and key sections not printed, both in *Straight*, 296, 306–8; *Harriman*, II, 28.

35. MacMurray to Rockhill, March 18, 1913, *Rockhill Mss.*; *Straight*, 296; J. G. Reid, *The Manchu Abdication and the Powers, 1908–1912* (Berkeley, 1925), 61.

36. Taft, Message of December 3, 1912, *Relations, 1912*, vii–xxvii; Taft, *Addresses*, XVII, 40–41; *The American Secretaries of State and Their Diplomacy*, edited by S. F. Bemis (10 vols., New York, 1927–29), IX, 303, 307, 320–25; Taft, *Address Before the Americus Club, Pittsburgh, Pennsylvania, May 2, 1910* (Pittsburgh, n.d.), 22; Carr to Straight, May 1, 1909, *NA*, RG 59; Griswold, *Far Eastern Policy*, 135.

37. *HAF*, 303; *LHA*, 520; Mott, *Military Attaché*, 140; *Register, 1917*, 128; *Register, 1924*, 176; *Register, August 1, 1944*, 173; B. D. Harlan, *Inside the Department of State* (New York, 1939), 66, 100, 257; G. H. Stuart, *The Department of State* (New York, 1949), 210, 233, 234, 235, and *American Diplomatic and Consular Practice* (New York, 1936), 89.

38. Phillips to Rockhill, July 16, 1908, same to same, September 19, 1908, *Rockhill Mss.*; "Memorandum of Assistant Secretary of State Phillips, May 10, 1909," Griswold, *Far Eastern Policy*, 140; *LHA*, 520; *Straight*, 270, 282; Bemis, *Secretaries*, IX, 325.

39. Phillips to Rockhill, April 27, 1909, *Rockhill Mss.*; Wilson to Rockhill, October 19, 1909, Wilson to Schuyler, October 30, 1909, Knox to Rockhill, October 30, 1909, all in *NA*, RG 59.

40. Bemis, *Secretaries*, IX, 328.

41. State Department Memorandum, January 6, 1910, *NA*, RG 59.

42. Phillips to Rockhill, January 9, 1909, *Rockhill Mss.*

43. *Straight*, 282, 292–93.

44. Taft to Prince Chun, July 15, 1909, Wilson to Reid, July 9, 1909, both in *NA*, RG 59; *Straight*, 295.

45. Rockhill to Izvolski, June 23, 1909, *Amerika*, 187; Morgan to Straight, October 8, 1909, *Straight*, 305–6.

46. Straight to Morgan, October 4, 1909, Fletcher to Knox, October 4, 1909 (with note by Phillips on conference with Davison), Morgan to Adee, October 19, 1909, Fletcher to Knox, October 10, 1909, all in *NA*, RG 59; *Straight*, 306, 320, 306, 308; *Schiff*, I, 252.

47. Fisher to Root, May 19, 1908, Schuyler to Knox, September 27, 1909, Rockhill to Knox, October 2, 1909, Heintzleman to Hoyt, October 14, 1909, Snodgrass to Knox, October 19, 1909, Wilson to Schuyler, October 30, 1909, all in *NA*, RG 59; Fletcher to Knox, November 2, 1909, *NA*, RG 84; Rockhill to Knox, November 6, 1909, Knox to Russian Embassy, February 8, 1910, both in *NA*, RG 59.

48. Krupensky to Izvolski, November 8, 1909, *Amerika*, 188; Schuyler to Knox, September 27, 1909, Schuyler to Root, April 25, 1908, Rockhill to Knox, December 31, 1909, Schuyler to Izvolski, December [?], 1909 (in Schuyler to Knox, December 20, 1909) all in *NA*, RG 59; *R v M*, 566; *Diplomacy*, 13–15.

49. Fletcher to Knox, November 2, 1909, *NA*, RG 84; *Straight*, 321, 306.

50. Reid, *Manchu Abdication*, 61.

51. Wilson to Rockhill, October 19, 1909, Wilson to Schuyler, October 30, 1909, Knox to Rockhill, November 9, 1909, same to same, November 16, 1909 (instructions to refrain from any "written or formal statement"), all in *NA*, RG 59; Phillips to Rockhill, June 3, 1908, Fletcher to Knox, June 19, 1909, *Rockhill Mss.*; Knox to Hoyt, October 9, 1908, same to same, October 18, 1909, both in *Papers of Philander Chase Knox*, materials courtesy of Professor Paul Varg; State Department, "Memo on the Chin-Ai Contract," January 16, 1911, Phillips to Wilson, May 25, 1908, Wilson to Fletcher, October 20, 1909, Wilson to O'Brien, October 30, 1909, Knox to Reid, November 6, 1909, Knox to O'Brien, January 20, 1910, Knox to Rockhill, February 8, 1910, Grey to Reid, November 25, 1909, Reid to Knox, November 26, 1909, Reid to Knox, February 16, 1910, all in *NA*, RG 59.

52. Knox to O'Brien and Reid, December 14, 1909, both in *NA*, RG 59.

53. Heenan to Knox, December 18, 1909, Wilson to Rockhill, December 23, 1909, Schuyler to Knox, December 15, 1909, O'Brien to Knox [2], December 24, 1909, Moses to Knox, December 28, 1909, all in *NA*, RG 59; *Straight*, 310; *Harriman*, II, 28; Price, *Treaties*, 51; *Diplomacy*, 8–9.

54. Knox to Rockhill, November 10, 1909, Rockhill to Knox, November 13, 1909, both in *NA*, RG 59; *R v M*, 566–67.

55. *Amerika*, 299; *R v M*, 566; Avarin, *Imperialism v. Manchzhurii* (2 vols., Moscow, 1934), I, 118.

56. *Rivalry*, 157, n143, reviews the argument in this vein.

57. Rockhill to Knox, January 30, 1911, *NA*, RG 59.

58. Rockhill to Knox, December 31, 1909, Rockhill to Knox, January 20, 1910, both in *NA*, RG 59. See Note 51.

59. Knox to Rockhill, January 3, 1910, *NA*, RG 84.

60. Rockhill to Knox of January 20, 1910, of January 21, 1910, of January 29, 1910, of February 18, 1910, all in *NA*, RG 59; Wilson to Knox, May 2, 1910, *NA*, RG 84; *Diplomacy*, 8–13; Price, *Treaties*, 139–40, n39; Izvolski to Knox, January 21, 1910, *NA*, RG 59; *Digest*, V 40(February 5, 1910), 214; (February 12, 1910), 271; (February 19, 1910), 338.

61. Schuyler to Rockhill, February 15, 1910, *Rockhill Mss.*; Izvolski to Knox of January 21, 1910, of February 2, 1910, both in *NA*, RG 59; Knox to Rockhill, February 14, 1910, *NA*, RG 84.

62. Reid, *Manchu Abdication*, 93, 98, 104; "Memorandum from the Russian Embassy, February 24, 1910," *NA*, RG 59.

63. Price, *Treaties*, 53.

64. Wheeler to Knox, June 26, 1910, *NA*, RG 59.

65. Knox to Izvolski, April 18, 1910, Rockhill to Knox, April 24, 1910, both in *NA*, RG 59; *Straight*, 326–27; *Rivalry*, 167–68; Price, *Treaties*, 53–56.

66. *Diplomacy*, 19; Grey's note on MacDonald to Grey, July 2, 1910, *British Documents on the Origins of the World War, 1898–1914*, edited by G. P. Gooch and H. W. V. Temperley (London, 1926–38), VIII, 485; New York *Times*, July 7, 8, 12, 14, 1910; London *Times*, June 16, July 17, 1910.

67. Wilenkin, Report of March 1, 1910, *Amerika*, 195; for Schiff's disillusionment with Japan see *Schiff*, II, 254–56; *Novoye Vremya*, March 10, 1910; Rockhill to Knox, March 11, 1910, O'Brien to Knox, March 16, 1910, both in *NA*, RG 59. By 1914, however, Schiff was ready to cooperate with Japan once again, see undated New York *Times* clipping, Sakatani to Schiff, March 9, 1918, Schiff to Sakatani, April 10, 1918, Sakatani to Schiff, June 2, 1918, all in *Schiff Mss.*

68. Rockhill to Knox of March 2, 1910, of March 26, 1910, Menocal to Morgan, May 31, 1910, Einstein to Knox, June 27, 1910, all in *NA*, RG 59; Miller to Rockhill, June 14, 1910, *NA*, RG 84; Williams to Rockhill of June 4, 1910, of June 25, 1910, *Rockhill Mss.*

69. Wright to Brown of February 12, 1907, of February 20, 1907, unsigned memorandum [probably written by Huntington Wilson], February 18, 1910, Wilson to O'Brien, February 19, 1910, O'Brien to Knox of February 21, 1910, of February 25, 1910, all in *NA*, RG 59.

70. J. H. Hammond, *The Autobiography of John Hays Hammond* (2 vols., New York, 1935), II, 454–56, 466, 467–68; Hammond, earlier associated with Cecil Rhodes, also had ties with the Guggenheim interests; and see Hammond's testimony, *Conditions in Russia. Hearings on House Res. No. 635* (Washington, 1921), 202–14; *Novoye Vremya*, December 9, 1910.

71. Hammond to N. D. Harris, February 4, 1924, *Rockhill Mss.*; Rockhill to Knox, December 10, 1910, *NA*, RG 59; *Novoye Vremya*, December 13, 20, 1910; Rockhill to Knox of December 22, 1910, of December 24, 1910, both in *NA*, RG 84; Rockhill to Knox, December 24, 1910, *NA*, RG 59; Nyvkov to Rockhill, July 11, 1911, *NA*, RG 84.

72. Rockhill to Knox, December 22, 1910, *NA*, RG 59.

73. Knox to Rockhill, July 13, 1910, Straus to Knox, July 15, 1910, J. R. MacArthur to Knox, July 29, 1910, Straus to Knox, August 4, 1910, all in *NA*, RG 84.

74. Commander of the Atlantic Fleet to Rockhill of March 20, April 26, April 29, June 13, June 16, 1911, all in *NA*, RG 59; Rear Admiral C. J. Badger to Rockhill, June 17, 1911, *NA*, RG 84; Wilson to Guild, July 1, 1911, *NA*, RG 84; MacMurray to Wilson, July 11, 1911, MacMurray, "Memorandum on Relations with Russia, June 3, 1911," both in *NA*, RG 59.

75. Guild to Knox, August 22, 1911, MacMurray, "Memorandum of June 3, 1911," both in *NA*, RG 59.

76. A. C. Millspaugh, *Americans in Persia* (Washington, D.C., 1924), 13–14; R. P. Churchill, *The Anglo-Russian Convention of 1907* (Cedar Rapids, Iowa, 1939).

77. *Diplomacy*, 61; E. M. Earle, *Turkey, the Great Powers, and the Bagdad Railway*

(New York, 1923), 199; P. E. Mosely, "Russian Policy in 1911–1912," *JMH*, V 12:1(March, 1940), 78.

78. *Diplomacy*, 85–86, 96, 104.

79. Unsigned Memorandum to Knox, September 13, 1910, *NA*, RG 59.

80. Wilson, Memorandum of September 14, 1910, Wilson to Reid, September 21, 1910, both in *NA*, RG 59.

81. Russell to Knox of May 14, 1910, of September 29, 1910, Adee to Russell of October 28, 1910, of November 10, 1910, Egan to Knox, November 9, 1910, all in *NA*, RG 59.

82. Hussum Kuli to Mirzu Ali-Kuil Khan, December 25, 1910, Reid to Taft, November 29, 1911, Schuster to Taft, December 28, 1910, Taft to Knox, December 28, 1910, MacVeagh to Taft, January 17, 1911, all in *NA*, RG 59.

83. Russell to Knox, September 27, 1911, *NA*, RG 59; W. M. Schuster, *The Strangling of Persia* (New York, 1912), Appendix B, 356–58.

84. Schuster, in *Annals*, V 54(July, 1914), 291; Guild to Knox, November 1, 1911, Seligman to Knox, February 10, 1911, both in *NA*, RG 59; *Rossaya*, December 5, 1912.

85. Reid, "Memorandum of a Conversation with Sir Edward Grey, November 23, 1911," *NA*, RG 59.

86. Russell to Knox, December 28, 1911, *NA*, RG 59; *Digest* (January 6, 1912), 1.

87. Russell to Knox, October 30, 1911, Guild to Knox, December 15, 1911, both in *NA*, RG 59.

88. *Schiff*, II, 136–39; Straus, *Under Four Administrations*, 191; Jessup, *Root*, II, 58, 65.

89. Adee, memorandum of October 4, 1906, Adee to Schiff, October 9, 1906, Schiff to Adee, October 10, 1906, Schiff to Roosevelt, October 22, 1906, same to same, November 1, 1906, all in *NA*, RG 59; Jessup, *Root*, II, 66; *Relations, 1906*, 1296–1314; *Outlook* (September 16, 1905), 94–95, (June 23, 1906), 394–95.

90. Schiff to Root, April 29, 1907, Sulzberger to Taft, May 18, 1908, Sulzberger to Roosevelt, May 18, 1908, Guild to Knox, June 29, 1911, all in *NA*, RG 59; *Record*, V 48:1:319; *House Report No. 179* (Washington, 1912), 4.

91. T. A. Bailey, *America Faces Russia* (Ithaca, New York, 1951), 219, 215.

92. *Schiff*, II, 116; *Outlook* (June 27, 1915), 171–75, (November 8, 1913), 529–35.

93. Parsons to Taft, January 16, 1911, Ritter to Taft, March 25, 1911, both in *NA*, RG 59; Wilson to Guild, September 5, 1911, *NA*, RG 84; Straus to Taft, December 19, 1911, *NA*, RG 59; C. Alder and A. M. Margalith, *With Firmness in the Right* (New York, 1946), 286.

94. New York *Times*, November 20, December 4, 5, 6, 7, 1911; *Record*, V 48:1:343; *Independent*, V 71(November 23, 1911), 1155–56; *Outlook* (December 16, 1911), 888–89; *Wilson Papers*, II, 318–22.

95. *Record*, V 48:1:311–54, V 47:97, 657, 1067, 1873, 1948, 2000, 2274, 2062, 2492, 2791, 2888, 2946, 3288, 3790, 3858; V 48:534, 181–82.

96. *Ibid.*, V 48:327–28, Appendix, 17, 335–56.

97. Rockhill to Knox of January 21, 1911, of January 30, 1911, both in *NA*, RG 59.

98. Guild to Knox, September 25, 1911, *NA*, RG 59.

99. Knox to Taft, November 28, 1911, *NA*, RG 84.

100. Guild to Knox of December 17, 1911, of December 19, 1911, both in *NA*, RG 59.

101. Wigmore to War College Staff, Report 1162, November 23, 1912, *NA*, RG 59.

102. Hammond, *Autobiography*, II, 475; Wilenkin to Schiff, September 6, 1914, *Schiff Mss.*

103. *Straight*, 325, 328, 244, 266–403; *Relations*, 1912, 88–92; *1913*, 192–98.

104. Adee to Rockhill, November 1, 1910, *NA*, RG 84; *Novoye Vremya*, November 2, 1910; *Rossia*, November 3, 1910; Rockhill to Knox, November 17, 1910, *NA*, RG 84.

105. Genfeld to Davison, November 11, 1911, Calhoun to Knox, December 5, 1911, both in *NA*, RG 59; *Straight*, 382; *Rivalry*, 174–87, 160.

106. *Relations, 1909*, 519.

107. *Robins; The Public* (Chicago), V 10:494:580–81; Progressive party of Illinois, *Raymond Robins. The Story of Raymond Robins' Life* (Chicago, 1914), 6.

108. Chicago *Daily News*, September 12, 1932; C. E. Merriam, *Chicago. A More Intimate View of Urban Politics* (New York, 1929), 209.

109. Robins, *Address at the National Protest Meeting of the Chicago Federation of Labor, April 19, 1908* (Chicago, 1908), 9; F. L. Hayes, "Standby Obituary on Raymond Robins," Robins File, Chicago *Daily News* Library; *Robins*.

110. Chicago *Tribune*, February 18, 1906; Robins, *Address . . . April 19, 1908*.

111. Chicago *Tribune*, November 29, 1908; *Public*, V 11:557:843; *Robins*.

112. *Digest*, V 43 (December 30, 1911), 1214, V 44 (April 20, 1912), 804–5; Laserson, *Impact*, 359–69.

113. R. M. Odell, *Cotton Goods in Russia* (Commerce, 1912), 11, 23, 41; *Commerce, 1908*, I, 327, 335; *Russia. Trade for the Year 1907* (Commerce, 1908), 17, 23; *Consular*, (October 14, 1911), 229.

114. *Commerce, 1901*, II, 602; A. J. Wolfe, *Foreign Credits* (Commerce, 1913), 181; *Consular*, (December, 1881), 561.

115. *Consular*, (March, 1899), 510; G. L. Carden, *Supplementary Report on Machine-Tool Trade in Russia* (Commerce, n. d.), 1–7; *Consular*, (April, 1910), 197, (January, 1910), 44, (February, 1910), 24, 28; *Commerce, 1901*, II, 599–602; *Consular*, (July, 1893), 471, (November, 1899), 404–8.

116. *Railroad Gazette*, V 28 (1896), 438, 485.

117. *Iron Age* (January 28, 1904), 11; Meyer to Root, January 6, 1906, *NA*, RG 59; G. S. Queen, "An American Employer and Russian Labor in 1905," *JMH*, V 15:2 (June, 1943), 120–26.

118. Coleman to Hughes, April 27, 1923, *NA*, RG 59; J. H. Snodgrass, *Russia. A Handbook on Commercial and Industrial Conditions* (Commerce, 1913), 179, 278, 242–43; U.S. Commissioner of Corporations, *The International Harvester Company*

(Washington, 1913), 147; R. R. Dennis, *American Agricultural Implements in Europe, Asia, and Africa* (Commerce, 1909), 82–83; *Consular,* (May, 1909), 43; Carden, *Machine Tool Trade,* 134–37.

119. H. Baker to Bureau of Foreign and Domestic Commerce, February 14, 1916, *NA,* RG 151: Records of the Bureau of Foreign and Domestic Commerce.

120. *NA,* RG 151: File No. 620, "American Investment Possibilities—Russia;" Tripp to Guild, May 31, 1912, *NA,* RG 84; Rockhill to Knox of April 13, of April 19, 1911, Perkins to Knox, February 14, 1910, all in *NA,* RG 59; Kennedy to Rockhill, March 14, 1910, Kingsley to Knox, October 17, 1910, Guggenheim to Guild, May 8, 1912, all in *NA,* RG 84; *Outlook* (January 23, 1904), 211, 216; *A New Estimate of American Investments Abroad* (Commerce, 1931), 15; *NA,* RG 59: File 861.51-Moorres, H. P.

121. Kenaston to Senator K. Nelson, March 8, 1912, *NA,* RG 59.

122. C. H. McCormick to Knox, January 13, 1912, Knox to McCormick, January 26, 1912, both in *NA,* RG 84; Guild to Knox, December 22, 1911, *NA,* RG 59.

123. Straus to Hilles, February 3, 1912, *NA,* RG 59; Knox to Wilson, May 20, 1912, *NA,* RG 84; Marshall to Taft, November 15, 1912, Knox to Bakhmeteff, December 16, 1912, both in *NA,* RG 59; Schiff to Wolf, May 24, 1918, *Schiff Mss.*

124. H. Notter, *The Origins of the Foreign Policy of Woodrow Wilson* (Baltimore, 1937), 203.

125. *Hearings,* III, 935; Francis to Jones, October 26, 1916: Francis, *Russia from the American Embassy, April, 1916—November, 1918* (New York, 1921), 25; Snodgrass, *Russia,* 9, 10; *Century,* V 85(1913), 296–310; *Digest* (October 3, 1914), 617–18.

126. Francis to Lansing, April 14, 1916, *NA,* RG 59; Francis to Wilson, April 8, 1916, *House,* II, 173. For background see D. C. De Young's unpublished Master's thesis, "David Roland Francis: American in Russia," University of Wisconsin, Madison, 1949.

127. *Trade of the United States with the World, 1912–1913* (Commerce, 1914), 34, 114; *Trade, 1914–1915,* 60–61, 215; *Trade, 1916–1917, Part 2, Exports,* 48, 264; *Trade, 1917–1918, Part 2, Exports,* 51, 289.

128. Francis to Lansing, June 16, 1916, Lansing to Page, April 30, 1918, Page to Lansing, May 2, 1918, Bakhmeteff to Morgan, April 30, 1918, all in *NA,* RG 59; *Russian Bonds* (Washington, 1919), 17–18, 21; *To Provide Revenue for War Purposes* (Washington, 1918), 85–87, 122; *Loans to Foreign Governments* (Washington, 1921), 89, 92–94.

129. Snodgrass to Knox, of January 17, 1913, of February 17, 19, 1913, Zarochentzev to Snodgrass, January 21, 1913, all in *NA,* RG 59; Brand to McKee, November 30, 1915, *NA,* RG 151; *Outlook* (May 24, 1916), 177.

130. *Digest,* V 53(July 1, 1916), 15.

131. Francis to Wilson, February 11, 1917, *NA,* RG 59; *Munitions Industry. Report on Existing Legislation* (Washington, 1936), Part 5, 61.

132. *KA,* V 2(1922), 143, 147, V 26(1928), 29–31, 32–33.

133. *Ibid.*, V 2(1922), 143–47, V 3(1922), 71–72, V 27(1928), 3.

134. N. N. Golovine, *The Russian Army in the World War* (New Haven, 1931), 238; *KA*, V 9(1926), 105.

135. *KA*, V 17(1926), 10.

136. *Ibid.*, V 21(1927), 4–5, 56.

137. *Ibid.*, V 10(1925), 67–94.

138. House to Wilson of January 11, 1916, February 3, 1916, House, diary entry of February 11, 1916, all in *House*, II, 121, 129, 157, 174–75; Page to Wilson, October 29, 1914: B. J. Hendrick, *The Life and Letters of Walter H. Page* (3 vols., New York, 1925), III, 168; House to Wilson, January 22, 1917, *Wilson Mss.*

139. House to Wilson, January 30, 1917, *Wilson Mss.*

140. D. Lloyd George, *War Memoirs of David Lloyd George* (6 vols., Boston, 1936), III, 463.

141. Morris to Lansing, March 19, 1917, Francis to Lansing of March 19, 1917, of March 22, 1917, all in *NA*, RG 59; McAdoo to Lansing, March 29, 1917, *Lansing Mss.*

142. Straus to Lansing, April 6, 1917, Wadsworth to Lansing, both in *NA*, RG 59; Morgenthau to Lansing, April 5, 1917, *Lansing Mss.*; Lodge to Wilson, April 13, 1917, Fling to Wilson, April 15, 1917, both in *Wilson Mss.*

143. House to Wilson, April 10, 1917, McAdoo to Wilson, April 17, 1917, Wilson to McCormick, April 22, 1917, Lansing to Wilson, April 12, 1917, McCormick to Wilson, May 9, 1917, all in *Wilson Mss.*; Lansing to Wilson, April 23, 1917, *NA*, RG 59; Harper, *Memoirs*, 202.

144. Harper, *Memoirs*, 9; Williams to Davison, February 14, 1917, *Harper Mss.*; Judson to Harper, June 7, 1918, *Harper Mss.*; Mrs. Maddin Summers, quoted by A. Parry, "Charles R. Crane, Friend of Russia," *Russian Review*, V 6:2 (Spring, 1947), 20–36.

145. Harper, *Memoirs*, 202; Crane to Harper of March 15, 1917, of May 22, 1917, both in *Harper Mss.*; Lansing to Wilson, April 23, 1917, *NA*, RG 59; Lansing, *War Memoirs of Robert Lansing* (New York, 1935), 331–32.

146. Harper, *Memoirs*, 91; Crane to Harper, March 15, Lansing to Wilson, March 16, 1917, both in *NA*, RG 59; Harper, "Memo on the Russian Commission," *Harper Mss.*

147. Wilson to Wise, April 28, 1917, *Wilson Mss.*, Root to Mott, July 8, 1917, Jessup, *Root*, 366, 360.

148. McCormick, quoted in *Outlook* (September 23, 1914), 196–201; *America's Message to the Russian People* (Boston, 1918), 119.

149. Howe, *George von Lengerke Meyer*, 273; Burleson to Wilson, May 3, 1917, Wilson to Baker, May 3, 1917, Baker to Wilson, May 5, 1917, all in *Wilson Mss.*; Judson to his wife, May 5, 1917, *Judson Mss.*; Harper to Williams of May 1, May 13, 1917, Crane to Harper, May 22, 1917, Harper to McCormick, May 14, 1917, all in *Harper Mss.*

150. M. M. Podolsky (Member of the Labor Committee of the Provisional Government) to Wilson, May 4, 1917, *Wilson Mss.*

151. Harper to Allen, May 17, 1917, *Harper Mss.*

152. Dixon to Harper, April 29, 1917, Harper to Dixon, May 12, 1917, Howard to Harper, May 7, 1917, all in *Harper Mss.*

153. Harper to Crane, May 17, 1917, Howard to Harper, May 21, 1917, both in *Harper Mss.*

154. C. P. I., *Preliminary Statement to the Press* (Washington, 1917), 11–13; Harper to Bullard, May 17, 1917, *Harper Mss.; Outlook* (December 23, 1917), 893.

155. Crane to Harper, May 22, 1917, *Harper Mss.*

156. W. Lippmann and C. Merz, *A Test of the News. Special Supplement, New Republic* (August 4, 1920) ; *Digest* (March 31, 1917), 799, 885, (March 31, 1917), 959, (April 7, 1917), 1001, (August 8, 1917), 16.

157. Hurley to Hagedorn, May 3, 1932, Platte to Hagedorn, June 19, 1931, both in *Thompson Mss.*

158. Dodge to House, April 28, 1917, House to Wilson, May 8, 1917, Davison to Wilson, May 10, 1917, all in *Wilson Mss.*

159. Wadsworth to Wilson, May 7, 1917, Phillips to Wilson, May 8, 1917, Wilson to Phillips, May 10, 1917, all in *Wilson Mss.*

160. Red Cross War Council Minutes, Volume I, May 29, 1917, *ARC;* Davison to Phillips, June 8, 1917, Wilson to Phillips, June 9, 1917, Phillips to Wilson, June 8, 1917, Phillips to Wilson, June 15, 1917, Wilson to Phillips, June 16, 1917, all in *Wilson Mss.*

161. Hagedorn memo, *Thompson Mss.;* Phillips to Wilson, June 8, 1917, *Wilson Mss.;* Roosevelt to Robins, June 28, 1917, *TR Mss.;* Chicago *Daily News,* April 28, 1917; Roosevelt to Davison, June [?], 1917, in War Council Minutes, June 18, 1917, *ARC.*

162. *Robins.*

163. *Robins;* Ickes, *Curmudgeon,* 234 (and conversation) ; Progressive party, *Robins,* 12; Chicago *Daily News,* July 16, September 9, October 7, 31, 1914; Chicago *Tribune,* October 2, 3, 25, 27, 29, 30, 31, November 1, 2, 3, 1914; New York *Times,* October 9, 1914; *Public,* V 17:726, 958, 965–66, 1165; "Campaign Information Sheet," Robins File, Chicago *Daily News* Library.

164. G. E. Mowry, *Theodore Roosevelt and the Progressive Movement* (Madison, 1947), 358–59; New York *Times,* July 16, August 14, 1916.

165. Davison to Billings, June 22, 1917, *ARC;* Davison to Roosevelt, June 28, 1917, Robins to Roosevelt of May 20, June 22, 1917, Roosevelt to Robins, June 28, 1917, all in *TR Mss.*

166. Kelleher to Hagedorn, April 29, 1931, *Thompson Mss.*

167. Platte to Hagedorn, June 19, 1931, Hagedorn memo, both in *Thompson Mss.;* Thompson to Davison, July 4, 1917, Davison to Thompson, July 4, 1917, War Council Minutes, August 6, 15, 1917, Billings to Davison, July 27, 1917, Finch to Thompson, August 20, 1917, Bain to Ruffin, August 11, 1917, all in *ARC; Robins.*

168. See *RAR*, 32, 34–36.
169. Root to Billings, July 21, 1917, McCormick to Billings, July 21, 1917, Miles to Billings, July 21, 1917, all in *ARC*.

Chapter IV: A TOKEN OF SYMPATHY

1. Lansing, "Memorandum on the Russian Situation and the Root Mission, August 9, 1917," *Lansing Mss.*
2. New York *Times*, May 10, 1917; Secretary of the Treasury, *Annual Report for 1920*, 325–30; and see note 104, Chapter III above.
3. Francis to Summers, March 15, 1917, Francis, *Embassy*, 71.
4. Francis to Lansing, May 4, 1917, *NA*, RG 59.
5. Francis to Lansing, June 9, 1917, Morris to Lansing, June 11, 1917, both in *NA*, RG 59; Sir G. Buchanan, *My Mission to Russia and Other Diplomatic Memoirs* (2 vols., Boston, 1923), II, 119; *Embassy*, 141; Francis to Lansing of May 4, 1917, of June 23, 1917, of July 19, 1917, of July 20, 1917, of February 13, 1918, all in *NA*, RG 59; Francis to Borah, April 7, 1923, *Borah Mss.*; below, Chapter V.
6. Kennan to Lansing, May 22, 1917, *Lansing Mss.*; Kennan to Lansing of May 30, 1917, of June 18, 1917, both in *NA*, RG 59.
7. Lansing to Francis, April 21, 1917, in *KA*, V 24(1927), 132; Lansing to Wilson, June 8, 1917, *NA*, RG 59; Francis to Lansing of June 20, 1917, sent to Wilson, *Wilson Mss.*, of June 11, 1917, *NA*, RG 59; Lansing to Wilson, June 25, 1917, *Wilson Mss.*; McCormick to Lansing, June 12, 1917, Lansing to McCormick, June 14, 1917, both in *NA*, RG 59.
8. *KA*, V 20(1927), 66, V 20(1927), 74, V 30(1928), 36–37, 39, V 10(1925), 139, 147; Kerensky, quoted in Harper, *Memoirs*, 108; J. Bunyan and H. H. Fisher, *The Bolshevik Revolution, 1917–1918. Documents and Materials* (Stanford, 1934), 11; L. Trotsky, *The History of the Russian Revolution* (3 vols., New York, 1932), II, 84.
9. House to Wilson, July 23, 1917, Frazier to House, June 22, 1917, sent to Wilson, both in *Wilson Mss.*
10. C. E. Russell to Lansing, June 22, 1917, *Russell Mss.*; Francis to Lansing of July 3, 1917, of July 10, 1917, both in *NA*, RG 59; Baker to Lansing, July 17, 1917, *NA*, RG 59; Scott to Judson, July 19, 1917 (orders of July 9, 1917), *NA*, RG 165: Records of the War Department General Staff.
11. Thompson to Davison, July 2, 1917, *ARC*; Root to Lansing, July 1, 1917, *NA*, RG 59; Billings to Davison, July 27, 1917, Bain to Ruffin, August 11, 1917, Ruffin to Bain, August 16, 1917, Finch to Thompson, August 20, 1917, all in *ARC*; Lansing to Francis, July 3, 1917, *NA*, RG 59; Thompson to Morrow, July 27, 1917, *ARC*.
12. Francis to Lansing, August 8, 1917, *NA*, RG 59; "Undated Memo by David Francis [probably written August 18, 1917]," *NA*, RG 84; Thompson to Kerensky, August 10, 1917, *Thompson Mss.*; Thompson to Morgan and McAdoo, August 10, 1917,

NA, RG 59; Kerensky to Thompson, August 11, 1917, *Thompson Mss.*

13. Lansing, "Memorandum on the Russian Situation and the Root Mission, August 9, 1917," *Lansing Mss.*

14. Lord Reading to Wilson, August 5, 1917, House to Wilson, August 9, 1917, Lansing to Wilson, August 9, 1917, Wilson to Creel, August 10, 1917, Lane to Wilson, August 10, 1917, Lansing to Wilson, August 27, 1917, all in *Wilson Mss.*; McCormick to Lansing, August 29, 1917, *Lansing Mss.*

15. Wilson to Lansing, August 14, 1917, *Wilson Mss.*; Judson, "Monthly Resumé (October 10 to November 13, 1917) to War College," *Judson Mss.*; Judson to Burleson, October 1, 1917, *Burleson Mss.*; Gibbs, "Memo on the Railroad Commission," *Papers of George Gibbs*; C. H. Smith, "What Happened in Siberia," *Asia*, V 22 (May, 1922), 373–78, 402–3.

16. Robins, "Extracts from Letters of Raymond Robins, August 14 to August 27, 1917," *TR Mss.*; "Report of the Red Cross Commission to Survey Civilian Needs," *ARC.*

17. Robins, "Extracts," *TR Mss.*

18. *Ibid.*; Robins to Billings, "Report on Refugees in the Ekaterinaslov Province," *ARC*; Billings to Davison of August 27, 29, 1917, both in *NA*, RG 59.

19. Harper, *Memoirs*, 101; Francis to Lansing, August 16, 1917, Crane to Crane, September 1, 1917, both in *NA*, RG 59; Baker to Wilson, August 13, 1917, *Wilson Mss.*; Baker to Lansing, September 6, 1917, *Judson Mss.*

20. R. S. Baker argues in this manner in note 1, p. 208, Vol. VII of *Woodrow Wilson. Life and Letters* (New York, 1939); House to Wilson, August 15, 1917, *Wilson Mss.*; Francis to Lansing, August 22, 1917, *NA*, RG 59; Judson to Burleson of August 3, 5, 1917, *Burleson Mss.*

21. Davison to Billings, September 7, 1917, Morgan to Lansing, August 23, 1917, both in *NA*, RG 59.

22. Thompson to Morgan, August 31, 1917, Thompson to Morrow, August 31, 1917, both in *Thompson Mss.*; Billings to Davison, September 4, 1917, Thompson to Davison, September 15, 1917, both in *NA*, RG 59; War Council Minutes, meetings of August 15, 30, September 4, 11, 1917, October 17, 1917, *ARC*; Judson to Burleson, August 3, 1917, *Burleson Mss.*

23. Robins, "Report," *ARC*; *Robins*; Robins and Thompson, Memoranda, *Thompson Mss.*; *Hearings*, III, 764ff.; Robins, "Some Observations on the Present Condition in Russia, September 10, 1917," *TR Mss.*; Thompson to Robins, August [?], 1917, *Robins Mss.*

24. Judson to Baker, "Report of Certain Events in Russia, 1917, 1918, dated June 18, 1919," July 23, 1919, *Judson Mss.*; Francis to Lansing, September 11, 12, 1917, both in *NA*, RG 59; *KA*, V 9 (1925), 160–62; Golovine, *Russian Army*, 280.

25. Robins, "Some Observations," *TR Mss.*; *Hearings*, III, 768–69.

26. *Hearings*, III, 768–69; Memo, *Thompson Mss.*

27. Lenin, quoted in E. H. Carr, *The Bolshevik Revolution, 1917–1923* (New York, 1951), 95; *V. I. Lenin. Selected Works* (12 vols., New York, annotated edition), VI, 206.

28. Robins, "Some Observations," *TR Mss.; Hearings*, III, 765.

29. *Hearings*, III, 781–82.

30. Billings, "Memo from Dr. Billings re Publicity Work in Petrograd," *ARC; Hearings*, III, 370; Thacher to Hagedorn, June 1, 1932, *Thompson Mss.*

31. Robins to Hagedorn, January 31, 1931, Thacher to Hagedorn, June 1, 1932, Billings to Davison, September 4, 7, 1917, Kelleher to Hagedorn, February 4, 1931, all in *Thompson Mss.*; Francis to Lansing, September 7, 1917, *NA*, RG 59; Pobrarissi to Francis, October 4, 1917, *NA*, RG 84; *Hearings*, III, 486–87; *Pravda*, December 9, 1917; Francis to Lansing, December 8, 1917, *NA*, RG 59.

32. *Hearings*, III, 764–67.

33. Thompson, "Memorandum on the Russian Period," *Thompson Mss.*; Thompson to Davison, September 24, 1917, *NA*, RG 59; Robins to Roosevelt, September 18, 1917, *TR Mss.*

34. Thompson, "Russian Period," *Thompson Mss.*; Davison to Thompson, September 27, 1917, *NA*, RG 59.

35. Thompson, "Russian Period," Thompson, memo, both in *Thompson Mss.*; *Robins.*

36. Thompson, "Russian Period," *Thompson Mss.*; Thompson to Davison, October 7, 1917, Judson to War College, October 6, 1917, both in *NA*, RG 165; *Hearings*, III, 767–68.

37. Thompson to Davison, October 7, 1917, *NA*, RG 165; Thompson to Hutchins, October 4, 1917, *Thompson Mss.*; Wardwell to Stetson, Thacher to Thacher, both quoted in Thompson, "Russian Period," *Thompson Mss.*

38. Breshkovsky to Wilson, September 20, 1917, *Thompson Mss.*; Thompson to Davison, September 22, 1917, sent to Wilson, *Wilson Mss.*; Thompson to Davison, September 23, 1917, Wilson to Breshkovsky, October 18, 1917, both in *Thompson Mss.*

39. Francis to Lansing of September 19, 23, of October 15, 24, 1917, all in *NA*, RG 59, of October 22, 26, 1917, both in *NA*, RG 84; Lansing to Wilson, October 3, 1917, House to Wilson, October 15, 1917, both in *Wilson Mss.*; Judson to Burleson, September 25, 1917, *Burleson Mss.*; Judson to War College, October 7, 1917, *NA*, RG 59; "Memorandum on Strategy of the Present War, Prepared at the Army War College, October 17, 1917," *NA*, RG 165; *RAR*, 37.

40. Thompson, "Russian Period," Wilson to Thompson, October 24, 1917, both in *Thompson Mss.*; Creel to Wilson, October 22, 1917, *Creel Mss.*, Vol. II.

41. E. Sisson, *One Hundred Red Days* (New Haven, 1931), 8–9; Francis to Lansing, October 22, 1917, *NA*, RG 84; Wilson to Sisson, October 24, 1917, *Wilson Mss.*; Lansing to Francis, October 29, 1917, *NA*, RG 59; Hutchins to Thompson, October 27, 1917, *Thompson Mss.*

42. Thompson to Hutchins, October 18, 1917, *Thompson Mss.*; *RAR*, 39–41; New York *Times*, November 3, 1917; Thompson to Hutchins, November 5, 1917, *Thompson Mss.*; Judson, "Report of Certain Events in Russia, 1917 to 1918, dated June 6, 1919," sent to Baker, July 23, 1919, *Judson Mss.*

43. *Hearings,* III, 778–81; Thompson, "Russian Period," *Thompson Mss.; Robins;* confidential witness, March 22, 1950.
44. Summers to Polk, November 2, 1917, *NA,* RG 59.
45. Bunyan and Fisher, *Bolshevik Revolution,* 170, 139, 172; *KA,* V 6(1924), 195–221, V 9(1925), 171–94, V 24(1927), 92, 93, 95–97.

Chapter V: THE BIRTH OF CONTAINMENT

1. Lansing, "Memorandum on the Russian Situation, December 7, 1917," *Lansing Mss.*
2. "X" [George Frost Kennan, distant relative of George Kennan, and State Department Official], "The Sources of Soviet Conduct," *Foreign Affairs,* V 25(July, 1947), 582.
3. *Relations, Russia, 1919,* 13; Wilson, *Mere Literature and Other Essays* (New York, 1896), 155–56; *Wilson Papers,* II, 2; Wilson, "The Road Away From Revolution," *Atlantic,* V 132(August, 1923), 145–46.
4. *Register, December 19, 1917,* 128, 129, 121; Howe, *George von Lengerke Meyer,* 306–7; De Witte Clinton Poole to author, April 18, 1950; Mott, *Attaché,* 140; Francis to Lansing, May [?], 1916, *NA,* RG 59; Wilson to Creel, September 4, 1917, *Creel Mss.,* Vol. II.
5. Mott (on duty in the Chief of Staff's Office) to Judson of September 15, 25, 1917, *Judson Mss.;* Phillips to author, August 19, 1950; for the drafting of messages see, for example, decimal file 861.00.
6. Judson to War College, November 14, 1917, Judson to Burleson, November [?], 1917, Francis to Lansing, November 7, 1917, all sent to Wilson, *Wilson Mss.;* Francis to Lansing, November 20, 1917, *Lansing Mss.;* Summers to Lansing, November 26, 1917, *NA,* RG 59.
7. Davison to Thompson, November 23, 1917, *NA,* RG 59; Miles to Van Sinderen, March 8, 1918, *NA,* RG 59; G. B. Clarkson, *Industrial America and the World War. The Strategy Behind the Lines, 1917–1918* (Boston, 1923), 195.
8. Lansing to Francis, November 24, 1917, *NA,* RG 59; Lansing, "Memorandum on Jules J. Jusserand," *Lansing Mss.*
9. Thompson, "Russian Period," *Thompson Mss.;* "Memo Approved by Wardwell, Thacher, and Robins, February 6, 1919," *ARC;* Thacher, "Economic Force and the Russian Problem," *Annals,* V 84(July, 1919), 125; Thacher to author, June 27, 1950; Wardwell to author, June 27, 1950.
10. *Hearings,* III, 782; *Robins; Bolshevik Revolution,* 119–39; Note No. 9 above.
11. Storms to Gumberg, April 5, 1917, Russell to Gumberg of July 20, 1917, of December 15, 1918, all in *Gumberg Mss.;* Robins to Borah, December 9, 1922, *Borah Mss.; Hearings,* III, 887–88; Thacher and Wardwell, conversations; Brodney to author, May 25, 1950; confidential witnesses, March 23, 1950, November 24, 1951.
12. *Robins.*
13. Thacher, "Russia and the War, dated June 4, 1918," *Thacher Papers* in *Rand School of Social Science Papers; Annals,* V 84:124–25; Thacher and Wardwell

to author, June 27, 1950; *Robins;* Thompson to Davison, November 19, 1917, *NA*, RG 165.

14. Francis, *Embassy*, 173–77; Summers to Lansing, sent to Wilson November 7, 1917, *NA*, RG 165; Judson to War College, November 25, 1917, *NA*, RG 59; *Izvestia*, December 1, 1917; *KA*, V 23(1927), 232–33; Francis to Lansing of November 28, December 1, 1917, both in *NA*, RG 59.

15. Thacher to Hagedorn, June 1, 1932, *Thompson Mss.*; Robins to Roosevelt, November 19, 1917, *TR Mss.*; Robins to Hagedorn, January 31, 1931, *Thompson Mss.*; Sisson, *Red Days*, 44–50; *RAR*, 48; M. P. Price, *My Reminiscences of the Russian Revolution* (London, 1921), 179.

16. Judson to War College, November 27, 1917, *NA*, RG 59; Judson to Trotsky, November 27, 1917, *RAR*, 48–49; Trotsky, speech of November 30, 1917, in J. DeGras, *Soviet Documents on Foreign Policy, 1917–1924* (New York, 1951), 12–13; Judson, Diary, November 27, 1917, *Judson Mss.*

17. Sisson, *Red Days*, 87–89; Buchanan, *My Memoirs*, II, 225; Huntington to Harper, November 27, 1917, *Harper Mss.*

18. *Register*, 142; Sisson, *Red Days*, 118; and see below.

19. *Diaries of Vance C. McCormick*, 7; Harper, *Memoirs*, 92–93.

20. Judson to Burleson, July 6, 1918, *Burleson Mss.*; Whightman to Hagedorn, May 8, 1931, *Thompson Mss.*; Judson, "Memo on Madame de Cram," Judson to Baker, June 18, 1918, both in *Judson Mss.*; Lansing, Diary, December 10, 1917, *Lansing Mss.*; Imbrie to Francis, May 28, 1918, Francis, "Undated Memo, August 18, 1917," both in *NA*, RG 84; Francis to Miss Karin Sante, November 29, 1918, Polk to Lansing, January 24, 1919, both in *NA*, RG 59.

21. Thacher, "Russia and the War," *Thacher Mss.*; *Hearings*, III, 787–89; L. Trotsky, *Stalin. An Appraisal of the Man and His Influence* (New York, 1941), 252.

22. Francis to Judson, November 20, 1917, *Lansing Mss.*; Judson to Francis, November 21, 1917, *Judson Mss.*; Judson to War College, November 29, 1917, *NA*, RG 165.

23. Francis to Lansing, December 1, 1917, *NA*, RG 59.

24. Judson to Francis, December 26, 1917, *Judson Mss.*

25. Judson to War College, December 1, 1917, *NA*, RG 165; Judson to Francis, December 26, 1917, *Judson Mss.*; DeGras, *Documents*, I, 14–15.

26. Judson to War College, December 2, 6, 1917, both in *NA*, RG 165; Judson to War College, December 1, 1917, Francis to Lansing of December 1, 2, 1917, Judson to War College, November 30, 1917, all in *NA*, RG 59.

27. Lansing to Francis, November 30, 1917, Francis to Lansing, December 9, 1917, both in *NA*, RG 59; Judson to Francis, December 3, 1917, *Judson Mss.*

28. *Russian Bonds*, 21; Lansing to Wilson, December 4, 1917, in Lansing, *War Memoirs of Robert Lansing* (New York, 1935), 343–45; Baker, *Wilson, Life and Letters*, VII, 391; E. B. Wilson, *My Memoirs* (Indianapolis, 1938), 138–39.

29. Lansing, Diary, December 6, 1917, *Lansing Mss.*; Lansing to Francis, December 6, 1917, *NA*, RG 59 (and *Wilson Mss.*).

30. Lansing, Diary, December 7, 1917, Lansing, "Memorandum on the Russian Situation, December 7, 1917," both in *Lansing Mss.*

31. Phillips to Miles, December 1, 1917, *NA*, RG 59; Lansing, Diary, December 26, 1917, *Lansing Mss.*; Phillips to Harper, December 8, 1917, *Harper Mss.*; Lansing to Wilson, December 10, 1917, *NA*, RG 59.

32. Lansing to Crosby, "Confidential. Not for Distribution," December 12, 1917, *NA*, RG 59; Lansing, Diary, December 11, 12, 1917, *Lansing Mss.*; McAdoo to Lansing, December 12, 1917, Wilson to Lansing, December 12, 1917, both in *NA*, RG 59.

33. Thompson, "Russian Situation," Lamont to Hagedorn, June 4, 1932, both in *Thompson Mss.*; Thompson to Wilson, January 3, 1918, *Wilson Mss.*

34. Thompson, "Memorandum to David Lloyd George, December, 1917," *Thompson Mss.*

35. Material in notes Nos. 33 and 34.

36. London *Times*, December 13, 1917; R. B. Lockhart, *Memoirs of a British Agent* (London, 1932), 200–1; Page to Lansing, December 29, 1917, sending "Memo Prepared for Lord Milner and Lord R. Cecil on Suggested Policy in Russia and Accepted by M. Clemenceau and M. Pichon on December 22, 1917," *NA*, RG 59; and see L. Fischer, *The Soviets in World Affairs* (2 vols., London, 1930), 837.

37. Sisson, *Red Days*, 85–86, 88–90; Creel to Sisson, December 3, 1917, Francis to Lansing, December 15, 1917, Creel to Wilson, December 27, 1917, all in *Wilson Mss.*

38. Sisson to Gumberg, February 25, 1918, *Gumberg Mss.*; *Hearings*, III, 88, 485–86, 566, 572, 629; Robins, "Some Considerations of the Present Situation in Russia, November 20, 1917," *Thompson Mss.*; Sisson, *Red Days*, 95.

39. Summers to Lansing, December 9, 1917, sent to Wilson, *Wilson Mss.*; Summers to Lansing, December 29, 1917, Summers to Francis, January 16, 1918, Poole to Summers of December 30, 31, 1917, Poole to Francis, February 6, 1918, all in *NA*, RG 84.

40. Lansing to Smith, December 27, 1917, Summers to Lansing, December 29, 1917, both in *NA*, RG 59.

41. *Hearings*, III, 956; Francis to Lansing of December 12, 1917, Lansing to Francis of December 20, 21, 1917, all in *NA*, RG 84.

42. Judson to Acting Chief of Staff, March 14, 1918, Judson to War College, December 23, 1917, both in *Judson Mss.*; Judson to War College, December 17, 1917, *NA*, RG 165; Robins, "Some Considerations," *Thompson Mss.*

43. Francis to Lansing, December 24, 1917, *NA*, RG 59; Judson to Francis, December 26, 1917, *Judson Mss.*

44. Judson, Diary, December 24, 1917, *Judson Mss.*; Francis to Lansing, December 27, 1917, Phillips to Lansing, December 27, 1917, Lansing to Francis, December 29, 1917, all in *NA*, RG 59.

45. *Bolshevik Revolution*, 484.

46. Francis to Lansing, January 1, 1918, *NA*, RG 59; Judson, Diary, December 31,

1917, *Judson Mss.*; Judson to War College, three cables of December 31, 1917, all in *NA*, RG 165.

47. Judson, Diary, January 1, 1918, *Judson Mss.*; Francis to Lansing, January 1, 1918, *NA*, RG 59; Sisson, *Red Days*, 196.

48. Francis to Lansing, January 1, 1918, *NA*, RG 59; and on the same document (in pencil) Miles to Phillips, January 4, 1918.

49. Judson, Diary, January 1, 1918, *Judson Mss.*; Baker to Lansing, December 24, 1917, *NA*, RG 165; Judson to Thompson, December 3, 1921, *Judson Mss.*

50. Francis to Lansing, January 2, 1918, *NA*, RG 59.

51. Robins to Francis, January 2, 1918, Francis to Robins, January 2, 1918, *Robins Mss.*, italics added; Francis to Lansing, January 2, 1918, *NA*, RG 59.

52. *Bolshevik Revolution*, 487; L. Trotsky, *My Life. An Attempt at an Autobiography* (New York, 1930), 363.

53. Sisson to Creel, January 3, 1918, *Creel Mss.*; Baker, *Wilson. Life and Letters*, VII, 447–48, 450–56; Lansing to Wilson, January 10, 1918, *NA*, RG 59.

54. Wilson, Fourteen Points Speech, *Wilson Mss.*

55. Lansing to Wilson, January 2, 1918, *NA*, RG 59; DeGras, *Documents*, I, 18–21; Lansing's reaction was delayed because Francis did not transmit the document until December 31, 1917.

56. Lenin and Trotsky, *The Proletarian Revolution in Russia* (New York, 1920), 355–60; Sisson, *Red Days*, 206–9; Francis to Lansing, January 12, 1918, *NA*, RG 59. Lenin's argument for peace was not published immediately.

57. Sisson, *Red Days*, 206–9, but see entire chapter.

58. *Ibid.*, 214–15; Lenin to A. R. Williams, April, 1918, in Williams, *Lenin. The Man and His Work* (New York, 1919), 97.

59. *Bolshevik Revolution*, 495–96, 498–500.

60. *Pravda*, February 24, 1918; Stalin, quoted by Trotsky, *Stalin*, 250; also see I. Deutscher, *Stalin. A Political Biography* (New York, 1949), 188–89.

61. D. Shub, *Lenin* (Garden City, New York, 1948), 280, 282; Carr, *Bolshevik Revolution*, 119–21.

62. Robins to Thompson, Sisson concurring, January 23, 1918, *Robins Mss.*; Carr, *Bolshevik Revolution*, 119–21; *KA*, V 28(1927), 76; Florinsky, *End of the Russian Empire*, 255.

63. Judson to War College, January 27, 1918, *Judson Mss.* (also RG 165).

64. Wilson to Lamont, January 31, 1918, *Wilson Mss.*

65. Robins to Davison, January 3, 1918, sent to Wilson, *Wilson Mss.*; Bullitt to Phillips, sent to Lansing, January 4, 1918, *NA*, RG 59; House to Wilson, January 2, 1918, *Wilson Mss.*; *House*, III, 389; Thompson to Wilson, January 3, 1918, *Wilson Mss.*; Creel to Wilson, December 31, 1917, *Creel Mss.*

66. Caldwell to Lansing, January 1, 1918, Cecil to Lansing, January 1, 1918, Child to House, December [?], 1917, Miles, "Memorandum for the Secretary of State, January 1, 1918," all sent to Wilson, *Wilson Mss.*; Chief of Naval Operations to

Commander in Chief of the Asiatic Fleet, January 3, 1918, Phillips to Polk, January [?], 1918, both in *Wilson Mss.* Miles' memorandum was returned by Wilson and is *NA*, RG 59:861.00/935.5.

67. Jusserand to Lansing, January 8, 1918, Lansing to Jusserand, January 16, 1918, both in *NA*, RG 59; Hill to Wadsworth, January 14, 1918, *ARC*.

68. Creel to Wilson, December 31, 1917, *Creel Mss.;* Wilson to Lamont, January 11, 1918, *Wilson Mss.*

69. Roosevelt to Robins, January 14, 1918, *TR Mss.;* Pringle, *The Life and Times of William Howard Taft* (2 vols., New York, 1939), II, 909.

70. Biddle to Hagedorn, April 26, 1932, *Thompson Mss.;* Borah to Kebabian, December 11, 1917, Borah to Hunt, January 10, 1918, both in *Borah Mss.;* Slemp to Wilson, "Memorandum on visit of Senators R. L. Owen, W. J. Stone, W. M. Calder, W. E. Borah to White House," *Wilson Mss.;* Sands to Lansing, January 16, 1918, *NA*, RG 59; *Record*, V 65:2:1408-10; New York *Times*, January 27, 1918.

71. Owen to Wilson, January 22, 1918, *NA*, RG 59; Miles, "Memo for Secretary of State on Owen's Letter Concerning Russia," *NA*, RG 59; Wilson to Tumulty (re his "cold"), February 1, 1918, *Wilson Mss.;* Lansing, Diary, January 31, 1918, *Lansing Mss.;* Thompson, memo, *Thompson Mss.*

72. Francis to Lansing of January 19, 20, 31, February 4, 1918, all in *NA*, RG 59; Sisson to Creel, January 21, 1918, *NA*, RG 63; Lockhart, *Memoirs*, 219.

73. N. D. Baker, "Foreword," in W. W. Graves, *America's Siberian Adventure, 1918–1920* (New York, 1931), ix.

Chapter VI: SOWING DRAGON'S TEETH IN EASTERN EUROPE

1. De Witt Clinton Poole, quoted in New York *Times*, February 19, 1933; M. Hoffman, *The War of Lost Opportunities* (London, 1924), 226; Ludendorff, *My War Memories* (London, 1919), II, 557–59.

2. *Pravda*, February 28, 1918; Francis to Lansing, February 20, 1918, *NA*, RG 59; *Bolshevik Revolution*, 512–13.

3. J. Sadoul, *Notes sur la révolution bolshevique* (Paris, 1919), 241–43; J. Noulens, *Mon ambassade en Russie sovietique* (2 vols., Paris, 1933), I, 233; Francis to Lansing, February 22, 1918, *NA*, RG 59.

4. *Pravda*, February 28, 1918; *Krasnaia Lietopis*, No. 1/28 (1929), 5–6; Robins to Lenin, February 28, 1918, Lenin to Robins, February 28, 1918, Robins to Francis, March 3, 1918, all in *Robins Mss.* (much of this correspondence between Robins and the Soviets and Francis is also in *NA*, RG 84:File 800); Memorandum from Earl Johnson, no date, *NA*, RG 84; *Hearings*, III, 799–800; Sisson, *Red Days*, 351–55.

5. Lockhart, *Memoirs*, 239; Riggs, memorandum of March 5, 1918, *NA*, RG 84; Francis to Lansing, March 5, 1918, *NA*, RG 59.

6. Lockhart to Balfour, March 5, 1918, *Gumberg Mss.;* Lockhart, *Memoirs*, 240.

7. Lenin and Trotsky to Robins, March 5, 1918, copy in *Robins Mss.*, original in *NA*,

RG 84: 1918 Correspondence, Confidential (not printed in *Relations*) ; Francis to Lansing, March 10, 1918, *NA*, RG 59.

8. Robins to Francis, March 6, 1918, *NA*, RG 84; Williams to Balfour and the London *Chronicle*, March 5, 1918, Stevens to Vanderlip, March 5, 1918, all in *Gumberg Mss.*; Stevens to Vanderlip, March 16, 1918, sent to Wilson, *Wilson Mss.*; Lockhart to author, April 18, 1950.

9. Francis to Robins, March 6, 1918, *NA*, RG 84; Francis to Lansing of March 10, 12, 1918, both in *NA*, RG 59.

10. Trotsky to Robins, March 9, 1918, Francis to Robins, March 10, 1918, Chicherin to Robins, March 9, 1918, all in *Robins Mss.*; Francis to Lansing, March 12, 1918, *NA*, RG 59; Francis to Robins, March 11, 1918, *NA*, RG 84; Ruggles to War College, March 8, 1918, *NA*, RG 165; Sadoul, *Notes*, 259; *Robins*; Lockhart to author, April 18, 1950.

11. Sisson, *Red Days*, 291, 294, 298, 307–8; Francis to Lansing, February 8, 9, 1918, both in *NA*, RG 59; Francis to Lansing, February 13, 1918, sent to Wilson, *Wilson Mss.*; Francis to Lansing, March 26, 1918, *NA*, RG 59; Gumberg obtained the first set of documents for Sisson.

12. Francis to Lansing, February 8, 1918, *NA*, RG 59; Robins to Thompson, February 15, 1918, *NA*, RG 59; Bullard to House, February 20, 1918, sent to Harper, *Harper Mss.*

13. Sisson, *Red Days*, 405; Imbrie to Treadwell, April 13, 1918, Armour to Treadwell, April 22, 1918, Imbrie to Francis, May 9, 1918, all in *NA*, RG 84; Cole to Poole, May 17, 1918, *NA*, RG 63.

14. Francis, *Embassy*, 236; Sisson, *Red Days*, 295, 343, 352–53; Francis to Lansing, March 26, 1918, Francis to Polk, January 22, 1919, both in *NA*, RG 59; Sisson to Creel, February 19, 1918, *NA*, RG 84.

15. Lansing to Francis (drafted by Phillips), February 1, 1918, Francis to Lansing, February 5, 1918 (on which is Miles to Phillips, February [?5], in pencil), both in *NA*, RG 59.

16. Thompson, articles in New York *Evening Post*, February 2–21, 1918; Washington *Post*, February 3, 1918; New York *Times*, February 25, 1918; Eames to Harper, February 24, 1918, *Harper Mss.*; see *ARC*, File 948.9.

17. Bullard to House, February 4, 1918 ("Memo on the Bolshevik Movement in Russia" with notes by Robins), Bullard to House, March 7, 1918, both in *NA*, RG 59; House to Wilson, February 2, 1918, Judson to Chief of Staff of February 26, March 5, 1918 (both marked "Urgent"), both sent to Wilson, *Wilson Mss.*; Davison to Wilson, February 21, 1918, *Wilson Mss.*; Wilson to Davison, January 22, 1918, *ARC*.

18. On Gompers and the A. F. of L. see M. Lovenstein, *American Opinion of Soviet Russia* (Washington, D.C., 1941), 8–9, 10, 51, 103–4; B. Gronert, "The Impact of the Russian Revolution upon the American Federation of Labor, 1918–1928," and D. F. Wieland, "American Labor and Russia, 1917–1925," both unpublished Master's theses, University of Wisconsin, 1948. Lansing to Smith, December 29,

1917, *Lansing Mss.*; Lansing to Wilson, February 2, 1918, Gompers to Wilson, February 9, 1918, Lansing to Wilson, February 15, 1918, all in *Wilson Mss.*

19. Miles, "Department of State Confidential Periodical Report on Matters Relating to Russia, No. 9, February 19, 1918," *NA*, RG 59:861.00/1125.

20. Frazier to Lansing, February 19, 1918, Sharp to Lansing, February 20, 1918, both in *NA*, RG 59; Wilson's Note of February 28, 1918, *House*, III, 419; Polk to Lansing, March 15, 1918, Balfour to Lockhart of March 4, 6, 1918, all in *NA*, RG 59; McFadden to Chief of Staff, February 14, 1918, *NA*, RG 165; General R. S. Spiers, "Secret. Russian-Japanese Intervention, February 14, 1918," sent to Wilson, *Wilson Mss.*; Lansing, Diary, February 20, 1918, *Lansing Mss.*

21. Wilson to Lansing, January 20, 1918, Wilson to Bryan, February 25, 1915, Lansing to Bryan, March 1, 1915, all in *NA*, RG 59; *Relations, 1917*, 264; Lansing, "Memo of an Interview with the Chinese Minister, November 2, 1917," *NA*, RG 59 (which compare with *Relations, 1914, Supplement*, 189–90).

22. J. A. White, *The Siberian Intervention* (Princeton, 1950), 155–57, 169.

23. House to Wilson, March 3, 1918, *Wilson Mss.*; *House*, III, 392–93, 394–95, 387–88.

24. White, *Intervention*, 160.

25. Wilson to U.S. Embassies, March 5, 1918, *NA*, RG 59; House to Wilson of March 5, 7, 1918, both in *Wilson Mss.*

26. Francis to Lansing, March 9, 12, 1918, both in *NA*, RG 59.

27. Polk to Summers, March 11, 1918, *NA*, RG 59; House to Wilson, March 10, 1918, *Wilson Mss.*; *House*, III, 399.

28. Harper, *Memoirs*, 112–13; Francis to Lansing, March 12, 1918 (note by Miles on margin), Lansing to Francis, March 19, 1918, both in *NA*, RG 59; Baker, *Wilson, Life and Letters*, VIII, 12.

29. Robins to Francis of March 11, 14, 1918, both in *Robins Mss.*; *Hearings*, III, 807; Williams, *Lenin*, 171; Lockhart to author, April 18, 1950.

30. See Y. Stekloff's editorial, "For More Realism," in *Izvestia*, cited here from copy in *Rand Social Science Papers*; Price, *Reminiscences*, 252; Lockhart, *Memoirs*, 250–51; Bullard to House, March 17, 1918, *NA*, RG 165; *Izvestia*, March 22, 1918 ("only the United States" dealt honestly with the Soviets); Lansing to Francis, March 23, 1918, Francis to Lansing of March 20, 23, November 1, 1918 (enclosing an Army report on Soviet cooperation), all in *NA*, RG 59; *RAR*, 103–7.

31. Trotsky to Ruggles, March 21, 1918, *NA*, RG 84; Francis to Lansing, March 25, 1918, Lansing to Francis, March 30, 1918, both in *NA*, RG 59; *RAR*, 107–14; Clarkson, *Industrial America*, 364, 370–71.

32. McAllister to Robins, April 4, 1918 (2 cables), *Gumberg Mss.*; McAllister to International Harvester Home Office, April 18, 1918, *NA*, RG 59; Fischer, *Soviets in World Affairs*, I, 300.

33. Lenin to Robins, May 14, 1918, *Robins Mss.* (*RAR*, 204–12); for a later Soviet view of this plan see *Foreign Affairs*, V 4(July, 1926), 574–84; Robins to Francis, March 22, 23, 1918, both in *Robins Mss.*; Francis to Lansing, March 22, 1918, *NA*, RG 59; *Hearings*, III, 813–14.

34. Francis to Lansing of April 1, March 26, 29, May 6, 1918, all in *NA*, RG 59; Francis to Lansing, May 28, 1918 (2 cables), Summers to Lansing, April 1, 1918, Francis to Robins, March 22, 1918, Robins to Francis, March 23, 1918, all in *NA*, RG 84; Lockhart, *Memoirs*, 213, 273; Lockhart to author, April 18, 1950; Armour to author, June 16, 22, 1950; Poole to author, April 10, 18, 1950; Johnson to author, September 22, 1950.

35. MacGowan to Francis, March 16, 1918, *NA*, RG 84.

36. Francis to Lansing, March 21, 22, 1918, Summers to Lansing, March 31, 1918, Lansing to Francis, April 5, 1918, all in *NA*, RG 59; *RAR*, 104–9, 165–87; Fischer, *Soviets in World Affairs*, I, 104.

37. Robins to Francis, March 25, 27, April 1, 6, 1918, Francis to Robins (and Lansing), April 4, 1918, *Robins Mss.* (*RAR*, 116–35).

38. Francis to Lansing, April 15, 1918, *NA*, RG 59; Robins to Francis, April 15, 1918, Chicherin to Robins for Francis, April 25, 1918, both in *Robins Mss.* (*NA*, RG 84) ; Robins to Thompson, April 18, 1918, *NA*, RG 59.

39. Ruggles to Military Staff, April 7, 8, 1918, both in *NA*, RG 165; Kerth to Chief of Staff, March 29, 1918, *Bliss Mss.;* Lockhart, *Memoirs*, 230, 289; Lockhart to Balfour, May 21, 1918, sent to Lansing, *NA*, RG 59; Lockhart to Balfour, May 7, 1918, sent to Wilson, *Wilson Mss.;* Francis to Lansing, May 2, 11, 1918, *NA*, RG 59.

40. Lansing to Francis, April 16, 23, 1918, Francis to Lansing, April 15, 29, 1918, all in *NA*, RG 59; Summers to Lansing, April 21, 1918, sent to Wilson, *Wilson Mss.* (*NA*, RG 59) ; Francis to Summers, April 15, 1918, MacGowan to Summers, April 18, 1918, both in *NA*, RG 84; *Izvestia*, September 19, 1922.

41. Francis to Summers, April 24, 1918, *NA*, RG 84; Lansing, Diary, April 25, 1918, *Lansing Mss.;* Lansing to Summers, April 30, 1918, *NA*, RG 59; Bliss to Davison, April 24, 1918, Dunn to Breckenridge, March 6, 1919, both in *ARC;* Poole to Lansing, May 5, 1918, *NA*, RG 59.

42. Francis to Lansing of May 16, of May 27, 1918, Davison to Robins, May 9, 1918, Lansing to Francis, June 1, 1918, all in *NA*, RG 59; unsigned memo on trip, *ARC;* Lenin to Robins, May 11, 1918, *Robins Mss.;* Trotsky to Robins, May 13, 1918, *Gumberg Mss.;* Francis to Robins, May 14, 1918, Robins to Francis, May 24, 1918, Francis to Consul at Vladivostok, May 25, 1918, all in *NA*, RG 84; L. E. Brown, *New Russia in the Balance* (Chicago, n.d.).

43. Francis to Stone, May 23, 1918, Francis to Russian Press, June 2, 1918, Francis to Lansing, May 11, 1918, all in *NA*, RG 59; Poole to Bullard, May 11, 1918, *NA*, RG 63.

44. *Asia* (May, 1920), 479–80; *Relations 1918, Russia*, III, 120.

45. Thacher to Morrow, February 14, 1918, *NA*, RG 84; Thacher, "Memo on the Russian Situation, London, April 12, 1918," *Bliss Mss.;* Kent to Wilson, May 22, 1918, sent to Lansing, Wilson to Kent, May 23, 1918, both in *Lansing Mss.;* Thacher to Lansing, June 4, 1918, *NA*, RG 59.

46. Lansing, Diary, June 21, 1918, *Lansing Mss.;* Chicago *Daily News*, June 20, 1918;

Chicago *Tribune*, June 24, 1918; Robins to Hagedorn, February 1, 1931, *Thompson Mss.; Robins.*

47. *Ibid.;* Lansing, Diary, June 26, 1918, *Lansing Mss.*

48. Robins to Lansing, July 1, 1918, *NA*, RG 59; Borah to Knott, January 16, 1919, *Borah Mss.;* C. O. Johnson, *Borah of Idaho* (New York, 1936), 387, 356; *Record,* V 56:9:9055–57; *Robins;* and see below.

49. Roosevelt to Robins, July 17, 1918, *TR Mss.;* Colcord to Wilson, July 4, 13, 1918, *Wilson Mss.;* F. Palmer, *Newton D. Baker* (New York, 1931), 302, 317–18; Thacher to Hagedorn, June 1, 1932, *Thompson Mss.*

50. Kent to Wilson, July 22, 1918, *Wilson Mss.;* Harper to Crane, March 23, 1918, Harper to Eames, May 9, 1918, Harper to Porter of July 4, 17, 1918, Harper to Rogers, July 15, 1918, Harper to Corse, July 29, 1918, all in *Harper Mss.;* Charles Merriam to author, January 12, 1950.

51. Robins to Lansing, July 1, 1918, Wilson to Lansing, July 3, 1918, *NA*, RG 59 (also *Wilson Mss.*) ; *Robins.*

52. Wilson to Lansing, April 18, 1918, *NA*, RG 59; Lansing to Wilson, May 10, 1918, Wilson to Lansing, May 20, 1918 (2 items), *NA*, RG 59 (also *Wilson Mss.*).

53. *Iron Age* (January 4, 1917), 36; *Banker's Magazine* (May, 1917), 563, (June, 1917), 693, (August, 1917), 231, (October, 1917), 49; *Electric World* (February 24, 1917), 359, (September 8, 1917), 489; *Annalist* (April 16, 1917), 529; *Commercial and Financial Chronicle,* March 3, April 7, 1917; *Journal of the American Banker's Association* (March, 1917), 710.

54. *Annalist* (October 15, 1917), 488; *Machinery* (November, 1917), 205; *Iron Age* (January 10, 1918), 144; *Digest* (October 5, 1918), 25; *Banker's Magazine* (June, 1918), 657–61, (January, 1919), 73; New York *Times,* November 25, December 29, 1918.

55. Rockhill to Knox, November 10, 1910, *NA*, RG 84; Russell to McCormick, April 5, 1918, Harper to Russell, April 22, 1918, Corse to Harper, May 6, 1918, all in *Harper Mss.;* McCormick to Wilson, May 17, 1918, *Wilson Mss.;* American-Russian League, brochure, September 19, 1918, *Harper Mss.*

56. Harper to Crane, May 30, 1918, Harper to Lippmann, May 30, June 11, 1918, Harper to Carpenter, May 30, June 10, 15, 1918, Crane to Harper, June 13, 1918, Harper to Robins, June 15, 1918, all in *Harper Mss.*

57. Crane to Harper, June 13, 1918, *Harper Mss.;* Redfield to Wilson, June 8, 1918 (2 items), *NA*, RG 59 (also *Wilson Mss.*) ; House to Wilson, June 13, 1918, *Wilson Mss.; House*, III, 409; Lansing, "Memorandum on Intervention in Russia, June 12, 1918," *Lansing Mss.;* Thacher to Hagedorn, June 1, 1932, *Thompson Mss.*

58. *Record,* V 56:1:1030, V 56:2:1408–9, V 56:3:3030; New York *Times,* April 20, May 26, June 6, 8, 9, 11, 12, 27, 1918; Lansing to Wilson, June 13, 1918, *NA*, RG 59; Jones to Wilson, June 12, 1918, Wilson to Jones, June 13, 1918, Wilson to Redfield, June 13, 1918, Redfield to Wilson, July 9, 1918, all in *Wilson Mss.*

59. Goodwin to Miles, April 6, 1918, *NA*, RG 59; *PPC*, II, 472; Morgan and Vance Thompson to Wilson, June 28, 1918, Redfield to Wilson, June 26, 1918, Barringer

to Wilson, June 29, 1918, enclosing McCarter's letter, "Memo from August Heid, Manager of the Vladivostok Office of International Harvester Company in Russia to General Office in Moscow, July 1, 15, 1918," Wilson to Redfield, June 27, 1918, Wilson to Morgan, July 1, 1918, Redfield to Wilson, July 9, 1918, Baruch to Wilson, July 13, 1918, Wilson to Baruch, July 15, 1918, all in *Wilson Mss.*; American-Russian Chamber of Commerce, *Partial List of Members* (New York, 1918); Kinley to Tumulty, August 5, 1918, Long to National Association of Manufacturers, July 9, 1919, *NA*, RG 59.

60. Lansing to Wilson, June 29, 1918, *Wilson Mss.*; "Memo on the Murman Coast Expedition, August 7, 1918," *ARC.*

61. Wilson to Lewis, July 24, 1918, Horvall to Wilson, June 11, 1918, Bertron to Wilson, June 24, 1918, Jusserand to Lansing, May 28, 1918, sent to Wilson, Jusserand to Wilson, June 24, 1918, all in *Wilson Mss.*; Lansing to Kennan, May 28, 1918, *Lansing Mss.*; Burleson to Wilson, June 17, 1918, *Burleson Mss.*; "Agreement of Allied Ambassadors, May 29, 1918, Confidential," Francis to Lansing, May 29, 1918, both in *NA*, RG 84; *House*, III, 410–16; *Record*, V 56:2:11177–79, V 56:8:7557; Thacher, conversation, March 23, 1950; *Robins.*

62. Baker to Wilson, June 19, 1918, House to Wilson, June 21, 1918, Daniels to Wilson, June 24, 1918, March to Wilson, June 24, 1918, all in *Wilson Mss.*; J. J. Pershing, *My Experiences in the World War* (2 vols., New York, 1931), II, 148–49; Washington *Evening Star*, March 7, 1931.

63. Francis, *Embassy*, 303; C. W. Ackerman, *Trailing the Bolshevik* (New York, 1919), 134–35; Lockhart, *Memoirs*, 288–89; White, *Intervention*, 246, 253; J. Bunyan, *Intervention, Civil War, and Communism in Russia* (Baltimore, 1936), 87–88, 336; Reinsch to Lansing, June 13, 1918, *NA*, RG 59.

64. Wilson to Lansing, June 17, 1918, Frazier to Lansing, June 10, 1918, Lansing, memorandum of June 3, 1918, all in *NA*, RG 59; Frazier to Lansing, June 10, 2, 1918, sent to Wilson, House to Wilson, July 6, 1918, Lansing to Wilson, July 8, 1918, Daniels to Wilson, July 5, 1918, Baker to Wilson, July 2, 1918, Reading to Wilson, July 2, 1918, Wilson to Jusserand, June 25, 1918, all in *Wilson Mss.*; Kennan to Lansing, August 9, 1918, Lansing to Kennan, May 28, August 15, 1918, Lansing, "Memo of a Conference at the White House in re to the Siberian Situation, July 6, 1918," Lansing, "Memo on the Siberian Situation, July 4, 1918," all in *Lansing Mss.*; F. Palmer, *Bliss, Peacemaker. The Life and Letters of Tasker H. Bliss* (New York, 1924), 296–97; *House*, III, 415; Bunyan, *Intervention*, 316.

65. Wilson's Aide Mémoire, distributed July 17, published August 3, 1918, Wilson to House, July 8, 1918, both in *Wilson Mss.*; *House*, III, 386, 415; *Record*, V 56:9:9054–58, 9125; Price, *Reminiscences*, 331.

66. Carpenter to Harper, July 26, 1918, Harper to Mott, August 15, 1918, House to Harper, August 29, September 9, 1918, Harper to McCormick, August 30, 1918, Carpenter to Harper, August 12, 1918, all in *Harper Mss.*; McCormick to Wilson, September 13, 1918, Wilson to McCormick, September 21, 1918, both in *Wilson Mss.*; *House*, III, 417; *PPC*, II, 472. For Batolin's arrival and later events see

Lansing to Stevens, September 5, 13, 1918, Stevens to Lansing, September 18, 1918, all in *NA*, RG 59; Corse to Harper, September 17, October 16, 24, December 4, 1918, House to Harper, September 20, 1918, Harper to Eames, October 1, 1918, Harper to Huntington, October 4, 11, 1918, Harper to Corse, October 14, 1918, "Minutes of a Meeting of the Executive Committee of the American Russian League, Washington, D.C., August 8, 1918," all in *Harper Mss.*

67. Polk to Morris, July 17, 1918, Press Release of the War Trade Bureau, Russian Bureau, December 5, 1918, Lansing to Morris, September 9, 1918, all in *NA*, RG 59; McCormick to Wilson, September 13, 1918, November 29, 1918, Lansing to Wilson, November 5, 1918, Baker to Wilson, November 27, 1918, Baker to Wilson (enclosing Graves to Baker of October 18, 1918), October 19, 1918, Wilson to Baker, October 21, 1918, all in *Wilson Mss.*; *PPC*, II, 472–75, 483; New York *Times*, October 7, 18, November 6, 24, December 9, 13, 15, 24, 1918.

68. Carpenter to Harper, July 26, August 12, 1918, Harper to Huntington, October 4, 11, 1918, Harper to Landfield, October 19, 1918, Corse to Harper, October 24, 1918, Harper to Corse, October 24, 1918, all in *Harper Mss.*; *ARC*, Robins File and Thompson File; *Record*, V 56:11:11177–78, V 56:9:9055, V 57:1:342.

69. Thompson, undated memo to Hagedorn, Robins to Hagedorn, December 5, 1930, February 1, 1931, Hays to Hagedorn, March 26, 1931, Lamont to Hagedorn, June 4, 1932, Biddle to Hagedorn, October 23, 1931, April 25, 1932, Ayer to Hagedorn, February 16, 1931, Lamont, "Speech of December 6, 1931," Wallace to Hagedorn, July 7, 1931, all in *Thompson Mss.*; Hays to author, November 3, 1950.

70. Lovenstein, *American Opinion*, 43.

71. Z. Chafee, Jr., *Free Speech in the United States* (Cambridge, 1946), 109–11, Chapter III; *NA*, RG 63:CPI File 17-D1; *Lansing Mss.*, V 39:6837; New York *Times* and Chicago *Tribune*, September 15–24, 1918; Robins to Roosevelt, October 15, 1918, *TR Mss.*; on the trial see New York *Times*, New York *Tribune*, New York *Post*, New York *World*, October 15–28, 1918; Lansing to Wilson, October 5, 1918, *Wilson Mss.*; Patchin to Creel, September 20, 1918, in J. R. Mock and C. Larson, *Words That Won the War* (Princeton, 1939), 319.

72. Harper to G. S. Ford, November 15, 1918, *Harper Mss.*

73. *Holmes-Pollock Letters. The Correspondence of Mr. Justice Holmes and Sir Frederick Pollock, 1874–1932*, edited by M. De Wolfe Howe (Cambridge, 1946), II, 29, 32; *Abrams v. U.S.*, 250 U.S. 616 (1919), in *U.S. Book 63. Lawyers Edition* (Rochester, New York, 1919), 1177, 1179.

74. *Outlook* (December 25, 1918), 650; Polk to Lansing, January 11, 1919, *NA*, RG 59; *Record*, V 57:1:342, V 57:3:3140–41.

75. R. S. Baker, *Woodrow Wilson and World Settlement: Written from His Unpublished and Personal Material* (3 vols., London, 1923), II, 64; W. S. Churchill, *The Aftermath* (New York, 1929), 171.

76. *PPC*, III, 1044.

77. Wilson, "The Road Away From Revolution," *Atlantic*, V 132 (August, 1923), 145–

46; but see first W. Bolitho [Ryall], *Twelve Against the Gods* (New York, 1929), Chapter XII.

78. Lansing, "Memorandum on Absolutism and Bolshevism, October 26, 1918," Lansing, "Memorandum on Absolutism and Bolshevism, October 28, 1918," Lansing to Root, October 28, 1918 ("Very Confidential"), Lansing to Parmelee, November 13, 1918 ("Confidential"), Lansing to Smith, November 14, 1918, all in *Lansing Mss.*

79. House to Wilson, May 24, June 4, 1918, both in *Wilson Mss.*

80. Lansing to Wilson, November 7, November 9 (enclosing Bullitt's memorandum of November 8), November 18, 1918, all in *Wilson Mss.*; Lansing to Hungerford, November 14, 1918, *Lansing Mss.*; *PPC*, I, 270–72.

81. *The Letters of Franklin K. Lane. Personal and Political*, edited by A. W. Lane and L. H. Wall (New York, 1922), 295; Squires to Wilson, November 9, 1918, Wilson to Squires, November 12, 1918, Lansing to Wilson, November 18, 1918, all in *Wilson Mss.*; *PPC*, II, 680; D. H. Miller, *The Drafting of the Covenant* (2 vols., New York, 1928), I, 43.

82. Lansing to House, December 2, 1918, *NA*, RG 59; *PPC*, II, 483, 517–18, 484; Borah to Shinkle, December 11, 1918, *Borah Mss.*

83. Litvinov to Morris, December 23, 1918, Litvinov to Wilson, December 24, 1918, Lansing to Polk, January 4, 1918, all in *NA*, RG 59.

84. *Relations, Russia, 1919*, 4; for French action see *Le Temps; Annales de la Chambre, Session Ordinaire de 1919. Debats Parlementaires* (Paris, 1920), 3250, 3335; and G. B. Noble, *Policies and Opinions at Paris, 1919. Wilsonian Diplomacy, the Versailles Peace, and French Public Opinion* (New York, 1935), 289–92.

85. Bliss, "Peace Conference Diary, January 7, 1919," *Bliss Mss.*; Wilson to Lansing, January 10, 1919, *Wilson Mss.*

86. *PPC*, III, 472, 473; *Relations, Russia, 1919*, 5, 6; *PPC*, III, 516, 581–83.

87. *Relations, Russia, 1919*, 5–6; *PPC*, III, 581–84, 589–93.

88. *Relations, Russia, 1919*, 13–14; *PPC*, III, 591–93.

89. Smith, "What Happened in Siberia," *Asia*, V 5:402–3; H. H. Douglas, "A Bit of American History—Successful Embargo Against Japan in 1918," *Amerasia*, V 4(1940):258–60; White, *Intervention*, 163–65; Ishii to Polk, January 15, 1919, Morris to Lansing, October 31, 1918, both in *NA*, RG 59.

90. White, *Intervention*, 149; Lansing to Polk, January 21, 1919, *NA*, RG 59.

91. *PPC*, III, 643, 630, 624, 638.

92. *Relations, Russia, 1919*, 15–17, 18; "Notes by W. H. Buckler of Conversation with Mr. Litvinov in Stockholm, January 14, 15, 16, 1919," *Lansing Mss.*; *PPC*, III, 643–46.

93. *PPC*, III, 648, 649, 650, 651, 653, 691–93; Lansing to Polk, January 27, 1919, *NA*, RG 59.

94. Polk to Lansing, January 24, 1919, *NA*, RG 59; *Record*, V 57:2:1876, 1878, 1880, V 57:3:2261–70; New York *Times*, January 1, 10, February 18, 1919.

95. Polk to Lansing, January 24, 1919, Lansing to Polk, January 31, 1919, Polk to Lansing, February 4, 1919, Lansing to Polk, February 9, 1919, all in *NA*, RG 59.

96. Polk to Morgan, December 18, 1918, Morgan to Polk, January 3, 1919, Long to Wallace, May 31, 1919, Lamont to Morgan, June 18, 1919, Lansing to Dawes, August 27, 1919, Lansing to Dawes, October 11, 1919, all in *NA*, RG 59; *Robins*.

97. Morris to Lansing, January 9, 1919, Chinese Legation to Lansing, January 26, 30, 1919, Polk to Reinsch, February 21, 27, 1919, Reinsch to Polk, February 28, March 18, 1919, all in *NA*, RG 59.

98. Noble, *Policies and Opinions at Paris*, 277–79; Miller, *My Diary at the Conference of Paris* (21 vols., New York, 1924), IV, 178; Straus, *Under Four Administrations*, 411, 417.

99. *Outlook* (February 5, 1919), 215–16; Levinson, *American Opinion*, 43–44; M. P. Briggs, *George D. Herron and the European Settlement* (Stanford, 1932), 13, 136–39, 145; *Outlook* (February 26, 1919), 340–41.

100. *Relations, Russia, 1919*, 39–42; Poole to Polk, January 30, 1919, Reinsch to Polk, February 6, 1919 [date of receipt], *NA*, RG 59; *Relations, Russia, 1919*, 53, 69–70; Urget to Polk, February 19, 1919, *NA*, RG 59; *PPC*, III, 1042–44; Miller; *Diary*, XIV, 423.

101. *PPC*, IV, 14, 16–18; Miller, *Diary*, XIV, 445.

102. *PPC*, XI, 44; *Relations, Russia, 1919*, 72.

103. L. Steffens, *The Autobiography of Lincoln Steffens* (2 vols., New York, 1931), II, 764–65, 799–800; *PPC*, XI, 10; Lansing to Polk, January 10, February 24, 1919, both in *NA*, RG 59; *Relations, Russia, 1919*, 76–77, 97.

104. Chicherin to Rakovsky, March 13, 1919, quoted in Fischer, *Soviets in World Affairs*, I, 171; *Relations, Russia, 1919*, 77–80, 81–84, 85–95; *Diplomatichesky Slovar*, ed. by A. Y. Vyshinsky (2 vols., Moscow, 1948–50), I, 306–7.

105. W. C. Bullitt, *The Bullitt Mission to Russia* (New York, 1919), 65, 73; Pettit to Bullitt, May 3, 1919, *NA*, RG 59; F. Hunt, *One American and His Attempt at Education* (New York, 1938), 166–68; *Relations, Russia, 1919*, 85.

106. *PPC*, XI, 573.

107. *Relations, Russia, 1919*, 101, 102, 110; *PPC*, V, 143, 744–47, 747–48, 735.

108. White, *Intervention*, 153, 196–99, 265.

109. *PPC*, V, 528–30, 497; V. McCormick, entries of April 21, May 15, 1919, *Diary*, 72, 85.

110. *PPC*, V, 522, X, 248, 335–36, VI, 530–31, VII, 644–45, X, 578–79; Phillips to Polk, September 9, 1919, Phillips to Wadsworth, November 1, 1919, both in *NA*, RG 59; *PPC*, VIII, 9.

111. *PPC*, V, 725; White, *Intervention*, 117, 347–50; J. Maynard, *Russia in Flux* (New York, 1948), 242–45; *PPC*, V, 737, VI, 15, 26; Lansing to Polk, May 26, 1919, *Loans to Foreign Governments*, 146; V. McCormick, entry of June 23, 1919 (quoting Wilson), *Diary*, 110–11; *PPC*, VI, 233.

112. McCormick to Phillips, July 2, 1919, Lansing to Harris, September 30, 1919, both in *NA*, RG 59; Lansing to Kennan, "Personal and Secret," February 2,

1920, *Papers of George Kennan; PPC,* XI, 591–92; Phillips to Polk and Hoover, September 9, 1919, *NA,* RG 59; Adee to Baker, August 22, 1919, *NA,* RG 94, Records of the Adjutant General's Office; on the loan to Kolchak, see Polk to Sharp, February 17, 1919, Polk to Lansing, April 24, 1919, Phillips to Stevens, June 28, 1919, Reinsch to Phillips, [?], Polk to Miles, August 23, 1919, Miles to Polk, August 25, 1919, Lansing to Grey, October 21, 1919, all in *NA,* RG 59.

113. Hoover to G. S. Queen, November 14, 1940, summarized in Queen, "American Employer and Russian Labor in 1905," *JMH,* V 15 (June, 1943), 123, note 14.

114. *Relations, Russia, 1919,* 101, 117; *PPC,* X, 461–62; Polk to Lansing, August 12, 1919, *NA,* RG 59.

115. *PPC,* V, 18, 817, XI, 259–60.

116. *PPC,* VII, 23, 21, 29, XII, 539, 616, XI, 348–49.

117. *PPC,* VII, 306, 321, XII, 619, 623, VII, 504, 505, Polk to Lansing, August 12, 1919, *NA,* RG 59.

118. Borah to Short, October 11, 1919, *Borah Mss.;* Colby to Davis, November 28, 1919, August 6, 1920, Polk to Baker, January 28, 1920, Colby to Baron Avezzano, August 10, 1920, Colby to Lubomirski, August 21, 1920, Colby to Wallace, August 25, 1920, Colby to Gibson, August 23, 1920, all in *NA,* RG 59; *Record,* V 58:5:4898– 4902, V 76:5:5486, V 77:5:4242–43; Polk to Baker, January 22, 1920, *NA,* RG 94.

119. *Hearings,* III, 878; J. M. Dunn (Director of the War Department's Division of Intelligence) to M. S. Breckenridge (Chairman of the Red Cross Loyalty Investigation Division) March 6, 1919, *ARC;* Robins to Gumberg, April 11, 1919, *Gumberg Mss.;* Anderson to Borah, December 8, 1922, *Borah Mss.*

120. *Robins;* Ingles to Hagedorn, October 20, 1931, Robins to Hagedorn, February 1, 1931, June 3, 1930, all in *Thompson Mss.*

121. Robins to Gumberg, September 30, 1921, February 21, 1921, both in *Gumberg Mss.; Robins;* E. A. Ross, conversation, April 12, 1950; New York *Times,* December 11, 25, 29, 1919, January 5, 11, July 13, 16, 24, August 30, December 16, 1920; Chicago *Tribune,* July 7, 1920; Chicago *Daily News,* August 31, November 4, December 15, 1920.

122. *Iron Age* (February 5, 1920), 417, (April 8, 1920), 1033; *Struggling Russia* (April 3, 1920), 22–27; New York *Times,* June 4, 1920; State Department Press Release, July 7, 1920; H. Heyman, *We Can Do Business with Russia* (New York, 1945), 77–78.

Chapter VII: THE LONG, LEAN YEARS

1. Colby to Wright, March 24, 1920, Hughes to Shipping Board, April 13, 1921, American Commercial Association to Promote Trade to Lansing, January 27, 1920, all in *NA,* RG 59.

2. *Izvestia,* quoted in *Digest* (February 9, 1924), 19.

3. Redfield to Polk, March 3, 1920, *NA,* RG 59; New York *Times,* March 7, June 4, 7, 1920; MacGowan to Colby, March 9, 1920, Legge to Polk, April 20, 1920, Land-

field to Kliefoth, January 18, 1921, Parker to Tumulty, January 18, 1921, Poole to Hughes, November 20, 1922, Kliefoth to Hughes, August 1, 1922, all in *NA*, RG 59.

4. Jennings and Boyer to Lansing, January 27, 28, February 4, 1920, all in *NA*, RG 59; New York *Times*, January 26, 27, February 4, 16, March 7, 1920; Arnow to Colby, March 3, 1920, Long, "Memorandum, March 4, 1920," Chicherin to Morris, February 25, 1920, all in *NA*, RG 59.

5. McCully to Colby, April 29, 1920, Caldwell to Colby, June 27, 1920, both in *NA*, RG 59.

6. All quotations are taken from the petitions in *NA*, RG 59:661.1115 P81/16 to 661.11175/205; see Poole to Hughes, May 25, 1922, *NA*, RG 59:661.1115 P81/205.

7. Morris to Hughes, April 11, 1921, Rockwell to Bliss, April 12, 1921, Kahn to Hughes, April 15, 1921 ("Private"), Oudin to Fletcher, May 3, 1921, all in *NA*, RG 59; *Relations with Russia. Hearings on Senate Joint Resolution 164 for the Reestablishment of Trade with Russia* (Washington, 1921).

8. Landfield to Bullard, January 19, 1921, *NA*, RG 59.

9. Cigar Makers' Union, No. 447 of Kenosha, Wisconsin, to Colby, January 22, 1921, Gompers to Hughes, March 15, 1921, Spargo to Hughes, March 24, 1921, all in *NA*, RG 59.

10. Poole to Hughes, May 25, 1922, Hoover to Hughes, March 16, 1921, both in *NA*, RG 59.

11. Litvinov to Harding, March 20, 1921, *NA*, RG 59; Hoover, quoted in New York *Times*, March 22, 1921, Hughes to Litvinov, March 25, 1921, Hughes to Gompers, April 4, 18, 1921, all in *NA*, RG 59; *Independent* (April 9, 1921), 369–70.

12. This conclusion is based on a complete search of the file cited in note 6 above.

13. Poole to Hughes, "Confidential Memorandum for the Secretary Concerning Raymond Robins, May 24, 1921 [the interview was on May 25]," *NA*, RG 59; *Robins*.

14. Robins to Gumberg, February 21, March 8, August 19, 21, 1922, Hoover to Mrs. Robins, June 28, 1922, Gumberg to Robins, August 21, 1922, all in *Gumberg Mss.*; White House Memorandum to Hughes, February 2, 1922, *NA*, RG 59.

15. *Loans to Foreign Governments*, 97, 115–22, 133–38, 142–43, 153–56, 163–75; *Record*, V 57:3:2638–43, V 60:4:3913–14, V 62:6:6295–6303, V 62:8:7911; New York *Times*, April 2, 5, 18, 30, May 6, 9, June 6, 9, 12, 20, 24, 30, 1922; Hoover, remarks before Washington, D.C. Chamber of Commerce, May 15, 1922, *New Republic* (May 31, 1922), 4–5; *Independent* (January 14, 1922), 25.

16. Davis to Colby, May 22, 1920, *NA*, RG 59.

17. MacMurray, "Memorandum of Conversation with British Counselor Lindsay, June 15, 1920," *NA*, RG 59.

18. Morgan to Yokohama Specie Bank, July 23, 1920, Yokohama Specie Bank to Lamont, August 2, 1920, Lamont to Morris, August 4, 1920, Wallace to Colby, August 26, 1920, Lamont to Davis, October 18, 1920, Jameson to MacMurray, no date [probably October 26, 1920], all in *NA*, RG 59.

19. MacMurray to Hughes, May 25, 1921, Naval Intelligence to Hughes, May 7,

1921 (a report on Lamont's pro-Japanese position), Morgan to Hughes, August 2, 23, all in *NA*, RG 59.

20. P. Tompkins takes this view in *American-Russian Relations in the Far East* (New York, 1949), 146, 162.

21. *Izvestia*, December 6, 1921, August 21, 1924; *Pravda*, June 18, 1922; and see *Protokoly zasedanii Vserossiiskogo Tsentralnogo Ispolnitelnogo Komileta 4-go sozyva* (Moscow, 1920), 263–70.

22. Trotsky, quoted in *Living Age*, V 318(1923), 486.

23. See here M. Beloff, *The Foreign Policy of Soviet Russia 1929–1941* (2 vols., New York, 1947–49), II, Chapter XV.

24. Lenin, quoted by A. Parry, "Washington B. Vanderlip, the 'Khan of Kamchatka,'" *Pacific Historical Review* (August, 1948), 315.

25. Anderson to Colby, November 2, 1920, Albrecht to Hughes, May 27, 1921, both in *NA*, RG 59.

26. White, *Intervention*, 387–89.

27. I. Maiski, *The Foreign Policy of the Russian Soviet Federated Socialist Republic, 1917–1922* (Moscow, 1922, in Russian), 177–79; Coolidge to Hughes, March 14, 1921, *NA*, RG 59.

28. Hughes to Bell, April 6, 1921, Smith to Hughes, March 8, 1921 (with comment in pencil by Jameson), both in *NA*, RG 59.

29. Harvey to Hughes, July 8, 1921, RG 43: Records of the United States Participation in International Conferences, Commissions, and Expositions, Hughes to Harvey, July 9, 1921, *NA*, RG 43.

30. Chicherin to Hughes, July 19, 1921, *NA*, RG 43.

31. Bell to Hughes, September 15, 1921, Hughes to Bell, October 4, 1921, both in *NA*, RG 59.

32. Warren to Hughes, January 17, 1922, Hughes to Stevens, February 9, 1922, Mac-Murray, "Memorandum of Interview with Mr. de Laboulage, Counsel of the French Embassy, March 22, 1924," all in *NA*, RG 59; *Izvestia*, September 7, 1922.

33. White, *Intervention*, 413.

34. Ruddock to Hughes, October 7, 1920, enclosing text of agreement of October 2, 1920, *NA*, RG 59.

35. Poole to Hughes, "Confidential," December 19, 1921, Hughes to Schurman, December 24, 31, 1921, all in *NA*, RG 59.

36. Schurman to Hughes, January 22, 1921, January 7, 1922, Chicherin to Hughes, December 8, 1921, all in *NA*, RG 59; *Conference on the Limitation of Armament* (Washington, 1922), 690–91.

37. *Conference on the Limitation of Armament*, 751, 862.

38. Ruddock to Hughes, March 1, 1922 (reporting an Anglo-American interview with the Chinese Minister of Foreign Affairs, February 22, 1922), Schurman to Hughes, March 29, 1922, September 14, 1923, Harrison to Schurman, July 24, 1924, all in *NA*, RG 59.

39. Hughes to Schurman, August 2, 1923, *NA*, RG 59.

40. *Izvestia*, July 6, 1922, March 21, 1923, May 31, 1923; *Pravda*, July 20, 1923, July 23, 1923; Kelley, "Memorandum on Conversation with Mr. Wasserman of Dillon, Read and Company, October 16, 1923," Kliefoth to Phillips, June 20, 1923, both in *NA*, RG 59.

41. Hughes to Schurman, August 2, 1923, *NA*, RG 59.

42. *Izvestia*, October 25, 1922; M. Beloff, *Foreign Policy of Soviet Russia*, I, Appendix C, "Russia and the Chinese Revolution."

43. Karakhan, Declaration of July 25, 1919, Karakhan to the Ministry of Foreign Affairs of the Chinese Republic, September 27, 1920, both in DeGras, *Documents*, I, 158–61, 212–15.

44. Karakhan to the Chinese Commission, November 30, 1923, in *China Year Book, 1924*, 873.

45. *China Year Book, 1924*, 879, 880; Sino-Soviet Agreements of May 31, 1924, in *Russian Review* (Washington, D.C.), October 15, and November 1, 1925; Young, *International Relations of Manchuria*, 295–300; *Lytton Report*, 35.

46. Hughes to Hoover, December 1, 1921, enclosing a "Memorandum by the Division of Russian Affairs, November 28, 1921," *NA*, RG 59.

47. Hoover to Hughes, December 6, 1921, *NA*, RG 59.

48. *Resolutions Adopted by the Supreme Council at Cannes, January, 1922, as the Basis of the Genoa Conference* (Cmd. 1621, London, 1922), 2; Hughes to Child, May 2, 1922, *NA*, RG 59.

49. Teagle to Colby, August 19, 1920, Caldwell to Colby, January 6, 1921, Smith to Millspaugh, December 24, 1920, all in *NA*, RG 59.

50. A. C. Millspaugh, *Americans in Persia* (Washington, 1946), 21–22; G. Lenczowski, *Russia and the West in Iran 1918–1948* (Ithaca, 1949), 49.

51. Millspaugh, "Memorandum of Conversation with the Persian Minister and the Counselor of the Persian Legation, December 16 [written December 17, 1920]," American-Russian Industrial Syndicate (Schuster) to Hughes, January 11, 1922, Fletcher, "Memorandum on Dinner at the Persian Legation, November 28, 1921 [written November 29, 1921]," all in *NA*, RG 59.

52. Dearing to Chilton, March 21, 1922, Millspaugh, memorandum of December 17, 1920, Memorandum by the Chief of Near Eastern Affairs, March 26, 1923, all in *NA*, RG 59.

53. Engert to Hughes, November 22, 1921, *NA*, RG 59.

54. Engert to Hughes, December 9, 1921, Kornfeld to Hughes, January 5, 1924, Gotlieb to Hughes, June 27, October 21, 1923, Chief of Near Eastern Affairs, memorandum of March 26, 1923, all in *NA*, RG 59 .

55. Millspaugh, *Americans in Persia*, 21–24; Lenczowski, *Russia and the West*, 85–86.

56. Teagle to Colby, August 19, 1920, Swain, "Memorandum on Russian Matters, December 20, 1920," A. C. Bedford, "The Russian Situation," left at the Department of State "early in December, 1920," Fletcher, "Memorandum of Conference with A. C. Bedford of Standard Oil," January 31, 1922, all in *NA*, RG 59.

57. Skinner to Hughes, January 20, 1922, Bedford, "Memorandum of December 1, 1920," Adee to London, December 21, 1920, all in *NA*, RG 59; *Record*, V 62:7:7440.

58. Bedford to Hughes, March 10, 1922, Bedford, quoted by the London *Times*, April 12, 1922.

59. Child to Hughes, May 4, 1922 (transmitting the British Note of May 2), Bedford to Hughes, May 5, 1922, both in *NA*, RG 59; London *Times*, May 7, 1922.

60. British Note of May 2, 1922, *NA*, RG 59.

61. Millspaugh to Hughes, May 3, 1922, *NA*, RG 59.

62. Bedford to Hughes, May 5, 1922 (a review of their conversation on May 4, 1922), Hughes to Child, May 4, 1922, both in *NA*, RG 59; Child, quoted in New York *Times*, May 12, 1922; Bedford, quoted in London *News of the World*, May 6, 1922; *Record*, V 62:7:7440.

63. Hughes to Child, May 15, 1922, Child to Hughes, May 11, 1922, both in *NA*, RG 59. During this same period Hughes refused to help Sinclair in Asia, opposed the efforts of the International Barnsdall Corporation to negotiate an understanding with Moscow, and refused to help Henry Mason Day in his project to penetrate the Caucasus: see *NA*, RG 59, files 861.6363; and see *Diplomatichesky Slovar*, II, 663.

64. *Record*, V 62:7:7363, V 62:8:7904.

65. Poole to Hughes, October 6, 1922, *NA*, RG 59.

66. Hoover to Hughes, July 14, 1922, Hughes to Harding, July 15, 1922 ("Personal and Confidential"), July 22, 1922 ("Confidential"), Harding to Hughes, July 24, 1922, all in *NA*, RG 59.

67. Hughes to Houghton, July 24, 1922, *NA*, RG 59.

68. Hughes to Child, May 17, 1922, Houghton to Hughes, July 29, 1922, Chicherin to Houghton, August 28, September 16, 1922, all in *NA*, RG 59.

69. Houghton to Hughes, August 29, 1922, Phillips to Houghton, August 30, 1922, Harding to Phillips, August 30, 1922, Kliefoth to Hughes, July 31, 1922, all in *NA*, RG 59; New York *Times*, August 22, 1922; *Izvestia*, September 15, 1922.

70. Hughes to Child, November 15, 1922, *NA*, RG 59.

71. Hughes to Child, November 15, 1922, *NA*, RG 59.

72. Bristol to Hughes, October 5, 1922, *NA*, RG 59.

73. *PPC*, VI, 212–13; Harvey to Hughes, October 12, 1922, *NA*, RG 59.

74. Rogers to Denby, October 10, 1922 (forwarded to Child in Hughes to Child, December 3, 1922), *NA*, RG 59.

75. Hughes to Herrick, October 27, 1922, Child to Hughes, December 6, 1922 (2 cables), December 8, 1922, December 22, 1922, all in *NA*, RG 59.

76. Grew to Hughes, February 3, 1923, *NA*, RG 59.

77. H. H. Fisher, *The Famine in Soviet Russia, 1919–1923* (New York, 1927); League of Nations, *Report on Economic Conditions in Russia, with Special Reference to the Famine of 1921–22* (Paris, 1922).

78. The Chicago *Tribune* gave Welles' reports frontpage display.

79. *Relief for the Starving People of Russia, House Report No. 512* (Washington,

1922); *Russian Relief. Senate Document No. 277* (Washington, 1923); *Record*, V 61:5:4854, V 62:1:40–51, 455–90, V 62:2:1220–23, 1271–72, 1495; Hughes to Mellon, January 10, 1922, *NA*, RG 59; and see *Gumberg Mss.*, Goodrich File.

80. Hughes to Herrick, September 2, 1921, Bertron to Hughes, November 17, 23, 1922, all in *NA*, RG 59.

81. F. A. Golder and L. Hutchinson, *On the Trail of the Russian Famine* (Stanford, 1927), viii; *Outlook* (January 11, 1922), 66–68.

82. F. G. Barghoorn, *The Soviet Image of the United States* (New York, 1950), 3, 32–33.

83. Gumberg to Durant, June 21, 1922, Hoover to Mrs. Robins, June 28, 1922, Gumberg to Robins, July 16, 1922, January 1, 1923, Robins to Gumberg, August 19, 21, 1922, Goodrich to Gumberg, October 1, 1922, all in *Gumberg Mss.*; Robins to Borah, December 9, 1922, *Borah Mss.*; confidential witness, March 23, 1950.

84. Gumberg to Borah, November 21, 1929 (introducing Fischer), *Gumberg Mss.*

85. Hughes to King, January 10, 1923, *NA*, RG 59; *Record*, V 64:4:4154–62; Goodrich to Gumberg, March 7, 16, April 23, 1923, all in *Gumberg Mss.*

86. Poole to Hughes, March 14, 20, 1923, Bannerman to Sharp, Special Agent in Charge, March 19, 1923 (report "requested on behalf of Mr. Poole"), all in *NA*, RG 59.

87. Monowi, Nebraska, State Bank to Borah, March 23, 1923, Dudley to Borah, April 13, 1923, Borah to Dudley, April 18, 1923, Francis to Borah, April 7, 1923, Borah to Francis, April 24, 1923, Borah to Good, May 7 1923, all in *Borah Mss.*

88. *Relations, 1923*, II, 755–58; New York *Times*, March 23, 1923.

89. Borah to Harding ("written by Raymond Robins"), June 5, 1923, Gumberg to Borah, June 18, 1923, both in *Borah Mss.*; Robins to Goodrich, May 31, 1923, Gumberg to Goodrich, June 15, 1923, Goodrich to Gumberg, June 18, 1923, all in *Gumberg Mss.*

90. Hapgood to Borah, July 11, 1923, Gumberg to Borah, July 23, 1923, both in *Borah Mss.*; and see *Gumberg Mss.*, Robins and Goodrich Files. For a clear indication of this tug of war between Borah and Hughes see Harding's last (undelivered) speech, *Record*, V 62:1:398–400.

91. Gumberg to Goodrich, July 5, 1923, Robins to Gumberg, August 5, 6, 1923, all in *Gumberg Mss.*

92. Johnson to Robins, telegram not dated, *Levinson Mss.*; Robins to Levinson, August 9, 1923, and other materials in *Levinson Mss.*, Box 76.

93. Borah to Robins, August 25, 1923, Coolidge to Robins, November 13, 1923, *Levinson Mss.*; Robins to Gumberg, September 21, December 1, 1923, both in *Gumberg Mss.*; Snyder to Coolidge, October 10, 1923, *NA*, RG 59.

94. Robins to Borah, December 1, 1923, *Borah Mss.*; Robins to Gumberg, December 1, 1923, *Gumberg Mss.*

95. Robins to Levinson, December 7, 15, 1923, both in *Levinson Mss.*; Robins to Borah, December 6, 15, 1923, both in *Borah Mss.*; *Record*, V 65:1:228.

96. Chicherin to Coolidge, December 16, 1923, *Coolidge Mss.; Pravda,* December 8, 1923.

97. Hughes to Coolidge, December 18, 1923, *Coolidge Mss.;* Hughes to Chicherin, December 18, 1923, *NA,* RG 59; Gumberg to Goodrich, December 19, 1923, *Gumberg Mss.;* this writer found no record of a phone call by Hughes to Coolidge.

98. Anderson to Coolidge, December 18, 1923, Coolidge to Anderson, December 24, 1923, Davis to Coolidge, December 22, 1923, Slemp to Davis, January 19, 1924, all in *Coolidge Mss.*

99. Borah to Robins, December 20, 1923, *Borah Mss.;* and see *Gumberg Mss.*

100. Robins to Borah, December 24, 1923, *Borah Mss.;* Levinson to Robins, December 27, 1923, Robins to Levinson, December 29, 1923, both in *Levinson Mss.; Gumberg Mss.,* Goodrich File; *Record,* V 65:1:445ff.; V 65:1:592–614; *Recognition of Russia. Hearings on Senate Resolution 50* (Washington, 1924).

101. Hughes to Coolidge and the President of the Senate, January 31, 1924, *NA,* RG 59; Borah to Coyle, January 30, 1924, *Borah Mss.*

102. Robins to Levinson, January 27, 28, 1924, both in *Levinson Mss.;* New York *Times,* January 28, 1924; Henry W. Temple, Chairman of the House Committee on Foreign Affairs in 1924, conversation, February 8, 1951; Spargo to Hughes, January 19, 1924, *NA,* RG 59; Coolidge to Gompers, February 19, 1924, *Coolidge Mss.*

103. Robins to Levinson, February 25, 1924, *Levinson Mss.*

104. Robins to Levinson, March 4, 5, 6, 7, 9, 1924, all in *Levinson Mss.*

105. *Robins;* Robins to Borah, March 18, June 16, 1924, Borah to Robins, June 18, 1924, all in *Borah Mss.;* Robins to Levinson, November 13, 1924, *Levinson Mss.*

106. Robins to Borah, December 4, 1924, *Borah Mss.;* W. R. Castle, quoted in New York *Times,* July 31, 1925; and see *Levinson Mss.,* and *Gumberg Mss.*

107. Robins, "United States Recognition of Soviet Russia Essential to World Peace and Stabilization," *Annals,* V 126(July, 1926), 100–4; Robins engineered a reconciliation between Thompson and Hoover in 1928 when the Republican Party was again short of funds, see *Thompson Mss.,* Boxes 2 and 10.

108. Confidential witness, July, 1951; *Relations, Soviet Union, 1933–39,* 249.

109. Kelley, "International Relations of the Soviet Government Since 1920, December 11, 1923," *NA,* RG 59.

110. Kelley, "The Essential Factors Involved in Establishing Normal Relations with the Soviet Regime, February 26, 1925 (sent on to Hoover by Hughes on February 28)," *NA,* RG 59.

111. Young to Hughes, August 31, 1922, Coleman to Kellogg, May 11, 1925, both in *NA,* RG 59.

112. Ludlow to Kellogg, June 15, 1920, *NA,* RG 59; *Izvestia,* May 31, July 6, 1923; *Economic Life* (Moscow), July 29, 1923; *Pravda,* August 11, 1923; *NA,* RG 151: File 531/23; Coleman to Kellogg, October 15, 1925, NA, RG 59. *Russian Review,* V 1(March 1, 1924), 255; *Nation* (June 14, 1922), 730–32, (November 7, 1923), 524–25.

113. Young to Hughes, October 25, 1923, *NA,* RG 59; Gumberg to Borah, March 4,

Borah Mss.; Russian Review, V 2(December 15, 1924), 239; *Gumberg Mss.*

114. Jenkins and Dulles, memorandum of January 19, 1923, *NA*, RG 59; *Russian Review*, V 2(July 1, 1924), 19; New York *Times*, June 19, 1924.

115. C. D. Martin, *Foreign Markets for Agricultural Implements* (Commerce, 1927), 14.

116. *Izvestia*, June 8, 1927; Stuart to Roosevelt, June 14, 1938, June 29, 1942, both in *FDR Mss.; Trade and Industry Gazette* (Moscow), October 24, 1929; and see H. Heyman, *We Can Do Business with Russia* (Chicago, 1945).

117. Material drawn from *NA*, RG 59:861.637 and 861.637 Harriman; *Izvestia*, May 14, 1925; *Economic Life*, June 13, 1925, November 15, 1928; *Pravda*, January 29, 1927, February 1, 1927.

118. Gumberg to Borah, December 11, 1925, *Borah Mss.; Economic Life*, January 3, 1926; New York *Times*, December 11, 13, 14, 1925, October 7, 1926.

119. Principal source for the R-A Chamber of Commerce is *Gumberg Mss.*, Schley and Chamber Files; but see New York *Times*, April 5, May 8, June 24, 25, 26, 1926; Schley to Kellogg, December 19, 1927, *NA*, RG 59; and below.

120. Material drawn from *NA*, RG 59:861.6363 and 861.6363 Std. Oil; but see Tobin to Kellogg, June 18, 1928, Atherton to Kellogg, October 9, 1928, both in *NA*, RG 59.

121. Material from *Gumberg Mss.*, Cooper File; *Pravda*, July 28, 1926; Cooper, "Observations of Present-Day Russia," *Annals*, V 138(July, 1928), 117–19; Cooper, letter to the New York *Times*, July 11, 1933.

122. This account is based on materials in the *National Archives* and the considerable number of personal memoirs of those who worked in Russia.

123. MacGowan to Kellogg, August 5, 1929, Sussdorff to Stimson, February 18, 1930, both in *NA*, RG 59; *New Republic* (May 6, 1931), 317–19; *Record*, V 71:3:2305; *Trade and Industry Gazette*, May 16, 1929.

124. W. H. Chamberlain, "Missionaries of American Techniques in Russia," *Asia*, V 32(1932), 422–27, 460–63; Heyman, *Business*, 30, 34, 38, 50; W. C. White, "American Big Business and the Soviet Market," *Asia*, V 30(1930), 746–53.

125. Fischer, *Soviets in World Affairs*, II, 766; other material from *NA*, RG 59: 661.1115 General Electric/Amtorg, 661.1115 GE-State Electrical Trust Contract, 861.6463 Westinghouse; *Gumberg Mss.*, Schley File.

126. *NA*, RG 151: Index No. 531, File No. 27; MacGowan to Kellogg, August 5, 1929, *NA*, RG 59; Bryant to Cooper, April 19, 1932, *Gumberg Mss.; R of R* (January, 1931), 44–48; *Outlook* (June 29, 1927), 280–83.

127. Gumberg, "Memo on Technical Assistance Contracts with American Firms as of July 18, 1930," *Gumberg Mss.; Izvestia*, July 3, 1929; *Harpers*, V 159 (September, 1929), 437–53; W. C. White, "Americans in Soviet Russia," *Scribner's*, V 89(February, 1931), 171–82.

128. *Pravda*, March 2, April, 1930; Stalin, remarks to Churchill, August, 1942, in W. S. Churchill, *The Hinge of Fate* (Boston, 1951), 498.

129. *Forum*, V 86(July, 1931), 18–22; *Bank for Russian Trade Review* (London), V 2(February, 1929), 16; *Digest*, V 114(July, 1932), 35–37.

130. *Outlook* (July 10, 1929), 405–7; Coleman to Stimson, May 22, August 20, September 9, 1929, Poole to Stimson, August 21, 1929, all in *NA*, RG 59.

131. Borah to Gumberg, November 16, 1925, *Borah Mss.*

132. Borah to Hays, October 8, 1925, *Borah Mss.*

133. Borah to Mooney, December 31, 1930, Borah to Barnes Drill Co., January 11, 1932, *Borah Mss.*, but see Boxes 416/G and 331/B; "What Business with Russia," *Fortune*, V 31(January, 1945), 156.

134. Gumberg to Borah, August 13, 1931, *Borah Mss.*; *Gumberg Mss.*, Chase Securities File; *NA*, RG 59:861.51 State Bank; Schley to Castle, October 24, 1928, Kelley, "Memorandum on Schley Letter," November 3, 1928, Castle to Schley, November 8, 1928, all in *NA*, RG 59.

135. Borah to Morton, May 24, 1932, *Borah Mss.*

136. MacMurray to Kellogg, April 3, 1926, *NA*, RG 59.

137. D. Borg, *American Policy and the Chinese Revolution, 1925–1928* (New York, 1947), 423; M. Beloff, "Soviet Policy in China," *International Affairs*, V 27(July, 1951), 252–53.

138. MacMurray to Stimson, July 11, 22, 1929, *NA*, RG 59.

139. Stimson to MacMurray, July 18, 1929, "The Obligations of Russia and China Under the Treaty for the Renunciation of War," unsigned memorandum of July 18, 1929, both in *NA*, RG 59.

140. This writer has searched the relevant material on the Outlawry Campaign in the *Levinson Mss.*, *Borah Mss.*, *Robins Mss.*, and the *NA*. None of the students of the subject has yet noted Robins' economic difficulties which tied him to Levinson. Robins later acknowledged (July 29, 1949) that this campaign was "less than realistic."

141. Stimson to MacMurray, July 19, 1929, Stimson, "Memorandum of Conversation with the Chinese Minister, August 20, 1929," both in *NA*, RG 59.

142. Coleman to Stimson, July 23, 1929, Poole to Stimson, October 12, 1928, both in *NA*, RG 59.

143. Johnson, "Memo of Conversation with Bronson Rea in re U.S. Loan to Purchase the Chinese Eastern," September 3, 1929, Stimson to Geneva, September 23, 1929, Stimson to MacMurray, July 26, 1929, Schurman to Stimson, July 30, 1929, Stimson to Schurman, July 26, 1929, all in *NA*, RG 59.

144. *Izvestia*, August 6, 1929; Schurman to Stimson, August 14, 1929, *NA*, RG 59; Gumberg to Schley, December 4, 1929, Gumberg to State Department, December 23, 1929, Gumberg to Goodrich, December 26, 1929, all in *Gumberg Mss.*

145. Neville to Stimson, November 27, 1929, *NA*, RG 59; Thompkins, *Relations in the Far East*, 220–46.

146. Stimson to Neville, November 26, 1929, Stimson to Paris, November 30, 1929, Armour to Stimson, December 7, 1929, all in *NA*, RG 59.

147. Borah to Davis, March 20, 1929, *Borah Mss.*; Stimson to Woll, May 1, 1929, in *United States Daily*, May 1, 1929; *Record*, V 71:1:120, V 71:4:4411, V 70:2:1570, V 72:6:5675, V 74:4:3785, V 74:4:4006–7, V 74:5:4671.

148. *Congressional Directory* (Washington, 1932), 63; *Record,* V 72:11:12089; W. C. White, "Economics vs. Politics in American Soviet Business," *Asia,* V 30 (December, 1930), 846–52.

149. *Hearings Before a Special Committee to Investigate Communist Activities in the United States* (19 vols., Washington, 1930); *Hearings on the Embargo on Soviet Products* (Washington, 1931); *United States Daily,* May 2, September 24, December 3, 1930, February 6, 13, 21, 1931; New York *Times,* July 24, 26, 28, 1930.

150. R. H. Ridgway, *Manganese and Manganiferous Ores in 1931* (Commerce, 1932), 154; *Economic Life,* September 7, 1929; Mellon, statement of February 24, 1931, in *United States Daily,* February 25, 1931; and see *NA,* RG 151, File 312.

151. *Annals,* V 156 (July, 1931), 54–61; National Civic Federation, press release of February 21, 1931 (and others), *Robins Mss.;* *Record,* V 71:5:5339, 5528–29, V 72:4:4347, V 72:6:5678–80, V 72:8:8075–77, V 74:1:627, V 74:4:3785, V 74:5:4694, 4830, 4999–5000, 5148, 5918, V 74:7:7273–85, V 75:6:6090–6147.

152. *Outlook* (October 15, 1930), 248, (April 15, 1931), 520–21.

153. *Record,* V 71:4:4411, V 74:1:314, V 74:1:671; for Borah's efforts in behalf of Americans in Russia see *Borah Mss.,* B331/G, B409/G, *United States Daily,* February 25, 1930; for Moscow's view of Borah see Coleman to Kellogg, September 17, 1925, *NA,* RG 59; K. Radek, "America Discovers the U.S.S.R.," in *Podgotovka Borby za Novy Perdel Mira* (Moscow, 1934), 149–55.

154. "Minutes of Conference, December 18, 1930," *Gumberg Mss.*

155. Bertron to Hoover, August 8, 13, 1930, Hoover to Bertron, August 11, 1930, Schley to Stimson, March 19, 1931, Stimson to Schley, March 25, 1931, all in *NA,* RG 59; Gumberg to Goodrich, April 30, 1929, Gumberg to Borah, May 29, 1930, *Gumberg Mss.*

156. Poole to Stimson, December 5, 1928, Fullerton to Stimson, November 19, 1931, Cole to Stimson, November 27, 1931, Kelley to Stimson, June 18, 1931, Borah to Stimson, August 25, 1932, Stimson to Borah, September 8, 1932, all in *NA,* RG 59; *Economic Life,* September 15, 1928.

157. Hoover, quoted by the San Francisco *News,* August 13, 1931; the Soviets immediately published this declaration of antagonism, Coleman to Stimson, September 18, 1931, *NA,* RG 59.

158. *War and Peace, United States Foreign Policy, 1931–1941* (Washington, 1945), 159–60.

159. *Lytton Report,* 63–71.

160. *War and Peace,* 155–56; *Conditions in Manchuria* (Washington, 1933), 4–5.

161. See S. R. Smith, *The Manchurian Crisis, 1931–1932* (New York, 1948).

162. W. S. Meyers, *The Foreign Policies of Herbert Hoover, 1929–1933* (New York, 1940), 157–58.

163. London *Times,* January 11, 1932; J. W. Wheeler-Bennett, *Munich: Prologue to Tragedy* (New York, 1948), 354.

164. Smith, *Manchurian Crisis,* 235.

165. Johnson to Stimson, October 2, 1931, *NA*, RG 59.
166. *Izvestia*, September 21, 1931.
167. Beloff, *Foreign Policy of Soviet Russia*, I, 79, 81.
168. Beyond the *NA* material cited above, the best published account of this Soviet overture is J. B. Powell, *My Twenty-Five Years in China* (New York, 1945), 193–95; but see *Izvestia*, August 16, 1932; Rogers, "Memorandum of a Conversation with A. M. Creighton, December 1, 1932," McIroy to Smith, February 23, 1933, *NA*, RG 59; and below.
169. Borah to Stimson, August 25, 1932, Stimson to Borah, September 8, 1932, both in *NA*, RG 59 (also *Borah Mss.*). For verification that the State Department was well aware of the Soviet overture see Kelley to Castle, Rogers, Klots, and Hornbeck, December 22, 1931, *NA*, RG 59.
170. Borah to Davis, January 19, 1932, *Borah Mss.*

Chapter VIII: THE TRAGEDY OF THE THIRTIES

1. B. Mitchell, *Depression Decade* (New York, 1947), 368.
2. C. W. Mills, *White Collar* (New York, 1951), xvii.
3. E. S. Corwin, *Constitutional Revolution, Ltd.* (Claremont, 1941), 107–17.
4. D. Lynch, *The Concentration of Economic Power* (New York, 1946), 362, 73; Mitchell, *Depression Decade*, 369.
5. Lynch, *Concentration of Economic Power*, 363.
6. F. Kuh to Gumberg, August 11, 1931, *Gumberg Mss.*
7. Borah to Gumberg, November 9, 1932, Gumberg to Borah, November 21, 1932, both in *Borah Mss.*; Gumberg to Duranty, July 22, 1932, *Gumberg Mss.*
8. Robins to Borah, February 10, 1933, *Borah Mss.*; Robins to Levinson, March 30, April 2, 9, 11, 13, 1933, all in *Levinson Mss.*; confidential witness to author, December 16, 1949.
9. Hull, *Memoirs*, I, 192, 292; "Memo to Mr. Castle, February 13, 1931," *NA*, RG 59.
10. Mitchell, *Depression Decade*, Chapter VII; L. H. Chamberlain, *The President, Congress, and Legislation* (New York, 1946), 46–58.
11. Kelley to Stimson, January 28, 1933, *NA*, RG 59.
12. Jones to Roosevelt, June 24, 1933, Shaman to McIntyre, August 12, 1933, both in *FDR Mss.*; Jones to Hull, September 26, 1933, *NA*, RG 59; *Saturday Evening Post* (August 26, 1933), 22.
13. Material drawn from *FDR Mss.*, File 220-A/Russia Misc.; *NA*, RG 59:711.61.
14. Bertron to Hull, March 21, 1933, A-R Chamber of Commerce to Roosevelt, October 22, 1933, both in *NA*, RG 59; Gumberg to Perkins, June 22, 1934, Barnes, Sullivan, Rockford, Sunstrand Machine Tool Companies to Roosevelt, July 8, 1933, both in *Gumberg Mss.*
15. Lape to Roosevelt, October [?], 1933, *FDR Mss.*
16. Material cited in Notes 156, 168, Chapter VII; Poole to Stimson, December 28, 1928.

17. Grew to Hull, March 6, 1933, Skinner to Stimson, March 21, 1932, both in *NA*, RG 59; *Izvestia*, October 21, 1933, March 14, 1932; *Pravda*, October 21, 1932.

18. Hull, *Memoirs*, I, 293; K. K. Kawakami, "Japan Seeks Economic Empire in Manchuria," *Current History*, V 39 (September, 1939), 1111–18; Hornbeck to Phillips, October 28, 31, 1933, both in *NA*, RG 59.

19. Allied Patriotic Societies to Kellogg, February 2, 1928, Phillips, "Memo of Conversation with Representative H. Fish, Jr., November 13, 1933," Phillips to Hull, March 24, 1933, Catholic Women to Hull, April 7, 1933, D. A. R. to Hull, April 7, 1933, "Memorandum on Bondholder's Protective Committee, October 20, 1933," all in *NA*, RG 59; Polk to Roosevelt, October 20, 1933, L. A. Johnson to Roosevelt, June 17, 1933, Brown to Roosevelt, July 11, 1933, all in *FDR Mss.; Record*, V 77:2:1366.

20. Material on Robins' trip to Russia collected from *Robins Mss., Levinson Mss., Borah Mss., Gumberg Mss., FDR Mss., Robins*, and confidential witnesses. The Stalin-Robins quotes from "A Conversation with Colonel Raymond Robins," *Labour Monthly*, V 33 (London, December, 1951), 574–82.

21. Hull to author, December 19, 1949.

22. Packer to Bullitt, August 31, 1933, Roosevelt to Polk, October 28, 1933, Kelley, "Problems Pertaining to Russian-American Relations Which in the Interest of Friendly Relations Between the United States and Russia, Should Be Settled Prior to the Recognition of the Soviet Government," dated July 27, 1933, forwarded to Bullitt and Roosevelt on July 27, 1933, all in *FDR Mss.* (also *NA*, RG 59) ; Hull, *Memoirs*, I, 299.

23. Kelley, memorandum of July 27, 1933, *NA*, RG 59.

24. Hull to Roosevelt, September 21, 1933, Kelley to Phillips, September 25, 1933, Moore to Hull, October 4, 1933, Bullitt to Hull, October 4, 1933 (sent to Roosevelt, October 5), all in *NA*, RG 59.

25. A. J. Toynbee, *Survey of International Affairs, 1933* (London, 1934), 185, 186, 180–81.

26. *Documents on International Affairs, 1933*, edited by J. W. Wheeler-Bennett (London, 1934), 219–23.

27. R. W. Moore, *State Department Press Releases, No. 529* (November 25, 1933), stated that "there were no stenographers present and no reports made." This is a bit misleading, see Bullitt to Roosevelt, November 15, 1933, *FDR Mss.;* Summary of Confidential Memorandum "A" on talks between Litvinov and Roosevelt, not dated, *NA*, RG 59; Bullitt to Hull, July 17, 1934, *NA*, RG 59, which makes clear that both words, *credit* and *loan*, were used. Also see Bullitt to Hull, April 2, 1934, Hull to Bullitt, April 5, 1934, both in *NA*, RG 59; *Relations, Soviet Union, 1933–39*, 104–5, 118, 158, 160, 577–78.

28. *Documents for 1933*, 462–63, 221–22, 231.

29. See *Record*, V 79:7:7526–34, V 79:8:9080, New York *Times*, June 23, 1935; Sterling, quoted in Washington *Herald*, June 9, 1935; *Relations, Soviet Union, 1933–39*, 111.

30. Roosevelt to Moore, August 23, 1935, *FDR Mss.; Report of the Seventh World Congress of the Communist International* (London, 1936), 7.

31. Bullitt to Hull, August 30, 1935, *NA*, RG 59; L. Fischer, *Men and Politics* (London, 1941), 292; *Relations, Soviet Union, 1933–39*, 227, 229.

32. Soviet policy is well reviewed in Beloff, *The Foreign Policy of Soviet Russia;* L. E. Namier, *Diplomatic Prelude 1938–1939* (London, 1948), *Europe in Decay. A Study in Disintegration 1936–1940* (London, 1950); and J. W. Wheeler-Bennett, *Munich: Prologue to Tragedy* (New York, 1948).

33. J. Maynard, *Russia in Flux* (New York, 1948), 285.

34. A. Baykov, *The Development of the Soviet Economic System* (New York, 1947), 309, 335; B. J. Moore, *Soviet Politics—The Dilemma of Power* (Cambridge, 1950), 221.

35. Maynard, *Russia in Flux*, 322, 509; I. Deutscher, *Stalin. A Political Biography* (New York, 1949), 358; *Relations, Soviet Union, 1933–39*, 379.

36. Deutscher, *Stalin*, 566–70.

37. Baykov, *Soviet Economic System*, 309, 277; *Survey for 1936*, 365; Wiley to Hull, December 14, 1934, *NA*, RG 59; Williams to Gumberg, November 17, 1934, June 23, 1935, *Gumberg Mss.*

38. Baykov, *Soviet Economic System*, 349, 335, 342.

39. Maynard, *Russia in Flux*, Chapters XXV and XXVII.

40. Wiley to Hull, December 14, 1934, Kelley, "Memo on Kirov, December 7, 1934," both in *NA*, RG 59; *Relations, Soviet Union, 1933–39*, 301.

41. Summary of Confidential Memorandum "A" on talks between Litvinov and Roosevelt, not dated, *NA*, RG 59.

42. R. T. Pollard, "Russo-Japanese Tension," *Annals*, V 175:101–9.

43. New York *Times*, December 28, 1933; *Documents for 1933*, 436–40; Bullitt to Hull, March 14, 23, July 27, 1934, all in *NA*, RG 59; *Relations, 1934*, III, 34, 68; Bullitt to Hull, December 24, 1933 (sent to FDR, December 26), *FDR Mss.*

44. Hull to Bullitt, March 17, 1934, Bullitt to Hull, March 21, 23, 1934, all in *NA*, RG 59.

45. "Memorandum of the Secretary's Press Conference, April 6, 1934," *NA*, RG 59; New York *Times*, March 16, April 5, 6, 7, 1934.

46. Bullitt to Hull, March 21, 1934, *NA*, RG 59.

47. "Memorandum of Secretary Hull's Conversation with Troyanovsky," Kelley, "Memorandum of Conversation with Troyanovsky, February 21, 1934," both in *NA*, RG 59.

48. Bullitt to Hull, April 2, 1934, Roosevelt to Moore, August 31, 1934, both in *NA*, RG 59.

49. Hull to Bullitt, April 5, 7, 1934, both in *NA*, RG 59.

50. Bullitt to Hull, April 8, May 5, 1934, both in *NA*, RG 59.

51. Hull to Bullitt, April 8, May 3, 1934, Bullitt to Hull, May 2, 1934, all in *NA*, RG 59.

52. Hull to Bullitt, May 7, 11, 12, 1934, Bullitt to Hull May 9, 1934, all in *NA*, RG 59.

53. Bullitt to Hull, May 13, June 14, 1934, Hull to Bullitt, May 15, 1934, all in *NA*, RG 59.
54. Beloff, *Foreign Policy of Soviet Russia*, I, Chapter IX.
55. *Izvestia*, May 28, 1934; Beloff, *Foreign Policy of Soviet Russia*, I, 135, 141–43; *Survey for 1934*, 339–45.
56. Litvinov, quoted in Bullitt to Hull, July 9, 1934, *NA*, RG 59; *Relations, Soviet Union, 1933–39*, 144, 146–48, 155, 159, 165, 177, 314–15, 447.
57. Bullitt to Hull, July 27, 1934, *NA*, RG 59.
58. New York *Times*, March 29, April 29, 1934; *Nation*, V 138(June 20, 1934), 690; Thompson to Roosevelt, July 2, 1934, Coyle to Howe, August 22, 1934, both in *NA*, RG 59; *Relations, Soviet Union, 1933–39*, 357.
59. Kelley to Hull and Moore, August 24, 1934, Kelley, "Questions on the Length of Credits, September 4, 1934," Kelley, "Considerations with Respect to the Amount of Credits, September 5, 1934," all in *NA*, RG 59.
60. Bullitt to Hull, September 15, 1934, *NA*, RG 59.
61. Hull to Bullitt, September 15, 17, 1934, both in *NA*, RG 59.
62. Hull, "Memo of Conversation with Troyanovsky, January 28, 1935," Wiley to Hull, February 2, 1935, both in *NA*, RG 59.
63. New York *Times*, February 1, 2, 1935; Hull to Bullitt, January 31, 1935, *NA*, RG 59.
64. Bertron to Howe, February 4, 1935, *FDR Mss.*; New York *Times*, March 23, 1935; *Relations, Soviet Union, 1933–39*, 192–218, 322–45, 405–40, 601–24, 809–37.
65. Wiley to Hull, February 3, 1935, *NA*, RG 59; *Relations, Soviet Union, 1933–39*, 124, 143, 164, 175, 319.
66. Bullitt to Hull, October 26, 1935, *NA*, RG 59; *Relations, Soviet Union, 1933–39*, 265, 311–12.
67. Bullitt to M. de Kalb Brogley, December 5, 1947, in Brogley, William C. Bullitt and Russian-American Relations, unpublished Master's thesis, University of Wisconsin, 1949, 62–63; *Ambassador Dodd's Diary, 1933–1938*, edited by W. E. and M. Dodd (London, 1941), 277–78, 285, 309, 316, 371–72; S. Welles, *The Time for Decision* (New York, 1944), 246.
68. See D. D. Young, "American Labor's Attitude Toward Soviet Russia, 1933–1941," unpublished Master's thesis, University of Wisconsin, 1949; New York *Times*, September 18, 26, 1935, June 8, 10, July 17, August 16, September 20, 1936; *Relations, Soviet Union, 1933–39*, 131, 132.
69. Moore to Roosevelt, January 16, 1937, Davies to Roosevelt, February 17, 1937, both in *FDR Mss.*; J. E. Davies, *Mission to Moscow* (New York, 1944), 2, 55–59, 70–71, 75–78.
70. H. Feis, *The Road to Pearl Harbor. The Coming of the War Between the United States and Japan* (Princeton, 1950), 9.
71. State Department, *Press Releases*, July 16, August 14, 1937; *Pravda*, July 22, 1937; *Izvestia*, July 22, 1937.
72. *The Public Papers and Addresses of Franklin D. Roosevelt, 1937* (New York, 1941), 423.

73. S. R. Smith, *The Manchurian Crisis, 1931–1932* (New York, 1948), 139–55; Stimson, letter to the New York *Times,* October 7, 1937.

74. Quoted by Feis, *Road to Pearl Harbor,* 10.

75. W. H. Shepardson, *The United States in World Affairs, 1937* (New York, 1938), 224.

76. A. Cooke, *A Generation on Trial, U.S.A.* vs. *Alger Hiss* (New York, 1950), 27.

77. *Survey for 1937,* I, 276, says this was done "prudently;" Welles, *Seven Decisions,* calls it the act of a "skilled politician." Both the argument from necessity and the use of public opinion polls to defend Roosevelt's behind-the-scene maneuvers evade the central issue: Roosevelt did not pose the question candidly and openly. This may be considered of importance to a society concerned with the exercise of democratic precepts.

78. Phrases, in order, from Feis, *Road to Pearl Harbor;* Welles, *Seven Decisions;* Namier, *Europe in Decay;* and Churchill, *The Gathering Storm* (Boston, 1947).

79. *Documents on British Foreign Policy, 1919–1939,* edited by E. L. Woodward and R. Butler (London, 1946–.), Third Series, II (1938), 623–24.

80. Hull, *Memoirs,* I, 659–60; A. Barth, *The Loyalty of Free Men* (New York, 1951), 89; Cooke, *A Generation on Trial,* 30; Welles, *Seven Decisions,* 14–23; Feis, *Road to Pearl Harbor,* 13, 6–7.

81. *Relations, 1904,* 2; Roosevelt to Griscom, October 22, 1937, *FDR Mss.;* R. G. Swing, "How We Lost the Peace in 1937," *Atlantic,* V 179(February, 1947), 33–37; Swing, "Is History Bunk?" *The Saturday Review of Literature,* V 33 (June 3, 1950), 38–39; Swing to author, July 23, 1950.

82. Welles, *Seven Decisions,* 76; Swing, "How We Lost the Peace," *Atlantic,* V 179:33–37; W. L. Langer and S. Everett Gleason, *The Challenge to Isolation 1937–1940* (New York, 1952), 18–32; *Relations, Soviet Union, 1933–39,* 285–86, 516–17, 591–93.

83. Mitchell, *Depression Decade,* 44–45; B. Rauch, *The History of the New Deal* (New York, 1944), 297, 314.

84. Morris to Hull, September 28, 1937, Hull to Morris, November 3, 1937, both in New York *Times,* November 22, 1937.

85. These moves can be followed in the *Levinson Mss.,* Box 76–77.

86. Beloff, *Foreign Policy of Soviet Russia,* II, 184–85.

87. Roosevelt to Callaghan, July 6, 1939, *FDR Mss.;* Langer and Gleason, *Challenge,* 127–28; *Relations, Soviet Union, 1933–39,* 457 ff., 670 ff., 869 ff.

88. Davies, *Mission,* 300–9, 325–28, 275–77; *Relations, Soviet Union, 1933–39,* 580–81, 594–601.

89. Confidential witnesses; *Relations, Soviet Union, 1933–39,* 504–5.

90. Hull, *Memoirs,* I, 657–58; *Record,* V 82:2:1329; *Relations, Soviet Union, 1933–39,* 491 ff., 708 ff., 904 ff.

91. Stalin, *Report on the Work of the Central Committee to the Eighteenth Congress of the C.P.S.U. (B)* (Moscow, 1939), 24.

92. G. A. Craig, "High Tide of Appeasement: The Road to Munich, 1937–38," *Political*

Science Quarterly, V 65:1:36–37; *Relations, Soviet Union, 1933–39,* 591–92, 593.

93. Hull, *Memoirs,* I, 655–56.

94. New York *Times,* March 6, August 8, 1939.

95. Stalin, *Report to the Eighteenth Congress,* 15, 16, 17, 18–19; New York *Times,* September 4, 1939.

96. Namier, *Europe in Decay,* 245; *Relations, Soviet Union, 1933–39,* 767–68, 777, 779.

97. Langer and Gleason, *Challenge,* 35, 161, 163.

98. *Ibid.,* 97.

99. Roosevelt, remarks to press conference, August 15, 1944, *FDR Mss.,* conference No. 963–15; Feis, *Road to Pearl Harbor,* 38ff.

100. H. Moore, *Soviet Far Eastern Policy 1931–1945* (Princeton, 1945), 118; Langer and Gleason, *Challenge,* 295.

101. Langer and Gleason, *Challenge,* 29, 55, 320.

102. *Finland and World War II, 1939–1944,* edited by J. H. Wuorinen (New York, 1948), 44–45. Italics added.

103. Wuorinen, *Finland,* 50; Namier, *Diplomatic Prelude,* 195–96, 200, 203.

104. Wuorinen, *Finland,* 50.

105. Stalin, quoted in *Latvia in 1939–1942* (Washington, 1942), 100–2.

106. Langer and Gleason, *Challenge,* 326.

107. Roosevelt, Embargo Statement of December 2, 1939, *FDR Mss.*

108. Langer and Gleason, *Challenge,* 328, n. 55.

109. *Ibid.,* 331, 332.

110. New York *Times,* December 3, 1939.

111. Shakespeare, *Macbeth,* Act IV, Scene 2, Line 3.

Chapter 9: Coda: THE SOPHISTRY OF SUPER-REALISM

1. S. Welles, *The Time for Decision* (New York, 1944), 74; Roosevelt to Berle, January 27, 30, 1940, Berle to Roosevelt, January 30, 1940, all in *FDR Mss.*

2. Hull, *Memoirs,* I, 742.

3. *Nazi Soviet Relations, 1939–1941: Documents from the Archives of the German Foreign Office,* edited by R. J. Sontag and J. S. Beddie (Washington, 1948), 134, 139; Wourinen, *Finland,* 73–80.

4. R. E. Sherwood, *Roosevelt and Hopkins. An Intimate History* (New York, 1948), 299–300.

5. *Ibid.,* 300; Hull, *Memoirs,* I, 743; Langer and Gleason, *Challenge,* 723.

6. Hull, *Memoirs,* I, 807.

7. Langer and Gleason, *Challenge,* 389.

8. Hull, *Memoirs,* I, 807, 809.

9. *Ibid.,* 812, 807, 811; Welles to Roosevelt of August 19, 1940, of January 9, 1941, *FDR Mss.*

10. Langer and Gleason, *Challenge,* 726–27.

11. Hull, *Memoirs,* II, 971, 969.

12. *Ibid.*, 972–73.
13. Sherwood, *Roosevelt*, 264, 308, 384–85, 391–96, 400–1; Hull, *Memoirs*, II, 973, 977.
14. Sherwood, *Roosevelt*, 308, 317–19, 384–85, 321; Roosevelt to Coy, August 2, 1941, Roosevelt to Harriman, August 29, 1941, Harriman to Roosevelt, October 29, 1941, all in *FDR Mss.*
15. The Atlantic Charter, White House Press Release, August 14, 1941.
16. Welles, *Where Are We Heading?* (New York, 1946), 15.
17. *Ibid.*, 5–6.
18. Sherwood, *Roosevelt*, 309, 350, 359, 339, 344.
19. *Ibid.*, 321–22, 306–7.
20. Compare Welles, *Where?*, 5–6, with Sherwood, *Roosevelt*, 317, 354–65, Welles, *Seven Decisions*, 127, and with Welles's testimony before the Pearl Harbor Investigating Committee, Part 4.
21. Hull, *Memoirs*, II, 1165–67; Sherwood, *Roosevelt*, 387; W. S. Churchill, *The Grand Alliance* (Boston, 1950), 628–29; Welles, *Seven Decisions*, 126–30.
22. Sherwood, *Roosevelt*, 867, 834.
23. Hull, *Memoirs*, II, 1165–67; Churchill, *Grand Alliance*, 629–30.
24. W. S. Churchill, *The Hinge of Fate* (Boston, 1951), 327.
25. Hull, *Memoirs*, II, 1172, 1165–73.
26. *Ibid.*, 1173–74; Churchill, *Grand Alliance*, 383–84; Sherwood, *Roosevelt*, 558–60; Vice-Admiral K. Assman, "The Battle for Moscow, Turning Point of the War," *Foreign Affairs*, V 28 (January, 1950), 309–26.
27. Sherwood, *Roosevelt*, 563; Hull, *Memoirs*, II, 1173–74.
28. Churchill, *Hinge of Fate*, 479, 487; Sherwood, *Roosevelt*, 619–20.
29. Sherwood, *Roosevelt*, 616.
30. *Ibid.*, 705, 640–41; Churchill, *Hinge of Fate*, 750; Hull, *Memoirs*, II, 1264.
31. Sherwood, *Roosevelt*, 705.
32. Welles, *Seven Decisions*, 173, 186; Sherwood, *Roosevelt*, 572–73, 716.
33. Hull, *Memoirs*, II, 1247–48; Sherwood, *Roosevelt*, 709–17, 733; Churchill, *Grand Alliance*, 391.
34. Sherwood, *Roosevelt*, 733, 734; Hull, *Memoirs*, II, 1250.
35. Sherwood, *Roosevelt*, 748–49.
36. Hull, *Memoirs*, II, 1171, 1254–55; Welles, *Seven Decisions*, 126–27.
37. Hull, *Memoirs*, II, 1294. See H. L. Stimson, *On Active Service in Peace and War* (New York, 1946), 603–5, and his report of January 20, 1945, in *The Forrestal Diaries*, edited by W. Millis and E. S. Duffield (New York, 1951), 28–29.
38. Hull, *Memoirs*, II, 1256–58, 1281, 1309.
39. Sherwood, *Roosevelt*, 710.
40. Hull, *Memoirs*, II, 1271–72, 1438–39.
41. *Ibid.*, II, 1439, 1441–48; W. W. Kulsi, "The Lost Opportunity for Russian-Polish Friendship," *Foreign Affairs*, V 25 (July, 1947), 667–84.
42. Sherwood, *Roosevelt*, 797; Hull, *Memoirs*, II, 1269, 1436; for Roosevelt's view of the Atlantic Charter see his press conference remarks of December 22, 1944 and

February 23, 1945, *FDR Mss.*, conferences No. 985–5, 992–16.

43. W. S. Churchill, *Closing the Ring* (Boston, 1951), 361–62.

44. *Ibid.*, 394–97, 450–51.

45. *Soviet Foreign Policy During the Patriotic War. Documents and Materials,* edited by A. Rothstein (2 vols., London, 1945), II, 39–41.

46. *Parliamentary Debates, House of Commons,* February 22, 1944, Cols. 697–98; Churchill, *Closing the Ring,* 452, 403.

47. Roosevelt to Bohlen, November 30, 1943, *FDR Mss.*; Welles, *Seven Decisions,* 190; Sherwood, *Roosevelt,* 799.

48. *Record,* V 90:1:55–57.

49. Churchill, *Closing the Ring,* 452.

50. Hull, *Memoirs,* II, 1270–71, 1436–41.

51. *Ibid.*, 1451.

52. *Ibid.*, 1451–53; for background, see Churchill, *Closing the Ring,* 708–9.

53. Hull, *Memoirs,* II, 1453–59.

54. *Ibid.*, 1455.

55. *Ibid.*, 1453.

56. *Ibid.*, 1454–55, 1461; *Record,* V 93:5:1999–2000.

57. Rothstein, *Soviet Foreign Policy,* 160, 162; Hull, *Memoirs,* II, 1458.

58. Sherwood, *Roosevelt,* 834.

59. Hull, *Memoirs,* II, 1458–59.

60. Churchill to Roosevelt, March 8, 1945, in New York *Times,* October 18, 1947.

61. J. F. Byrnes, *Speaking Frankly* (New York, 1947), 53; Sherwood, *Roosevelt,* 875; Roosevelt, press conference remarks, *FDR Mss.*, conference 995–5.

62. For Soviet emphasis on reparations and the close relationship between the charges and counter-charges over events in the Balkans and the Stalin-Churchill talks of 1944 see: Churchill, *Closing the Ring,* 359–61, 401–2; Byrnes, *Speaking Frankly,* 74, 82, 98, 124, 132, 135; Smith, *My Three Years in Moscow* (New York, 1950), 212; Forrestal, *Diaries,* 266; Sherwood, *Roosevelt,* 861–62, 894.

63. New York *Times,* March 15, 1945.

64. Byrnes, *Speaking Frankly,* 56; E. R. Stettinius, Jr., *Roosevelt and the Russians. The Yalta Conference,* edited by W. Johnson (Garden City, 1949), 300–3; Sherwood, *Roosevelt,* 875.

65. Roosevelt to Harriman, December 1, 1943, *FDR Mss.*; Sherwood, *Roosevelt,* 777.

66. Sherwood, *Roosevelt,* 782, 786–87, 853; but see Roosevelt, press conference of February 19, 1945, *FDR Mss.*, conference No. 991-2: "Q. What can they [the Russians] do about getting reparations in kind from the Germans? *The President:* Get all they can."

67. Stettinius, *Roosevelt and the Russians,* 120.

68. New York *Times,* February 15, 1950.

69. Though differing in detail, both W. D. Leahy, *I Was There* (New York, 1950), 351–52, and Forrestal, *Diaries,* 50–51, present the same review of this conference.

70. Forrestal, *Diaries,* 41; Leahy, *I Was There,* 351–52.

71. Forrestal, *Diaries*, 49–50.
72. *Ibid.*, 50, notes by C. E. Bohen.
73. Sherwood, *Roosevelt*, 887–902.
74. *Ibid.*
75. Churchill, *Closing the Ring*, 713.
76. *United States Relations with China. With Special Reference to the Period 1944–1949* (Washington, 1949), 550; Welles, *Where?*, 71; M. Beloff, "Soviet Policy in China," *International Affairs*, V 27:3 (July, 1951), 293; G. W. Atkinson, "The Sino-Soviet Treaty of Friendship and Alliance," *International Affairs*, V 23:3 (July, 1947), 362; New York *Times*, May 30, 1949.
77. Sherwood, *Roosevelt*, 792, 866.
78. Welles, *Seven Decisions*, 157.
79. *Ibid.*, 159–62; W. H. Chamberlain, *America's Second Crusade* (Chicago, 1950), Chapter IX, 206–31.
80. Stettinius, *Roosevelt and the Russians*, 351; Sherwood, *Roosevelt*, 867.
81. Chinese Memorandum of March 18, 1935, in *China Year Book, 1935* (Shanghai, 1935), 139.
82. Sino-Soviet Agreement of September 20, 1924, in V. A. Yakhontoff, *Russia and the Soviet Union in the Far East* (New York, 1931), 398–400; Sino-Soviet Agreement of August 14, 1945, in *United States Relations With China*, 593–94; G. F. Kennan, *American Diplomacy 1900–1950* (Chicago, 1951), 85.
83. *United States Relations with China*, 97.
84. Forrestal, *Diaries*, 107; but on July 28, 1945, Byrnes told Forrestal (according to the latter) that "he was most anxious to get the Japanese affair over with before the Russians got in," *Diaries*, 78.
85. State Department, *Bulletin*, January 19, 1947, 83–85.
86. Forrestal, *Diaries*, 132; Byrnes, *Speaking Frankly*, 151–52.
87. Smith, *Three Years in Moscow*, 220–22.
88. P. E. Mosely, "Soviet-American Relations Since the War," *Annals*, V 263 (May, 1949), 209; Hull, *Memoirs*, II, 1465.
89. Welles, *Where?*, 67, 70.
90. D. E. Lillienthal and D. Acheson, *A Report on the International Control of Atomic Energy* (Washington, 1946); Welles, *Where?*, 349–50.
91. G. F. Kennan, "The Sources of Soviet Conduct," *Foreign Relations*, V 25 (July, 1947), 566–82; for Russian reaction to the Truman Doctrine see E. Varga, "Anglo-American Rivalry and Partnership: A Marxist View," *Foreign Affairs*, V 25 (July, 1947), 594; Deutscher, *Stalin*, 536–37, 540–43; *Diplomatichesky Slovar*, II, 829.
92. Forrestal, *Diaries*, 135–40; Kennan to author, January 23, 1952.
93. Forrestal, *Diaries*, 136, 139, 171, 182, 195, 210.
94. *Record*, V 93:5:1999–2000; Department of State, *Bulletin*, XVI, 395.
95. Kennan, "Soviet Conduct," *Foreign Affairs*, V 25:4:566–82.
96. *Webster's New International Dictionary of the English Language* (2d. edition, Revised, Springfield, Massachusetts, 1935), 1616, 2928.

INDEX

As used in this index, the terms Russia, Russian, and Russo refer to Tsarist Russia; Soviet and U.S.S.R. to the Soviet Union.

Abrams vs. U.S., 155–57

Abrogation of U.S.-Russian Commercial Treaty of 1832, 77–78, 80–82, 83 ff., (*see* Kennan, G. F.; Schiff, J.)

Acheson, Assistant Secretary of State Dean, 279

Adams, Brooks
background of, 32–33
influence of, 32–33, 34, 35, 39–40, 41–42, 44, 46, 50
policy of, 23, 40, 41–42, 46, 50

Adams, Henry, influence of, 32, 34, 39, 42, 46, 64

Adams, Secretary of State John Quincy, 3, 6, 8, 12
and expansion, 7, 9, 10, 12, 13, 14–15, 16
and Russia, 3, 6–7, 9–11, 12, 13–16

Addams, Jane, 43, 80

advisors, State Department, role in policy-making, 10, 29, 30, 32, 34–37, 51, 59, 60, 62 ff., 78, 86–87, 89, 93, 103, 107–09, 113, 117, 122, 126, 127, 128, 137 ff., 159–60, 165–66, 180, 197, 208, 209–10, 224, 228, 239 ff., 250, 259, 266, 277, 279 ff.

agricultural-machinery interest, U.S.
role in U.S.-Russian and U.S.S.R. relations, 83–84, 211 ff., 216, 236

Alaska, purchase of by U.S.
motivation of Tsarist sale, 21–22
pressures for purchase, 21–22

Alexander I, and U.S.-Russian relations, 3, 5, 6, 8, 9, 10–11, 12, 14, 16, 18

Alexander II, 21

Alexeev, Mikhail, intervention, role in, 117, 119–20

Alexeiev, E. I., and Russian policy in the Far East, 38, 39, 43

Allen, Minister Horace N., views on U.S.-Russian relations, 43–44, 46, 56, 62

Allied-American Company, 211

Allied Memorandum to U.S.S.R. of 2 May 1922, character and purpose, 196–97

Allied Patriotic Societies, Inc., 237

Allies, Western, pressure on Provisional Government for military offensive, 1917, 91–92, 93

All-Russian Democratic Congress, September, 1917, 100–01

All-Russian Textile Syndicate, 211–12
(*see* cotton exporters, U.S.; Gumberg, Alexander)

American-China Development Company, 29, 35, 41

America First Committee, 234

American Chamber of Commerce in Shanghai, China, 220

American-Chinese relations
antagonism and rivalry, 106, 139, 166, 178 ff., 219 ff.
economic ties, 35, 36, 58 ff. (*see* Chinese Eastern Railroad; Extraterritoriality; Manchuria; Sino-Soviet Dispute of 1929; Washington Conference; and central personalities of these relations)

American Civil War, Russian policy during, 19–20, 21

American Commercial Association to Promote Trade in Russia, 180

American Committee of Creditors of the Soviet Union, 237

American Farm Bureau Federation, 223

American Federation of Labor, 82, 137
leadership of, 138, 203
policy of, 138, 148, 179, 181, 203

American-Finnish relations, role in of U.S.S.R., 254–55, 260–1

American Geographical Society, 24

American Historical Review, 156

American Iron and Steel Institute, 223, 224

American-Japanese relations
antagonism and rivalry, 50–51, 71 ff., 136 ff., 161 ff., 178 ff.
collaboration, 38, 46
third nations, role in
Russia, 37, 59
U.S.S.R., 139 ff. (*see* Chinese Eastern Railway; Manchuria; Washington Conference; and central personalities of these relations)

American Legion, 238, 247

American Locomotive Company, 150, 224

American Manganese Producers Association, 223

American-Persian relations
economic ties, 76 ff., 194 ff. (*see* Anglo-Persian Oil Co.; oil; Royal Dutch Shell Oil Co.; Schuster; W. Morgan; Standard Oil Company; and central personalities of these relations)
American Red Cross Commission to Russia
and Provisional Government, 94 ff.
origin and character, 88–90
(*see* Davison, Henry P.; Robins, Raymond; Thompson, William Boyce)
American Red Cross War Council, 88–89, 97, 127
American Relief Administration, aid to U.S.S.R., 193, 198, 200–01
American-Russian Chamber of Commerce
policy and leadership, 85, 148 ff., 174, 180, 217, 224, 236, 246
reorganization, 213–14 (*see* Gumberg, Alexander; Schley, Reeve)
American-Russian Industrial Syndicate, 194
American-Russian League, 148, 153
American-Russian relations
antagonism and rivalry, 4, 7, 8–9, 10–11, 12, 25–27, 30–31, 36–37, 38, 40–41, 44–47, 49–50, 51–52
collaboration and decreased tension, 4, 5, 6, 7, 15–16, 18–19, 20–21, 30, 37
economic ties, 5, 7, 35–36, 51 ff., 82 ff., 92, 94 ff.
third nations, role of
France, 5, 7, 18, 57
Germany, 82
Great Britain, 5, 13, 18, 20, 30–31, 32, 34, 82, 84
Japan, 28, 30–31, 47, 49–50, 51–52, 61–62, 94, 95, 106
Persia, 76 ff.
Spain, 9
(*see* Anglo-Japanese Alliance; Chinese Eastern Railroad; Manchuria; and central personalities of these relations)
American-Soviet Negotiations of 1922, 197–98, 199, 202
American-Soviet relations
antagonism and rivalry, Ch. V ff.
economic ties, 178 ff., 208 ff.
third nations, role of
China, 178 ff., 219 ff., 231, 233, 237 ff.
France, 178 ff.

American-Soviet relations (*continued*)
Germany, 132 ff., 159–60, 231, 233, 237 ff., 261 ff.
Great Britain, 178 ff., 261 ff.
Japan, 132 ff., 178 ff., 225 ff., 261 ff.
Persia, 194 ff.
Poland, 267–68, 270–71, 273 ff.
(*see* Chinese Eastern Railroad; intervention in Bolshevik Revolution; Manchuria; Paris Peace Conference; Recognition of U.S.S.R.; Soviet Union, overtures to the U.S.; and central personalities of these relations)
American Sugar Refining Company, 29
American Telephone and Telegraph Company, 83
American Trading Company, 29, 57
American Tool Works, 224
Amtorg Trading Corporation, 212
Amur River, 21, 22, 24, 28
Amur River Basin, concessions for the development of, 41, 189
Anaconda Copper Company, 100
Anglo-American relations (*see* American-Russian and Soviet relations, third nations, role of)
Anglo-French Agreement on Russia of 23 December 1917, 119
Anglo-French-Soviet Negotiations of 1939, 254 (*see* Eighteenth Congress of the Communist Party; Munich Crisis; Nazi-Soviet Pact)
Anglo-Japanese Alliance of 1902, 39, 58, 186, 191
Anglo-Japanese relations
antagonism and rivalry, 186 ff.
collaboration, 46, 58, 70 (*see* Chinese Eastern Railroad; Manchuria; neutralization of Manchurian Railways)
Anglo-Persian Oil Company, 194, 195
Anglo-Persian relations, 74, 194 ff.
Anglophilism, in U.S. policy-making, 31, 39, 40, 43, 64–65 (*see* Russophobia)
Anglo-Russian Convention of 1907, 58, 75–76, 194
Anglo-Saxonism, 27, 34–35, 45
Anglo-Soviet Talks, 1941, 263, of 1942, 264
Anti-Comintern Pact, 248, 252
Anti-Japanese agitation in the U.S., 57
Appeal to the Toiling, Oppressed, and Exhausted Peoples of Europe, view of held by Lansing, Robert, 123

appeasement, policy of (*see* Munich Crisis)

Araki, Japanese General, 243

Arcos-American Company, 212

Arcos Corporation, 212

Army War College, 96, 101, 135 (*see* Judson, William V.)

Associated Press, 24, 111, 135, 145

Association of American Creditors, 250–51

Atlantic Conference, significance of in U.S.-U.S.S.R. relations, 262–63, 264

Atlantic Fleet, U.S., visit to Russia, 75

atom bomb, diplomacy of by U.S., 258, 279

Baker, Secretary of War Newton D., 96, 109, 116, 127, 129, 147, 151, 173

Bakery and Confectionery Workers, 180

Bakhmeteff, Russian Ambassador Boris, 182

balance of power, concept of in policy of major powers, 3–4, 5–6, 7–9, 12, 20, 21–22, 28, 31, 32, 38, 44–47, 50, 51, 59, 65, 68 ff., 184 (*see* intervention, in Bolshevik Revolution; Marxism, revision of by; Sino-Japanese War, 1931–45; Soviet Union, overtures to the U.S.; Washington Conference; policy-making personalities)

Baldwin Locomotive Works, 36, 83, 180, 213

Balfour, Sir Arthur J., 95, 123, 126, 168

Baltimore *American*, 43

Baltimore *Chronicle*, 12

Banker's Club of America, trade with U.S.S.R., discussion of, 213, 217

Barnes Drill Company, 218

Barthou, French Foreign Minister Louis, 242–43

Batolin, P. P., 100, 152–53, 198

Bedford, A. C., chairman of the Board of Directors of Standard Oil of New Jersey, policy and influence, 194 ff.

Behind the Urals, 215

Bela Kun, Bolshevik leader of Austria policies of, 170
overthrow of, by Allies, 171 ff.

Belmont, August, 43

Berle, Adolf A., Jr., 171

Bertron, Samuel R., 87, 94

Bethlehem Iron Works, 29

Bethlehem Steel Company, 213

Bezobrazov, Captain A. M.
economic interests of, 37, 55

Bezobrazov, Captain A. M. (*continued*)
influence of, 38, 39, 43
policy of, 30, 37–39, 43, 73

Billings, Dr. Frank C., 89–90, 94

Black Tom Plot, 114

Bliss, General Tasker H., policy toward intervention, 144, 162, 168

Blockade and embargoes, economic, against the Soviet Union, 109, 127, 170–71, 174, 179, 211, 219, 255, 260

Bolshevik Party of Russia, 93–94, 98, 100
seizure of power, 102–4 (*now see* Soviet Union)

Bolshevik Revolution, problem posed by for the West, 4, 91, 105 ff., 159 ff., 189–91, 220, 227–29, 231 ff., 269, 278 ff.

Bonaparte, Napoleon, 5, 7, 8

Bondholder's Protective Committee, 237

Bone, Helen Wilson, 100

Borah, United States Senator William E.
general policy of, 128, 146 ff., 217 ff.
influence of, 128, 154, 157, 182
policy toward
Chinese Revolution, 220
intervention, in Bolshevik Revolution, 146 ff., 197
U.S.S.R., recognition of, 128, 146 ff., 175, 177, 179, 182, 197, 201 ff., 217 ff., 228, 234
U.S.S.R., trade with, 174, 179, 182, 217 ff.
relationships with
Gumberg, Alexander, 179, 202 ff., 234
Robins, Raymond, 132, 146 ff., 173–74, 179, 182, 201 ff.
Stimson, Henry L., 228
Thompson, William Boyce, 128, 202, 206

Borodin, Michael, Soviet representative in China, 190

Boston Steamship Company, 57

Boxer Rebellion, 36, 38

Brandeis, Supreme Court Justice Louis D., 127, 156, 241

Breshko-Breshkovsky, Ekaterina Konstantinova, 99, 100, 101

Brest-Litovsk, negotiations and Treaty of
background, 112, 115
crisis in, 121, 122 ff., 133, 134
policy toward
Lenin, 122–23, 125, 133, 134, 140–41
Stalin, 125
State Department, 116–17, 126
Trotsky, 115 ff., 122 ff., 133 ff.

Brest-Litovsk (*continued*)
ratification of, 140–41
Robins group, efforts to influence, 112, 115 ff., 133 ff.
sequel to, 135, 141 ff., 155
Wilson's Fourteen Point Speech, relation to, 123–24, 126–27
Brookhart, United States Senator William, 222, 236
Brooklyn, cruiser U.S.S., 127
Brotherhood of Railway Clerks, Station Employees and Freight Handlers, 180
Brown, Lewis Edgar, 144
Brusilov, General A. A., 119
Brussels Conference of 1937, character and significance of, 249 ff., 254
Bryan, William Jennings, 81, 108, 226
Buchanan, Sir George, British Ambassador to Russia, 92, 112, 115
Buchanan, James, 18
Buchanan, John, 118
Buckler Mission to the U.S.S.R., 1918–1919 (*see* Buckler, William H.)
Buckler, William H., mission to U.S.S.R., 1918–1919, 160 ff.
Budd, Ralph, 216
Buick automobiles, 216
Bulgaria, 271, 272, 276
Bullard, Arthur, U.S. representative in Russia and the U.S.S.R., 88, 99, 111, 136, 137, 141
Bullard Machine Tool Company, 83
Bullitt, William Christian
as Ambassador to U.S.S.R., 241 ff.
background of, 159, 160
general policy of, 1918–19, 126, 159–60, 236
influence of, in 1933, 236, 238, 239 ff.
policy toward Franco-Soviet Pact, 247
U.S.S.R., mission to of 1919, 168 ff.

Cadillac automobiles, 216
Calder, John, 215
Calder, William M., 128
Caldwell, John K., 127
Campbell, Thomas, 216, 236
Cannes Resolution of 1922, 193, 196
Capitalism, response to Marxism (*see* Bolshevik Revolution problem posed by for the West)
Carpenter, Herbert L., policy and influence, 148, 153
Carr, Edward Hallett, 258
Carson, Lord, 118, 126

Cassini, Count, 53
Castlereagh, Viscount, 8, 14
Catherine II, 4–5
Cecil, Robert, 127
Century Magazine, 25, 27
Chadbourne, Thomas L., 100
Chaikovsky, Nikolai, 100
Chamberlain, Joseph, 32
Chang Tso Lin, 220, 221
Chase National Bank, U.S.-Russian and U.S.S.R. trade, role in, 29, 85, 211, 213 (*see* American-Russian Chamber of Commerce; Gumberg, Alexander; Schley, Reeve)
Chester, Rear Admiral Colby M., 75
Chiang Kai-shek
power, loss of, 219, 220 ff., 276 ff.
Sino-Soviet Dispute of 1929, policies in, 220 ff. (*see* China)
Chicago *Daily News,* 89, 144
Chicago Pneumatic Co., 224
Chicago *Tribune,* 93, 102, 234, 249
Chicherin, Soviet Foreign Commissar Georgii Vasilevich, 135, 143, 186, 187
Child, Richard Washburn, 127, 194, 197
China, economic penetration of, 22, 28, 29, 30, 35, 40–41, 58, 183 ff.
internal politics, 190, 219, 276 ff.
policy toward
Chinese Eastern Railroad, 166, 178, 188 ff., 219 ff.
Extraterritoriality, 178, 219 ff.
(*see* expansion; Manchuria; Washington Conference; and central personalities involved in Chinese affairs)
Chinchow-Aigun Railroad Project
origin and character of, 58, 60, 62, 63, 66 ff.
sequel to, 189
(*see* Neutralization of Manchurian Railways)
Chinese Eastern Railroad, control of, struggle for, 4, 55 ff., 83, 95, 106, 140 ff., 161 ff., 178, 183 ff., 219, 220 ff., 277
sale of, proposed, to U.S., 59–60, 62, 63, 65–69, 190
sale of, to Japan, 277
Chita, Government of (*see* Far Eastern Republic)
Choate, Joseph H., 64
Choate, William G., 43
Christian Science Monitor, 88
Churchill, Winston Spencer, 216, 242, 249

Churchill, Winston Spencer (*continued*)
  intervention, in Bolshevik Revolution, 167–68
U.S.S.R., policy toward during World War II, 262 ff.
U.S.S.R., policy toward settlement with after World War II, 262, 263 ff., 270 ff.
Churchill-Stalin Agreement of 1944
  character and purpose of, 271–72
  disruption of, and sequel to, 272 ff.
  origin of, 271
  views of, held by U.S., 272
  Yalta Conference, relation to, 272 ff.
Cigar Maker's Union, 181
City of Flint, 255
Civil War, American, 19–20
Civil War, Russian (*see* intervention, in Bolshevik Revolution)
Clark, Sir George, 118
Clay, Cassius M., 3
Clay, General Lucius M., 280
Clayton, Henry D., 156
Clemenceau, Georges, policy at the Paris Peace Conference, 162 ff., 168
Cleveland, Grover, 43
co-existence, Soviet theory of, 184–85
  (*see* Marxism, revision of; Soviet Union, overtures to the U.S.)
Colby, Bainbridge, 89, 147, 173–74
collective security, concept of (*see* Barthou, Louis; Litvinov, Maxim M.; Marxism, revision of; Soviet Union, overtures to the U.S.)
collectivization of agriculture, in Soviet Union, 216, 221, 243
Collins, Perry McD., 23
Colt, Samuel, 82
Columbia River Valley, 10
Commerce Department (*see* Hoover, Herbert)
Committee on Public Information, 88, 99, 101, 102, 136, 137, 156, 157
Committee of Workmen and Soldiers, 94
Communism (*see* Bolshevik Revolution)
Communist International (*see* Marxism, revision of; propaganda; Seventh Congress of the Communist International)
concession contracts, by U.S.S.R. to U.S. firms and individuals, 185, 211 ff.
  (*see* firms and individuals)
Congress of Soviets, 110
Congressional Elections of 1918, 132, 154
  (*see* Hays, Will; Robins, Ray-

Congressional Elections of 1918 (*cont.*)
  mond; Thompson, William Boyce)
Consolidated Machine Tool Corporation, 218
Consortium, First (1909)
  origin and original purpose, 62 ff.
  U.S. participation in, view held of by Taft, William Howard, and State Department, 63, 65–67
  U.S. withdrawal from, 79–80
Consortium, Second (1918)
  U.S. participation in, reason for, 166 ff.
Consortium, proposed (1929)
  (*see* Lamont, Thomas; Sino-Soviet Dispute of 1929)
Constituent Assembly, Russian, dissolution of, 125–26
containment, U.S. policy of
  origin of, 1917, Chapter V, 105–7, 116–18, 123–24, 127 ff.
  nature of, 279 ff.
  revival of, 1945–47, 279 ff.
Continental Congress, 4
continental expansion (*see* expansion)
Continental System, Napoleon's, 6–7
Convention of 1824, Russo-American, 16–17
Coolidge, President Calvin, 173, 177, 204 ff. (*see* Borah, William E.; Hughes, Charles Evans; recognition of U.S.S.R.; Robins, Raymond)
Cooper, Hugh A., U.S. engineer
  background, 128, 214–15
  U.S.S.R., relations with, 214–15
Cordon Sanitaire (*see* Clemenceau, Georges; containment; intervention in Bolshevik Revolution)
Corse, Frederick M., 100, 148–53, 159
cotton exporters, U.S., 35, 82
  Russia, trade with, 36
  U.S.S.R., role in recognition of, 211–12
  U.S.S.R., trade with, 211–12, 213, 236
Cox, U.S. Representative Samuel S., 26
de Cram, Madame Matilda, 113–14
Cramp Shipbuilding Company, 29
Crane, Charles R., U.S.-Russian and U.S.S.R. relations, role in, 86 ff., 96, 113
Crane, Richard, 107, 108, 149
Creel, George, 88, 119
  Bolshevik Revolution, policy toward, 123, 126
  Provisional Government, policy toward, 101–2

Creel, George (*continued*)
German-Agent theory of Bolshevik Revolution, role in, 157
Crimean War, 18, 20, 21
Crosby, Oscar T., intervention, role in, 117, 120
Cuba, U.S. interest in, 13–14
Curtiss Wright Corporation, 237
Curzon Line, 267–68 (*see* Polish Question)
Cutting, Bronson, 223
Czech Legion in Russia, intervention, role in, 151–52
Czechoslovakia, 158, 263 (*see* Munich Crisis)

Dairen (*see* Port Arthur)
Dairen Conference, 1921–22, 187
Dalny, 56, 57
Dana, Minister to Russia Francis, 4–5
Danbury Hatter's Case, 82
Daniels, Josephus, 127
Dardanelles, Straits of, 92, 167 (*see* Lausanne Conference; Wilson, Woodrow)
Darrow, Clarence, 43, 80
Daugherty, Harry S. (*see* Daugherty Scandal)
Daugherty Scandal, significance of in U.S.-U.S.S.R. relations, 207
Davies, Ambassador to Soviet Union Joseph E., 248, 251, 266
Davis, Arthur Powell, 217
Davis, Jerome, 167
Davis, Norman H., role in and views of Brussels Conference, 250
Davison, Henry P., 63, 67
Red Cross Mission to Russia, role in, 88–90, 96, 97, 100–1, 111, 144
Debs, Eugene, 155
debts, Tsarist and Provisional Government's
to U.S., issue of in U.S.-U.S.S.R. relations, 179–80, 219, 224, 234, 237 ff., 241 ff.
U.S.S.R., view of, 179–80, 244 ff.
Dekansov, Soviet Ambassador to Nazi Germany, 231
Denby, Charles, Jr., 34, 58, 62
Denikin, Anton Ivanovich, intervention, role in, 171
depression of 1921, significance of in U.S.-U.S.S.R. relations, 179, 180–81
depression of 1929, significance of in U.S.-U.S.S.R. relations, 179, 217 ff., 233

Dilke, Sir Charles W., 41
Dillon, John F., 43
Dillon, Reed and Company, 190
Dingley Tariff, 45
Dixon, Frederick H., 88
Dixon, Walter F., 150
Dodge, Cleveland H., 88
Dollar Diplomacy (*see* expansion; Harriman, Edward H.; Straight, Willard)
Dolliver, Senator Jonathan P., 42
Donetz State Coal Trust, 212
Duane, William, 6
Duncan, James, 87
du Pont de Nemours Corporation, 216
Duranty, Walter, 179, 235, 238

Easley, Ralph, 137, 153
economic imperialism (*see* expansion)
Economic Bill of Rights, relation of to Teheran Conference, 269–70
Eden, Foreign Secretary Anthony, 263–64, 266–67, 271
Eighteenth Congress of the Communist Party of the Soviet Union, 251–52
Eisenhower, General Dwight D., 280
ELAS, 273
Emery, Enoch, 35
Equitable Trust Company, 171
Equitable Trust and Life Insurance Company, 83
Erie Central Labor Union, 180
expansion
France, economic, 66
France, territorial, 5, 13–14, 20
Germany, economic, 29, 66, 75–76, 132, 234 ff.
Germany, territorial, 132, 234 ff.
Great Britain, economic, 14, 19, 66, 75–77
Great Britain, territorial, 4 ff.
Japan, economic, 46–47, 61–62, 132, 138–39, 178 ff., 225, 234
Japan, territorial, 43, 46–47, 60, 61–62, 132, 138–39, 178 ff., 219, 225, 234
Russian, economic, 3, 28–29, 49, 75–77
Russian, territorial, 3–4, 10, 21–22, 41, 43
U.S., economic, 3, 16, 19, 23, 28, 29, 30, 31, 33–34, 35, 40–41, 49, 51 ff., 76–77, 148, 177, 178 ff.
U.S., territorial, 3, 9, 11–13, 15–17, 21–22, 31, 177–78
(*see* Chinese Eastern Railroad; Man-

expansion (*continued*)
    churia; oil; personalities involved)
Export–Import Bank, First, origin and
    purpose of, 244–46
exports, U.S.
    to Russia, 36, 82 ff.
    to U.S.S.R., 124, 179, 202 ff., 208 ff.,
        217 ff., 236
    (*see* specific commodities, companies,
        and items)
extraterritoriality, 178, 219 ff.

famines, Russian, U.S. aid in, 27, 42 (*see*
    American Relief Administration)
Far Eastern Republic, character and
    policies of, 185, 186 ff.
Federal Bureau of Investigation, 174
finance capitalism, development of in U.S.,
    83 (*see* Morgan, House of)
Finance Ministry, Russian, policy toward
    U.S. (*see* Kokovtzev, V. N.; Witte,
    S. U.)
financial interests (*see* expansion; firms;
    personalities involved)
Finland (*see* Soviet-Finnish War)
First National Bank, 66, 85
Fischer, Louis, 179
Fish, Senator Hamilton, 19
Fish, Representative Hamilton Jr., 223 ff.
Flint, Charles R., 86
food, as anti-Bolshevik weapon, 159 ff.
Ford Motor Company, 216
Foreign Affairs, 227, 279, 280
Forrestal, Secretary of Defense James,
    275, 278, 279, 280
Forsyth, John, 17
Fort Sumter, 20
Foster, John W., 32
Fourteen Points of Woodrow Wilson,
    origin of and references to U.S.S.R.
    in, 123, 126–27
Fourth All-Russian Soviet, 135, 140–41
Fox, Gustavus V., 21
Francis, Ambassador to Russia David Ro-
    land
    appointment and background, 84, 108
    general policy, 85, 108
    German-agent theory of Bolshevik Revo-
        lution, role in development of, 92,
        136
    policies toward
        Bolshevik Revolution and U.S.S.R.,
            111 ff., 115 ff., 135 ff.
        intervention, 136 ff.
        Provisional Government, 92, 94 ff.

Francis, David (*continued*)
    relationship with
        de Cram, Madame Matilda, 113–14,
            165
        Judson, William V., 94, 113–14, 115 ff.
        Robins, Raymond, 114 ff., 120 ff., 131,
            136 ff., 142, 144–45, 203
        Summers, Maddin, 92, 120, 142, 144–
            45
Franco-Japanese Treaty of 1907, 57
Franco-Soviet Pact, 247 ff.
Frazier, Arthur H., 94
Free Russia, 77
Freyn Engineering Company, 215
Frick, Henry Clay, 28
Friends of Russian Freedom, 25, 45, 80
fur trade, role in U.S.-Russian relations,
    6 ff.

Gay, E. F., 85
General Electric Company, role in U.S.-
    Russian and U.S.S.R. relations, 83,
    150, 181, 210, 215, 237
General Motors Corporation, role in U.S.-
    U.S.S.R. relations, 218, 224
Geneva Disarmament Conference of 1927,
    191
Genoa Conference of 1922
    oil, role of in, 194 ff.
    origin, 193–94
    policies of, at
        Great Britain, 195 ff.
        Standard Oil Company, 194 ff.
        U.S., 178, 193 ff., 199
        U.S.S.R., 196 ff.
German-agent theory of Bolshevik Revo-
    lution
    intervention, use of to explain, 92, 105,
        117, 127, 139, 142–43, 154–57
    origin of, 92, 105, 109–11, 114, 116–18,
        124, 127, 136, 139, 142–47
    Sisson Documents, relation to, 124, 136,
        154–57
    red scare, relation to, 136, 154–57
Golder, Professor Frank A., views on
    American Relief Administration,
    201
Goldfogle, Representative Henry M., 77
Gompers, Samuel
    influence of, 137, 138, 153, 206
    U.S.S.R., policy toward, 137, 138, 181,
        182, 206 (*see* American Federation
        of Labor)
Goodrich, James P., efforts to secure
    recognition of U.S.S.R., 202 ff.

Goraynoff, Natalie, 113
Gorky, Maxim, 200
Greece, agreement concerning made by Stalin and Churchill, 271–72, 273
Gregory, T. T. C., 172
Grew, Joseph C., 237
Grey, Sir Edward, 73
Griscom, Lloyd C., 55, 250
Guaranty Trust Company, 85
Guchkov, Minister of War Alexander, 92
Gumberg, Alexander
  background of, 110–11
  general policy of, 111, 179, 202, 204, 234
  influence of, 110–11, 124, 179, 202 ff., 217, 234, 236 ff.
  relationships with
    American-Russian Chamber of Commerce, 213, 217, 236
    Borah, William E., 202 ff., 234
    Hoover, Herbert, 202
    Robins, Raymond, 110–11, 124, 144, 179, 202 ff.
    Schley, Reeve, 211 ff.
    Thacher, Judge Thomas D., 211
  U.S.-U.S.S.R. economic relations, role in, 124, 179, 202 ff., 208 ff., 217 ff., 236

Hague Conference of 1922, 178, 197
Halifax, Lord, 249
Hall, Admiral, 118
Hamilton, Alexander, 5
Hammer, A. J., 211
Hammond, John Hays
  Abrogation of Treaty of 1832, view of, 79
  U.S.-Russian economic relations, 74–75
Hanna, Marcus A., 137
Harbin, city of, in U.S.-Russian relations, 68, 70, 72
Harding, President Warren G., 173, 177
  Robins, Raymond, agreement with, 174, 182, 201, 204
  U.S.S.R., views on, 174, 190, 198
Harding Scandals (see Daugherty Scandal)
Harper, Professor Samuel N.
  background of, 86–87
  U.S.-Russian and U.S.S.R. relations, 86 ff., 93, 107–8, 132, 137, 142, 147, 149, 152–53, 156, 159
Harper's Weekly, 41
Harriman, Edward H., role in U.S.-Russian relations, 44, 51 ff.
Harriman, W. Averell

Harriman, W. Averell (continued)
  U.S.S.R., ambassador to, 272, 275
  U.S.S.R., economic concession contract with, 212–13, 219
  U.S.S.R., policy toward after World War II, 275, 279, 280
Harris, Levett, 5, 9
Harrison, President Benjamin, 27
Hawaii, U.S. control of, 31, 32, 44
Hay, Secretary of State John
  Adams, Henry, relationship with, 32, 34, 39
  background of, 31–32, 39
  general policy of, 31–32, 36, 39
  Open Door Notes of, 32, 33, 36, 38, 65
  Russia, policy toward, 31–32, 36–37, 38–39, 43
Haymarket Riot, 28
Hays, Will, 154, 174, 217
Heid, August, 150, 153
Heine, Heinrich, 242
Hempy-Cooper Manufacturing Company, 218
Herron, Professor George, 167
Hill, George W., 127
Hill, James J., 44
Hippisley, Alfred E., 32
Hitchcock, Eathan A., 35
Hitler, Adolf, 231
Hoffman, Max, 124
Holmes, Supreme Court Justice Oliver Wendell, 156, 241
Holy Alliance, 8, 9, 14–15
Homestead Strike, 28
Hoover, Herbert Clarke
  background of, 150, 170–71
  policies toward
    Bela Kun, 171 ff.
    Bolshevik Revolution, 149, 160, 166, 170, 177–78, 229
    Japan, attack on Manchuria of 1931, 219, 222, 225 ff., 255
    U.S.S.R., famine aid to, 193, 198, 200–1
    U.S.S.R., relations with, 173, 175, 177, 178, 179, 181 ff., 193 ff., 197 ff., 200–1, 202 ff., 219 ff., 222, 255, 280
  relationships with
    Gumberg, Alexander, 202
    Hughes, Charles Evans, 178, 181–82, 191 ff., 202 ff.
    Robins, Raymond, 182, 208
Hopkins, Harry
  Atlantic Conference, role at, 262
  Stalin, conversations with, 1941, 262

Hopkins, Harry (*continued*)
  Stalin, conversations with, 1945, 275–76
Houghton, Ambassador to Germany Alanson B., 198
House, Colonel Edward M.
  policies toward
    Bolshevik Revolution, 109, 118, 123, 126, 132, 136, 144, 149, 151, 158, 168, 169
    Japan, 137, 139–40, 149, 151, 152
    Provisional Government, 86 ff., 94, 95, 96, 100, 101
Howard, Roy W., 88
Howe, Julia Ward, 25
Hsinmintun-Fakumen Railway Project, 57–58 (*see* Chinchow-Aigun Railway)
Hughes, Secretary of State Charles E., 114, 173, 175, 217
  general policy of, 177–78, 191–92
  influence of, 198, 202 ff.
  policies toward
    China, 183, 184, 185, 186 ff., 219
    Chinese Eastern Railway, 178, 183, 188 ff.
    Genoa Conference, 178, 193 ff.
    Hague Conference, 178, 197
    Japan, 185, 186 ff.
    Lausanne Conference, 178, 199–200
    Washington Conference, 178, 183–84, 186 ff.
    U.S.S.R., overtures from and recognition of, 178, 179, 181 ff., 189–90, 193 ff., 197–98, 200, 202 ff., 280
  relationships with
    Bedford, A. C., 195 ff.
    Hoover, H. C., 178, 181–82, 191 ff., 202 ff.
    Robins, Raymond, 182
Hukuang Railways Loan, 51, 62–63, 65–66 (*see* Harriman, Edward H.; Straight, Willard; Taft, William Howard)
Hull, Secretary of State Cordell
  policies of toward U.S.S.R. and debt negotiations, 239 ff.
  international collaboration with, 246, 251, 252, 255, 260, 261, 263, 271–72
  negotiations with, 246, 247, 248, 251, 261, 263, 270, 273
  World War II, 260–61, 263, 270–73
  Troyanovsky, Soviet Ambassador Alexander, conversations with, 231, 244 ff.
  views on

Hull, Secretary of State Cordell (*cont.*)
  Churchill-Stalin Agreement of 1945, 271–72
  U.S.S.R., recognition of, 3, 235, 237 ff., 243
Hungary, 272
Huntington, William Chapin, 112–13, 142
Hutchins, H. Grosvenor, role in American Red Cross Commission to Russia, 100–1

Ickes, Harold, 89
Illiador, Monk, 93
imperialism (*see* expansion)
Independent Order of B'nai B'rith, 43
Industrial Bank of Moscow, 211
Inter-Allied Finance Council, 117
Inter-Allied Passport Bureau, 114
Inter-Allied Railway Agreement and Committee, origin and purpose, 163, 166, 173
  control of, struggle for between Japan and the U.S., 186, 187 ff. (*see* Chinese Eastern Railroad)
International Association of Machinists, 180
International Banking Corporation, 63
International Garment Worker's Union, 211
International General Electric, 224 (*see* General Electric)
International Harvester Company, U.S.-Russian and U.S.S.R. relations, role in, 83, 141, 150, 153, 210, 215, 216 (*see* Agricultural Machinery interests)
International Paper Company, 224
International Securities Corporation, 219
International Workers of the World, 155
intervention in Bolshevik Revolution
  Allied pressure for, 118–19, 131, 135 ff., 143 ff.
  British, 118–19, 127, 131, 132, 135 ff.
  Bolsheviks, view of, 143, 151, 161
  efforts to forestall, 118 ff., 133 ff.
  efforts to terminate, 157 ff.
  French, 118–19, 127, 131, 132, 135 ff.
  German-Agent theory of Bolshevik Revolution, role in, of U.S., 116–18, 124, 127, 136, 139, 142–43, 154–57
  Japanese, 120, 131, 132, 143 ff.
  Paris Peace Conference, role of, at, 157 ff.
  U.S.
    character of, 105–7, 116–18, 119, 123,

intervention in Bolshevik Rev. (*cont.*)
127–29, 131–32, 138, 148 ff., 160 ff.,
280
economic interests, pressure for, by,
132, 142–43, 145, 148 ff., 171
(*see* containment; central personalities)
intervention, principle of in U.S. foreign
policy, 157–58, 177–78, 183, 191–92,
219, 272 ff.
Iranian Crisis of 1946, 276 (*see* Persia)
Iron Age, 148
Isaak, Abraham, 81
isolation, U.S. policy of
actual character of contrasted with traditional view of, 158, 178, 183,
190 ff.
Izvestia, 184, 228, 248
Izvolsky, Russian Foreign Minister A.,
general policy of, 49, 58, 63
policies of toward
Chinchow-Aigun Railway Project, 60,
67 ff.
Knox Neutralization Plan, 67 ff.
U.S., collaboration with, 58, 60, 63,
67 ff.

Jackson, Andrew, 10
Jameson, John F., 156
Japan (*see* American-Russian and
U.S.S.R. relations; Chinese East-
ern Railroad; expansion; interven-
tion; neutralization; Russo-Japan-
ese War; Washington Conference)
Jefferson, Thomas, and relations with
Russia, 5, 6, 7, 8
Jewish Publication Society, 43
Joffe, Adolf, 121
Johnson Act, significance of in U.S.-
U.S.S.R. relations, 244–45
Johnson, U.S. Senator Hiram, 174, 223
influence of, 154, 157, 161, 165 ff.
intervention, policy toward, 152, 153–
54, 161, 164
relationships with
Borah, William E., 132, 146 ff.
Robins, Raymond, 146 ff., 174
Johnson, Louis A., 238
Jones, Jesse, 236, 261
Judson, Colonel William V., 138
background, 87, 94
Bolshevik Revolution, policy toward,
112 ff., 126
recall of, 116–17, 122
Robins, Raymond, collaboration with,
112 ff.

Judson, Colonel William V. (*continued*)
U.S.-U.S.S.R. relations, role in, 87, 94,
96, 101, 102, 109, 112, 113–14, 126
(*see* Brest Litovsk, Intervention)
July Offensive, Russian of 1917, 93

Kahn, Albert Inc., 215
Kaledin, Alexei Maximovich, 103
intervention, role in, 117, 119–20
Kalgan to Kiakhta Railroad Proposal, 73,
75
Kamchatka, peninsula of, 185
Kawamoto, Japanese Army Lieutenant,
225
Kelley, Robert F., 280
influence and policy recommendations
of, 208–9, 219, 224, 228, 239 ff., 243
Kellogg, Secretary of State Frank B., 208,
219
Kellogg-Briand Peace Pact, 220–21, 222,
226, 227
Kellor, Frances A., 89
Kennan, George, 171
background of, 24–25, 27
general policy of, 24–25, 26–27, 45–47
influence of, 24–25, 27, 34, 45, 80, 93
policies of toward
Abrogation of Treaty of 1832, 26–27,
28, 77, 80
Russo-Japanese War, 45–47
U.S.-Russian and U.S.S.R. relations,
24–25, 26, 27, 28, 34, 45, 93
Kennan, George Frost, influence and
policy of, 258, 259, 270, 277, 279 ff.
Kent, U.S. Tariff Commissioner William,
145, 147
Kerensky, Alexander
Provisional Government of, 91, 94 ff.,
109, 110
Thompson, William Boyce, 91, 94–95
Kerth, Monroe C., 111, 113
King, Rufus, 5
King, William H., 203
Kirov, Sergei Mironovich, assasination of,
significance of, 242, 243
Kishineff Pogrom, 42–43
Knox, British General Alfred, 102–3, 115
Knox, Secretary of State Philander C.,
174
background of, 64
general policy of, 62, 63–65, 66 ff.
policies toward
Neutralization of Manchurian Rail-
ways, 68 ff., 74, 163, 221
Treaty of 1832, abrogation of, 79, 84

Kokovtzev, Russian Finance Minister V. N., policy of collaboration with U.S., 54–55, 60, 66 ff.
Kolchak, Admiral Aleksander, intervention, role in, 106, 158, 170 ff.
Komura, Japanese Foreign Minister, 56
Konoye, Prince, 248, 249
Koppers Construction Company, 215
Korea, struggle for control of, 21, 28, 29, 30, 37–39, 43, 56, 84
  Kennan, George, view of, 44
Kornilov, Lavr Georgievich, 120
  Provisional Government, attempted coup against, 97–98, 99, 103
Kropotkin, Prince Peter, 99
Kropotkin, Sasha, 99
von Kuhlmann, Richard, 121, 122
Kuhn, Loeb and Company, 27, 51, 107, 180–81 (see Harriman, Edward H.; Schiff, Jacob)
Kurile Islands, 10
Kuropatkin, Russian General, 38, 39, 93
Kuznets Basin, 211

La Follette, Robert M., Sr., 223
La Follette's Seaman Act, 174
La Guardia, Fiorello, 165, 222
Lamont, Thomas W., 194–95
  background of, 112
  influence of, 112, 118, 126
  Japan, supports against U.S.S.R., 166, 183, 221
Lamsdorf, Vladimir Nicholas, 37
land question, Russian, 103 (see collectivization of agriculture)
Lansing, Secretary of State Robert
  influence of, 86, 89, 93, 137 ff.
  Judson, William V., recall of, 122
  policies toward
    Bolshevik Revolution, 105 ff., 116 ff., 137 ff.
    intervention in Bolshevik Revolution, 105–7, 116–18, 119, 123, 124, 127–29, 131–32, 138, 148 ff., 159 ff.
    Provisional Government, 87, 91 ff., 109
  relationships with
    advisors in State Department, 86–87, 93, 107, 121, 137 ff.
    Robins, Raymond, 120–21, 144–45
    Summers, Maddin, 144–45
    Wilson, Woodrow, 116, 117, 123–24, 137 ff., 145–47, 159–60
  social philosophy of, 91, 107, 116–17, 123, 159

Lausanne Conference on the Near East, 1922
  U.S. policy at, 178, 199–200
  U.S. Navy, recommendations for, 199–200
Law of Civilization and Decay, The, 33, 40
Lawson, Victor F., 89
League of Armed Neutrality, 4
Leahy, Admiral William D., 274
Lehigh Machine Company, 180
loan, U.S.S.R., request for, 275, 278–79
Leningrad Electrical Institute, 215
Lend Lease to U.S.S.R.
  authorization for, 261
  termination of, 275, 278
Lenin, Vladimir Ilich, 92, 103–4, 109
  foreign policy, cornerstone of, 114, 125, 134 ff., 169, 184, 191, 208, 227, 252
  general policy of, 93–94, 98, 122–23, 133, 211
  German agent, portrayal of as (see German-agent theory of Bolshevik Revolution)
  intervention, view of, 143
  Twenty-One Theses on Peace, January, 1918, 124–25
  relationship with Robins, Raymond, 124 ff., 128, 133, 134 ff., 238
  U.S., proposes collaboration with, 106, 114, 128, 133, 134 ff., 169, 184–85, 227, 252
Lenin-Robins Plan for U.S.-U.S.S.R. Economic Collaboration, 141–42, 147, 206
Liaotung Peninsula, 28
Lilienthal, David, 279
Litvinov, Soviet Foreign Commissar Maxim M., 190, 222, 236
  broad policy of, 169, 181, 185, 239 ff., 245 ff.
  Wilson, Woodrow, message to, 1918, 161 (see debt; recognition of the U.S.S.R.)
Litvinov-Roosevelt Negotiations of 1933, 239–41, 244
Lloyd George, British Prime Minister David, 186, 199
  intervention, policy toward prior to the Paris Peace Conference, 118–19
  intervention, policy toward at Paris Peace Conference, 162 ff.
Lockhart, Robert Bruce, 128
  appointment, circumstances of, 118–19
  intervention, role in, 133 ff.
Lodge, U.S. Senator Henry Cabot, 86, 203

Lodge, U.S. Senator Henry Cabot (cont.)
background of, 32
expansion, policy toward, 32, 34, 42
relationship with Adams, Brooks, 42
Logan Act of 1798, 9
London Economic Conference, 1933 (see Bullitt, William C.; Moley, Raymond)
London Times, 19, 226
Los Angeles Times (see Vanderlip, Washington B.)
Lowden, Frank, 174
Lowell, James Russell, 25
Lvov, Prince Georgii Eugenevich
Provisional Government of, 85–86, 93
Provisional Government, crisis of, view of, 148

MacDonald Engineering Company, 236
MacDowell, George, 217
MacDowell, Howard J., 217
MacGowan, David B.
German-agent theory of Bolshevik Revolution, role in, 142–43
Robins, Raymond, role in recall of, 144–45
machine tool industry, U.S.
trade, with Russia, 36, 83
trade, with U.S.S.R., 211, 218, 224, 261
role in recognition of U.S.S.R., 218, 236 ff.
Madison, President James, 8
Madison, Wisconsin, Federation of Labor, 180
Magnitogorsk steel center, 215, 238
Mahan, Captain Alfred Thayer, 39, 47
Manchester Guardian, 152
Manchu Dynasty, 21–22
Manchukuo, 228 (see expansion, Japan; Manchuria)
Manchuria, 19
economic life of, domination of by Japan, 51, 56 ff., 139–40
economic life of, domination of by U.S., 37, 38–39, 43–44, 47
Mukden Incident, 1931, 225 ff.
penetration of and struggle for control of by Japan, Russia, U.S. and U.S.S.R., 23, 28–30, 36 ff., 51 ff., 56ff., 106, 128–29, 138 ff., 151 ff., 163 ff., 170, 175, 219 ff., 225 ff., 237, 276–77
Russo-Japanese War, sequel to, in, 46–47, 51 ff., 140
(see Chinese Eastern Railroad; Harri-

Manchuria (continued)
man, Edward H.; neutralization of Manchurian Railways; Straight, Willard)
Manchurian Bank, proposals for, 58–59, 60–61, 63, 65
manganese deposits in U.S.S.R., development of (see Harriman, W. Averell)
manganese interests, U.S., oppose U.S. recognition of U.S.S.R., 223
March, General Peyton C., 151
Marcy, Secretary of State William L., 18, 19
Marshall, General George C., 265, 278
Marx, Karl, 114, 283 (see Marxism; Soviet Union, overtures to U.S.)
Marxism
classical theory of, 114
classical, revision of by Lenin and Stalin, 125, 184–85, 208, 227, 252
Masaryk, Thomas G., 145, 159
Mayer, Judge Charles, 54
McAdoo, Secretary of the Treasury William Gibbs, 78, 86, 127
McCall, Representative Samuel W., 78
McCarter, R. D., 150
McCormick, Cyrus, role in U.S.-Russian and U.S.S.R. relations, 84, 86, 87, 94, 95, 149, 152–53, 159, 165
McCormick, Vance, 118
intervention, policy toward, 153, 166
Provisional Government, policy toward, 100, 101
McKee, Arthur G. and Company, 215
McKinley, President William, 31, 32, 81
Mellon, Secretary of the Treasury Andrew J., 223
Merchant's Association of New York, 150, 246
Meyer, George von L., 46, 87, 108
Miles, Basil
background, 87, 108
policies and influence of in U.S.-U.S.S.R. relations, 87, 90, 117, 122, 127, 128, 137, 138, 141, 146, 147, 280
Miliukov, Pavel Nikolaevich, general policy of, 92, 167
Miller, Arthur, 231
Millspaugh, Arthur S., 76 ff. (see oil; Persia)
Milner, Lord Alfred, 118–19
missionaries, role in U.S. expansion
Russian view of, 45

Mitchell, John, 81
Mitsui Bussan Karsha, Japanese cotton export syndicate, 57
Mohamed Ali, 77
Moley, Raymond, 236
Molotov, Vyacheslav, 252, 265
  U.S.-U.S.S.R. relations, view of, 253
Molotov-Roosevelt Talks, 1942, 264–65
Monroe Doctrine, 20
  Russia, relation to, 13, 16
Monroe, President James, 14
  U.S.-Russian relations, view of, 8, 11, 16
Montague, Charles Edward, 1
Mooney, James D., 237
Moore, John Bassett, 28
Morgan, Edward V., 56
Morgan, House of, 107, 118, 194–95, 216
  Asia, expansion into, 51 ff.
  intervention in Bolshevik Revolution, role in, 171
  U.S.-Russian and U.S.S.R. relations, role in, 51 ff., 80 ff., 88–90, 148, 149, 180, 183, 185
  (see American Red Cross Commission to Russia; Chinese Eastern Railway; expansion; Harriman, Edward H.; Hukuang Railway Loan; Manchuria; Persia; Straight, Willard; Washington Conference)
Morgan, Thomas A., 236
Morgenthau, Henry, 86
Morgenthau, Henry, Jr., 255, 274
Morris, George W., 180
Morris, U.S. Minister to Sweden Ira N., 86, 87
Morrison, Samuel E., 171
Morrow, Dwight, 94, 97, 100, 101
Motono, Baron, 49
Mott, John R., 87
Muchnic, Charles M., 150
Munich Crisis
  sequel to, in policy of U.S.S.R., 252 ff., 254–55, 263, 271
  Western Powers, policy of in, 226, 232, 234, 249, 251, 254–55
  U.S.S.R., policy of in, 234, 254–55
Mukden, city and administrative center of, struggle for control of in U.S.-Russian relations, 47 (see Knox, Philander C.)
Mukden Incident, 1931 (see Manchuria)
Mussolini, Benito, 241
Mutual Life Insurance Company (see Morgan, House of)

Naphtha Syndicate of U.S.S.R., 214
National Association of Manufacturers, 213
National Citizen's Committee for Abrogation of the Treaty of 1832, 78
National City Bank, 171
  U.S.-Russian economic relations, role in, 66, 85, 88, 224
  U.S.-U.S.S.R. economic relations, role in, 135, 136, 153, 224
  (see Gumberg, Alexander; Schley, Reeve)
National Civic Federation, 137, 153
  U.S.-U.S.S.R. relations, role in, 137, 181, 223, 238
National Council of Catholic Women, 238
National Industrial Recovery Act, 232, 236
National Intelligencer, Washington, D.C., 11, 12
Nationalist Party, Chinese, division within, 219 (see Chiang Kai-shek)
Navy, United States, policy concerning Dardenelles Straits, 199–200
Nazi Germany, 215
  domestic policy, 233–34
  foreign policy, 192, 233–34
Nazi-Soviet Pact, 1939, 252 ff., 259
Nazi-Soviet War, 1941, 261 ff.
Nelson, H. L., 41
Netzlin, Eduard, of the Bank of Paris, 54–55, 63
Neutral Rights, in U.S.-Russian relations, 5, 6, 8, 9–10, 18–19
neutralization of Manchurian Railways, plan for
  character and purpose, 68 ff., 163
  (see Harriman, Edward H.; Knox, Philander C.; Straight, Willard; Sino-Soviet Dispute of 1929)
Nevslakovsky, Russian General, 102, 103
Newburyport Herald, 12
New Deal, character of, 232–34
Newport News Shipbuilding and Dry Dock Company, 215
newspapers, U.S., treatment of Russian Revolutions of 1917, 87–88 (see German-agent theory of Bolshevik Revolution, specific newspapers)
New York Air Brake Company, 83
New York Bank of Commerce, 100
New York Chamber of Commerce, 29–30, 35
New York Herald, 22, 23
New York Life Insurance Company, 83, 85, 100, 148, 218

New York *Spectator*, 16
New York *Times*, 156, 198, 248, 252
New York *World*, 167
Nicholas I, 18
Nicholas II, 27, 38, 53, 55, 93
Niles' *Weekly Register*, 11, 12, 16, 17
Nitrogen Engineering Company, 216
Norris, U.S. Senator George W., 89
Northwest Coast of North America, competing claims to, 10–11, 12–13, 13 ff.
Novoye Vremya, 45
Nueselle, French General, 102

Oddie, U.S. Senator Tasker L., 223 ff.
Oil
diplomacy of, 75, 194 ff.
open door in U.S.S.R. and, 197
Persia, struggle for in, 75, 194 ff.
U.S.S.R., struggle for in, 194 ff.
Okuma, Count, views on significance of Russo-Japanese War, 56
Olney, Secretary of State Richard, 32
Open Door Policy
Germany, use of by, 76
U.S., development and use of by, 32, 33–34, 36, 38, 65, 69, 106, 219, 225, 228
U.S.S.R., attempt to apply to by U.S., 165, 166, 197
Oregon Territory, competition for, 7, 13, 16, 17, 21
Oudin, M. A., 150
Oumansky, Soviet Ambassador to the U.S., 261
outlawry of war (*see* Kellogg-Briand Pact)
Outlook Magazine, 41, 44, 88, 167, 224
overseas economic expansion (*see* expansion)
overseas territorial expansion (*see* expansion)
Owen, U.S. Senator Robert L., 89, 128

Pact of Paris (*see* Kellogg-Briand Pact)
Page, U.S. Ambassador to Great Britain Walter H., 86, 118
Panic of 1907, 57
Paris Exposition of 1900, plan to transfer U.S. exhibits from there to Russia, 35
Parsons, William B., 41
Patriotic Alliance, opposition to recognition of U.S.S.R., 247
peace societies, U.S., 9
Penrose, Boies, 174

Pepperell Manufacturing Company, pressure for expansion into Asia, 35, 36
Pershing, General John J., 151
Persia
economic penetration of, by
Germany, 75–76
Great Britain, 19, 75–77, 194 ff.
Russia, 49, 75–77
U.S., 49, 76–77, 194 ff.
financial difficulties of, 77–78, 194 ff.
(*see* Iranian Crisis; Schuster, W. Morgan)
Pettit, Walter, 168
Philadelphia *National Gazette and Literary Register*, 16
Philippine Islands, 31 (*see* expansion)
Phillips, William, 122, 239, 280
background of, 64
influence of, 64, 70, 89, 107–8, 116, 117, 121, 126, 137
Pierce, Herbert H. D., 35, 36, 37
Podolsky, Michael M., of Provisional Government, 87
pogroms, Russian
policies toward, of
Kennan, George, 26, 27
Russian Government, 26–27, 42, 43, 49
Schiff, Jacob, 27, 43, 61, 79
Straus, Oscar, 27, 43
U.S.-Russian relations, impact upon, 26–27, 41, 42–43
(*see* Abrogation of the Commercial Treaty of 1832)
Poletica, Pierre de, 9
Polish Government-in-Exile of World War II, policy of, 266, 267–68, 270–71, 273
Polish Question
U.S.-Russian relations, role in, 17–18, 20
U.S.-U.S.S.R. relations, role in, 266–68, 273 ff.
Polish Revolt of 1830, 17–18
Polish Revolt of 1863, 20
Polish-Soviet War, 1920, policy of U.S. during, 173
Political Refugees Defense League, 80
Polk, Frank, 103
background and influence of, 93, 107–8, 111, 127
policies of, toward
Bolshevik Revolution, 122
intervention, 154, 157, 165–66
Poole, de Witt Clinton
policies toward

Poole, de Witt Clinton (*continued*)
Bolshevik Revolution, 119, 145
intervention, 151
Poole, Frederick C., 111
Porter, E. C., 150
Port Arthur, control of, issue of in Far Eastern politics, 28, 30, 36, 38, 56, 276–77
Portsmouth Treaty of 1905 (*see* Russo-Japanese War)
Potsdam Conference, 276
Pouren Defense Committee, 80
Pouren, Jan Janoff, issue of extradition of, 80–82
Prinkipo Conference
origin and purpose of, 164
collapse of, 166 ff.
Products Exchange corporation, 212
propaganda, issue of in U.S.-U.S.S.R. relations, 208–9, 240 ff.
Provisional Government of March, 1917 of Russian Revolution, 49, 80, 85 ff.
character of, 92 ff.
difficulties of, 92 ff.
July, 1917, crisis of, 93
Kornilov Crisis of, 97–98
policies toward, of
American Red Cross Commission to Russia, 93 ff.
Francis, David R., 92, 94 ff.
Great Britain, 91, 93
Lansing, Robert, 91 ff.
Robins, Raymond, 94 ff.
Root Mission, 92, 93–95
Thompson, William Boyce, 91, 94 ff.
U.S., 91 ff., 109, 148
Wilson, Woodrow, 86 ff., 92 ff.
Putnam's Magazine, 24

Quincy, Josiah, 41

Rada, Ukranian Government of, 122, 133
Radek, Karl, 190, 227, 228, 238
Radio Corporation of America, 216
Railways (*see* Chinese Eastern Railroad; Harriman, Edward H.; and other specific railroads and personalities)
Rasputin, Gregory, 93
Reading, Lord, 118
Recession of 1937, significance of in U.S.-U.S.S.R. relations, 249–50
recognition of the U.S.S.R., by U.S., 235 ff.
opposition to, 203 ff., 223 ff., 237 ff., 247–48

recognition of the U.S.S.R. (*continued*)
pressure for, 179, 180, 202 ff., 217 ff., 222 ff., 227–28, 235 ff.
U.S.S.R., overtures for, 179, 180, 181–82, 184–85, 205, 214, 227–28, 237 ff.
(*see* Soviet Union, overtures to the U.S.)
Reconstruction Finance Corporation, 232, 261
finances U.S.-U.S.S.R. cotton trade, 236
Red Cross and Red Cross Commission to Russia (*see* American Red Cross)
Redfield, William
policy toward intervention, 151–52
relationship with American-Russian Chamber of Commerce, 149–52, 180
Red Scare of 1918–1920
relationship to German-agent theory of the Bolshevik Revolution and U.S.-U.S.S.R. relations, 132, 136, 154–57, 174
Reed, John, 128
Reid, Reverend Gilbert, 41
Reid, Whitelaw, 32
Reinsch, Paul, 44, 151
reparations, importance of in U.S.-U.S.S.R. relations, 270, 273 ff., 277, 344 note 65
Republican League, 74
Review of Reviews, 41, 44
Revolution, Russian of 1905, 46, 55, 83
Revolution, Russian of March, 1917 (*see* Provisional Government)
Revolution, Russian, of November, 1917 (*see* Bolshevik Revolution; intervention)
von Ribbentrop, Nazi Foreign Minister, 231
Riggs, E. Francis, 113, 133, 135, 137, 141
Robins, Mrs. Margaret Dreier, 82, 153
Robins, Raymond
background, 50, 80–82, 89–90
general policy of, 50, 80–82, 89–90, 98–100, 102–3, 105, 109–10, 131–32, 141 ff., 151, 173–74, 179 ff.
Harding, President Warren G., agreement with, 174, 182, 201, 204
influence of, 50, 80–82, 89–90, 96 ff., 126, 132, 133 ff., 146 ff., 179 ff., 201 ff.
policies toward
Bolshevik Revolution, 105, 114 ff., 131–32, 133 ff.
intervention, 134 ff.
Provisional Government, 96 ff.

Robins, Raymond (*continued*)
recall of, 144–45
relationships with
Lenin, 124 ff., 128, 133 ff.
Stalin, 238
Trotsky, 111 ff., 126, 133 ff.
U.S.S.R., recognition of, efforts to
secure, 174, 179, 182, 201 ff., 235 ff.
(*see* Borah, William E.; Gumberg,
Alexander)
Robins-Lenin plan for U.S.-U.S.S.R. eco-
nomic collaboration, 141–42, 147,
206
Robins-Stalin Talk of 1933, 238
Robins-Summers Dispute, 142, 144–45
Rockhill, William Woodville, 64
background, 32, 34, 42
policies toward
Japan, 44, 57
Russia, 42, 44, 49, 62, 69, 71–72, 74–
75, 78–79
Roosevelt-Eden Talks, 265–66
Roosevelt, President Franklin Delano, 81,
229
Atlantic Conference, views at, 262–63
China policy of, 276 ff.
Crisis of 1937, views during, 248 ff.
domestic policy of, 232–34, 268–70
general policy of, 192, 232–34, 248 ff.,
253 ff., 268–70
reparations, views on, 270, 273, 344 note
65
U.S.-U.S.S.R. relations, views on, 3, 235,
238–40, 244, 246, 248, 253, 255, 259,
260 ff., 271 ff.
Roosevelt-Litvinov Negotiations of 1933,
239–41, 244
Roosevelt-Molotov Talks, 1942, 264–65
Roosevelt, President Theodore, 49, 56, 64,
80, 81, 82, 87, 89, 100, 108, 112, 114,
140, 147, 188
general policy of, 22, 39, 40–41, 42, 44,
51, 65
policies toward
expansion, 32, 39, 42, 44, 51, 62–63
Japan, 43–44, 51, 53, 57–58, 59, 62–
63
Russia, 40–41, 42, 43–47, 77
relationship with Adams, Brooks, 40,
41–42, 44–46, 57
Russo-Japanese War, views on, 42, 43–
47
Root, Elihu, 57, 58, 59, 77, 82, 89, 188
general policy, 62, 64, 94
Root Mission to Russia, 1917

Root Mission to Russia (*continued*)
origin and character of, 87, 89, 90, 93–
95, 110, 139
report of, 151
Root-Takahira Agreement, 50, 59
Rosen, Baron R. R., 67, 85
Rosenstrauss, Theodore, 26–27
Ross, Edward A., 174
Royal Dutch Shell Oil Company, oil diplo-
macy of, 194 ff.
Rudowitz, Christian, issue of extradition
of, 80–82
Ruggles, James A., 133, 135, 137, 141
Rumiantzov, Count, 3
Russell, Charles Edward, 87, 94, 113
Russia
domestic policies, 24–26
economic life, 85–86
economic penetration of, by
France, 54
Germany, 36, 54
Great Britain, 36
U.S., 35, 49, 51 ff., 82 ff.
foreign policy, broad, 49–50
general policy, 3–4
U.S. overtures to, 52 ff., 58, 60 ff., 75, 84
Russian-American Chamber of Commerce,
85, 148, 150
Russian American Company, 6, 7, 16, 21
Russian American Mining and Engineer-
ing Company, 211
Russian Bureau, Incorporated, of the War
Trade Board, 153, 165
Russian Fleet, visit to the U.S., 20
Russian Oil Products, Ltd., 214
Russo Asiatic Bank, 188
Russo Chinese Bank, 29, 39
Russo-Japanese relations
antagonism and rivalry, 51 ff., 68 ff.
third nations, role in
France, 28
Germany, 28
Great Britain, 28, 46, 51, 58
U.S., 51 ff.
Russo-Japanese War, 31, 74
origin, 43, 45–47
legacy of, 228
sequel to, 51 ff.
Russo-Persian Relations
antagonism and rivalry, 75–77
economic ties, 75–77
third nations, role in
Great Britain, 75–77
U.S., 75–77
Russophobia, role in U.S.-Russian rela-

Russophobia (*continued*)
    tions, 31, 32, 37, 40–41, 65 (*see*
    Anglophilism)
Ryan, John, 100

Sadoul, Jacques, role in Bolshevik Revo-
    lution and intervention, 133, 134,
    135
Sakhalin Island, in U.S.-Russian relations,
    19, 52–53, 185, 189
San Francisco *News*, 224
Santo Domingo, 20
Saturday Evening Post, 236
Sazonov, Russian Foreign Minister Serge,
    49, 77
Schiff, Jacob
    Abrogation of Treaty of 1832, role in,
        27, 43, 61, 77–79
    Kuhn, Loeb and Company, role in, 27
    U.S.-Japanese relations, role in, 74
    U.S.-Russian relations, role in, 51 ff.,
        74–75, 77–79
    (*see* Harriman, Edward H.; Wilenkin,
        Gregory)
Schley, Reeve
    U.S.-U.S.S.R. economic relations, role
        in, 211, 213–14, 218, 224 (*see* Gum-
        berg, Alexander)
Schurman, Dr. Jacob G., 32
Schurz, Carl, 43
Schuster, W. Morgan, 76
    U.S. Persian relations, 76–77, 194–95
Schuyler, Montgomery, 73
Schwab, Charles M., 213
Scott, John, 215
Seasongood, General Lewis, 27
Second Front, issue of in U.S.-U.S.S.R. re-
    lations, 264–65
Seligman Brothers of London, 76–77
Seligman, Jesse, 27
Semenov, General Grigorii Mikhailovich,
    147, 182
Seventh Congress of the Communist Inter-
    national, 1935, 240–41
Seward, Secretary of State William H., 3,
    19, 20, 21–22, 23
Shakespeare, William, 242
Shantung Province, 29
Siberia and the Exile System, 25
Simon, Sir John, 226
Simpson, Thacher and Bartless, 101
Sinclair, Henry Ford, 189–90, 194 ff.
Sinclair Oil Company (*see* Sinclair,
    Henry Ford)
Singer Sewing Machine Company, invest-

Singer Sewing Machine Company (*cont.*)
    ments of, in Russia, 26, 83, 141, 150
Sino-Japanese War, 1895, 28, 29
Sino-Japanese War, 1931–1945, 225 ff.
Sino-Soviet Agreement of 1924, 190–91,
    277
Sino-Soviet Agreement of 1945, 277
Sino-Soviet Dispute, 1929, policy of U.S.
    and U.S.S.R., 220 ff.
Sino-Soviet Relations
    collaboration, 190–91, 192, 227, 253–54
    economic ties, World War II and after,
        276 ff.
    (*see* Chinese Eastern Railway; inter-
        vention, Washington Conference)
Sisson Documents
    origins, 136
    U.S.-U.S.S.R. relations, significance of
        in, 154–55
    (*see* German-agent theory of Bolshevik
        Revolution)
Sisson, Edgar, 112
    background, 102
    U.S.S.R., policy toward, 115 ff., 119 ff.,
        123
    U.S.S.R., policy toward, shift in, 124 ff.,
        136 ff.
    (*see* German-agent theory of Bolshevik
        Revolution)
Smith, General Bedell, 278
Smith, Charles
    background, 111
    Bolshevik Revolution and intervention,
        policy recommendations concern-
        ing, 111, 135, 145, 159
    U.S.-U.S.S.R. economic relations, role
        in, 186, 189–90, 202
Smith, F. Willoboughy, 120
Social Darwinism, 39 (*see* Anglophilism,
    Anglo-Saxonism, Russophobia)
Socialist Party of the United States,
    155
Society for the Abrogation of the Russian
    Extradition Treaty, 28
Sormovo Machine Works, 83
Soskice, David, 102, 103
South Manchurian Railway, 4, 57, 277
    control of, struggle for, 56, 60, 74, 166
    (*see* Harriman, Edward H.)
Soviet Far Eastern Army, 227
Soviet-Finnish relations
    negotiations of 1938–39, 254–55
    third nations, role of in
        Germany, 254
        U.S., 254–55

Soviet-Finnish War, policy toward of U.S., 254–55, 260–61
Soviet-Iranian relations, after World War II, 276, 279
Soviet-Japanese Border War, 1937–1939, significance of, 252–53
Soviet overture to the U.S. and Allied Powers of March 5, 1917, 134 ff., 140 ff.
Soviet-Persian relations, 194
Soviet Union
  overtures to the U.S., 106, 111, 112 ff., 120 ff., 128, 131, 133–37, 140–48, 161, 164, 167, 169, 179, 181–82, 184–85, 189–91, 200, 205, 214, 227–28, 237 ff., 248 ff., 260–61, 263
  (see American-Soviet Relations; collectivization of agriculture; Kirov, S.; Lenin, V. I.; Litvinov, M. M.; Stalin, J.; Trotsky, L.; Bolshevik Revolution; intervention)
Spain, 9, 10, 11, 20
Spanish American War, 31
Spanish Colonies in Latin America, 9, 13, 14–15, 16
Spargo, John, role in U.S.-U.S.S.R. relations, 181, 182, 206
Sperry Gyroscope Company, 216
Spheres of Influence (see balance of power; Churchill-Stalin Agreement of 1944)
Stalin, Iosif Visarionovich
  domestic policies of, 216, 221, 234, 242–43
  foreign policy of, 125, 208, 251 ff.
  speech of March 10, 1939, 251–52
Stalingrad Tractor Factory, 215
Stalin-Robins Talk of 1933, 238
Standard Oil Company of New Jersey, 57
  agreement with Royal Dutch Shell of July 24, 1922, 197, 214
  influence of, 44–45, 194
  investments of, in U.S.S.R., 195
  policies of, 44–45, 194 ff.
  U.S.S.R., policy toward, 195 ff., 214
Standard Oil Company of New York, 214
State Department, policy-making role (see advisors)
Steffens, Lincoln, 168
Steinhardt, Ambassador to the U.S.S.R. Laurence, 251–52
Sterling, Admiral Yates Jr., 241
Sterne, Laurence, 257
Stetson, Francis, 101
Stetson, Jennings and Russell, 101

Stevens, John F.
  intervention, role in, 152, 163, 165, 173
  mission to Russia, 1917, 92, 95, 110, 139, 145
  (see Batolin)
Stevens Railroad Commission to Russia, 1917, 92, 95, 110, 139, 145
Stevens, R. R., 135
Stiemer, Molly, 155–56
Stimson, Secretary of State and War Henry L., 178
  Manchurian Crisis of 1931, 219, 225 ff., 248
  Sino-Soviet Dispute, role in, 220 ff.
  U.S.S.R., policies toward, 22, 218, 224, 228–29, 274
St. Louis Republic, 84
Stockholm Socialist Conference, 1917, 93, 155
Stone, Melville, 145
Stone, William J., 128
Straight, Willard, 107
  U.S.-Russian relations, role in, 51, 56 ff.
  (see Chinese Eastern Railroad; Harriman, Edward H.; Manchuria; neutralization of Manchurian Railways; Schiff, Jacob)
Straus, Oscar, 86
  Abrogation of the Commercial Treaty of 1832, role in, 27, 43, 44, 84
  Paris Peace Conference, role at, 166
Stuart, Charles, 212
Stuart, James, and Cooke, Engineers, 212
Sulzer, Representative William, 78
Summers, Maddin, 92
  background, 113
  general policy of, 103, 113, 119–20
  influence, 120, 142 ff.
  intervention, role in, 119–20, 131–32, 141 ff.
Summers-Robins Dispute, 142, 144–45
Sumner, Charles, 19, 20
Sunstrand Machine Tool Company, role in recognition of U.S.S.R., 218, 236
Sun Yat-sen, 190
Supreme Economic Council, 179, 193

Taft, President William Howard, 51, 76
  policies toward
    Abrogation of Treaty of 1832, 79
    Consortium, 62 ff., 166
    Manchuria, 63 ff., 178
    Russia, 58, 63–64, 77–78, 149

Taft-Katsura Agreement, character of, 46, 50
T'ai P'ing Rebellion, 22, 28
Takahashi, Baron, 61
Tariff of 1828, Russian view of, 18
technical assistance contracts of U.S. firms with the U.S.S.R., 211 ff.
Technical Sub-Committee on the Chinese Eastern Railway of the Washington Conference, 188 ff. (see Washington Conference)
Teheran Conference, 1943, 274
  decisions of
    general, 276–77
    Poland, 267–68
  Roosevelt, Franklin D., report on, 268–69
  significance of, 268–70
Temporary National Economic Committee, 233
Tennessee Valley Authority, 232–33
Tent Life in Siberia, 24
Texas, U.S. expansion into, 17, 44
Thacher, Judge Thomas D., 224
  background of, 101
  intervention, view of, 144–45, 159
  Gumberg, Alexander, relationship with, 211
  Red Cross Commission to Russia, role in, 101, 145
  U.S.-U.S.S.R. relations, economic plan to facilitate, 144–45, 149, 211
Thompson, William Boyce, 80, 180, 202, 206, 217
  background of, 88
  Bolshevik Revolution, policy toward, 109–10, 111–12, 118–19, 126, 127–28, 135, 143, 145, 146, 153, 154, 166, 169, 174
  Congressional election of 1918, role in, 132, 154
  Provisional Government, attempts to aid, 91, 94 ff.
  Red Cross Commission to Russia, role in, 88–90, 91, 94 ff.
  relationships with
    Borah, William E., 128
    Robins, Raymond, 90 ff., 174
Tolstoy, Count Leo, 242
  appeal to, by U.S. citizens in Russia, 26–27
Tower, Charlemagne, 36
trade unions, role in policy-making (see American Federation of Labor; Depression of 1921)

Trans-Siberian Railway, 28
  construction of, use of U.S. materials in, 83
  control of, 29, 55–56
  (see Harriman, Edward H.)
Treasury Department, U.S., role in U.S.-U.S.S.R. relations, 109, 117
Treaty of Ghent, 11
Trident Conference, World War II, 266
Trotsky, Lev Davidovich, 92, 101, 111, 112 ff.
  Brest Litovsk Treaty, role in, 115 ff., 122 ff., 133
  intervention, view of, 151
  Judson, William V., relationship with, 112
  Robins, Raymond, relationship with, 111 ff., 133 ff.
  U.S., collaboration with, view of, 111, 114 ff., 120 ff., 128, 133 ff.
  U.S. society, view of, 184
Troyanovsky, Soviet Ambassador Alexander, 3
  Hull, Cordell, negotiations with, 231, 244 ff.
Truman Doctrine, character of, 280
Truman, President Harry S., 238, 270
  UNRRA, policy toward, 280
  U.S.S.R., views on relations with, 273 ff., 278, 279
Turkey
  economic penetration of by
    Germany, 75–76
    Great Britain, 4, 75–77, 199
    U.S., 75–77, 199
Tuyll, Baron de, 12, 13, 14, 15
Twain, Mark, 25
Twenty-One Demands, Japanese on China, 138–39

Union Iron Works, 29
Union of Soviet Socialist Republics (see Soviet Union)
United Brotherhood of Carpenters and Joiners of America, 180
United Engineering and Foundry Company, 215
United Mine Workers, 81, 180
United Nations Organization, organization and original concept of, 265, 269, 274–75, 279
United Press, 88
United States
  general policy of in 1920s, 177 ff.
  general policy of in 1930s, 231 ff., 253 ff.

United States (*continued*)
  (*see* entries under specific events, personalities, and policies)
United States Board of Trade, 236
United States Chamber of Commerce, 108, 148
United States Rubber Company, 219
United States Steel Company, 213, 223
Urquhart, Leslie B., 210–11

Vanderlip, Frank A., 185
Vanderlip, Washington B., background of and efforts to negotiate economic concession with the U.S.S.R., 185
Venezuelan Crisis of 1895–97, 31
Versailles Peace Conference (*see* Paris Peace Conference)
Vrooman, Carl S., 89
Vzestnik Europy, 45

Wadsworth, Eliot, 86
  Red Cross Commission to Russia, relationship with, 89
Wardwell, Allen, Red Cross Commission to Russia, role in, 101
War Department Division of Intelligence, shadows Robins, Raymond, 174
War of 1812, 8
War Trade Board of World War I, Russian Division, Inc. of, origin and role in intervention, 100, 101, 153
Washington Conference
  character and purpose of, 183–84, 186, 187 ff., 219
  decisions of, concerning
    Chinese Eastern Railroad, 184, 187 ff.
    Japanese expansion in Asia, 185, 186 ff.
  Far Eastern Republic of China, role in, 186 ff.
Washington *Globe*, 18
Welles, Sumner
  Atlantic Conference, views on, 262, 263
  Hull, Cordell, differences with, 266
  Oumansky, C., neogiations with, 261
  U.S.S.R., views on relations with, 261, 262
Wells, H. G., 201
Western Electric Company, 215
Western Union Telegraph Company, 24
Westinghouse Air Brake Co., investments in Russia, 36, 83, 142, 150; in U.S.-U.S.S.R. economic relations, 210, 215, 224
whaling interests, U.S., 12

Wheeler, Senator Burton K., 222
White, Ambassador Andrew D., 44, 78
White, Henry, 32
Wilenkin, Gregory
  influence, 60
  policy toward, U.S., 60 ff.
  relationships with
    Hammond, John Hays, 79
    Knox, Philander C., 74
    Schiff, Jacob, 60 ff., 73, 79
Williams, E. T., 49
Williams, Harold, 135
Wilson, Huntington, 76
Wilson, President Woodrow, 78, 81
  general policy of, 84, 116–18, 129, 157–58, 162 ff., 177–78
  policies toward
    Bolshevik Revolution, 116 ff., 131, 132, 137 ff.
    Buckler Mission to U.S.S.R., 160 ff.
    Bullitt Mission to U.S.S.R., 168 ff.
    Dardenelles Straits, 199
    intervention in Bolshevik Revolution, 105–7, 116–19, 123, 124, 127–29, 131, 132, 147, 148 ff., 162 ff.
    Japan, 106, 129, 132, 138–40, 149, 151–52, 162 ff.
    Paris Peace Conference, 157 ff.
    Prinkipo Conference, 164, 166 ff.
    Provisional Government, 86 ff., 92, 94 ff., 100 ff.
  relationships with
    Lansing, Robert, 116–18, 123–24, 137 ff., 145–47, 159–60
    Robins, Raymond, 89, 147
    Thompson, William Boyce, 128
  social philosophy of, 107, 116–18
  tragedy of, 87, 88, 158, 159, 162–63, 166
Wilson's Memorandum of February 28, 1918, on Intervention, 138–39
Witte, Sergius U.
  Bezobrazov Group, conflict with, 30, 37, 38, 39
  general policy of, 29, 30, 37, 55
  influence of, 39
  U.S., collaboration with, policy of, 53–54, 61, 74, 77, 83
Woll, Mathew, policy toward U.S.S.R., 222, 224
Women's Trade Union League, 81
Wood, Leonard, 174
World Disarmament Conference, 1932, 227, 239
World Economic Conference, 1933, 236, 240

Worthington Pump Company, 36, 82
Wrangel, Petr Nikolaevich, role in intervention, 167
Wright, J. Butler, 113

Yalta Conference, 1945, 267
  Churchill-Stalin Agreement of 1944, significance of at, 272 ff.
  decisions of, 273 ff.

Yokohama Specie Bank, role in U.S.-Japanese relations, 61 (*see* Schiff, Jacob; Lamont, Thomas)
Young, John Russell, 32
Yuan-Shih-Kai, 190
Yugoslavia, 271, 272

Zaklind, Ivan A., 128